Historic Preservation

Michael A. Tomlan

Historic Preservation

Caring for Our Expanding Legacy

With contributions by David Listokin

 Springer

Michael A. Tomlan
Cornell University
Ithaca
New York
USA

ISBN 978-3-319-04974-8   ISBN 978-3-319-04975-5 (eBook)
DOI 10.1007/978-3-319-04975-5
Springer Cham Heidelberg New York Dordrecht London

Library of Congress Control Number: 2014946614

Printed on acid-free paper

Springer is part of Springer Science + Business Media (www.springer.com)

Introduction

At its core, historic preservation is a social campaign concerned with the character, condition, use, and treatment of the physical world around us. The items of concern are large and small, and found everywhere. They are in the water and in landscapes of every kind—rural, urban, suburban, and even sparsely settled forests and deserts. This social campaign enlists and engages people who are dedicated to extending the legacy and the usefulness of existing buildings, structures, and sites.

This definition reflects the Greek philosophical view that culture and nature are largely different entities, with overlapping concerns for animals and plants. The roots of historic preservation lie largely in European activities, and many are associated with a Judeo-Christian idea that distinguishes the thoughts and activities of the corporal world from the spiritual nature of things. Various rulers and religious leaders throughout history invoked the ideas and images of their predecessors to gain legitimacy, but the transformation of Western civilization that embraced Positivism as a concept with the growth of the Industrial Revolution provided new platforms for change and reactions against that change.

Contemporary American thinking has moved beyond this, just as the humanistic concept of natural rights declared during the Revolution and inscribed in the Constitution continues to be refined and expanded. Even more important, the concept of "property" is being re-defined. In 1776, most people and everything on the land fell within the description of "property." In the early nineteenth century, some states outlawed slavery but, even after the Civil War, many people were skeptical that all African Americans should be emancipated. For advocates, social change came slowly. Federal legislation guaranteed Civil Rights only in 1964. In a similar fashion, The Declaration of Sentiments and Resolutions drafted for the women's rights convention at Seneca Falls, New York in 1848, demanded equality with men before the law, in education and employment. It was not until 1920, however, that the nineteenth amendment to the Constitution provided all women the right to vote. Growing nineteenth century recognition of the disenfranchised Native Americans led to the passage of the Indian Citizen Act in 1924. In short, the American Revolution started a process that spawned successive waves of ethical reevaluation, and they continue. Alongside the need to redefine the rights of certain groups and classes of people rose the concern for the prevention of cruelty to animals and, in time, a growing sensitivity to the need for healthy trees and plants. The rising interest in what was, at the turn of the twentieth century, dubbed "conservation," centered on forests and streams, evolved after World War II to become the environmentalism we know today. Forest management was not enough for those who believe that Nature has a rightful place in the cosmic order. Hence, the expanding concept of rights now includes not only concerns for the role of the person, family, tribe, race, region, and nation, but also the relationship between them and animals and plants. Although agreement upon the best the path to follow has not always been clear to everyone, in hindsight, the contributions of the federal legislation of the 1960s and early 1970s are clear. This included not only the National Historic Preservation Act, but also the National Environmental Policy Act, and closely linked legislation regulating water pollution, ocean dumping, coastal zone management, and endangered species.

In recent decades, the growing recognition of the intrinsic value of the tangible and intangible character of places and objects has continued in the United States of America (USA), so that historic preservation has flowered. More people have become involved, the total number of projects completed and programs implemented has increased, the approaches have become more thoughtful, and the general quality of the work has improved. Public advocacy has led to more legislation at the state and local levels, and preservation education has attracted more resources. In many ways this improvement and maturing is to be expected. The United States has provided the best grounds for the maturation of historic preservation, aided by a comparatively well educated population, generally well-intended government, and an interested business community. No other country has so successfully fostered and funded contemporary preservation activity. We have even linked our social agenda to the tax code, providing historic properties with some of the same financial advantages as desirable social goals such as low-income housing.

Just as the United States is continually reexamining its motivations and beliefs, it is appropriate to revisit our historical and aesthetic ideas. Like all communal, political activities, the historic preservation movement is a product of, and supported by, our changing society. Still, at the root of all historic preservation efforts is the basic belief that we should save things. The reasons follow.

First, we save things because they have immediate personal or social usefulness. If the object is found to be helpful, it is put aside for use again. In agrarian life, experience showed that the careful selection of the most prolific seeds advanced the goals of the farmer by providing the best crops. Selecting the best animals for breeding followed the same logic. In industrial production, the model that produces the best result is imitated, with immediate social impact. The act of putting aside anything often increases its value, whether an archaeological location, a landscape, structure, site, or object.

Second, we save things because it is economically prudent. Simply put, our wants often outstrip our needs. By saving what we have acquired or been given, it is possible to shift our resources and time elsewhere. Saving, rather than replacing, often leads individuals and groups to value more highly what has been put in reserve. It is axiomatic that poverty is frequently a major reason for preservation. In fact, poverty may be among the most powerful reasons for what has remained.

Third, we save things because they are important to us as remembrances of people, events, and periods in the past. The Romans were sensitive to this. They wanted to recall the glory of the past and passed legislation that forbade using or abusing ancient temples. As more nations grew increasingly sensitive, this legislation was copied in spirit, if not in fact. Places of historic and religious significance spurred some of the most important preservation advocacy of the nineteenth and early twentieth centuries in Western Europe. In a similar way, early historic preservation efforts in the USA were pietistic, centered on saving Independence Hall and the home of George Washington, to mark the place of the country's founders in history.

Fourth, we save things because they are aesthetically exceptional. Our society no longer insists, as de Tocqueville wrote, that democratic nations "prefer the useful to the beautiful." No longer simply the province of art connoisseurs and the privileged classes, the expanding and ever changing concepts of aesthetics and the social relevance of design ideas has challenged old interpretations of just what is artistically significant. In this regard, it is a comparatively easy step from the rise of art collections and history museums in the nineteenth century to the recognition and designation of objects and properties of merit beyond museum walls.

And fifth, we save things because they have contemporary spiritual or religious value, calling to mind the relationship of a supernatural creative or governing force. God, representing either the sole deity in a monotheism, or one of the gods in a polytheism, has held the attention of people who regard particular objects, properties, or locations as sacred. In spiritual or religious rituals, beliefs and activities may dictate that a particular location has special meaning, segregating its faith-based use from other uses.

Each of these rationales plays a role in preservation efforts today, although some are more apparent than others at any given time. It is also important to recognize that any of these arguments are useful alongside the others. Yet, the choice of what we need to save is not often ours alone. Natural disasters continue to affect our ability to save anything. Fires, floods, landslides, earthquakes, and dozens of other forces accelerate decay, and play havoc with our legacy. Although some advance notice of disasters is possible, they often strike without warning, and lives and property are lost. At the same time, the slow deterioration of our physical fabric, due to the changing climate, seasons, and elements, while not as cataclysmic, can be just as damaging with the passage of time.

Often more traumatic than the forces of Nature is human intervention. Destruction of a highly regarded object, property, district, or region can take place at a surprisingly swift pace. In some cases, there is little public reaction. While thousands of people over the globe may understand and sympathize with the rationales for saving, several billion others are not readily convinced and want to know why they should care. "New" is widely seen as better than the "old." In fact, in the USA, the urge to create and start afresh seems a constant refrain. The nation is ever changing, with cities continually rebuilt, the suburbs made over, and rural areas constantly transformed. Structures of all kinds are added at the periphery of urbanized areas, with older properties torn down and still others arising in their place. New shopping centers and malls open while others lie surprisingly vacant, and still others changed to serve new functions. Companies announce a new headquarters while leaving aside their former location, with only a sign indicating that they have moved. Small homes on large lots fall victim to large houses or mansions, as the countryside's farms and ranches are underutilized, some only a step away from passing into history.

Who is it, then, that prefers change, while others relish the status quo? Why is it that some communities and properties are considered "historic" and apparently treated with care, while others are subjected to continual rebuilding? What is it that triggers the population in one municipality to urge the government to designate one area as special while so many others are overlooked and defenseless against change?

Historic preservation is saving and caring for the legacy we have come to call our "cultural heritage." Heritage is not synonymous with "history," nor is it simply based on "tradition." It includes both of these to various degrees, and considerably more. The physical properties of the "object," regardless of how large or small, are often the focus of initial attention, but the intangible aspects are equally important. They include the wide range of artistic practices and religious rituals that support the value a society places on the property. Culture is composed of the pattern of ways of thinking, feeling, reacting, and acquiring associations, beliefs, attitudes, and values. These are shared and learned among people who, in turn, create and shape objects and places that symbolize their common understandings.

The growing awareness of Americans to the fast pace of change, spurred on by technological improvements such as the telephone, television, and internet, has led many to take action to modify the definition of "progress." In addition to this increasing awareness, proposed changes may disrupt familiar patterns of life. It is for these reasons that the need for this book is clear: to guide students of preservation—professional or amateur—so they may extend our legacy to all those who will follow us.

To address these problems, this text draws on a wide range of scholarship, experience, and information, concentrating on the last 50 years. As such, this work is only secondarily an historical study, only briefly reviewing the history of the historic preservation movement before World War II. This chronological history is deliberately restrained to allow attention to be paid to a broad range of contemporary topics. This is needed because the boom in preservation activities throughout the country during the last several decades almost defies description, let alone analysis and direction. Yet, the challenges continue.

The reader who is familiar with any one of these topics may find that only a few case studies are included. This is deliberate because specific examples are used to exemplify a theoretical position, illustrate a program, and provoke thought, rather than address all of the concepts and questions that arise. This text, like any introduction to the field, can only be suggestive. This is not a how-to manual that can be followed step-by-step, resulting in a predetermined outcome. References to the most helpful material of that kind, including online government publications, are available in the footnotes and references. In addition, this work is neither an explicit call for government action, nor a demand for increased funding, although admittedly both are implied. Instead the purpose is to redefine historic preservation activity as a course of action, incorporating more explicitly the socially progressive goals that have come to characterize the movement.

This text is unusual because it deliberately embraces almost all of the disciplines involved in the field of historic preservation.[1] It includes, but is not limited to, topics ranging from American studies to urban affairs. Indeed, a number of fields that have not previously been included in preservation discussions will spur greater consideration. For example, faith-based initiatives and their role in rebuilding communities to save properties are all but completely absent in previous preservation works. They are examined closely in this text.

In addition, by re-thinking past and current ideas in preservation, this is a more contemporary view of the field. It challenges readers to see not only how each of the related disciplines is connected, but also how preservation influenced each of them. Ideally, anyone who reads this text will be able to find included some aspect of their own interests and be able to see how he or she can contribute their knowledge, and learn more. Students of all ages will see this book not simply as a starting point and handy reference, but as a document open to discussion and critical examination. It should help everyone understand what previous generations have held important, and see how he or she can connect that to our contemporary ideas.

Other caveats are in order. Natural curiosity leads to speculation about how the historic preservation in this country compares to efforts outside of the United States, particularly with the policies, programs, and projects that seem similar in other parts of the English-speaking world. This text is not attempting to draw these comparisons. Although mention of examples from other countries are included in some instances, to do justice to efforts in other countries would require extended discussions about the people, history, and customs in these locations to reach a parallel level of understanding. Given the differences in the societies and the variations in governments, legal frameworks, political structure, economics, financing, and common practices around the world, this is simply not possible within this work.

One of the unusual aspects of this book is that it deliberately moves away

---

[1] The history and conservation of building materials has been omitted in the interests of space and so as not to compete with texts by other authors. These include: Martin E. Weaver and Frank G. Matero, *Conserving Buildings: A Guide to Techniques and Materials*, New York: John Wiley, 1993; Theodore H.M. Prudon, *Preservation of Modern Architecture*, Hoboken, NJ: Wiley, 2008; and Robert A. Young, *Historic Preservation Technology*, New York: John Wiley, 2008. Also important are: Frederick A. Stahl, *A Guide to the Maintenance, Repair and Alteration of Historic Buildings*, New York: Van Nostrand Reinhold Company, 1984; and Swanke Hayden Connell Architects, *Historic Preservation: Project Planning & Estimating*, New York: R. S. Means, 2000. Comparable texts in Great Britain include: Bernard M. Feilden, *Conservation of Historic Buildings*, London: Butterworth Heinemann, 1982, 1994; and the series edited by Michael Forsyth, including: *Materials and Skills for Historic Building Conservation*, Oxford, UK and Malden, MA, Blackwell Pub., 2008; and *Structures & Construction in Historic Buildings Conservation*, Oxford, UK and Malden, MA, Blackwell Pub., 2007. Some of my own contributions to this area are contained in: Thomas C. Jester, (Ed.), *Twentieth-Century Building Materials.History and Conservation*, New York: McGraw-Hill Companies, 1995.

from historic preservation as an "artifact-centered" discussion. This text considers the importance of "what" is significant only after considering "who" is involved, which begins to answer the question of "why" anyone should care. After considering "who," "why," and "what," it is suitable to address the questions of "when" and "how" to proceed. The discussion begins with the view that historic preservation is a social activity first, and proceeds to examine the organization of the movement and its accomplishments, and the particulars of the government response. Only after that does it become clear how to go forward.

In the opening chapter, "who we are" and why it matters is at the center of the discussion. It is understood that the people who become involved in any social movement make deliberate decisions about—and influence—what they believe is important. During the nineteenth and early twentieth centuries, the men and women who held high pietistic ideals and aesthetic concerns were secure and well educated by comparison to most Americans. They were different because, as advocates, they began to organize in societies that would not accept the continuous change around them as "progress." The early preservationists had a larger vision of improvement, of which historic properties were a part. To accomplish their goals they gained additional financial and political support. By the end of the nineteenth century, a wave of romanticism gave rise to a host of new organizations in historic preservation, embracing archaeology, museology, and scenic conservation. In succeeding decades, the people who become involved were not only amateurs but also an increasing number of professionals, exploring how science and better management could make a difference. In many cases, their decisions become very pragmatic in order to gain maximum advantage as the role of the state and federal government slowly increased.

The second chapter extends the historical review through the mid-1980s to provide a basis for discussion in the seven other chapters of the book, which are thematic. After World War II, historic preservation efforts across the country were stimulated in reaction to the widespread destruction caused by federally sponsored urban renewal and highway improvement. As the number of objections to these ill-planned initiatives rose during the late 1950s, widespread local advocacy struggled to create what became the national preservation movement. Influenced by the Modern movement in architecture and planning, preservation became part of the ferment in the 1960s that characterized the environmental movement. Civil Rights reform also affected the preservation movement, as it did many social movements of the period. Then, the Bicentennial and tax reform initiatives strengthened both the historical and economic rationales for historic preservation in a way that the framers of the 1966 National Historic Preservation Act had envisioned.

Chapter 3 lays out the broad intellectual basis and the fundamental legal framework at the federal, state, and local levels. It also provides an overview of the role that chief executives play as leaders, setting out goals in a variety of directives affecting the treatment of government property. The third part of this chapter deals with the important judicial decisions that have influenced historic preservation practice. Key is the famous *Penn Central* case of 1978, in which the U.S. Supreme Court affirmed the applicability of local landmarks legislation. Granted, the balance between individual rights and responsibilities and the concerns for the larger community in the treatment of property seems to be a never-ending source of controversy and tension. This text views this ongoing discussion as a healthy dialogue. Included in this section is consideration of the separation of church and state, sometimes a hot-button issue in urban areas, where the future use of historic religious buildings are at issue.

Chapter 4 investigates the economic factors that influence the continued use of all properties. This begins with a discussion of the major demographic changes taking place in the USA, focusing on the economic and social characteristics that have given rise to the country's population relocation. The shift from a largely agrarian economy, through the twentieth century's industrialization, into the twenty-first century's dependence on the service sector carries with it tremendous implications, and directly affects extending the legacy in all areas of the country. Arguments about obsolescence used to support demolition are rarely justified, particularly when the economic contribution made by rehabilitation projects clearly boost local public revenues. Programs to revive main streets, heritage areas, and housing complexes also play a key role in meeting some of the disinvestment that leads to the threat of demolition. Additionally, heritage tourism activities provide an often-needed economic boost, leading to the consideration of the "multiplier effects" of preservation initiatives.

Chapter 5 addresses financial challenges by examining three sources of revenue. First are income tax credits. These include the federal and state historic rehabilitation tax credit programs, which are recognized as a powerful incentive for investors interested in income-producing properties. Low-income housing tax credits are considered because they are also used in commercial housing ventures. Second are the New Market Tax Credits, introduced by federal legislation in 2000, also targeted to low-income communities. Third is a wide range of supports dedicated to historic preservation projects, including property-tax reduction, tax-increment financing, special bonds, and the funding made available for transportation improvement and enhancement. It is important to point out that, although private support by individuals, groups, foundations, and corporations continues to provide a sizable lift to preservation efforts, charitable gifts are by no means the only manner in which projects are made financially viable.

Chapter 6 focuses on the importance of providing a vision that respects the history of the property and the existing character of the place. This begins with seeing and recording, and then organizing and interpreting information, respecting the value of the context. Designing successful alternatives requires information from community members. Design review boards, historic district commissions, and conservation advisory groups all have a role to play. The renewed interest in "sustainability" presents special questions, because not all "green" alternatives are preservation-friendly. Likewise, special care must be taken to understand the preservation "treatments," specifically restoration, reconstruction, and rehabilitation. The exciting projects that have reused former train stations have led to re-conceiving entire rail beds, including the warehouses alongside them. Transit corridors and transportation facilities have, in some cases, gone underground. In other cases, baseball stadia, military bases, and naval yards have been re-purposed and integrated into their surroundings, suggesting even greater successes are possible in the future.

Ethics and advocacy are the subjects of Chapter 7. Given that historic preservation is a social campaign that concerns the future of our cultural heritage, it is important to set out a clear definition of just what encompasses those patterns of thinking, feeling, and reacting, with its beliefs, attitudes, and shared values. Taking care to be ethically coherent, yet being alert to the need to enlist the public and build a stronger constituency with sound professional guidance, is essential. After these introductory sections, a series of cases provide more insight, because conflicts arise within preservation organizations, between preservation organizations, and with other powerful social groups, often leading to the loss of the cultural landscape, historic district, property, archaeological site, object, or artifact. In short, the preservation rationales— aesthetic, social, historic, spiritual, and economic—come up against other goals of society, and the questions of how to best proceed becomes troubling for policy makers and local officials who sit in judgment.

Chapter 8 considers the importance of religion, arguably our most important intangible values as they relate to historic preservation activities. It addresses the long-held arms-length distance between preservation activities and faith-based ideas, and spells out how more people are becoming aware of the need to bridge this gap. Unlike most other nations, the USA reacted against adopting or preferring any specific religion. This country holds firmly to the positivist view that no single faith should hold sway over others, preferring to put its faith in the accumulation of knowledge and the proper application of science. Social and economic change would therefore follow. Yet, the urban gospel movement of the late nineteenth and early twentieth century formed the platform for social reform that led to Civil Rights and Womens' Rights initiatives, and a range of reforms in sanitation, housing, and recreation. True, fundamentalism rose in the twentieth century at several points, and mid-century federalism attempted to take on the tasks of organized religion. Since the late 1970s, however, decentralization in government has led to a reevaluation of faith-based initiatives, with a number of new preservation partnerships. In addition, while this country is becoming less Protestant and more Catholic, it also continues to attract immigrants from abroad who often hold faiths that influence our collective sense of values.

The conclusion briefly evaluates some of the key accomplishments of the recent historic preservation movement. It also provides a synthesis that draws on the lessons of each of the chapters, sketching out some of the hurdles that remain and are likely to occupy the agendas of preservationists in the decades ahead. The development of the historic preservation movement is, in itself, evidence of our particular American culture, as it changes. All of the evidence strongly suggests, however, that this social campaign will continue and our legacy will extend to future generations.

Acknowledgements

Every book has a story. This work began with an idea that a much better text about the historic preservation field in the United States should be made available for students and colleagues everywhere. That idea blossomed through a friendship with my colleague and friend Professor David Listokin, of Rutgers University. David provided not only the substance of two chapters on economics and finance, but also contributed mightily to a chapter on legal concerns. He remains an ideal collaborator and his assistance is greatly appreciated.

Because the scope of this work is so broad, several readers were enlisted for their specializations and perspectives on specific chapters. These include Emily Bergeron, Jeffrey Chusid, Joyce Clark, Emily Goldstein, A. Robert Jaeger, and Kristin Olson. Two reviewers, Julee Johnson and Peter Wissoker, read the entire work at different points and offered very helpful editorial suggestions. Teaching assistants and alumni conducted image searches, among them Jessica Evans, Jonathan Gunderlach, Caitlin Kolb, Ashima Krishna, Thomas Richmond, Charles Uhl, and Casey Woster. All must be recognized for their contributions. The primary author captured the majority of the images both old and new, but professional photographers supplied a few of the important pictures, including the late Jack Boucher, who worked for the Historic American Buildings Survey and the Historic American Engineering Record in the National Park Service. Jack was always generous with his time and expertise.

Although writing and revising the text has taken almost eight years, the research for some segments of the chapters began over three decades ago. Several essays were initially prepared for and delivered at conferences and seminars sponsored by agencies and organizations. These include the General Services Administration, National Park Service, National Trust for Historic Preservation, General Services Administration, Association for Preservation Technology International, and Preservation Trades Network. I thank the organizers of these events for inviting me, providing the opportunity to share my thoughts. A summer term teaching public history graduate students at Middle Tennessee State University was particularly helpful in renewing my familiarity with the changing nature of the Bible Belt. Experiences elsewhere in this country and abroad have also been helpful, especially when making comments about advocacy, personnel issues, project funding, government approvals, scientific investigations, evaluative metrics, and heritage management.

The editors at Springer have been tremendously helpful, supporting the work at every turn. Special thanks are due to Teresa Kraus and Hana Nagdimov, who brought the manuscript into fruition with more color illustrations than this author ever thought possible, making it a more attractive product.

Lastly, Cornell University has permitted me sabbatical leaves for a term on two occasions. In this regard, my thanks go the Department Chairs, Kenneth Reardon and Kieran Donaghy, and the Deans, Mohsen Mostafavi and Kent Kleinman. I thank them for their cooperation and support.

Ithaca, NY   M.A.T.

Contents

List of Figures

List of Tables

Author's Biography

Michael A. Tomlan is the Director of the Graduate Program in Historic Preservation Planning in the College of Architecture, Art and Planning at Cornell University, in Ithaca, New York. With nearly four decades of teaching and field experience, Professor Tomlan serves students pursuing degrees not only in historic preservation but also in archaeology, architecture, city and regional planning, history, public administration, real estate, and urban studies. A published author with a wide range of interests, he also edited *Preservation of What? For Whom? A Critical Look at Historical Significance* (1998). He currently serves as a Project Director for the National Council for Preservation Education, having established a cooperative agreement for that organization with the National Park Service in 1995 that supports the longest-running preservation internship program in the country. Dr. Tomlan is a Fellow of the Association for Preservation Technology, a former board member of the Society of Architectural Historians, former consultant to the World Monuments Fund and advisor to the Global Heritage Fund, working on significant sites in India, China and Cambodia. He regularly travels abroad as the Treasurer of Heritage Watch International, based in Siem Reap, and the President of *Yosothor*, a publishing firm in Phnom Penh, in Cambodia. He also remains the Chair of the New York State Barn Alliance, and the President of Historic Urban Plans, Inc.

Introduction

Most of the ideas held by residents of the United States that are the basis for historic preservation thought originated in Western Europe. Americans generally believe that logical thought is preferable to chance and look forward to a better future. Although many believe that spiritual guidance is necessary, the search continues for reason, linking cause and effect. There is also a fundamental understanding that an individual's rights are generally as important as the society's as a whole in governing specific actions. These ideas developed as industrialization spread in the late eighteenth and nineteenth centuries, and the rapid change was embraced as a sign of progress. The French social theorist Auguste Comte claimed that careful study of the facts would generate positive laws in society, and this "positivism" became a fundamental axiom in the search for a better way of life, individually and collectively. The English philosopher John Stuart Mill went further in his belief that society would improve, and intensified the advocacy for women's rights, forecasting that they would take an increasingly important role in all aspects of society. In reviewing historic preservation activity, it becomes clear that women have always been coequal in the field, even though not always recognized by historians. At the same time, the rise and application of the natural and physical sciences brought about improvement in what is today sometimes termed the "quality of life." With concerted effort, progress was all a matter of time.

The rise of Positivism in the nineteenth and early twentieth century is breathtaking because Americans embraced it at every turn. It provided the basis for this country's transformation from an agrarian nation to an industrial one, based in urban centers. It lies at the root of planning and progress, especially as defined in Progressivism. In cities, towns, and villages, the immediate need to provide adequate water supply, better sanitation, more housing, and recreational open space became an almost continuous dedication to improvement. Most members of the rising middle-class endorsed these physical enhancements, and increasingly accessible public education transformed thinking about the future. Although there were countervailing beliefs that slavery was an appropriate social institution and human rights were subservient to economic expansion, modernization through the City Beautiful movement and into the mid-twentieth century increased the pressure for social reform in housing, women's rights, more equitable minority treatment, and improved labor conditions. At the same time, religion was gradually less of a requirement for success in civic affairs, and Christian teaching competed in governance with a secular, more general respect for humanity.

Amidst these strong prevailing ideas, during the nineteenth and early twentieth centuries, still other undercurrents developed. They called into question just what "progress" was all about, and these eventually provided alternative ideas and viewpoints. Romanticism held that the imagination should determine the form and substance

M. A. Tomlan, *Historic Preservation*, DOI 10.1007/978-3-319-04975-5_1,
© Springer International Publishing Switzerland 2015

of the world, an artistic view that treasured the spontaneity, diversity, and soul of individual expression. Jean Jacques Rousseau posited that reason alone was not sufficient for life. Rather, folk traditions, legends, native languages, and songs provide a continuous source of inspiration, in many ways awakening nationalist thinking. And the Pragmatism spelled out by John Dewey and others tempered both Positivism and Romanticism. Historic preservation drew on all of these ideas to varying degrees, sometimes simultaneously.

This chapter provides a broad picture of who became involved in saving things, that is, in collecting artifacts and art objects, in preserving our built heritage, and in conserving our most important natural areas in the early years of this country. It also explains why. The early preservation advocates were better educated and wealthier than the average resident. In several instances, preservation pioneers were more progressive socially and openly questioned the prevailing attitudes and norms. In other cases, their motivations lay in a patriotic dedication to the homes of the country's founding fathers, or war heroes, or the appreciation of a regional colonial heritage (Jacobs 1966; Jokilehto 1999)[1]. The ideas of Europeans would change in the New World, just as they would evolve in the Old World.

A Culture of Collecting: Museums Get Started

The social and cultural change associated with the Enlightenment would have far-reaching impacts in Europe and the USA. New learned societies explored topics previously restricted to the aristocracy. In this context, the advantages of travel were obvious, and collecting objects for discussion and examination was an extension of historic, artistic, and scientific inquiry. Previous generations had led the way: almost all major conquerors of foreign lands brought

back mementos and military souvenirs, sometimes including plants, animals, and humans to mark their exploration.[2] Perhaps this is no surprise, given the long Christian custom of regarding relics as sacred objects, carefully housed in special cases and handled only by those anointed to touch them. Just as cathedrals often collected special religious objects, many imperial treasuries served as museums. The origins of the European museum as an institution lie in the activities of wealthy, comparatively well-educated amateurs who selected and collected fauna, flora, and artifacts of all kinds, sharing them with others of refined taste. Shared tastes and curiosity among upper-class youth in the recently discovered ruins of Greece and Italy in the late eighteenth century aroused interests in later life in a wide range of artistic and architectural fragments. Whether the objects were freely given, salvaged, purchased, or purloined, they formed part of "exotic" collections that were often secured in cabinets, accessible only to those who gained permission. In part, these private and personal treasures served to reassure the adventurer that their travel was real and substantive, even life changing. Furniture and antiques were specially arranged, while art works were mounted in long, narrow rooms, preferably with windows on one side, suitable for viewing painting and sculpture.

In the early American Republic, perhaps the most notable collection that became accessible was painter Charles Willson Peale's Philadelphia Museum, founded in 1786 and housed in what came to be known as "Independence Hall." (Fig. 1.1) It stressed natural history with more than 250 portraits, paintings, historical objects, inventions, devices, and stuffed animals (Alexander 1983). As the second largest English-speaking city in the world, Philadelphia followed the latest London fashions, but the ideas associated with collecting were already spreading among

---

[1] Both works survey the development of the field, Jacobs from the perspective of the USA and Jokilehto from a European view.

[2] Several recent studies (Patterson 1995) explore the historical evidence for the changing Euro-American ideas about "exotic" peoples. Despite the frequent use of the term "postcolonial" to describe the present, when examining the formation of museums in developing countries, often colonialism is so enduring that its meaning merits continued reinterpretation.

Fig. 1.1 Painter Charles Willson Peale's Philadelphia Museum, located in Independence Hall, was one of the best known collections of curiosities in Colonial America. Here the wonders of the natural history museum were accessible to like-minded gentry. (Library of Congress)

the gentry. The discussion rose from the parlors into the academies, and local and state historical societies throughout the East coast.[3] From the start, then, the property now revered as having witnessed the signing of the Declaration of Independence was also considered the best location for housing and explaining the objects associated with our past. Independence Hall was saved from demolition in 1813 when a citizens' petition was presented to the City fathers. Three years later the City of Philadelphia purchased the building and the square on which it sits for $70,000, although elements of the property were already lost. The initial major campaign for its first restoration occurred in 1829, when architect William Strickland attempted to replicate the original steeple, removed before the Revolution.

The embryonic development of New World archaeology provided added impetus for collecting. The goal of locating, excavating, and examining artifacts to reconstruct the development of early human societies brought to light thousands of artifacts. These, then, need cataloguing and curation, always a slow process. Thomas Jefferson seems to have been the first prominent American citizen to dig with such purposes. He investigated a mound near his home seeking to determine when, why, and how the human remains were placed in the manner they were found. Jefferson believed that different people buried the remains at different times. In spite of his views, however, there arose a number of alternative theories about the mysterious mound builders, as westward explorers reached places like Cahokia, Illinois, and found dozens of other examples of earthworks in the USA (Milner 2004, p. 873).[4]

In the mid-nineteenth century museum, sponsorship of archaeological investigations not only produced thousands of artifacts, but also some of the most significant early publications calling for preservation. In Washington D.C., the first book issued by the Smithsonian Institution, *Ancient Monuments of the Mississippi Valley*, was the archaeological work of E. G. Squier and E. H. Davis (Squier and Davis 1847) (Fig. 1.2). The survey included a wealth of information about the size, shape, construction, materials, stratigraphy, age, and possible functions of hundreds of Indian mounds and earthworks. Although most sites were located in Ohio, others in the upland and Deep South, and Upper Midwest led to widespread interest and speculation about their origin and purpose. Early excavations took the form of irregular tunnels and trenches, and lacked any horizontal or vertical controls, but the interests of the first archeological explorers centered on the artifacts as products, rather than the information that might be gained by careful attention to processes or contexts. Squier and Davis took particular pride in their work, suggesting that the mounds were sacrificial, sepulchral, temple,

[3] The Massachusetts Historical Society was the earliest (1791), followed by the New-York Historical Society (1804), and the American Antiquarian Society (1812).

[4] The Cahokia Mound is noted as being endangered in 1890, for "it has already had a narrow escape from being used for ballast on a railway." (Putnam 1890).

Fig. 1.2 Ephraim
G. Squier and Edwin
H. Davis were the
first professionals
who, when surveying
archaeological
sites in much of the
center of the country,
appealed to the public
to save and protect
historic sites, shown
in their book *Ancient
Monuments* (1848).
(Library of Congress)

ANCIENT WORKS, MARIETTA, OHIO.

and observation-related, although it remained an open question whether the artifacts suggested a truly advanced civilization. What was worthy of protection grew from the objects discovered. More important, perhaps, these authors raised issues that ethnologists would soon take further.

Squier and Davis left no doubt that these sites were endangered and needed protection. Throughout the pages of *Ancient Monuments*, they noted the destruction of many mounds and earthworks, caused by agriculture, public improvements, and Nature. Farmers seemed to disturb the graves routinely, and road improvements such as the Chillicothe Turnpike became the first of many public works projects that destroyed these and similar curious monuments.[5]

The extensive book review of *Ancient Monuments* by Charles Eliot Norton opened up a discussion among people who were concerned about the future of these artifacts. Norton is important because of his influence over the direction that preservation would take. The son of a Harvard theologian, he graduated from the same institu-

tion, briefly went into foreign trading and soon had sufficient security to pursue his archaeological interests. After traveling widely in India and Europe, and writing eloquently on a number of literary topics, in 1875 Norton became the first professor of Fine Arts in the USA, at Harvard University. He helped to shape the history of art and architecture by linking them to literature and social, political, and cultural developments (Will 2002). His familiarity with European intellectual developments has generally gone underappreciated, in both historic preservation and archaeology. His students became active in saving properties and establishing museums, and he himself played an active role in founding the Archaeological Institute of America in 1879, becoming its first President.[6] While many members of this organization preferred supporting classical studies in Europe, under Norton's leadership they also backed Adolph Bandelier's exploration of the pueblos in Pecos and other sites in the Southwest and Mexico. Meanwhile, Squier's appeals

---

[5] Squier and Davis were not as concerned about these artifacts remaining in their country of origin; their archaeological collections were purchased by a London buyer and are now held by the British Museum.

[6] Norton's chief motive in establishing the society was to advance the interest in classical studies, particularly in Athens, in part as an antidote to what was perceived as the barbarian materialism of contemporary American thinking (Turner 1999).

Fig. 1.3 Archaeologist Alice Cunningham Fletcher gathered subscriptions to purchase the Serpent Mound, in Adams County, Ohio. (Lithograph, Author's collection)

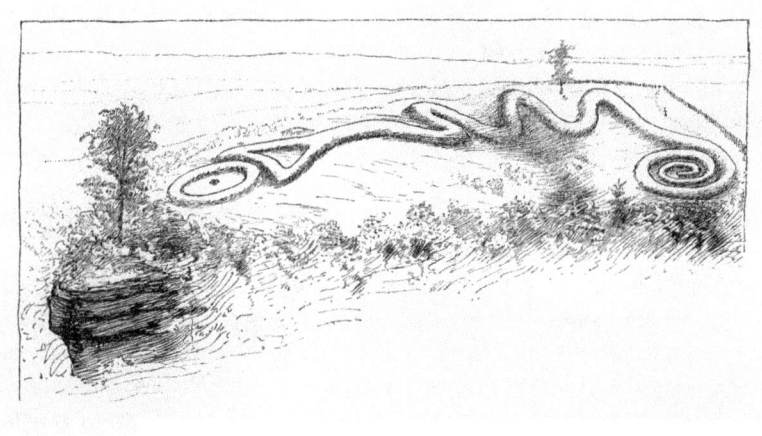

in *Ancient Monuments* remained vital. Harvard ethnologist Frederic W. Putnam recognized the 1886 initiative of archaeologist Alice Cunningham Fletcher for gathering subscriptions to purchase the Serpent Mound, in Adams County, Ohio. It was given in trust to Harvard's Peabody Museum as a 60 acre park (Putnam 1890; Mark 1988, pp. 32–34) (Fig. 1.3).

From a contemporary perspective, it is important to note that, after this initial period the trend to build museums continued with increasing fervor for decades. The museum backers in Philadelphia and Washington were only the first of many interested in art, archaeology, and natural history. As the population and wealth of Manhattan began to supersede that of other cities, it became a preeminent center of collecting. The Tammany Society may be the first organization in the country to support a museum, whose collection included a full-length portrait of George Washington, one of four painted by Gilbert Stuart (Howe 1913).[7] The American Academy of Fine Arts, established in 1802, went further by holding exhibitions of sculpture, paintings, and fine miniatures. Following the custom of relatively secure Europeans, many of its esteemed members traveled widely. For example, Ambassador to France Robert Livingston chose the Academy's first

collection of casts in Paris, and shipped them to New York in 1803. The idea of the French artist's salon was soon duplicated. The New-York Historical Society, founded in 1804, collected not only historical documents but also drawings and paintings, again, tending to extol European fashions in art. In part as a deliberate attempt to feature American work more aggressively, in 1825 the Historical Society gave birth to the National Academy of Design. Remarkably enough, by the late 1840s, several thousand schoolchildren were visiting the facilities in a mock Venetian palace with suitable galleries, one of the first new buildings in the USA deliberately conceived for public display of art (Howe 1913). Temporary exhibits are also worthy of note. The Crystal Palace Exhibition in Manhattan, held in 1853, though it was destroyed by fire a few years later, provided a broad nave, aisles, and galleries filled with art and manufactured goods from all corners of the globe, including 675 sculptures and paintings.

The contemporary art museums in New York, Boston, Philadelphia, Cincinnati, Chicago, and St. Louis sprang up in the years from 1870 to 1890. In New York, the idea to form a national institution and gallery of art originated with John Jay, grandson of the first Chief Justice of the US Supreme Court, who turned for help to members of the Union League Club. William Cullen Bryant and George Fiske Comfort of Princeton outlined the scheme in 1869, and the new Metropolitan Museum of Art was incorporated the following April (Hibberd 1980; Tomkins 1970). In 1870,

---

[7] The Society was established before April 30, 1787. Although that museum did not survive, a portion of it was housed later in Phineaus T. Barnum's Museum of Wonders (Howe 1913, p. 5).

when the Historical Society did not seize the initiative to move to Central Park, the newly formed Metropolitan Museum took its place. Although it took 10 years before the new building was ready for occupancy, the collections grew with casts and models of Egyptian, Greek, Roman, and Gothic monuments. The Art Institute in Chicago, organized in 1879, was one of the only early art museums open to the public and free of charge on Sunday afternoons and evenings. Shortly after the turn of the century, the list of notable early art museums grew to include Detroit, Washington, Pittsburgh, Providence, Springfield, Worcester, Buffalo, Toledo, Milwaukee, Syracuse, and Minneapolis.

The widespread study of art was in its infancy, but collectors, curators, taxidermists, and artists often worked largely behind closed doors to create museums, visual libraries to excite the relatively well-educated visitor. In the latter half of the nineteenth century in the USA, the fashions of Paris and London seem to have prevailed in the museum world, with an emphasis on the high style rather than the homemade or handmade.

In this context, it is important to keep in mind the tremendous changes in thinking made by the widespread adoption of the common school system (Cubberley 1934) and the rise of the private and public library in accelerating the culture of collecting. Field exercises expanded the chalk and slate exercises in the classroom in almost every village, town, and city, where young boys were sent out to collect samples of rocks, woods, and insects, while girls sought dozens of seeds, herbs, and fabric samples, which were mounted and labeled in displays. Mechanics' institutes and literary clubs reinforced these activities, as more ideas about archaeology, history, and art history were introduced soon after reading, writing, and arithmetic. The tendency to boast about recent inventions, scientific and mechanical improvements spurred an exhibition fever, and those collections, too, became part of museums. The first museum to establish a branch exclusively for children was the Brooklyn Institute of Arts and Sciences, established in 1899, reportedly enjoying over 100,000 visitors per year (Zueblin 1916, pp. 250–251). At the same time children's books

were available that explained the reasons for saving historic properties, hoping that by interesting boys and girls, the adults might become involved.[8]

Organizing for Historic Preservation

Although isolated examples of efforts to preserve buildings occurred in the early nineteenth century, and museums provided an appropriate immediate use, by the 1850s the number of structures of historical interest began to rise and the pressure for commemoration increased. In some cases, petitions to the government would be successful, but in most cases, the men and women who cared would first mount campaigns for popular support.

Historical connections to the life of George Washington held considerable attention. As Commander in Chief of the Continental Army, Washington spent 16 and a half months in Newburgh, New York in a farmhouse overlooking the Hudson. The Jonathan Hasbrouck House, dating from 1722 according to the date cut in stone over the east door, was little transformed by Washington, but his stay there is well documented. When the property passed from Hasbrouck's descendents by default to the State of New York, the county commissioners were forced to sell the property. One of them, Andrew J. Caldwell, stirred by the connections to the first President and frustrated by the local residents' lack of interest, presented the case to Governor Hamilton Fish. In turn, Fish appealed to the state legislature, citing that the associations were more important than "dollars and cents," and urged that this Revolutionary War site receive special treatment. The dedication and opening to the public of the country's first house museum took place on July 4, 1850 (Anthony 1927; Caldwell 1887; Corning 1950) (Fig. 1.4).

---

[8] Laura Bride Powers, author of *The Story of the Old Missions of California* (1893), produced a children's edition, *Historic Tales of the Old Missions for Boys and Girls* (1902). These were used in the San Francisco public school system.

Fig. 1.4 George Washington spent sixteen and a half months in the Jonathan Hasbrouck House (1722), in Newburgh, NY. Concern for the future of the property surfaced by the 1830s; by default it fell to the State of New York in 1849 and the following year it became the first publicly owned historic site in the country. (Author's photograph)

MOUNT VERNON.

Fig. 1.5 Saving Mt. Vernon, the home of President George Washington, was the passion of Ann Pamela Cunningham, one of hundreds of visitors stopping to see the ruins of the plantation. (Lithograph, Author's collection)

In Virginia, the story was remarkably different because the state legislature showed little interest in saving Mt. Vernon, the home of President Washington (Fig. 1.5). While on a steamboat trip on the Potomac River, Ann Pamela Cunningham became alarmed at the neglect the plantation suffered and set in motion the crusade to save it (Thane 1966; King 1929). Miss Cunningham wrote a letter published in 1853 in the *Charleston Mercury* calling upon the "Ladies of the South" to rescue the property because it was already apparent the men governing the commonwealth in Richmond, and the men in Congress would not rise to the occasion. In a period when white women were only beginning to voice their concerns about the need to hold property in their own name, the idea that an organization such as the Mt. Vernon Ladies Association of the Union (MVLA) would be the owner and curator of Washington's home was, to some, a bit of lunacy. Nevertheless, MVLA members would organize with vice regents in every state and began a national campaign to save Mt. Vernon. True, most of the women associated with this project were better educated and connected than many, but the well-coordinated nation-wide campaign was the most impressive preservation effort of the nineteenth century.[9] Remarkably, the government played no direct role in supporting this historic site.

Just as important, MVLA provided an organizational template that other women followed. In Nashville, for example, Mrs. Andrew Jackson, wife of the grandson of President Andrew Jackson, wrote to Miss Cunningham for advice on how to create a similar organization to care for The Hermitage, the home of Andrew and Rachel Jackson (Dorris 1915; Hosmer 1965).[10] (Fig. 1.6)

Although early historic preservation activities in the USA first became widely recognized from a pride in the political accomplishments of our country's founders, not all of the efforts were successful. In Boston, John Hancock's home was demolished on Beacon Hill in 1863. Although Hancock had intended to bequeath the house to the Commonwealth, the value of the land for re-

Fig. 1.6 The Hermitage, the home of President Andrew Jackson, was in the hands of the State of Tennessee before an organization arose to protect and care for it. It ranks among the first "friends group" to help a government-owned historic site. (Author's photograph)

development adjacent to the State House spelled its doom. The city's Common Council appointed a committee that recommended the house be moved, and some pledges were secured to make it a reality, but there were insufficient funds to complete the project. In a community well aware of the role its heroes played in attaining independence, the house haunted the minds of architects, historians, and patrons of the arts for years to come. In part, this is due to the measured drawings made in anticipation of the demolition by the young architect John Hubbard Sturgis, and the published memorial tribute to the house by prominent local architect Arthur Gilman, and the inspiration it served for subsequent Colonial Revival designs (Floyd 1979). Years later, a replica of the Hancock House would be used to represent the Commonwealth at the World's Columbian Exposition in Chicago. However, as often happens, the loss raised interest in the next campaign, the preservation of the Old South Meetinghouse, as well as efforts to save the Charles Bulfinch-designed Massachusetts "new" State House and the old Boston State House.

Mention of the effort to save the Old South Meetinghouse is important for at least three reasons (Fig. 1.7). First, it was a significant early preservation success story and provided a model for other campaigns, some outside of New England. Second, the discussions revolved around

---

[9] The role of Edward Everett, preacher and tireless lecturer, should not be overlooked. His lecture on the character of Washington, revised in various forms in 139 venues across the nation, raised nearly $500 per appearance, making it possible for the Association to secure the property.

[10] Hosmer's work remains the basis for almost all of the historic preservation movement's nineteenth and early twentieth century history, a testament to his thorough research. For example, he noted that the cases are not identical because the state of Tennessee already owned The Hermitage, whereas Mt. Vernon was not purchased by the Commonwealth of Virginia.

Old South Church, Boston.

Fig. 1.7 The Old South Meetinghouse, Boston, MA, was the first major urban success story in New England, with women organizing the necessary political and financial support to undertake the re-use of a redundant religious property. (Stereoview, author's collection)

the role a redundant "church" could play in the community, which led to the development of an acceptable alternative use. As we will see in upcoming chapters, this remains an ongoing issue. Third, like Mt. Vernon, it demonstrated that while men might provide public leadership, women would play a major role in saving the property by providing almost all of the financial support.

After the threat to "Old South" was recognized, the first step in the campaign was assembling a history of the site, in this case published to benefit the Old South Fund. The structure, which dated from 1730, gained considerable importance as being the venue for the most animated town meetings during the Revolutionary War era, when other buildings could not hold the enormous crowds. The history also recalled the petitions drawn up, the orations delivered, and the desecration of the church during the siege of Boston by the British, who burned the pulpit and pews, spread dirt on the floor, and turned it into a riding school. General Washington viewed its poor condition and commented that it was "strange that the British, who so venerated their own churches, should thus have desecrated ours" (History 1876, p. 68). That said, the location was growing noisier and more crowded, some members of the congregation wanted to move to a more fashionable location nearer their suburban homes, and the opportunity to use the structure to address other purposes arose in the aftermath of the Great Fire of 1871, which destroyed the immediate area. Although the dispute between the majority bent on relocating and the minority who wished to continue the religious use of the structure was brought to court, the justices considered the conflict an internal issue to the Old South Society. The congregation proceeded with the plans to auction-off the building and contents. At the 11th hour, in July 1876, Bostonians rallied at a meeting led off with an appeal by abolitionist preacher Wendell Philips, an event that marked the US Centennial. That gathering appointed a committee chaired by the Governor to raise funds and secure the building's future. Boston women did most of the canvassing for funds, and the wealthiest woman in New England, Mary Hemenway, anonymously offered $100,000 to the effort. While it was a few years before the property's future was secure, the controversy diminished.

Fig. 1.8 Although the first preservation efforts were dedicated to saving properties for their historical important, aesthetics began to play a major role with the campaign waged by Boston architects to save the Massachusetts State House. (Author's photograph)

Along with this historical recognition of sites, a rising interest in artistic affairs was evident in the greater Boston community. This is closely associated with the Romanticism of John Ruskin, and supported by commercial publishing ties to England. If the number of imprints of Ruskin's books in the USA is any indication, no other nineteenth century European author was so widely read. To Ruskin, structures were chiefly artifacts to be protected and the characteristics they acquired over time should be safeguarded, not removed to achieve a stylistic unity or to evoke a particular period (Ruskin 1849). Ruskin decried the idea of "restoration," particularly the practice of scraping down the walls to reveal the stone beneath, destroying the look of age. Given the nearly 40 year correspondence between Ruskin and Harvard Professor Charles Eliot Norton, it was no wonder that Harvard students were among the first to believe that by studying the beauty of architecture and art, truth could be found and moral virtue could be reclaimed (Bradley and Ousby 1987). The first successful organized effort to save a major government property for its aesthetic importance was the rescue of the Massachusetts State House, a controversy that raged in the mid-1890s, largely due to the advocacy of the Boston Society of Architects (Holleran 1998, pp. 135–150; Fig. 1.8). Two years later, the American Institute of Architects renovated

the 1801 Tayloe House, called the "Octagon," in Washington, D.C. for their national headquarters. It lays claim to being the oldest house museum dedicated to architecture in the country. Just as important, the discussion about the future of this property brought preservation issues to the attention of architecture professionals throughout the country[11] (Fig. 1.9).

Outside of academic and professional circles, an increasing number of periodicals carried these aesthetic ideas, where they became widely reinterpreted by dozens of artists, architects, historians, poets, novelists, and social commentators. Magazines such as *Appleton's, Harper's, Scribner's,* and the *Century,* produced for the parlors of the rising middle-class, spurred women to participate in a wide range of artistic activities (Tomlan 1983, pp. 265–266). Travel, romance, and local history were at the core of *Appleton's* "Picturesque America" series, with most of these "wayside relics," such as the old Van Rensselaer House in Greenbush, located only a short carriage drive away from Manhattan. Benson Lossing's sketching and writing gave way to Martha

---

[11] Thanks to the persuasiveness of architect Charles F. McKim, the property was not only secured, but paid for by 1907. To judge by the Proceedings of the Conventions, however, it was by no means clear for years how the building would be treated.

Fig. 1.9 The American Institute of Architects adopted the 1801 Tayloe House, called the "Octagon," in Washington, D.C. for their national headquarters. This site lays claim to being the oldest house museum dedicated to architecture in the USA. (Author's photograph)

Lamb's "Historic Homes of America," later collected in a book. Meanwhile, the growing suburban readership of *Scribner's* first learned from Norton about the "Lack of Old Homes in America" in 1889, just as they read a few months later that "It was in the old historic homes of downtown that the tenement was born of ignorance and greed…" in an article on "How the Other Half Lives" by Jacob Riis. Progressive era journalism would build on these themes, differentiating the old with the new, the high class with the working class living conditions.

Just as the professionals and the public became aware of Ruskin, they also learned about William Morris's advocacy of the Arts and Crafts Movement, which emphasized spiritual unity and functional sincerity, rejecting the mechanical repetition so often associated with the factory, and celebrating the worker as artisan. In England, Charles Robert Ashbee's Arts and Crafts workshop, the Guild of Handicraft, was perhaps the most radical example of the movement, for it emphasized the needs of the worker, rather than the consumer. In a similar fashion, artistic and social reformers in the USA began to embrace a fusion of art, labor, and social relations, often reinforced by historical references.

It is important to remember that, despite a vigorous amount of preservation advocacy, no systematic methods existed to protect historic and architectural landmarks. In England, the Society for the Protection of Ancient Buildings, founded in 1877 by William Morris and his Pre-Raphaelite colleagues, provided a forceful lobby for the rescue and proper repair of medieval churches and some secular buildings that were in imminent danger, but the group did not survey or acquire structures. The only government-protected sites were the 68 prehistoric monuments specified in the Ancient Monuments Protection Act of 1882. When Ashbee's Watch Committee began in 1894, it was the first attempt at surveying London's wealth of historic buildings (Ashbee 1900).[12] The English National Trust for Places of Historic Interest or Natural Beauty was established in the same year, noteworthy for becoming the first organization in that country to acquire, hold, and preserve old buildings of many types, and unspoiled scenery. These included medieval half-timbered houses, guild and market halls, and scenic stretches in the Lake District and Cornwall. With only 200 members, however, the Trust had limited personnel and financial support. As will be explained further below, to expand its support, the group proposed establishing local committees in all of the former and then current colonies. The honorary secretary of the National Trust traveled to the USA in 1899, and Charles Ashbee followed in 1900, all with an idea of

---

[12] The Watch Committee can be seen as the forerunner of the Survey of London, now available online.

forming a corresponding "American Council" (Ashbee 1901; Crawford 2005).

The 1876 Centennial Exhibition in Philadelphia helped spur a renewal of interest in the study of colonial history, as more local historical societies formed. Journalism dedicated to biography and history, such as the San Jose *Pioneer*, a monthly magazine established in 1877, provided additional material. The Daughters of the American Revolution alone numbered 45,000 members (Hall 1903, pp. 284–295). Like the MVLA, private organizations memorialized colonial-era heroes. The Sons of the American Revolution, founded in 1889, the Daughters of the American Revolution founded in 1890, and the National Society of Colonial Dames established in 1891 (Hunter 1991, p. 3), all focused their attention on the role of pioneer ancestors or Revolutionary War heroes, erecting monuments and improving cemeteries.[13] By one estimate, at least one hundred thousand people were members of two dozen national historical organizations by 1903, not including children.

The western portion of the country, although more recently settled by European and Asian immigrants, was almost immediately involved in historical activity. The first preservation efforts arose in California, a state that initially appears to have wanted to ignore the original Mexican land grants and the Indian land claims, and to overlook the role of the missions in providing any social structure. By the 1870s, of the 21 great missions built in California, only four remained intact, the others having suffered earthquakes, fire, and neglect (Weinberg 1974). When repairs took place through the late 1880s, it was simply by the padres involved who wanted to make the properties available for worship. The work of Father Angelo D. Casanova at Carmel's Mission San Carlos Borromeo highlighted the need for a broader program of mission restoration (Know-

land 1941, p. 4; Fig. 1.10). Seeing the need, the novelist Robert Louis Stevenson wrote compellingly in the local press about the problem and sparked a fundraising campaign (Hata 1992, p. 258). Helen Hunt Jackson's advocacy for the equal treatment of Indians in the Southwest also brought attention to the Spanish heritage of the region, most famously in her novel *Ramona*, published in 1884, which led to an annual pageant (Phillips 2003, p. 4). The Los Angeles city librarian Tessa L. Kelso assembled and promoted stereopticon exhibits of the mission sites and founded the Association for the Preservation of Missions in 1888 (Hata 1992; James 1927, pp. 383–384; Thompson 2001, p. 182; Fiske 1975). Although this group lost initiative when its leader took another job, the idea remained and provided a platform for Charles F. Lummis, best known for his tramp from Chillicothe, Ohio to Los Angeles, to relaunch the advocacy effort in the Landmarks Club of Southern California. Its most notable repairs were at the Mission San Juan Capistrano and the Mission San Fernando Rey, under the direction of Los Angeles architect Arthur B. Benton. Lummis's position as editor of the low-priced *Land of Sunshine*, a Chamber of Commerce-supported monthly periodical, brought considerable attention to the "preserve the missions" crusade, especially outside of California.[14] Much of what Lummis wrote is almost mythical, but he was effective. Just as important, while his Methodist upbringing taught him to disregard Indian religions as superstitious, his experience living among the Pueblos in New Mexico led him to appreciate how their society worked, and to decry the government's approach in "re-educating" them. It also allowed Lummis to compare the prevailing Protestant view with the traditional approach of the Catholic missionaries, who were more sympathetic to tribal culture, and led the missions to be more than a place of worship.

---

[13] The Civil War initiated a new interest in war commemoration. New York was the first state in the country to recognize Memorial Day officially, with the village of Waterloo, in Seneca County, claiming to be the holiday's birthplace.

[14] Established in 1890, it claimed to hold "The largest certified regular circulation of any kind, but one, in Southern California," with 7468 copies. (Rowell 1894, p. 117).

Fig. 1.10 Opening the grave of Father Junipero Serra at Mission San Carlos Borromeo, in Carmel, CA, on July 3, 1882 was an event of considerable importance. Early mission stabilization projects were often in the hands of the padres left in charge. (Powers, *Old Monterey*, 1934, opp. 204; Author's collection)

Similar to the fashion in which patriotic civic associations developed in the East, in 1886 the Native Sons of the Golden West proposed to honor James W. Marshall, the man whose discovery of gold led to the fever that transformed the West. The Sons also launched the successful initiative to preserve Sacramento's decaying Sutter's Fort, reconstructed in 1894, and in campaigning for the preservation of the Custom's House in Monterey, the city where Father Junipero Serra first landed and the location where the Constitution was drafted under which the state joined the Union (Knowland 1941, pp. 106, 157; Figs. 1.11 and 1.12)

California's best-known preservation advocates during the early twentieth century were John Knowland and Laura Bride Powers. Knowland's activities with the Native Sons, which he joined in 1891, led him to establish and lead a historic landmarks committee to survey the state and determine the condition of its remaining historic properties so as "to perpetuate the memory of men and events intimately associated with the romantic history of California." (Knowland 1941, p. vi). Powers is best known for her 1893 book on California missions, but she also convened an important 1902 meeting in San Francisco of representatives of the Society of California Pioneers, Pioneer Women, Daughters of California Pioneers, Women's Press Association, the California Club, and other groups to form the California Landmarks League. She served as secretary and Knowland became the first president of the League, a remarkable alliance at the time. He went on to serve as state legislator, Congressman, chair of the State Park Commission, and, beginning in 1915, became the publisher of the *Oakland Tribune* (Wyatt 1982).

Fig. 1.11 The Native Sons of the Golden West launched the successful initiative to preserve Sacramento's decaying Sutter's Fort, reconstructed in 1894. ("Sutter's Fort," View of 1857, Author's collection)

Fig. 1.12 The campaign for the preservation of the Custom's House in Monterey also began in the late nineteenth century and continued until it was restored in 1905. (Historic American Buildings Survey, Library of Congress)

People, Parks, Monuments, and Antiquities

The differences between preservation activity in the largely rural South, the urbanizing East—so often concerned with civic improvement and parkways in an era of Progressive reform—and the relatively small but rapidly growing cities in the vast open spaces of the West left many ques-

tions for organizers. Some were skeptical about how the power of the government could stretch to recognize, designate, and preserve property in trust (Lee 2000). Yet, the connections across the country were beginning to be made by a few far-sighted individuals.

The western wilderness was widely viewed as a region to be explored, logged, mined, ranched, and farmed. Forests and mineral rights were of

Fig. 1.13 John Muir's advocacy led to a relationship with President Theodore Roosevelt that gave added public weight to the views of early conservationists. Here the two men are at Yosemite. (Library of Congress)

considerable value so that, only by getting the members of Congress to agree that some characteristics merited special consideration could any major area of land be reserved, and perhaps serve as a national monument or park. Many critics observed that Europe was far ahead in setting aside parks and antiquities (Robinson 1903, pp. 130–131).

The special nature of the scenic vistas and landscapes led to the reservation of the Yosemite Valley, including the Mariposa Grove of Giant Sequoias. Congress recognized the unique characteristics of the place and deeded it to the State of California to be used as a park. Like the reporters, painters, photographers and so many visitors before him, landscape architect Frederick Law Olmsted, co-designer of Central Park in New York City, became enamored of the place when he first visited in 1863 (Roper 1974). He and I. W. Raymond, among others, petitioned Congress for the creation of a public park, and the bill was signed by President Abraham Lincoln on June 30, 1864. Olmsted subsequently served as the chair of the state management commission.

In succeeding years, the difficulty defending the park against prospectors, poachers, shepherds and their "hoofed locusts," led others, including the celebrated naturalist John Muir to enlist Robert Underwood Johnson, the well-connected editor of the *Century* magazine in New York, to push for added federal protection, which occurred in 1890 (Ise 1961, pp. 59–61; Fig. 1.13).

The campaign to designate Yosemite as a national park came in the wake of the creation of Yellowstone National Park in 1872. Located in Wyoming Territory, Yellowstone became the first reserve in the country to be formally set aside with explicit provisions for protecting a remarkable amount of land: 1 million acres containing hundreds of geysers, hot water ponds, rivers, and abundant wildlife.[15] Exploration by scouts and various explorers led to a government-sponsored

---

[15] Mackinac Island, designated the second national park in 1875, caused Congress to reconsider the wisdom of allowing the states to manage federally designated reserves because the site was largely serving wealthy summer vacationers.

expedition to Yellowstone under the leadership of Henry D. Washburn, Surveyor General of Montana Territory, in 1870. With a military escort to protect 19 relatively wealthy and politically well-connected advocates, the party traveled deep into the southeast portion of what would be the park. Subsequently, bank president Nathaniel P. Langford delivered a series of lectures to press the case in Washington, D.C., including one that attracted the attention of Dr. Ferdinand V. Hayden, head of the US Geological Survey. Having gained sufficient backing, the following year Langford and Hayden thoroughly surveyed Yellowstone with prominent geologists, zoologists, botanists, photographer William H. Jackson and artist Thomas Moran (Senate 1871, 1872). In addition to the specimens and notes, the romantic images of the landscapes emphasized the special character of the place.

The legislation to set aside Yellowstone called for preservation of the forests, fish and wildlife, and natural wonders, retaining their natural conditions, while giving to the Secretary of the Interior the discretion to grant leases to accommodate visitors, and the responsibility of managing the roads and bridle paths. These provisions became the template for all other parks.

With increased exploration and railroad travel to the West, the ruins on federal land and on Indian reservations began to receive increased Anglo attention. Occupied for centuries by native peoples, the buildings and fields of previous tribes remained intact. Remarkably enough, the Spanish explorers seeking gold found them relatively uninteresting. However, the explorations of Adolph Bandelier, mentioned earlier, alerted many to the condition of the ancient remains and the threat posed by treasure hunters. In fact, the New England Historic Genealogical Society turned to one of its former trustees, Massachusetts Senator George Frisbie Hoar, to present a petition on the Senate floor. He called attention to the ruins in the territories of Arizona and New Mexico, citing Bandelier's belief that the "ancient Spanish cathedral of Pecos" was a building older than any standing within the 13 original States (Lange and Riley 2008, pp. 27–28). Its graves were being robbed and its timber used for campfires, sold as relics, and used in stable construction.

Although Hoar was unsuccessful in moving the Senate to take action, the problem received more attention and Bandelier's work was increasingly attracting notice. In Boston, yet another project led to the establishment of the first federally designated archaeological reservation. The woman who was so important in the campaign to save Old South Meetinghouse, Mary Hemenway, sponsored an expedition intended to be a comprehensive exploration of Pueblo culture in the Americas. Frank H. Cushing, of the Bureau of Ethnography at the Smithsonian, had already visited the Zuni and Hopi tribes. Enlisted as the leader of the expedition, he wrote newspaper reports that brought widespread attention to the roofless four-story great house, known as Casa Grande, located southeast of Phoenix (Fig. 1.14).

Again, at the request of 14 prominent members of the New England Historic Genealogical Society, in 1889 Massachusetts Senator George F. Hoar presented a petition to set aside the Casa Grande ruins. Congress agreed, and President Benjamin Harrison established the Casa Grande Ruins Reservation in 1892 (Rothman 1985, 1989).

As remarkable as the site was, the establishment of a single reservation made it even more obvious that many other sites remained completely unprotected. Looting and vandalism increased, perversely stimulated by the growth and the establishment of more natural history museums. The Peabody Museum at Harvard and the Smithsonian Institution in Washington, D.C. employed field explorer Edward Palmer to collect artifacts. Nativist pride labeled very negatively any explorers who collected for foreign museums (Jeter 1999). In fact, Smithsonian Secretary Spencer F. Baird pushed to collect material before English, French, and German museums had the chance to scoop up and export Indian work. Thousands of artifacts changed hands, bringing attention to the collecting habits of Easterners. This came to a head with the activities of the ranching Wetherill family in the famous Chaco Canyon case, in New Mexico. This was widely reported in the newspapers from 1900 to 1907, when it came to light that the wealthy philanthropic collectors Benjamin Talbot Hyde and Frederick Hyde of New York acquired material

Fig. 1.14 In Arizona, Casa Grande Ruins Reservation was set aside in 1892 primarily through the actions of the New England Historic Genealogical Society. The large communal settlements of the Ancestral People of the Salt and Gila Rivers and their Great Houses were largely gone by the time the Spanish arrived in the late 1600s. The National Park Service erected the protective shelter in 1932. (Author's photograph)

from the Wetherills, taken from 198 rooms and kivas at Pueblo Bonito, to donate to the American Museum of Natural History.

The growth of interest in American Indians and American Indian artifacts accelerated with the 1893 World's Columbian Exposition in Chicago, where thousands of artifacts were displayed, and ultimately donated to the Field Museum in that city. About the same time, popular journalism carried news of the vandalism at sites in Mesa Verde, resulting in the Colorado Cliff-Dwellings Association voicing its concerns about the eventual future of these sites (Fig. 1.15).

The specter of the Wetherill family's activity in the Southwest was probably the most important impetus for the consensus around preserving the ruins. Perhaps the most forceful single advocate was the Reverend Henry Mason Baum, former editor of the *American Church Review*, who established a new organization, The Records of the Past Exploration Society. He assembled the foremost scholars and professionals of the day, facing down Wetherill, and enthusiastically testifying before Congress. While Baum's forcefulness was helpful, the western archaeologist Edgar L. Hewitt quietly went about mapping many of the significant sites and gathering the support in the Department of Interior and the Congressional committees necessary to make a difference. Hewett's bill, "An Act for the Preservation of

Fig. 1.15 Mesa Verde and other similar sites became the focus of the Colorado Cliff Dwelling Association, eventually leading to their acquisition and the management of the National Park Service. (Author's photograph)

American Antiquities," first presented at a joint meeting of the American Anthropological Association and the Archaeological Institute of America in December 1905, had broad appeal, and quickly became law (Rothman 1989, pp. 34–51).

Good intentions were not enough, however. The stipulations of the 1906 Antiquities Act that permits be required and some archaeological expertise be demonstrated before excavation was approved went ignored for years. The undesignated, less spectacular sites still in private hands remained completely unprotected. With growing recognition, the more pressing concern became the need to unify the approach to managing a growing number of national parks and national monuments. This led to the creation of the National Park Service (NPS) in 1916 (Albright and Cahn 1985). Landscape architect Frederick Law Olmsted and J. Harland McFarland, a key advocate in the American Civic Association, played an enormous role in enlisting the needed support and, with the establishment of the NPS, the government had its first federal level preservation agency (Huth 1957; Roper 1974).

While the Antiquities Act was legislation that applied to sites across the country, it was primarily a federal response to a regional problem. The creation of an organization dedicated to preserving sites of natural importance in the East had a parallel regional impact. The Boston landscape architect Charles Eliot led this effort. In the research he conducted for a series of articles on "Old American Country Seats," Eliot provided the outline of a plan for preserving "fine bits of natural scenery" in the midst of the growing suburbs (Eliot 1903, p. 239; Moga 2009). Having studied in Europe, collaborated with Frederick Law Olmsted, and worked with several New England communities, Eliot recognized the importance of creating parks for the enjoyment and good health of the general public. Backed by a distinguished group of academics and professionals, the Commonwealth's legislature passed the act and the governor signed the bill in May 1891, which allowed the Trustees of Public Reservations to acquire real estate by gift or purchase, acting in the spirit of a public trust. Virginia Wood, a 20-acre diversified woodland in Stoneham, Massachusetts, was the first to be accepted, and five more parks were set aside in the next decade. The organization spurred other communities, most notably Boston, to expand its Metropolitan Park Commission (Eliot 1890, 1903, pp. 316–350).

The establishment of the Trustees of Public Reservations also inspired Andrew Haswell Green, President of the Commissioners of the State Reservation at Niagara Falls, to address the New York State legislature on the subject of preserving natural and historic sites (Fig. 1.16). To get the broadest possible perspective, Green studied the activities of the National Trust in England and the Monuments Historiques in France. This led him to propose a union of natural conservation and preservation interests in an organization composed of individuals that could own and manage property.[16] The American Scenic and Historic Preservation Society (ASHPS) was formed in 1895, with this remarkably broad scope. It promoted the preservation of properties with scenic beauty, archaeological or historic interest.

As a civic leader, Andrew Haswell Green was without peer (Ford 1913). He was the Central Park Commissioner most influential in guiding its development and played a significant role in locating the Bronx Zoo. In addition to his advocacy on behalf of the ASHPS to further protect Niagara Falls, Green fought to save threatened historic forts and battlefield sites, and to create the Pallisades, Riverside, and Morningside Parks. The most important local project of ASHPS was Fraunces Tavern in lower Manhattan, most celebrated for being the site where Washington bade farewell to his troops on December 4, 1783. The building had undergone several significant changes. Mrs. M. F. Pierce is credited for first proposing its restoration, laboring unsuccessfully since 1894 to save the structure. When the plans for a skyscraper on the site became public, she appealed to Green and they established a Women's Auxiliary to the Society (Pierce 1901). Only a bird's-eye view of the building existed to guide the architect William Mersereau, showing a gambrel roofed structure; he used 15,000 bricks imported from Holland in his reconstruction, one of the most complete at the time[17] (Fig. 1.17).

As suggested above, in the late nineteenth century aesthetic criteria were the concern of only a comparatively minor segment of the population,

---

[16] There is ample evidence to show the organization was also aware of developments in Italy, Greece, and Turkey, and much of the historical understanding about preservation and conservation during the nineteenth century dates from this research.

[17] William H. Mersereau also worked on the restorations of Westover, on the James River, Virginia, on Sunnyside, in Tarrytown, N.Y., and on Old Swedes Church, in Wilmington, Delaware (Schuyler 1908; Pierce 1901; Drowne 1925).

Fig. 1.16 Andrew Haswell Green, President of the Commissioners of the State Reservation at Niagara Falls, led the early campaign to save this natural wonder from an increasing amount of industrialization that sought to divert the river's water for power. This *Harper's Weekly* advertisement is one of several that influenced the public and built political backing. (*Harper's Weekly*, 1884, Author's collection)

Fig. 1.17 Fraunces Tavern, in lower Manhattan, is the site where Washington bade farewell to his troops on December 4, 1783. The early twentieth century restoration by the American Scenic and Historic Preservation Society is now interpreted as part of the site's history. (Author's photograph)

generally the civic-minded business leaders who held City Beautiful ideals. Despite the rising interest in colonial architecture, in general, archi-tects played a minor role in preservation. In New York, a battle raged over the proposed demolition of the old City Hall to make way for a new municipal building and the newly established Municipal Arts Society, concerned with the aesthetic improvement of the city, supported the idea of an architectural competition. Unfortunately, the effort failed to produce a consensus regarding the future of the site (Gilmartin 1995, pp. 331–332). Perhaps more important, the ASHPS was the first organization that could claim to have connections nation-wide, recording preservation activities that stretched from Massachusetts to California, although its board membership was largely based on the East Coast.

By contrast, as both architect and advocate, Charles R. Ashbee's turn of the century lectures for the National Trust and his itinerary throughout the northeast USA are very revealing because they show how personal connections made a difference. Ashbee presented English architecture as the symbol of a legacy shared by all English speaking people, so that churches, abbeys, and

Elizabethan estates belonged to British-descended Americans as much as to the residents of England. In his view, the American Constitution was an extension of the revolution begun with the Magna Carta and any former political differences between the countries should be minimal in light of the greater goal of preserving a common aesthetic heritage. His call for help was answered positively with the establishment in Concord, Massachusetts of the first local chapter of the National Trust's American Council. The host of societies and clubs that Ashbee subsequently visited in Boston is lengthy, but it is important to emphasize the introductions and endorsements he gained. These included such prominent thinkers as abolitionist, suffragist, and temperance activist Colonel Thomas Wentworth Higginson; Miss Alice Longfellow, daughter of the poet and former Vice Regent for Massachusetts in the Mount Vernon Ladies' Association; and landscape architects Frederick Law Olmstead, Jr. and Warren H. Manning, both of whom offered support on behalf of the American Park and Outdoor Art Association. Philadelphia offered an even greater sense of aesthetic civic mindedness, and, in his remarks at the Civic Club, he openly admired the effective organization of women in American society, indicating that the English would do well to follow their example. In New York, Ashbee solicited Columbia University President Seth Low, diplomat John Bigelow, and financier J. Pierpont Morgan. He lectured at Barnard College, the National Society of Colonial Dames, and the American Scenic and Historic Preservation Society, where he found a friend in its president Andrew Greene (Benjamin 1989).

As Ashbee traveled to the industrial centers of the Midwest, he shifted ground from the concern for a common English heritage to civic aesthetics. In his view, municipal progress fostered historic preservation and was measured by the treatment of the arts in museums, libraries, clubs, and a wide variety of educational and cultural institutions. This emphasis found considerable interest and support. In Cincinnati, he addressed the Municipal Arts Society, while in Pittsburgh he spoke to the Academy of Arts and Sciences at the Carnegie Institute. In Chicago, Ashbee lectured

on ten separate occasions, meeting leaders of the Art Institute, Architectural Club, Art Association, Antiquarian Society, Christian Socialist League, Hull House Lewis Institute, Municipal Art League, Public School Art Society, and University of Chicago. Prominent philanthropist Charles Hutchinson, educator John Dewey, and architect Frank Lloyd Wright all pledged their support. In short, Ashbee's tour fused together the Romanticism of historic preservation with the Positivist civic improvement and progressive era thinking.

Ashbee's views did encounter criticism, however, particularly in Chicago, because there his discussion was rather high-toned, even condescending (Fig. 1.18). It was not clear to some American civic leaders that an emphasis on history provided a viable approach to improvement but representatives of 15 local organizations pledged support to the idea that they could find places of beauty and historical interest in the city (Chicago 1900). From a twenty-first century perspective, it appears that the well-educated and nouveux riche formed a social union, a clique, to press for civic improvement and often employed City Beautiful ideals, recalling the past to foster an "American renaissance." One of the most well-known Chicago philosophers, John Dewey, held that human understanding was more based on day-to-day experience, and that was ever changing. At the same time, for those who became involved in political life, a political pragmatism tempered their aesthetic concerns. This pragmatism was often missing from Ashbee's lectures. Social theory and practice had to be modified to meet the conditions at hand, a position that many preservationists would adopt in the years ahead.

Even in Boston, pragmatic solutions would arise with new preservation leadership. Born of Brahmin stock, William Sumner Appleton enjoyed a considerable amount of privilege. Educated at Harvard, he attended the classes offered by Charles Eliot Norton, George Santayana, and a number of other prominent teachers. His education was furthered by travel to India and Europe, and his security assured by a trust fund. At 29, he joined two older men in the formation of an organization to raise money to make a permanent patriotic memorial of Paul Revere's home

during the Revolutionary War (Fig. 1.19). What
began as a pietistic initiative, to rescue the house
in North Square from its tenement condition and
turn it into a museum, soon became an exercise
in restoration. With the support of Appleton and
his colleagues, architect Joseph Everett Chandler
removed most of the later additions and returned
the house to its 1680 appearance—ignoring the
fact that Paul Revere would never have known it
as such (Little 1965).

Appleton's longstanding appreciation of history and growing familiarity with colonial architecture led him to tour Europe again in 1909,
learning all that he could about historic buildings
and the organizations that were making a difference to their future (Brown 1905). He admired
the restorations in France, especially the walled
city of Carcassonne, France's most aggressive
early twentieth century project. The career of
French restoration architect Eugene Emmanuel
Viollet-le-Duc was widely known by this point.
The next year Appleton formed the Society for

Fig. 1.19 William Sumner Appleton and two other men
formed an organization to save Paul Revere's home, in
Boston, which was a tenement at the time. Today the
house is a museum, operated by the National Park Service. (Photograph: Thomas Richmond)

the Protection of New England Antiquities, a
departure from previous organizations for being
regionally based, with specific representatives
in the adjoining states. SPNEA's claim to fame
rested on the idea that, with this arrangement, it

Fig. 1.20 The Society for the Protection of New England Antiquities gained title to the first town house of Harrison Gray Otis, a former senator and mayor of Boston. The organization has grown to become the largest regional preservation force, recently renaming itself Historic New England. (Author's photograph)

would be better able to rescue and maintain historic sites with consistent policy and treatment procedures. Appleton also continued to employ curators, architects, and archaeologists who specialized in the scientific examination of the building fabric to supplement and corroborate where possible whatever documentary evidence historians could discover. In addition to Chandler, Appleton favored the work of architects J. Frederick Kelly and Norman Isham.

The cover of the first issue of SPNEA's *Bulletin* carried a picture of the Hancock House, reminding subscribers of the loss and subtly projecting a better future. Upper class individuals and institutions gave Appleton access to influence and money when needed. Like many other Brahmin-dominated organizations, SPNEA was a private society with an avowed public mission, often considered progressive, but just as often acting as an outlet for conservative ideals. In contrast, the Association for the Preservation of Virginia Antiquities (APVA) was created by a traditional elite that was primarily composed of women. SPNEA grew to 1500 members in five years, and acquired several houses. The office and library soon outgrew its space, so on August 1, 1916, SPNEA acquired title to the first town house of Harrison Gray Otis, a former senator and mayor of Boston (Fig. 1.20). Appleton convinced the board that this would serve as the future headquarters of the organization, a house worthy of preservation. Its restoration was assured by his

foresight when the widening of Cambridge Street truncated the property and the structure was moved back 43 feet (Lindgren 1984). By the time the organization was 20 years old, about 3000 members supported 16 properties, the majority of which were in Eastern Massachusetts.

The Titans of Industry Turn to Restoration

Committed activist-amateurs, many of them women, continued to dominate the preservation field throughout the nineteen teens and twenties by maintaining house museums. On the other hand, two titans of industry, John D. Rockefeller, Jr. and Henry Ford, provided the backing for what would become not only the largest but also the most influential outdoor museums in the USA, and they employed an increasing number of professionals in their endeavors.

The story of what became the largest restoration effort of the twentieth century, at Williamsburg, Virginia, begins with its church and a women's group. The first preservation organization in the community was the Bruton Parish Church women's auxiliary, the Catherine Memorial Society, organized by Cynthia Beverley Tucker Colemen in 1884. It raised money through bake sales to restore the gravestones in the churchyard and help maintain the church. Coleman became well known in Williamsburg for raising the funds to repair the Old Powder Magazine, which was eventually purchased by the Association for the Preservation of Virginia Antiquities (APVA). Coleman was also instrumental in APVA's acquisition of the church ruin at Jamestown and she became involved in the first archaeological investigations there in 1897 (Montgomery 1998, p. 57; Lindgren 1993).

Coleman's extended her influence on the future of the community by her contact with the Reverend Doctor William Archer Rutherfoord Goodwin, a handsome, forceful preacher. A native Virginian and graduate of Virginia Theological Seminary, Goodwin had already distinguished himself as a clergyman when, in February 1903, he came to Williamsburg as the rector of the old Bruton Parish Church (Montgomery

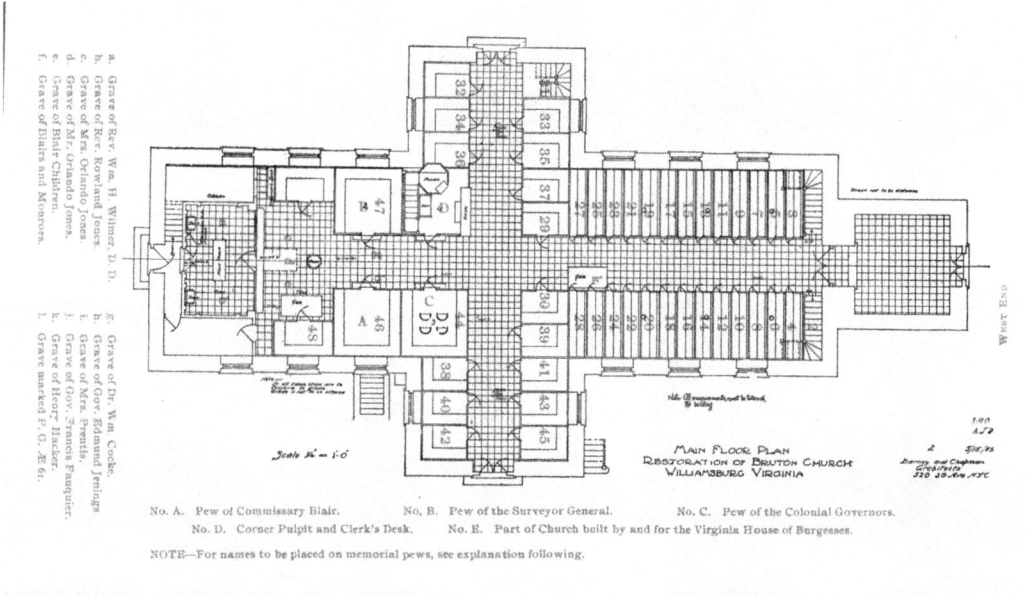

Fig. 1.21 The restoration efforts in Williamsburg, VA, began with the efforts of the woman's auxiliary of Bruton Parish Church. Here, the main floor restoration plan prepared by New York architects Barney and Chapman indicates the proposed location of the graves inside the structure. (Goodwin, *Bruton Parish Church, Restored* (1907), p. 129, Author's collection)

1998, p. 61). With some funds to restore and repair the church already in hand, Goodwin lost no time in gaining a consensus from his parishioners to move ahead. In the first few months, Goodwin wrote a promotional pamphlet and began active fundraising that took him north to visit church leaders in other parts of the country. In so doing, he was referred to and enlisted the New York-based church architect J. Stewart Barney, a Richmond, Virginia native, to direct the restoration of the old Bruton Parish building, which began in 1905 (Goodwin 1907; Montgomery 1998, p. 70) (Fig. 1.21). Barney's familiarity with the site and the academic models of European architectural styles was comprehensive. As a graduate of Columbia University and the École des Beaux Arts in Paris, and with more than 10 years of practice, he was thoroughly prepared to take on the project in the colonial mode, further attuned to the project by his familiarity with the views of French restoration architect Viollet-le-Duc and his work at Carcassonne (Schuyler 1904). To learn more, Goodwin assembled an advisory committee, but the decisions to remove an old partition wall, floor, and old plastering, as well as archaeologi-

cal investigation provided considerable evidence for the restoration in the colonial interior, complete with new lighting fixtures, organ, carpet, pews, and roof. The completed work became a feature attraction of the 300th anniversary of the Jamestown settlement in 1907.

Although Goodwin enjoyed a considerable amount of success, two years later he left for upstate New York, to head Rochester's St. Paul's parish, one of the wealthiest in the region. He subsequently volunteered to minister to the American troops in the USA during World War I, under the auspices of the YMCA. As years passed, however, Goodwin suffered from his overactive schedule and believed that he should turn to a quieter life, writing a history of the Theological Seminary in Virginia. He returned to Williamsburg to accept a professorship at the College of William and Mary in 1923, although his chief responsibility was writing letters to potential donors. Through a relentless campaign to raise money for the College, he became convinced that the entire community could be saved. Automobile garages, pharmacies, tourist cabins, and chain grocery stores had no place in the colonial town. All of

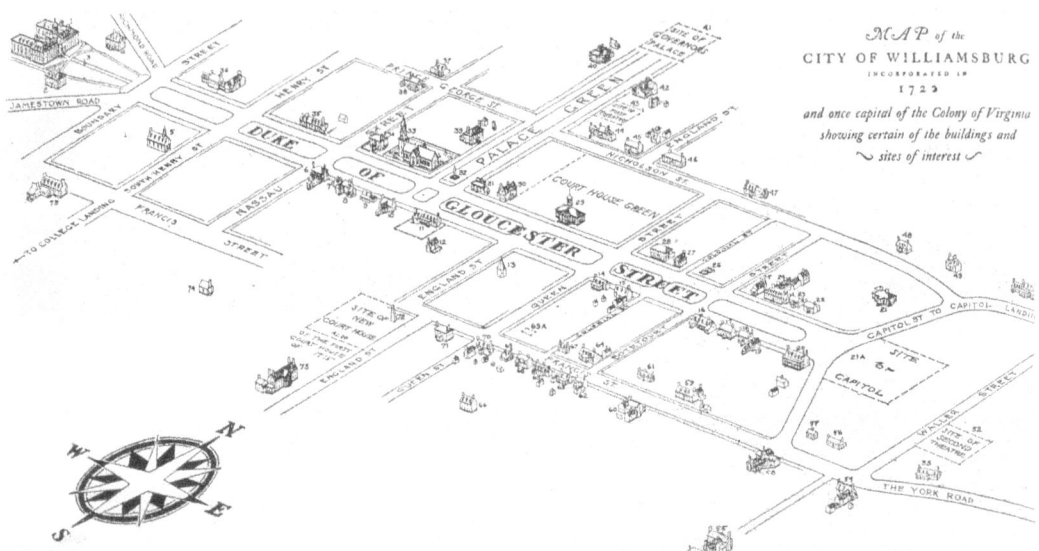

Fig. 1.22 The Reverend Doctor William Archer Ruth-erfoord Goodwin, rector of Bruton Parish Church, was instrumental in enticing John D. Rockefeller to purchase dozens of properties for what became Colonial Williams-burg. (Birdseye drawing, c.1947 version, Courtesy of Colonial Williamsburg Foundation)

these intrusions should be restored to their original form or be replaced by replicas in the spirit of the past, made evident through the reconstruction of the Capitol, the Palace, and the Raleigh Tavern (Fig. 1.22).

The idea was a daunting one, but Goodwin dedicated himself to the cause. Through a regional Ford automobile dealership, he first approached millionaire Henry Ford, without success. By repeatedly addressing possible donors and newspapermen, however, the idea of restoring the oldest colonial capital in the USA began to get more attention.

Rockefeller and Goodwin first met in 1924, when the latter spoke at a Phi Beta Kappa celebration, where the Reverend mentioned the idea of restoring the colonial town. Although several subsequent meetings failed to occur, when Rockefeller visited the location in late March of 1926, he was impressed. Subsequently, Goodwin prepared a map of the colonial buildings and put forth a set of broad goals. He enlisted the help of the architect Barney who outlined six points that the restoration project should follow: secure an option on each colonial house in the town; establish a holding corporation; rebuild the Capitol and Raleigh Tavern; remove the telephone poles and create a park around the Palace site; replace the homes occupied by African Americans with reconstructed colonial housing for the use of faculty and students, giving the rents to the College of William and Mary; and remove the through roads to Jamestown and Richmond, so the land could also be given to that educational institution. To this list, Goodwin seems to have added the restoration of the Wren Building at William and Mary. In short, the plan of action unfolded, built on the idea that the community would be oriented to educational needs.

William and Mary College President Chandler did not want to deal with consultants, and proposed hiring Barney, but when he withdrew, it became possible to hire architect William Perry of Boston. He was already involved with the Wythe House on the Palace Green and came highly recommended. This began the more than half century-long involvement of his firm with the site.

Between 1926, when Goodwin purchased the first property in Williamsburg for Rockefeller and 1934, the Reverend could count 63 buildings restored, 72 reconstructed, and 345 removed or destroyed. The French restoration architect Viollet-le-Duc would have been pleased, for the transformation of the entire area conformed to a single vision, with a unity of style (Hearn 1990). While archaeologists dug in one area, other buildings were relocated blocks away. One of the most important effects of Colonial Williamsburg is that it provided a proving ground for young architects, engineers, historians, and archeologists, working together on a complex project with a common goal. With the assistance of the architectural firm of Perry, Shaw and Hepburn, with Kenneth Chorley serving as administrative head and their new draftsmen, including Ed Kendrew—who became the first resident architect—work proceeded with Harold Shurtleff and Rutherfoord Goodwin in the Colonial Williamsburg research department (Hosmer 1981, pp. 61–73). The remarkable discovery of contemporary cuts of the original government structures, for which only the foundations survived, in the Bodleian Library at Oxford, reemphasized the necessity of studying original sources before rebuilding. When the reconstructed town first opened in the early 1930s, it included not only the residences and public buildings, but also 28 shops with colonial facades along the western end of the Duke of Gloucester Street (Montgomery 1998, p. 6). In 1935, the telephone and power lines began "disappearing" underground, and the asphalt and concrete pavements were replaced with gravel and appropriate sidewalks.

Historians who examine historic preservation initiatives for evidence that the well-educated upper and middle classes are attempting to consolidate its identity and status often find considerable evidence to support this view. Colonial Williamsburg was one of many examples. By contrast, Henry Ford was dedicated to anything but the celebration of the elite, preferring the story of American inventors and invention. The influence of his collections had a profound effect on the direction other collectors followed. His first goal was to assemble a complete set of tools, from the earliest to the present day. It was not simply a fascination with fast disappearing handicrafts. It was also a passion for recording changing processes and solutions to uniquely American problems.

Ford's friendship with Thomas Edison revolved around their common interest in invention. By 1905, Ford's collection of experimental phonographs and electrical apparatus was considerable. His displeasure with schoolbooks and rote memorization aside, Ford preferred museums and exhibits that illustrated everyday life. Ford's fascination with the common person let him to collect commonplace elements of small, rural town life. Ironically, the automobile entrepreneur found his own birthplace threatened by road widening, so he hired a local draftsman, Edward J. Cutler, to help him move it 200 feet and launched his Edison Institute, planning it as a New England village with a combination of old buildings restored around a green. Announced in late 1928, it was under construction from April through October, 1929. Expansion has concerned the Institute ever since, with more than one hundred structures occupying the Henry Ford Museum and Greenfield Village complex (Upward 1979).

The rise of several other outdoor museum "villages" followed the models set by Rockefeller and Ford. For example, early members of what became the New York State Historical Association, founded in 1899, were influenced by its sister organization in Massachusetts. In fact, the Association built a replica of the demolished John Hancock house in Ticonderoga, New York, as its first headquarters. The prospect of presenting an interpretative setting at village scale in New York State occurred later, when Stephen C. Clarke, a principal of the Singer Company who served as a founding trustee of the Museum of Modern Art, and a director of the Metropolitan Museum of Art, launched two museums in Cooperstown, New York, where he maintained a rural home. The first, the National Baseball Hall of Fame, was one of the earliest collections dedicated to a recreational activity in the country. The second was an outdoor museum, somewhat like Stockholm's Skansen, although influenced more

Fig. 1.23 In Cooperstown, NY, millionaire George Clark provided the New York State Historical Association with an early twentieth century model dairy farm as a new home. The Association added a village collection of early nineteenth century houses and shops with period rooms, opened in 1943 as the Farmer's Museum, recently updated. (Author's photograph)

directly by Ford's Greenfield Village and Colonial Williamsburg (Edenheim 1995; McClean 1998) (Fig. 1.23). The original layout revolved around Cooper Park in the village and included an exhibition hall, houses, and shops with period rooms, including wax figures and dioramas. By the time the Association established its presence in Cooperstown in 1938, however, the collections were too large so the trustees decided to move everything to the model Fenimore farm on the western shore of Otsego Lake. The transformation of Clark's former dairy farm was complete by the time the museum opened in 1943, while a hunt began for additional buildings to create a pre-Civil War New York State Village. This included a one-room schoolhouse, a gristmill, bandstand, old country inn, schoolhouse, cobblers shop, and a bank (Donofrio 2001).

Although the most celebrated new museums were outdoors and soon attracted school groups, indoor museums continued to spur the revision of history by using a wide range of techniques and materials. This was evident at both the primary and secondary level. Margaret E. Wells, supervisor of third and fourth grades at the Speyer School in New York City, was fascinated by the potential of the anthropological and zoological collections. Her 1921 book, *How the Present Came From the Past*, is "written for the boys and girls of the Present, in the hope that this digging into the Past may make them better planters of

the Future." The use of history to throw light on the future included visits to the Museum of Natural History in New York City, to "make the life of these tribes almost as real to you as a trip to their country would." (Wells 1921, p. 6). The opening illustrations contrast Neanderthal man with a modern four-door touring car, an African elephant, and a fist hatchet with a typewriter, dynamo, and an aeroplane. Clearly, with the application of science, faster communication and travel would make a difference in the lives of the young readers (Fig. 1.24).

In a similar fashion, the history of art and architecture became the foundation for introductory "appreciation" courses. Emily Ann Barnes, sixth grade teacher at Lincoln School of Barnard College in New York City, explored the architectural world by making use of the collections of the Metropolitan Museum of Art. Her curriculum centered around a wide variety of activities to bring the children into direct contact with architecture by visiting sites, making sketches, modeling in clay, constructing stage sets, performing in historical costumes, vocabulary building exercises, and selecting architectural elements (Barnes 1932, p. 34). Barnes' scheme, first designed in 1929, at the height of the skyscraper boom in Manhattan, makes direct references to scholars and writers, from John Ruskin, Banister Fletcher, Frank Lloyd Wright, and Russell Sturgis, through Helen Gardner, to Lewis Mumford and Henry-Russell Hitchcock.

Fig. 1.24 The contrast of the old with the new becomes the basis for one of the first "then and now" books dedicated to educating children. The faster communication provided by a profusion of telephone wires was already seen as an eyesore to some adults. (*How the Present (1921)*, p. 11, Author's collection)

Living Cities Left Behind or Ahead of Their Time?

In the early 1920s, a remarkable number of small cities became urban while the largest cities blossomed. Industrial productivity spurred satellite communities in Boston, Chicago, Cincinnati, St. Louis, and Birmingham, to name a few (Taylor 1915), while Los Angeles boomed horizontally. However, some old commercial centers declined. The relatively stagnant economies of Charleston, New Orleans, and San Antonio provide the context for the earliest neighborhood and community-wide preservation efforts. These efforts led to city-based nonprofit organizations, and the first historic district zoning, historic preservation commissions, and broad survey efforts.

Somewhat like Williamsburg, Charleston was so remote from other urban centers that when the forces of progress arrived, in the form of gasoline stations, tourist hotels, and parking lots, they were immediately noticeable. Susan Pringle Frost is recognized as the first individual to make a difference by saving properties as a professional realtor.[18] Although well educated and

---

[18] This does not overlook the contributions made previously by the National Society of Colonial Dames in South Carolina for saving the Powder Magazine, or the Daughters of the American Revolution, which acquired Charleston's Old Exchange Building, both of which served as museums. Neither of these two examples, however, illustrate broader preservation issues, with city-wide implications.

well connected, her family bankruptcy forced her to earn a living, which she did by learning typing and stenography. Her misfortune proved to be an opportunity because, by serving as the private secretary for New York architect Bradford Lee Gilbert, who was responsible for supervising the South Carolina Interstate and West Indian Exposition of 1901–1902, Frost learned more than many women about the importance of civic leadership, Progressive era thinking, and the vision needed for architectural projects. Subsequently working as a court stenographer, she observed firsthand the workings of the judicial system, and became increasingly interested in the salary inequalities between men and women. Always energetic, and irrepressible at times, she wrote and spoke out at women's clubs, social circles, newspapers, and business meetings. As president of the Charleston Equal Suffrage League, formed in 1915, Frost was a tireless advocate for equal opportunity for women, and formed connections with other leaders at the national level. Ultimately, her knowledge of the legal system and political processes, her willingness to challenge the local power structure, and her organizational capacity all came to serve the cause of preservation. The death of her aunt in 1917 curtailed Frost's further involvement with suffrage, when, as co-executor of her aunt's estate, she became preoccupied with the future of the ancestral home, the Pringle (Miles Brewton) House (Fig. 1.25). In 1918, Frost hung out her shingle as a professional

Fig. 1.25 When the Miles Brewton House, in Charleston, came into the hands of Susan Pringle Frost she was best known from her involvement with the suffrage movement. In 1918 she became the first woman real estate agent in the city, specializing in historic properties. (Author's photograph)

real estate agent, the first woman in the community to do so.

Frost's views about her activity are important to understand. She employed a very talented African American stair builder and contractor, Thomas Mayhem Pinkney, to insert modern plumbing, lighting and heating in the houses she "restored," taking special care to save and install period hardware and fixtures. On the other hand, the poor African Americans who occupied most of the buildings she purchased were displaced because, she believed, whites would be better renters.

The idea of forming a preservation society appears to have arisen due to the threat to the Joseph Manigault House, a three-story brick mansion built in 1802–1803 on the highest elevation in Charleston, already flanked by a brand new gasoline station (Fig. 1.26). "Miss Sue" gathered almost three dozen individuals, mostly women, to form the Society for the Preservation of Old Dwellings in 1920.

As a leader in the Society and in the local real estate community, Frost was one of the first citizens to approach local officials about using the authority of government to prevent demolition. Little legal precedent existed for taking action that would restrict a private property owner's actions. True, in Charleston, as in most communities, the first building regulations were primarily concerned with preventing fires and controlling the use of construction materials. This stemmed from the development of regulations that forbade erecting wooden buildings within defined fire limits. These districts are a form of zoning if only because different areas of the community came under different building regulations. Across the country, concerns about building placement and construction methods were growing. Density was a particular concern of late nineteenth century tenement reformers and the use of a property became an issue when some California cities outlawed Chinese laundries. The setback of buildings also raised issues. In Massachusetts, the State legislature prescribed the allowable heights for buildings fronting on certain streets in Boston (Weiss 1987). In Illinois, particularly in Chicago, and in the District of Columbia, building height was becoming a concern. In general, however, municipalities were doing little to control the placement and design of skyscrapers (Krueckenberg 1983, p. 112; Bassett 1936). Many cities looked to New York City's Zoning Ordinance of 1916 as the most sophisticated and comprehensive, dealing with height, use, setback, and density, even treating auxiliary structures. By the end of the 1920s, more than 750 communities adopted some variety of it, with increasing segregation of the residential, commercial, industrial, and public areas.

Promoting zoning at the national level also helped win acceptance locally. The Standard State Zoning Enabling Act and the Standard City Planning Enabling Act were prepared by committees of the US Department of Commerce for distribution nationwide. The Zoning Act was first released in 1922, then revised and released again in 1926. The Planning Act was issued in 1927 and 1928 (Bassett et al. 1935). At first, many local lawyers questioned whether the Constitution had provided the states with the power to regulate land use with zoning, but in 1926 the concept was upheld by the US Supreme Court in the case Village of Euclid, Ohio, vs. Ambler Realty Company.

As a result, in 1929, when the Charleston City Council established a special zoning committee,

Fig. 1.26 The threat to the Joseph Manigault House stimulated the formation in 1920 of the Society for the Preservation of Old Dwellings, in Charleston. (Author's photograph)

it was in the vanguard, although the city was more unusual for having selected as the chair of that committee Alston Deas, a president of the Society for the Preservation of Old Dwellings. Deas and his colleagues on the committee made sure the special concerns about the incursion of gasoline stations, automobile repair shops, and other recent commercial developments were considered in the ordinance by the planning consultants from Morris Knowles' firm in Pittsburgh. The conflict between the kind of development that automobile tourism spurred and the need to protect the historic structures and their context was already very evident. By working with local architect Albert Simons to identify the oldest buildings at the tip of the peninsula, the zoning ordinance included the "Old and Historic Charleston District," as a special zone, at the time a unique invention in American land use ideas (Weyeneth 2000).

To guide changes being made to the properties in the district, the new ordinance established a "Board of Architectural Review" composed of representatives of the concerned organizations and agencies of city government. These included the local chapters of the American Institute of Architects and American Society of Civil Engineers, the Carolina Art Association, the Real Estate Exchange, and the planning and zoning com-

mission. In October 1931, after seven neighborhood meetings throughout the city, the Charleston City Council approved and Mayor Thomas P. Stoney signed the new bill into law (Young 1990, pp. 1–2). The "ordinance and review board model" soon became the guide for the wave of commissions to be established in other historic cities, including New Orleans.

The "Crescent City" retained its vivid French character and complex social history. French Creoles tended to live in the Vieux Carre, while the new immigrants, both American and European, settled in outlying neighborhoods. The French culture manifested itself in a number of ways. The city was bilingual during the first half of the nineteenth century and there are many examples of building contracts and advertisements in city directories written entirely in French. By the end of the century, however, the city core was declining and sorely in need of attention. By the early twentieth century, the famous St. Louis Cathedral had deteriorated to such an extent that the bishop ordered it closed to the public. It did not reopen until 1918, after repairs were completed (Huber and Wilson 1965).

Although Charleston was the first city to pass local preservation legislation, there is ample evidence that New Orleans witnessed remarkable advocacy even earlier. This is due to Allison Owen, who carried forward his family's very prominent name in military service, architectural practice, and a wide range of civic affairs. A graduate of Tulane University and the School of Architecture at the Massachusetts Institute of Technology, as early as 1895 Owen introduced the idea of forming a preservation society not unlike those operating elsewhere (Chambers 1925, vol. 2, p. 14). Although no evidence of such a group has surfaced, his advocacy is obvious 10 years later when he began editing the journal *Architectural Art and Its Allies* under the auspices of the Louisiana Architectural Association. There he voiced his opinion and supported others who wished to improve the city with better code enforcement, streets, lighting and sidewalks, while celebrating the carnivals and artistic activities of the Old Quarter. Editorials included comments on the "misdirection of honest and well intended effort" regarding the restoration of the Cabildo, the seat of French colonial government, and the problems associated with the continued use of the camel-back cottages that so characterized the city (Editorial 1906). If World War I had not intervened perhaps Owen could have influenced the city even more, but he left for Europe, ever after known as General Owen. By the early 1920s he would be in full evidence again, serving as the president of the New Orleans Round Table Club, president of the Lions Club, and vice president of the City Planning and Zoning Commission, as well as the vice president of the city Parking Commission. With all of his activity it is easy to see how, in November 1925, he became an advisor to the Vieux Carre Commission and the City Council on preservation questions.

About that time, German-born photographer Arnold Genthe arrived in New Orleans and captured over 100 romantically realistic images of the city (Fig. 1.27). He wrote how, only in the last few years, were residents beginning to understand the importance of the Old French Quarter, and he urged that competent architects be "given official authority to direct and supervise all restorations and repairs" (Genthe 1926, pp. 32–33).

Fig. 1.27 During the 1920s the German photographer Arnold Genthe's romantic images captured the beauty of the Old French Quarter in New Orleans. He featured the shadows produced by the cast and wrought iron grilles of balconies and urged that competent architects be given authority to oversee restorations and repairs. (Library of Congress)

Although qualified architects were in short supply, a private organization incorporated as the Vieux Carre Association stepped up to encourage preservation, led by its executive director Theodore A. Waltners, and backed by a number of local businessmen. This organization worked to improve the area by prodding the city to install historically appropriate street lamps and restore the 1806 Absinthe House. At the same time, a new group, La Renaissance du Vieux Carre, led by Stanley C. Arthur, amplified the crusade to save the Old French Market on the riverfront, which the city "restored" (Arthur 1936).[19] In 1936, a coalition of these organizations and others successfully campaigned to amend the Louisiana Constitution to allow the city to create a

---

[19] The restoration was really a transformation, caused in part by the decline of the stock market and the funds made available by the Works Progress Administration.

The Fortified Building.

The Main Building of the Alamo where the heroes died, as it looked originally.

(Made from description in old manuscript, plans, pictures draw ings, and descriptions of old settlers and pioneers.)

The Church in The Alamo.

Towers, Dome and Arched Roof fell in previous to or about 1762. Never restored or fully rebuilt.

Fig. 1.28 In San Antonio, the Mission San Antonio de Valero, known as the Alamo, was the most important symbol of independence. When the Catholic Church began to dispose of the property, an active campaign thwarted de- molition. Here, the site is illustrated in the first authoritative guide by Adina De Zavala, the woman who led the campaign to save the property. (Author's collection)

Vieux Carre Commission that would be more than advisory, an effort accompanied by a publication, Arthur's *Old New Orleans*. Even after the city adopted the local ordinance in 1937, however, there was no initiative to survey and document the properties as there was in Charleston (Owen 1938, pp. 10–13).

Just as English and French colonial development captured the public imagination, equally inspiring was the Spanish colonial influence. In the Southwest, the Texas Revolution was the single-most important event to spur commemoration. In San Antonio, the Mission San Antonio de Valero, known as the Alamo, was the most important symbol of independence. When the US Army vacated the structure in 1877, the Catholic Church began to dispose of the property, selling off the adjacent dormitory and convent. The uncertain future of the Alamo stimulated the creation of a fund-raising memorial association, the Alamo Monument Association, formed under the leadership of Mary Adams Maverick, widow of one of the signers of the Texas Declaration of Independence, at Washington-on-the-Brazos (Fig. 1.28).

The work of Maverick, which was endorsed by the Texas Veterans' Association and the political leadership of San Antonio, convinced the state legislature to purchase the property. Texas stands as the first state to set aside a memorial to its independence, in 1905 (Fisher 1996, p. 56).

While the call for restoration of the Alamo was almost immediate and the city promised to assume maintenance of the site, and the Mayor announced that he was ready to contribute a collection of stuffed animals and birds to a museum on the property, the officials did comparatively little, while the number of visitors increased. Into the breach stepped Adina Emilia De Zavala, the granddaughter of the first vice president of the Texas Republic, Lorenzo de Zavala. As president of the new local chapter of the Daughters of the Republic of Texas, and in a number of succeeding roles in San Antonio and the state, she greatly expanded preservation activity (De Zavala 1917, p. 212; Ables 1965, pp. 203–214; Zesch 2008). Her role became, literally, "to hold the fort" by barring entrance to developers reputedly intent on altering the church, thereby providing almost legendary power to her organization.

Saving the Alamo was part of an even more ambitious goal: the purchase and restoration of all four of the remaining missions held by the Catholic Church in San Antonio. All were in need of repair and restoration. Even the best maintained, Nuestra Senora de la Purisma Concepcion de Acuna, suffered the decay of its outbuildings, while San Jose y San Miguel de Aguayo's dome and roof had collapsed, and San Juan Capistrano, the most deteriorated, was nearly a ruin (Fig. 1.29). Under an agreement between the De Zavala Chapter of the Daughters of the Republic of Texas and the Diocese, the former would raise the funds and conduct the restoration provided the latter could continue to use the buildings for religious purposes and the church did not assume responsibility for any debts or contractor's liens. De Zavala set about the work of soliciting funds from businesses and collecting money with representatives of allied groups, including the Texas Federation of Women's Clubs (De Zavala 1917, p. 47; Howard 1935; Almaraz 1994). She distinguished herself as one of the earliest and most civic minded Hispanic women in the preservation field.

She was not alone in these efforts, however. Clara Driscoll, treasurer of the Daughters, conducted a nationwide campaign soliciting funds and ultimately stepped up to purchase the expanded Alamo property, which included both the church and the convent. In early 1905, when the State reimbursed her and acquired the site, it agreed to allow the Daughters to serve as custodian.

As the largest city in the state, San Antonio's economy spurred the construction of taller commercial buildings, and fostered street widening improvements. It also precipitated a considerable amount of demolition as the old Spanish era town gave way to a brash, new city. Then, in 1921, disaster struck when the San Antonio River rose up 12 ft above its banks, inundating downtown. To avoid the possibility of a reoccurrence, the Olmos Dam was constructed upstream and a new cutoff channel was dug to eliminate the possibility of floodwaters ever reaching downtown.

As often is the case, the public works projects came at a cost. Due to street widening and the need to create a new channel, the 1859 Greek Revival Market House was sacrificed. Long abandoned as an outdoor market, the announce-

Fig. 1.29 In addition to the Alamo, the other four extant missions needed considerable repair and restoration. San Jose y San Miguel de Aguayo's dome and roof collapsed and the Daughters of the Republic of Texas worked with the Catholic Diocese to raise needed funds. (Author's photograph)

ment of the impending demolition early in 1924 spurred to action Rena Maverick Green and Emily Edwards. Both women were accomplished artists and had lived in other parts of the country, and instantly recognized the charm of the only Doric columned front in San Antonio (Fig. 1.30). Gathering their friends and associates, 13 women met on a Saturday in March to organize the San Antonio Conservation Society. Advancing the study and conservation of the "distinctive" aspects of San Antonio, their concerns not only included residences and commercial structures, but pecan trees and playgrounds in parks, legends, and Spanish nomenclature and art (Fisher 1996, p. 95). Thanks to the Society's efforts, by the early 1930s, San Antonio's preservation advocacy was relatively well established. In 1939, it became the third city in the nation to pass a local historic preservation ordinance.

Fig. 1.30 The 1858 Greek Revival Market in San Antonio was removed for river improvements, but served as the rallying point for the early members of the local preservation organization, and was incorporated in the San Pedro Park Playhouse. (Author's photograph)

The Expansion of the Federal Government

The local struggles of Charleston, New Orleans, San Antonio, and other cities such as St. Augustine, Natchez, and Santa Fe (Wilson 1997) to remake themselves are even more valiant when considering that the USA was suffering from a massive economic depression. The record number of business and bank failures, the decline in housing construction, and soaring unemployment took their toll on the country during the early 1930s. In some cities, such as Chicago and Detroit, 50% of the labor force was without a job. The resounding call for economic and political reform led to the election of President Franklin D. Roosevelt and promises of recovery won from the Congress extraordinary measures to jumpstart the nation's economy under the guidance of new federal planning agencies. The National Recovery Administration put in place industry-wide compacts to control production levels, prices, and wages, with authority never before attempted. In the land-use arena, the Tennessee Valley Authority became the model public corporation charged with rural electrification, flood control, industrialization, recreation, and education. Just as important, the 1935 Emergency Relief Appropriations Act provided over 8 million jobs through the Civilian Conservation Corps, the Public Works Administration (PWA), and the new Works Progress Administration (WPA) (Kennedy 1999).

Under the guidance of director Horace Albright, the National Park Service took advantage of the PWA and the subsequent Emergency Relief and WPA programs to make long sought after acquisitions and expand its staff. In late 1932 and early 1933, Charles E. Peterson, an architect who had worked at Yorktown and with Colonial Williamsburg staff, began an appeal for the creation of measured drawing teams to record historic structures (Peterson 1976). Originally designed as a work relief program to employ 1000 men for six months, the program became the Historic American Buildings Survey. To spur interest, the *Journal of the American Institute of Architects* contained a fill-in-the-blank form, the first nation-wide survey form for use by subscribers to record pre-1850 buildings of merit. In 1934, a formal memorandum of agreement was worked out between the American Institute of Architects, the Library of Congress, and the National Park Service, and an Advisory Board was created to guide the development of the program. Structures to be recorded had to have architectural interest due to age or form, integrity of design, and be imminently endangered. A lesser-known, parallel effort began to record historic sailing vessels, located primarily in the Chesapeake Bay (Warren 1986). Conceived by naval architect Eric Steinlein, the Historic American Merchant Marine Survey existed only from 1936 to 1937, with the cosponsorship of the Smithsonian Institution.

The National Park Service was not able to choose and purchase appropriate historic sites with federal government funds, however. The process generally worked in reverse, with advocates pressuring members of Congress to purchase sites and, after the fact, give them to the National Park Service to protect and administer. On the other hand, some sites were in the hands of the War Department. An Executive Order signed by President Roosevelt on June 10, 1933 ordered all battlefields, parks, monuments, cemeteries, and Indian sites to be immediately transferred to the Department of the Interior, then headed by Secretary Harold Ickes (Albright and Cahn 1985). Horace Albright found it difficult to work with the new secretary, and left the NPS. He remained influential however, for he joined the Board of Colonial Williamsburg and convinced John D. Rockefeller to back a detailed study of European preservation, which would provide more of the rationale for the expansion of the role of the Service. In addition, interest in drafting legislation by the NPS Chief Historian Verne Chatelain and his expanding staff, and other initiatives, all came together in what ultimately became the Historic Sites Act of 1935 (Hosmer 1981, pp. 563–575).

Appearing before the House Committee on Public Lands in early April, Secretary Ickes began his testimony noting that England, France, Italy, Germany, Spain, Switzerland, and the Scandinavian countries had well-established national policies expressed in legislation (Ickes

1935). He then recounted the expansion of the National Park Service's responsibilities formerly under the War Department, the initiatives taken by the Historic American Buildings Survey, and the new national parks as ample justification. Distinguished visitors, such as the Rev. W. A. R. Goodwin, added to the testimony for what became known as the Historic Sites Act.

This legislation declared it "a national policy to preserve for public use historic sites, buildings, and objects of national significance for the inspiration and benefit of the people…" (Public Law 1935–1936, pp. 666–668). Acquisition of these resources could occur by gift or bequest in unison with a state or local agency, or eminent domain. Representative Stubbs, whose California district contained seven historic missions, questioned the provisions of the bill that called for taking an historic property by eminent domain, and led a discussion about the effect of the legislation on the Catholic Church, which would not give up these historic missions to the National Park Service. The Representative responsible for introducing the legislation, Maury Maverick of Texas, later mayor of San Antonio, reassured his colleague that he had only the best intentions for the Catholic missions and that, in San Antonio, $167,000 was spent on these properties with the title in no way affected (Public Law 1935–1936, pp. 8–12).

From 1935 until 1951, an additional 44 historic sites passed into the care of the National Park Service, 20 through the Historic Sites Act. The remarkable pressure to expand, however, with hundreds of requests for studies, bogged down the agency and often delayed protection. After the WPA archaeology program began in 1934, field supervisors were in short supply, one of the reasons that led to the formation of the Society for American Archaeology, founded the same year.

Perversely, the Historic Sites Act was the legislation used to speed demolition in some instances. One of the most obvious examples of this was the creation of the Jefferson National Expansion Park in St. Louis. St. Louis attorney Luther Ely Smith, backed by the Mayor, spearheaded the effort to demolish the derelict waterfront warehouse district to make way for a new park dedicated to Thomas Jefferson and the Pioneers of National Expansion. Congress used the Historic Sites Act to purchase 40 city blocks and, with the backing of the federal, state, and local governments, obliterate the warehouses and historic street pattern. In 1946, Charles Peterson of HABS was called upon to record the area before demolition, during which time he advocated for an architectural museum on the river including whole buildings, architectural fragments, scale models, photographs, and drawings. This request was denied, and only the St. Louis Courthouse and Cathedral were saved. Today, the perseverance of Smith is evident in the competition-winning waterfront design provided by architect Eero Saarinen and landscape architect Dan Kiley, with its great arch and grassy plane. The original vision included museums, forests, and an evocative frontier ensemble, but it was never funded (Peterson 2009; Toft and Josse 2002; Fig. 1.31).

A similar story was underway in Philadelphia. Because of the fear that Independence Hall might be destroyed either by a direct hit from a bomb or by other buildings falling on it, the idea of demolishing the commercial structures around it was promoted, especially by Judge Irvin Lewis (Greiff 1987). The "Independence Hall and Old Philadelphia Association, Inc.," founded for the beautification of the city, joined with the city and the National Park Service to pressure the Commonwealth legislature to purchase the three block area north of the Hall. The state put up $4 million, an amount originally earmarked to promote Philadelphia as the site of the United Nations. In 1948, Charles Peterson conducted another architectural survey, and the federal government pledged another $5 million. By mid-1948, over 100 buildings were removed to provide for another park, in this case erecting no new monument (Cotter et al. 1992, pp. 74–151; Fig. 1.32).

Although both these projects were for parks, the domestic federal programs that would have the greatest impact on the built environment were devoted to housing. As a rule, housing policy and programs were at the periphery of preservation advocacy, although in Charleston, Susan Pringle

Fig. 1.31 Congress used the Historic Sites Act to purchase 40 city blocks for the Jefferson National Expansion Park in St. Louis, demolishing hundreds of properties. Only the St. Louis Courthouse and Cathedral remain. (Library of Congress)

Frost stands as a notable exception. The roots of the housing reform movement are generally traced to the muckrakers, such as Jacob Riis, who focused on the need for minimum housing standards—specifically for light and air, less overcrowding, and proper sanitary facilities—for immigrants and laborers. Local and state government responses resulted in the first zoning ordinances and building codes, and local planning legislation. In 1926, for example, the New York State Housing Board created corporations that agreed to its standards, and these "limited dividend" entities were given partial tax exemptions and the right to exercise eminent domain. At the federal level, in 1932, the economic imperatives during the Depression led to the passage of the National Emergency Relief and Construction Act, permitting the Reconstruction Finance Corporation to make loans to housing corporations when they agreed to similar stipulations. More

Fig. 1.32 In a fashion similar to St. Louis, many of the intervening properties in Philadelphia were removed from the historic core to provide what was believed to be a fitting setting for the more historic buildings. The National Park Service has subsequently changed and enlarged the Mall layout completed in the early 1950s, seen here. (Library of Congress)

generally, federal funding would support legislation, all with the single object: to eliminate "blight and slums." At the time, blight is defined as "an insidious malady," that first appears as "barely noticeable deterioration, and then progresses gradually toward a final condition known as the slum."

By contrast, new construction was a panacea, especially when backed by the real estate and construction industries. The provisions of the President's Conference on Home Building and Home Ownership, contained in an 11-volume report issued in 1932–1933, became the Holy Grail in finance circles, emphasizing the role of local government and the private sector. With the establishment of the Federal Housing Administration (FHA) in 1934, minimum property standards were provided for federally backed projects, and the agency offered ongoing services to developers and the public in the form of mortgage insurance. The FHA endorsed the ideas of progressive planners who favored suburban design ideals, including cul-de-sacs, looped streets, and arterial streets, and disapproved of the traditional grid-iron layout of cities, forecasting the preferences of post-World War II suburban expansion.

Bombing Cities to Save Western Civilization

Although most Americans were relatively uninformed about the theory and practice of conserving major historic sites, this changed to some degree as conflict arose and destruction increased in Europe as a result of World War II. The attention given to the progress of the war in the daily newspapers and magazines, and on the radio, re-educated the USA about the geography of the world, even as the country served as the "arsenal of democracy." The expansion of the federal government's role in planning superseded anything conceived by the Depression era programs.

Unlike previous wars, which were fought on the ground and in the sea, World War II was also fought from the air. Bombing was considered not only strategically preferable but psychologically damaging to the enemy. Compared to many European countries, the USA came into the war officially rather late, but its effects could hardly go unnoticed as it provided massive amounts of war material, including aircraft. Beginning in May 1943, the US Army Air Force joined the Royal Air Force in dropping hundreds of thousands of pounds of bombs in the effort to reclaim Europe.

Given the widespread use of aerial photography, the identification of military and industrial targets seemed considerably advanced and American bombing precision was applauded (Roerich Museum website n.d.),[20]. Unfortunately, often due to negligence, lack of skill, and panic in the air, the casualties mounted and historic properties were destroyed and damaged. In fact, both German and English air raids focused on cities known for their rich architectural heritage. In an ironic twist, the attacks became known as "Baedeker Raids" because the cities were important destinations in the European travel guides published by Karl Baedeker (Verrier 1968, pp. 164, 207). In addition to London, Exeter, Bath, Norwich, and Canterbury suffered from bombing raids and this hardened the resolve of the British, sparking retaliatory strikes. True, some cities were sacrosanct. Bombing Rome would provide the enemy with an irresistible opportunity to paint the Allies as assaulting Christendom. Other pilgrimage sites served as sanctuaries. By contrast, occupied cities like Paris, Amsterdam, Nantes, and German cities like Frankfort were subject to repeated Allied military scrutiny and bombing, endangering historic properties above and below ground (Schaffer 1985). As the war continued, the significance of such sites paled by comparison to the need to save human life and additional property. A Gallup poll conducted in the USA during March and April in 1944 asked residents "If military leaders believe it will be necessary to bomb historic religious buildings and shrines in Europe, do you approve or disapprove of their bombing them?" Remarkably, of the 1500 respondents, 74% approved, and 19% disapproved, while 7% had no opinion (Gallop 1944). Seen in the context of the war, it is perhaps no surprise that so many Americans were willing to accept the destruction of the culture of their forebears. The obvious military targets, such as airfields, munitions plants, staging compounds, shipping and harbor facilities, train depots, refineries and bridges were easiest to comprehend, but as the American casualties mounted, the difficulties of winning became harder to ignore.

There was an attempt to safeguard the monuments, however. At the outset of the War, scholars and museum officials became alarmed at the level of destruction (Nicholas 1994). Among the academics were Harvard professors Ralph Barton Perry, Paul J. Sachs, and George Chase, best known as the American Defense-Harvard Group (AD-HG). Columbia University professor and Greek scholar William Bell Dinsmoor formed another group under the auspices of the American Council of Learned Societies that had access to art historians and archaeologists throughout the country. Both pressed for the formation of a high-level group of advisers to safeguard cultural property in Europe and volunteered to provide lists, maps, and handbooks of recognized monuments. Dinsmoor also enlisted David E. Finley, Director of the National Gallery of Art, who in turn approached Supreme Court Chief Justice Harlan Fiske Stone with the proposal that the federal government create a commission (Doheny 2006, pp. 205–235). Stone agreed that it was needed and, although he declined to chair it, suggested his associate Justice Owen Roberts. More important, Justice Stone forwarded the proposal to President Roosevelt. When the "Roberts Commission" was officially announced in 1944—officially known as the "American Commission for the Protection and Salvage of Artistic and Historic Monuments in Europe" (ACPS)—its chief responsibility was to pass along the information from the AD-HG in the US and the newly formed Monuments, Fine Arts and Archives (MFA&A) units to the European and Asian theaters. The Commission also provided recommendations of appropriate personnel to staff MFA&A units and instructions to military personnel regarding the protection and salvage of monuments, largely though the School of Military Government at the University of Virginia (US Government Historical Reports on War Administration 1946; Woolley 1947; Grevstad-Nordbrock 2007). The results were, at best, mixed. Often the 200 officers in the

---

[20] The previous agreements under which cultural property was treated in war include: the Lieber Instructions (1863); the Brussels Declaration (1874); the Hague Regulations (1899, 1907); and the Hague Rules of Air Warfare (1922–1923). The Roerick Pact was signed by President Roosevelt on April 15, 1935.

Fig. 1.33 The destruction in Europe was epitomized not only in the damage to historic buildings in England, France, Germany, and Italy, but also in Poland. General Dwight D. Eisenhower toured the ruins in Warsaw in 1945. (Library of Congress)

field were not of appropriate rank, even if they had been sufficient in numbers. At the front, Allied forces found that the German city centers, often built of wood, would burn until stopped by stone party walls. Rarely could the damage be contained; the collateral damage was not easy to avoid.

Hence, a considerable amount of destruction took place due to the occupation of Europe and in East Asia. The story of the Nazi destruction and rebuilding of Warsaw is legendary (Ciborowski 1969). Although Coventry, Hiroshima, Rotterdam, and Stalingrad all suffered considerable damage, Warsaw was the city that the Nazis deliberately set out to destroy. The destruction began in September 1939, when 12% of the buildings were ruined and 50,000 people perished. By the time Soviet forces freed the city in 1945, one fifth of the population had died and Warsaw was completely leveled (Fig. 1.33). After the War, before beginning to rebuild, the removal of mines, unexploded bombs, and live ammunition took months. The exhumation and burial of the dead also took more time, as millions of tons of rubble were slowly removed by hand and horse cart. Warsaw would be rebuilt, and the plans were quickly implemented. The restoration of the Old Town Market Square became a remarkable source of community pride, a protest against the attempt to wipe out a culture.

On the other side of the globe, the damage by fire induced by the incendiary bombing in Japanese cities received less attention largely because of rush to end the war and relatively minor historical roots of the Japanese in the Eurocentric thinking of the USA.

Conclusion

It is clear that the connections between Europe and the USA existed in who we were, what we believed, and why we mounted campaigns to save objects, sites, buildings, and neighborhoods. The prevailing Positivism continued to hold that expansion and growth could solve most common problems and lead to social and economic improvement, even though the costs and benefits were distributed unevenly. For many, with a belief in hard work and additional industrial and scientific advances, improvement became an end in itself. In a young country, dependent on the land for its wealth—a nation that was still attempting to establish law and order in some regions—the amount of time for history was limited. While Americans could cherish their heroes, patriotic memories, and battles, the compelling message was to grow, expand, and continually rebuild. Progress became a historical characteristic of the country.

By contrast, a small number of people held a different, admittedly romantic outlook, calling for history to be remembered and revered. In part this was due to the limited number of people who had a basic historical sensitivity. It was also due to the small number who had the time and financial ability to care for and understand the past by interpreting artifacts and properties. The culture of collecting was cast by the predilections of wealthy amateurs, some of whom would come to share their views with larger audiences in museums, which in turn gradually made collections accessible to the public. Likewise, the leaders in the preservation movement were relatively well-educated and financially secure members of society. Ann Pamela Cunningham, Mary Hemenway, Andrew Haswell Green are the most obvious leaders in the nineteenth century, while the romantic Charles Lummis, adventurous Susan Pringle Frost, and courageous Adina Emilia De Zavala are notable in the early twentieth century.

While individuals and groups in the South often proved successful, Boston's intellectual contribution was as substantial, largely owing to the influence of educators like Charles Norton and professionals such as Frederick Law Olmsted, Charles Eliot, and William Sumner Appleton. The influence of Boston's thinking on Williamsburg also spurred more scientific and professional activity, and provided a preservation "school" of sorts for both architects and archaeologists. The work of professionals in New Orleans and Charleston with surveys and building treatment also contributed to a broader understanding. Surveys became the primary activity that would provide the legal basis for preservation as a part of zoning and planning. The treatments were often either the stabilization of ruins or restoration, with the conversion of sites to museum use. In short, scientific thought that rested on data collection was put into service to support preservation rationales.

Almost from the start, museums paid attention to American artifacts and the links to native tribes, if only because Europeans found the "foreign" material of interest. Museums were the first to study American agriculture, focused as many were on interpreting the colonial era and pioneer period, as were the wide range of patriotic associations. In light of subsequent rethinking, it is clear that the overwhelming theme of the "march of progress" led to misrepresentation of ethnic groups and social communities. Among some native tribes, for example, the concept of a past, present, and future is not separate and distinct. On the other hand, early ethnographers and archaeologists learned a considerable amount when faced with the interpretation of their findings. Meanwhile, garden clubs extended the idea of caring for the great estates, mansions, and town houses into the landscape, always looking over their shoulder at what was taking place in Europe. Until the Depression, however, the comparisons of American preservation activity with the initiatives in Europe were comparatively few. What appears to have occurred is that the passion for collecting led to accomplishments in other areas, serving as an inspiration to others across the country.

Against all of these developments, it is comparatively easy to understand why, after the Depression and World War II, when it was discovered that the neglected downtown business districts and inner city neighborhoods were in need of substantial rehabilitation, urban renewal seemed like the answer. Yet historic preservationists would need to rally a considerably broader constituency to provide an alternative view of "progress."

References

Ables, L. R. (1965). Adina De Zavala. In C. L. Lord (Ed.), *Keepers of the past.* Chapel Hill: University of North Carolina Press.

Albright, H. M., & Cahn, R. (1985). *The birth of the National Park Service: The founding years, 1913–33.* Salt Lake City: Howe Brothers.

Alexander, E. P. (1983). *Charles Willson Peale and his Philadelphia museum. Museum masters: Their museums and their influence* (pp. 43–78). Nashville: American Association of State and Local History.

Almaraz, F. D. Jr. (8 May 1994). De Zavala made historical mark. *San Antonio Express-News*, 61.

Anthony, W. C. (1927). *Washington's headquarters, Newburgh, New York. A history of its construction and its various occupants.* New York: Historical Society of Newburgh Bay and the Highlands.

Arthur, S. C. (1936). *Old new Orleans*. New Orleans: Hermansan.

Ashbee, C. R. (1900). *The survey of London: volume I: The Parish of Bromley-by-Bo*. London: London County Council.

Ashbee, C. R. (1901). *American sheaves & English seed corn: Being a series of addresses mainly delivered in the United States, 1900–1901*. London: E. Arnold.

Barnes, E. A. (1932). *Children and architecture*. New York: Bureau of Publications, Teachers College, Columbia University.

Bassett, E. M., et al. (1935). *Model laws for planning cities, counties and state*. Cambridge: Harvard University Press.

Bassett, E. M. (1936). *Zoning: The laws, administration, and court decisions during the first twenty years*. New York: Russell Sage.

Benjamin, J. E. (1989). *C.R. Ashbee in America: An Englishman's observations on the arts and crafts movement, architecture, and culture 1896–1916*. Master of Arts thesis, Graduate Field of History of Architecture and Urban Development, Cornell University.

Bradley, J. L., & Ousby, I. (Eds.) (1987). *The correspondence of John Ruskin and Charles Eliot Norton*. Cambridge: Cambridge University Press.

Brown, G. B. (1905). *The care of ancient monuments: An account of the legislative and other measures adopted in European countries for protecting ancient monuments and objects and scenes of natural beauty, and for preserving the aspect of historical cities*. Cambridge: Cambridge University Press.

Caldwell, R. (1887). *A true history of the acquisition of Washington's headquarters at Newburgh by the State of New York*. Middletown: Stivers, Slauson & Boyd.

Chambers, H. E. (1925). *A history of Louisiana* (Vol. 2). Chicago: The American Historical Society.

Chicago. (8 Dec 1900). Save local historic ruins. English apostle of beauty in art organizes an association. *Chicago Daily News*, 1.

Ciborowski, A. (1969). *Warsaw: A city destroyed and rebuilt*. Warsaw: Interpress Publishers.

Corning, A. E. (1950). *The story of the Hasbrouck House, Washington's headquarters*. NY: Board of Trustees, Washington's Headquarters.

Cotter, J. C., Roberts, D. G., & Parrington, M. (1992). *The buried past. An archaeological history of Philadelphia*. Philadelphia: Temple University Press.

Crawford, A. (2005). *C.R. Ashbee: Architect, designer & romantic socialist*. New Haven: Yale University Press.

Cubberley, E. P. (1934). *Public education in the United States, a study and interpretation of American educational history*. Boston: Houghton Mifflin Company.

De Zavala, A. (1917). *The De Zavala daughters. History and legends of the Alamo and others missions in and around San Antonio*. San Antonio.

Doheny, D. A. (2006). *David finley: Quiet force for American arts*. Washington: National Trust for Historic Preservation.

Donofrio, G. A. (2001). *Building the farmer's museum, 1943–1965*. Master of Arts thesis, Graduate Field of City and Regional Planning, Cornell University.

Dorris, M. (1915). *Preservation of the hermitage 1889–1915: Annals, history and stories. The acquisition, restoration, and care of the home of General Andrew Jackson by the Ladies' hermitage association for over a quarter of a century*. Nashville: Ladies' Hermitage Association.

Drowne, H. R. (1925). *Sketch of Fraunces Tavern and those connected with its history*. New York: Fraunces Tavern.

Edenheim, R. (1995). *Skansen: Traditional Swedish style*. London: Scala Books.

Editorial. (1906). Architectural art and its Allies, January, 8.

Eliot, C. (5 March 1890). Waverly Oaks. *Garden and Forest*.

Eliot, C. W. (1903). *Charles Eliot, landscape architect*. Boston: Houghton Mifflin and Company.

Fisher, L. F. (1996). *Saving San Antonio: The precarious preservation of a heritage*. Lubbock: Texas Tech University Press.

Fiske, T. L. (1975). *Charles F. Lummis: The man and his west*. Norman: University of Oklahoma Press.

Floyd, M. H. (1979). Measured drawings of the Hancock House by John Hubbard Sturgis: A Legacy to the Colonial Revival. *Architecture in Colonial Massachusetts, 60*, 87–110.

Ford, J. (1913). *The life and public services of Andrew Haswell Green*. Garden City: Doubleday, Page & Company.

Gallop, G. (19 April 1944). Religious buildings: Gallop finds 74% of those questioned back army chiefs. *The New York Times*.

Genthe, A. (1926). *Impressions of old New Orleans: A book of pictures*. New York: George H. Doran.

Gilmartin, G. F. (1995). *Shaping the city; New York and the municipal art society*. New York: Clarkson Potter.

Goodwin, Rev. W. A. R. (1907). *Bruton Parish Church restored and its historic environment*. Petersburg: The Franklin Press.

Greiff, C. M. (1987). *Independence. The creation of a National Park*. Philadelphia: University of Pennsylvania Press.

Grevstad-Nordbrock, T. E. (2007). *The American Commission for the protection and salvage of artistic and historic monuments in war areas: Historic preservation in Europe during World War II*. Master of Arts thesis, Program in Historic Preservation Planning, Cornell University.

Hall, E. H. (1903). Historic and scenic preservation in America. *Chautauquan, 20*(3), 284–295.

Hata, N. I. (1992). *The historic preservation movement in California, 1940–1976*. Sacramento: California Department of Parks and Recreation.

Hearn, M. F. (Ed.). (1990). *The architectural theory of Viollet-le-Duc. Readings and commentary*. Cambridge: MIT Press.

Hibberd, H. (1980). *The metropolitan museum of art*. New York: Harper & Row.

Holleran, M. (1998). *Boston's 'Changeful Times': Origins of preservation and planning in America*. Baltimore: Johns Hopkins University Press.

Hosmer, C. B. Jr. (1965). *Presence of the past, a history of the preservation movement in the United States before Williamsburg.* New York: G. P. Putnam's Sons.

Hosmer, C. B. Jr. (1981). *Preservation comes of age* (Vol. 1). Charlottesville: The University Press of Virginia.

Howard, P. (1935). Southern Personalities-Adina De Zavala, Patriot-Historian. *Holland's, The Magazine of the South, 64*(7), 36.

Howe, W. E. (1913). *A history of the metropolitan museum of art, with a chapter on the early institutions of art in New York.* New York: The Metropolitan Museum of Art.

Huber, L. V., & Wilson, S. Jr. (1965). *The Basilica on Jackson Square: The history of the St. Louis Cathedral and its predecessors, 1727–1965.* New Orleans: St. Louis Cathedral.

Hunter, A. A. (1991). *A century of service: The story of the DAR.* Washington: National Society Daughters of the American Revolution.

Huth, H. (1957). *Nature and the American.* Berkeley: University of California Press.

Ickes, H. (1935). Preservation of historic American sites, buildings, objects, and antiquities of National significance. Hearings before the United States House Committee on Public Lands. 74th Congress, 1st Session, 1–2 April.

Ise, J. (1961). *Our National park policy: A critical history.* Baltimore: Johns Hopkins University Press.

Jacobs, S. W. (1966). *Architectural preservation: American development and antecedents Abroad.* Doctoral dissertation, Department of Art and Archaeology, Princeton University.

James, G. W. (1927). *In and out of the old missions of California.* Boston: Grosset & Dunlap.

Jeter, M. D. (1999). Edward Palmer: Present before the creation of archaeological stratigraphy and associations. *Journal of the Southwest, 41,* 335–358.

Jokilehto, J. (1999). *A history of architectural conservation.* Oxford: Butterworth-Heinemann.

Kennedy, D. M. (1999). *Freedom from fear: The American people in depression and war, 1929–1945.* New York: Oxford University Press.

King, G. (1929). *Mount Vernon on the Potomac. History of the Mt. Vernon Ladies Association of the Union,* New York: MacMillan.

Knowland, J. R. (1941). *California: A landmark history.* Oakland: Tribune.

Krueckenberg, D. A. (Ed.) (1983). *From the autobiography of Edward M. Bassett. The American planner.* New York: Methuen.

Lange, C. H., & Riley, C. L. (Eds.). (2008). *The Southwest journals of Adolph F. Bandelier* (Vol. 1). Albuquerque: University of New Mexico Press.

Lee, R. F. (2000). The antiquities act of 1906. *Journal of the Southwest, 42*(2), 198–269.

Lindgren, J. M. (1984). *The gospel of preservation in Virginia and New England: Historic preservation and the regeneration of traditionalism.* Doctoral dissertation, Department of History, College of William and Mary.

Lindgren, J. M. (1993). *Preserving the old dominion: Historic preservation and Virginia traditionalism.* Charlottesville: The University Press of Virginia.

Little, B. L. (1965). William Sumner Appleton. In C. L. Lord (Ed.), *Keepers of the past* (pp. 215–222). Chapel Hill: University of North Carolina Press.

Mark, J. (1988). *A stranger in her native land: Alice Fletcher and the American Indians.* Lincoln: University of Nebraska Press.

McClean, T. (1998). The making of public history: A comparative study of Skansen open air museum, Colonial Williamsburg, Virginia; and the Fortress of Louisbourg, National historic site, Nova Scotia. *Material History Review, 47,* 21–32.

Milner, G. R. (2004). *The Moundbuilders: Ancient peoples of eastern North America.* London: Thames & Hudson.

Moga, S. T. (2009). Marginal lands and suburban nature. *Journal of Planning History, 8,* 308–330.

Montgomery, D. (1998). *A link among the days: The life and times of the Reverend Doctor W.A.R. Goodwin, The Father of Colonial Williamsburg.* Richmond: Dietz Press.

Nicholas, L. H. (1994). *The rape of Europa: The fate of Europe's treasures in the third Reich and the Second World War.* New York: Knopf.

Owen, C. A. (1938). Les Anciens. The Octagon. *Journal of the American Institute of Architects,* (3), 10–13.

Patterson, T. C. (1995). *Toward a social history of archaeology in the United States.* Fort Worth: Harcourt Brace & Company.

Peterson, C. E. (1976). HABS-In and out of Philadelphia. In R. Webster (Ed.), *Philadelphia preserved. Catalog of the Historic American buildings survey* (pp. xxi–xxvi). Philadelphia: Temple University Press.

Peterson, C. E. (2009). Before the Arch: Some early architects and engineers on the St. Louis Waterfront. In D. Ames & R. Wagner (Eds.), *Design & historic preservation: The challenge of compatibility.* Newark: University of Delaware Press.

Phillips, K. (2003). *Helen Hunt Jackson: A literary life.* Berkeley: University of California Press.

Pierce, M. F. (1901). *The landmark of Fraunces' Tavern.* New York: Women's Auxiliary to the Society for the Preservation of Scenic and Historic Places and Objects.

Powers, L. B. (1893). *The story of the old missions of California: Their establishment, progress and decay.* San Francisco: W. Doxey.

Powers, L. B. (1902). *Historic tales of the old missions for boys and girls.* San Francisco: Walter N. Brunt.

Public Law 74-292. (1935–1936). United States statutes at large.

Putnam, F. W. (1890). The serpent Mound of Ohio, *Century, 39*(6), 871–883.

Robinson, C. M. (1903). *Modern civic art or the city made beautiful.* New York: G.P. Putman's Sons.

Roerich Museum Website. (n.d.). http://www.roerich.org/roerich-pact-publications-archival-materials.php. Accessed 8 Feb 2014.

Roper, L. W. (1974). *FLO: A biography of Frederick Law Olmsted*. Baltimore: Johns Hopkins Press.

Rothman, H. (1985). *Protected by a gold fence with diamond tips: A cultural history of the American National Monuments*. Doctoral dissertation, Department of American Studies, University of Texas at Austin.

Rothman, H. (1989). *Preserving different pasts: The American National Monuments*. Urbana and Chicago: University of Illinois Press.

Rowell, George P. & Co. (1894). *Rowell's American newspaper directory*. New York: Rowell's.

Ruskin, J. (1849). *The seven lamps of architecture. With illustrations, drawn and etched by the author*. London: Smith, Elder, and Co.

Schaffer, R. (1985). *Wings of judgment: American Bombing in world War II*. New York: Oxford University Press.

Schuyler, M. (1904). The works of Messrs. Barney & Chapman. *Architectural Record*, September, pp. 203–296.

Schuyler, M. (1908). The restoration of Fraunces Tavern. *Architectural Record, 24*(6).

Senate (1871). Executive Document No. 51, 3rd Session

Senate (1872). Executive Document No. 26, 2nd Session.

Sohier, E. P. (1876). *History of the Old South Church, Published for the benefit of the Old South fund*. Boston: Printed by Reuben Hildreth.

Squier, E. G., & Davis, E. H. (1847). *Ancient monuments of the Mississippi Valley, comprising the results of extensive original surveys and explorations*. Washington, DC: The Smithsonian Institution.

Taylor, G. R. (1915). *Satellite cities: A study of industrial suburbs*. New York: D. Appleton and Company.

Thane, E. (1966). *Mt. Vernon is ours. The story of its preservation*. New York: Duell, Sloan, Pearce.

Thompson, M. (2001). *American character: The curious life of Charles Fletcher Lummis and the rediscovery of the southwest*. New York: Arcade.

Toft, C. H., & Josse, L. (2002). *St. Louis: Landmarks & historic districts*. St. Louis: Landmarks Association of St. Louis.

Tomkins, C. (1970). *Merchants and masterpieces: The story of the metropolitan museum of art*. New York: Henry Holt and Company.

Tomlan, M. A. (1983). *Popular and Professional American Architectural Literature in the late nineteenth century*. Doctoral dissertation, Graduate Field of History of Architecture and Urban Development, Cornell University.

Turner, J. T. (1999). *The liberal education of Charles Eliot Norton*. Baltimore: Johns Hopkins Press.

Upward, G. C. (Ed.). (1979). *A home for our heritage: The building and growth of greenfield village and Henry Ford Museum, 1929–1979*. Dearborn: Henry Ford Museum Press.

U.S. Government Historical Reports on War Administration (1946). *Report of the American commission for the protection and salvage of artistic and Historic monuments in war areas*. Washington, DC: U.S. Government Printing Office.

Verrier, A. (1968). *The bomber offensive*. London: Batsford.

Warren, J. P. (1986). *The historic American merchant marine survey*. Master of Arts thesis, Graduate Field of History of Architecture and Urban Development, Cornell University.

Weinberg, N. (1974). *Historic preservation and tradition in California: The restoration of the missions and the Spanish-colonial revival*. Doctoral dissertation, University of California, Davis.

Weiss, M. A. (1987). *The rise of the community builders: the American real estate industry and urban land planning*. New York: Columbia University Press.

Wells, M. E. (1921). *How the present came from the past, book I: The seeds in primitive life*. New York: Macmillan.

Weyeneth, R. R. (2000). *Historic preservation for a living city: Historic Charleston foundation, 1947–1997*. Columbia: University of South Carolina Press.

Will, E. L. (2002). Charles Eliot Norton and the Archaeological Institute of America. In Susan Heuck Allen (Ed.), *Excavating our past: Perspectives on the history of the archaeological institute of America* (pp. 52–53). Boston: Archaeological Institute of America.

Wilson, C. (1997). *The Myth of Sante Fe: Creating a modern tradition*. Albuquerque: University of New Mexico Press.

Woolley, Lt.-Col. Sir Leonard. (1947). *A record of the work done by the military authorities for the protection of the treasures of art & history in war areas*. London: His Majesty's Stationery Office.

Wyatt, D. E. (1982). *Joseph R. Knowland: The political years, 1899–1915*. San Francisco: D. Wyatt.

Young, D. (1990). Charleston's 1931 ordinance still hard at work. *The Alliance Review. Newsletter of the National Alliance of Preservation Commissions, Summer*.

Zesch, S. (2008). Adina De Zavala and the second Siege of the Alamo. *CRM: The Journal of Heritage Stewardship, Winter, 5*(1), 31–44.

Zueblin, C. (1916). *American municipal progress*. New York: Macmillan.

A Different Way of Thinking

2

Introduction

At the conclusion of World War II, most Americans agreed with the views of Henry Luce in *Life* magazine that the USA would lead the world into the next century. With little concern for what other people in the world might think, Americans believed that, just as their country had come to the rescue of Europe, it would forge ahead as the very epitome of progress. With a deep and abiding positivist belief in a future guided by the most advanced science and technology, Americans shifted gears from marching in step in war to the cadences of industrial expansion. Government activity swelled.

Cold War rhetoric reinforced the idea that the way of life in the USA was the best path to follow, to be celebrated, and to be defended. American flags were displayed proudly, even in bomb shelters below ground. Conformity was important to veterans and their new families, who looked forward to a good life in the rapidly growing suburbs. There, "similar" people viewed the world from similar houses in a similar manner. Men and, gradually, more women entered colleges and universities. The veterans were encouraged to learn more while the country's economy shifted from a wartime engine to a peacetime model. Women who had served as the mainstay for military production were encouraged to return to homemaking, while young "coeds" were guided into traditional careers in nursing, home economics, and education. They would find the right man, one who would wear a grey flannel suit and be proud to be a member of a corporation. The security of marriage would to lead to happy children. The new family was the hallmark of success, just as obvious as the new car in the driveway and the new television in the "rec room." Freedom increasingly became synonymous with mobility, guaranteed by an automobile-centered culture.

Even during the 1950s, however, it was clear that this was an incomplete and sometimes very misleading picture. Artists and writers captured the discontent in the suburbs, seeing the "crack in the picture window." Sputnik's launch in 1957 shook the American view that their leadership in science was unbeatable. Urban renewal schemes and new interstate transportation improvements spelled massive destruction and dislocation in cities. By the early 1960s, social movements erupted that, at first, seemed to characterize only a few disaffected individuals. As the number of these individuals increased, however, their disruptions became more worrisome. The structure of the social movements began to challenge established society with demonstrations, protests, and riots that contradicted any image of a single, monolithic viewpoint on a wide range of issues.

Many of the same fractures would be found in the historic preservation movement, although the authors involved with creating the 1966 National Historic Preservation Act did not comment upon contemporary social activities. Some preservation leaders were convinced the Modern Movement in architecture and planning offered a better way, while others instinctively reacted against it. Preservationists were also aware of the

M. A. Tomlan, *Historic Preservation,* DOI 10.1007/978-3-319-04975-5_2,
© Springer International Publishing Switzerland 2015

expanding Civil Rights Movement. Indeed, on-the-street preservation activists often embraced some of the same protest techniques as African Americans, and alongside them insisted on a reversal of the top–down approach to planning. At the same time, most preservationists embraced the growing environmental movement, emphasizing recycling and ecological consciousness, embedding these ideas into the "new" historic preservation. In short, these three movements influenced the next generation of thinking as the preservation field expanded. Subsequently, advocacy for women's rights, gay and lesbian initiatives, and Native American concerns provided added impetus.

The genius of the National Historic Preservation Act remains that it allowed a growing number of local interests to catalyze some important basic goals into a national policy. It legitimized widespread local advocacy and, while often challenged by those in authority, it remained flexible enough to continue to serve a broadening constituency with only relatively minor amendments. Although the traditional artifact-centered approach that preservationists had favored remained important, the range of objects of attention increased and the frontiers of the movement reached into the most remote communities across the country. From neighborhood conservation and main-street rehabilitation, the preservation community learned the political necessity of creating a coalition of all local interests, not just some. And, after the spotlights of the Bicentennial in 1976 were turned off, the political shift away from Washington and toward local interests increased. The American melting pot was transformed into a mosaic, celebrating roots and learning more about the differences among people.

By the mid-1980s, as edge cities sprang up across the country, preservation focus also shifted from city cores to the first and second ring suburbs, some of which were experiencing disinvestment and scattered depopulation. Preservation adopted the then-current "indirect" financial initiatives, rather than direct government funding. Tax incentives more truly demonstrated the public's social priorities. The positivism that impelled the post-War era's ambitions—characterized by unity, predictability, and certainty—was thrown into question by "post-modern" relativism, much of it based on identity politics. New initiatives that began with a strategic assessment of the available options supplanted comprehensive planning with more timely, politically calculated objectives. Postmodern planning attempted to understand but not resolve differences in culture, race, class, gender, and religion, leaving the solution to any problem to those working at the local level. In this context, the historic preservation movement continues to serve as a different way of thinking, influencing Americans in a manner that most early advocates would never have conceived. This chapter takes the history of the preservation movement from World War II to the end of the twentieth century. Subsequent chapters discuss themes introduced here in greater detail.

Changes in Historic Preservation in the Post-War Era

Early in the twentieth century, Charles Ashbee had introduced the English National Trust to the USA with the idea of enlarging the public willing to advocate for significant monuments. William Sumner Appleton had suggested that a nationwide nongovernment organization was needed to save endangered historic properties, and the American Scenic and Historic Preservation Society had held out the idea that a countrywide preservation network was possible. Unfortunately, the Depression and then World War II made the establishment of a unified private sector initiative across the country a low national priority. The American Scenic and Historic Preservation Society's membership rolls dropped precipitously by mid-century. Similar dips in attendance in other nonprofit professional and volunteer organizations were common until peace returned.

The clearest sign of a resurgence of interest in historic preservation centered around the founding the National Trust for Historic Preservation. In late 1946, David E. Finley, Director of the National Gallery of Art, invited George McAneny, President of the American Scenic and Historic Preservation Society; Christopher Crittenden,

Fig. 2.1 The need to protect "Hampton," the remarkable eighteenth century mansion north of Baltimore, and other estates like it, was one impetus for the creation of the National Trust for Historic Preservation. (Author's photograph)

from the North Carolina Department of Archives and History; and Ronald F. Lee, a historian in the National Park Service, to a meeting to discuss the common problems they faced saving historic properties (Doheny 2006). Finley was frustrated by having failed to get the National Park Service to accept the responsibility for "Hampton," a splendid, intact eighteenth-century mansion north of Baltimore (Fig. 2.1). Finley also faced the prospect that Oak Hill, the former home of President Monroe, would be sold. The National Park Service was reluctant to become involved in these cases because so many similar estates across the country were on the market, and the agency could not take care of them all (Hosmer 1981, pp. 814–820).[1] What the country needed, the four men agreed, was a new nongovernmental organization that could quickly become involved in saving buildings of architectural and historic importance and open them up to the public, with a mission statement modeled after the National Trust in England (Finley 1965).

Subsequent meetings with a number of interested parties broadened interest in the idea. Under Finley's leadership, in early 1947, 41 representatives of a wide range of allied groups assembled and formed the National Council for Historic Sites and Buildings. The Council would increase public awareness and give birth to the National Trust, which would deal with the acquisition and operation of historic properties. By October, the Council had as its president Maj. General US Grant 3rd and a young, Harvard-trained National Park Service historian, Frederick L. Rath, Jr., loaned to the new organization as the first Executive Secretary. Rath's office was in what became the first headquarters of the organization, Ford's Theatre in Washington, D.C. With the continued support of allied, historically minded groups, bills were introduced and passed in the Senate and the House, and President Truman signed the legislation approving a Congressional charter for the National Trust for Historic Preservation on October 26, 1949.

Initially the National Trust was to hold and administer such properties and encourage public participation in their preservation.[2] However, Ex-

[1] In the case of Hampton, ultimately the Avalon Foundation and Mrs. Ailsa Mellon Bruce provided the funding that led to the transfer of the property to the National Park Service. Both were also early financial supporters of the nascent National Trust.

[2] The National Trust adopted a policy of accepting gifts of important architectural and historic monuments if some means could be found for their support, either by income from endowments or operation by other qualified organizations.

Fig. 2.2 "Woodlawn," another historic estate, was to be sold to Belgian monks until the Historic Woodlawn Public Foundation stepped in to save it, transferring it to the National Trust as the organization's first house museum. (Author's photograph)

ecutive Director Rath saw the nascent organization as more than a steward of great estates and townhouses. To him, the organization was the center of a network of likeminded advocates. He believed the National Trust should be a "clearinghouse" for information, applying the phrase used by staff and many of the organization's members until the 1990s. In hundreds of letters to people in every corner of the country, he advised advocates on how they could learn from one another to save properties.

Large estates in the Tidewater region of Virginia continued to demand immediate attention. "Woodlawn," the estate near Mt. Vernon given by George Washington to his foster daughter and his nephew, seemed destined to be sold to an order of Belgian monks (Fig. 2.2). A young lawyer, Armistead Wood, and a small group of associates stepped up to attempt to raise sufficient funds on behalf of the newly established Woodlawn Public Foundation. While Rath was skilled in house museum administration because of his National Park Service work, he also found himself involved with fundraising. It was not until wealthy collector Paul Mellon assisted the organization by providing a matching grant that it became possible to tender an offer that ultimately led to the first

house museum owned and operated by the National Trust (Hosmer 1981, pp. 842, 845).[3]

Although the initial decision-makers in and around Washington were men, women would soon make contributions to the Trust. Helen Bullock, who joined the staff in 1950, shaped the organization and its early views more than any other employee. Bullock coordinated regional meetings and house tours to build a preservation constituency, and edited and wrote many of the early publications. As a researcher of colonial recipes, she became an acknowledged expert on early American cooking. By gaining the interest of a division of the National Biscuit Company in a line of historical recipes that could be adapted to a ready-mix method, she was able to provide financial support to the Trust and allied organizations, such as the Thomas Jefferson Memorial Foundation at Monticello (Mulloy 1976; Pilot 1995; Thomas 1956).

After the Trust acquired Woodlawn in 1951 and the Decatur House on Jackson Square in Washington, D.C. 3 years later, the word spread

---

[3] The site would later serve as the home of an additional building, the Pope Leighey House, designed by Frank Lloyd Wright.

to potential donors.[4] Mrs. Frances Adler Elkins bequeathed her property, "Casa Amesti," in Monterey, California, a site the organization accepted in 1955. Clearly, the first years of the National Trust were house-museum oriented. Fred Rath resigned in 1956 and, although Helen Bullock managed the affairs of the Trust, it was under the executive direction of the President of the Board for 4 years. In 1958, the president gained a new assistant, William J. Murtagh, who carried the Trust's message to dozens of communities around the country. The next executive director, Robert Garvey, would expand the activities of the organization with even more vigor. Garvey's career in historic preservation had begun in 1955, managing Old Salem, the outdoor museum of the Moravian community in the Piedmont of North Carolina.[5] His skill as a manager was important, but his ability as a fund-raiser was the chief reason he was valued at the Trust. Garvey had come to the attention of Christopher Crittendon, head of the North Carolina Department of Archives and History, who was also a founding board member of the National Trust.[6] Garvey joined the National Trust during the early fall of 1960 and quickly began to expand the staff (Author's Papers August 4, 1981). As will be shown, the Trust's employees became extremely important when implementing the "new preservation" nearly a decade later. Although most members of the team were familiar with museums, they were all eager to go beyond them to spread the ideas of the preservation movement.

From "Do It Yourself Digs" to "New" Archaeology

The post World War II changes taking place in the preservation community ran parallel to the transformations in archaeology, eventually affecting the Office of Archaeology and Historic Preservation, established by the National Historic Preservation Act in 1966. When the American Anthropological Association reorganized in 1946, the prevailing idea among its membership was to present the field as an integrated scientific discipline, despite the humanistic orientation from which it had grown. Archaeologists in the country were keenly aware that, to become involved with the rising number of public improvements projects, they needed to demonstrate rigorous scholarship that would be useful in planning viable alternatives to the destruction of valued sites. During the 1950s, the US Army Corps of Engineers focused its efforts on flood control in the heartland of the USA by building dams. It soon became apparent to anthropologists and archaeologists that the resulting flooding behind the dams would cover several major prehistoric sites. The alarm was an urgent one, and an informal agreement reached between the Smithsonian Institution and the National Park Service became formal in the adoption of the 1960 Reservoir Salvage Act, whereby Congress would make available funds for subsurface investigations by a wide variety of public institutions.

At the same time, a number of popular books stimulated the rising interest in archaeology and increase the number of amateur archaeologists. Exciting stories of archaeologists' great discoveries in Crete, Egypt, Assyria, Babylon, and Yucatan were penned by the German journalist Kurt W. Marek, writing under the pseudonym C.W. Ceram. He produced *Gods, Graves, and Scholars,* his first book, in 1951, and over 10,000 copies sold every year during the ensuing decades (Books in Print 1951). The marked increase in

---

[4] The fact that the Decatur House was designed by architect Benjamin Henry Latrobe added a note of distinction.

[5] In later life Garvey was proud of the fact that, when he arrived at Old Salem, only one building was open to the public, but by the time he left, seven exhibit structures were operating (Author's Papers 1981).

[6] Crittendon's role was also important earlier, for he transformed the American Association of State and Local History (AASLH). Although it can trace its origins to the early twentieth century, under his leadership the organization rededicated itself to advancing many ideas well known in the local history field that would later have a significant influence on the National Trust. These included teaching in schools and colleges, issuing press releases and communicating with the general public, serving as a clearinghouse for information among members and nonmembers, creating radio programs and magazine articles, and, whenever possible, preserving historic buildings (Alexander 1991).

local and regionally based archaeological organizations was noticed, and would often be helpful when a dam or highway was about to be constructed. In all but three states, the recognized associations noticed a surge in their numbers, as legions of amateurs got down to the earth, guided by state archaeologists and enthusiastic spokesmen, such as Roland Wells Robbins. He led teams of "dig-it-yourself" archaeologists on sites at the Saugus Iron Works in Massachusetts and at Philipse Manor in Tarrytown, New York (Jones 1958; Linebaugh 2005). Schoolteachers, housewives, and family parties were attracted to the Philipse site so that they could experience the excitement of discovery.

With more sites explored and more information available, an increasing number of archaeologists began to ask embarrassing questions about what was *not* being explored. Like preservationists, archaeologists were becoming simultaneously more precise and broader in their interests. Although scientific tools such as dendrochronology (Hawley 1937; Schulman 1956; Vivian and Kletso 1964; and Stokes 1968) and radiocarbon dating were more commonplace in highly structured academic archaeological digs (Johnson 1951; Libby 1955), a growing sensitivity arose toward the need for the study of settlement patterns, community organization, crop patterns, subsistence practices, fauna and flora, artifact distribution, and statistics. This "new archaeology" placed much greater emphasis on the vernacular or common activities of people and, with time, affected others disciplines, such as history, art history, and architectural history (Sabloff 1998).[7]

With these developments, the distance grew even further between classical archaeology, with its iconic attitudes about the interpretation of high-style artifacts and major sites of interest to Europeans, and American archaeologists, who were increasingly inter- and multi-disciplinary, interested in applying high technology and science to their investigations. For many archae-

Fig. 2.3 Charles Peterson and Ivor Noel Hume shaped the work of young professionals for decades, raising questions about the appropriate course of action. (Author's photograph)

ologists, particularly academics, the growing amount of information tended to create specialization and distanced them from the amateurs (King et al. 1997). By contrast, museum interpretation provided a connection to the public. The most visible exponent was Ivor Noel Hume (Fig. 2.3). Although trained in theatre in England and coming to archaeology as a second career, he was the most influential historical archaeologist of the period, guiding the development and interpretation of Colonial Williamsburg at the same time he wrote some of the most easily accessible texts, spelling out methods and techniques to guide investigations (Hume 1969, 1974; Hume and Miller 2011).

While archaeology on the vast federal and state lands in the Midwest and West became widespread, only rarely did a city employ an archaeologist. The city of Alexandria, Virginia, was the first to hire an urban archaeologist outside of the museum setting provided by Colonial Williamsburg. The need arose in 1960–1961 when their urban renewal program, centered on the old

---

[7] "New archaeology" is understood to begin with the publication of Lewis Binford's *Archaeology as Anthropology* in 1962.

town, uncovered hundreds of Civil War artifacts. When the city failed to pick up the expenses for the work, a committee of 100 citizens supported the project for a few years. The city created the permanent position of city archaeologist in 1973, and it served as a model for other communities to broaden their programs (AllianceLetter 1983; Cressey 1979). Subsequently, city archaeology programs began in New York, Philadelphia, Baltimore, and Boston.[8]

Preservation as an Alternative to Urban Renewal

After World War II, the poor condition of American housing caused by long-deferred maintenance demanded immediate attention. Housing specialists stated that the unsatisfactory units occupied by tenants were twice as likely as owner-occupied units to witness continued social and economic problems. In 1949, an improved and expanded version of the Housing Act of 1937 attempted to relieve the postwar housing shortage with new apartments (Foard and Fefferman 1967; Bauman 1987; Schuyler 2002). In both laws, federal urban redevelopment efforts focused predominantly on residential uses.

In the mid-1950s, inner city rental properties were almost two thirds of the nation's housing inventory. As the decade wore on, the decline in manufacturing and problems associated with the transition to a peacetime economy riveted the attention of policy makers. Obsolescent structures of all kinds, not only houses but also factories and entire commercial blocks, became candidates for demolition and removal, particularly if they were in poor condition. At the same time, it was already clear that the nonwhite population of the inner city was growing, and African Americans were increasingly segregated in certain downtown neighborhoods (Frieden 1964).

Post-World War II federal urban renewal legislation often worked against saving historic structures, particularly in locations designated as "blighted," that is, targeted for demolition. The structures most in need of maintenance, repair, and improvement were some of the most significant examples of architectural or historical merit. Although the long period of neglect during the Depression and the national priorities of wartime left inner city housing with many problems, to some there was no apparent way to reconcile housing needs with the goal of saving historic properties, and often the areas immediately adjacent to an urban renewal project continued to experience decline.

In early historic districts, in Charleston and New Orleans, the role of the architectural survey was critical to determining the character of the properties and districts. The surveys also provided guidance about the procedure for designating properties as important for their architectural and historical significance. In Charleston, for example, a rating system differentiated the properties deemed most significant, and the published survey results became well known (Carolina Art Association 1944).

To explore alternatives to demolition, the Housing Act of 1954 contained a new provision, Section 314, which allowed urban renewal demonstration grants to be used to match funds raised from the community. This spurred a recognizable pattern in historic preservation planning that combined the characteristics of a housing study with an architectural historical survey, and rated buildings on a weighted numerical scale (Kalman 1976).[9] Urban renewal in Providence, Rhode Island provided an early template that many cities would follow. The transformation began with advocacy in the state legislature, where enabling legislation was passed that allowed municipalities to establish redevelopment agencies, and the city adopted a master plan focusing on residen-

---

[8] For example, Dr. Sherene Baugher was hired in August 1980 as the first archaeologist for New York City and Stephen Mrozowski was hired in Boston the following year (Author's Papers 2007).

[9] Kalman provides a comparison of the advantages and disadvantages of qualitative and quantitative techniques, theorizing the need for more dynamic systems of evaluation. Further examination of these ideas can be found in Chapter 6.

tial properties. By early in 1948, the city council had designated 17 areas suffering from blight and dilapidation, and, in November, the voters approved city bonds to establish a redevelopment revolving fund. Questions arose about the constitutionality of the legislation, but planning proceeded so that the Providence Redevelopment Agency could begin demolition. The Agency and a mayor's advisory committee held over 60 public meetings in the following 2 years, discussing the proposed clearance legislation.

Critical flashpoints arose when Brown University wished to expand its dormitories, demolishing 13 residential properties in 1952 with more targeted for removal in 1955. Continued destruction by Brown seemed certain. The reaction among concerned citizens was swift. In April 1956, the Providence Preservation Society was founded to stem the rapid loss of historically and architecturally significant property on College Hill, immediately adjacent to Brown University (Woodward 1982; Woodward and Sanderson 1986). Encouraged by John Howland, chairman of the Board of the National Trust for Historic Preservation, the organization attempted—in vain—to stop the University's plan to demolish 30 historic structures south of its existing campus for a new residential quadrangle. Although this was not the first time that the residents of this city had fought to save residential and commercial buildings and lost, never before had so much real estate been at issue at one time (Wright 1964).[10]

Mrs. William Slater Allen, the first president of the Providence Preservation Society, and John Nicholas Brown, the chairman of the board, quickly approached the Providence City Plan Commission and the Redevelopment Agency, seeking information about how to halt the destruction. At the same time, they lobbied the State legislature for historic zoning (Wright 1964, pp. 20–21). Previous studies regarding the future of the area included a Master Plan for Land Use and Population, a controversial Mas-

ter Plan for Thoroughfares that was revised as an official transportation plan (1950), and several central area studies financed by the US Housing and Home Finance Agency. All of the proposals included considerable demolition and clearance, but none of these studies mentioned the architectural or historic character of the city, or College Hill, the home of Brown University.

The city contracted with Lachlan Blair, the former head of the state planning division and deputy planner of Providence, to write the grant for the College Hill Urban Renewal Project, originally covering 120 acres.[11] (Fig. 2.4) Blair's success netted the city ample funds to create a plan, and he formed a private consulting group with planner Stuart Stein in 1957. More important to the young firm was the addition of local advocate and architectural historian Antoinette Downing and architect and planner William Warner. In an explicit attempt to conduct a demonstration study aimed at improving urban renewal techniques in an historic area, they created a rating system by which an historic district could become part of a comprehensive master plan.[12] (Fig. 2.5)

The College Hill Plan also demonstrated how to integrate contemporary architecture in the historic neighborhoods in an aesthetically pleasing fashion. The program included guidance on developing an historic trail, a park and museum, street improvements, historic area zoning, a program for cooperative planning, methods of encouraging private investment, and citizen involvement (Providence 1959).

The publication of the report became the basis for other studies and future development. The specific proposals involved clearance, rehabilitation, and conservation, with an historic trail and National Park status for the Roger Williams' Spring site. Other ideas included a long-range

---

[10] Russell Wright, Jr. worked for Lachlan Blair and Stuart Stein on the College Hill Plan and took the time to review the background of his work with his former employers, local officials and advocates when writing his thesis in 1964.

[11] Lachlan Blair went on to become a well-known preservation planner and educator at the University of Illinois, Urbana from 1966 to 1988, serving on Urbana's first preservation commission (NCPE 2001).

[12] The criteria for evaluating the significance of historic buildings were more extensive than previous studies. From approximately 1700 College Hill buildings, about 1350 were surveyed and maps were created to visualize the areas in need of protection, private investment, and renewal.

Fig. 2.4 The College Hill Plan, in Providence, RI, the first historic preservation plan developed with the support of federal urban renewal funds, became a well-known model for providing an approach to specifying a range of preservation treatments, especially rehabilitation. (Author's photograph)

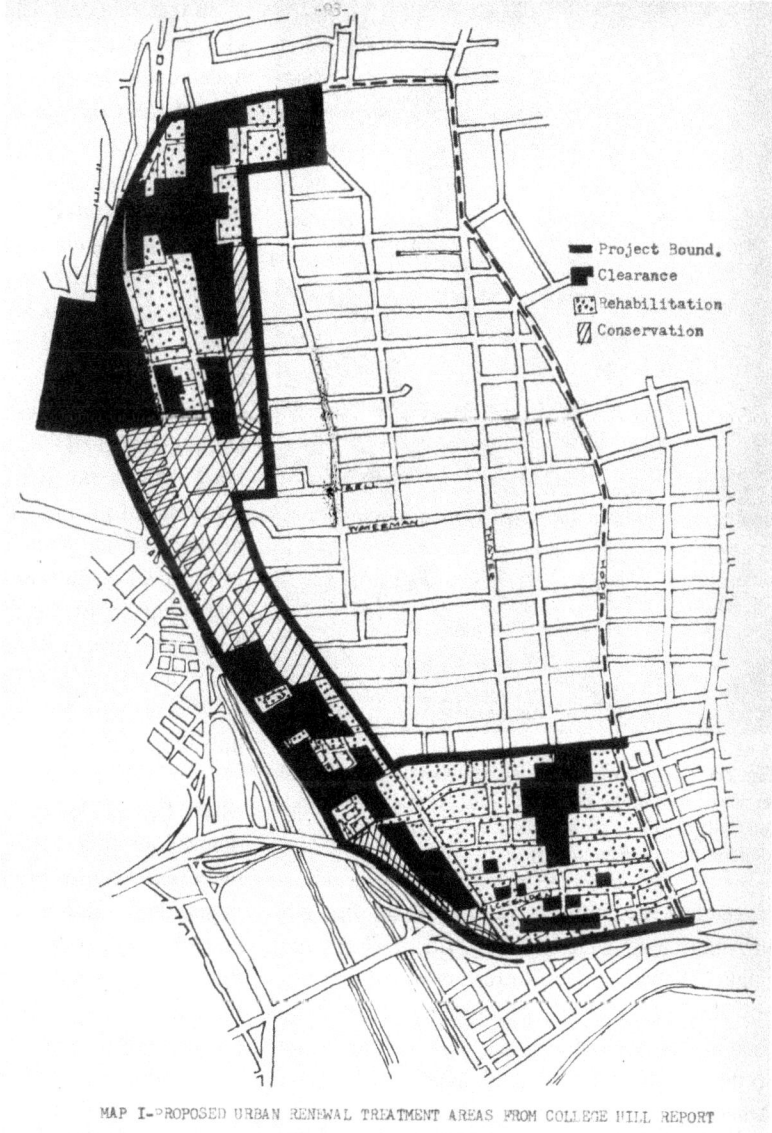

MAP I–PROPOSED URBAN RENEWAL TREATMENT AREAS FROM COLLEGE HILL REPORT

plan for the growth of educational institutions in College Hill, recommendations for community facilities such as a school, park space, playgrounds, an historic area-zoning ordinance, and changes in the current zoning ordinance. Key was the reduction of traffic, intersection improvement, and increased off-street parking. At the same time, local realtor Beatrice "Happy" Chace purchased and restored 15 structures and built new infill housing in College Hill.

Although this initiative provided a positive preservation alternative, most urban renewal project directors had no compunction about proceeding as quickly as possible to accomplish much more destructive goals. For example, in 1958 Edward J. Logue, then urban redevelopment director in New Haven, Connecticut, quoted the words of Federal Housing Administrator Albert M. Cole, who said that "Any city that does not set in motion a comprehensive program to halt blight will be flirting with municipal ruin by 1965" (Logue 1958). Logue was proud of his city's demolition initiative and, without any apparent fear of contradiction, stated that "New

Fig. 2.5 Architectural historian Antoinette Downing took an active role in the preservation of several properties in the College Hill historic district, and the Providence City Hall. (Author's photograph)

Haven believes it will have become the first city in America to be completely rid of slums and blight" (Logue 1958). He further noted that big-city representatives in Congress supported the rebuilding of Europe under the Marshall Plan so that it "was time" to recognize the 18 million Americans living in "slum saturated cities" who could be helped by Federal aid "just as great and urgent as any nation of Europe and Asia." And Logue was later noted as having said "the best thing that could happen to San Francisco would be another earthquake and fire."[13] It was precisely this kind of "macho" behavior and the fear that it instilled that stimulated preservation advocacy.

In the southeast, Charleston continued to provide preservation leadership but Savannah also became increasingly well known. The demolition of the City Market in 1954-1955 provided the initial stimulus for the founding of a citywide preservation organization, the Historic Savannah Foundation (HSF; Morning News 1955). Artist–writer Anna Colquitt Hunter led a group of women to rally to save the Isaiah Davenport House, slated to make way for a funeral parlor parking lot.[14] The Davenport House was saved, eventually opening as a house museum in 1963; in the meantime, energetic members of HSF set about learning all they could and enlisting outside help. Among the first invited to Savannah was professor of planning Carl Feiss, an early trustee of the National Trust for Historic Preservation. In his 1958 lecture to HSF, Feiss recommended that a survey of the historic and architecturally significant properties in the old city should be an immediate priority (Feiss 2011).

The survey effort was put on the back burner, however, when it became known in 1959 that "Marshall Row," four Savannah grey brick houses on East Oglethorpe Avenue, were slated for demolition (Fig. 2.6). The property owner sold the Savannah grey bricks to a contractor who had begun demolition with the carriage houses at the rear of the properties. HSF stepped in and asked that further demolition be stopped, offering to purchase the bricks from the contractor. This is the first instance in which the young stockbroker Lee Adler became involved with the new organization that ultimately secured and rehabilitated the properties.

HSF began to get on its feet with a staff and a corps of volunteers by 1961. As president of the organization, Adler formed a broad structure that included a steering committee composed of the presidents of a local bank and the gas company. Together, they developed the financial approaches needed to advance the ideas of the

---

[13] Jane Jacobs recalled this attitude when discussing the research for her book *Death and Life of Great American Cities* in an interview by James Howard Kunstler (Kunstler 2001).

[14] The others were Elinor Grunsfeid Adler, Katharine Judkins Clark, Lucy Barrow McIntire, Dorothy Ripley Roebling, Noia Roos, and Jane Adair Wright. Harvard educated historian Walter Hartridge served as a trusted advisor to the group.

Fig. 2.6 The 1959 threats to the brick Marshall Row in Savannah, GA, provided yet another stimulus for the young preservationist Lee Adler to step forward with Historic Savannah Foundation, the city-wide preservation organization, thwarting demolition. (Historic American Buildings Survey, Library of Congress)

Foundation. The preservation efforts in Charleston were a model, and the Historic Charleston Foundation had enormous influence because its published survey and local revolving fund were much-admired goals. Following Feiss's suggestions, in 1962 University of Virginia professors Frederick Doveton Nichols[15] and Paul Dulaney led the inventory team that surveyed 2000 buildings in downtown Savannah, 1100 of which were recognized as having architectural or historical significance. Russell Wright, the chief technician in Providence's College Hill study, assisted in drafting the final publication.[16]

As the previous examples demonstrate, historic preservation was gaining attention in relatively

---

[15] Nichols was the first preservation educator to offer a regular academic class in historic preservation, beginning in 1957.

[16] Additional assistance was provided by Cary Langhorne, professor of architecture (HSF 1968).

small communities that sought tourist attention. This is also shown by the distribution of the size of cities that passed local landmarks legislation: Alexandria (1946) and Williamsburg, Virginia (1947); Winston-Salem, North Carolina (1948); Santa Barbara, California (1950); Georgetown, in Washington, D.C. (1950); Natchez, Mississippi (1951); Annapolis, Maryland (1951); and St. Augustine, Florida (1953). All followed the model first adopted by Charleston. In many ways so did Beacon Hill in Boston in early 1955 (NYT 1955, 1956) and Nantucket in 1956 (Dennis 1993). It was not long before advocates in larger cities took note.

Preservationists in Philadelphia made an important contribution during the 1950s by pressing for a preservation ordinance covering the entire city, rather than a carefully defined district in the city (Tinkcom 1971). Architect Grant M. Simon and Judge Harold D. Saylor, members of the Philadelphia Historic Buildings Committee, led the local advocates. Simon and veteran National Parks Service crusader Charles Peterson were among the first to be appointed members of the new Philadelphia Historic Preservation Commission in the spring of 1956. The commission staff surveyed structures and included a three-tier grading system from most to least important—A to C—but commission members declined to use the last two classifications for fear of losing more of the vernacular structures in the city.

The need to become involved in a much larger framework to anticipate large-scale plans soon became evident. Philadelphia city planner Edmund Bacon and his close friend architect Oscar Stonorov, both backed by the local government, launched an urban renewal scheme along the major east-west axis of the city's grid. Bacon called on his memories of the axial plan of Beijing, where he worked as a young man, for the justification for clearance and a new design (Salisbury and Boasberg 2005; Saffron 2005; Bacon 1967; Knowles 2009). It complemented the transformation of the "cluttered" blocks of the city that obscured views of Independence Hall. They were cleared to create the formal garden to the north, named Independence Hall Mall, allowing the visitor to admire the "historic relic"

Fig. 2.7 The architect
of the Frederick C.
Robie House, Frank
Lloyd Wright, stepped
forward in 1957 to
pronounce the house
completely sound,
commenting further
that only the kitchen
was out of date.
(Historic American
Buildings Survey,
Library of Congress)

in a fashion never before possible. Bacon and his associates also focused their attention immediately to the south, on Society Hill, taking special efforts to rid the city of the blight of old housing. In addition, the Pennsylvania Railroad station and its tracks that created a 15 block long "Chinese wall" through the heart of downtown to the old station near City Hall were also removed. In their place, rose Penn Center, which included tall office buildings, a transportation center, parking garage, and a circular glass and steel welcome center (Levine 1957; NYT 1960). Although Philadelphia had a preservation ordinance, urban renewal was hard to stop.

By contrast, Chicago's preservation history stands somewhat apart because the threat to a single architecturally significant residence produced an unusual immediate response. Rumors that the Chicago Theological Seminary planned to demolish architect Frank Lloyd Wright's famous Robie House near the University of Chicago campus surfaced as early as 1955 (Robertson 1955), but when the news became public in early March of 1957, prompt protests arose, near and far (Fig. 2.7). Earl Reed, chair of the American Institute of Architects (AIA) committee on preservation, led the outcry (Chicago Tribune 1957b). Only two months earlier, as two west-side slum redevelopment projects became known, the city's planning and housing committee recommended that an architectural advisory commission be established to designate Chicago landmarks and

establish policies for preservation (Chicago Tribune 1957a). Now, the commission's attention was riveted to an immediate problem. Adding fuel to the fire, in mid-March the 87-year old master architect himself visited the site, declaring the house completely sound, frowning only at the kitchen for being out of date! (Chicago Tribune 1957c) A committee of interested parties met repeatedly during the following months so that, just before Christmas in 1957, Chicago Mayor Daley and William Hartmann, of the Commission on Chicago Architectural Landmarks, announced the stop-gap solution. William Zeckendorff, of the real estate firm of Webb and Knapp, purchased the Robie House to use for offices, but he promised to turn the property over to any educational organization once the firm no longer needed the space (Chicago Tribune 1957d). Subsequently, the University of Chicago took ownership with the condition that a restoration fund would be created (Preservation News 1962).

The Commission's official landmark designations soon went beyond the Robie House to include the Auditorium Building, the Monadnock block, the Carson Pirie Scott department store, and the Rookery, all legendary structures in the architectural history of the high rise office building (Chicago Tribune 1958). The focus clearly was on the "Chicago School" of architects, those who had gained recognition during the late nineteenth and early twentieth centuries. Photographer Richard Nickel, already recording

Fig. 2.8 The demolition of the Garrick Theater was recalled whenever buildings were threatened throughout the 1960s, until the Chicago City Council passed local preservation legislation in January 1968. (Historic American Buildings Survey, Library of Congress)

on film the work of the Chicago firm of Adler and Sullivan, became fascinated with the decorative ornament of their buildings and aghast that so many of their structures were threatened. In January 1960, the Garrick Theater and office block seemed doomed as unprofitable and too expensive to restore (Fig. 2.8). Through public hearings, court appearances, and the popular and professional press, the Garrick fight reached a nation-wide audience. However, when the state appellate court judges decided that the city could issue a demolition permit, lacking a strong city political consensus, the site was cleared for a parking garage in early 1961 (Cahan 1994; Chicago Tribune 1961a).[17]

Conscious of the battle over the Garrick, later that year Alderman Leon M. Depres introduced an ordinance that would delay issuance of a permit

to raze any building identified by the Commission on Architectural Landmarks by 6 months, to allow alternative proposals to be developed (Chicago Tribune 1961b). Yet, in the years following, two additional important skyscrapers in "the Loop" of the center city fell, the Cable Building and the Republic Building, both designed by the firm of Holabird and Roche. A renewed effort to draft an improved local ordinance began in August 1963, after the Illinois General Assembly passed state enabling legislation (Chicago Tribune 1963). Remarkably, Depres continued to press on with ever more sophisticated local landmarks ordinances, repeatedly reminding everyone of the loss of the Garrick until the City passed the new law in January 1968 (Frederick 1966; Chicago Tribune 1967).[18]

Efforts to stem the tide of destruction on the West Coast ran a similar course. In 1957, for example, the Los Angeles Renewal Agency set out to acquire over 250 parcels near downtown to clear for redevelopment, and a $300 million project was soon underway (Blake 1958). The necessity of saving more than a single building became clear as the rumors proved true: there were definitive city-led plans to demolish many of the large Victorian mansions on Bunker Hill, the residential district on the low hills west of downtown. In response, on May 15, 1958 the Los Angeles Committee of the American Institute of Architects launched a plan to survey historic structures in the city. Local architect William Woollett, chairman of the committee, began the initiative by preparing a map (LA Times 1958).[19] A year later, the six-man survey team reported that, of the 200 residences studied, it was clear that about a dozen had varying historic value, although whether they should be kept or moved remained unclear (LA Times 1959).

As the demolition plans became a reality, behind the scenes considerable pressure upon local

---

[17] Originally named the Schiller Theater and briefly the Dearborn, the structure gained its last name in 1903.

[18] The subsequent story of preservation in the city, and the controversy over the Chicago Stock Exchange, are discussed in several books and articles (Costonis 1974; Miller 2000; Gapp 1984).

[19] The other committee members included Martin Fuller, Ray Girvigian, Roger Nissen, and Henry Withey.

city representatives led the notorious Mayor
Samuel Yorty to appoint a committee to look into
the possibility of a landmarks board (LA Times
1961). In early January of 1962, the Los Angeles
City Council decided to draft an ordinance for a
five-member advisory "Cultural Heritage Board"
that would have the responsibility of cataloguing
historic buildings. Architect Woollett and a representative of the Board of Municipal Art Commissioners testified on behalf of the need, indicating
that it would also be wise to include a provision
in the ordinance for demolition delay of up to 6
months (Herbert 1962). This would cover "any
site (including trees or plant life located thereon),
building, or structure of particular historic or
cultural significance..." and the focus included
properties "inherently valuable for a study of a
period, style, or method of construction, or a notable work of master builder, designer, or architect whose individual genius influenced his age."
In that context, not only the work of high-style
architects but Simon Rodia's Watts Towers merited designation (LA Times 1963b).

The local legislation adopted in June 1962 was
a big step forward in California (Garrigues 1962).
The immediate designation of the adobe Miguel
Leonis Residence in Calabasas, the Bolton Hall
community building in Tujunga, the Andreas Pico
House in Mission Hills, the funicular to Bunker
Hill known as "Angels Flight," and the Brad-
bury Building in downtown, all brought attention
to their plight (Fig. 2.9). In fact, in the first year
the Cultural Heritage Board designated 21 sites
as cultural and historic monuments, including
houses, a church, a fig tree, a group of towers,
and a railroad (LA Times 1963c). The AIA Historic Buildings Committee continued to serve as
the principal advocate (LA Times 1963a), but it
proved unequal to the task of saving Irving Gill's
Dodge House from demolition by the Board of
Education, primarily because of its location in
West Hollywood, outside city's jurisdiction (Ainsworth 1963; Terence 1965) (Fig. 2.10). By the
mid-1960s, plans to demolish Bertram Goodhue's
1926 Los Angeles Central Library were in the
news (West 1967; Hata 1992).

The discussion about urban renewal also surfaced in San Francisco during the late 1950s and

Fig. 2.9 Recognized among the first properties to be designated at local landmark in Los Angeles, the funicular to
Bunker Hill, "Angels Flight," remains in place today in a
radically different downtown. (Author's photograph)

Fig. 2.10 Architect Irving Gill's Walter Dodge House
was outside Los Angeles and thus was afforded no protection from demolition by the local preservation legislation. (Historic American Buildings Survey, Library of
Congress)

1960s. In contrast to many large cities around the
country, however, San Francisco was very slow
to become involved in urban redevelopment. In

Fig. 2.11 The 1963 demolition of San Francisco's Fox Theater is remembered annually in the city even today, however its destruction can be said to have saved structures such as the Old Mint, illustrated here, and the Presidio, discussed in Chapter 5. (Author's photograph)

1959 Philadelphia-based planning consultant Aaron Levine reported the city was badly in need of leadership, staff, and commitment from the business community. A committee formed 3 years earlier by Hewlett Packard director Charles Blyth and pulp and paper magnate J.D. Zellerbach was poised to act on a large urban renewal plan with additional financial backing of New York developer William Zeckendorf (Wirt 1974; Hartman 1983).[20] The proposed project included the five-block Embarcadero Center, the Alcoa Building, and elevated pedestrian linkages to serve luxury apartments and townhouses. In this context, a pilot architectural survey focused on the northeast sector and a section of the South of Market area. This included about 10% of the city's features, a pioneering effort in the spring of 1959 led by University of California, Berkeley Professor of Architecture Stephen W. Jacobs (Jacobs and Jones 1960).[21]

Regrettably, the buildings in the downtown core had few defenders. For example, despite years of warning about the closing of the Fox Theater, no opposition arose. No demonstration or any resistance appeared even as the end was near in February 1963 (Chronicle 1963a), although 5000 people attended the farewell concert prior to demolition for a steel and glass office building (Chronicle 1963d; Craig 1963). The Wurlitzer organ was the first piece to be sold, and the auctioneer disposed of most of the interior elements, although not before some of them were stolen (Chronicle 1963b, c). "What's worth saving?" was the question the *San Francisco Examiner* asked its readers later that year. The response "ran the gamut from the sensible to the absurd" according to the editors, although it discovered that the residents had a strong sense of their heritage (Preservation News 1964a). Questions continued regarding the future of the Palace of Fine Arts, the Old Mint, and the Presidio.[22] (Fig. 2.11)

In 1964, in reaction to "the indiscriminate leveling of buildings," the Junior League of San Francisco began to survey the historically and architecturally significant pre-1920 properties in San Francisco, San Mateo and Marin counties. Enlisting over 100 interviewers who went door-to-door and canvassed by telephone, the League

---

[20] The Blyth–Zellerbach Committee was considered a shadow government for years.

[21] Jacobs found the efforts of the local AIA very modest with the exception of a list of works provided by the Wurster, Bernardi and Emmons firm. John and Sally Woodbridge assisted Jacobs, and produced their guide shortly thereafter (Woodbridge et al. 1960). The Woodbridges provided guidance for Berkeley's nonprofit environmental group, Urban Care. January 1968 marked the first meeting of its Architectural Heritage Committee, which evolved into the Berkeley Architectural Heritage Association in 1974 (Bruce 1994).

---

[22] The Presidio became a National Historic Landmark in 1963. Further discussion of its preservation and redevelopment is included in Chapter 6.

Fig. 2.12 A distinctive landmark overlooking the San Francisco waterfront, Ghirardelli Square was the earliest major industrial property in the city to be rehabilitated. Its giant sign is a distinctive feature of waterfront views. (Author's photograph)

began by studying the available histories and attending lectures by knowledgeable architects and local scholars (Preservation News 1964b). The results of the survey, published in 1968 as *Here Today: San Francisco's Architectural Heritage*, went further afield than the guidebooks for the city and previous unpublished survey efforts (Olmsted and Watkins 1968). Largely due to the Junior League's efforts in the field, the city approved a local landmarks ordinance in 1967 (Hata 1992).[23] The Foundation for San Francisco's Architectural Heritage was established in 1971.

Just as important for the recognition of the effort being put into preservation activities was the example provided by one of the country's best known waterfront projects launched at this time. San Francisco developer William M. Roth was impressed with the size and potential of abandoned harbor buildings, and decided to purchase those centered on the Ghirardelli chocolate factory in 1962 (Preservation News 1974b).[24] Opened

in 1964 as Ghirardelli Square, with over 30 shops and restaurants, it received instant recognition.[25] As a celebrated early privately financed commercial rehabilitation, it influenced dozens of subsequent initiatives (Fig. 2.12).

Jane Jacobs and the Reaction to Modernism

The reaction against urban renewal was sharper in the Northeast. No single late twentieth century American author gave more life to the preservation movement than Jane Butzner Jacobs. Although at the outset it was not her intent to be a preservationist, her thinking helped broaden the movement like no other author. One of the few women contributors to architectural journal-

[23] The Junior League was assisted by the California Heritage Council, the California Historical Society, and the San Francisco Landmarks Council.

[24] Landscape architect Lawrence Halrpin and architects Wurster, Bernardi and Emmons won an AIA award for

the conversion. The buildings included the Woolen Building, 1864 (part of the old San Francisco Pioneer Woolen Factory); Mustard Building 1899; Cocoa Building 1900, 1911; Clock Tower 1916; Powerhouse 1918; and the Wurster Building 1864 (eastern portion) and 1868 (western portion).

[25] The complex has been refinanced on several occasions, transforming into a high-end residential complex.

ism, she initially reviewed new school, hospital, and shopping mall construction for *Architectural Forum*. Through her travel and writing on redevelopment in New Orleans, Cleveland, Fort Worth, Philadelphia, and Washington she met several planners and architects involved in urban renewal, as well as preservation advocates (Laurence 2007; Flint 2009; Gratz 2010). Jacobs was disturbed by the pattern by which urban renewal would often ignore the social life of neighborhoods and demolish residences that contained the diversity characteristic of the city in order to advance the visions of planners who promised a more profitable and pleasant core. The downtown San Francisco that planner Ed Logue believed should be demolished was exactly what Jacobs' featured in her first article in *Fortune* magazine, "The Downtown Is for People." "If the downtown of tomorrow looks like most of the redevelopment projects being planned for it today, it will end up being a monumental bore" (Jacobs 1958).[26] In what was the most important critique of urban thinking in the post-World War II period, *The Death and Life of Great American Cities* (Jacobs 1961, 1969; Gans 1962), Jacobs argued persuasively for a small-scale, incremental approach to urban development that values the diversity of people and housing stock, and encourages informal commercial activities. She attempted to represent the disenfranchised, lower class workers and extended immigrant families, borrowing ideas from labor organizers, including Sol Alinsky.

Although Jacobs traveled widely, her personal experiences influenced her thinking just as profoundly. She was a vocal Greenwich Village resident dedicated to defending her New York City neighborhood against the powerful planner Robert Moses as well as those in local government and the business sector promoting urban renewal. By 1955, she joined the Greenwich Village activ-

Fig. 2.13 Jane Jacobs, here pictured in 1961 as the Chair of the Committee to Save the West Village, informed the city and the country of the plight of urban neighborhoods in *The Death and Life of Great American Cities*. (Library of Congress)

ists opposing the plan to insert a sunken highway through Washington Square (Fig. 2.13). She and her architect husband wrote the Mayor about how discouraged they were, having just renovated the building they were living in, only to be threatened by questionable rebuilding schemes. The residents, lacking a voice at the outset (Grutzner 1958; Burlingham 1958), formed the Committee to Save the West Village and Jacobs cochaired the group.

Their opposition was easy to identify. The tendency to centralize power in the hands of master planners is nowhere more obvious in the USA than in the career of Robert Moses. With extraordinary drive, in the pre-War years he conceived and executed some of the metropolitan region's most imaginative public works, including Jones Beach, the Long Island state park and parkway system, and the Triborough Bridge. In the postwar years, as chairman of bridge authorities and as park commissioner, he became the "power broker," building for the sake of building, plotting one expressway after another through dense communities, and exploiting vast new federal powers and funding sources to flatten neighborhoods for immense yet often bland urban renewal projects. Although Moses arranged much of the financial structure and physical infrastructure that is essential to the metropolitan region today,

---

[26] Jacobs credited her editor, urban sociologist William H. Whyte, for providing the initial opportunity to deliver her views, and in backing her efforts. Whyte's own writing influenced Jacobs, especially by questioning the direction in which American society was headed (Whyte 1956).

objections arose when the social cost grew too high (Caro 1974; Kreig 1989; Schwartz 1993).

In *The Death and Life*, Jacobs also assembled the first critical history of the Modern Movement as it developed before World War II and gradually spread in postwar design. European ideas first made their way to the USA largely through exhibits and publications in New York. At the 1932 architectural exhibition held at the Museum of Modern Art in Manhattan, historian Henry-Russell Hitchcock and young architect Philip Johnson introduced the works of designers such as Walter Gropius and Charles Édouard Jeanneret, known as Le Corbusier. Hitchcock and Johnson's exhibition catalogue, *The International Style*, brought the new emphasis on transparency and spatial dynamics to a wider design audience (Hitchcock and Johnson 1932). Also in 1932, the most popular and widely distributed architectural journal, the *Architectural Forum*, began to feature contemporary European designers in its "International Section," with examples from countries including Austria, Germany, France, and Italy (Tomlan 1988). In October 1935, the journal featured the "Coming of Le Corbusier," the "prophetic French architect" who was "known throughout the world as the founder of the International Style" (Architectural Forum 1935).

A few years later, elite university programs began to change with the appointment of Walter Gropius to Harvard's School of Architecture and Ludwig Mies van der Rohe's move to the Illinois Institute of Technology. These teachers ensured that upcoming designers were knowledgeable about *avant garde* European thinking (Alofsin 2002). Swiss art and architectural historian Sigfried Gideon's 1939 lectures at Harvard, published as *Space, Time, and Architecture* in 1941, became the equivalent of the Bible in architectural theory during the post-World War II era. In planning, the American roots of the Modern Movement stemmed from the transformations proposed and built by designers such as Clarence Stein and Henry Wright. These architect-planners adopted an English garden-city model, guided by critic and historian Lewis Mumford. While Le Corbusier saw the future of the city as high-rise towers set among public gardens, the low-rise alternatives arranged around cul-de-sacs in suburban new towns became a more appealing vision for most Americans.

Jacobs rejected both European and American modernism as paternalistic, misguided thinking. All positivist planning was suspect because, in her view, government did not have all the answers. To Jacobs, while government could insist that the city should be neat and clean, it was never meant to be a work of art (Fishman 1980). She valued the inefficiencies and impracticalities of cities. Critics held that she was not scientific and that her bias against planners was clouding her view (Allen 1997)[27]. What was more difficult for architects and urban designers, however, was that, in Jacobs' eyes, aesthetics had so little meaning. In New York, a city that prided itself as the most important center of fashion and style in the country, she was clearly striking out on a different path.

By contrast, the principal preservation organization in Manhattan at the time, the Municipal Arts Society, was concerned with saving the masterpieces of architectural history. In this more limited view, it was essential to preserve the most outstanding examples of each of the respective periods. Leading tours of the city, for example, historian Henry Hope Reed wanted to recover the sensibilities of the turn of the century American Renaissance and considered the buildings constructed through World War I to be the best, attacking anything built by modernists thereafter. Yet, there was a need for more than lists. While Reed began his walking tours to sensitize the public, advocate Nathalie Dana repeatedly brought new people and their energies to the Municipal Arts Society, and sponsored a weekly radio program to spur the preservation of particular buildings, beginning in 1955. Scholars such as the senior architectural historian at Columbia University, Talbot Hamlin, reinforced the

---

[27] Lewis Mumford, when reviewing Ebenezer Howard's *Garden Cities of Tomorrow* in the *New York Review of Books* (April 8, 1965) wrote "… Jane Jacobs preposterous mass of historic misinformation and contemporary misinterpretation in her *The Life and Death of Great American Cities* exposed her ignorance of the whole planning movement".

Fig. 2.14 Manhattan lost Pennsylvania Station, but not before many people, including celebrities such as Jackie Kennedy Onassis and Architect Philip Johnson gathered to demonstrate against the plans to demolish the structure. (Library of Congress)

connoisseurship of the period by limiting his list of important buildings to the architecture before 1860 (Gilmartin 1995).

Compared to activity in the most preservation friendly cities, the initiatives in New York were late. The relatively feeble responses to some fabled demolitions tell the story. For example, through the late 1950s and early 1960s, it was clear that the Pennsylvania Railroad was in financial trouble, exacerbated by strikes that left its stunning Manhattan station almost completely empty (Fig. 2.14). Plans for the future of the facility were alternately bright and bleak as various schemes proposed and then failed to bring about extended railroad use. The proposal that the New York Central Railroad would use the Penn Station facility for long distance service, if the merger of the two companies was approved, led

preservationists to believe there was hope (Lee 1962). Unfortunately, the federal government opposed the merger. As a design and engineering feat, Pennsylvania Station was in many ways unsurpassed. McKim, Mead and White, one of New York's largest and most influential architectural firms, had provided the city with a publicly accessible monument modeled on the Baths of Caracalla in Rome. In early 1962, working against a demolition deadline set by the sponsors of the new Madison Square Garden, Parks Commissioner Newbold Morriss recognized the beauty of the façade and proposed saving the 84 colossal order Doric columns by using them in a new garden in Flushing Meadows Park (Fowle 1962). The site and design were easy to agree upon; the question, never answered, was where to find the money. Only as the "eleventh hour" approached did those concerned get organized. Despite the public protests, enhanced by the visible support of Jacqueline Kennedy Onassis and architect Philip Johnson, the demolition proceeded apace (Wood 2007).

It is curious that, although the New York State legislature passed an enabling law in 1956 to permit cities to adopt historic preservation ordinances, little came of the initiative. The long tradition of "home rule," in which local communities in the state were given free reign to govern themselves, and a lack of court decisions, placed the onus for preservation advocacy on the private sector.[28] It was 1962 before Schenectady's Stockade Association pressed that city into passing the first local landmarks law in the state (Ritter 2008). The new ordinance forbade the demolition of all of the pre-1825 buildings in that district and it intended to regulate alterations to the others. In New York City, meanwhile, scattered local advocacy slowly focused on the steps made by municipal decision-makers.[29] In 1959, the campaign to save Carnegie Hall provided one critical focus (NYT 1964; Martin 2008), while Ruth Wittenberg and Margot Gayle's campaign to save Jefferson Market Courthouse and the longer effort to establish the Friends of Cast Iron were notable organizational efforts. In 1961, Mayor Robert F. Wagner approved the appointment of an exploratory committee, but it was 3 years before the city council received the local landmarks bill, signed in April 1965, over the vociferous objections of real estate industry representatives (O'Kane 1964; Ennis 1965).

Still, demolition was in the wind. Harry Avirom, Vice President of the Wrecking Corporation of America, declared that "We are entering a great new era of demolition" because "All of the little garbage has been torn down, so now we are sinking our teeth into the big stuff." In New York City, Penn Station, the Grand Central Palace, Belmont Race Track, the Polo Grounds, and

the Raymond Street Jail would soon be demolished. The Savoy Plaza, the Park Lane Hotel, and all but a few elements of the 1964 World's Fair followed, courtesy of the 50 wrecking firms in the metropolitan area, with dozens of pneumatic hob-knockers, derricks and cranes, some 30 stories tall (Blum 1964).

That said, the new landmarks law was quickly used. The first designated structure was the Pieter Claesen Wychoff House in Brooklyn, but the first major preservation success occurred when the commission designated the Old Astor Library, a red brick and brownstone Victorian monument, and imposed a demolition delay to allow those concerned about its future to develop an alternative (Huxtable 1966; Hawthorne 2013) (Fig. 2.15). Joseph Papp's plan to adapt the Library as the home of the "Public Theater" provided a kind of "spot renewal" scheme that demonstrated the community value of the historic preservation ordinance and simultaneously helped spark renewed life in the Astor Square area. It also challenged advocates to be continually ready to provide a range of creative solutions whenever the threat of demolition arose (Gray 2002).

The Highway and the City's Image

By the late 1950s, threats to historic properties across the country were frequent, often described as downtown improvement plans, suburban development schemes, waterfront enhancement, suburban industrial expansion, and highway construction (Brown 1958b). Although alarms sounded repeatedly in all of these arenas, transportation improvements became the most thorny in the following decades. As preservationists in Charleston knew, the very highways that allowed tourists to see more of the country than ever before were often laid out with little regard for the preservation of America's history. The threats mounted. In Morristown, New Jersey, Washington's Headquarters was scheduled to have a federal highway constructed within 100 yards of the mansion. In Santa Fe, the "Pink Adobe" and several hundred other adobe residences faced likely damage by road widening. There the parking lots

---

[28] See Chapter 3 for the legislative responses to Berman vs. Parker, of which the "Bard Act" in New York was one.

[29] This was despite the fact that New York preservationists were alerted to the initiatives taken by the Beacon Hill Civic Association (NYT 1956).

Fig. 2.15 The first designated local structure under New York City's new landmarks law was the Pieter Claesen Wychoff House, in Brooklyn. (Historic American Buildings Survey, Library of Congress)

for the expansion of the state Capitol also elicited protests (LeViness 1956; Wilson 1997).

In a country that gave birth to the automobile and where every activity seemed to require driving further and further distances, a government-sponsored initiative to speed traffic spelled progress. In his 1956 State of the Union message, President Dwight Eisenhower requested legislation to create a modern interstate highway system, in part to facilitate civil defense. Congress responded with the Federal-Aid Highway Act of 1956, authorizing the largest joint federal-state activity in American history: a 41,000-mile national system of interstate defense highways, costing over $31.5 billion to be spent over 13 years. The federal government would pay 90% of the total cost of the highway while the state was responsible for only 10%.[30]

With billions of dollars becoming available through the states, the impact upon historic landmarks and districts was felt immediately. In Washington, D.C., Helen Bullock, writing from her editor's desk at *Historic Preservation*, the voice of the National Trust, noted in 1957 that she was receiving reports of destruction from the impending highway projects (Bullock 1957). At the 1957 annual meeting of the Trust, Michael Fromme, travel editor of the American Automobile Association, spelled out the likely impact of the 1956 highway legislation, stating that the "roads should be regarded as an accessory rather than a deterrent to historic preservation" (Fenton 1957). The 400 National Trust conference attendees who were busy visiting the Essex County, Massachusetts house museums could not have anticipated the amount of destruction that soon followed. Newspapers and magazines took notice. "Extinction by Throughway" in *Harper's*, and "The Wanton Disregard of Our National Heritage" in *The Diplomat*, both reprinted in *Reader's Digest*, fueled the discontent (Clark 1959; Prater 1958).

Unfortunately, preservationists were unfamiliar with how to deal with highway engineers or transportation projects and so lacked a clear strat-

---

[30] The Department of Agriculture oversaw early road construction, spawning the Public Roads Administration. The 1916 Federal-Aid Road Act cast the basic pattern for federal-state cooperation whereby Washington provided 50% of the cost of approved projects to states that would establish highway departments to conform to national road standards. The Federal Highway Act of 1934 started the process of continuous highway planning. Conceptually, the Federal-Aid Highway Act of 1944 authorized the enormous National System of Interstate and Defense Highways but lack of funding forestalled implementation. In 1949, the reconstituted Bureau of Public Roads was relocated to the Department of Commerce. In turn,

it became the Federal Highway Administration in 1966, a component of the new Department of Transportation.

Fig. 2.16 Paths, nodes, edges, districts, and landmarks entered the lexicon of urban design and preservation with the work of MIT planning professor Kevin Lynch. (Author's illustration)

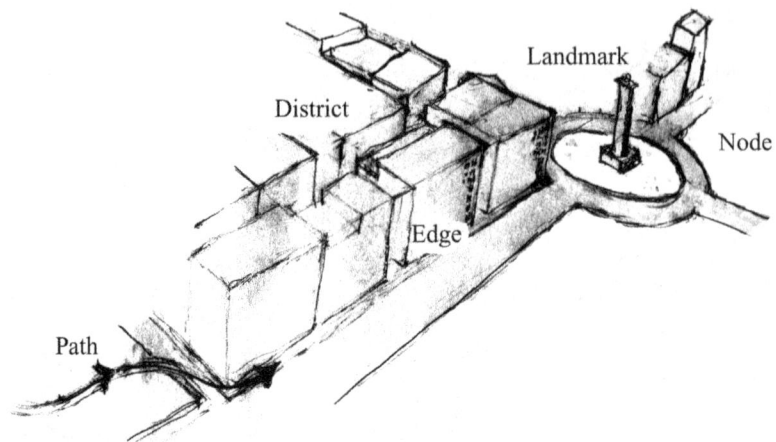

egy to protect threatened properties and neighborhoods. In this regard, the "place making" ideas of M.I.T. planning Professor Kevin Lynch ultimately proved very important.

Throughout the 1950s, Boston was attempting to find a way to relieve congestion in its historic urban core, located at the end of a narrow peninsula. The construction of the new elevated highway termed the "Central Artery" divided neighborhoods and demolished buildings. These were among the problems that Jane Jacobs and others had noted, but in *The Image of the City*, first published in book form in 1960, Professor Lynch set out a defense. He explained what gives cities their "sense of place" and how people function within it, starting with the concept of "imageability": "that quality in a physical object which gives it a high probability of evoking a strong image" (Lynch 1960, p. 9).[31] This idea is important for city design because, instead of mimicking an abstract artistic concept, it offered an alternative. Lynch maintained that the city dweller needs only "a pattern of high continuity with many distinct parts clearly interconnected" (Lynch 1960, p. 10), which could be crafted in almost any context. He explained his urban language with a grammar of five "parts" or "elements" that make up a city: paths, edges, districts, nodes, and landmarks (Fig. 2.16). For the city dweller, these five elements are important as a means of recognizing and understanding the place in which they live. In this way, the experience of the city is enhanced. Lynch demonstrated his views by using examples in three very different cities: Boston, Los Angeles, and Jersey City. In the process of studying these places, he conducted interviews with residents and asked them to draw maps in order to see how they viewed their city. He also interviewed people to get a better sense of how they function and move around in the city.

Perhaps the most important piece for preservationists was the element of paths. Like Jane Jacobs, who saw that people will start to identify certain streets based on their use, Lynch pointed out that when it came to how people understand their city, it is often due to how they see particular streets and what associations they make with them. Paths are important because when placed in good form, that is, a not very complex system, they increase the city resident's knowledge and perception of the city space. From his interviews, Lynch determined that the size of the street and its façade characteristics are important for the identity of the route as well (Lynch 1960, p. 51).

Moving beyond the importance of paths, Lynch also explained how observers need a certain amount of conceptual reinforcement to understand their city. This may come from the architecture, the history, the residents, or the use of the area or "thematic unit." It is here that the ele-

---

[31] Lynch openly acknowledged that the underlying concepts of his book were developed from his exchanges with M.I.T. professor Gyorgy Kepes, a connection established in the early 1950s. This ardent modernist, a Hungarian born teacher, painter, photographer, and author, taught visual design in Cambridge from 1946 until 1974 (Raynsford 2011).

ment of edges becomes important (Lynch 1960, p. 68). The edge of an area works to give it definition, but, as he points out, the lines do not actually define the area. For some people the different districts with definite edges added to a sense of disorganization of the city design. It is the use of edges to define space that Lynch sees "a striking opportunity for change in the urban landscape." If districts are needed for people to define their city and help orient them, then edges are essential to give the districts boundaries.

Hence, the reaction to the Modern Movement in architecture and planning was taking place at the same time that the preservation movement was coalescing. Both Jacobs and Lynch questioned the manner in which architects, planners and government decision makers proposed to redevelop the city. Neither author was widely recognized for contributing to the preservation field at the time, but both provided intellectual guidance that echoed repeatedly and became apparent years later.

Developing the New National Preservation Agenda

Congressional representatives were well aware of local preservation advocates as they battled city hall, regional authorities, and state and federal transportation officials. Often, when controversies arose, senators and representatives received petitions. They responded in turn by sponsoring more than 30 bills for the broader protection of historic lands, buildings, and works of art between 1959 and 1965, over and above the individual proposals to add historic properties to the National Park system. In Washington, D.C., the attempt to change the West Front of the Capitol galvanized opposition literally at its doors (Preservation News 1969c). Because the federal government, which was often the largest single "landlord" of commercial office space in some downtowns, was also increasingly abandoning some of the most obvious civic landmarks around the country, voices of protest rose in Congress with considerable frequency. The General Services Administration's intentions caused ad-

ditional concern, because it wanted to demolish massive monuments of nineteenth-century public architecture, such as the old State, War, and Navy Building (the Old Executive Office Building) in Washington, D.C.; the US Post Office and Courthouse in Saint Louis; and the US Mint in San Francisco (Preservation News 1970).

The small staffs of the National Trust and the National Park Service gradually began to orchestrate the preservation movement more actively. In order to catalyze professionals, a conference was held at Colonial Williamsburg, a natural venue, as the Washington, D.C. bureaucracy often returned to the restored city to host official visits (Brown 1958a). About 160 activists assembled for 3 days in early September, 1963, to review the status of American preservation and its European antecedents, and to discuss the philosophical basis, current effectiveness and best way of directing its future. By mid-1964, the "Principles and Guidelines for Historic Preservation in the USA" were compiled under a committee headed by National Park Service historian Ronald F. Lee (NTHP 1966, 1967).

The role of aesthetics mentioned in the "Principles" received even greater national attention at the time through the efforts of the First Lady, Lady Bird Johnson. President Johnson's Task Force on the Preservation of Natural Beauty, chaired by Harvard lawyer Charles Haar, submitted its report in November 1964 outlining a number of recommendations concerning the need to clean up lakes and rivers, improve access to public transit, and provide increased attention to urban design (Journal of Urban History 1998). With contributors including Jane Jacobs and sociologist William H. Whyte, the report also conveyed ideas on how to advance historic preservation. Building on previous work, the report indicated that the National Park Service should prepare a comprehensive inventory of historic sites in cooperation with state governments and private organizations. The recommendations stipulated that a workable system for the protection of those assets would include a federal board established to veto expenditures that could damage historic properties. To stimulate preservation activities, federal loans and matching grants could be given to states and municipalities, and the National Trust would play a more active role paid for with an annual appropriation that would be matched by private contributions. Housing regulations were to be revised that would allow suitable repairs and additions to old buildings. A federal income-tax deduction could cover the expenses.

On February 8, 1965, President Johnson issued a message on "Natural Beauty," complementing the citizens who rallied "to save landmarks of beauty and history" and stating that the federal government would make an effort to assist. Pledging support for the National Trust, he added, "I shall propose legislation to authorize supplementary grants to help local authorities acquire, develop, and manage private properties for such purposes." He also commended the Registry of National Historic Landmarks as "a fine federal program with virtually no federal cost."

In the White House Conference on Natural Beauty, held in May 1965, Edmund N. Bacon, who represented the Philadelphia City Planning Commission, chaired the panel labeled "The Townscape." The "action proposals for historic preservation" listed in his committee report reiterated the basic recommendations of the earlier task force, but with a specific provision to create historic districts, including some entire historic towns. In addition, it was suggested that tax policies be overhauled "to encourage greater private investment in the preservation of approved historic and landmark structures and areas" (GPO 1965). Secretary Morris K. Udall's response was to direct the National Park Service, in conjunction with its sister agency, the Bureau of Outdoor Recreation, to draft legislation authorizing grants to assist local authorities to protect "landmarks of beauty and history."

Local advocacy played a role in gaining the attention of the Executive branch of government. The next problem was to attract the attention of Congress to support new legislation and the necessary appropriations. To gain greater publicity and prestige, Laurance G. Henderson, then Director of the Joint Council on Housing and Urban Development, began a collaboration in mid-1965 with noted planner Carl Feiss, John J. Gunther,

Executive Director of the US Conference of Mayors, Robert R. Garvey, Jr. of the National Trust, and Ronald F. Lee of the National Park Service. The Special Committee on Historic Preservation set out to tour Europe, examining preservation practices in several leading countries.[32] Completing its review in November, staff members of the Special Committee produced a well-illustrated book to be ready for Congress when it reconvened in January 1966. The work, *With Heritage So Rich*, contained a foreword by the First Lady and concluded with the Committee's findings and recommendations (Feiss 2011).[33] Chiefly, it recommended legislation to affirm a strong national policy of historic preservation, indicating that the National Park Service be empowered to consolidate federal inventory and survey programs in a national register. The Committee also proposed that the National Park Service have the authority to make grants to state and local governments to carry out the survey and inventory program.[34]

The two prominent leaders who provided the final push were extremely important. Gordon Gray, Chairman of the National Trust for Historic Preservation, sensed the important role his organization had to play, and George Hartzog, the National Park Service leader, saw the opportunity to expand the base of support for his agency by intro-

---

[32] This is often called the "Rains Committee" named for its lead sponsor, Congressman Albert Rains, Chairman of the Subcommittee on Housing, Committee on Banking and Currency. The other members were Senator Edmund S. Muskie of Maine, Representative William B. Widnall of New Jersey, Governor Philip H. Hoff of Vermont, Professor Raymond R. Tucker of Washington University (formerly Mayor of Saint Louis), Gordon Gray, Chairman of the Board of Trustees of the National Trust, and Laurance G. Henderson. Members ex officio were the heads of federal agencies with programs involving historic properties: Interior, Commerce, Housing and Urban Development, and General Services. The Ford Foundation and an anonymous donor provided financing. The visits included stops in Austria, Czechoslovakia, France, Great Britain, Italy, the Netherlands, Poland, and West Germany (Mayors 1966).

[33] Helen D. Bullock and Carl Feiss both played a major role in refining the essays and recommendations.

[34] The specifics of the legislation and the development of federal agency responsibilities are discussed in the following chapter.

ducing a new urban program in the context of the proactive changes in Congress. The *Congressional Record* shows that Edmund Muskie of Maine introduced the new preservation legislation in the Senate and Leo O'Brien of New York in the House of Representatives. It stalled in the House for several weeks, in part by representatives who held that Washington was faced with rising indebtedness due to the Vietnam War, and should not interfere in what was deemed a local matter. Representative Craig Hosmer of California closed his remarks with a reference to the comic strip "Li'l Abner," "In short, if Jubilation T. Cornpone's birthplace is to be preserved, Dogpatch should do it" (Congressional Record 1966).[35] When the bill languished, Gordon Gray intervened by approaching the Speaker of the House, who praised the bill and asked his colleagues that it be passed as a tribute to the very popular Representative O'Brien, who was soon retiring. As a result, the House passed the bill, the Senate concurred, and the new law was signed by President Johnson on October 15, 1966.

In 1966, NPS historian Ronald Lee asked Ernest Allen Connally to work in Washington with J.O. Brew, a Harvard University archeologist, on a task force that would implement the National Historic Preservation Act.[36] In 1967, Connally became the director of the newly created Office of Archaeology and Historic Preservation in the National Park Service, with a core staff, including architect and architectural historians Russell Keune and William J. Murtagh, and historian Jerry Rogers. Together, they went about the task

of setting up the National Register, the grants program, and assisting the newly forming state preservation offices (Glass 1987). The marriage of archaeology and historic preservation would prove important to the development of both fields in the decades ahead, as they learned from one another.

Museum Salvage; Cultural Resource Management

As suburbs continued to grow and air conditioned supermarkets eclipsed open-air markets in most cities, and migration from farms, ranches, and plantations to urban centers continued, American's understanding of agrarian life began to fade. Faith in scientific management led to consolidation of the family farm and the rise of what became known as agribusiness. Against this background, a renewed interest in the rural past took hold in outdoor museums, which saved and interpreted vanishing agricultural and early industrial village life. The prolific and influential agricultural resource economist Robert Marion Clawson provided an intellectual framework. He stimulated the beginning of the living historical farms movement in the USA by proposing a national system of 25 to 50 living historical farms. In a 1965 article, he emphasized that the wide variety of American agriculture—derived from climate and geography, crops and livestock, cultural differences, and technological advances— was deserving of broader recognition (Clawson 1965). Subsequently, a group of professionals in Washington representing the NPS, the Smithsonian, and the Department of Agriculture provided additional guidance by spelling out the need for a professional organization that might serve as an appropriate network, saving and interpreting representative examples of agrarian life and early industry.

In response, the Association for Living History, Farms and Agricultural Museums (ALHFAM) was founded at a symposium on American agriculture held at Old Sturbridge Village in eastern Massachusetts in September 1970

---

[35] The humor was directed at President Johnson, who was often portrayed as an unsophisticated country bumpkin by members of the opposite political party, critics, and by members of the press.

[36] Ernest Allen Connally studied architecture at Rice University, served in World War II, and received his bachelor of architecture degree from the University of Texas in 1950. He earned a doctorate in art history at Harvard University and began teaching at Miami University in Oxford, Ohio, followed by stints at Washington University in St. Louis, Missouri, and at the University of Illinois, Urbana-Champaign. During this period, he began his association with the National Park Service while leading summer teams for the Historic American Buildings Survey.

Fig. 2.17 Plimouth Plantation, the reconstruction of the colonial English and Native American settlements near the presumed original locations, provides instruction and historical amusement with a range of facsimiles and first-person interpretation. (Author's photograph)

(Hawes 1975). The innovative mission of Old Sturbridge, which adopted the theme of a pre-industrial textile village, caused other outdoor museum advocates to rethink their interpretative missions. The Association's first annual meeting, held in at the Farmer's Museum in Cooperstown, New York in June 1972, assembled a broader group of representatives from agricultural, folk life, and living history farms to discuss common concerns. The fundamental agreement among the participants was that they needed to go well beyond static displays of artifacts and place the emphasis on "living history," that is, on demonstrating the processes of everyday life. By performing the everyday tasks of early Americans, the docents could explain to the public what each of the chores involved. Historic restored villages such as Colonial Williamsburg and Plimoth Plantation in Plymouth, Massachusetts already had created a new, special type of museum, with goals less centered on the artifact and more dedicated to providing education through demonstration (Fig. 2.17). Whether the museum was sufficiently "real" or its material "authentic" was secondary to whether it accurately presented history so that the visitor learned from the past. In venues such as these, museum professionals worked out the most common rationales for restoration, replication, and interpretation.

The prolific, popular anthropologist and archaeologist James Deetz of Plimoth Plantation also played an important role in this reimagining of the outdoor museum. Deetz approached site interpretation by appealing to the senses. He wanted the visitor to see, touch, smell, and hear the animals and human activity. Likewise, he sought to keep the amount of written information relatively limited, with few signs and written comments. With his emphasis on first-person interpretation, Deetz opened up the eyes and ears of visitors in a new way (Anderson 1984). Although ALHFAM can be seen as an outgrowth of older house museum cooking and garden programs and open-air collections, many of the programs were also a product of the 1960s, with an emphasis on understanding social and environmental realities. These participatory activities mirrored the teaching at free schools, sit-ins, and community events.[37] The emphasis on the commonplace agrarian settings during this period served as an antidote to the rediscovery of Victorian architecture occurring at the same time among architectural historians (Watkins 1965; SHA 2001). Folklore could provide answers to questions like why the sod house was better for human habitation on the Nebraska prairie than the frame alternative—

---

[37] These included theoretical papers, field trips to a wide variety of museums, discussions about costumes, interpretation, old tools and equipment, collections, food-ways programs, seeds, livestock, and the restoration of buildings

Fig. 2.18 In Los Angeles, Heritage Square became the new home of the Valley Knudsen Garden Residence (on the *right*) and several other buildings moved from Bunker Hill and other locations in the face of urban renewal. (Author's photograph)

it provided better thermal protection in an era before insulation—proving to be a sound "Whole Earth" technology.

In the face of urban renewal and widespread modernization, several outdoor museums took on the role of salvage operators, doing their best to demonstrate their environmental concerns as well as their interest in history by collecting and storing threatened structures in various cities. The most striking example in the USA was "Strawbery Banke," in Portsmouth, New Hampshire, an area of the community that was threatened by destruction in 1957 by the local housing authority, which wanted to demolish several nineteenth- and early twentieth-century structures. Perry, Dean, Hepburn and Stewart, the architects of Colonial Williamsburg, worked on both the recreation and restoration of the site. Opened in 1965, it was a remarkable success (Fenton 1961; Morgan 1965; Garvin 1971). In Los Angeles, working with the city's Cultural Heritage Board, the Cultural Heritage Foundation was founded in 1969 to relocate dozens of Victorian houses from Bunker Hill to a vacant 10-acre parcel in Highland Park, alongside the Pasadena Freeway, creating "Heritage Square" (Preservation News 1969b; LA Times 1974; Fig. 2.18). The moving progress was slow, and shortly after reaching their new site arsonists damaged two buildings, but the complex opened as a cultural park in the early 1970s. In a similar fashion, in 1969, the most influential pres-

ervation organization in San Diego, Saving Our Heritage Organization (SOHO), formed largely to save Victorian buildings (Giebner 1971; Moss and Fintselberg 1971). The need for urban preservation broadened the focus of historical interest to center more on the properties of the late nineteenth century.

As the number of archaeology projects grew, the sheer number of artifacts uncovered created a major curatorial problem. Museums could not expand fast enough to acquire, inventory, and treat, let alone interpret, the amount of new material. Although federal and an increasing number of state mandates stipulated that archaeologists provide the needed due-diligence when considering the options on how to proceed with a government sponsored or licensed project, because of a shortage of qualified personnel, the number of incomplete reports increased.[38] Against this reality, others raised the prospect of a computerized inventory that would improve the ability to make informed decisions. All of this led professionals to question whether current practices were likely to meet immediate needs, let alone anticipating the discovery of new cultural resources. These

---

[38] This dilemma was spurred by passage of the Archaeological Resources Protection Act in 1979 and the reauthorization of the National Historic Preservation Act in 1980 with Executive Order 11593.

concerns swirled around in the discussions at the 1974 Arlie House Conference in Warrenton, Virginia, sponsored by the Society of American Archaeologists (McGimsey and Davis 1977). The ideas were centered on the management of archaeological resources, although the thinking of the participants embraced a broader range of cultural issues. In this context, the term "cultural resource management" (CRM) came to be defined as a branch of archaeology primarily concerned with the identification, maintenance, and preservation of cultural sites that are facing threats. As such, CRM work went beyond exploration and investigation, shaping the future of professional archeological practice as largely a private-sector activity, recognizing that the various levels of government were never likely to be able to support the personnel required to meet the needs.

At about the same time William D. Lipe circulated a paper in archaeological circles that presented a more aggressive conservation model, influenced by environmental advocates, wherein emergency salvage to be a last resort, "to be undertaken only after all other avenues of protecting the resource have failed." Lipe held that archaeological sites comprise a finite, nonrenewable resource, one rapidly being obliterated (Lipe 1974). If this position was to be maintained, the public policies that spurred project directors to proceed with a "dig and destroy" approach to reach a "mitigation solution" were headed in a distinctly compromised path. The Society of Professional Archaeologists, founded in 1976, and the Archaeological Conservancy, begun 3 years later, continued these discussions. The latter attempted to raise funds to purchase endangered prehistoric sites with the intent of putting them into the hands of a public entity.

The National Trust Programs Develop

Although house museum properties continued to preoccupy the National Trust for Historic Preservation, a pronounced shift began when Russell V. Keune left his position as assistant to the Keeper of the National Register of Historic Places in

January 1969 to join the organization and began to develop its field services.[39] Following ideas detailed in a memo to the new President of the Trust, James Biddle, Keune was given free reign to create field services. He began in the Western states, hiring John L. Frisbee III in 1971 to become the director of the first regional office, in San Francisco, which served all states west of the Mississippi (Ainslee 1981).[40] When Frisbee arrived there were 1085 members of the Trust, but his widespread speaking engagements and numerous meetings increased the ranks of the organization quickly.

The Trust quickly acknowledged the importance of this first field office, leading to the launch of the second, in Chicago, with Mary Means as its director. Other offices soon followed, spreading the idea that organizing was the key to influencing change at the local level (Preservation News 1976).[41] Indeed, the staffs in the regional offices were often the first and only contact that members of the public had with the embryonic preservation structure.

Means is especially important as the developer and promoter of the National Trust's Main Street Program, the most successful initiative the organization has undertaken in business revitalization. Begun in 1978, it is widely emulated for

---

[39] Russell V. Keune's interest in historic preservation stemmed from his student days pursuing a degree in architecture at the University of Illinois, Urbana, where he came under the tutelage of Professor Ernest Allen Connally, who referred him to Charles Peterson in 1957. Keune was assigned to a HABS measured drawing team in Harper's Ferry, West Virginia headed by University of Florida Professor Blair Reeves. His short stints with the NPS in Puerto Rico and Massachusetts provided him with a range of contacts, allowing him to be hired to implement elements of the National Historic Preservation program, under Robert Utley, in 1966 (Glass Papers 1981; Preservation News 1969a). Field services experienced a setback in 2011 when the new President, Stephanie Meeks, closed several field offices in a major restructuring plan (Talmquist 2011).

[40] A 3-year $65,000 grant from the San Francisco Foundation made it possible, additional funds being made available by trustees (Glass Papers 1981).

[41] Cynthia Emrick became the director of the Southwest Plains Office, in Oklahoma City, and Samuel N. Stokes, the director of the Mid-Atlantic office.

its effectiveness in combining public and private support, with thousands of small towns successfully adopting its marketing formula (Walters 1981; Keister 1990).[42]

One of the principal goals of the regional directors was to set up state-wide preservation advocacy organizations, akin to "miniature" national trusts. For example, Charles Black, president of the Hawaiian Mission Children's Society, attended the NTHP annual meeting in San Diego and solicited the Western Regional Office's help in setting up the Historic Hawaii Foundation, which was founded in 1974.

In addition to annual meetings held around the country, the Trust began to hold conferences on special topics. The first, timed to begin on Law Day, 1971, was also the first time attorneys gathered to discuss the growing body of regulations, restrictions, less-than-fee interests, and tax inducements (Morten 1971; Preservation News 1971; Duke 1971). Over 80 lawyers and 60 others attended the meeting in Washington, D.C. The emphasis on the growing number of preservation commissions led the Trust to announce a new division of legal services and hire the recent Harvard Law school graduate Roger Holt to create an assistance program (Biddle 1971). This, in turn, allowed Keune to gain the support of the Department of Housing and Urban Development to hire attorney and former secretary to the New York City Landmarks Commission, Frank B. Gilbert.

Just as important, the National Trust staff learned more about attitudes on the street, particularly in depressed neighborhoods. The only African American man at the Law Day conference, Chicagoan Michael Newsom, addressed the question "How Can Blacks Stop a Historic Preservation Project: Or, the Preservationists Meets the Militant." "Historic preservation work has been too often seen as a plaything for the wealthy," he offered. "To the extent that blacks get hurt by the process, then preservationists must reconsider

their position in light of the black man's struggle for control over his own destiny." Forecasting the "ground-up" discussion of the next decade, Newsom continued, "The rules of the game will have to be changed so as to accommodate legitimate black aspirations. Preservation is not a bad idea, mind you. I personally think it is great. But where we are vitally concerned it could give you a great deal of soul" (Preservation News 1971).

The Only Way to Go Is Up: "Grass Roots" Neighborhood Conservation

The contrast between the development of historic preservation thinking in Washington, D.C., and the violent and destructive outbreaks in Harlem, Bedford-Stuyvesant, Rochester, Chicago, Philadelphia, Watts, and dozens of other smaller communities could not be more profound. While most municipalities struggled with civil rights issues and declining property revenue as the white middle class left the city, the progressive leadership in Washington pressed for greater environmental consciousness and civil rights. During the early 1960s, prominent liberal Democrats distinguished themselves as environmental leaders (Schneider 2005).[43] As the decade ended, Senator Gaylord A. Nelson announced that a "teach-in," a grass roots protest to emphasize the importance of environmental issues, would take place to catalyze support. On April 22, 1970, more than 20 million Americans assembled on the Mall in the District of Columbia, and elsewhere, to mark the first "Earth Day." Congress closed to allow lawmakers to participate in local events and 42 State legislatures passed Earth Day resolutions to mark the date. Only months later, President Richard M. Nixon established the Environmental

---

[42] Downtown revitalization programs begun earlier in Corning, New York, and Chillicothe, Ohio, were expanded in three pilot Midwest towns: Galesburg, Illinois, Hot Springs, South Dakota, and Madison, Indiana. The history and development of the program is treated in depth in Chapters 4 and 6.

[43] The independent minded Senator from Wisconsin, Gaylord A. Nelson, was among the first to declare the declining quality of our air and water as a national issue. He was one of a group of legislators who sponsored the Wilderness Act and worked to pass the Wild and Scenic Rivers Act in 1968. Further discussion of the gestation and development of environmental legislation continues in Chapter 3.

Protection Agency, and the Clean Air Act and Endangered Species Act followed in 1970.

At the same time, the rise of the environmental movement provided moral and ethical strength to neighborhood and civic groups who sought to use new tools against large-scale construction. A key factor was the ability of the residents to build a community organization and give voice to local concerns, particularly centered on the need for safe residential areas. Legal challenges could stall projects for years, increasing their costs, effectively killing them. In Manhattan, the Westway—an ambitious plan to reclaim 5 miles of Hudson River waterfront for housing, parks and a submerged highway—was one of the last serious attempts at the old manner of grand planning. Eco-centric thinking played a large role in rallying support. Meanwhile, "urban homesteading," the idea of Philadelphia city council member Joseph E. Coleman in 1968, was adopted by the National Association of Housing and Redevelopment Officials and the National Urban Coalition. Those interested in adopting abandoned inner city residential properties could, if they improved them, gain title in cities like Baltimore and Washington, D.C. (Preservation News 1974a).

Although the shift to a more community-oriented and socially conscious approach to rehabilitation was a much-needed corrective, it was far easier to reject than approve any large public project—good, bad or mixed. It was scarcely surprising that most cities did little to maintain their existing inventory of major public projects in subsequent years. Money was tight; some cities teetered on the brink of bankruptcy. Parks and public facilities were in poor condition. In the face of growing financial strains on the inner city, new alliances formed of necessity, some unwittingly.

Like most writers during the preceding decades, Jane Jacobs and Kevin Lynch did not explicitly address the racial prejudice that was widespread. In 1963, sociologist Nathan Glazer and the young legislator Daniel Patrick Moynihan reexamined the need for a viable political base, and some Americans begin to discuss the end of the concept of the Melting Pot (Glazer and Moynihan 1963). It took some time, however, for the study of demographics to demonstrate to politicians just how immigration made a difference because many recent immigrants did not vote or participate in civic affairs.

Most urban critics were silent on the most publicly discussed issue—race—often retreating to environmental concerns. Although it is true that Jacobs' platform for urban life included a wide range of housing choices, something preservation leaders well understood, more often than not, they were relatively silent in the Civil Rights Movement. Yet, its influence on preservation was to inject a new concern for equity and sensitivity to gentrification, increasing recognition of the vernacular housing that plays a crucial role in providing shelter for low-income residents. As the 1970s advanced, preservationists worked on the street with people of all races and economic levels, often first in the housing arena. A new set of preservation pioneers, more interested in bringing life back to the city in minority neighborhoods in Brooklyn, Pittsburgh, and Savannah, began to make a difference.

In Brooklyn, the "overwhelmingly Negro" Bedford-Stuyvesant section was regularly depicted "as being among the nation's worst centers of poverty and decayed housing; an area which unemployment, infant mortality and school dropout rates" regularly exceed the norms, and where "alienation among young people is matched only be a sense of crushing defeat among many of their elders" (Fried 1969). Local civic leaders resented this picture, however, and emphasized its well-preserved neighborhoods, pointing to approximately 100 block associations fostering community spirit. Tracing the early settlement pattern of African Americans, many New Yorkers were surprised just how deep their roots went. The most outstanding advocate was Joan Maynard, commercial artist, writer, and teacher. She became widely recognized as the driving force behind the preservation of historic Weeksville, the pre-Civil War community founded by freed slaves in Brooklyn's Bedford-Stuyvesant neighborhood.[44]

---

[44] Designated as local landmarks in 1970, in December 1972, the houses were placed on the National Register and, in June 1973, the Bedford-Stuyvesant Restoration

Fig. 2.19 The Bedford-Stuyvesant neighborhood has seen a considerable amount of preservation activity. The Weeksville Heritage Center is actively interpreting the local history. (Author's photograph)

The Society for the Preservation of Weeksville focused on a small area, bounded by present-day St. John's Place, Albany Avenue, Fulton Street, and Buffalo Avenue. The pride in this neighborhood was palpable. The organization began with three buildings dedicated to a community historical museum to house artifacts, documents, and pictures, and the oral histories collected by a broad cross section of residents, focusing on programs for schoolchildren (Fig. 2.19).

The role that Brooklyn played in expanding neighborhood preservation cannot be overstated. The story of Evelyn and Everett Ortner, who moved to the Park Slope neighborhood of Brooklyn in 1967, became legendary. Attracted by the potential the brownstone row houses held, they also saw the park, the museum, and the library as valuable assets. Inviting other young couples to explore the area, the Ortners served as restoration and renovation advocates. At their cocktail parties they would persuade bankers to stop "redlining" the neighborhood, the practice in which lenders drew "no-lending lines" around high-risk areas, and offer mortgages to more young buyers. Before long, they persuaded the Brooklyn Gas

Company to rehabilitate a brownstone to feature modern gas fixtures, and the model home served as the center for the ambitious brownstone housing fair that attracted thousands to appreciate the transformative nature of the local renaissance (Dominus 2006).

One of the most influential Brooklyn residents was chemical engineer Clem Labine. Labine left his job at McGraw-Hill publishers in 1967 when he bought and restored an 1883 brownstone townhouse in Park Slope, which also provided an outlet for his writing and editing talents. With his wife Claire, a television producer, Labine began the *Old-House Journal* (*OHJ*) in October 1973. At first, this short, inexpensive subscription-based newsletter was illustrated with black and white line drawings and occasional photographs accompanying folksy advice on sealing drafty windows, staircase surgery, stiffening sagging floors, and "how to get plastered." Readers contributed some articles (OHJ 1973/1974). Later, the *OHJ* became a magazine with historic product advertising and a color cover, but practical application remained a key focus (Yarrow 1987). For many people, there was no better guide to materials and methods in the "renovation and maintenance" of the "antique house," originally defined as built before 1914. Labine and his first associate editor, Carolyn Flaherty, sold *OHJ* 14 years later, starting *Traditional Buildings*, a magazine that serves primarily as a source guide for

---

Corporation purchased the properties and began restoration. A commercial artist for African American comic books and inveterate educator, Maynard was the first African American to become a member of the Board of the National Trust for Historic Preservation (Martin 2006).

Fig. 2.20 Arthur P.
Ziegler, cofounder of
the Pittsburgh History
and Landmarks Foun-
dation, lecturing on
"Pittsburgh as People
and Place," key in-
gredients for the work
of his organization.
(Author's photograph)

products and services.[45] With the increase in the number of young professionals who were willing to put the time and energy into their neighborhoods, more policy makers and politicians saw their future changing.

The "gritty city" in the rapidly deindustrializing Great Lakes region that attracted the most attention was Pittsburgh. A few members of the Pittsburgh Architectural Club led the way in the mid-1950s, writing about preservation in the *Charette*. James D. Van Trump, Arthur Ziegler, and Charles Shane assumed publishing responsibility for the newsletter in 1965, bringing attention to preservation challenges through the late 1960s (Van Trump et al. 1971). In 1971, the old Penn Theatre was transformed into Heinz Hall for the Performing Arts and the old Post Office was rescued by the Urban Development Authority of Pittsburgh to become a museum of Pittsburgh and Allegheny County history (Van Trump 1971). The agent of many of these changes was the Pittsburgh History and Landmarks Foundation, founded in 1964 by Ziegler and Van Trump. They learned that the local urban renewal agency intended to demolish blocks of the Manchester neighborhood and to throw its weight toward the

installation of a new elevated highway. Proactively, Ziegler and Trump began surveying the area in 1965, and established a revolving fund in 1966 to help residents purchase and revitalize buildings in a manner that set the tone for other preservationists throughout the country (Ziegler 1967; Ziegler et al. 1975; Fig. 2.20).

Just as important is Pittsburgh Neighborhood Housing Services (PNHS), founded in 1968 by Dorothy Richardson. She set out to help low and moderate-income African American residents, many of whom were viewed as poor credit risks by local banks, by providing money from a revolving loan fund for rehabilitation services. PNHS also encouraged more financial literacy through homebuyer education programs to specific North Pittsburgh neighborhoods. The Federal Home Loan Bank Board and the Department of Housing and Urban Development (HUD) sponsored a study of the most imaginative and successful initiatives in neighborhood reinvestment. PNHS's idea of loaning money to people otherwise classified as a poor risk in a targeted area became a model (Urban Reinvestment Task Force 1976). HUD's Urban Reinvestment Task Force adopted the technique, and it became a standard procedure used by not only neighborhood conservationists, but also banking networks. When the President signed the Housing and Community Development Act of 1974, the formulas to fund urban renewal, open space, planning, and historic preservation, among other

---

[45] By the time he began this publishing venture in 1988, Labine recognized that the historic craft skills and products were being used in new construction, and neo-traditional buildings often referred to historical antecedents in a respectful manner (Lockwood 2003).

programs, were replaced with a community de-velopment block grant (CDBG) program that al-lowed municipalities to decide largely for them-selves how to distribute this funding.[46] Although the attitude of local residents may be improved by cleaning up the neighborhood, the injection of more money raised fears of displacement and relocation.[47]

Broadening the preservation movement to in-clude neighborhood conservation is apparent in the smaller historic cities. For example, a local foundation provided a $75,000 challenge grant to Historic Savannah Foundation (HSF)'s capi-tal campaign to establish a revolving fund. In the absence of local historic district regulations and design guidelines, when the organization gained control of a property, HSF placed a restrictive covenant on the property to require that the pres-ent and future owners and tenants would maintain its historic character. With an increasing sense that the revitalization of residential property was only the beginning, the HSF eyed the commercial blocks on West Congress Street. In turn, several Foundation decisions prompted the city to make improvements to streets with improved lighting, sidewalks, and road surfaces. On River Street, the city even retained the old Belgian block pav-ing. A number of individuals began to see the wisdom of investing in undervalued real estate and the legendary squares and streets of the city's unique plan began to come alive again (Hodder 1993; Historic Savannah Foundation 1964).

To promote the advantages of the city, the HSF enlisted staff members from Colonial Wil-liamsburg and the local Chamber of Commerce. Together they developed plans to expand tourism, emphasizing that the historic properties were as important as the hotels, motels, restaurants, and recreational opportunities. The annual Georgia Day celebration provided the opportunity to in-vite federal, regional, and state officials, cement-ing the Savannah renaissance in the minds of the public. Emma Adler, president of the Junior League during the mid-1960s, played a crucial role coordinating joint volunteer activities with the Foundation (Adler and Adler 2003).

In 1965, Reid Williamson, employed with the Atlanta Chamber of Commerce, was hired as HSF's executive director and served the next 7 years, effectively promoting the wide range of activities of the Foundation. Following Charles-ton's example, the Historic Savannah Foundation acquired options on property to hold them for re-development. Often the organization become in-volved in complex projects but, because historic district zoning legislation was not approved until 1972, when securing property the organization often relied upon covenants attached to the deeds to ensure that future owners would properly maintain and preserve them. Lee Adler attempted to prod the Foundation into a more aggressive role to deal with absentee owners who were not maintaining the wooden Victorian architecture of the city. To meet the needs of local low-income residents, he formed the Savannah Landmark Rehabilitation Project in 1974, a separate entity from HSF. With Ford Foundation support and job training funds, people were put to work (Adler and Adler 2003).

Although significant progress in rehabilitat-ing the historic core and the work in the Victorian district was impressive, civil rights advocate and historian Westley Wallace Law still saw historic preservation as an elitist activity that "turned off" African Americans who should become involved in reclaiming their neighborhoods (Meyerson 1989). Law and others at HSF worked to help re-locate the King-Tisedell Cottage and turn it into a house museum, to interpret the life of local resi-dents in the 1890s. He also worked to keep over

---

[46] This approach subsumed the Department of Housing and Development's categorical grant programs.

[47] During the early 1970s, an emphasis arose on identify-ing and protecting these resources on a scale never before undertaken, with considerable financial assistance from the US Department of Housing and Urban Development. One percent of the budget of that agency applied to his-toric preservation projects surpassed the entire Depart-ment of the Interior appropriations for the State Historic Preservation Offices, the National Trust for Historic Pres-ervation, and the National Park Service's cultural resource programs. The belief that the government would continue to provide direct financial aid to assist in solving urban problems continued in some quarters for another decade or more (Fullilove 2004).

Fig. 2.21 The plan
to renew the central
business district of
Seattle by demolishing
Pike Place Market led
preservationists to rise
in opposition and call
for the retention of not
only the architectural
form but also the range
of functions of the
location, as a "living
thing." (Author's
photograph)

2 dozen row houses in the hands of low-income residents.[48]

The stories of community-based advocacy in Pittsburgh, Brooklyn, and Savannah were placed in a broader context when, in September of 1975, the National Endowment of the Arts sponsored a major Neighborhood Conservation Conference (McNulty and Kliment 1976). Initiatives like Pike Place Market and Pioneer Square in Seattle, Washington; others in the Mt. Auburn and Mt. Adams neighborhoods in Cincinnati, Ohio; and still others that emphasized the importance of socially sensitive preservation were showcased, indicating that hope was possible even in some of the most depressed city cores (Link 2005; Fig. 2.21). In fact, because so many renovation efforts were taking place outside of the relatively limited number of historic preservation districts, neighborhood conservation in the revised housing and urban redevelopment framework began to supersede the older method of historic district designation. Overlay zones designated these neighborhoods. Although the neighborhood con-

servation movement was not yet evident in all cities, the work was beginning from the ground-up.

Bicentennial Fever and the "Mosaic" Paradigm

The Bicentennial spurred a immense amount of historical and preservation-minded activity and shifted the vision of some intellectuals interested in leaving behind the idea of America as a "melting pot" to a country celebrating the features in its social "mosaic." Across the USA from Alaska to Florida and Puerto Rico, and from Massachusetts to Hawaii, Guam and American Samoa, in about a dozen Indian reservations and in 22 foreign countries, people mounted exhibits, restored houses, reenacted battles, organized conferences, planted trees, and planned festivals in red, white and blue. In addition to federal, state, and local government funds, the sponsors included corporations, unions, foundations, educational institutions, religious groups, and ethnic societies. The chance to feature historic districts as well as to build parks and monuments provided historic preservation with a remarkable boost (Hornblower 1975). The "Tall Ships" that sailed into New York harbor on July 4th provided perhaps the most memorable romantic vision, although the burst of patriotism was seen in fireworks throughout the nation. The Mall in Washington,

---

[48] Law founded the Beach Institute Historic Neighborhood Association in 1980. In this case, the organization attracted sufficient funds from the city's community development block grant program and private donors, and rehabilitated the oldest African American area in downtown.

Fig. 2.22 Representative John Seiberling of Ohio, and Loretta Neumann, senior staff assistant, played a role in a number of significant preservation initiatives, including the 1980 NHPA amendments. (Author's collection)

D.C. opened the Air and Space Museum, a National Visitor's Center, and 34 nations participated in the Festival of Folklife during its 3-month stay in the Capital (Darling 1977).

Washington's zeal to become the most obvious tourist destination continued when preservationists launched a project to create a museum dedicated to building and construction. When the General Services Administration deemed the old Pension Building a surplus structure in 1976, the agency commissioned local architect Chloethiel Woodward Smith to evaluate potential uses for the property. Although various combinations of commercial, recreational, and professional offices were proposed, a museum seemed to be the most appropriate. Architectural historian Cynthia Field pushed this idea in a series of public lectures and formed a nonprofit organization that included developer James Rouse and architecture critic for the *Washington Post*, Wolf von Eckardt. By enlisting the support of the General Services Administration, the Smithsonian, and the Nation-

al Endowment for the Arts, and with the help of Loretta Neumann, senior staff assistant to Representative John Seiberling, the National Building Museum took a step closer to reality when a provision supporting it was included in the National Historic Preservation Act amendments of 1980 (Franklin and Field 2005/2006) (Fig. 2.22).

As opposed to an emphasis on assimilation, Bicentennial history celebrated diversity and led to self-examination in several ways. Author and researcher Alex Haley began to share the results of his own African family's origins in the early 1970s, but his work, *Roots: The Saga of an American Family*, became an overnight best seller when it was published in 1976. The novel was loosely based on his family's history, beginning with the 1767 kidnapping of Kunta Kinte in Gambia (Terrell 1976; Haley 1976). Haley claimed to be a seventh generation descendent of Kinte, who was sold into slavery. The story of his ancestors and his tale of visiting the African village where Kinte was raised, where he learned more from a tribal historian, captured the imagination in a television miniseries in 1977. The narrative was also the basis for a film, reaching an estimated 130 million viewers. *Roots* emphasized the long history that African Americans share and renewed a deep interest in genealogy (Lescaze and Saperstein 1978).

Nicodemus, a pioneer free Black community in Western Kansas, also became a center of interest, so much so that the Historic American Buildings Survey fielded a team to record it in the early 1980s (Fig. 2.23). The Black communities in Northeastern Montgomery County, Maryland, many of them already gone and barely leaving a trace, also received attention. More generally, the search for sites associated with the Underground Railroad spread throughout the eastern half of the nation.

Yet, at the neighborhood level, historic preservation efforts remained uneven as the rhetoric of the Bicentennial cooled. By contrast, in 1978 the cries of gentrification against preservationists reached a fevered pitch, most notably in Baltimore, where the difference was apparent between the income levels of long time inner city African American residents and the wealth displayed by

Fig. 2.23 Nicodemus, Kansas, recognized as a National Historic Landmark for being the earliest and most prosperous Midwestern African American settlement, formed in 1877 by settlers from Kentucky and Tennessee. (Historic American Buildings Survey, Library of Congress)

their new neighbors. As housing rehabilitation became an increasingly viable option, preservationists, used to being the underdog, found that their intervention was decried as harmful to the low-income residents who could not afford to live in the newly improved areas. While they had fought and often succeeded in bringing new lines of credit to the residents of the neighborhood, and although the improvement was more a matter of sweat equity than outside investment, preservationists were caught defending their intentions and being criticized as "no more than" injecting middle class values in the historic core of some cities (Nelson 1988). Subsequent research indicated that residents already living in the city who had relocated to adjacent neighborhoods made most of the small-scale investments, but in the early 1980s this became a matter of considerable concern among members of the National Trust for Historic Preservation.[49]

Ironically, some of those who had moved into the city did so to *escape* the prevailing values of suburbia. Gays and lesbians moved to the inner city largely to affirm their identity and mobilize to gain political influence (Haeberle 1996). By settling areas of lower Manhattan around Christopher Street and the Castro District in San Francisco, they provided a remarkable difference in the life of formerly blighted neighborhoods. Restaurants, bars, bookstores, museums, art galleries, literary and publishing firms, music and dance studios were but a few vital businesses that provided "eyes on the street," very much in keeping with the ideals espoused by Jane Jacobs. With articulate voices, their talent and considerable organizational skill made a difference, gradually affecting political decisions. Networks of gay advocates were evident around Dupont Circle in Washington, D.C. and Pike Place in Seattle (Adkins 2003), while in cities like Philadelphia, Savannah (Berendt 1994), and Birmingham, others contributed to the preservation movement informally, lending strength to the gradual change from concerns for diversity to a focus on identity politics (Bailey 1999). Sadly, the leadership gay men provided was overshadowed by the rise of AIDS in the 1980s, diminishing their ranks (Fellows 2004).[50]

---

[49] This is confirmed by a review of the number of articles on the topic in *Preservation News* and the newspapers of the period. See Chapter 7 for further discussion of the misuse of this term.

[50] Unfortunately, the leadership of lesbian women, so obvious in renovation projects and advocacy efforts, remains largely understudied.

The Struggle Continues, the Base of Support Grows

The 1976 election of Jimmy Carter as President, a populist Southern conservative Democrat, proved to be a watershed for the expansion of the federal government. Carter held high his faith in God and promised the electorate to end the rancorous politics in Washington. From his experience as governor of Georgia, Carter brought several ideas to federal government, one of which was to join natural area conservation and historic preservation in a single agency, the Heritage Conservation and Recreation Service, combining elements of the Bureau of Outdoor Recreation and the National Park Service. The initiative was short-lived, rejected by the state historic preservation officers, among others. It spurred more discussion between archaeologists and historic preservation specialists, however, and continued to broaden the relationship between these disciplines. Potentially more helpful was the Department of Housing and Urban Development's Urban Development Action Grant program, at first criticized by preservationists as a "new urban renewal" for the sweeping destruction it sponsored (Satterthwaite 1979). While the federal government searched for a way in which to reposition itself to be helpful in a deindustrializing country, with declining state aid, many cities were left to fend for themselves. Despite this, preservation efforts in several large cities would ramp up in the late 1970s.

In Atlanta, preservationists saw the demolition of the historic commercial and residential urban core for transportation arteries and new corporate offices. In particular, the 1892 Equitable Building, designed by Chicago architect John Wellborn Root, was torn down in 1971 to make way for the new Trust Company of Georgia headquarters. In a scant gesture to preservationists, the original columns from the Equitable Building became a sculptural arrangement in front of the new building. The center of this "New" Southern city rapidly changed, as most of the white residents moved to the suburbs. Other important buildings that were lost include

the Forsyth Building, the Atlanta National Bank, Loew's Grand Theatre, and the Carnegie Library, which was torn town in 1980 (Auchmutey 1986).[51]

The dispute over the Fox Theater on Peachtree Street was the first major preservation battle in Atlanta in the post-National Historic Preservation Act era. The Fox, a 1920s movie palace with lavish Moorish architectural detailing, was to be demolished when a small group of Atlantans recognized the importance of the structure and challenged the owner, the Southern Bell Telephone Company, to reconsider its plans to demolish it. The nonprofit Atlanta Landmarks, Inc., formed to "Save the Fox" during the mid-1970s, proved remarkably successful, providing the metro area preservation community with its first major victory (Upward 1975; Zarafonetis 2010; Fig. 2.24).

Many more properties needed attention, however. The fits and starts provided by the two original entrepreneurs in Underground Atlanta, the commercial section of the city below grade near the state Capitol, have been variously described since 1969 with euphoria and disdain (Galphin 1969; Green 1977; Lohmann 1985; Crane 1977). The low level of revenue it generated so long beleaguered the efforts and the city that Underground Atlanta best serves as a lesson for why commercial revitalization can repeatedly fail (Degross 2003; Stafford and Bond 2007). Meanwhile, preservation efforts took hold elsewhere in the city. In response to the threat of demolition of an early twentieth century structure known as "The Castle," Eileen Rhea Brown founded the Atlanta Preservation Center in 1980. The Castle, located in upper midtown, was in poor condition and vacant by the time it came into the hands of AT&T. When the new group attempted to intervene, Mayor Andrew Young dismissed the structure as a "hunk of junk." In retrospect, the quote catalyzed the local movement as no other threat had previously and the Center persisted, turning Mayor Young's derogatory comment into

---

[51] Another significant controversy surrounded construction of the Presidential Parkway, a narrative deserving of further study.

Fig. 2.24 The Fox Theater, Atlanta, a lavishly decorated Moorish monument, was saved by preservationists who went on to form Atlanta Landmarks, Inc. (Historic American Buildings Survey, Library of Congress)

a campaign slogan: "Save Our Hunk of Junk." The Atlanta Preservation Center negotiated with AT&T and convinced the company to carry out an extensive restoration of the structure's exterior even though its setting was compromised by the soaring AT&T towers immediately adjacent (Preservation News 1986).

In comparison to Atlanta, the largest community in the Southwest should have been well advanced. Los Angeles had established an ordinance and witnessed advocacy campaigns earlier. Yet, its downtown also suffered disinvestment. In response, neighborhood groups organized. One of the best known was the Carroll Avenue Restoration Foundation, established in 1975. Its efforts began informally 2 years earlier, focusing on the 1300 block of Carroll Avenue, which included Queen Anne, Eastlake and bungalow residences, most in very poor repair (Murray 1973).[52] As an all-volunteer organization, the Carroll Avenue group raised funds to purchase period street lamps, bury overhead wiring, and plant trees. Yet another group, Keep Old Los Angeles (KOLA), formed in 1977, decried the increasing rate of de-

molition, effectively using the press to advocate their position. Claiming 1900 members, KOLA's leader, commercial artist Douglas Carlton, attempted to save the Ozro William Childs Mansion from demolition by the Board of Education. The group went to court with the Greater West Adams neighborhood association, but the effort to save the house failed (Decker 1978; Merl 1980).

The intensity of the discussion surrounding the demolition of the Childs residence was important for providing the impetus for the founding of the Los Angeles Conservancy (LAC). By May 1978, it became involved with urban and neighborhood issues, including the proposed multimillion dollar people mover project and the fate of the Central Library. From the start, it welcomed as members a broad cross section of architects, municipal officials, neighborhood representatives, planners, and preservationists (Herbert 1978). Chair Margaret Bach and the founding board recognized the need to embrace a broader than average constituency. Saving more than an occasional building, however, would remain difficult for some years to come.

Somewhat like the LAC, on the other side of the country another loose association of preservation organizations was founded in 1978, the Boston Preservation Alliance (AllianceLetter 1980). By that time, to judge by the membership rolls, the regional strength of preservation organizations in eastern Massachusetts far outweighed most other metropolitan centers.[53] The city's reputation as a center for historic preservation activities was made in reaction to several Boston Redevelopment Authority projects. Boston also indirectly benefited by the creation of the most popular television program specifically developed for residential rehabilitation, "This Old House." The 1978 brainchild of Russell Morash, well known for "how to" programming at the public broadcasting station WGBH in Boston, the star of the show was energetic Bob Vila. Morash boosted the number of television viewers by demonstrating every week for 3

---

[52] Tom and Priscilla Morales at 1300 Carroll Avenue and Barbara Thornburg at 1316 Carroll Avenue played pivotal roles.

[53] At its outset, the Boston Preservation Alliance communicated with the Society for the Preservation of New England Antiquities and a number of other smaller organizations.

months a step in the renovation of an inexpensive old house in Dorchester. Neither Clem Labine nor Bob Vila ever made claims to be following national historic preservation standards, but both went a long way toward repopularizing residential investment. In Vila's case, in his 10 years at WGBH he reached cult hero status, endorsing *Time-Life* home repair books and a wide range of products. At its peak in 1988, "This Old House" reached 22 million viewers, 66 % of whom were 35 years old or older, with an average income of $25,534. Another television series, Maryland Public Broadcasting's "Old Houseworks," with host Bob Callahan and woodworker Gilbert Brooks, began at the same time and included notable preservation experts, so that the words rehabilitation and renovation became commonplace through hundreds of affiliate stations across the country (Preservation News 1980).

Features on the work done in New York and Boston set the tone for other locations in the USA. Television reports about the condition of the urban core of Washington, D.C. in the 1960s and 1970s, by contrast, were often bleak. It would take another 20 years for preservation activities to become successful. In 1960, newly elected President John F. Kennedy was so embarrassed by the condition of the buildings and streets along Pennsylvania Avenue, the inaugural parade route from the Capitol to the White House, that he immediately ordered a study to investigate options for improvement. An Ad Hoc Committee on Federal Office Space recommended in May 1962 the establishment of a President's Advisory Council on Pennsylvania Avenue. Architect Nathaniel A. Owings and Senator Daniel Patrick Moynihan were among the first appointments and both men provided strong direction. Indeed, Moynihan's role in formulating subsequent legislation earns him a place in preservation history few lawmakers can match. However, the 1968 riots left Washington's downtown further damaged. Not until the election of Mayor Walter Washington did the District begin to gain some measure of direction and, with his successor Marion Barry, hope (Gillette 1995). Large areas deemed blighted required rebuilding, but urban renewal came at a cost. The most vocal preservation voice was

Don't Tear It Down, organized in 1971 to oppose demolition of the Old Post Office. Although the founding president, Karen Gordon, the first executive director, Judith Sobol, and the skilled attorney David Bonderman,[54] found themselves in a number of local battles that ended in demolition, they gained an increasing amount of attention. The turning point came when rallying against the planned destruction of the massive Romanesque Old Post Office Building on Pennsylvania Avenue, which stood in the way of completing a Neoclassical axis from the Capitol to the White House. The local controversy led to a Congressional hearing on the future of surplus public buildings, called by Senator Mike Gravel, the Public Works Subcommittee chair, just 2 days after the rally, which provided advocates a timely opportunity to press their case for regulatory reform (Maddex 1971a, b; Fig. 2.25).

Don't Tear It Down also fought against the Pennsylvania Avenue Development Commission (PADC) when it pursued the demolition of the all but completely abandoned Willard Hotel (ICH 1986). The owner-developer of the famed hostelry, located immediately adjacent to the White House, stripped it of its exquisite interiors and held an auction with the expectation that the land would be seized by PADC for a National Square. When the Commission abandoned this idea, the rehabilitation of the hostelry became a possibility and in 1981 was identified as a signature property of a major hotel chain (Knight 1979; Greer 1986; Gamarekian 1986). By the early 1980s, Don't Tear It Down changed its name to the D.C. Preservation League, in part to avoid being labeled obstructionist by the business community, and began to work alongside those inside government and in the private sector.

Atlanta, Los Angeles, Boston, and Washington, D.C. were not the only cities to see local preservation initiatives, as advocates in dozens

---

[54] Bonderman's 1978 brief filed by the National Trust for Historic Preservation on behalf of Grand Central Station was applied by the Supreme Court in its decision to uphold the New York City Landmarks ordinance. He was also a principal author of DC Law 2–144, the local legislation in the District (Greve 1983).

Fig. 2.25 On Pennsylvania Avenue in Washington, D.C., the Romanesque Old Post Office was threatened with demolition but preservationists led a campaign not only to save it, but other surplus public buildings. (Historic American Buildings Survey, Library of Congress)

of other smaller communities sprang into action. Because it was clear that the federal government would provide less direct financial support than it had in the past, the private sector would need to contribute more to preservation.

A Change in the Wind: The "Business" of Preservation

In an era when one of the most viable new uses for an historic structure was a museum, it was common to measure the level of support for preservation in terms of the direct governmental appropriations for bricks and mortar projects. As housing rehabilitation become the focus of the movement during the 1970s, revolving funds and foundation grants often supplemented private financing. With the Bicentennial, corporate support increased. In 1976, an idea proposed in the mid-1960s became more viable and provided a new and exciting approach to financing commercial historic preservation projects: altering the federal tax code to favor rehabilitation.

In 1973, a bill introduced in the US Senate proposed several incentives to encourage rehabilitation of historic buildings in an attempt to equalize the tax breaks already given new construction. The measure was referred to the Senate Finance Committee where it remained until 1975. When reintroduced, the new bill's sponsor, Senator J. Glenn Beall of Maryland, stated "it is important for us to update our tax system so as to help redirect and achieve socially desirable goals" (Congressional Record 1975). Beall's legislation provided a special deduction for specific renovation expenses and accelerated depreciation for rehabilitated historic buildings (Washington Post 1976).

This bill became part of a larger tax reform bill adopted in 1976, although the favorable provisions came as a surprise to the preservation community, few of whom participated in the lobbying effort. The most controversial feature was the prohibition against allowing demolition expenses associated with destroying a "certified historic property," including those that contributed to an historic district (IRC 1976). Objections to this provision incorporated in subsequent tax legislation eliminated it, but the broader idea that historic preservation was a social goal resonated in subsequent discussions at every level of government (Thatcher 1995). The Tax Reform Act of 1976 seemed to provide the key to stimulate private sector investment that would offset the loss of federal aid. New provisions in the Economic Recovery Tax Act of 1981, passed under President Reagan, attracted developers and financiers who had more money, eclipsing the work of smaller investors (Urban Conservation Report (UCR) 1982).

Projects such as the rehabilitation of the Willard Hotel in Washington, D.C. were attributable to this new means of raising capital, and soon the economics of urban preservation in the USA changed. It was apparent that "public–private" partnerships could stimulate downtown revitalization (Frieden and Sagalyn 1989) and maverick developers and enterprising mayors joined hands to undertake what seemed to be an impossible task of bringing people back to the inner city. As part of the much greater building boom in the suburbs, the early 1980s became the period in which it became possible to not only dream about the revival of the city's commercial core, but actually do something about it. While "edge cities" formed at transportation nodes in the suburbs, the renewal of dozens of commercial fronts, train stations, early skyscrapers, and scores of vacant school buildings proceeded apace. Preservationists joined other city watchers in applauding James Rouse who, in 1981, was canonized "an urban visionary" (Demarest 1981; Pawlyna 1981; Olsen 2004; Bloom 2004). His career as a shopping mall and new town backer behind him, Rouse's festival marketplaces were important to reintroducing the ideas of contemporary retailing in downtown. Although his marketplaces were not intended to be primarily historic preservation projects and, occasionally were decried as simply bringing the suburban mall to core areas (Landers 1985; Gregerson 1988),[55] many preservationists and developers learned by his example how to play a more active role in urban redevelopment (Walter 1987; Opsata 1987; Shashaty 1983). By the mid-1980s, the preservation industry had expanded to include a wide variety of business activities, such as masonry cleaning, product manufacturing, publishing, and merchandising (Chittendon and Gordon 1983; Oldham 1990). In November 1987, a *Time* magazine cover story remarked that the preservation ethic sweeping the country was "so complete that it is difficult today to remember how recently people were blithely ripping out and throwing away the warp and woof of America's cities" (Anderson 1987). [56]

Problems arose, however, when the urban redevelopment agenda got ahead of other concerns. San Francisco's overheated market for office space led to the construction of ubiquitous high-rises and the prospect of more building threatened the image and function of the city. A number of protests led to popular initiatives that effectively halted vertical growth. Two years in the making, the Board of Supervisors adopted a new downtown plan in 1985. San Franciscans for Reasonable Growth promoted a measure in late 1986 that effectively made it the most restrictive of any in the USA with regard to height and bulk of new construction (UCR 1985). On the other end of the country, by 1984, Boston was overbuilt with new towers sponsored by commercial developers and banks entering the real estate industry, amid widespread talk of reaching record-breaking prices (Campbell 1984a). A report issued by the Chamber of Commerce and the Boston Society of Architects called for controls on the growth of the downtown hub (Yudis 1984). At the same time the city seemed to be suffering from what critic Robert Campbell called "parachute architecture," that is, buildings that seemed to be dropped by parachute into the city by a famous and busy out-of-town architects from a plane flying overhead (Campbell 1984b). More troubling news came from New York City, where the local preservation commission, once cited as a model for other cities in the nation, was repeatedly attacked by members of the real estate community, various church groups, and politicians as being inefficient, elitist, and obstructionist. As the studies of commission activities demonstrated, citizen activists were alternately exhausted by their own efforts and frustrated by what they read and heard (Village Views 1987; Conklin 1989; Tung 1989).

Uneasy Successes and Compromises

The possibility of revitalizing commercial buildings that gave new economic life to underutilized urban areas and provided a reasonable return on the investment in historic property was incredibly energizing for preservationists, but it also precipitated ethical questions. The heated real estate market and preservationist's willingness

---

[55] The most notable projects are Faneuil Hall in Boston (1976), South Street Seaport in New York (1983), Harborplace in Baltimore (1980); Jacksonville Landing, Jacksonville, Florida (1987); Bayside Marketplace in Miami (1987), and Riverwalk in New Orleans (1984).

[56] This is in contrast to other major cities, such as Detroit and Buffalo, which continued to see their populations decrease and their economic condition worsen.

to embrace the business community led to a tendency to "switch rather than fight," that is, accept compromise from the start of a project rather than question whether the solution was the best one at the time. The most obvious result was a rash of "facadism," the deliberate demolition of all but one or more elevations of an old building that are then held in place while a larger new structure is erected behind. Some preservationists defended the procedure as saving half a loaf rather than none, but others recognized that facadism is demolition by another name. Today, examples of these "compromises" are evident in almost every large city in the country. In San Francisco, the diminutive White Investment Company Building and Crocker Bank; in Boston, the Stock Exchange Building; and in New York, the Villard Houses-turned-Helmsley-Palace Hotel, all mark the beginning of this unfortunate tendency, often justified as a "special case." (Fig. 2.26) In Washington, D.C., the Congressionally-mandated height limits, the marshy soil, and an unusually strong local preservation ordinance forced local developers to negotiate with various community interests before seeking local approvals and permits, but the discussion of aesthetic solutions rarely extended to consider social implications.[57]

The ethical problems of the 1980s that were associated with big money began to subside only when the funding for preservation projects declined at the end of the decade. In 1984 and 1985, growing dissatisfaction among the public with the perceived unfairness of the tax system and the continued prevailing belief in supply-side economics—emphasizing tax cuts to restrict income, rather than tax increases—to control the federal budget led to change once more (Treasury 1984). The alteration of the internal revenue code in the Tax Reform Act of 1986, first crafted in secret by the Treasury Department and then deftly moved through Congress with the support of the press (Conlan 1990) so thoroughly altered the passive investment rules that the downturn in the number and size of certified historic rehabilitations was almost immediate (UCR 1986). The

Fig. 2.26 In San Francisco, the White Investment Building was one of the first to be all but completely destroyed, despite the best efforts of the preservation community. Saving only the fronts gave rise to the term "facadism." (Author's photograph)

cooling economy and difficulties in the banking industry further sharply decreased the number of compromised projects.

Ethical questions also seemed to arise when dealing with intangible values, especially when spiritual and social ideals came up against aesthetics and economics. Churches, meetinghouses, synagogues, temples, and mosques are obvious candidates for local landmark status, and their social organizations are major stakeholders in the city and suburbs. Yet, those religious leaders who focused on the "higher" purpose of serving God and their organization's human spiritual needs saw preservationists, who generally centered their concerns upon keeping intact the physical fabric of a religious property, as obstructionists. One of the hottest cases in the 1980s began when St. Bartholomew's Episcopal Church in Manhattan submitted an application to the Landmark

---

[57] This discussion is extended in Chapter 7.

Preservation Commission to demolish part of their property to further what their leaders argued was their religious mission. The decision of the US Supreme Court, affirming the right of the Commission to control St. Bart's options in this matter, was widely hailed in the preservation community as a cause for celebration (Greenhouse 1991; Goldberger 1991; Purdum 1991). However, state court decisions in other parts of the country were not as favorable and subsequent federal legislation seemed to call into question just what direction acceptable compromises should follow.[58]

Outside of the courts, the problems of saving and extending the use of so many sacred sites often seems too large to handle. Every year, dozens of religious sites are put on the auction block. In Detroit, the Roman Catholic archdiocese targeted several churches for closing (Holusha 1988). In Chicago, the diocese proposed that about 30 churches and six schools would cease operations (The New York Times (NYT) 1990). The story is similar in New York City and Boston where the mounting deficits in poor neighborhoods led church administrators to predict that as high as 10% of their properties would be deconsecrated and sold. Even relatively recently established religions, such as the Christian Scientists, suffer from declining congregations, in some cases having lost more than 60% of their numbers from their peak. The effect is particularly telling because some of these groups have been committed to the importance of an urban ministry, sustaining social services where otherwise none would exist. Only in the late 1980s did preservation partnerships begin to form to address these problems.

Reclaiming and Reconceiving Landscapes

As the preservation constituency grew, the range of projects increased. Neighborhood improvement linked to nearby parks, commons, squares, and cemeteries became a point of pride and civic consciousness. During the 1970s, the creation and development of "friends of the park" and "friends of the cemetery" organizations repeatedly worked to improve their respective areas, often in an attempt to reduce crime and increase public safety.

In New York City, the parks administration recognized the special nature of the principal parks in 1966, when it named two well-known historians, Henry Hope Reed, Jr., and Clay Lancaster, as the first curators of Central Park and Prospect Park, respectively. While these historians offered tours, the marked decline of the condition of these landscapes was a greater problem than the city could fix (Blumenthal 1966). Graffiti on the rocks, bridges, pavilions, and buildings was commonplace, and liquor bottles and garbage was strewn everywhere. Although loitering along Central Park West remained a problem, the rising drug use and open thievery in the early 1970s made the general public dread visiting the parks. The crime statistics shocked most residents, as the figures for 1969 were topped by those in 1970, and became even higher in 1971. Nearly 800 robberies occurred in the first 8 months of 1971, with over 1100 felonies, including 24 rapes, double the number in the previous year (Pace 1971). Financier Arthur Ross began to plant pine trees near the northwest edge of the Great Lawn in 1971 in an effort to instigate a turnaround. This private initiative made it apparent that without noteworthy generosity and dogged determination, the city's public parks would become no-go zones (Martin 2007). Rising to the fore was Elizabeth Browning Barlow, who supplied the necessary zeal by spearheading the Central Park Task Force in 1975, becoming the first Central Park Administrator in 1979. Working with a new Parks Commissioner, Gordon Davis, they created a private–public relationship, the Central Park Conservancy, with its own board, which included Chairman Bill Beinecke (Dembart 1979; Glueck 1980). That board, with the help of the Conservancy's Womens' Committee, gradually made a difference. With the help of thousands of volunteers, the change became noticeable with the restoration of the Great Lawn,

---

[58] The legal issues are discussed in Chapter 3, ethical concerns in Chapter 7, and the contributions of faith-based organizations are examined in Chapter 8.

Fig. 2.27 The
campaign to reclaim
the beauty of Central
Park began with a task
force that eventually
blossomed into a
broad scale effort
to assist the city's
Parks Department.
Today, a remarkable
set of cooperative
arrangements
continue to support
the management
and maintenance.
(Author's photograph)

the Sheep Meadow, the Bethesda and Cherry Hill fountains, and dozens of paths and pavilions. Just as important, a master plan was discussed, published, and disseminated, spurring other cities to take a more aggressive stance (Carmody 1985; Rosenzweig and Blackmar 1992; Fig. 2.27).

Similar efforts began in other cities. Friends of the (Chicago) Parks, established in 1975, began with an adopt a park program, while the Philadelphia Parks Alliance built coalitions and educated the public in order to rid the area of crime and revitalize the parks and other open spaces of that city. In Seattle, the Friends of Discovery Park formed in 1974 to defend the integrity of that amenity and to keep man-made objects to a minimum. In this case, the organization vigilantly resisted several proposals by various interests to appropriate "just a piece" of the Park. By the 1980s, the movement to rehabilitate parks became a feature of the annual meetings of the National Trust for Historic Preservation, giving strength to the growing concern for cultural landscapes of much larger scope, and presaging crusades during the 1990s for increased attention to local recreation sites and facilities. In succeeding years, cultural landscape evaluation became more widely understood as a methodology, alongside historic preservation planning, cultural resource management assessments, and the study of building problems.

The most obvious landscapes were some of the most sacred, claimed by Civil War reenactors and enthusiasts. Among the issues that galvanized national attention was the rising need to protect battlefields against suburbanization, especially in the South. The campaign to save Civil War battlefields began in earnest after commercial development on the site of the Battle of Ox Hill in Fairfax County, Virginia. The most celebrated controversy was the struggle to protect the land surrounding the Manassas Battlefield Park from mall development during the late 1980s and early 1990s (Colin 1988; Rankin and Snyder 1989; Zenzen 1997; Boge and Boge 1993). Walt Disney Company's planned mammoth theme park in the area, projected to include the "slave experience," drew particular scorn (Styron 1994).[59] (Fig. 2.28)

---

[59] In this context, Brian C. Pohanka's passion to preserve Civil War battlefields is worth special mention. In 1987, Pohanka convened some of the first meetings of the Association for the Preservation of Civil War Sites, later known as the Civil War Preservation Trust. His work included writing dozens of books and articles, appearing on documentaries like "Civil War Journal" on the History Channel and advising makers of period movies. For "Glory," a 1989 film that portrayed soldiers in the first black regiment in the Union Army, the 54th Massachusetts, he recruited and instructed actors portraying soldiers. For "Cold Mountain," released in 2003, he used original drill manuals to teach Civil War tactics to about 1000 Romanian soldiers hired as extras.

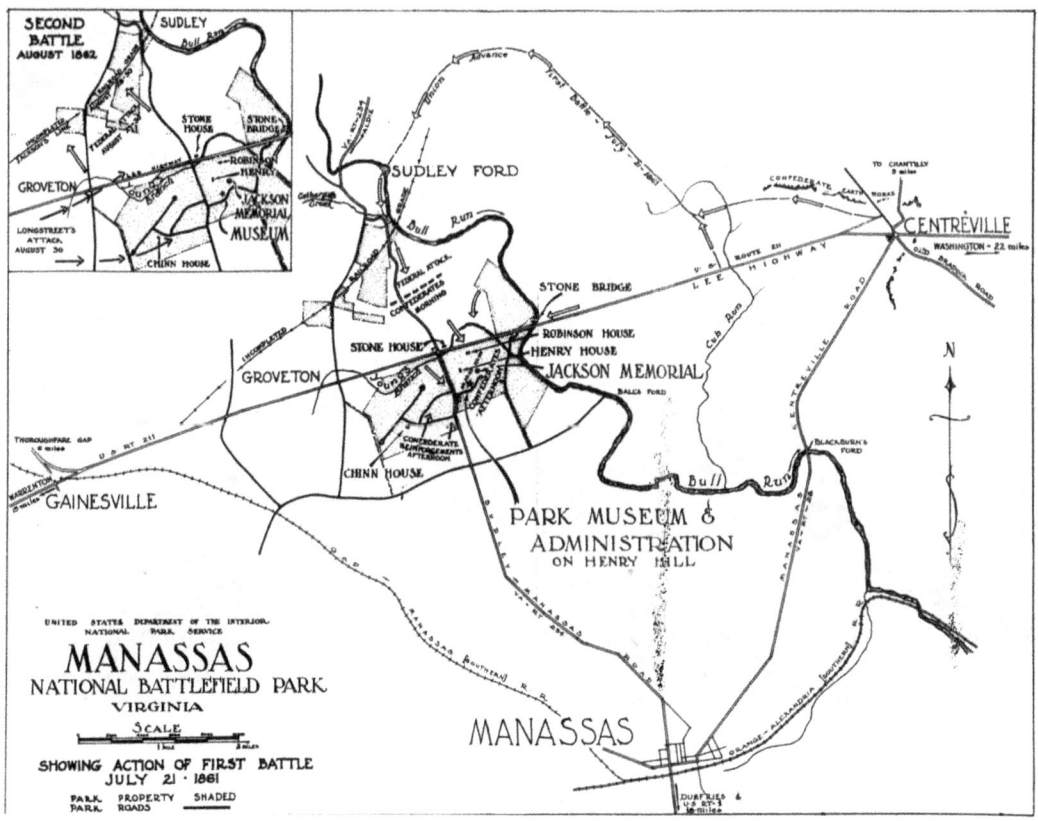

Fig. 2.28 The boundaries of the Manassas Battlefield as shown here in a 1943 map of the grounds encompassed a relatively limited area. The threat posed to the adjacent battlefield areas by a Walt Disney theme park spurred a campaign to save more of hallowed ground. (Library of Congress)

In saving battlefield sites, the National Trust for Historic Preservation took a leading role. In 1993, its president, J. Jackson Walter, stepped down and lawyer Richard Moe succeeded.[60] Earlier Moe became interested in historic preservation while conducting research for a book about the activities of a Minnesota regiment in the Civil War. He discovered many of the Civil War battlefields were threatened by neglect and development, and he joined the board of the Civil War Trust to learn more about how to help. As a result of his interest, although the National Trust invited Moe to head the organization with the idea of diversifying the properties under its control and to

shape federal, state and local policies in housing and transportation, the organization's first preservation victories were against the sprawl that was becoming so evident in Northern Virginia (Christian Science Monitor (CSM) 1993). This sprawl signals broader changes in the agrarian economy. Although the disappearance of the family farm became a rallying cry, the reasons for the abandonment of farmsteads and ranches in rural sections of the country are myriad. The problems led the National Trust to launch a pilot study of rural preservation initiatives in the late 1970s (Stokes et al. 1989). However, the organization had difficulty sustaining interest (Benson 1993). Attempting to stem the losses, in 1987 Trust field representative Mary M. Humstone renewed the effort to gather advocates and mounted an awards program to recognize special preservation ini-

---

[60] A native of Minnesota, Moe served as a staff aide and later chief of staff for Vice President Walter Mondale. He retired in 2010 (Schwartz 2010).

Fig. 2.29 The National Trust's Barn Again program and the initiatives of similar state-level barn organizations emphasize the need to connect the continued use of the land and its economic productivity to the aesthetic enjoyment the agricultural landscape provides. (Author's photograph)

tiatives. Her Mountains/Plains office, actively working in cooperation with *Successful Farming Magazine*,[61] launched the "Barn Again!" Farm Heritage program, focusing more attention on the preservation of older barns, farmhouses, ranches, and related buildings; the conservation of significant natural features, such as windbreaks, prairies, timber and wetlands; and historical developments in agricultural technology and archaeological significance. Examples such as the 1100 acre Arnold Farm in Rush County, Indiana, were recognized for having remained in the family since 1820, with a range of structures that span a log cabin through a Gothic Revival farm-

house, corn cribs, milk house, pole barn and machine shed (Preservation News 1990). Although the National Trust's program did not survive, several state barn preservation programs began, the most active being those in Illinois, Iowa, Indiana, Michigan, Minnesota, New York, Ohio, and Wisconsin (Fig. 2.29). All became members of the National Barn Alliance and most conduct joint activities with the cooperative extension offices through the land grant universities in their respective states, the 4-H chapters, and maintain a presence at their annual state fairs. Others play a roll in providing grants, offering technical assistance, and restoration awards.

---

[61] John Conrick, publisher of *Successful Farming*, expressed his interest in fostering stewardship and economic development. Grants from John Deere and Co. and Pioneer Hi-Bred International, a seed production and research firm, were very helpful (Preservation News 1987; Hoffman 1989).

Conclusion

By the end of the twentieth century, the continued growth of the urban and suburban communities in the southern and southwestern USA reshuffled their relative importance to the national economy. California and Texas superseded New York in population, with Florida nearing third place. "New" cities, like Phoenix, were largely post-World War II creations, adding their own history to the story of a developed nation. Meanwhile, some old cities continued to have difficulty while others were making a profound "come back," with new residents and investments, largely geared to making downtown a center of recreation and culture. Urban areas in the Great Lakes region and the Mississippi heartland continued to experience depopulation and declining property values. With declining tax revenues, Buffalo, Detroit, Milwaukee, St. Louis, and St. Paul posed difficult challenges, while most sections of Boston, Manhattan, Washington, Chicago, Denver, Los Angeles, and San Francisco saw remarkable positive transformation. The inner city residents of previous decades saw new waves of immigrants from South and Central America, Asia, and Africa, creating new enclaves, each with their own class structure, religions, and economic initiatives. The former urban cores of several of these cities became home to relatively well-educated and affluent professionals who purchased lofts and invested in inner-city suburbs. The coffee shops, outdoor restaurants, and theater districts that combined a bit of European café atmosphere with a Disney-like family friendly environment are the latest changes in conserved neighborhoods, recycled industrial warehouses, and refurbished waterfronts. No one observing the urban and suburban scene since passage of the National Historic Preservation Act in 1966 could doubt that historic preservation had demonstrated the merits of a different way of thinking about historic resources.

In retrospect, it is possible to identify the strong roots in house museum thinking. For some preservationists, the upper and upper middle class roots of the aging Eurocentric majority remain a motivating interest. At the same time, however, younger preservationists readily accept and evaluate whether to pursue the Main Street approach or tax advantaged rehabilitation, or a new heritage area initiative. The discussion about how to approach the integration of the new

and the old buildings has changed. The Modern Movement in architecture, art, and planning gave way in the late 1970s and 1980s to "postmodern" and "neo-urban" ideas, allowing contemporary designers more freedom to work on their own terms with community groups. The idea of saving post-War era design, now history to another generation, has led to the historic designation of entire suburbs and shopping centers, themselves character-defining features of American cities.

Parallel to the changes in the people and their attitudes toward buildings and landscapes are the thoughts that continue to propel preservationists. One of the most prominent critical texts, *The Power of Place* written by critic and historian Dolores Hayden, fused the ideas of Kevin Lynch and Jane Jacobs, going beyond the sociological studies of William Whyte to embrace African American, Latino, East Asian, and Native American diversity in public art, museum, and civic projects in Los Angeles (Hayden 1995). Despite the conflicts that inevitably arise—socially, economically, aesthetically, culturally, and technologically—historic preservationists accept the challenge and follow the basic concept of sustainability as it is currently defined, that is, proceed with ideas that are environmentally sound, economically viable, and socially equitable.

References

Adkins, G. L. (2003). *Gay seattle. Stories of exile and belonging* (pp. 56–58). Seattle: University of Washington Press.

Adler, L., & Adler, E. (2003). *Savannah renaissance*. Charleston: Wyrick.

Ainslee, M. L. (1981). President's column: 10th anniversary. *Preservation News, 21*(6), 2.

Ainsworth. (Ed.). (29 Sep 1963). Effort speeded to save mansion. *Los Angeles Times,* J7.

Alexander, E. P. (1991). *Valiant efforts and good intentions: AASLH's beginning years, 1940–1956. Local history, national heritage: Reflections on the history of AASLH* (pp. 37–77). Nashville: American Association for State and Local History.

Allen, M. (Ed.). (1997). *Ideas that matter: The worlds of Jane Jacobs*. Owen Sound: The Ginger Press.

AllianceLetter. (April 1980). BPA reorganization. *AllianceLetter, 1*(1), 1.

AllianceLetter. (March 1983). Urban archaeology. *AllianceLetter, 4*(2), 3.

Alofsin, A. (2002). *The struggle for modernism: Architecture, landscape architecture, and city planning at Harvard*. New York: Norton.

Anderson, J. A. (1984). *Time machines: The world of living history*. Nashville: American Association of State and Local History.

Anderson, K. (23 Nov 1987). Spiffing up the urban heritage. *Time*, 73.

Architectural Forum. (1935). Coming of Le Corbusier. *Architectural Forum, 63*(4), 34.

Auchmutey, J. (17 Feb 1986). The way we were: Downtown Atlanta's lost landmarks. *Atlanta Constitution*, A6.

Author's Papers. (4 Aug 1981). Transcript. Robert Garvey interview by Charles Hosmer, Jr. Sponsored by the Eastern National Parks and Monuments Association.

Author's Papers. (July 2007). Transcript. Sherene Baugher interview by Michael A. Tomlan.

Bacon, E. (1967). *Design of cities*. New York: Viking.

Bailey, R. W. (1999). *Gay politics, urban politics*. New York: Columbia University Press.

Bauman, J. F. (1987). *Public housing, race, and renewal: Urban planning in Philadelphia, 1920–1974*. Philadelphia: Temple University Press.

Benson, T. E. (1993). Barns: Seeing, feeling-and saving-our rural roots. *Preservation News, 33*(5), 6.

Berendt, J. (1994). *Midnight in the garden of good and evil: A savannah story*. New York: Random House.

Biddle, J. (1971). Preservation law at the trust: A new service. *Preservation News, 11*(5), 5.

Blake, G. (28 April 1958). Bunker Hill to be jewel again. *Los Angeles Times*, 2.

Bloom, N. D. (2004). *Merchant of illusion: America's salesman of the businessman's Utopia*. Columbus: Ohio State University Press.

Blum, S. (27 Dec 1964). What goes up must come down. *The New York Times*.

Blumenthal, R. (20 Jan 1966). 2 City Parks get first curators. *The New York Times*.

Boge, G., & Boge, M. H. (1993). *Paving over the past: A history and guide to civil war battlefield preservation*. Washington: Island Press.

Books in Print. (17 Nov 1951). *Nation, 173*(20), 430.

Brown, N. (15 June 1958a). When the very important visit Williamsburg. *The New York Times*.

Brown, N. (28 Sep 1958b). The fight to save the nation's landmarks. *The New York Times*.

Bruce, A. (1994). How BAHA began. *BAHA Newsletter, Fall, 7*, 10.

Bullock, H. D. (1957). 41,000 miles to…? *Historic Preservation, 9*(2), 30.

Burlingham, C. C. (14 April 1958). To preserve park. Plans for roads to run through Washington square opposed. In Letter to the Editor, *The New York Times*.

Cahan, R. (1994). *They all fall down. Richard Nickel's struggle to save America's architecture*. Washington, DC: Preservation Press.

Campbell, R. (19 Feb 1984a). Overbuilt Boston. *Boston Globe Magazine*, 58.

Campbell, R. (1984b). Parachute plans landing in Boston. *Boston Globe, 11*, 13.

Carmody, D. (28 April 1985). The city unveils a blueprint. *The New York Times*.

Caro, R. (1974). *The power broker: Robert Moses and the fall of New York*. New York: Alfred A. Knopf.

Carolina Art Association. (1944). *This is Charleston: A survey of the architectural heritage of a unique American City*. Charleston: Carolina Art Association.

Chicago Tribune. (15 Jan 1957a). Urge listing 2 west side areas for clearance. *Chicago Tribune*, 12.

Chicago Tribune. (2 March 1957b). Plan cemetery dormitory. *Chicago Tribune*, 7.

Chicago Tribune. (19 March 1957c). Wright terms doomed Robie house sound. *Chicago Tribune*, B10.

Chicago Tribune. (21 Dec 1957d). New York builder offers $ 125,000 for Robie House. *Chicago Tribune*.

Chicago Tribune. (7 May 1958). Pick 4 loop buildings as landmarks. *Chicago Tribune*, 10.

Chicago Tribune. (12 Feb 1961a). City posts $ 10,000, saves Garrick items. *Chicago Tribune*.

Chicago Tribune. (6 Dec 1961b). Proposes law to help save 38 landmarks. *Chicago Tribune*, 6.

Chicago Tribune. (17 Aug 1963). City to draft law. *Chicago Tribune*, p. S-A10.

Chicago Tribune. (16 Nov 1967). Daley seeks law. *Chicago Tribune*, 2.

Chittendon, B., & Gordon, J. (1983). *Older and historic buildings*. Washington, DC: National Trust for Historic Preservation.

Chronicle. (4 Feb 1963a). Farewell recital. *San Francisco Chronicle*, 39.

Chronicle. (9 Feb 1963b). Auction set at fox. *San Francisco Chronicle*, 9.

Chronicle. (10 Feb 1963c). Farewell fling. *Sunday Bonanza, San Francisco Chronicle*, 5.

Chronicle. (17 Feb 1963d). Farewell to the fox. *San Francisco Chronicle*, 1, 16.

Clark, B. (1959). The Wanton disregard of our national heritage. *The Diplomat* (January 1959) Reprinted in *Reader's Digest, 74*, 119–124.

Clawson, M. (1965). Living historical farms: A proposal for action. *Agricultural History, 39*(2), 110–111.

Colin, T. J. (1988). Mall mentality at Manassas. *Historic Preservation, 40*(4), 2.

Congressional Record. (19 Sep 1966). 112 *Congressional record*, part 116, 22027–22031.

Congressional Record. (12 Feb 1975). 121 *Congressional record*, part 3, 3004.

Conklin, W. J. (1989). New York, The historic city. New York: A report prepared for the New York City landmarks commission, n.p.

Conlan, T. J., et al. (1990). *Taxing choices. The politics of tax reform* (pp. 232, 250). Washington, DC: CQ Press.

Costonis, J. (1974). *Space Adrift: Landmark preservation and the marketplace*. Urbana: University of Illinois Press.

Crane, C. (Comp.). (1977). *Atlanta, Georgia, today*. Washington, DC: Urban Land Institute.

Craig, J. (18. February 1963). A rush to buy part of the fox. *San Francisco Chronicle*, 1, 9.

Cressey, P. J. (1979). The city as a site: The Alexandria model for urban archaeology. *Conference on Historic Site Archaeology Papers 1978-Raleigh, NC, 13*, 204–227.

CSM. (14 May 1993). The trust's new president, a Washington insider, has ambitious plans. *Christian Science Monitor*, 12.

Darling, L. (1 Jan 1977). Bicentennial hailed for its legacies. *Washington Post*, A1.

Decker, C. (27 March 1978). A city landmark falls. *Los Angeles Times*, B3.

Demarest, M. (24 Aug 1981). He digs downtown. *Time, 118*, 42–44.

Degross, R. (2 June 2003). Underground atlanta faces new hurdle. *Atlanta Journal-Constitution*, E1.

Dembart, L. (28 Feb 1979). New central park overseer, Elizabeth browning Barlow. *The New York Times*.

Dennis, S. N. (1 Feb 1993). Did Richmond, Virginia nearly lead the nation into landmarking? *Preservation Law Update*, 1–2.

Doheny, D. A. (2006). *David Finley: Quiet force for American arts* (pp. 245–285). Washington, DC: National Trust for Historic Preservation.

Dominus, S. (31 Dec 2006). Evelyn Ortner, B. 1924. Mothering Brooklyn. *The New York Times*.

OHJ. (1973/1974). Index to the old-house journal. *The Old-House Journal*, October 1973 to December 1974, 1–4.

Duke. (1971). *Law and Contemporary Problems, 36*(3), 309 –441. Summer. Duke University Law School.

Ennis, T. W. (20 April 1965). Landmark Bill Signed by Mayor. *The New York Times*.

Feiss, C. (2011). *Remaking American places: The vision of Carl Feiss, architect, planner, preservationist* (pp. 332–361). North Charleston: CreateSpace.

Fellows, W. (2004). *A passion to preserve: Gay men as keepers of culture*. Madison: University of Wisconsin Press.

Fenton, J. (20 Oct 1957). Roads and historic sites. *The New York Times*.

Fenton, J. H. (19 Feb 1961). Renewal project to revive history; Project at Portsmouth, N.H., to stress restoration of colonial structures. *The New York Times*, 78

Finley, D. E. (1965). *History of the national trust for historic preservation* (pp. 1–6). Washington, DC: National Trust for Historic Preservation.

Fishman, R (1980). The anti planners: The contemporary revolt against planning and its significance for planning history. In G. Cherry (Ed.), *Shaping an urban world: Aspects of twentieth century planning*. New York, St. Martin's Press.

Flint, A. (2009). *Wrestling with Moses*. New York: Random House.

Foard, A. A., & Fefferman, H. (1967). Federal urban renewal legislation. In J. Q. Wilson (Ed.), *Urban renewal: The record and the controversy* (pp. 71–125). Cambridge: MIT Press.

Fowle, F. (20 Feb 1962). 84 Penn station columns may be moved. *The New York Times*.

Franklin, H., & Field, C. R. (2005/2006). Birth of a museum. *Blueprints, 24*(1), 8–11.

Frederick, L. (16 Oct 1966). Depres acts. *Chicago Tribune*, S4.

Fried, J. P. (1 Feb 1969). Bedford-Stuyvesant has bright side, too. *The New York Times*, C31.

Frieden, B. J. (1964). *The future of old neighborhoods. Rebuilding for a changing population*. Cambridge: MIT Press.

Frieden, B. J., & Sagalyn, L. (1989). *Downtown. Inc.: How America rebuilds cities*. Cambridge: MIT Press.

Fullilove, M. (2004). *Root shock: How tearing up city neighborhoods hurts America, and what we can do about it*. New York: Random House.

Galphin, B. (12 April 1969). Atlanta underground to sparkle. *Washington Post*, C1.

Gamarekian, B. (4 Sep 1986). The Willard is restored as a jewel of Pennsylvania avenue. *The New York Times*, C10.

Gans, H. J. (1962). *The urban villagers: Group and class in the life of Italian-Americans*. New York: Free Press.

Gapp, P. (2 Dec 1984). Preservation or porkopolis? A new focus on protecting our built heritage. *Chicago Tribune*, p. S13-8.

Garrigues, G. (11 Oct 1962). City takes big step forward with law on historic sites. *Los Angeles Times*, E8.

Garvin, J. L. (1971). Strawbery banke. *Early American Life, 2*(3), 6–9, 35, 36.

Giebner, R. C. (1971). Historic American building survey San Diego 1971. *Journal of San Diego History, 17*(4), 21–24.

Gillette, H. Jr. (1995). *Between justice and beauty: Race, planning, and the failure of urban policy in Washington, DC*. Baltimore: The Johns Hopkins University Press.

Gilmartin, G. F. (1995). *Shaping the city. New York and the municipal arts society* (p. 344). New York: Clarkson Potter.

Glass Papers. (1981). Transcript. Russell Keune interview, 3 Aug. Cornell University Archives.

Glass, J. A. (1987). *The national historic preservation program, 1957–1969*. Doctoral dissertation, Graduate Field of History of Architecture and Urban Development, Cornell University.

Glazer, N., & Moynihan, D. P. (1963). *Beyond the melting pot; The Negroes, Puerto Ricans, Jews, Italians, and Irish of New York City*. Cambridge: MIT Press.

Glueck, G. (16 Aug 1980). Conservancy will seek private central park aid. *The New York Times*.

Goldberger, P. (17 March 1991). Two reasons for dancing in the streets. *The New York Times*, H36, H42.

GPO. (1965). *Beauty for America*. Washington, DC: U.S. Government Printing Office.

Gratz, R. B. (2010). *The battle for Gotham: New York in the shadow of Robert Moses and Jane Jacobs*. New York: Nation Books.

Gray, C. (10 Feb 2002). The old Astor library. *The New York Times*.

Green, C. (4 July 1977). Crime, rails deal blow to underground. *Washington Post*, A1.

Greenhouse, L. (5 March 1991). Court ends tower plan at St. Bart's. *The New York Times*, Bl-4.

Greer, N. R. (Nov 1986). Grande dame makes a comeback. *Architecture*, 49

Gregerson, J. (1988). The evolution and growth of the festival marketplace. *Building Design and Construction*, 29(2), 72–77.

Greve, F. (1983). David bonderman, esq., preservation's unsentimental hero. *Historic Preservation*, 35(1), 24–27.

Grutzner, C. (30 March 1958). Strategy revamped on Washington square. *The New York Times*, 1, 58.

Haeberle, S. (1996). Gay Men and Lesbians at City Hall. *Social Science Quarterly, Spring*, 190–197.

Haley, A. (1976). *Roots: The saga of an American family*. Garden City: Doubleday.

Hartman, C. (12 Oct 1983). Just how secretive Is SF's invisible government. *San Francisco Bay Guardian*.

Hata, N. I. H. (1992). *The historic preservation movement in California, 1940–1976*. Sacramento: California Department of Parks and Recreation.

Hawes, E. L. (1975). *The living historical farm in North America: New directions in research and interpretation*. Proceedings of the annual meeting, April 1975, national museum of history of technology. Washington, DC: Annual Association for Living Historical Farms and Agricultural Museums, pp. 41–42.

Hawley, F. (May 1937). *Tree ring analysis and dating in the Mississippi valley*. Chicago: University of Chicago Press.

Hawthorne, C. (8 Jan 2013). Ada Louise Huxtable Dies at 91: Renown architecture critic. *Los Angeles Times*.

Hayden, D. (1995). *The power of place: Urban landscapes as public history*. Cambridge: MIT Press.

Herbert, R. (16 Jan 1962). City acts to save historic monuments. *Los Angeles Times*, B2.

Herbert, R. (6 June 1978). Group to preserve landmarks formed. *Los Angeles Times*, C5.

Historic Savannah Foundation. (1964). *Historic Savannah*. Savannah: Historic Savannah Foundation, Inc.

Hitchcock, H.-R., & Johnson, P. (1932). *The international style*. New York: Museum of Modern Art.

Hodder, R. S. (1993). *Savannah's changing past: A generation of planning in a southern city, 1955–1985*. Doctoral dissertation, Graduate Field of City and Regional Planning, Cornell University.

Hoffman, M. (18 Jan 1989). Barns reborn! *Christian Science Monitor*, 12.

Hornblower, M. (16 Feb 1975). Bicentennial fever spreads across US. *Washington Post*, A1, A14.

Holusha, J. (5 Oct 1988). Detroit catholics wary on closing. *The New York Times*, A23.

Hosmer, C. B. Jr. (1981). *Preservation comes of age* (Vol. 1). Charlottesville: The University Press of Virginia.

HSF. (1968). *Historic Savannah*. Savannah: Historic Savannah Foundation and the Savannah Junior League.

Hume, I. N. (1969). *Historical archaeology*. New York: Knopf.

Hume, I. N. (1974). *All the best rubbish*. New York: Harper Row.

Hume, I. N., & Miller, H. M. (2011). Ivor Noel Hume: Historical archaeologist. *Public Historian*, 33(1), 9–32.

Huxtable, A. L. (6 Jan 1966). A landmark is saved. *The New York Times*, 29, 53.

ICH. (1986). *The history of the Willard inter-continental*. New York: Inter-Continental Hotels.

IRC. (1976). Section 250(B) of the internal revenue code of 1954.

Jacobs, J. (1958). The downtown is for people. *Fortune Magazine*, April.

Jacobs, J. (1961). *Death and life of great American cities*. New York: Random House.

Jacobs, J. (1969). *The economy of cities*. New York: Random House.

Jacobs, S. W., & Jones, B. G. (1960). City design through conservation. unpublished typescript. University of California, Berkeley, 3, 60–148.

Johnson, F. (Comp.), (1951). *Radiocarbon dating*. Salt Lake City: Society for American Archaeology.

Jones, E. (16 Feb 1958). Dig-it-yourself archaeologists. *The New York Times*.

Journal of Urban History. (1998). A conversation with Charles M. Haar: Urban history and the great society. *Journal of Urban History*, 25(1), 57–75.

Kalman, H. (1976). An evaluation system for architectural surveys. *APT Bulletin*, 8(3), 3–27.

Keister, K. (1990). Main street makes good. *Historic Preservation*, 42(5), 44–50, 83.

King, T. F., King, P. P., & Berg, G. (1977). *Anthropology in historic preservation: Caring for culture's clutter*. New York: Academic.

Knight, C. III (Feb 1979). Post-Modernism strikes it rich on Pennsylvania avenue. *Progressive Architecture*, 22.

Knowles, S. G. (Ed.). (2009). *Imagining Philadelphia. Ed Bacon and the future of the city*. Philadelphia: University of Pennsylvania Press.

Kreig, J. P. (Ed.). (1989). *Robert Moses: Single minded genius*. Interlaken: Heart of the Lakes Publishing.

Kunstler, J. H. (2001). *Jane Jacobs Interviewed by Jim Kunstler For Metropolis Magazine, March 2001*. 6 Sep 2000, Toronto, Canada. http://www.kunstler.com/mags_jacobs1.htm . Accessed 24 Feb 2014.

Landers, R. K. (1985). The conscience of James Rouse. *Historic Preservation*, 37(6), 60–63.

LA Times. (16 May 1958). Drive on to save buildings. *Los Angeles Times*, B3.

LA Times. (16 April 1959). Bunker Hill survey made by architects. *Los Angeles Times*, B7.

LA Times. (8 Dec 1961). LA landmark board proposed by Yorty. *Los Angeles Times*, 6.

LA Times. (3 March 1963a). Civic groups seeks to preserve landmarks. *Los Angeles Times*, A13.

LA Times. (8 March 1963b). Watts towers called historic. *Los Angeles Times*, 6.

LA Times. (20 Sep 1963c). Cultural unit celebrates its first year. *Los Angeles Times, 33*.

LA Times. (19 May 1974). Talk slated on heritage square. *Los Angeles Times*, A10.

Laurence, P. J. (2007). Jane Jacobs before death and life. *Journal of the Society of Architectural Historians, 66*(1), 5–15.

Lee, J. M. (18 July 1962). Central considers using station after merger. *The New York Times*, 1, 33.

Lescaze, L., & Saperstein, S. (15 Dec 1978). Bethesda author settles 'Roots' suit for $ 500,000. *Washington Post*, A1.

Levine, A. (14 July 1957). Philadelphia story: A new look. *The New York Times*.

LeViness, W. T. (21 Oct 1956). Santa Fe's historic sites facing destruction. *The New York Times*.

Libby, W. F. (1955). *Radiocarbon dating*. Chicago: University of Chicago Press.

Linebaugh, D. W. (2005). *The man who found Thoreau. Roland W. Robbins and the rise of historical archaeology in America*. Durham: The University of New Hampshire.

Link, K. (2005). Preservation and the era of civic revival. In M. A. Tanner (Ed.), *Pioneer square: Seattle's oldest neighborhood*. Seattle: University of Washington Press.

Lipe, W. D. (1974). A conservation model for American archaeology. *Kiva, 39*, 213–245.

Lockwood, C. (4 Dec 2003). House proud: The 6-month makeover, 36 years later. *The New York Times*.

Logue, E. J. (9 Nov 1958). Urban ruin-Or urban renewal? The time for decision is now, if we are to save our blighted cities from themselves. *The New York Times Magazine, 17*(28), 30–33.

Lohmann, B. (30 March 1985). Atlanta may revive old district. *Washington Post*, F12.

Lynch, K. (1960). *The image of the city*. Cambridge: The MIT Press.

Maddex, D. (March 1971a). 'Save D.C. post office' heard again. *Preservation News, 11*(3), 3.

Maddex, D. (June 1971b). Rally held round the old D.C. post office. *Preservation News, 11*(6), 3.

Martin, D. (24 Jan 2006). Joan Maynard Dies at 77; Preserved a black settlement. *The New York Times*.

Martin, D. (11 Sep 2007). Arthur Ross, investor and philanthropist who left mark on the park, dies at 96. *The New York Times*.

Martin, D. (30 Sep 2008). Margot Gayle, urban preservationist and crusader with style, dies at 100. *The New York Times*.

Mayors. (1966). United states conference of Mayors, Special Committee on historic preservation. *With Heritage So Rich. A Report*. New York: Random House.

McGimsey, C. R. III, & Davis, H. A. (Eds.). (1977). *The management of archeological resources: The Airlie house report*. Lawrence: Society for American Archaeology.

McNulty, R. H., & Kliment, S. A. (1976). *Neighborhood conservation. A handbook of methods and techniques*.

New York: Whitney Library of Design, Watson-Guptill Publications.

Merl, J. (12 Jan 1980). Artist outbids developers for historic house. *Los Angeles Times*, B5.

Meyerson, A. (1989). Preservation or profit. *Georgia Trend, 5*(1), 46.

Miller, R. A. (2000). *Landmark preservation council. The Early Years, 1971–1976*. Chicago: Illinois Landmarks Preservation Council.

Morgan, S. (16 Feb 1965). New Hampshire to unveil restoration project. *The New York Times*, Travel Section, 26.

Morning News. (28 June 1955). Preservation of historic sites to be discussed. *Savannah Morning News*, 24.

Morten, T. B. (1971). Editorial: Conference on preservation law, 1971. *Preservation News, 11*(5), 1, 4, 7.

Moss, J., & Fintselberg, N. (1971). San Diego saving adobes alongside queen anne. *Preservation News, 11*(8), 6.

Mulloy, E. D. (1976). *The history of the national trust for historic preservation, 1963–1973* (p. 21). Washington, DC: The Preservation Press.

Murray, C. S. (30 Dec 1973). The remembered houses of Carroll avenue. *Los Angeles Times*, F22.

NCPE. (2001). Remembering lock Blair. *National Council for Preservation Education News, Fall*, 2.

Nelson, K. P. (1988). *Gentrification and distressed cities*. Madison: University of Wisconsin Press.

NTHP. (1966). *Historic preservation today. Essays presented to the seminar on preservation and restoration, Williamsburg, Virginia*. Washington, DC: National Trust for Historic Preservation and Colonial Williamsburg, Inc.

NTHP. (1967). *Historic preservation tomorrow*. Washington, DC: National Trust for Historic Preservation and Colonial Williamsburg.

NYT. (1 Feb 1955). Beacon Hill Backs law to preserve its Façade. *The New York Times*, 10.

NYT. (4 Nov 1956). Historic places rescued by law. *New York Times*.

NYT. (30 Oct 1960). Philadelphia Hall ready for tourists. *The New York Times*.

NYT. (7 Nov 1964). Carnegie hall designated as a 'national landmark'. *The New York Times*.

NYT. (22 Jan 1990). Churches to close in Chicago. *The New York Times*, A10.

OHJ. (1973/1974). Indexes. *The Old-House Journal*, October 1973–December 1974, 1–4.

O'Kane, L. (7 Oct 1964). City gets landmark bill. *The New York Times*, 49.

Oldham, S. (1990). The business of preservation is bullish and diverse. *Preservation Forum, 3*(4), 14–19.

Olmsted, R., & Watkins, T. H. (1968). *Here today: San Francisco's architectural heritage*. San Francisco: Chronicle Books.

Olsen, J. (2004). *Better places, better lives. A Biography of James Rouse*. Washington, DC: Urban Land Institute.

Opsata, M. (1987). How pros play the Rehab game. *Historic Preservation, 39*(3), 34–37.

Pace, E. (31 Oct 1971). East meadow area is center of central park's increase in violent crime. *The New York Times*, 73.

Pawlyna, A. (1981). James Rouse, A pioneer of the suburban shopping center, now sets his sights on saving cities. *People, 16*, 63–64.

Pilot. (Nov 1995). Colonial cooking historian, Dies. *Virginian Pilot*, 11.

Prater, P. (Feb 1958). Extinction by throughway. *Harper's magazine, 216*, December. Reprinted in *Reader's Digest, 74*, 182–186.

Preservation News. (Sept 1962). A nation-wide campaign. *Preservation News, 2*(9), 2.

Preservation News. (Jan 1964a). What's worth saving in San Francisco? *Preservation News, 4*(1), 1.

Preservation News. (Feb 1964b). The indiscriminate leveling of buildings. *Preservation News, 4*(2), 1.

Preservation News. (Jan 1969a). National trust opens field services division. *Preservation News, 9*(1), 1, 7.

Preservation News. (March 1969b). Bunker Hill, in Los Angeles. *Preservation News, 9*(3), 2.

Preservation News. (Nov 1969c). Senate safeguards U.S. capitol. *Preservation News, 9*(11), 1.

Preservation News. (Oct 1970). Reprieve awarded old post office in St. Louis, Missouri. *Preservation News, 10*(10), 1, 4.

Preservation News. (June 1971). Trust sponsors 1st conference on preservation law problems. *Preservation News, 11*(5), 2.

Preservation News. (April 1974a). Homesteading seminar. *Preservation News, 14*(4), 2.

Preservation News. (June 1974b). Honor awards 1974. *Preservation News, 14*(5), 12.

Preservation News. (July 1976). Trust opens two new regional offices. *Preservation News, 19*(7), 3.

Preservation News. (March 1980). Old houses make hit TV series. *Preservation News, 20*(3), 7.

Preservation News. (Nov 1986). Young vs. Old. *Preservation News, 26*(11), 1, 15.

Preservation News. (July 1987). Trust boosts "Barn Again!" *Preservation News, 27*(7), 6, 13.

Preservation News. (May 1990). Indiana farm wins in trust's BARN AGAIN! program. *Preservation News, 30*(5), 16, 19.

Providence. (1959). *College hill. A demonstration study of historic area renewal*. City of Providence, Rhode Island.

Purdum, T. S. (13 April 1991). Church as landmark: Battle rejoined. *The New York Times*, 27.

Rankin, B., & Snyder, A. (1989). The third battle of Manassas. *Preservation Forum, 3*(1), 2–7.

Raynsford, A. (2011). Civic art in an age of cultural relativism: The aesthetic origins of Kevin Lynch's *Image of the City. Journal of Urban Design, 16*(1), 43–65.

Ritter, D. (2008). *Schenectady's stockade: New York's first historic district*. Charleston: Arcadia.

Robertson, R. W. K. C. (13 July 1955). Plea for the Robie house. *Chicago Tribune*, 20.

Rosenzweig, R., & Blackmar, E. (1992). *The park and the people: A history of central park*. New York: Henry Holt and Company.

Sabloff, P. L.W. (1998). *Conversations with Lew Binford: Drafting the new archaeology*. Norman: University of Oklahoma Press.

Saffron, I. (23 Oct 2005). Flaws and all, Bacon molded a modern Phila. *Philadelphia Inquirer*.

Salisbury, S., & Boasberg, L. W. (14 Oct 2005). City visionary Edmund Bacon, 95, Dies. *Philadelphia Inquirer*.

Satterthwaite, A. (1979). UDAG: Is it the new urban renewal? *Preservation News, 19*(12), 1–2.

Schneider, K. (3 July 2005). Gaylord Nelson, former senator who founded earth day, Dies at 89. *The New York Times*.

Schulman, E. (1956). *Dendroclimatic changes in Semiarid America*. Tucson: University of Arizona Press.

Schuyler, D. (2002). *A city transformed: Redevelopment, race, and suburbanization in lancaster, Pennsylvania*. University Park: Pennsylvania State University Press.

Schwartz, J. (1993). *The New York approach: Robert Moses, urban liberals and redevelopment of the inner city*. Columbus: Ohio State University Press.

Schwartz, J. (May–June 2010). The view from the top. *Preservation Magazine*, 32–33, A23.

SHA. (2001). Notice of death. *Society for Historical Archaeology Newsletter, Spring*, 9.

Shashaty, A. (1983). The deal makers. *Historic Preservation, 35*(3), 14–23.

Stafford, L., & Bond, P. (7 April 2007). Underground Atlanta: Lost its fizz? *Atlanta Journal-Constitution*, A1.

Stokes, M. (1968). *An introduction to tree ring dating*. Chicago: University of Chicago Press.

Stokes, S. N., et al. (1989). *Saving America's countryside*. Baltimore: The Johns Hopkins University Press.

Styron, W. (4 Aug 1994). Slavery's pain, Disney's gain. *The New York Times*.

Talmquist. (21 Sep 2011). The national trust for historic preservation. Toward a new level of success. PDF issued by the National Trust for Historic Preservation.

Terence, M. (5 Sep 1965). The battle to save the past. *Los Angeles Times*, WS1.

Terrell, A. (8 Dec 1976). Tracing his past. *Washington Post*.

Thatcher, J. (1995). Historic rehabilitation tax credits: An effective policy in perspective, Master of Public Administration thesis, Cornell University.

Thomas, R. McG. Jr. (20 Oct 1956). Old recipes save U.S. landmarks. *The New York Times*, B3.

Tinkcom, M. B. (1971). The Philadelphia Historical Commission: Organizations and procedures. *Law and Contemporary Problems, 36*(3), 386–397.

Tomlan, M. A. (1988). Architectural Press, U.S. In J. A. Wilkes (Ed.), *Encyclopedia of architecture, design, engineering and construction* (pp. 281–282) New York: Wiley.

Treasury. (1984). *Tax reform for fairness, simplicity and growth: The treasury department report to the president*. Washington, DC: Office of the Secretary, Department of the Treasury.

Tung, A. M. (1989). The Historic city report: Ignoring the lessons of history. *Village Views, 5*(4), 3–6.

UCR. (15 April 1982). Rehab tax credits attract big money, shut out the little guys. *Urban Conservation Report, 6*(7), 1.

UCR. (10 Sep 1985). San Francisco curbs development, Outlaws Glass Box. *Urban Conservation Report, 9*(8), 2.

UCR. (31 Oct 1986). Passive investor rules. *Urban Conservation Report, 10*(10), 4.

Upward, G. C. (1975). Fox productions presents a night at the opera. *Preservation News, 14*(11), 12.

Urban Reinvestment Task Force. (1976). *Neighborhood partnerships-The urban reinvestment task force in 1976.* Washington: U.S. Department of Housing and Urban Development.

Van Trump, J. D. (Sep/Oct 1971). Autumn wine and preservation: The Heinz hall and the old post office at Pittsburgh. *Charette,* 7–10.

Van Trump, J. D., et al. (Sep/Oct 1971). A new publisher for Charette; Farewell and Hello. *Charette,* 5.

Village Views. (1987). Is landmark designation finished? *Village Views, 4*(1), 39–44.

Vivian, G., & Kletso, K. (1964). *A Pueblo III community in Chaco Canyon, New Mexico.* Globe: Southwestern Monuments Association.

Walter, J. J. (1987). Introduction: Preservation is everybody's business. *Historic Preservation, 39*(3), 33.

Walters, J. (1981). Main street turns the corner. *Historic Preservation, 24*(11), 37–45.

Washington Post. (15 Feb 1976). Taxation and preservation. *Washington Post.*

Watkins, C. M. (1965). The central role of the commonplace in the history museum. *Western Museums Quarterly,* III.

West, R. (31 March 1967). Central library to be razed, commission says. *Los Angeles Times,* E7.

Whyte, W. H. (1956). *The organization man.* New York: Simon & Schuster.

Wilson, C. (1997). *The myth of Santa Fe: Creating a modern regional tradition.* Albuquerque: University of New Mexico Press.

Wirt, F. (1974). *Power in the city: Decision making in San Francisco* (p. 190). Berkeley: University of California Press.

Wood, A. C. (2007). *Preserving New York: Winning the Right to protect a city's landmarks.* New York: Routledge.

Woodbridge, J., Woodbridge, S., Okomoto, R., & Theil, P. (1960). *Guide to Bay area architecture.* New York: Grove.

Woodward, W. M. (1982). *1956–1981, 25th anniversary, providence preservation society.* Providence.

Woodward, W. M., & Sanderson, E. F. (1986). *Providence: A citywide survey of historic resources.* Providence: Rhode Island Historical Preservation Commission.

Wright, R. J. Jr. (1964). *College hill five years later.* Master of Regional Planning thesis, Graduate Field of City and Regional Planning, Cornell University.

Yarrow, A. L. (5 Feb 1987). The *old-house journal* comes of age. *The New York Times.*

Yudis, A. J. (10 May 1984). Curbs urged on hub growth. *Boston Globe,* 1.

Zarafonetis, M. J. (2010). *The 'Fabulous' fox theatre and Atlanta, 1929–1975.* Doctoral dissertation, Department of History, Auburn University, 218.

Zenzen, J. M. (1997). *Battling for Manassas.* State College: Pennsylvania State University Press.

Ziegler, A. Jr. (1967). An introduction. Both personal and programmatic. In J. D. Van Trump & A. Ziegler Jr. (Eds.), *Landmark architecture of Allegheny County Pennsylvania.* Pittsburgh: Pittsburgh History and Landmarks Foundation.

Ziegler, A, Jr., Adler II, L., & Kidney, W. C. (1975). *Revolving funds for historic preservation: A manual of practice.* Pittsburgh: Ober Park Associates.

The Legal Framework

3

Introduction

As a social campaign, the historic preservation movement reminds the public and our government representatives and administrators of the need to think ahead, to view themselves as stewards of our common legacy. To implement this goal, a broad array of federal, state, and local legislation sets forth the goals and parameters for advancing the recognition of important districts, sites, and objects; providing funding; reviewing changes; and granting licenses and permissions. The executive branch of government also plays an important role in the day-to-day management of properties in a wide variety of ways. In addition, the role of the courts that interpret actions of governments becomes an important indicator of what the appropriate course of preservation action should be.

After a brief review of some of the fundamental thinking that went into the Constitution of the United States, the first section of this chapter considers preservation's legislative framework. This begins with an overview of the most important federal legislation, the National Historic Preservation Act (NHPA) of 1966. This act created a National Register of Historic Places, administered by the National Park Service (NPS) in the Department of the Interior, and a review process (Section 106) to evaluate federal undertakings that threaten National Register resources. Federal funds from the NHPA channeled to the State Historic Preservation Offices (SHPOs) helped hire staff to identify appropriate properties to be placed on the National Register and the state registers. Many states further enacted "mini-106" procedures to evaluate state and local government actions threatening properties on the state or local registers. Of equal significance is the establishment of many more local preservation commissions than had existed previously, local bodies that would sponsor surveys to identify historic resources, act to designate those resources, and follow-up with residents to ensure properties were being well-treated. Other federal preservation legislation complemented the NHPA, such as the 1966 Transportation Act, which guards against federal transportation projects affecting historic resources inappropriately, and the 1969 National Environmental Policy Act (NEPA) and its amendments, which requires impact assessments of major federal actions affecting the environment, including historic resources.

The second section contains a review of the Executive Orders (EO) issued by various presidents. Hundreds of specific administrative decisions have hinged on the decisions of executives who have responsibilities for landscapes, properties with cultural significance above and below ground.

The third section of this chapter examines the most prominent federal level judicial decisions. The analysis of key court decisions is linked to the activities of local historic district commissions in addressing some of the principal legal challenges. Most prominent is the advocacy that arises among those concerned with the private property rights of religious organizations.

M. A. Tomlan, *Historic Preservation*, DOI 10.1007/978-3-319-04975-5_3,
© Springer International Publishing Switzerland 2015

In much the same way that the country's social goals have evolved and the preservation movement shifted in emphasis, so has the courts' reception and interpretation changed over time.

Some Basic Concepts in the US Constitution

For those familiar with the history of Europe, it is easy to understand how the New World would be appealing, in that it offered thousands of people a chance for a better life. The motivations for emigrating were varied but reacting to the social, religious, and political upheaval in England and France, the seventeenth century philosopher John Locke captured, developed, and presented what became the most important ideas in American government. His central idea was that all persons possess natural rights. They are free and equal; that is, they are free to do as they wished without being required to ask the permission of any other person, while at the same time there should be no natural political power of one man over the other. Further, Locke held that the legitimate role of governments is the protection of these rights, as government derives its limited authority from the consent of the governed. In this political framework, the government has no role in religious affairs, unlike England where the church and state were joined (Mack 2009).[1]

By the time that the framers of the Constitution began to gather, these ideas were generally known (Becker 1922; Zuckert 2002). By that point, certain rights are fundamental, among them the right to life, liberty, and the pursuit of happiness. The last is linked to being secure in one's free use of property, as Samuel Adams wrote in 1772, bearing in mind that during the period property included slaves (Eicholz 2001). In 1774, George Mason composed the Virginia Constitution, reiterating the same concepts, so

that when Thomas Jefferson crafted the US Constitution, he could not have helped but reiterate the core ideas of Locke's thinking. In the largely Protestant world in which Americans conceived their activities, where the individual's success was defined largely in his own efforts to succeed, this moral philosophy provided much of the needed framework for legal and governmental affairs.

In addition to being familiar with the Constitution, preservationists need to understand the key provisions in the Bill of Rights that arise in legal disputes over the use of historic properties. The Fifth and the Fourteenth Amendments are important because they contain phrases around which arguments and judicial opinions are framed. The Fifth Amendment begins by addressing the concerns about criminal and civil courts, ending in the clause that no person should "… be deprived of life, liberty, or property, without due process of law; nor shall private property be taken for public use, without just compensation." The discussion of the "takings clause," which includes "due process," "eminent domain," and "just compensation" appears in many preservation laws and disputes, as will become apparent in this and other chapters. The interpretations of this clause have affected the actions of millions of people and at least as many properties (Duerkson and Roddewig 1994).[2]

Because the rights of all citizens include the right to own land and all of the improvements upon it, as civil rights have been extended to all residents in United States, including African Americans and women, the disposition of property is one of the most important features of our system of laws and administrative procedures. Property rights are a legal form of wealth, and the concerns regarding them influence the relationships between people throughout the nation. Yet, "nuisance law," wherein no one has the right to use their property in a manner that is detrimental to others, so "that the good of the many may require imposition on the few" inevitably

---

[1] Locke was not the only person in that period to hold some of these views, as others, such as Thomas Hobbes and Robert Filmer, also contributed to the public discussion. Locke's *Two Treatises of Government* (1689) and *Essay Concerning Human Understanding* (1689) are the principal responses to both.

[2] Although slightly dated, the jargon-free nature of Duerkson and Roddewig's text is an excellent starting point for those unfamiliar with legal discussions.

Fig. 3.1 Gettysburg Battlefield reunions, such as the one in 1865 pictured here, remained commonplace for decades, largely involving veterans. However, by the end of the nineteenth century it took the threat of a railroad to spur Congress to take action and begin to acquire the land. (Library of Congress)

supports the idea that overarching concerns for the public good rise in consideration. Just where the lines are drawn becomes somewhat murky when taking into account the stricture of the Tenth Amendment, which reinforces the idea that the Constitution's principle of federalism is limited by the powers provided by the states. And it is the states alone that have the power to enable city and county zoning codes, landmark commissions, and building regulations. So, while the federal government can encourage the states to adopt regulations by offering financial support that are tied to conditions, or through its commerce power, Congress cannot compel states to enforce federal laws and regulations.

More fundamentally, the generally agreed-upon, prevailing Judeo-Christian theism that provides the moral framework for the Constitution and the majority of our legislative and judicial proceedings produces inevitable conflicts with minorities, such as Native Americans, who do not hold the same views of the natural rights of man. Remembering that our founding fathers also stipulated the "free exercise" of religion, the spiritual views of all must be respected. Hence, whether or not Native Americans can gather eagle feathers (Hugs 1997), or smoke the mild hallucinatory drug peyote (Oregon 1990), or hold

a mountain sacred is critical to their identity and way of life (Wilson 1983), often running counter to the prevailing land-use management policies and programs (Burton 2002; Ross et al. 2011). Conflicts inherent in the social basis for the law will continue to arise, particularly as other "foreign" cognitive social frameworks become evident with more immigrants from Asia and the Middle East finding their way in our ever-changing nation.

The Importance of Federal Actions

Chapter 1 described the manner in which Congress, made conscious of the special nature of certain places, withdrew from development lands in the Western States to create reservations that became national monuments and national parks. Congress was also stirred by the threatened defacement of the Civil War battlefield at Gettysburg to purchase it and similar sites in the late 1800s (Gettysburg 1896; Fig. 3.1). In part because battlefield and cemetery maintenance fell to the War Department, these properties were seen as hallowed locations, sites of heroic importance that emphasized the victors and the vanquished. As historical sensitivity increased, concerns broadened.

The 1906 Antiquities Act authorized the President to designate as national monuments those areas of the public domain containing historic landmarks, historic and prehistoric structures, and objects of historic or scientific interest. Such national treasures as the Grand Canyon and Grand Tetons became national monuments (USC 1906).[3]

Then, when President Franklin D. Roosevelt signed the Historic Sites Act in 1935, federal participation in historic preservation broadened again. The Act empowered the NPS to inventory the nation's most significant historic resources held in private and public hands. By authorizing a survey of historic and archaeological sites, buildings, and objects for the purposes of determining resources possessing exceptional value, it became possible to designate them as National Historic Landmarks (NHLs). The ensuing National Survey of Historic Sites and Buildings adopted several themes in American history, conceived in terms of the "stages of American progress," focusing on military and political figures to guide further study and recognition. The NHL program was formalized by the NPS in 1960, and revisions to this framework in 1970, 1987, and more recently have re-conceptualized ideas of national significance, all in attempts to provide a more inclusive nominations process (Chambers 2000; Macintosh 1985).[4] About 2500 historic places bear this national distinction, including the White House and Monticello. More recently constructed NHLs include the planned communities of Radburn, New Jersey and Baldwin Hills Village, in Los Angeles. Listing provides protection from adverse federal actions, and the NHL staff in the NPS is required to be in continuous contact with the owners facilitating condition assessments and offer limited financial assistance (Fig. 3.2).

While many of these premier NHL treasures are in safe governmental or vigilant nonprofit care, others are not. The Edwin H. Armstrong House designation recognized the electronics engineer who invented the frequency modulation (FM) radio. The structure was virtually intact in 1976, but an owner who anticipated developing the site in Yonkers allowed it to deteriorate, suffer a fire, and it was demolished in 1983. Philadelphia's Eastern State Penitentiary became the model of American prison construction for most of the nineteenth century but it remains closed as a penal institution and only survives because of an active friends group. The uneven fate of the NHLs across the Nation points to the ongoing struggle to preserve resources.

Federal designation is important because of the broad goals that were set, and then expanded to meet the needs of an increasing number of local advocates. The federal legislation in the 1960s went even further by setting out a more aggressive surveying apparatus, outlining a federal-state-local partnership to implement review and compliance, and grants procedures. A framework has remained in place for decades, broadly enough interpreted to serve people throughout the country at every level.

---

[3] Even with this special legislation, the actions of a President to designate a site can become controversial. The 1.7 million acre Grand Staircase-Escalante region in Utah—the size of Yellowstone National Park—was designated and protected as a national monument, but critics of the action bemoaned the potential loss of 900 jobs in the area connected with a Dutch mining company that proposed extracting 7 billion tons of coal (*NYT* October 13, 1997).

[4] The Program was fully implemented in 1983 with NPS regulations under the authority of the Historic Sites Act of 1935 (16 U.S.C. § 461–467 (2006)) and the 1980 Amendments. For more about the National Historic Landmarks Program, see 36 C.F.R. § 65.1 (2001). The review of NHL nominations takes place in Washington, with a specially constituted board.

The National Historic Preservation Act and Its Amendments

The 1966 NHPA declared that "… the historical and cultural foundations of the nation should be preserved," and established four ways to achieve this goal. It created: (1) the National Register of Historic Places to inventory the Nation's cultural resources; (2) a national Historic Preservation Fund (HPF) to provide financial aid; (3) a new executive-level body, the Advisory Council on Historic Preservation (ACHP), to advise the President and federal agencies on preservation;

Fig. 3.2 National Historic Landmarks can be relatively recently built. Radburn, New Jersey, conceived in 1928 by architect Henry Wright and planner Clarence Stein, did not have a green belt around it as they migh have hoped, but nevertheless provided a mid-twentieth century template for subsequent suburban layouts. (Library of Congress)

and (4) a review process, "Section 106," to evaluate federal actions affecting National Register properties. Each plays a major role at the federal, state, and local level.[5]

Section 101(a) of the NHPA authorizes the creation of a National Register of Historic Places, defined by statute as "composed of districts, sites, buildings, and objects significant in American history, architecture, archaeology, engineering, and culture." Thus, many categories of resources are eligible. A *building* is a structure created to shelter any form of human activity, such as a house, barn, church, factory, or a hotel. A *district* is a geographically definable area possessing a significant concentration, linkage, or continuity of sites, buildings, structures, or objects united by past events or aesthetically by plan or physical development. Charleston and New Orleans were among the first cities to designate historic districts and dozens have followed. An *object* is a material thing of functional, aesthetic, cultural, historical, or scientific value that may be, by nature or design, movable yet related to a specific setting or environment. Steamboats, railroad engines, and aircraft are just a few types of objects. A *site* is the location of a significant event, a prehistoric or historic occupation or activity, or a building or structure, whether standing, ruined, or vanished,

---

[5] This Act became law on October 15, 1966 (Public Law 89–665; 16 U.S.C. 470 et seq.). The subsequent amendments to the Act include: Public Law 91–243, Public Law 93–54, Public Law 94–422, Public Law 94–458, Public Law 96–199, Public Law 96–244, Public Law 96–515, Public Law 98–483, Public Law 99–514, Public Law 100–127, Public Law 102–575, Public Law 103–437, Public Law 104–333, Public Law 106–113, Public Law 106–176, Public Law 106–208, Public Law 106–355, and Public Law 109–453.

Fig. 3.3 The Schoharie Creek Aqueduct, Fort Hunter, NY, a portion of the historic Erie Canal, is a National Historic Landmark. Constructed from 1838 to 1841, the Army Corps of Engineers demolished six arches in the 1940s to alleviate ice jams; a seventh arch collapsed during a 1977 flood, and an eighth fell in 1988. (Photograph: Thomas Hahn)

where the location itself maintains historical or archaeological value regardless of the value of any existing structure. Often these are properties of archaeological interest, such as battlefields or burial mounds. In addition, a *structure* is a work constructed by humans made up of interdependent and interrelated parts in a definitive pattern or organization. Examples include covered bridges, railroad bridges, lighthouses, and aqueducts, such as that at Schoharie Creek in Fort Hunter, New York (Fig. 3.3).

To help decision makers determine what kind of historic resources can be placed on the National Register for its significance in American history, architecture, archaeology, engineering, and culture, the districts, sites, buildings, structures, and objects must have at least one of four characteristics. They must be: (A) associated with events that have made a significant contribution to the broad patterns of our history; or (B) are associated with the lives of persons significant in our past; or (C) embody the distinctive characteristics of a type, period, or method of construction, or that represent the work of a master, or that possess high artistic values, or that represent a significant and distinguishable entity whose components may lack individual distinction; or (D) have yielded, or may be likely to yield, information important in prehistory or history.

In general, category C is the most common, comprising about 70 % of the total number of properties nominated. Of the (A) event, (B) persons, (C) architecture-engineering and (D) archaeological criteria, the record shows that, after C, A dominates followed by B and D, respectively. Typically, however, a property will be listed based on more than one criterion.

In addition to meeting the criteria for inclusion, the properties are required to possess integrity of location, design, setting, materials, workmanship, feeling, and association. The majority of these characteristics must be present. Where natural features or landscape designs containing living plants, or human practices are part of the nominations, however, the changing character of the property often require special attention (NRB 1995; Howett 2001).

Generally, certain kinds of properties are not considered eligible for National Register listing. These include religious, moved, reconstructed, or commemorative properties; birthplaces, graves, and cemeteries; and properties less than 50 years

Fig. 3.4 The Six-teenth Street Baptist Church in Birmingham is one of two locations intimately associated with Dr. Martin Luther King, easily recognized for the historical associations with the Civil Rights movement. (Historic American Buildings Survey, Library of Congress)

Fig. 3.5 The Edgar J. Kaufmann, Sr., House, "Fallingwater," was listed on the National Register of Historic Places well before the half-century mark that is generally requested before designation, largely because of its well known, dramatic design and its architect, Frank Lloyd Wright. (Author's photograph)

old. Such properties, however, are listed if they satisfy the "criteria considerations," namely attributes that take them beyond the usually excluded characteristics. For instance, a religious property merits listing if it has primary significance from historic, architectural, or artistic importance—the "standard" National Register "A," "B," and "C" criteria noted above. The Sixteenth Street Baptist Church in Birmingham, Alabama, and the Abyssinian Baptist Church in New York City, both pulpits of Dr. Martin Luther King, Jr., are placed on the National Register for these reasons (Fig. 3.4). In a similar vein, reconstructed properties can move from the excluded group if they retain architectural or other significance. The dozens of structures at Colonial Williamsburg fall into that category.

Properties less than 50 years old are generally not eligible, unless they possess exceptional significance (Sprinkle 2007). Frank Lloyd Wright's masterpiece, "Fallingwater" in Bull Run, Pennsylvania was placed on the National Register before the half-century mark because of its importance to architecture and history (Fig. 3.5).

The importance of a National Register entry, as opposed to a listing in its predecessor, the National Survey of Historic Sites and Buildings, is that the 1966 legislation made it possible to list with the same level of protection not only for resources of national significance, but also for those having state and local merit. Over time, the changes in the characteristics of the National Register listings have come to mirror this shift. While most of the early entries were of national significance, in the last several decades a much greater emphasis has been place on local importance. Of the 1929 National Register listings between 1967 and 1970, 70% were nationally significant and only 22% and 8% were of state and local significance, respectively. Two decades later, of the 10,536 National Register listings between 1987 and 1990, only 5% were nationally significant while the state and local significant listings had climbed to 24% and 90%, respectively. Today, about 70% of all resources on the National Register are locally significant and it appears this is the likely trajectory for the foreseeable future.[6]

As of 2011, approximately 80,000 entries have been placed on the National Register, with an average of about 2000 new nominations, submissions and other reports per year. About 70% of the properties are in private ownership, reflecting to some degree the attractiveness of financial incentives tied to listing income-producing properties.

Significant amendments to the NHPA in 1980 and 1992 revised some of the NPS procedures. The rising number of controversies about the manner in which the provisions of the NHPA were used to slow or halt development projects led to changes. After December 1980, a property could be included on the National Register only if its owner, or a majority of the owners within a proposed historic district, consented to its nomination.[7] In addition, local government participa-

tion was encouraged by a provision that set up the possibility of a parallel system of review to that maintained by the states. If the local government maintained a qualified historic commission, with qualified staff, it became eligible to apply for pass-through funds from the State office.[8]

The 1992 Amendments to the NHPA included important provisions for Tribes and Native Hawaiians by emphasizing the creation of Tribal Historic Preservation Officers (THPO) and funding mechanisms (PL 1966, 1992). The Tribal Historic Preservation Officers are officially designated by a federally recognized Indian tribe to direct a program approved by the NPS, and assume some or all of the functions of State Historic Preservation Officers (SHPO) on Tribal lands.[9] Rather than beginning with an emphasis on physical resources from the perspective of Western civilization, THPOs emphasize the importance of oral traditions, consulting the tribal elders and spiritual leaders to respect the traditions of the tribe. THPOs also give emphasis to the importance of protecting "traditional cultural properties," places that are eligible to be included on the National Register of Historic Places because of their association with cultural practices and beliefs, based in the history of their community. Often these are essential to the maintenance of traditional practices. The THPO also reviews Federal actions that may affect the historic properties. Hence, archaeological survey work is an important part of the work in that office. In 1996, some American Indian tribal governments began to reach agreements to assume responsibility for the vast number of artifacts on thousands of square miles in tribal hands. At that time, the first

---

[6] The annual reports provided by the National Register staff to the National Park Service show remarkable consistency.

[7] The owner receives notification of the impending hearing, but in practice, the preservation office staff often spends considerable time in the attempt to obtain consent, particularly in the cases where multiple properties are under consideration, where a majority is required to approve.

[8] In 1980, Executive Order 11593 was institutionalized in law, so that each federal agency must take affirmative action toward the protection of its resources, and establish an agency historic preservation officer with adequate staff. In addition, NHL protections were strengthened against adversely designed federal projects; the Advisory Council was reduced in membership from 29 to 19, subsequently enlarged by later amendments.

[9] This program was made possible by the provisions of Section 101(d)(2) of the National Historic Preservation Act.

twelve THPOs received a total of $958,500 to help carry out their duties.

Several paths can lead to a listing on the National Register. The SHPO, the designated state official given lead preservation responsibilities, can nominate candidates, which are reviewed by a State Board of Review. Or, the Tribal Historic Preservation Officer (THPO) can nominate properties. As a third option, certified local governments (CLGs), which are local governments that meet SHPO-level preservation personnel and operating standards, may nominate properties in their purview.[10] Fourth, federal agencies can nominate buildings, sites, and other resources within their control, often via their agency preservation officer (APO). Fifth, items can be added by an act of Congress, in which case the NPS staff will likely facilitate the nomination. Sixth, the designation as a NHL by the Secretary of the Interior automatically places the object on the National Register, again the responsibility of the NPS staff in Washington, D.C. The first procedure described above is the most common method used.

Entry on the National Register has a number of implications because it is tied to other components of the NHPA: the National HPF and the activities of the Advisory Council on Historic Preservation (ACHP), particularly its regulatory oversight in the Section 106 process. In addition, as the following chapters will demonstrate, financial incentives exist, including federal and sometimes state income tax credits, to encourage the rehabilitation of the listed property.[11]

The HPF was created by the 1966 NHPA and is supported by annual revenues from Outer Continental Shelf oil leases. The policy remains that this assists the states, local governments, Indian tribes, and the Historically Black Colleges and Universities (HBCUs) with their historic preservation activities nationwide.

The money provided by the Department of the Interior is made available to the States on an annual competitive, matching basis, to support surveys for historic properties, preparation of historic preservation plans, acquisition, and preservation of properties listed on the Register, and staffing the SHPOs. Since its inception, this income has provided over $1 billion and, with the exception of two years in the late 1970s when the annual grant exceeded $50 million, the annual amount of the HPF has hovered in the $25 to 40 million range. Most of the funds are distributed to the SHPOs, each of which receives about $570,000. This is obviously not a large sum of money relative to national and state preservation needs; it simply provides the basis for a continued discussion between the preservation arms of the federal and state government.

The role of the Advisory Council for Historic Preservation (ACHP) is important as an independent federal agency that promotes preservation and provides advice to Congress and the executive branch regarding preservation policy. It has 21 designated members appointed by the President. These include four members of the public, four historic preservation experts, a member of an Indian tribe or Native Hawaiian organization, a governor, and a mayor. Two federal agency heads (the Secretaries of Interior and Agriculture) and the Architect of the Capitol are permanent members, and seven federal agency heads have designated terms.[12] In addition to these 21 members, two *ex officio* representatives are included in the discussions, one from the National Trust for Historic Preservation and second from the National Conference of SHPO.[13]

The principal activity of the ACHP staff is the administration of the "Section 106" review process.[14] This calls upon "The head of any Federal

---

[10] The definition of the certified local government is reviewed in more detail later in this chapter.

[11] These are discussed at length in Chapters 5, 6, and 7

[12] The seven agency heads are the Administrator of the General Services Administration, and the Secretaries of Defense, Transportation, Housing and Urban Development, Commerce, Education, and Veterans Affairs.

[13] The Chair of the Board of the National Trust regularly delegates the responsibility for attending ACHP meetings to the President of that organization or his representative, and the President of the Board of the National Conference likewise delegates his or her duties to the Executive Director of the organization.

[14] This is known as "Section 106," even though it is now technically Section 470f due to subsequent legislative

Agency having direct or indirect jurisdiction over a proposed Federal or federally assisted *undertaking* in any State and the head of any federal department or independent agency having authority to license any undertaking" to "*take into account* the *effect* of the undertaking upon any district, site, building, structure or object that is included in or eligible for inclusion in the National Register." Section 106 states that the head of that Federal Agency must provide the Advisory Council with "a reasonable opportunity to *comment* with regard to such undertaking" [*Emphasis added*] (USC 1966).

The key words from the Section 106 statutory language define its character—federal "undertaking," "effect," "take into account," and Advisory Council "comment." Section 106 review is triggered by a federal "undertaking," broadly defined to include "any federal, federally-assisted, or federally-licensed action, activity, or program or the approval, sanction, assistance, or support of any non-federal action, activity, or program." In practice, federal undertakings triggering Section 106 review range from ordinary highway and dam construction through the widening of utility corridors, to bank regulator approval of new branches or automated teller machines. Reviews take place when the General Services Administration builds and leases office space, or when a license is required from the Federal Communications Commission to construct a cell tower. Any of these actions could affect historic properties.

Following the determination that an activity constitutes a federal "undertaking," Section 106 requires that the responsible federal agency planning the undertaking identify existing or potential historic resources (i.e., on or eligible for the National Register) that may be impacted. Information gathering is very important. In practice, while the responsibility for complying with this review rests within all federal agencies, a wide range of consultants are often used to gather the information with the assistance of the SHPO staffs, local historic preservation commissions, and a variety of advocacy organizations (Advisory Council 2010).

The next step is to consider whether the undertaking will have an "adverse effect," i.e., whether the property is likely to suffer physical destruction, alteration, or relocation and suffer a substantial change of character. With a finding of "no adverse effect," the federal agency proceeds with the project, keeping a record of the finding. In the case of an "adverse" effect, a consultation process begins to resolve the adverse impact. In all instances, this process brings together the appropriate people, i.e., the "consulting parties." This is likely to include the representatives of the federal agency, the SHPO, and/or the tribal historic preservation officer, local government representatives, and other individuals and organizations with a demonstrated interest in the proposed project, particularly if they have a legal or an economic interest. Sometimes the ACHP staff may participate in the consultation, such as when Native American resources are involved. The result is typically a Memorandum of Agreement (MOA)—the product of compromise that outlines the agreed upon measures to avoid or limit adverse effects—signed by the agency, the Advisory Council, and the SHPO or THPO (King 2000, 2008).

As the number of resources potentially eligible for inclusion on the National Register increases, the pressure rises on all those who become involved to reach decisions quickly. Often this is difficult, simply due to the lack of information. For example, the Abandoned Shipwreck Act, passed in 1987 to stem the tide of highly publicized, privately backed treasure-hunters off the coast of Florida and in the Great Lakes, gives to the states title to abandoned shipwrecks that lie embedded in a State's submerged land. Consistent with the Act, the NPS has provided guidelines for including the properties on the National Register, but the limited number of specialists in the field and differing views of the consulting parties can make this difficult (PL 1988; USC 1987).[15]

---

revisions and amendments.

[15] The law does not protect military vessels that are owned by other countries, or the wrecks found on Native American land, or thousands of commercial and recreational vessels. In all cases, there is a rising need for protection (Earley 1982; Lobsenz 1983).

Fig. 3.6 "Poletown," named for the high concentration of Polish working class families in this Detroit neighborhood, was demolished for a new factory for General Motors. Over 1000 homes, 144 businesses, 16 churches, and dozens of other properties were leveled. (Historic American Buildings Survey, Library of Congress)

Each year, thousands of Federal actions undergo Section 106 review. The majority of cases are routine and do not undergo extensive discussion. When it becomes difficult to reach a MOA or a more general programmatic agreement, however, the issues are brought before the full Advisory Council membership, which may call for a public hearing, often on-site. This will often happen, for example, when the actual properties are yet unidentified. After an agreement is signed by all parties, the public may still play a role by making sure that the provisions are properly carried out, requesting status reports from the federal agency.

A heightened level of scrutiny is required when a federal undertaking bears on a NHL. Instead of the standard mandate that the federal agency simply "take into account," their actions must go further to the "maximum extent possible" and "undertake planning and actions to minimize harm." In these cases, the involvement of the ACHP is mandatory.

The Section 106 process has been revised several times to streamline the procedures and make the steps more meaningful. Examples of changes include simplifying the determination of "effects,"[16] encouraging more meaningful public participation and respectful dialogue with THPO, promoting early review and compliance with other federally mandated reviews, and directing ACHP staff involvement to more critical situations. Where a substantial impact to an NHL might occur, when the case presents important questions of policy or interpretation, or when there are issues of concern to tribal communities, extensive discussion follows before decisions are reached.

With all of this attention to process, those proposing a project often see the Advisory Council as standing in the way. Although a more complete public disclosure is often helpful, it cannot be the only thing standing in front of the bulldozer. In 1981, Poletown, a blue-collar area of Detroit, was leveled to make way for a new General Motors automobile plant. The city and the automaker reached an agreement that led to the demolition of over 1000 homes, 144 businesses, 16 churches, 2 schools, and a hospital. The Advisory Council weighed-in on this decision, which made use of millions of federal dollars, but it was powerless to change the overall direction of the project (Wylie 1989; Fig. 3.6).[17]

---

[16] This involved the change from a three-tier "no effect," "no adverse effect," and "adverse effect" to a two-tier "no adverse effect" or "adverse effect."

[17] The concept of taking private property for the public good, demonstrated in the case *Poletown Neighborhood Council v. City of Detroit* 304 N.W.2d 455, 410 Mich. 616

In short, Section 106 review does not guarantee preservation. It is triggered by a federal undertaking, and, even then, it only brings together affected parties with the hope of preserving the resource on, or deemed eligible for, the National Register.

Preservation in the Transportation Act of 1966

The strongest language in support of historic properties came in response to widespread criticism of federally aided highway construction. Municipal representatives, civic groups, and organizers in San Francisco, Seattle, Boston, New York, and Baltimore repeatedly called for more deliberation of neighborhood concerns, as highway engineers planned to seize property. In the historic Vieux Carre in New Orleans and in the Southwark area of Philadelphia, the proposed elevated highways seemed particularly egregious. Although the 1962 Federal Highway Act stipulated that after July 1, 1965, any federal highway programs in an urban area must be based on a continuous transportation planning process that was carried on cooperatively with the states and local communities, problems continued to arise (Highway 1962). In Washington, D.C. the radical group "Niggers Incorporated," which distributed handbills that stated flatly "No more white highways through black bedrooms," brought the message to the doorstep of Congress (Ayres 1967).[18]

On the same day that President Lyndon B. Johnson signed the NHPA, he approved the legislation that established the new cabinet-level Department of Transportation. The law stated that henceforth the office would maintain a policy to preserve historic sites as well as natural resources of scenic beauty and recreational

Fig. 3.7 One of the most celebrated US Supreme Court decisions was won by the Citizens to Preserve Overton Park, in Memphis. Twenty-six acres might have been lost to Interstate 40; the effect on the property and its old growth forest would have been disastrous. (Library of Congress)

value.[19] Section 4(f) of the act forbid the Secretary of Transportation from approving any project requiring the use of land from a public park, recreation area, wildlife and waterfowl refuge, or "land of an historic site of national, state, or local significance" unless "there was no feasible and prudent alternative" and "all possible planning [was done] to minimize harm."

The "no feasible and prudent" test has been interpreted as a stringent requirement. In a case in Memphis, *Citizens to Preserve Overton Park v. Volpe* (Overton 1971), the United States Supreme Court declared that "factors of [transportation] cost, route, and community disruption are not to be balanced against preservation values absent truly unusual factors of extraordinary important" (Fig. 3.7). Given this high bar of protection, Section 4(f) has stopped federal transportation projects from threatening historic resources. In the case of the proposed federally funded elevated expressway in New Orleans, the vigorous neighborhood opposition and application of the strin-

---

(1981) became an important benchmark in later legal decisions (Preservation News September 1983). The Poletown controversy is explored further in this chapter in the paragraphs regarding the "taking" issue.

[18] The protest was largely against the plan to build a large bridge across the Potomac to connect several superhighways.

---

[19] The so called "Yarborough Amendment" introduced by Democrat Ralph Yarborough of Texas provided the crucial language. An ardent conservationist, the Senator was co-author of the Endangered Species Act of 1969 (Cox 2001).

gent 4(f) test led to the defeat of that highway (Borah and Baumbach 1981).

In many respects, the provisions in Sections 106 and 4(f) have similar goals. As federally aided government action often led to the destruction of historic resources, a review procedure was put in place to limit harm. Because of the long history of federal government regulation in interstate commerce and political backlash against the deleterious impact of the interstate system on inner city neighborhoods and historic properties, the 4(f) mandate was set to a higher bar than that of Section 106 (Rose 1989). While the latter merely requires that the responsible federal agency "take into account" the consequences of their undertaking and affords the ACHP the ability to "comment" on the same, Section 4(f) more strongly sets the substantive "no prudent or feasible" standard.

Over time, some federal plans, appearing to violate the spirit if not the letter of Section 4(f), have arisen and created controversies, lasting decades. The Federal Highway Administration (FHWA) proposed a $1.4 billion Interstate 710 Freeway Extension in Southern California that would have cut through four National Register historic districts and skirted the boundaries of two others, and would have led to the demolition of almost 1000 historic homes and 6000 trees. It took decades of litigation to stop what appeared like a flagrant violation of the "no prudent and feasible" standard (Freeman 1992)[20] (Fig. 3.8).

In other instances, Interstate 710-type projects gain approval. While Section 4(f) does raise the preservation bar relative to Section 106, it too does not guarantee preservation. Yet, the importance of Section 4(f) cannot be overemphasized. With the gradual decline of urban renewal funding and other forms of federal inner-city aid, the appropriations to advance transportation have provided many of the major urban and suburban improvements, well beyond the survey boundaries of the highway right-of-way. The remarkable role of this subsequent aid in supporting

Fig. 3.8 The "Stop 710" button was created by preservation advocates who objected to a proposed superhighway that would cut through four historic districts in Los Angeles. (Author's Photograph)

a wide range of projects, explained in detail in Chapter 5, has meant transportation projects have affected thousands of preservation projects across the country.

The National Environmental Policy Act

The rise in environmental sensitivity in government during the early 1960s completed the shift from nineteenth century forest and wildlife management to much broader ecological thinking. The idea that Man should work in harmony with Nature, not against it, advanced by the early ecologist Aldo Leopold as the centerpiece of his "land ethic," gained more widespread attention in the post World War II era. However, environmental disasters were more effective in directing public opinion and creating political change (Leopold 1949). Several texts were influential. The plea for an end to the use of pesticides by biologist Rachel Carson, in her expose *Silent Spring*, was followed by a focus on the problems of population expansion highlighted by Paul Ehrlich in *The Population Bomb*. Then the need for more ecologically sensitive land use planning was promoted by landscape architect Ian McHarg in his *Design With Nature* (Carson 1962; Ehrlich 1968; McHarg 1969). Two oil spills off the coast of Santa Barbara, California, in early 1969, killing

[20] The litigation began in 1973 at the initiative of several environmental groups and the city of Pasadena. Current studies consider underground alternatives (LA Times March 23, 2007).

marine life and tarring birds and fauna, further highlighted the dangers of oil trans-shipment. The establishment of the World Wildlife Fund (1961), Environmental Defense Fund (1967), and Natural Resources Defense Council (1969) all helped by taking the discussion to the airwaves and press (Lindstrom and Smith 2001). All of these organizations demonstrated the confusion in government, which often sent mixed signals about the policy direction to follow, particularly when compared to specific projects. For example, Senator Henry "Scoop" Jackson held hearings during 1967 and 1968 that highlighted the cloudy future of Everglades National Park, where the Department of Transportation, the Corps of Engineers, and the NPS all had different plans (Kaufman 2000).

With Senator Jackson's leadership, the NEPA (NEPA) made its way through Congress in 1969 and became law January 1, 1970. It is distinguished for having created a policy that demanded the recognition of the interconnectedness of all aspects of the environment. The legislation charges the federal government with a broad mandate "to preserve and enhance the environment including the historic, cultural, and natural aspects of our national heritage" (NEPA 1969).

The implementation of NEPA takes place by means of the environmental impact statement (EIS), which bears similarities to the Section 106 process. Like the NHPA, NEPA is triggered by specified federal activity—namely, "major federal actions significantly affecting the quality of the human environment." The primary vehicle for assessment and public review is the environmental impact assessment. This detailed statement prepared by the federal agency undertaking the action consists of a description of the intended action and possible alternatives. It contains a description of the affected environment; an analysis of the environmental consequences, both that of the intended action and of the alternatives; and a discussion of measures to limit any harmful effects on the environment (Mayda 1993).[21] In the case of a federal action that will negatively affect a historic resource, the EIS, if properly prepared, will define the level and type of effect, consider alternative actions more amenable to the historic environment, and/or, if the original action is to be maintained, analyze how its adverse effects can be mitigated.[22]

An EIS process can protect historic resources, especially if there is vigorous public review. For example, the potential for a Kennedy Presidential Library in Harvard Square in Cambridge, Massachusetts, led to considerable public discussion. As this proposed construction was a major federal action that would significantly affect the quality of the human environment, a NEPA-mandated EIS was prepared. The study concluded that the anticipated additional 1,000,000 annual visitors to Harvard Square would have "no impact." That claim lost merit as the public began to understand more about the actual effect the project would have on the historic character of the Square. The heightened public scrutiny of impact, centered on likely traffic problems, catalyzed the EIS process, and led to another proposal. The facility was built in Dorchester, a location in Boston that could better handle the visitation. In this instance, NEPA furthered preservation (Allis 2005).

The preparation of an EIS is a procedural stipulation, however. Government agencies and courts that do not embrace the underlying rationale can frustrate the implementation of the law. NEPA does not halt activity harmful to the environment. It requires only that the effects are considered in an EIS with alternatives and mitigating actions noted (Kreske 1996). Having filed an EIS, a federal agency can demolish or in other ways adversely affect the historic environment. Thus, while both NEPA and the NHPA Section 106 process require that federal agencies

---

[21] The earliest call for an environmental impact assessment appears to have been by 30 university professors at the University of Puerto Rico and other professionals about the plans for copper mining in the highlands of the Island, questioning the underlying assumptions of decision makers.

[22] The Council on Environmental Quality and the environmental impact statement process are attributed to Lynton K. Caldwell, one of Senator Jackson's top advisors. A useful handbook prepared by The Harmonizing Workgroup of a NEPA Task Force, "Coordinating the National Environmental Policy Act With Other Federal Environmental Laws" (2008), compares Section 106 with the NEPA concepts.

pay attention to historic preservation, they do not prohibit destructive actions.

In yet another example, the FHWA proposed replacing an old six-lane drawbridge with a new twelve-lane model spanning the Potomac River that would carry the tremendous volume of Washington beltway traffic along the Maryland-Virginia stretch of Interstate 95 (Siew 1998).[23] While Sections 106, 4(f), and the NEPA-EIS reviews were all triggered, these procedures did not stop the construction of the bridge and the loss of National Register resources. Despite preservation group appeals that there were less destructive alternatives, such as construction of a ten-lane bridge and an underground tunnel, a determined federal agency will not easily be dissuaded.

Saving Tribal Culture?

Chapter 1 pointed out that early archaeologists became involved with excavating the work of the Mound builders. This led to pages of speculation about their origin and relationship to the existing American Indian tribes. The Antiquities Act was passed in 1906, but by the mid 1970s, that legislation's archaeological protections were declared unconstitutionally vague because the terms used, such as "objects of antiquity," were not adequately defined (Diaz 1974). Just as important, late twentieth century scholars argued that the nineteenth and early twentieth attitudes of the early archeologists were prejudicial, often marginalizing the concerns of Native Americans. Much of the policy and many of the early twentieth century practices requiring that the tribes were to be nativitized and made part of the Judeo-Christian majority prevailed, just beneath the surface, in administrative procedures in federal, state and local governments. At the same time, late twentieth century objections voiced by tribes about the treatment and display of human remains received a growing amount of public attention (Brown 2000; Watkins 2005).

In response to this court ruling and continued controversies, the 1979 Archaeological Resources Protection Act (AHPA) re-affirmed that the preservation of archaeological resources is important to the nation.[24] It went further by prohibiting the sale, purchase, transport, exchange, or receipt of any archaeological resources removed without permission from public or Indian land. It established a permit system for archaeological excavations and put in place penalties for violators of this law.[25] For all federally contracted or licensed construction that would harm archeological sites, AHPA required archaeological excavation and documentation. Considerable resources—up to 1 % of total project monies—can be made available for projects.

Native Americans and social advocates whose lands, culture, and even ancestral remains had been the "objects" of archaeology for decades continued to press for change. This led to the passage of the 1978 American Indian Religious Freedom Act (AIRFA 1978). Signed by President Jimmy Carter in August 1978, this legislation created the platform for Indian religious rights by declaring that the United States government will "protect and preserve" for American Indians their inherent right of freedom to believe, express, and exercise the traditional religions of the American Indians, Eskimo, Aleut, and Native Hawaiians.

How well does AIRFA work in practice? In the case of Devils Tower in Wyoming, should mountain climbers be allowed to climb it, as it is held in federal hands? (Fig. 3.9) Or, should "Mathó Thípila" and "Ptehé Ǧí," which means "Bear Lodge" and "brown buffalo horn," respectively to the Lakata Sioux, be reserved out of respect for Indian beliefs, consistent with the law? The 867-foot tall hulking butte, the country's first National Monument, featured at a stark monolith in the film "Close Encounters of the First Kind," is a popular Wyoming tourist attraction. Yet, the

---

[23] The new span was opened in 2006.

[24] The longstanding battle in Tellico, in Eastern Tennessee, is a prime example (Washington Post October 10, 1979; ARPA 1979).

[25] *United States v. Austin*, 902 F. 2d 743, 9th Cir. 1990 ruled the Act was not unconstitutionally vague and underscored the penalties (Hutt 1994).

Fig. 3.9 Known to the Indian tribes in the region as "Bear Lodge," and to others as "Devil's Tower," the 867 foot high butte was designated the first National Monument. The uses deemed appropriate for this property remain in question. (Library of Congress)

Lakata Sioux, Cheyenne, and Kiowa hold it sacred and several tribal leaders objected to the climbers ascending the monument, considering it a desecration. The compromise adopted is a voluntary climbing ban during the month of June when the tribes are conducting ceremonies around the monument.

Guaranteeing the practice of religion did little for the hundreds of thousands of artifacts associated with the tribes (Mihesuah 2000). In 1986, when several Northern Cheyenne leaders visited the Smithsonian Institution, they found 18,500 remains of their ancestors in the collection. This spurred the development of the National Museum of the American Indian Act, passed in November 1989, authorizing the repatriation of some of the Smithsonian's artifacts (NMAIA 1989; Williams 1986).

Then, with the AIRFA guaranteeing access of Native Americans to sacred places and new ideas being circulated about the treatment and interpretation of Tribal remains in museum settings, in 1990, Congress passed and President George H. W. Bush signed the Native American Graves Protection and Repatriation Act (NAGPRA 1990). This law requires that tribes be consulted before Native American graves are excavated. It also provides a process for protecting and distributing Indian cultural items found on federal or tribal lands through intentional excavation or inadvertent discovery, and it requires that Indian remains found in museums be repatriated to the appropriate tribal community (McManamon 2001). In addition, under NAGPRA, federal agencies and federally funded institutions were required to inventory and summarize all American sacred objects by 1993 and funerary objects by 1995.

The implementation of these laws has raised further questions, as seen in some well-publicized cases. In 1996, a 9500 year-old skeleton surfaced along the Columbia River in Kennewick, Washington (Downey 2000; Thomas 2001). Archaeologists intrigued by the rare, whole nature of the remains wanted to study the find further because it might provide a valuable clue as to the origin and developments of the first Americans. The Washington State Umatilla Tribe claimed, however, that they have controlling rights as mandated by NAGPA and they plan to rebury the skeleton within 30 days. Secretary of the Interior Bruce Babbitt agreed, and asked the US Corps of Engineers, which manages navigation in the Columbia River, to turn over the bones to the Umatilla, but archaeologists countered that scientific scrutiny should proceed and some scientists even questioned whether the tribe existed five millennia ago. After protracted litigation, in 2002 a federal judge sided with the scientists, and the five tribes that had become involved decided not to appeal to the Supreme Court. Despite NAGPRA, the skeleton of Kennewick Man remains in boxes in the University of Washington's Burke Museum and there is no scheduled date for a report of the findings. Moreover, the tribes have come to recognize the courts are not likely to see their values as inherent in the legislation.

Spurring Stewardship of Federal-Owned Properties: Executive Orders

Leadership in the executive branch often begins with the President, who is not only the Commander-in-Chief of the military forces and the chief diplomatic officer, but also heads all of the Cabinet departments. Because the staff members of these departments need direction and the authority to execute the laws and implement administrative procedure, ever since 1789 the President has issued "executive orders," which have the force of law.

This is important because Federal agencies own or lease vast amounts of property for grazing, forestry, and mining. They also care for thousands of structures and buildings. The Department of Interior has the largest responsibilities, largely due to the millions of acres under the Bureau of Land Management and the US Forest Service. The Department of Agriculture also plays a large role, with the Department of Defense in third place, with about 350,000 properties in its historic resources inventory, well ahead of the General Services Administration, which ranks fourth. In all cases, the appropriate stewardship mandates can potentially have a far-reaching preservation impact.

Of all of the EOs that have affected the disposition and treatment of historic properties, the first became the most important (Sprinkle 2001). Although all federal agencies were assumed to comply with the provisions of the NHPA, EO 11593, signed by President Richard Nixon in May 1971, went further by expecting more aggressive positive action. EO 11593 required each federal agency to identify, evaluate, and nominate *all eligible properties* to the National Register of Historic

Places within two years. The idea that a property would be placed on the National Register and receive protection was contained in the Act. That a property could be determined eligible for inclusion before the nomination was complete, and thus be protected from being transferred, sold, demolished, or altered, was an important concept. Because the survey of historic properties would not be complete in the near future, the *de facto* position of the Advisory Council was to recommend that federal agencies retain stewardship and explore alternatives for reuse whenever possible. An important test was the proposal of the General Services Administration to declare surplus the St. Louis Post Office and Custom House. In August 1970, the news that GSA intended to allow the building to be demolished unleashed a storm of protest. That and other problem cases ultimately led to revisions of the Surplus Property Act, other EOs, and revisions to the NHPA.

Other initiatives followed. EO 12072, signed in 1978, stipulated that federal facilities should be located in the central business district (CBD).[26] As historic properties are disproportionately located in CBDs, this EO gives added economic life to these properties. While federal agencies have sometimes located in the downtown, in other cases, administrators might attempt to dodge the mandate, arguing that they were compelled to locate in the distant suburbs. In this vein, EO 13006, signed in 1996, provided a slightly improved mandate that federal facilities be established in urban areas and gives first consideration to historic properties. This suggests the importance of reiterating preservation goals as the political dispositions change and new people assume public responsibilities.[27] The

---

[26] This Executive Order should be seen in the context of the 1976 Public Buildings Cooperative Use Act, where it is mandated that the General Services Administration should acquire space in historic buildings unless such space is not "feasible and prudent."

[27] Executive Order 13327, regarding Federal Real Property Asset Management, mandates a real property inventory. Real property is owned, leased, and otherwise managed property within and outside the USA. The EO stipulates that each federal department designate a Senior Real Property Officer who reports to the Office of Management and Budget (OMB) on issues such as the life-cycle costs,

2003 EO 13287 is similar, mandating protection, enhancement, and contemporary use of historic properties owned by the federal government

A number of other federal initiatives assist preservation. Most of them link to the core NHPA provisions, which are connected to the National Register, Sections 106, 4(f), and NEPA reviews. At the same time, the often-stated sentiment for less public intervention has led to more reliance upon the state and local preservation programs described below.

The Role of the Partners for the Federal and Local Governments

Although the role of the federal government is very important in historic preservation, by no means does it act alone. The State governments and Tribal Nations serve as the partners to implement many federal preservation programs, performing many important functions of their own, and serving as partners for local initiatives.[28] In addition, the District of Columbia, American Samoa, the Commonwealth of the Northern Mariana Islands, the Commonwealth of Puerto Rico, Guam, and the US Virgin Islands all have established preservation offices.

Hence, the SHPO, the Territorial Historic Preservation Officer, or the Tribal Historic Preservation Officer (THPO) is the individual whose staff leads in the partnership with both the federal and the local governments. Their offices must: (a) compile and maintain a statewide survey and inventory of historic properties; (b) identify and nominate eligible properties to the National Register; (c) implement a statewide historic pres-

ervation plan; (d) administer Federal assistance through grants-in-aid programs; (e) aid federal, state, and local governments in carrying out their historic preservation duties; (f) work with the Secretary of the Interior, the ACHP, and federal and state agencies to ensure that historic properties are considered throughout planning and development; and (g) serve as an information, education, training, and technical source for federal and state historic preservation programs.[29]

Many federal preservation programs require active "state level" participation. The historic preservation officer (HPO) is important in the National Register survey and nomination process; the review and compliance Section 106 process; identifying historic resources affected by federal agency activity and in determining the type of impact (No Adverse Effect or Adverse Effect); and facilitating financial incentives. The HPO also provides technical assistance, review, and approval in the federal historic rehabilitation tax credit program. There is a two-level test for eligibility: first, whether the property qualifies as historic; second, whether the planned rehabilitation is historically appropriate as per the guidelines established by the Secretary of the Interior. The federal historic tax credits are the most significant public financial incentive offered for historic preservation, and the HPO's review functions are extremely important to the smooth operation of this program.[30]

The SHPO also performs another federally related duty. The 1980 Amendments to the NHPA made local governments eligible to receive a minimum of 10 % of the federal HPFs allocated to the state, provided the local jurisdiction was "certified." The SHPO has the responsibility for certification. This means that if local governments can hire appropriate personnel, mount a comprehensive preservation program that includes activities such as surveying and inventorying historic properties, establish a qualified preservation review commission, and enforce

---

the purchase, condemnation, exchange, and leasing of real property, and related issues. The relationships between real property officers and federal preservation officers is key; rarely are they one and the same person or lodged in the same location.

[28] 16 U.S.C. 470a(b) describes the State Historic Preservation Programs and their responsibilities. The Code goes on in 47a(d) to stipulate that a tribe may assume all of any part of the functions of the SHPO, assuming the tribe's chief governing authority requests this, the tribe designates an official to administer the program, and other provisions are met.

[29] Items listed here are condensed for the sake of this discussion.

[30] See Chapter 5 for the specifics of this legislation.

appropriate state or local legislation, they can receive funding to support these activities.

Most states have State Registers of Historic Places—an official roster of resources important from history, culture, architecture, archaeology, and other perspectives that, in turn, have provisions similar to the NHPA. The criteria for state register designation often resemble, if not are identical, to the National Register, as is the procedure for placing resources on the state register. For example, the Virginia Landmarks Register, established in 1966, uses the same criteria as the National Register. Among the 4000 properties that have been so designated is Rosewell, the remnant of one of the state's largest colonial mansions dating from 1726; St. Peter's Church, built in 1701, where Martha Washington worshipped as a child; and such vernacular and more contemporary structures, as the Tastee 29, one of Virginia's few surviving art deco streamlined diners.

Once on the state register, a property affected by state and local government actions may be subject to varying types of review reminiscent of the provisions of NHPA, NEPA, and DOTA. Many states have a "mini-Section 106" process. Like its federal namesake, the state 106 review forestalls government action inimical to the historic environment, in this case state agency activity.[31] In some instances, entry on the State Register delays actions harmful to listed properties by both private and public agencies. For example,

the landowner of a State Register property in Hawaii cannot initiate demolition or other adverse redevelopment activity without first notifying the Department of Land and Natural Resources. Then, a 90-day discussion period begins during which the SHPO attempts to protect the State Register entry through purchase, negotiation, and other means. The discussion period varies: Illinois imposes a 210-day "cooling-off period."[32]

Some states also have "mini-NEPAs." As at the federal level, the state NEPA mandates that an EIS be prepared to examine the effect of major state actions. For instance, California requires all state agencies to prepare an EIS on any project, which has a significant effect on the environment. The statute defines this to include "objects of historic or aesthetic significance" (CA Proposition 50 2002; CA Proposition 65 1986; CEQA 1970). In California and other states, the EIS-identified effects are examined within the context of alternatives to the contemplated action as well as measures limiting the harmful effects on the environment.

State transportation legislation may also have a Section 4(f) requirement, although it is connected only infrequently to state 106 and EIS reviews. Alternatively, a Section 4(f)-like provision may be more broadly applicable than the federal Section 4(f) standard. For example, the Kansas Historic Preservation Act calls on "the state or any political subdivision of the state" (e.g., local or county government) to "not undertake any project" (not just a transportation undertaking) "which will encroach upon, damage or destroy any property" (a broad impact) "on the national and state registers" (both resources are included) "unless the SHPO is given an opportunity to comment." This is reminiscent of the ACHP's "comment" power. Further, the law requires that the SHPO has determined "that there is no feasible and prudent alternative to the proposal" and that the program includes "all possible planning to minimize harm." Again, this is verbatim language from the federal Section 4(f) (Kansas 1977).

---

[31] The state-federal Section 106 parallel is evident from the following description of the New York State procedure: The Notice and Comment provision of the (New York) 1980 Preservation Act are patterned after section 106 of the NHPA. The state review process is activated whenever a state agency is planning a project that may cause a change in the quality of a "state historic resource," namely, a property listed on the National Register or eligible whenever a state agency is planning to demolish, alter, or transfer any property under its jurisdiction that is listed on the statewide inventory. The agency preservation officer must give notice to the Commissioner "as early in the planning process as practicable." The commissioner then reviews the plans and comments as to whether the proposed project will have an adverse impact on any of the state's historic resources. If it is determined that an adverse impact will occur, the commissioner notifies the agency and works with it to examine alternatives.

[32] Illinois State Agency Historic Resources Preservation Act (20 ILCS 3420/).

Fig. 3.10 Building "Camden Yards," the stadium of the Baltimore Orioles, triggered historic preservation reviews, but the effect on the surrounding neighborhood was minimized. (Author's Photograph)

In a similar vein, the Minnesota Environmental Rights Act (MERA) incorporates a 4(f)-like standard. When an action affects "natural resources," including objects of historic value, the MERA requires that the adverse action be explained so that it is clear "there is no feasible and prudent alternative" (Beaumont 1996). Incorporating the stringent interpretation of such a standard enunciated in the *Citizens to Preserve Overton Park* decision, MERA further adds that "economic considerations alone shall not constitute a defense" of an action adversely affecting resources, both natural and historic.

There are many examples of state Sections 106, 4(f), and NEPA-EIS reviews that have helped to save historic resources and to mitigate problems. Some have been more successful than others.

The Baltimore Orioles' stadium has achieved fame as one of the first and most successful "retro-look" baseball parks. Its development also involved a successful application of Maryland Section 106. As the Maryland Stadium Authority helped finance construction, thus constituting a

state action, and the ballpark was located in Camden Yards, an historic neighborhood, Maryland's state 106 process was triggered. Often building a ballpark is detrimental to nearby neighborhoods because existing buildings are razed for parking lots and there is an increase in traffic and other adverse effects. In the case of Camden Yards, however, by encouraging mass transit as opposed to primarily automobile access to the stadium, much of the historic character remained untouched. This preservation-supportive outcome was fostered by Maryland's 106 review (Heller 1992) (Fig. 3.10).

The New Brunswick, New Jersey Hiram Street Market was a two-story structure built in 1811 that housed important mercantile and public uses for over 150 years. Because of its historical, cultural, and architectural contributions, it was placed on the New Jersey state register. Redevelopment of its downtown location for a new hotel and high-end townhouses threatened the future of the property. As this redevelopment involved state action, it prompted a state Section 106 review. The denouement: in this case the process was only a perfunctory 106 review and the Hiram Street Market was shortly thereafter demolished.

Hence, just as the federal processes have been helpful but do not guarantee preservation will follow in every instance; the state level reviews often encounter the same challenges.

Stewardship of State Owned Properties

State agencies mandated to identify and maintain with care the historic properties they control follow similar procedures. For example, in a requirement reminiscent of the federal EO 11593, each New York State agency must appoint a preservation officer who, amongst other obligations, is required to identify agency-owned historic properties and to bring such properties to the attention of the New York State SHPO. In a requirement echoing the federal Public Buildings Cooperative Use Act, state agencies in Arizona, California, New York, and Oregon, among other states, must give priority to restoring historic buildings under state control before leasing, buying, or constructing new space. In the same way as the 1992 NHPA amendments reminded federal agencies of the need to shepherd the disposition of surplus federal buildings, state agencies in New York, Pennsylvania, and elsewhere are similarly on notice. The resources may be transferred, but often only if their preservation is fostered through such means as an easement. Just as federal agencies give preference to urban locations for their space needs, so too do states such as Maryland, Massachusetts, Oregon, Texas, Vermont, and New Jersey have similar requirements.

These mandates help further preservation. For example, the University of Maryland sought to build a satellite campus in Hagerstown. It was offered a donated site for free on the outskirts of this community. This option was rejected in favor of putting the campus in Baldwin House— an abandoned yet historically important hotel and department store in the heart of the downtown (France 2008).

As at the federal level, state agency stewardship mandates do not guarantee a preservation outcome. The Texas Main Street Program encountered opposition from the Texas General Services Commission (GSC) when the former wanted to use a historic building for its headquarters (Beaumont 1996). The GSC argued that historic renovation would be too expensive but the Main Street group persevered in reclaiming the historic property. Often less preservation-minded agencies may have gone the traditional route of new construction. State agencies in Florida, Minnesota, and Arizona often disregard a requirement to give preference to the acquisition of space in historic properties on the grounds that such space does not meet their needs. In short, the state (as well as the federal) stewardship mandates are a useful albeit not foolproof tools in the preservation arsenal.

The state preservation actions described thus far—survey and designation on state registers, review of government action affecting resources so identified in state level Sections 106, 4(f), and NEPA-EIS procedures, and state stewardship mandates—all mirror federal programs in this arena. Yet forces that affect historic properties on a day-to-day basis typically have nothing to do with state action, nor are most historic resources owned or controlled by state or other governments. Of more importance besides the issue of financial resources for preservation (discussed in Chapter 5) are the influences on construction and land use. While the federal government has little influence on construction and even less on land use regulations, states are a major player in these arenas and increasingly are using their authority over construction and land use to foster preservation.

State Regulation of Construction to Foster Preservation

State enabling legislation also provides municipalities with the power to regulate construction within their boundaries. Communities look to the state to provide model regulations and to set out basic guidance for local building inspectors. These, in turn, affect the rehabilitation of existing structures. The primary traditional concerns arise from the need for fire protection. In the nineteenth century, maps of the "fire limits" marked the downtown areas where only fireproof construction materials were acceptable, to safeguard people and their property. Departments of public works generally had the responsibility for reviewing building plans and specifications so they would conform to building codes. In 1895, the National Fire Protection Association formed, principally to standardize sprinkler systems.

In the decades that followed the number of codes proliferated, specifying the permissible types of construction; quality of building materials; minimum floor and roof loads; electrical and mechanical equipment; and health and safety requirements pertaining to water pressure, fire ratings, and other considerations (Kaplan 2003). In addition to fire prevention, concerns about public health and housing conditions spurred ideas that ultimately formed the basis of state enabled zoning, which gradually became more acceptable after the adoption of New York City's "Comprehensive Zoning" law in 1916.[33]

Although these codes all regulate both new constriction and renovation, they are largely oriented to new construction, and that emphasis creates problems for renovation. The codes often mandate new-construction standards, so that retrofitting an existing building to the new-building standard is technically problematic and can be expensive. Two building code provisions in particular—the "25%–50% rule" and the "change-of-occupancy rule"—have often proved most difficult for renovations. The "25%–50% rule" suggests that a complete code-complying building (e.g., existing sections, renovated areas, and new additions) must be the result if the total cost of the proposed work (over some stated period of time) exceeds 50% of the estimated cost to replace the existing buildings.

Building and zoning codes also address a change of use or occupancy in existing buildings because such a change may introduce new or greater hazards. A code may require that the entire building comply with the new-construction requirements for the new occupancy. For instance, if industrial property is adapted for housing, then the new-construction standard for housing would have to be satisfied. Because local building officials are generally reluctant to issue waivers on their own authority, the professionals involved with a well-financed renovation project might approach the state review board for an exemption, anticipating local concerns. Unfortunately, many projects are not given that flexibility or the time to file an appeal.

This problem has led to corrective action on the part of both the model code groups and government, especially state government. Beginning with New Jersey, states began to develop new ways to regulate work in existing structures, using what are known as "rehabilitation codes," and in some jurisdictions as "smart codes." In May 1997, the US Department of Housing and Urban Development published the Nationally Applicable Recommended Rehabilitation Provisions (NARRP) to serve as a model for developing rehabilitation codes. In January 1998, New Jersey adopted its rehabilitation code. Since then, several states and local jurisdictions followed suit, including Maryland; New York; Rhode Island; Minnesota; Wilmington, Delaware; and Wichita, Kansas (Galvin 2006). These new codes recognize the need for predictability and proportionality. There is predictability in that clear rehabilitation code regulations foster the accurate prediction of improvement standards and costs. Proportionality establishes a sliding scale of requirements depending on the level and scope of the rehabilitation activity, from repairs to reconstruction. Proportionality has led to the elimination of the most onerous application of the "25%–50%" and "change of use" rules. The overall goal of the rehabilitation codes is to encourage the reuse of older buildings, with special sensitivity to historic buildings.

To illustrate, New Jersey's smart code includes special provisions applicable to structures that meet the Standards for Historic Buildings established by the US Secretary of the Interior. It allows for the use of replica materials, establishes special provisions for historic buildings used as museums, and identifies building elements that may meet relaxed code requirements to preserve the integrity of an historic structure. New Jersey

---

[33] See Chapter 1 for more background and references.

is not alone in allowing flexible building code requirements for historic properties. Section 635 of the Massachusetts Building Code (MBC) allows exceptions to the state building code for features that contribute to a property's historic distinctiveness. As with the interpretation of any codes and regulations, opening up a line of conversation with the local buildings department is the first step.

State Regulation of Land Use to Foster Preservation

Land use planning regulations also affect the viability of existing properties and their community setting. An important recent development is the increased use of growth management provisions in state land use planning and regulation. Although this initiative began in Hawaii in the early 1960s, at least four waves of interest have led a number of other states to adopt some form of growth management. These include Vermont, Florida, Oregon, New Jersey, Maine, Rhode Island, Georgia, Washington, and Maryland (Weitz 1999). Most of the statewide growth management strategies begin with an array of goals, such as reducing congestion and preserving natural resources. These goals set into motion a series of operating objectives that lead to the formulation of specific strategies and programs. Sometimes the objectives become reality, as future land designations on a map, and subsequent local land-use regulations draw their ultimate authority from the objectives. Programs, strategies, and maps indicate which land will be preserved and which areas will be available for limited, moderate, or active growth.

The implementation of growth management varies by state. Most commonly, growth management provides for the preparation of local/county/regional plans consistent with state goals. The plans are then submitted to the state or sub-state body for review, comment, and approval. Further incentives and/or disincentives can encourage compliance. For example, state infrastructure assistance is often offered only to jurisdictions that comply.

Because growth management shares many of the sentiments that have propelled historic preservation—such as preserving environmental resources and enhancing the quality of life—it is not surprising that an almost universal goal of growth management is the preservation of historic resources. A national survey of growth management and statewide comprehensive land-use planning acts in Delaware, Florida, Georgia, Hawaii, Maine, Maryland, New Hampshire, New Jersey, Oregon, Rhode Island, Vermont, and Washington found that *all* included historic preservation as a goal and/or a required planning element. In Maine, for instance, one of the ten state goals in the Comprehensive Planning and Land Use Regulation Act of 1998 is "preservation of the state's historic and archaeological resources." In Vermont, Goal nine of the state's sixteen planning goals is "to identify, protect, and preserve natural and historic features of the Vermont landscape." There is almost identical language calling for historic preservation in other states. Growth management can spur historic preservation by (1) enhancing the economic sustainability of historic resources, often reorienting the direction and location of development; (2) fostering the identification of historic resources; and (3) incorporating preservation into the planning and land use process (Burchell et al. 2000).

Growth management challenges outward sprawl. Toward that end, it often establishes "urban growth boundaries" within which most growth is encouraged, especially in older communities. Because most historic areas lie within these boundaries, they are reinvigorated by the economic and social changes.

Growth management may also foster the identification of historic resources. Oregon's statewide planning Goal five is illustrative. It calls for the conservation of open space and the protection of natural resources, including those of an historic nature. To accomplish this, it calls for "the locations, quality, and quantity of the following resources shall be inventoried, listing among other resources historic areas, sites, structures, and objects." Growth management can further help by bringing preservation into the master planning and land-use regulatory process. Goal nineteen of Florida's State Comprehensive Plan seeks the furtherance of "cultural and historic resources." In turn, local governments and regional councils are required to develop comprehensive plans that conform to the State Comprehensive Plan and are subject to approval by the state. Thus, Florida's local and regional plans must further historic preservation among other goals.

In sum, by changing where development occurs and by influencing the land use planning process, state growth management can potentially be a major force in fostering preservation. While the potential of this approach has yet to be fully realized, a promising start has occurred.

The Roles of Local Governments

Although federal and state legislation set the framework for police action, local government provides the greatest protection, much of it through the designation process. Designation may protect the landmark by delaying or prohibiting alterations to the entire exterior, façade (the portion viewable from the street), or interior (in the case of an interior landmark), and/or the demolition of the structure itself. Generally, changes are approved only if they conform to the prevailing architectural style or historic character.

As noted in Chapter 2, while about a dozen cities had local preservation laws in place before the NHPA was passed, most were enacted in the early-to mid-1970s. Today, over 2000 communities have local preservation commissions with a principal activity being the survey and designation of historic resources. In the paragraphs that follow, the processes in New York City are given particular attention because the following parts of this chapter discuss important court decisions that affect that municipality.

Designation, an application of the government's "police power," rests on the fundamental idea that the state has the authority to regulate social behavior and enforce order to further the public welfare. The statement of purpose for New York City's landmark ordinance refers to safeguarding "the city's historic, aesthetic, and cultural heritage." It also intends to "stabilize and

improve property values," "foster civic pride," and "protect and enhance the city's attractions and strengthen its economy." Similar goals and language echo in the Chicago landmark ordinance, which is deemed to "safeguard... Chicago's heritage... preserve the character and vitality of the neighborhoods and central area... foster civic pride... and protect and enhance the attractiveness of the City... to homeowners, homebuyers, tourists, visitors, businesses, and shoppers" (Chicago 2011).

A landmarks commission, usually with seven to fifteen members, makes decisions about the designation and disposition of historic properties. The individuals on the commission have expertise in such areas as architecture, history, art history, law, planning, and real estate. In New York City, the Landmarks Preservation Commission (LPC) comprises eleven members, including at least three architects, one historian, one city planner or landscape architect, and one realtor. In the small community of Litchfield, Connecticut, the historic commission is comprised of five members who only have to be "electors of the borough."

Day-to-day designation work rests on the shoulders of the commission's staff, which range in number and expertise depending on community size, resources, preservation commitment, and other factors. New York City has a 50 member, full time professional preservation staff organized into research, preservation, and other departments. Most commissions have one or two staff members, while others such as Litchfield have only one part-time staff person.[34]

In order to qualify for designation, the resource must be significant from an architectural, historical, cultural, or archaeological perspective. The local designation criteria may or may not mirror those for the National Register. The criteria for designation as a Chicago landmark, including a site of a "significant historic event, identification with [notable] persons, and exemplification of an architectural type or style" (Chi-

---

[34] The problems faced by historic district commissions, conservation overlay district review boards, and other public review bodies are discussed in Chapters 6 and 7, dealing with design, ethics, and advocacy.

cago 2011), greatly resemble the National Register (A) through (D) criteria. The Montgomery County, Maryland preservation ordinance and many others incorporate the National Register criteria verbatim. The New York City designation criteria are purposely broad and refer in the case of an historic district to an area "having a special character or special historical or aesthetic interest… represent one or more periods or styles… and that constitute a distinct section of the city" (NYC 2013). The Santa Fe, New Mexico designation criteria refer to the adobe style and Spanish heritage characteristics of that community.

Just as the criteria for designation differ, the minimum "age" of a property to qualify for designation varies. Often 50 years is the minimum, mirroring the half-century requirement for entry on the National Register of Historic Places. Yet, a number of exceptions exist. Los Angeles has no explicit age qualification, Seattle requires only 25 years to have passed, and in New York City 30 years is the minimum (Chao 1995).

The potentially eligible properties are identified through a formal historical resource inventory or survey, performed by a variety of parties, including outside consultants, municipal staff, or a non-profit historical society. Frequently the inventory or survey is not citywide but, rather, is limited to a number of promising areas, a limitation required by lack of funding. Resource constraints also limit the ability to update the original base inventory.[35]

In many cases, the preservation commission can designate without additional specific legislative approval. In other instances, the recommendation of the commission goes to the planning commission and it, too, must grant approval before the municipal elective body finally hears testimony and grants or denies the designation.

These activities should be coordinated with a community's overall land use and planning vision and controls in its master plan, and its zoning ordinance. The community's master (or comprehensive) plan provides long-range guidance

for the growth and development of a community in terms of population, economy, housing, transportation, community facilities, and land use. Communities implement their land-use vision through zoning, which controls the uses permitted and the intensity of development allowed, and through subdivision standards, which affect the division of land for sale, development, or lease. This land-use regulatory structure—zoning and subdivision—has a bearing on historic preservation. If the zoning code allows a high intensity of use, it imposes pressure for the demolition and redevelopment of historic buildings or districts, which typically reflect the lesser intensity of use of the past.

In New York City, the LPC first conducts research and a survey, and, if the evidence warrants, it holds a hearing on a potential designation. The hearing is advertised and notice is given to affected property owners. Following the hearing, the LPC can designate the resource as a landmark—an action that is then reviewed by the City Planning Department, which examines the documentation from a number of perspectives. The Planning Department then forwards a report to the City Council, which then votes on the matter. The Mayor can then accept or reject this vote, although the City Council can override the Mayor's veto with a two-thirds affirmative vote. In Chicago, the Historic Commission makes a preliminary determination of designation after careful survey, research, and property owner notification. That determination is reviewed by the Chicago Planning Department and the Chicago City Council provides further oversight, leading to passage of the designation.

Theoretically, the number of properties a community can designate has no limit, but practically the staff and financial resources restrict the administration of the programs. The categories vary widely. New York City has a broad array of landmark categories. Its groups of historic resources encompass: (1) individual (exterior) landmarks, such as Grand Central Station; (2) historic districts, such as Greenwich Village and Brooklyn Heights, (3) interior landmarks, such as the Woolworth Building Lobby; and (4) scenic landmarks on city owned property, such as the Central Park

---

[35] Further comments on the process of surveying historic properties and the landmarks commissions' procedures are contained in the following chapters.

Sheep Meadow. As of May 2010, the LPC had granted landmark status to over 27,000 buildings, including 100 historic districts, 1265 individual landmarks, 110 interior landmarks, and 10 scenic landmarks in all five boroughs. This number is less than 3 % of all the structures in the City.

Owner consent and/or initiation may be required in many cases before approving the designation, in part because of the property restrictions that follow designation. Chicago requires owner consent in the case of religious properties considered for designation. Following the lead of the federal and state preservation agencies, Chicago also will not designate if 51 % of the property owners in a district contemplated for designation object. Central City, Colorado; Coral Gables, Florida; Independence, Missouri; and other communities have owner consent requirements for religious structures. By comparison, New York City has no consent provisions for any potential landmark, religious or otherwise.

Considerable variation exists in the preservation commission's exact powers—that is, what action it can take with reference to planned demolition, moving a designated structure, and alterations, as well as new construction on vacant lots in a designated neighborhood. At the very least, the commission may intervene in an advisory capacity, recommending actions to another body such as a city planning agency, a building department, or the local legislature. Some commissions are also empowered to delay actions threatening a designated property, for instance, by providing for a mandatory 30-, 60-, or 90-day discussion period. The most stringent preservation commission intervention is to prohibit demolition, moving, and inappropriate alterations and/or new construction. Where there is stringent regulation, with the exception of minor maintenance, almost all work done on a designated building requires approval from the preservation commission, typically in the form of a "certificate of appropriateness" or comparable permit.

In New York City, the LPC reviews any work requiring a building permit to a designated property and all changes affecting protected features. There are three LPC permits. (1) *Certificate of No Effect (CNE)*. When the proposed work requires

a building permit but does not affect protected architectural features (e.g., interior renovations, such as new heating equipment). (2) *Permit for Minor Work (PMW)*. When the proposed work will affect significant protected architectural features but does not require a building permit (e.g., masonry cleaning or repair). (3) *Certificate of Appropriateness (CofA)*. When the work requires a building permit and affects protected features (e.g. additions, demolitions, new construction, and removal of architectural features).

Some preservation commissions impose affirmative maintenance obligations stipulating that owners of designated buildings must keep their properties in "good" or "sound" condition— a requirement over and above that imposed by the city's general housing code. Yet, few of the communities with this maintenance obligation have the staff to enforce it. In New York City, "demolition by neglect" is defined as the gradual deterioration of a property when routine maintenance is not performed, sometimes due to the owner's benign indifference and in other instances a deliberate attempt to avoid demolition procedures (Mayors 2006). Regardless of the intent, the result of this neglect creates an unwelcome appearance and may lead to a building open to vandals.[36] Without the authority to assess civil penalties directly, the New York Landmarks Commission must litigate to enforce maintenance requirements. By carefully following an established procedure, it has done so suc-

---

[36] State Codes across the country define "Demolition by Neglect" in various ways. For example: "Substantial deterioration of a historic structure that results from improper maintenance or lack of maintenance" (Historic Preservation Districts and Landmarks, Miss. Code Ann. § 39-13-2(e)(2007)); "Neglect in maintaining, repairing, or securing an historic landmark or a building or structure in an historic district that results in substantial deterioration of an exterior feature of the building or structure or the loss of the structural integrity of the building or structure" (Historic Landmark and Historic District Protection, Subchapter 1. General Provisions, D.C. Code § 6–1102(3A) (2007)); "Neglect in maintaining, repairing, or securing a resource that results in deterioration of an exterior feature of the resource or the loss of structural integrity of the resource" (Historical Records and Sites Local Historic Districts Act, Mich. Compile Law Service, § 399.201a(f) (2007)).

cessfully. One of the first designated buildings in New York was "Skidmore House," a 159-year old Greek Revival residence located in Manhattan. When the condition of the property became public knowledge, the owners were ordered to repair and restore the exterior of the building to the state of "good repair" (New York 2004). In this case, the building's roof, exterior, and interior needed attention. As the dispute led to litigation, ultimately the court ordered the owners to submit an application for approval of the actions required to bring the exterior of the building into good repair. The court also ordered that the owner grant access to the Commission so that the staff could determine what repairs were necessary for the interior. Finally, the court issued a permanent injunction that required the owners to maintain the interior and exterior in the future.

Penalties for violating designation controls can be sweeping and nominally quite stiff. Most preservation commissions can impose fines, issue injunctions to stop unauthorized work, issue orders requiring the replacement of unauthorized changes that were not caught in time (e.g., a cornice or other decorative item removed), and, in some cases, have violators imprisoned. Generally, however, these measures usually are not applied. This reluctance is due to the belief that property owners should be educated and act voluntarily because they recognize the value of protecting historic resources. On a practical level, the limited number of staff does not allow for the pursuit of minor violations through the courts.

By contrast, most enforcement of the preservation commissions' powers is informal, spurred by public complaints and monitored by windshield surveys taken by the commissions' staffs and/or preservation watchdog groups. Regular on-site inspection is comparatively rare because historic preservation commissions simply do not have the personnel to monitor the changes taking place in the buildings under their care. Notification by city departments when alterations are pending does occur, but this is not often done in a consistent manner.

A number of other local government preservation measures could provide property owners with financial compensation. Transfer of devel-

opment rights (TDR) is one such measure. In a fashion similar to that used in land conservation, a municipal TDR program permits the sale of a property's unused development potential in an area zoned for more intense use. Hence, if a designated historic building containing 5000 sq. ft. is located in a zone permitting a 20,000 sq. ft. structure, in a TDR scheme the owner is able to sell 15,000 sq. ft.[37]

By allowing the sale of the unused development potential, TDR alleviates some of the financial pressures on the property owner. When the Church of St. Jean Baptiste wished to restore its neo-Baroque limestone and brick façade and copper domes in Manhattan, the air rights for its rectory were sold to a developer who used them in an adjacent property (Architectural Record 1991). While a useful tool, comparatively few municipalities in the United States have the ability to administer a TDR program.

The Initial Judicial Reaction to Preservation: Restricted Application

As we have seen, the initiatives of the legislative and executive branches of government are extremely important in setting out the goals, objectives, and some procedures for historic preservation. In similar fashion, because disputes arise, the role of the courts has significantly influenced the disposition and treatment of historic properties. In 1893, the federal government acquired the Gettysburg Battlefield in Pennsylvania by condemnation. The railroad that owned the land brought suit, arguing that the government's "taking" was unconstitutional because the acquisition of the battlefield for commemorative purposes was not a valid "public purpose." The US Supreme Court decided otherwise. It held that the acquisition of the battlefield site served a public use and, therefore, was a valid application

---

[37] TDR schemes first received considerable notice in Chicago (Costonis 1974; Pruetz 1997). About 200 TDR programs in 33 states are underway, most preserving open space and farmland (Pruetz and Pruetz 2007).

Table 3.1 The Judicial Systems in the United States

The Federal Judicial System		
Supreme Court Nine Justices (Hearing appeals from the highest state courts and questions regarding the Constitutionality of Congressional legislation)		
United States Court of Appeals 12 Circuits and the Federal Circuit. (Three-judge panels hear almost all of the cases, not the entire Court.)		
U.S. Administrative Agencies	U.S. District Courts In 50 states, the District of Columbia, and territories.	U.S. Tax Court (Reviewing Internal Revenue Service decisions)

The State Judicial System
State Supreme Court Generally 5 to 9 justices
Appellate or Reviewing Court Three judge panels hear almost all of the cases
Trial or Superior Court
Lower Trial Courts

of the power of eminent domain (Gettysburg 1896). "Any act of Congress which plainly and directly tends to enhance the respect and love of the citizen for the institution of his country and to quicken and strengthen his motives to defend them… must be valid." State courts tended to follow this response. Illustrative is a 1929 decision, *Roe v. Kansas ex rel. Smith*, where the US Supreme Court upheld the propriety of the use of the eminent domain power by state government to condemn and take historic properties (Roe 1929), provided the owner receives "just compensation."

Left untested was the propriety of using the police power for preservation purposes without full compensation. Exceptional cases did arise, often tested at the state and local level. In the 1890s, Massachusetts passed a law limiting the height of buildings around Copley Square in Boston and provided for compensation for the restriction on development. To some property owners this was an inappropriate use of eminent domain. The matter went to the US Supreme Court, which affirmed the state's action (Williams 1899, 1903). In this case, the decision mentioned the distinguished buildings fronting Copley Square—Trinity Church, the Boston Public Library, "new" Old South Church—as well as the point that the protection of such resources "could have been achieved by imposing the same restrictions under the police power without compensation" (Williams 1983-Sup). The Copley Square decision on the application of police power for preservation was prescient and foreshadowed the direction of future judicial decisions.

As suggested by the table above, it is important to understand the basic framework of the court system at the federal, state, and local levels. As will be shown in the discussions that follow, disputes are often argued differently in light of the disposition of the court or courts being approached.

The Second Judicial Reaction: Cautious Acceptance

For most of the twentieth century, local governments applied designation criteria and other restrictions relying on the state's police power. The preservationist's scope expanded from objects solely of historical value to include those of aesthetic significance. Because the New Orleans Vieux Carre ordinance was one of the first, it was repeatedly subject to challenge. Three decisions by the Louisiana Supreme Court became key interpretations.

In the first case, a property owner claimed he could reconstruct a small outside lavatory without the Commission's approval because its control did not extend to such matters. The court in *City of New Orleans v. Impastato* decided otherwise, indicating that the Commission's control encompassed the full "exterior" of the buildings, not only their facades. The court also concluded that police power gave "full and complete authority with respect to the preservation of the architecture and historic value of buildings situated in the Vieux Carre" (Impastato 1941).

In a second case, an owner of a gasoline station erected a 560-square foot sign on his premises, ignoring the district's regulations limiting sign size to a maximum of eight square feet. The owner of the gas station argued that his *modern* building should not be subject to the Commission's controls. The court favored the Vieux Carre Commission (Pergament 1941). District controls were justified based on police power because they furthered the public's welfare on both aesthetic and economic grounds (Pergament 1941; Delafons 1990). The court also spoke of an important aspect of preservation: protecting the ambience of the *whole,* not just that of isolated buildings (Pergament 1941).

The third Louisiana State Supreme Court decision was the 1953 case *New Orleans v. Levy* (Levy 1953). Litigation arose when the owner of a restaurant placed a roof over a courtyard. When the city brought action to require the removal of the roof, the owner objected, stating that his addition was not specifically prohibited by the governing regulations. The court thought otherwise and concluded that the statutory language requiring that alterations in the Vieux Carre be appropriate from an "architectural and historical perspective," and be "quaint and distinctive," was sufficiently clear to provide guidance as to permissible construction activity (Williams 1974–1975). When the city moved for an injunction to force the removal of the roof, however, the court balked, arguing that there was considerable non-enforcement of similar regulations, such as never taking action to require the removal of the lavatory that was the subject of litigation in the *Impastato* decision. The *New Orleans v. Levy* decision foreshadowed some current legal issues, namely that while the legality of controls based on police power was upheld, attention had to be paid to equal and adequate enforcement.

In addition to the state court decisions affecting New Orleans, the city played a role in an important federal decision on preservation, *Maher v. City of New Orleans* (Maher 1975). Maher claimed that the Vieux Carre ordinance constituted a taking of property without just compensation and violated due process guarantees. The Court of Appeals found against both these charges (Maher 1975, at 1059–1061, 1066). It also found the administration of the Vieux Carre ordinance, including the guidelines followed by the Commission, did not violate due process standards (Maher 1975, at 1062).

Preservation controls in other cities were also tested and, for the most part, upheld. The Massachusetts Supreme Court affirmed historic district regulations in Nantucket and Beacon Hill in Boston on police power grounds (Opinion 1954, 1955). The decisions noted the expanding horizons of police power to include the public pursuit of aesthetic objectives. At the same time, the justices were not comfortable with upholding the preservation regulations entirely on an aesthetic basis and thus pointed to the numerous economic gains that would occur by protecting the special historic ambience of Nantucket and Beacon Hill. The New Mexico Supreme Court in upholding Santa Fe's historic district controls noted similar economic and aesthetic factors (Santa Fe 1955).

In sum, the judicial reception towards historic preservation at mid-century was different from during the initial period. In the early years, the major issue was the bounds of eminent domain,

Fig. 3.11 Grand
Central Station, one of
the best examples of
the French Beaux-
Arts architecture in
the nation, became
the focal point for
the US Supreme
Court decision that
legitimized local
landmarks legislation.
(Author's photograph)

and most courts upheld such application. At that
time, police power was not used as a preservation
tool, and it is likely that if it had been, the courts
would have struck down such measures. Later,
the issues went well beyond eminent domain to
the exercise of police power. Was historic preservation via police power a valid exercise of sov-
ereign authority, or were private property owners
so adversely affected that due process and taking prohibitions were violated? The court's response was to apply a "balancing test" in which
the interests of the public-at-large were weighed
against the hardships faced by the individual affected by the regulations. The overwhelming
consensus of the court was that preservation significantly furthered the public's welfare on both
aesthetic and economic grounds. The courts realized that public sensitivities were changing and
broadening to include an aesthetic dimension. In
this respect, many courts were influenced by, and
often cited, the US Supreme Court's dictum in a
1954 decision, *Berman v. Parker,* a case involving condemnation of property for urban renewal
purposes:

> The concept of the public welfare is broad and
> inclusive… The values it represents are spiritual as
> well as physical, aesthetic as well as monetary. It
> is within the power of the Legislature to determine
> that the community should be beautiful as well as
> healthy, spacious as well as clean, well-balanced as

well as carefully patrolled… If those who govern
the District of Columbia decide that the Nation's
Capital should be beautiful as well as sanitary,
there is nothing in the Fifth Amendment that stands
in the way. (Berman 1954)

Berman v. Parker gave measurable support for
governmental activity to protect the aesthetic
environment. Nonetheless, when considering the
legality of governmental intervention, the courts
hesitated to uphold these measures solely on aesthetic grounds. Instead, they tacked on other benefits, such as the economic gain from tourism that
a preserved French Quarter, Nantucket, and Santa
Fe would achieve. Using aesthetics as a basis for
preservation regulations did not come until later.

The courts in this second stage were guarded
in another manner: that of the equality of treatment. Underlying designation and related preservation activities is the question of whether all
parties are treated in a similar fashion, as opposed
to singling out some owners of historic resources
and some areas for special restrictions and protections while others are ignored. In considering
this issue of equality, there is always comfort in
numbers—it is better to designate an entire district than to single out individual buildings. This,
for the most part, was the format of designation
in the early years though mid-century. The legal
testing of the designation of individual properties
did not occur until later.

The Third Judicial Reaction: Stronger Affirmation

The year 1978 serves as an important benchmark because it is when the US Supreme Court upheld the landmark designation of Grand Central Station by the New York City LPC. This action is described with great attention because it demonstrates the degree to which the legal details make a difference in the courts' decisions and it is arguably the most influential decision to date (Fig. 3.11).

Occupying more than two full blocks of midtown Manhattan real estate, Grand Central Railroad Terminal, completed in 1913, is one of the best examples of French Beaux-Arts architecture in the nation. For the person arriving by train, its vast concourse provides an impressive entrance to New York City with a direct linkage to the suburban trains system and city subways. For those departing, the Terminal offers a refuge from the extremely high density of midtown Manhattan. For all of these reasons and more, Grand Central was one of the early buildings designated as a landmark under the 1965 New York City Landmarks Law. In the report describing the special value and significance of Grand Central, the LPC lavished praise on the property as a unique example of the designs of distinguished architects trained the Ecole des Beaux Arts (Gilmartin 1995, pp. 401–410). This report provided a basis for the designation of Grand Central by the LPC in August of 1967, which was confirmed by the City's Board of Estimate in September 1967.[38]

Even as these actions took place, the idea surfaced of redeveloping the site. In the 1960s, buildings in the Grand Central area had an allowable floor-to-area ratio (FAR) of eighteen.[39] By contrast, Grand Central used a FAR of two—one-ninth of that permitted—leaving an additional 2.6 million square feet of office and related space that could be constructed on the site. As the Terminal was located in one of the most valuable real estate areas in the world, its owners considered how to capitalize on the unused development potential.

In September 1967, the New York Central Railroad, the predecessor of Penn Central, proposed the construction of a multi-million square foot office tower above the Terminal. In the following January, a subsidiary of New York Central, holding a lease on Grand Central Terminal's air space, entered into a long-term agreement with a lessee, U.G.P. Properties. Under this agreement, U.G.P. would build the tower and pay the railroad a minimum of $3 million annually (Smith 1975).

The actors soon changed, but not the plan. New York Central would merge with the Pennsylvania Railroad Company and the lease with U.G.P. was assigned to Penn Central, which moved forward with the project. Internationally famous Modernist architect Marcel Breuer crafted two schematic plans. The first entailed a 55-story office building to be constructed on the roof of the Terminal (referred to as Breuer I); the second, a 53-story building, required the demolition of the 42nd Street facade of the Terminal (referred to as Breuer II).

As required by law, Penn Central submitted its plans to the LPC for review. It applied for a CofA for both Breuer I and II, holding that the changes contemplated in both designs were compatible with and therefore "appropriate" to the Terminal. The LPC thought otherwise. Its reaction to Breuer I was that "balancing a 55-story office tower above a flamboyant Beaux-Arts facade seems nothing more than an aesthetic joke." The Commission also rejected Breuer II because it felt "to protect a landmark, one does not tear it down" (Goldstone and Dalrymple 1974).

Even while the LPC was rejecting these proposals, it was working behind the scenes to mollify Penn Central's desire to capitalize on the unrealized development potential of its property. To this end, the Planning Commission proposed an amendment to the city's TDR mechanism. In 1968, New York City allowed owners of underdeveloped landmarks to sell their unused air

---

[38] The Board of Estimate functioned as the legislative body responsible for budget and land use decisions until 1989, when the US Supreme Court ruled that it violated the one man, one vote rule.

[39] Floor Area Ratio, or FAR, is a concept used to control the amount of building on a lot. The FAR number represents the multiple of the lot area, which produces the maximum allowable floor area in a development.

rights to adjacent lots.[40] The latter could then increase their allowable intensity of development by a maximum of 20%. These "adjacency" and intensity qualifications limited the application of TDR in the Grand Central situation because there were no adjacent lots that could absorb the full 2.6 million square feet of the Terminal's air rights. Consequently, New York City modified both of these TDR restrictions in order to make the air-rights mechanism more attractive to Penn Central. In 1969, the city removed the 20% density increase ceiling on landmark TDR sales occurring in the CBD. In the same year, it expanded the area over which development rights could be transferred by allowing movement over "chains of title," that is, over multiple building lots, provided these lots had a common owner. The removal of the 20% density increase ceiling worked to the advantage of Penn Central as well as other owners of landmark properties. The second change, allowing "chains of title," was almost custom-tailored for Penn Central because of the many nearby properties it then owned in the midtown area. By using this concept, Penn Central could transfer the 2.6 million sq. ft. of unused air rights over Grand Central to, in effect, a midtown zone over the many blocks in which it was a major landowner.

Despite this concession by the City, Penn Central challenged the denial of its redevelopment plans in the courts. Ultimately, litigation was to go through four courts. Three were at the state level: first at the Trial Court (Supreme Court); second, the Appellate Court; and third, the Court of Appeals. All but the first affirmed the landmark designation of Grand Central. The fourth and final judicial statement on the Grand Central matter was by the US Supreme Court, which also upheld the landmark designation of the Terminal. The significance of these decisions merits a brief consideration of the travails of the litigation and the resulting judicial decisions, with the goal of highlighting the arguments and decisions rather than delving into the many technical and legal points raised during litigation.

---

[40] The use of the transfer of development rights is discussed further in Chapter 5.

Penn Central at the Trial Court Level

In October 1969, Penn Central filed suit against the City, seeking declaratory judgment that designation of Grand Central was invalid; the railroad also sought damages for the delay in its Breuer redevelopment plans (Smith 1975). The plaintiffs did not bring their case to court until May 1972. Penn Central argued that the landmark designation of Grand Central Terminal constituted a taking of property without compensation. It also added that the landmark process violated equal treatment because the property was singled out, while owners of other historically significant buildings had not been subject to designation.

In January 1975, the Trial Court reached its decision; the verdict was a blow to the City's preservation efforts (Penn-TC 1975). The court decided that the municipal designation was so onerous a regulation that it constituted a taking, and property owners so affected were entitled to compensation. The Trial Court's decision was reminiscent of the judicial attitudes prevailing during the earliest period of preservation litigation. Governmental preservation efforts would take the form of eminent domain, with compensation given to property owners. Preservation regulations in the guise of police power would *not* be tolerated. The implication of the Trial Court's ruling was to declare unconstitutional the direction of local preservation of the prior two decades, but its finding was reversed at all subsequent levels of appeal.

Penn Central at the Appellate Division

Later that same year, the Appellate Division of the New York Supreme Court upheld the right of New York City to designate landmarks by a vote of three-to-two (Penn 1975). The Appellate Division also recognized the public welfare benefit realized by preservation controls.

> To summarize, in view of the nationwide burgeoning awareness that our heritage and culture are treasured national assets, New York City's landmarks preservation law is a valid exercise of its police power. The need to preserve structures worthy of landmark status is beyond dispute; and

Fig. 3.12 The interior of the Grand Central Station is one of the most striking interior public spaces in the country, recently restored and rehabilitated with comparatively minor changes. (Author's photograph)

the propriety of the landmark designation accorded Grand Central Terminal is essentially unchallenged. (Penn 1975 at 272)

While preservation might satisfy the welfare test for applying police power, the question remained whether its specific application in the form of landmark designation constitute so onerous a burden as to be a taking of property. The Appellate Court indicated that the "taking" test applied would be the same as in zoning cases: "Have the plaintiffs [owners] demonstrated that the regulation in issue deprives them of all reasonable beneficial use of their property?" Given that test, the Appellate Court declared that designation was not a taking, even though it could result in a reduction of value (Penn 1975 at 274).

Penn Central at the Court of Appeals

In 1977, the New York Court of Appeals unanimously affirmed the decision of the Appellate Division (Penn-NY 1977). The Court of Appeals also wrote about the many benefits to the public's welfare realized by preservation and noted the financial difficulty of effecting preservation via eminent domain as opposed to police power.

The Court of Appeals then addressed the taking issue. Was designation so onerous as to constitute an unlawful taking of property? The Court declared there was no taking on the grounds that much of the market value of the Grand Central site was "socially created" in the form of public streets, utility lines, and the like. Penn Central could legitimately calculate its rate of return only on "privately-created value," and on this basis, designation did not have a "taking" effect. The "public" versus "private" value concept pointed to by the Court of Appeals perplexed attorneys, both at the time of this decision in 1978 and subsequently.

Penn Central at the Supreme Court

The controversy had one more judicial hearing, before the US Supreme Court. In 1978, the Court affirmed the designation of the Terminal by a six-justice majority (Penn-US 1978). The highlights of the case are important. The first question was whether preservation regulations were a permissible application of police power in furthering the general welfare. The Court's response was that preservation was a growing activity of merit, and that cities had the right to enhance their quality of life by preserving aesthetic features (Penn-US 1978 at 2651, 2662). The decision recognized that States and cities could enact land use restrictions or controls to enhance the quality of life by preserving the character and desirable aesthetic features of a city (Fig. 3.12).

The Court then addressed whether the designation of Grand Central, with attendant restrictions on demolition and other changes, was a taking of property in violation of constitutional safeguards. The judges responded that the test on this matter followed that used when considering the effects of zoning, namely, that controls would be upheld if they allowed for some economic use, albeit not the most profitable one possible, in the absence of the land-use restrictions. Given this test, the Supreme Court declared that the designation of Grand Central did not constitute a taking (Penn-US 1978). The New York City law does not interfere in any way with the present uses of the Terminal. Its designation as a landmark not only permits but also expects the appellants to continue to use the property precisely as it has for the past as a railroad terminal, with ticket vending, waiting rooms, open meeting space, and concessions. More importantly, in instances in which a state tribunal reasonably concluded that "the health, safety, morals, or general welfare" would be promoted by prohibiting particular contemplated uses of land, this court upheld land use regulations that destroyed or severely affected recognized real property interests.

The Supreme Court said that the test for preserving a designated historic building was whether it could be put to "reasonable beneficial use." The Court added that if a landmark ceases to be "economically viable," the owner may then obtain relief. While the Court did not turn its decision on taking on Penn Central's ability to sell air rights under New York City's TDR provision, it noted this ability somewhat mitigated the designation restriction (Penn-US 1978 at 2666).

The Court also dealt with the charge by Penn Central that the designation of individual properties as landmarks constituted a discriminatory regulation as Penn Central argued that only selected property owners were singled out for attention and control. The Court thought otherwise, holding that the designation of individual buildings was part of a "comprehensive plan" in which all properties of historic note were under review by the LPC for possible designation (Penn-US 1978 at 2663–2664).

The *Penn Central* decision is the bellwether case of the judicial reception to preservation.

Numerous observers have equated *Penn Central* and preservation with the *Euclid* decision and zoning because the Supreme Court addressed a number of uncertainties about these regulations and fortified future discussion about planning issues (Kayden 2003). In addition, *Penn Central* clarified a "taking" test for preservation controls under which designation restrictions would be upheld. Hence, the question is no longer whether landmarks designation is legal, but rather, given that designation and related controls do not violate basic Constitutional safeguards, how best to refine the process.

Although the *Penn Central* decision answered many Constitutional issues regarding preservation, it surely did not quiet litigation in the years that followed. Three of these areas are discussed in the sections that follow: (1) the continuing debate regarding what constitutes a "taking;" (2) private sector preservation alternatives to public regulatory control; and (3) the affects of preservation commission decisions on properties owned by religious organizations.

The Quest for Balance in the "Taking" Definition at the State Level

One of the central legal issues of historic preservation is if and when it crosses the line between appropriate public regulation and the taking of property. This is part of a larger and continuing legal dynamic, and the courts have labored mightily on the appropriate definition. As the views of society change, so do the judicial rulings. The Penn Central decision may reflect a past US Supreme Court, more amenable to public control than today's judiciary or a future Court. In addition, legislatures will continue to respond to perceived challenges.

Some retrenchment by the Justices has come in rulings concerning public regulations. The 1981 *San Diego Gas & Electric* decision is illustrative in this regard (San Diego 1981). This case involved the purchase by a San Diego utility of a 200-acre site for its future expansion. At the time of purchase, the site was zoned for both industrial and agricultural purposes; after purchase, the city down-zoned the property, prohibiting any industrial use and reclassified a portion of the site as permanent open space. The utility, in turn, charged that the rezoning constituted a taking of its property and demanded compensation. Its suit argued that the city's regulation had gone "too far" and precluded "all reasonable use of the property." The US Supreme Court ultimately heard the case. A five-member majority voted to dismiss the case because final judgment had not been reached by the California courts.

Putting aside this technicality, what is most significant about the San Diego decision is Justice Brennan's dissent (Harr and Kayden 1989). Justice Brennan, who wrote the majority opinion in *Penn Central* upholding public controls, assumed a much more conservative posture vis-à-vis public regulation in San Diego. "It is only logical, then, that government action other than acquisition of title, occupancy, or physical invasion can be "taking," and therefore a *de facto* exercise of the power of eminent domain, where the effects completely deprive the owner of all, or most of his interest in the property" (San Diego 1981 at 651, 653). This dissent bears certain similarities to the Trial Court's opinion in *Penn Central,* namely that if regulation goes too far, the action becomes a taking of property and requires compensation. While the factual settings of the decisions are different in these two cases, the latter may herald a more conservative Supreme Court with respect to historic preservation.

Much more controversial are the cases surrounding the issue of "taking," often involving more than one property, ostensibly allowing a municipality to condemn land for a "public use." The 1981 Michigan Supreme Court ruling *Poletown Neighborhood Council v. Detroit* permitted the city to use eminent domain to seize and demolish a working class neighborhood so that General Motors could build an assembly plant to create jobs, strengthen the tax base, and promote economic development (Fischel 2005–2006). Roundly criticized at the time, the trend of cities to solicit developers willing to become involved in variously defined public projects is well known.

On the day before Thanksgiving 1998, Susette Kelo and six of her neighbors received an evic-

tion notice. They were given five months to move because their land was to be seized by the New London Development Corporation. As in Poletown, the properties were not "blighted." These properties were formerly part of a submarine base; the residents had purchased and improved them.

The private developer chosen to redevelop the site appealed to the city, wanting to demolish occupied, well-maintained waterfront homes in order to construct an office block and upper-income apartments. The owners did not want to sell, but the city, convinced that the action would increase the tax base and create new jobs, forced the sales. The Connecticut Supreme Court heard the case in 2002 and upheld the city's position. By the time the case reached the Supreme Court it carried with it 25 *amicus curie* briefs submitted by groups across the political spectrum.[41] In a 5 to 4 decision, Justice John Paul Stevens wrote for the majority that there was no "… literal requirement that condemned property be put to public use for the… public" (Kelo 2005).

The reaction against this decision by the public was immediate. Between 85% and 95% of those surveyed expressed the view that the government should not expand its power by using such a broad definition to seize property (Lexington 2010). The House of Representatives passed a bill with a 376 to 38 vote, forbidding the use of federal funds by any state or locality using eminent domain to obtain property for private commercial development, or failing to pay relocation costs (STOPP 2007). More important, this Supreme Court decision catalyzed property rights advocates across the country. The opposition to the *Kelo* decision became so strong among both Republicans and Democrats that 34 states passed legislation or constitutional amendments designed to curb the practice of city condemnation for the sole purpose of increasing revenue (Mer-

---

[41] These included New London Landmarks, the American Association of Retired People, the National Association for the Advancement of Colored People, and, speaking on behalf of the city, the American Planning Association. Well over 4000 articles have been written to date on the *Kelo* decision.

riam 2006; Main 2007). Some states took the occasion to forbid the transfer of private property from one owner to another for economic development, while others expressly state that the use of eminent domain is restricted to blighted parcels. Still others imposed a moratorium on this kind of project to allow closer study (Ross and Tolan 2006).

Also worthy of note, on the first anniversary of the Kelo decision President George W. Bush issued an EO stating that the federal government must limit its use of eminent domain for "public use" with "just compensation," mirroring the wording in the Constitution (EO 1988).

Property Rights and Private Preservation Controls

Easements and covenants are the most common restrictions on private property, in which certain "sticks" in the "bundle" of property rights are negotiated. An easement is a voluntary legal agreement between a property owner and a qualified easement holding organization used to protect some aspect of an historic property (Schofield 2003). An easement can be defined as a "less-than-fee" right or interest that is recorded in the public land office. This arrangement is "almost always held by a public agency, charitable trust, or corporation having as one of its purposes the conservation or preservation of environmental or historic resources" (Netherton 1980). Less-than-fee historic or conservation controls include scenic easements, which protect visual characteristics in the landscape in a field of view; façade easements, which protect exterior features and elements, generally those that are publicly prominent; and easements that cover the property's interior characteristics.[42] For example, a conservation easement on the land over an archaeological site might protect a view from being spoiled or limiting foot traffic. Whether these easements

are used in tandem or added incrementally, they can be very effective. In the Field-Hodges House in North Andover, Massachusetts, preservation easements have been placed on the grounds, barn, and fencing, as well as most interior features and finishes. An easement protects against development in Virginia's Civil War Cedar Creek Battlefield site (NPS 2007). The preservation easement offers a strong measure of protection to historic properties because it continues in perpetuity and has the force of law.

Another, traditionally more common private property control device is a restrictive covenant running with the land and stipulated in the deed or lease. This is often termed a deed restriction and has been in use since the earl twentieth century (Monchow 1928). Restrictive covenants are often used when designing new subdivisions to control subsequent additions and alterations, and were used in the past to limit owners or tenants by racial composition. The latter application has imbued covenants with a nefarious reputation. Yet from a purely technical perspective, a restrictive covenant prohibiting the destruction or alteration of historic properties can be an effective preservation device (Anderson 2003). By specifying lot sizes, building lines, architectural styles, paint color, and the uses to which the property may be put, deed restrictions legally bind the property owner to comply with a list of conditions for a specified length of time (Garner and Black 1999). If the deed restrictions are perpetual and "run with the land," successive owners are also bound to comply with the restrictions. The result is that property restrictions can last for several generations. In general, owners are not willing to restrict the use of their property for fear that it will harm the potential sales price or the value when passed along to heirs. In some cases, technical impediments stand in the way.[43]

---

[42] Valuation and the market value of the preservation easement are discussed further in Chapter 5. New standards for a "qualified appraisal" have been issued (Roddewig 2011).

[43] For instance, most less-than-fee historic preservation interests are in the form of an easement-in-gross, as opposed to an easement appurtenant; this runs headlong into common law restrictions against easements in gross. While a number of state statutory changes allow and encourage these easements, these are a recent development.

The relationship of preservation to the rights and operation of specially-favored groups will also continue to see a legal forum. For instance, the government bestows property-tax exemption and other benefits on charitable, non-profit groups. What is the proper relationship between these groups and preservation? This issue has often come to a head when buildings owned by charitable groups are designated as historic, with attendant restrictions on alterations and demolition.

Preservation Law and Religious Properties

As indicated at the beginning of the chapter, European social, political, and economic upheaval remained in the minds of colonists when they attempted to settle in the New World. This upheaval was also part of the prevailing religious disputes. Although the comparative ease with which religious groups could relocate in the Colonies worked against militant religious uprisings, it is little wonder that the free exercise of one's religious beliefs is stipulated in Maryland law as early as 1649 (McConnell 1990). One hundred and forty years later, James Madison wrote the Bill of Rights as part of the Constitution. The First Amendment to the US Constitution provides that Congress "shall make no law respecting an establishment of religion, or prohibiting the free exercise thereof."

In part because of the common Judeo-Christian heritage between Protestants, Catholics, and Jews, who formed the vast majority of the population at the time, religious groups, historical societies, and preservationists have generally worked cooperatively.[44] As indicated in Chapter 1, the earliest successful preservation effort was the campaign to save Old South Church, an early site of Revolutionary activity in Boston, in 1871. After the August 1886 earthquake in Charleston, South Carolina, restoring St. Philips

Fig. 3.13 St. Michael's Episcopal Church in Charleston is one of the most obviously visible landmarks, having been rebuilt repeatedly after every natural and man-made disaster in the city. (Author's Photograph)

Episcopal Church and St. Michael's Episcopal Church became a major effort[45] (Fig. 3.13). The Catholic missions of California and the Southwest declined to the point that they also stimulated concern, specifically for the artistic contributions made by the tribal, Anglo, and Mexican communities. The California Landmarks Club's mission "to conserve the missions and other historic landmarks of Southern California" led it to secure long-term leases on San Juan Capistrano, San Fernando, and San Diego missions, and raise money to remove debris, replace tile roofs, and repair crumbling masonry (Lummis 1903).

---

[44] The contributions made by all faith-based efforts will be discussed at greater length in Chapter 8. The discussion in this chapter revolves only on the legal issues.

[45] This was restored by architects W.B.W Howe, Jr. and John Gaillard Gourdin, respectively, with the assistance of William A. Potter, a ranking church architect from New York.

It is also important to remember the advocacy of Rev. Henry Mason Baum was essential in passing the 1906 Antiquities Act, and the leadership of Rev. Goodwin in saving Bruton Parish Church at the turn of the twentieth century served as the inspirational focus for the restoration of Williamsburg. During the Congressional hearings that led to the Historic Sites Act of 1935, a principal sponsor proudly asserted that $167,000 of federal funds were used in restoring the missions in San Antonio, and there was no attempt to usurp the power of the Catholic Church, nor wrest land from its control.[46]

As local zoning, planning, and historic preservation legislation became more commonplace, however, more attention centered on just how the regulations issued to protect the physical character of a place applied to religious organizations. As hundreds of communities passed historic preservation ordinances, with decisions made by over 2100 preservation commissions, conflicts have arisen over the interpretations of the Constitution's language. Those responsible for maintaining the designated religious properties question the role of government at the federal, state, and local levels.

Religious organizations often exist in older and often architecturally distinctive structures, and some are designated as historic landmarks with attendant demolition and alteration restrictions. Although the issue of preservation and religious organizations bears much the same relation as that of other charitable, non-profit groups, specific language in the First Amendment provides different protections. At the center of the discussion, then, lies the question of whether designation precludes the "free exercise" guarantee (Greenawalt 2006). Some religious leaders charge that a landmark designation forces them to remain in buildings that are no longer suitable to their needs. Even if the buildings are suitable, the argument follows that any designation may prohibit demolition and redevelopment of the property to a greater intensity of use, development that can sustain the religious ministries. In response, preservationists claim that designation typically has very little bearing on the suitability of a prop-

Fig. 3.14 St. Bartholomew's Episcopal Church in Manhattan proposed to demolish its adjacent community house and build a tower, in the face of a local landmarks commission decision that this action was not appropriate. The courts agreed that the action was not unconstitutional and, enforcing the law did not constitute "taking" the property. (Author's Photograph)

erty to a religious organization's needs and, in the cases where this might occur, the existing hardship relief provisions already part of the designation system permit exceptions (Gill 1984).

This issue has come to the courts. Almost as soon as the ink was dry on the landmarks ordinance in New York City, the United Lutheran Church in America challenged the designation of its Manhattan headquarters, located in the former home of J. P. Morgan, Jr., because it was deemed unsuitable (Gilmartin 1995, pp. 374–376). The New York Court of Appeals considered this charge and concluded that the landmarks designation should be lifted. The court believed the Morgan Mansion was inadequate to meet the administrative needs of the Church (Lutheran 1974). In another New York decision, however, the court found that the landmark designation of the meetinghouse of the Society for Ethical Culture did not seriously interfere with that organization's charitable purpose (Society 1980).

The question concerning the proper relationship of religious liberty and preservation continued to surface during the 1980s. As noted in the previous chapter, considerable publicity surrounded the case of St. Bartholomew's Church in midtown Manhattan, one of the most resplendent examples of Byzantine architecture and decorative arts in the country (Fig. 3.14). The Church

---

[46] See Chapter 1.

administration wanted to demolish the adjoining community house in order to permit construction of a 59-story office tower (Brolin 1988; Homer 1996; St. Bart 1990). The parish leadership claimed that it needed the annual rent it would receive from the office tower to continue its ministry, and designs were prepared for a new building to fit it into the surrounding context. Numerous preservationists and half the congregation discounted this cry of poverty and added that if St. Bartholomew's is financially pressed, it could seek redress under New York City's landmark hardship provision. This argument came before the US District Court, the US Court of Appeals, and the US Supreme Court, all of which upheld the Landmarks Commission's designation of St. Bartholomew's community house, rejecting the plaintiff's claim that landmarks laws unconstitutionally interfere with the free exercise of religion. Further, the Courts held there was no merit to the arguments that a "taking" had occurred. The final 1991 decision and a change in the parish administration led the surrounding corporate neighbors to support the Church's restoration, including the failing exterior mosaic tiles of the colorful dome, fixing faulty drains, and addressing the need for better lighting (Dunlap 2007).

In the US Supreme Court decision in *Employment Division, Department of Human Resources of Oregon v. Smith*, the justices rejected the claim of members of the Native American Church that they had the right to use peyote in their worship services. Curiously, this decision seemed to abandon the general principle that it was not necessary for government to have a "compelling interest" to intervene in the affairs of a religious group (Sherbert 1963). Instead, the Court held that striking a balance between protection of religious practices and the requirements imposed by laws of general application was a task for legislatures, not the courts.

In response to *Oregon v. Smith*, Congress passed the Religious Freedom Restoration Act (RFRA) in 1993 (Hamilton 2005). This imposed a strict scrutiny standard for religious freedom challenges, which, in turn, spurred further controversy because Congress relied on its broad power under the enforcement clause of the Fourteenth Amend-

ment in enacting RFRA. This caused problems, such as in Boerne, Texas, where the Roman Catholic archbishop sought to demolish St. Peter's Church, a major focus of an historic district, and replace it with a large box-like structure. Using RFRA, the church argued that the city interfered with its rights as a religious organization when it denied permission to demolish the 1923 Mission style church. The city contended that the Church should be denied the permit since RFRA is unconstitutional because it exceeds Congressional power. The US Supreme Court ruled in favor of the City of Boerne on October 14, 1997, allowing the city to refuse a permit for Archbishop P.F. Flores to tear down the historic St. Peter's Catholic Church. In the end, the religious organization and the city negotiated an agreement whereby 80% of the structure remained, and a sympathetic addition was located outside of the view of those in the historic district (Boerne 1997).

In siding with the city, however, the Supreme Court struck down RFRA, a law that could be interpreted as having given religious organizations an exemption from many zoning restrictions. The Court maintained that RFRA was an improper application of Congress' Fourteenth Amendment power to enforce constitutional values on the states, and was an unlawful usurpation of the judiciary's role as Constitutional arbiter.[47]

Although many states had similar laws, Congress went back to the drawing board and designed a "compelling state interest test," when passing the Religious Land Use and Institutionalized Persons Act (RLUIPA) in 2000 (Waltman 2011). In an effort to circumvent the Boerne decision, RLUIPA requires that local governments demonstrate that they have a compelling interest in the property and that they have taken the least restrictive means of furthering their interest when imposing or implementing a land use regulation which results in a "substantial burden" on religious exercise.

RLUIPA can be brought to bear on historic preservation efforts when local governments use land use, zoning, and historic preservation laws

---

[47] Matt Camp, a student in public policy at Rutgers University, initially prepared this section of the chapter.

to impede religious groups from acquiring, developing, or using worship space. On September 15, 2000 the City of Huntsville, Alabama ordered the Temple B'nai Sholom to "repair or demolish" a house on a lot that the religious organization purchased for expansion but had not maintained because the code enforcement officer said it was a danger to public health and safety. The home, on a parcel adjacent to the Temple, was of no historic significance but lay within an historic preservation district. When the Temple approached the Historic Preservation Commission, however, a demolition permit was denied. Hence, the religious organization seemed caught between two city agencies and sued them both in 2001 (Sholom 2001). Later that year, the Temple removed the case from county court and submitted it to US District Court for the Northern District of Alabama. The Becket Fund for Religious Liberty joined the case, and an amended complaint was filed, charging the city with violations of the Constitutions of Alabama and the United States and RLUIPA. The City and the Alabama Historic Preservation Alliance argued that RLUIPA and the Alabama Religious Freedom Amendment were not "valid laws." On June 26, 2003, however, the City council agreed to a settlement rather than to incur further legal costs, and paid for the house and its removal, approving the Temple's expansion plans.

In the future, RLUIPA may well be used in other cases, particularly as mega-churches continue to expand in the face of land use and historic preservation decisions (Evans-Cowley and Pearlman 2008). To what degree other religious organizations make use of it remains unknown.

Conclusion

It is evident that preservationists need to be familiar with the law to successfully protect cultural resources and enlist others in implementing appropriate policies and procedures. It should also be clear that social changes outside of government shape the responses of the legislative, executive, and judicial branches to varying degrees over time. Just as human rights campaigns in our largely Christian country have affected the expansion and interpretation of property rights, our legal thinking continues to change in considering the significance of historic properties and how best to save them. The growing recognition of the importance of historic sites, from cemeteries and military properties of national important, to a broader range of sites, more often than not including those of local significance, continually redefines the "official view" of our social understanding.

The fact that the NHPA recognized the significance of national, state, and local properties is also important because it tied governmental action to land use decision making. It influenced and was influenced by legislation in environmental policy and transportation, putting in place procedures that cause decision makers to pause and consider alternatives to achieve better outcomes.

The limitations of legislation and the courts, of executive orders and administrative approaches are obvious. Generally unrecognized is the manner in which decisions of the courts legitimize social activities. The Penn Central case is not only important for legitimizing the decisions of those in the New York City Landmarks Commission who played a role in the designation and decision to deny a project, but also for all who have become involved in historic preservation, with other commissions across the country. Likewise, the decisions of state and local courts can have an effect on the decision-making in any particular case.

It is important to understand that not all disputes should or will end up in court. Mediated settlements are also very important, and arguably more important when addressing minority rights and tribal affairs with questions that lie beyond the ability of the courts to address adequately. The comparatively "quiet" agreements reached about water rights and the ability to hunt and fish in a traditional manner are as important for some as the Penn Central case. As we have seen, the concepts of property held by traditional American Indians are not derived from positivist European views of land ownership. Many tribes have maintained that all land is spiritual and that the material universe has a direct relationship to the Creator or the spirit world. Certain locations are important spiritually, or held in reverence for having a special meaning for the faithful. In this sense, the tribes do not hold it is possible to own the land, any more than the air, water or any naturally occurring matter (O'Brien 1989). Many tribes also have adopted practices in which to give a gift is a mark of respect, with the more gifts the greater the honor. Hence, their cultures, based on sharing and distribution, are not interested in and do not condone individual accumulation. Often, when assigning land to clans or families, the tribe retains the right to recall and redistribute the property, as well as determine its use (Cronon 1983).

Hence, preservation law is a field that demands knowledge of the history of attitudes about property and the use of the land, as well as understanding the key pieces of legislation at the federal, state, and local levels, judicial decisions, and a wide range of administrative and procedural concerns. While some might find the changing mix confusing, the system of government we enjoy does require maintenance and attention to all of these details.

References

Advisory Council. (2010). *Protecting historic properties: Citizen's guide to section 106 review*. Washington: Advisory Council on Historic Preservation. http://www.achp.gov/docs/CitizenGuide.pdf. Accessed 28 Feb 2014.

AIRFA. (1978). American Indian Religious Freedom Act and amendments, 42 U.S.C., 1996.

Allis, S. (20 Nov 2005). A true American idol library. *Boston Globe*.

Anderson, R. M. (2003). *New York zoning law and practice* (Vol. I). Rochester: Lawyers Co-operative Publishing Company.

Architectural Record. (1991). Landmark Church in air-rights swap. *Architectural Record, 179*(2), 17.

ARPA. (1979). Archaeological resources protection act, 16 U.S.C., 470aa et. seq.

Ayres, B. D. (31 Dec 1967). Washington: White roads through black bedrooms. *The New York Times*.

Beaumont, C. (1996). *Smart states, better communities*. Washington, DC: National Trust for Historic Preservation.

Becker, C. (1922). *The declaration of independence. A study in the history of ideas*. New York: Harcourt Brace.

Berman. (1954). Berman v. Parker, 348 U.S. 26, 33.

Boerne. (1997). City of Boerne v. Flores, 521 U.S. 507.

Borah, W. E., & Baumbach, Jr. R. (1981). *The second battle of New Orleans: A history of the Vieux Carre Riverfront Expressway controversy*. Tuscaloosa: University of Alabama Press, for the Preservation Press.

Brolin, B. C. (1988). *The battle of St. Bart's: A tale of the material and the spiritual*. New York: William Morrow & Company.

Brown, M. F. (2000). *Who owns native culture?* Cambridge: Harvard University Press.

Burchell, R. W., Listokin, D., & Gallery, C. C. (2000). Smart growth: More than a ghost of Urban policy past, less than a bold New Horizon. *Housing Policy Debate, 11*(4), 821–879.

Burton, L. (2002). *Worship and wilderness: Culture, religion, and law in the management of public lands and resources*. Madison: University of Wisconsin Press.

CA Proposition 50. (2002). http://ballotpedia.org/California_Proposition_50,_Bonds_for_Water_Projects_2002. Accessed 1 Mar 2014

CA Proposition 65. (1986). http://ballotpedia.org/California_Proposition_65_1986. Accessed 1 Mar 2014

Carson, R. (1962). *Silent spring*. New York: Houghton Mifflin.

CEQA. (1970). https://www.dfg.ca.gov/habcon/ceqa/ceqapolicy.html. Accessed 1 Mar 2014.

Chambers, S. A. (Ed.). (2000). *National landmarks, America's treasurers: The National Park Foundation's complete guide to national historic landmarks*. New York: Wiley.

Chao, J. (19 Sept 1995). Seattle's landmarks aren't that old, but city isn't either. *Wall Street Journal*, A1, A10.

Chicago. (2011). *Commission on Chicago landmarks*. [City Code] Chapter 2–120, Article XVIII, 1.

Costonis, J. (1974). *Space adrift: Saving urban landmarks through the Chicago Plan*. Urbana: University of Illinois Press.

Cox, P. (2001). *Ralph W. Yarborough: The people's senator*. Austin: University of Texas Press.

Cronon, W. (1983). *Changes in the land: Indians, colonists, and the ecology of New England*. New York: Hill and Wang.

Delafons, J. (1990). *Aesthetic control: A report on methods used in the USA to control the design of buildings*. Berkeley: Institute of Urban and Regional Development, December.

Diaz. (1974). United States v. Diaz, 499 F. 2d 113, Fed. Cir.

Downey, R. (2000). *Riddle of the bones: Politics, science, race and the story of Kenniwick Man*. New York: Copernicus Springer-Verlag.

Duerkson, C. J., & Roddewig, R. J. (1994). *Takings law in plain English*. Chicago: Clarion Associates for the American Resources Information Network.

Dunlap, D. W. (18 Dec 2007). Seeking $30 M to renovate, church finds help in neighbors. *The New York Times*.

Earley, P. (14 Aug 1982). The Pinta? *Washington Post*, H1.

Ehrlich, P. R. (1968). *The population bomb*. New York: Ballantine Books.

Eicholz, H. L. (2001). *Harmonizing sentiments. The declaration of independence and the Jeffersonian idea of self government*. New York: Lang.

EO. (15 March 1988). Executive order 12630.

Evans-Cowley, J. S., & Pearlman, K. (2008). Six flags over Jesus: RLUIPA, Megachurches and Zoning. *Tulane Environmental Law Journal, 21*(2), 203–232.

Fischel, W. A. (2005–2006). Before Kelo. *Regulation, 28*(4), 32–36.

France, J. (1 Oct 2008). Rising from the Ruins. *Chesapeake Bay Journal*, 1.

Freeman, A. (1992). California freeway war erupts again. *Preservation News, 32*(9), 1–2.

Galvin, S. C. (2006). Rehabilitating rehab through state building codes. *Yale Law Journal, 115*(7), 1744–1782.

Garner, B. A., & Black, H. C. (1999). *Black's law dictionary* (7th ed.). St. Paul: West Group.

Gettysburg. (1896). United States v. Gettysburg Electric Railroad Co., 160 U.S. 668, 165, Ct 427.

Gill, B. (1984). *Fair land to build in: The architecture of New York State*. Albany: Preservation League of New York State.

Gilmartin, G. F. (1995). *Shaping the city. New York and the municipal arts society*. New York: Clarkson Potter.

Goldstone, H. H., & Dalrymple, M. (1974). *History preserved. A guide to New York City landmarks and historic districts* (p. 225). New York: Simon and Schuster.

Greenawalt, K. (2006). *Religion and the constitution. Volume 1: Free exercise and fairness* (pp. 234–235). Princeton: Princeton University Press.

Hamilton, M. A. (2005). *God vs. the Gavel: Religion and the rule of law*. New York: Cambridge University Press.

Harr, C. M., & Kayden, J. S. (1989). *Landmark justice: The influence of William J. Brennan on American Communities*. Washington: Preservation Press and the Lincoln Institute of Land Policy.

Heller, J. (1992). History triumphs at Camden Yards. *Preservation News, 32*(5), 10–11.

Highway. (7 and 8 Aug 1962). *United States. Congress. Senate. Committee on public works*. Federal-aid Highway Act of 1962. Hearings before the subcommittee of the committee on public works. Eighty-seventh congress, Second Session, G.P.O.

Homer, M. (1996). Landmarking religious institutions: The burden of rehabilitation and the loss of religious freedom. *Urban Lawyer, 28*(2), 327–347.

Howett, C. (2001). Integrity as a value in cultural landscape preservation. *Sage Urban Studies Abstracts, 29*(4), 411–568.

Hugs. (1997). United States v. Hugs, 109 F3d (9th Cir).

Hutt, S. (1994). *The civil prosecution process of the archaeological resources protection act. Technical brief no. 16*. Washington: U.S. Department of the Interior, National Park Service.

Impastato. (1941). City of New Orleans v. Impastato, 3 So. 2d 559.

Kansas. (1977). Kan. Stat. ANN., Chapter 75, 2715 to 2726.

Kaplan, M. E. (2003). Rehabilitation codes come of age: A search for alternative approaches. *APT Bulletin, 34*(4), 5–8.

Kaufman, R. G. (2000). *Henry M. Jackson. A life in politics* (pp. 102–103). Seattle: University of Washington Press.

Kayden, J. S. (2003). Celebrating how the Supreme Court's preservation of grand central terminal helped preserve planning nationwide. *Planning*, June, 21–23.

Kelo. (2005). Susette Kelo et al v. City of New London et al. (SC 16742).

King, T. F. (2000). *Federal planning and historic places: The section 106 process*. Walnut Creek: AltaMira Press.

King, T. F. (2008). *Cultural resource laws & practice*. Lanham: AltaMira Press.

Kreske, D. L. (1996). *Environmental impact statements: A practical guide for agencies, citizens, and consultants*. New York: Wiley.

LA Times. (23 March 2007). Freeway tunnels under S. Pasadena to be studied. *Los Angeles Times*, p. B4.

Laurence Baum. (2013). *American Courts. Process and Policy*. Boston, MA: Wadsworth.

Leopold, A. (1949). *A sand county almanac*. New York: Oxford University Press.

Levy. (1953). New Orleans v. Levy, 64 So. 2d 798, 1953, Rev. on other grounds, 98 So. 2d 210, 1957

Lexington. (14 April 2010). The worst decision of justice Stevens. *Economist*.

Lindstrom, M. J., & Smith, Z. A. (2001). *The national environmental policy act* (pp. 19–21). College Station: Texas A & M University Press.

Lobsenz, G. (28 Sept 1983). Maryland asks U.S. protection for historic shipwrecks. *Washington Post*, p. C9.

Lummis, C. F. (1903). *The landmarks club. The landmarks club cook book* (pp. v–vi). Los Angeles: The Out West Company.

Lutheran. (1974). Lutheran church in America v. city of New York, 35 N.Y. 2d 121 at 132, 316 N.E. 2d 305 at 311-312, 359 N.Y.S. 2d 7 at 17.

Macintosh, B. (1985). *The historic sites survey and national historic landmark program*. Washington: National Park Service.

Mack, E. (2009). *John Locke*. London: Continuum International Publishing Group.

Maher. (1975). Maher v. city of New Orleans, 516 F. 2d 1051, 5th Cir, 1975, Aff'd. 371 F. Supp. 653, E.D. La. 974, Reh'g. denied, 426 U.S. 905, 1976.

Main, C. T. (2007). *Bulldozed: "Kelo," eminent domain, and the American lust for land*. New York: Encounter Books.

Mayda, J. (1993). Historical roots of EIA. *Impact Assessment, 11*(4), 411–415.

Mayors. (2006). United States conference of Mayors. *Combating problems of vacant and abandoned properties: Best practices in 27 cities*. Washington, DC: City Policy Associates.

McConnell, M. (1990). The origins and historical understanding of the free exercise of religion. *Harvard Law Review, 103*(May), 421–425.

McHarg, I. (1969). *Design with nature*. Garden City: American Museum of Natural History.

McManamon, F. P. (2001). Cultural resources protection under United States Law. *Connecticut Journal of International Law, 16*(2), 272.

Merriam, D. H. (2006). *Eminent domain use and abuse: Kelo in context*. Chicago: American Bar Association.

Mihesuah, D. A. (Ed.). (2000). *Repatriation reader: Who owns American Indian remains?* Lincoln: University of Nebraska Press.

Monchow, H. C. (1928). *The use of deed restrictions in subdivision development*. Chicago: Institute for Research in Land Economics and Public Utilities.

NAGPRA. (1990). Native American graves protection and repatriation Act, 104 stat. 3048. *Public Law*, pp. 101–601.

NEPA. (1969). National environmental policy act 101(a), 42 U.S.C. 4331(a).

Netherton, R. D. (1980). Restrictive agreements for historic preservation. *Urban Lawyer, 12*(1), 55.

New York. (2004). City of New York et al., v. 10-12 cooper square, Inc., et al., 793 N.Y.S. 2d 688.

NMAIA. (1989). National museum of the American Indian act, 103 stat. 1336, *Public Law*, pp. 101–185.

NPS. (2007). *Budget justifications and performance information* (p. 1). Washington, DC: U.S. Dept. of the Interior.

NRB. (1995). National register bulletin 15: How to evaluate integrity. http://www.nps.gov/nr/publications/bulletins/pdfs/nrb15.pdf. Accessed 28 Feb 2014.

NYC. (2013). New York city landmarks commission rules (Title 63 of the Rules of the Code of New York City). http://www.nyc.gov/html/lpc/downloads/pdf/pubs/rules.pdf. Accessed 1 Mar 2014.

NYT. (13 Oct 1997). Utah is warming up to newest monument. *The New York Times*.

O'Brien, S. (1989). *American Indian tribal governments* (p. 217). Norman: University of Oklahoma Press.

Opinion. (1954, 1955). Opinion of the justices to the senate, 128 N.E. 2d, 55; 128 N.E. 2d, 563.

Oregon. (1990). Employment division, dept. of human resources of Oregon v. Smith, 494 U.S. 872.

Overton. (1971). Citizens to preserve Overton Park v. Volpe, 401 U.S. 402, 412-13.

Penn-TC. (13 Jan 1975). Penn central transp. co. v. City of New York, N.Y.L.J.

Penn. (1975). Penn central transp. co. v. City of New York, 50 App. Div. 2d 265, 377 N.Y.S. 2d 20.

Penn-NY. (1977). *Penn central transp. co. v. City of New York*, 42 N.Y. 2d 324, 366 N.E. 2d 1271, 397 N.Y.S. 2d 914.

Penn-US. (1978). Penn central transp. co. v. City of New York, 438 U.S. 104, 98 S. Ct., 2646.

Pergament. (1941). City of new Orleans v. Pergament, 5 So. 2d 129.

PL. (1966, 1992). Public law 102-575-16 U.S.C., 470.

PL. (1988). Public law 100-298

Preservation News. (Sept 1983). Midwest. *Preservation News, 23*(9), 8.

Pruetz, R. (1997). *Saved by development*. Burbank: Arie Press.

Pruetz, R., & Pruetz, E. (2007). Transfer of development rights turns 40. *Planning & Environmental Law, 59*(6), June, 3–11.

Roddewig, R. J. (2011). *Appraising conservation and historic preservation easements*. Chicago: Appraisal Institute.

Roe. (1929). Roe v. Kansas ex rel. Smith, 278 U.S. 191.

Rose, M. H. (1989). *Interstate: Express highway politics, 1939–1989*. Knoxville: University of Tennessee Press.

Ross, A., et al. (2011). *Indigenous peoples and the collaborative stewardship of nature*. Walnut Creek: Left Coast Press.

Ross, M. M., & Tolan, K. (2006). Legislative responses to *Kelo v. City of New London* and subsequent court decisions one year later. *Journal of Affordable Housing & Community Development, 16*(1), 52–85.

San Diego. (1981). San Diego Gas & Elec. Co. v. City of San Diego, 450 U.S. 621, 101 S.C.t.1287.

Santa Fe. (1955). Santa Fe v. Cruz, 389 P. 2d 17.

Schofield, C. (2003). *Historic preservation easements. A directory of historic preservation easement holding organizations* (p. 3). Washington, DC: U.S. Dept. of the Interior.

Sherbert. (1963). Sherbert v. Verner, 374 U.S. 398, (1963).

Sholom. (2001). Temple B'nai Sholom v. City of Huntsville, et al., CV-01-S-1412-NE.

Siew, W. (19 Nov 1998). New Wilson Bridge set to feature 12 lanes. *Washington Times*, p. A1.

Society. (1980). Society of ethical culture v. Spatt, New York Court of Appeals, 51 N.Y. 2d 449, 415 N.E. 2d 922, 434 N.Y.S. 2d 932.

Sprinkle, J. H. (2001). "A careful inventory and evaluation:" The origins of executive order 11593. *CRM Journal, 8*(1–2), 80–102.

Sprinkle, J. H. (2007). Of exceptional importance, The origins of the "fifty-year rule" in historic preservation. *Public Historian, 29*(2), 81–103.

Smith, L. (27 May 1975). *New model for land use: Development rights transfer as a devide [sic] to preserve open space*. Submitted to Professor Arval A. Morris, University of Washington, 97.

St. Bart. (1990). Rector of St. Bartholomew's Church v. City of New York, 914 F.2d 348, 354-55 (2d Cir.).

STOPP. (2007). H.R. 926: Strengthening the ownership of private property act.

Thomas, D. H. (2001). *Skull wars: Kenniwick man, archaeology, and the battle for Native American identity*. New York: Basic Books.

USC. (1906). 34 Stat. 225, 16 U.S.C., 431–433.

USC. (1966). 16 U.S.C., 470.

USC. (1987). 43 U.S.C., 2101–2106.

Waltman, J. L. (2011). *Religious free exercise and contemporary American Politics. The Saga of the religious land use and Institutionalized Persons Act*. London: Continuum International Publishing Group.

Washington Post. (10 Oct 1979). Cherokees will try to stop Tellico Dam, save burial grounds. *Washington Post*, p. A14.

Watkins, J. (2005). Representing and repatriating the past. In T. R. Pauketat & D. DiPaolo Loren (Eds.), *North American archaeology*. Malden: Blackwell Publishing.

Weitz, J. (1999). From quiet revolution to smart growth: State growth management programs, 1960-1999. *Journal of Planning Literature, 14*(14), 267–333.

Williams. (1899). Attorney General v. Williams, 174 Mass. 476, 55 N.E. 77, Aff.'d.

Williams. (1903). Williams v. Parker, 188 U.S. 491, 47, L. Ed. 2d 559, 23 S. Ct. 440.

Williams, J. (12 Feb 1986). Battle of the Indian heritage: Museum under fire for displaying bones. *Washington Post*.

Williams, Jr. N. (1974–1975). *American Planning Law: Land use and the Police power*. Chicago: Callaghan.

Williams, Jr. N. (1983). *American Planning Law: Land use and the Police power*. Chicago: Callaghan.

Wilson. (1983). Wilson v. Block, 708 F.2n 735, C.A.D.C.

Wylie, J. (1989). *Poletown: Community betrayed*. Urbana: University of Illinois Press.

Zuckert, M. P. (2002). *Launching liberalism: On Lockean political philosophy*. Lawrence: University of Kansas Press.

Changing Our Economic Outlook

4

Introduction

In 1849, a New York State legislative committee argued that the government should purchase Hasbrouck House, George Washington's headquarters in Newburgh. They recognized that the property was "associated ... with many delightful reminiscences with our early history and if the visitor has an American heart in his bosom, he will feel himself a better man [and] his patriotism will kindle with deeper emotion ..." (Caldwell 1887).

Today the rhetoric for preservation is often less florid and more economically pragmatic. Preservationists' growing awareness of the relationships between local activities and regional, countrywide, and global changes provides better guidance for the future of the existing built environment. Broadly defined, economics is the study of the appropriation of goods and services for the satisfaction of human wants. With this in mind, preservation economics examines how needs and wants relate to, and are influenced by, the activities in and around historic properties.

To demonstrate the power of preservation economics, this chapter begins by examining the broad macro influences in the social character of the country, linking demographic and economic changes to current and future property uses. Regional strengths and weaknesses demonstrate how population shifts provide the character of areas, many of which were once agricultural in a nation built on industrial expansion and, recently, more dependent on the service sector. These factors and the changing nature of the population's age, race, and ethnicity begin to suggest future challenges and opportunities.

Preservation economics also challenges the idea that an "obsolete" property needs to be demolished. The reality is that such sites are more accurately described as suffering from inattention, physical deterioration, functional inadequacy, dislocation, or social and aesthetic unacceptability. None of these characteristics presents insurmountable problems; all can be remedied cost effectively. Mindful of the continued desire for a wide range of existing property types that meet a broad range of human needs, the arguments for continued reuse are made even clearer by considering local job creation, and the energy, time, and materials saved in reusing historic properties (Kula 1998).[1] The public costs of abandonment and demolition are cause for serious concern. A vast amount of infrastructure already exists that can be better utilized to meet our needs, in effect minimizing the use of landfills and mitigate the need for ecological remediation.

The chapter then explains how the various players in the real estate industry regard property to help preservationists understand the differences in assumptions about potential uses. For example, real estate agents often differ in their views from real estate investors, and they both

---

[1] Chapter 7 deals more with these issues.

M. A. Tomlan, *Historic Preservation*, DOI 10.1007/978-3-319-04975-5_4,
© Springer International Publishing Switzerland 2015

can differ from the ideas held by lenders. In all this, the manner in which monetary value is assigned to property in marketing and appraising is key to seeing the limits often set by lenders and government agencies charged with fiscal oversight. The techniques are far from scientific or accurate, however. Because historic properties continue to defy easy classification, it often takes time to create an appropriate package in a particular economic context.

With greater understanding, it is possible to see that several alternatives exist. Some solutions are programmatic, following a pattern. The most celebrated is the Main Street initiative sponsored by the National Trust for Historic Preservation. This private sector program, repeatedly adjusted and applied in thousands of locations, stands as the most successful path for those involved in continuing commercial property use. Housing revitalization is also central to this discussion. As the amount of money in government programs available for low and moderate-income housing has declined, the use of indirect financing has increased, largely with tax credits.

Regional preservation programs also spur economic development. With the leadership of the National Park Service (NPS), the National Heritage Areas attempt to link federal, state, and local governmental partnerships, again with private sector assistance. These regional historical concepts extend over more than one existing political and governmental boundary, and draw on working relationships with businesses and nonprofit organizations to spur change. Heritage tourism is also very important. An examination of the number of visitors to museums, historic and archaeologically significant sites, battlefields, cemeteries, memorials, entertainment venues, reenactment sites, and religiously important locations underscores their economic impact.

All of these initiatives lead to the concluding section in which the multiplier effects of heritage work are considered. When one preservation project begins, others follow, often with direct linkages. Hence, by becoming aware of the economics at work, a variety of exciting options becomes evident.

Table 4.1 Growth of the regions of the USA

Region	1900 (%)	1950 (%)	2000 (%)	2010 (%)
Northeast	27.7	26.2	19.0	17.0
Midwest	34.7	29.5	22.9	21.7
South	32.3	31.3	35.6	37.1
West	5.4	13.0	22.5	23.3

Macro Influences

The standard economics textbook defines macro influences as employment, money, and interest. These factors, elements of theories meant to explain why the Great Depression occurred, are now regarded as only a few features in a much more complex picture. In this text, macro influences are the broad demographic and social changes that control the demand for all types of goods and services. This discussion is an important starting point because it places regional and municipal-level influences in a broader context.

The United States has grown rapidly in population, almost doubling in size every half century, or at about 9.7 % between 2000 and 2010. A considerable amount of this growth is due to immigration, as the birthrate after the World War II "baby boom" has remained relatively stable (Census 2009).[2]

With the widespread adoption of automobiles for passenger travel and trucks for freight transportation, in the latter half of the twentieth century the population began to shift from the Northeast and Midwest to the South and West. The 2010 Census is the first to show the West as more populous than the Midwest. Hence, the existing infrastructure of certain areas of the country—the water supply, sewers, roads, and electrical service need to facilitate the creation of goods and provide services—is larger than is needed in some areas, while it strains to meet demands in other locations (Table 4.1).

California and Texas have become the most populous states (numbers one and two in the

---

[2] The tables in this chapter rely on federal census statistics taken from several categories.

Table 4.2 The relative rank in population of selected states

State	1900	1950	2000	2010
Arizona	48	38	20	16
California	21	2	1	1
Florida	33	20	4	4
Iowa	10	22	30	30
Missouri	5	11	17	18
New York	1	1	3	3
Pennsylvania	2	3	6	6
Texas	6	6	2	2

table above), part of the Sunbelt expansion that stands in stark contrast to the shrinking or static Snowbelt states. In time, Florida may become more populous than New York, further reflecting the growth of the South. Table 4.2 highlights these changes by providing selected states, listed on the left, with their relative rank in population during the census years provided.

Along with the demographic changes, there are major economic shifts. The early American Republic was primarily an agrarian nation. During the nineteenth century, the majority of the people in the country made their living by taking part in agriculture, food product manufacturing, and food distribution, peaking in the early twentieth century. During the Depression and World War II, the decline in farm population began. Farming and ranching has become more efficient. As Table 4.3 demonstrates, today the number of people directly involved in growing crops and raising animals is less than 2 % of the population.[3] The depopulation of the center of the country has left some agricultural properties underutilized and many once-prosperous farming centers all but completely abandoned.

In the late nineteenth and early twentieth centuries, the United States became an industrial power with unmatched manufacturing capacity, particularly on the East and West Coasts and in the Great Lakes. Almost everything was "Made

in USA." By contrast, in the late twentieth and early twenty-first centuries, manufacturing has provided less employment, leaving many industrial properties underutilized. Meanwhile, the service sector is making an increasingly important contribution. Table 4.4 demonstrates the number and the percentage of jobs in producing goods and providing services. Today, the most important aspects of the American economy includes: banking, financial management, real estate, retail and wholesale sales, health care, transportation, education, travel, entertainment, personal and professional services, and religion. These economic activities are important to remember when attempting to find new uses for all existing properties.

Regional differences are also apparent by their traditional strengths and the current employment activities. Gross economic base studies often forecast population growth by determining "basic employment," examining the condition of export and nonexporting companies. However, much of the theory relies upon empirical evidence collected when the country was an industrial giant, exporting manufactured goods. Today, suburban centers provide the majority of the services for the surrounding areas.

Some communities continue to specialize in one or two economic activities, and allow all other activities to follow. For example, a former industrial city might also depend on a state university or a small college, assuming that the economic outlook will remain relatively unchanged. That city could be more proactive and convert the outdated and underutilized factories to other uses, perhaps including facilities for retirement, recreation, and additional transportation services that is important to tourism. This does not mean that a single, predominant activity cannot serve as the lynchpin of economic development. Some of the most successful communities are rooted in providing medical services, such as Rochester, Minnesota, the home of the Mayo Clinic. Hotels and restaurants in the area rely for their income on the number of patients and visitors to patients. Looking ahead, however, preservationists must become more knowledgeable about job training so that cities can successfully adjust what goods

---

[3] The exact number of people involved is a matter of discussion because the number of migrant workers is difficult to determine and the variation in who is employed solely in agricultural labor as opposed to other forms of income-income producing activities.

Table 4.3 Agricultural activity in the USA (in thousands)

	1900	1930	1950	1970	2000	2010
Number of farms	5740	6295	5388	2954	2150	2201
Farm population	29,875	30,529	23,048	9712	–	–
Farm population as percent of the total population	42	25	15	5	–	–
Agricultural workers	–	10,340	7160	3642	2464	2634
Nonagricultural workers	–	–	45,355	69,491	125,114	129,874

Table 4.4 Recent employment trends in goods and services (in millions)

	1960	1970	1980	1990	2000	2010
Goods producing jobs	19.2	22.1	24.3	23.7	24.6	17.8
Percentage of all jobs	35.3	31.1	26.9	21.6	18.7	13.7
Services producing jobs	35.1	48.8	66.3	85.8	107.1	112.1
Percentage of all jobs	64.6	68.7	73.3	78.4	81.3	86.2
All nonagricultural jobs	54.3	71.0	90.5	109.5	131.9	129.9
Percentage of all jobs	100.0	100.0	100.0	100.0	100.0	100.0

Table 4.5 Percentage of the US population by location

	1900	1950	2000	2010
Nonmetropolitan	71.6	43.9	19.3	16.3
Metropolitan	28.4	56.1	80.3	83.7
Central cities	21.2	32.8	30.3	32.6
Suburbs	7.2	23.3	50.0	51.1
Total	100.0	100.0	100.0	100.0

Table 4.6 Cities with significant losses and gains (in thousands)

Significant loss or gain	1950	2010	Change	Change (%)
Buffalo	580	261	−319	−55
Cleveland	915	397	−518	−57
Detroit	1850	714	−1136	−61
St. Louis	857	319	−538	−62
Albuquerque	97	546	+949	+463
Denver	416	600	+184	+44
Las Vegas	25	584	559	+2236
Phoenix	107	144	+1339	+1251

and services they offer, thereby facilitating the adaptation of properties.

The need to diversify and rediversify links changes to where people are located. Table 4.5 demonstrates how the population has shifted from rural areas to metropolitan regions, with the lion's share of metropolitan growth occurring in suburbs as opposed to the cities. Although the 2010 census showed 51 % of Americans live in the suburbs, they have been the center of the economic growth for decades. Throughout the United States, the growing suburban population has fueled the increasing importance of county governments in all areas of civic affairs.

Although cities as a group have slipped in relative economic importance, considerable differences exist between them. In some locations, such as San Francisco and New York, the percentage change in population over time has been relatively modest, at 4 and 6 % respectively, from 1950 to the present. In other cases, remarkable changes have taken place. The population of St.

Louis and some of the former industrial giants of the Great Lakes has significantly decreased, which has caused them to appear overbuilt and to suffer from property devaluation. Still other cities have been able to maintain or increase their population, generally with new immigrants from Mexico, Central and South America, and South and East Asia. The formerly lily-white Midwest and once "black and white" South are becoming the home to foreign-born Central and South Americans. Whereas in previous decades, European immigrants would first find employment in agriculture and industry, today a wide variety of new Americans are more often found working in the service sector (Massey 2008; Table 4.6).

In addition to changes in the large cities, most of which are watched closely by state legislatures,

Table 4.7 The US population: Age and household composition

	1900	1950	2000	2010
Median age	22.9	30.2	35.3	37.2
Persons 65+ (%)	4.1	8.1	12.4	13.0
Households 65+ (%)	–	15.2	21.0	24.9
Sex ratio (males/100 females)	104.4	98.6	96.3	96.9
Average household size	–	3.38	2.59	2.58
Percent of 1-person households	–	9.3	25.8	26.7
Percent of family households	–	84.9	68.1	66.4
Percent of nonfamily households	–	10.6	31.9	33.6

Table 4.8 Changing racial and ethnic character

	1900	1980	2000	2010
White (including Hispanic) (%)	87.9	83.1	75.2	72.4
Black (%)	11.6	11.7	12.3	12.6
Other (%)	0.5	5.2	12.5	15.0
Hispanic alone (%)	–	6.4	12.5	16.3
White (excluding Hispanic) (%)	–	76.7	62.7	63.7

it is important to emphasize that small cities also matter. Second-tier cities often suffer more rapid expansion and contraction than larger cities. In several areas of the country, what were once suburbs have become cities, and the growth at transportation nodes has spurred suburban business complexes, which has encouraged high-density housing, and replanning in the public and private sectors.

Other population characteristics, such as age, sex, and household composition, are also changing. The population is aging, a feature of the post-World War II baby boom that will continue to define the country in part because, with medical advances, the average life-span is increasing. As shown in Table 4.7, a growing share of single-person households and nontraditional (i.e. nonfamily) households are evident throughout the country. Household size is also declining and the number of single-person households is increasing, notwithstanding the increasing immigrant population. All of this suggests that home remodeling will continue in the near future, and changing social characteristics will continue to spur high demand for appropriate property uses.

The United States is further growing much more diverse with respect to race and ethnicity. Historically, the country's European roots predominated. Changes in recent immigration from

Table 4.9 Percentage of group population in central cities

	1980	2000
White (non-Hispanic)	24.6	22.6
Black	57.2	53.1
Hispanic	48.8	46.6

South and Central American countries, however, is increasing the Hispanic population, superseding the number of residents with African connections. The number of people of Asian descent has also increased. Soon, California will not be the only state in which the White population is in the minority (Table 4.8).

Historically, the minority population in the USA clustered disproportionately in central cities. Recently, an increasing number of recent immigrants are developing enclaves in the suburbs, where the jobs are located, sometimes miles from the traditional city center. This suggests that a broader, regional approach to economic issues is necessary to identify the possibilities for the future of historic properties (Table 4.9).

Because of the decline in the number of farmers and deindustrialization, and other social changes, the residents of many cities and older suburbs, and comparatively distant rural communities in the United States confront economic challenges. The problems are often greater for minorities because of their limited access to financial resources (Table 4.10).

Table 4.10 2000 median US family income by race and location

	Non metropolitan ($)	Metropolitan central city ($)	Metropolitan suburb ($)
All families	41,112	44,743	63,460
White families	42,597	50,173	65,586
Black families	23,861	32,172	47,081

The broad implications of these changes should be clear. Preservationists must be aware that any increase or relocation of the population is a major factor in how property is regarded. A precipitous decline in jobs can trigger a drop in population, which often leads to market devaluation of that area's housing and other properties, including stores, schools, and religious buildings. Property abandonment increases in these cases, and often the decline correlates to a rise in crime and other social problems. Likewise, any dramatic increase in jobs can complicate housing needs, stimulate commercial activity, and put pressure on educational and religious structures.

An increase in population also leads to calls for more effective transportation systems, with considerable investment in infrastructure. In fact, any shift in the routes that people take is important as it will facilitate or retard travel time, affecting property along the way. In addition, the changing nature of society itself in any location will have a profound effect on the possibilities for preservation efforts. As a result, it is essential to look beyond the site, neighborhood, and community to examine the region because people make a crucial difference in determining the future uses of an existing property (MacDonald and Peters 2011).

Micro Analysis, Market Studies, and Appraising

Finding the best new use for an historic property requires a keen understanding of market conditions. When real estate developers are thinking about the possibilities for a particular location, they often ask "what 'product' should I develop in this market?" That is, what kinds of uses should be built so that the property sells quickly and profitably? Some developers prefer to build housing, while others prefer to construct commercial structures. Others specialize in providing other kinds of property, often termed real estate "assets." Preservationists should follow the same thinking, involving a "micro-analysis," in order to discuss the possibilities with realtors, brokers, and lenders in their own language.

In some respects, everyone begins with the laws of "supply and demand." The "market" is where buyers and sellers of property meet to bargain and exchange items of value at negotiated prices. The total quantity that sellers are willing to sell is called the "supply," while the total quantity of anything buyers are willing to purchase is the "demand."[4] The law of supply indicates that producers will offer more products as the sales price increases, and fewer if the prices decrease. Hence, if the developer finds the sale of housing increasing, it is natural to see a widespread urge to create more housing of similar nature. Anticipated profit is a very strong motivation for redevelopment.

The law of demand stipulates that the lower the price, the more consumers will purchase, or, that higher prices will dampen consumer demand. In short, the price of real estate correlates to the assumed consumer demand. Shifts in demand are the result of a number of factors, including an increase or decrease in population, variation in income levels, changes in consumer taste, the amount of credit available, and the effects of advertising. In housing, the perception of a particularly good or poor school nearby will also influence demand, sometimes raising or lowering the price of a property by several thousand dollars. In commercial real estate, access to good transportation routes is among the

---

[4] The introduction and development of advanced degrees in real estate since the mid-1980s has led to an increasing number of specialized texts dealing with real estate "markets," in residential, office, retail, and industrial construction.

most important features. Information is available about the current possibilities for sale by using a wide range of demographic information, searching especially for "niche" markets that have yet to be addressed or fulfilled.

Real estate investors hope to capitalize on social and economic changes in a particular location to make a profit. In the same fashion, preservationists need to be aware of factors in their neighborhoods that could attract outside investment that is either consistent with, or harmful to, the community's overall goals and aspirations. Some of the most common indicators of real estate activity include the number of deeds recorded in the current month compared to the previous month and the same month in a previous year; the number of mortgages recorded; the trend in rent levels; the trends in construction costs; the number of vacancies; and the number of subdivisions being approved.

Because the best use of a property is the one for which it was originally designed, and the majority of the built environment is dedicated to housing, preservationists often find themselves studying the possibility of residential rehabilitation. To facilitate this, a housing marketing study will includes several factors that affect new housing supply, including the number of conversions and the number of demolitions. By contrast, commercial and industrial projects require review of a different set of factors. In studying commercial retail use, location is closely associated with automobile transportation routes, whereas the prospects for a wholesale warehouse would require truck, rail, and airport access. These market studies often take longer to assemble because they also reflect business cycles that, in turn, involve leases and extensive property management and security (McCoy 2008).

Religious sites are another class of properties that deserve special attention. Places of worship, whether they are forests, fields, or mountain tops, or whether they are meeting houses, churches, mosques, temples or synagogues, all have special characteristics. Some properties are designed for preaching or teaching, while others are primarily dedicated to meditation. In addition, auxiliary functions dedicated to food programs, medical care, retail sales, or broadcasting all require a careful understanding of the local, national, and international contexts. Unfortunately, because most of these properties are not large moneymakers, many members of the real estate industry ignore these remarkably important features of social, economic, and cultural life (Aaron and Wright 1997).[5]

Regardless of the location or intended use, no two properties are identical, which leads to the need for appraisals. Standardized appraisal methods became more commonplace in the late nineteenth century and early twentieth century (Moore 2009), as insurance companies, financial institutions, and local governments came to depend on a common standard for valuation or needed a basis for comparing one property to another to be able to levy taxes. Determining the best manner of appraising land and improvements was an area of almost continuous discussion, especially during the Depression (Hurd 1903; Fisher 1906; Zangerle 1924).

Appraisers generally use three methods to determine a residence's worth (Pagourtzi et al. 2004). The most common approach is by locating "comparable" properties or "comps" with like features that have sold recently, and adjusting the value of the subject property based on such differences as age, size, and location. Single-family residences are often appraised in this fashion.

Another method, often used for insurance purposes, attempts to compute what it would cost to replace or reproduce the home. Most homes are insured for replacement costs; that is, what would be spent to rebuild the home with comparable, but not necessarily the same, materials. For example, the residence of a Revolutionary War hero may be a one-of-a-kind home, and could be appraised and insured for the cost of creating a reproduction using similar materials and craftsmanship. Producing an exact replica, however, might be three times the cost of replacement. By the comparison of these approaches—finding the comparable market value, or determining the replacement or reproduction cost—it is clear that

---

[5] For a more thorough discussion of the changing nature for worship, see Chapter 8.

the viewpoint the appraiser adopts makes a considerable difference.

Another technique is to determine the value of a property by what the owner can charge in rental income. Although this approach is not helpful when determining the value of a single-family house, where no income is expected, it is preferred when dealing with real estate viewed as a business investment. This method divides the anticipated net operating income (NOI) by the rate of return for similar properties. If a property is expected to earn $100,000 per year in an area where the capitalization (or "cap" rate) is 10%, the appraiser would determine it would be worth $1,000,000 (Pagourtzi et al. 2004).

These techniques are widely accepted by banks, the financial services industry, and government regulators, influencing the cash value assigned to a property. It is important to bear in mind, however, that the intangible values of the site are rarely equivalent to any precise cash amount. It would be impossible to put a value on a "traditional home" held in the family for generations by comparison to a new house of the same size, or the rent that house might provide.

Although opinion polls show that the vast majority of people associate positive values with the historic environment and some buyers recognize the special character of a specific property, the amount the buyer will pay often remains an open question. Contingent valuation methods, which measure the potential consumer's stated willingness to pay more than "normal" for an historic or aesthetically striking property, are of limited help in providing an alternative perspective.

Another approach has arisen in the last few decades, as more research has led to the development of hedonic methods in pricing housing. Just as noise, pollution, and poor water quality negatively affect property value, so it is possible to evaluate the positive contributions to a home-buyer's view of a property with farmland, trees, and streams (Baranzini et al. 2010). Hedonic methods have begun to be accepted among appraisers, especially those who are familiar with the latest computer software. This technique can be used when examining the effects of historic preservation designation on residential property

(Clark and Herrin 1997), and a knowledgeable appraiser will consider all of these approaches and factors before "reconciling" an estimate.

The Price We Pay for Accepting the Term "Obsolescent"

Having briefly considered the manner in which the population of the country is changing and the various methods by which those involved in real estate transactions rationalize the cash value of a particular property when offering it for sale, it is appropriate to consider one of the most broadly held real estate preconceptions. The most common complaint leveled against old properties is that they are "obsolete" and "out of date." But just what *is* meant by these words? Obsolescence is generally defined by an implied comparison between existing conditions and the goals and aspirations of an occupant, resident, visitor, or professional. Ironically, almost the minute a new property is completed and put into service, it becomes "out of date" in comparison to new properties being built around it. Much of this comparison is fueled by advertising and perceptions, influenced by the fashions of the day. Often the comparison is not made by examining the facts, or a change in the property.

Obsolescence is one of four characteristics real estate agents and developers associate with an existing property:

1. As suggested in the previous section, transportation changes in the vicinity of a property often affect its relative value as a prime location. Introducing new forms of transport often affect the desirability of a property. For example, a new airport access road may create opportunities for existing properties. On the other hand, enhancing existing roads is often the key to reuse.

2. Functional obsolescence is also due to the expectations of users for more than basic shelter or support provided by the land. Often these expectations take the form of requirements and standards. For buildings, adequate heat, ventilation, light, hot and cold water, electrical service, an elevator, and handicapped

accessibility are common demands. Many properties have seen waves of additions and improvements. The recent reliance upon computer systems and enhanced communication is spurring additional updating. None of these functional needs are impossible to provide and this updating can be done economically with sensitivity to the historic character of a property.

3. Aesthetic and social preferences also spur the perception of obsolescence. Typical views were contained in a 1924 appraisal manual that decried the "profuse scroll work and gaudily detailed porches and cornices" as "no longer in good taste"; exactly the kind of features that would become highly desirable 50 years later (Zangerle 1924, p. 224). Advertising and marketing expected to emphasize a new or novel appearance. Likewise, real estate and financial professionals expect the consumer will be willing to pay a premium for the latest fashion. Conversely, some buyers are interested in the "tried and true," and the aesthetic of a previous age may be important to these buyers.

4. Economic obsolescence is further encouraged by the tax codes, where the expense of new buildings and equipment are deducted or "written off" against the taxes owed. Even here, however, the tide is changing, as changes in the tax code are increasing its flexibility at the federal and state level, acknowledging that the original "one size fits all" approach is not suitable for all properties.

Understanding that there is no reliable mathematical formula that can describe the relationships of these kinds of obsolescence, preservationists must be aware of how to link various new uses—for housing, commercial, industrial, religious, educational, and recreational—with existing properties. The idea that properties experience an inevitable "life cycle" of birth, middle age, and death is often a naïve attempt to justify unproven assumptions. The concept gained credence in the Depression in the activities associated with the Homeowners' Loan Corporation real estate valuation maps, and it was carried forward by planners and government officials who believed that straight-line population projections should be linked to property values in order to estimate public investment potential (Hillier 2005). Later, the concept of accelerated depreciation carried another host of implications for development (Hanchett 1996).

Approaches to Reclaiming Property

With an increased ability to look beyond traditional approaches, it is much easier to view an existing property as an asset rather than a liability. In addition to providing the property owner with an opportunity to make money, renewing and reclaiming the site is essential to the financial health of the community. This is because one of the fundamental functions of government is to raise revenue in order to finance public improvements. City, town, and state governments depend upon two principal sources of revenue to conduct their affairs: sales taxes and property taxes. An underutilized commercial or industrial building that is experiencing a drop in sales will experience a corresponding sales taxes decline. This shifts the burden for supporting a government's functions to tax revenue by property owners. Moreover, when residential, commercial, and industrial properties go underutilized or remain vacant for a number of years, the property values inevitably decrease, as do the property taxes that are collected. Hence, preservation embraces the idea that marketing the products and services of an existing business is crucial to the degree that it is compatible with the neighborhood and local needs.

In many cases, the failure to pay taxes leads to the public acquisition of parcels by the municipality. "Surplus" property inventory maintenance, control, and disposition is an on-going public responsibility that affects almost all cities and requires pro-active local governmental initiative (Burchell and Listokin 1981). In the District of Columbia, for example, the "Home Again" program introduced by Mayor Anthony Williams in 2002 attempts to transfer vacant and abandoned residential properties to single-family ownership in neighborhoods like Columbia Heights, Ivy City/Trinidad, and Shaw/Ledroit

Park (Stewart 2006; Combal 2007). In addition, in a number of communities around the country, "sweat equity" programs provide new residents with an opportunity to reclaim an abandoned house, and, by using their labor to rehabilitate it, eventually attain ownership.

The idea of "land banking" undervalued properties has gained considerable attention in recent years. A property seized by or donated to the municipality for back taxes is renovated with the idea that it can then be sold at a modest profit.[6] Land banking of this kind is largely for housing rehabilitation, making use of a variety of funding streams. It involves a streamlined eminent domain procedure, coordination with all city agencies, and often includes agreements with nonprofit organizations to facilitate portions of the work. New York, Cleveland, Atlanta, Baltimore, Philadelphia, St. Louis, and Portland all have viable programs, some having begun in the early 1970s (O'Brien and Toth 2005; Klein 2011). A broader approach is possible as well: In 2011, the governor of the State of New York announced the creation of 10 new regional land banks under the administration of the state development corporation (ESD 2011; Simpson 2012).

Some under utilized properties are easy to reclaim, while others require more analysis. Bridges, railroad lines, military property, state insane asylums, and contaminated waterfront structures often fall outside the real property inventory of local governments, in the hands of state and federal agencies. As shown in subsequent chapters, revitalizing large cultural landscapes that cross several governmental boundaries and involving dozens of owners, leases, tenants, and visitors often require extensive negotiations. Saving these properties may entail working with people using several languages and across several disciplines to build a constituency. Because these unique historic properties are valuable for more than their market price to more than one constituency or user group, they are often less likely than

newer structures to be abandoned when inflation costs rise, or mortgage rates fluctuate.

Perhaps just as important to note is that existing structures and landscapes contain a tremendous amount of "embodied energy" that might otherwise be shipped to the landfill or destroyed. Stone requires a considerable amount of energy to quarry, dress, and transport; brick requires tempering and working the clay, burning fuel and transporting it to the site; wooden elements are cut from logs, shaped, and installed. All of the energy has a present and future value. With thick, solid walls and high ceilings, the thermal mass and air volumes of an historic structure can be more energy efficient and comfortable than similar mass and space in contemporary construction. Likewise, the shelter and sustenance provided by existing trees and plants are valuable features to protect. By reusing existing structures and landscapes we reduce the cost of demolition, the transportation of debris, and the amount of waste storage, affecting not only the bottom line for the property owner, but also the costs borne by local government (Stein et al. 1981).

Advocates for environmentally sound new construction may insist that older properties are not as energy efficient. However, even if a new structure is designed to be "green," the embodied energy in an existing building will often more than offset any immediate gains to be made in the near future by an "energy-efficient" alternative. If the designers consider the total cost of energy-intensive building materials like aluminum and plastics, often local, natural materials are more economical. In short, the "greenest" building is often the one that already exists.[7]

Preservation-Related Construction Provides Jobs

Although the statistics commonly reported about the construction industry in the United States continue to emphasize the production of new

---

[6] In principle, this is similar to the process used to purchase a large inexpensive parcel of unimproved land and ready it for development by gaining permission to subdivide it into lots, offered for sale at an increased price (Flechner 1974).

[7] Further critical discussion of the Leadership in Energy & Environmental Design (LEED) criteria is provided in Chapter 6.

buildings, rehabilitation is an important component of the economy. Preservation provides a significant number of jobs, in some cities constituting about 40 % of all the construction activity reported by architects (Opperman 2008). In 1994, new construction amounted to $167 billion. In the same year, which is the last year for which census statistics are available, $44 billion was spent in rehabilitation, defined as all "permitted" additions, alterations, and improvements.[8] This shows that rehabilitation accounted for slightly more than one fifth of the officially recorded construction activity.

Yet, architectural work and census statistics grossly underestimate the economic contribution made by preservation because billions of dollars go unrecorded in minor housing renovation. This work is not monitored by any government agency; most is simply "home improvement," a level of work that does not require public safety review. Material and time involved in these projects fall well below the dollar threshold that requires residents or their contractors to secure a building permit. In addition, the activity of the "handyman" who makes home repairs at a reduced cost if he is paid in cash often goes unreported. In the mid-1980s, home repairs accounted for over $12 billion of the total estimated "informal economy," easily outranking food sales and childcare (Smith 1987).

As might be expected, rehabilitation is more evident in the areas in the United States with older properties. In the entire Northeast and Midwest, the expenses associated with renovation in 1994 were 31% and 22%, respectively, of the total amount in new construction. By comparison, renovation compared to total construction spending was 17% and 20 % in the South and West, respectively. These percentages are changing very rapidly, however, because the average age of all of the built fabric in the country is getting older, and the population shift to the South and West is increasing the amount of renovation and rehabilitation.

In the same fashion, in metropolitan areas with older structures, renovation is very significant. From 1990 to 1994, rehabilitation activity represented 50 % or more of the total construction in major cities like Atlanta, Baltimore, Boston, Chicago, Cleveland, Denver, Philadelphia, and San Francisco.

As might be expected, historic preservationists often take the lead in promoting appropriate roofing and siding materials, and wooden trim and window sash. These activities stimulate small businesses and some large product manufacturers to respond to the redeveloped market for traditional materials, such as historic paint colors. Many of these initiatives have created new jobs or sustained existing positions in ongoing businesses, while others have provided employment in relatively depressed areas. Because rehabilitation often involves a wider range of custom-crafts, skills, and materials than those required for new construction, a trades' worker is more highly valued. This labor-intensity promotes the economic viability of the traditional work patterns and preserves trade practices.[9]

Commercial Revitalization

The commercial activity around us often contains homogenized retail businesses, malls, and office parks; older downtowns; and near suburbs. Each has their own unique, compact assemblage of buildings and functions. These provide natural assets that can be featured by communities trying to bolster their economies. As noted in Chapter 2, downtown revitalization is the centerpiece of the widely recognized National Trust for Historic Preservation's Main Street Program. No other initiative in historic preservation in the United States has had a more lasting or more pervasive influence than this program, and none so successfully used in other countries.

The impetus for this program originated in the Midwestern United States. Shopping centers and malls seemed to draw all of the customers to the suburbs. With the firm belief that

---

[8] This discussion is derived from the statistics in the US Census, which does not define rehabilitation work, nor does it track rehabilitation as "certified" or reviewed by any federal, state, or local historic preservation agency, and thus might be more appropriately termed renovation.

[9] As mentioned in Chapter 2, the trend began in the 1970s.

Fig. 4.1 Market Street in Corning, NY, faced the tremendous challenge of rebuilding its businesses after a flood caused by Hurricane Agnes. It provided the most viable means for partnering local initiatives at the time, and proved to be an inspiration for the National Trust's Main Street program. (Author's photograph)

another alternative had to be developed, Mary Means, then the director of the Chicago office of the National Trust for Historic Preservation, began to examine the techniques used in urban renewal programs for rehabilitating stores and shops in the traditional downtown business districts. Most of the examples were inappropriate in size and scale, and few of the people involved were members of the business community. The most celebrated example at the time was the program begun in Corning, New York (Fig. 4.1). Like many small industrial towns, Corning had boomed in the late nineteenth through the mid-twentieth century. Then, with the opening of a local four-lane bypass, suburbanization accelerated and the principal shopping streets in the central business district faced decline. This was so severe that the local government and concerned citizens embraced urban renewal and demolished commercial blocks, in part to create more parking and compete with the regional mall (Campbell 1995). In a story typical of the period, hope for the future was pinned on a new civic center and library, making use of federal funds. Eventually, a new city hall, library, and apartments rose on the cleared land.

A reaction began in 1964 when a local group formed, dubbing itself "Care about Corning." Mrs. Gene Wozinski led the public awareness campaign, and Paul Perrot, director of the Corning Museum of Glass and chair of the Area Beautification Committee of the Chamber of Commerce, worked together to provide a positive alternative. They pushed for a preservation scheme for the main commercial area centered on Market Street, focusing on façade rehabilitation. The Chamber of Commerce launched a "facades program" in cooperation with merchants in 1970, but it met with lukewarm interest, as the city continued to be preoccupied with rebuilding in the urban renewal area. Against this tide, Thomas Buechner, head of the Corning Foundation, provided strong leadership by convincing the city and merchants of the value of a Market Street Restoration program. As a result, when a disastrous flood caused by Hurricane Agnes occurred in June 1972, revitalization plans were already afoot. Following the ideas presented by the architectural firm of John Milner in 1973, the Corning Foundation backed the creation of the Market Street Restoration Agency to specialize in façade and streetscape improvements, marketing and promotion, and new business recruitment. Norman Mintz, the program's first director, was deeply committed to making design improvements that would help characterize the special nature of the place, and he provided design guidelines more in keeping with the original character of the city.[10]

With the Market Street Restoration Agency as a leading example, in 1977 Mary Means

---

[10] The politics of creating guidelines for historic districts and overlay zones is discussed further in Chapters 6 and 7.

Fig. 4.2 Mary Means, the creator of the Main Street Program, developed the most successful initiative that the National Trust for Historic Preservation has ever offered, applicable in thousands of communities in this country and abroad. (Photograph, author's collection)

embarked on a campaign to reinvigorate traditional downtowns in similar small communities in the Midwest (Fig. 4.2). The pilot programs in Galesburg, Illinois; Madison, Indiana; and Hot Springs, South Dakota became examples (Skelcher 1990; Gerloff 1995). The National Trust paid for the director in each town. Each leader had the responsibility of building private sector financial support for a wide range of promotional activities. These activities became the four-point Main Street approach: organization, promotion, design, and economic restructuring. Building on the experience of the three-pilot programs, the approach demands that community leaders, building owners, business owners, and residents are involved from the outset. In addition, eight principles guide the activities. Each program must be comprehensive, incremental, committed to

self-help, involve private-public partnerships, aware of existing assets to capitalize upon them, high quality, unafraid of change, and action oriented (Smith 1995). The experiences of the program managers provided continuous feedback and allowed the Main Street specialists to develop an extremely successful training program.

Recognizing the potential for a nationwide program with similar goals, Means moved to Washington to head the Trust's National Main Street Center in 1980. Work began toward establishing a network of state programs. Soon, of 38 applicants, eight were chosen.[11] Each of these state programs was required to choose five communities to form their network. Support from Washington for a trial period of three years ensured a strong start. Generally, these statewide networks were housed in departments of commerce or tourism; rarely were they tied directly to the state historic preservation offices. One of the highpoints of the Center's efforts occurred in 1984, when satellite hookups beamed interactive programming to 21,000 people in over 400 city halls and villages (Hoffman 1989; Joynt 1989). As the Main Street programs expanded, they began to play an important role in Sunbelt locations. One of the largest is in Texas, where over 100 cities have participated. Florida has witnessed a growth spurt from 35 Main Street communities in 1995 to more than 60 twelve years later (*USFNS* 2009).[12]

Despite its age, the Main Street program has not been static. While the original program was designed for small communities of generally under 50,000 people, it was determined that great gains could be made in cities of larger size. The National Trust's Washington staff launched an Urban Demonstration Project in 1985 in which four cities with a population under 250,000 were selected based on their commercial downtown core, and four cities with a population over 250,000 were chosen for their neighborhood commercial centers (Dane 1988). This, in turn,

---

[11] These included Colorado, Georgia, North Carolina, Pennsylvania, Massachusetts, and Texas.

[12] Florida's Main Street Program benefits from the Secretary's office by announcements tied to a monthly competition.

led to the first urban Main Street program, officially launched in Boston in 1995, a network of 19 neighborhood business districts. Many of these minor commercial centers are at the core of former trolley car suburbs, facilitating more pedestrian travel and alternative means of transportation to the automobile. San Diego, Chicago, and Baltimore have developed citywide programs, and plans are under development in several other cities (Kemp 2000).

The economic activity of these programs continues to make a considerable difference. Over 1500 communities in 43 states and Puerto Rico have adopted the Main Street model.

Providing Assistance in Housing Rehabilitation

Traditional commercial business districts are important, but so too are the neighborhoods that support them. The original goals of the federal urban development program were to provide decent housing, stimulate construction, and improve the economy.[13] After World War II, the federal government expanded its production and ownership of public housing, providing money to local authorities for slum clearance, expecting local housing authorities to take up the planning, building and maintenance of the then-new facilities, and renting the units to the poor. When these approaches became too expensive, too socially objectionable, and too destructive, the focus shifted from clearance to rehabilitation. The cessation of demolition in urban renewal projects sponsored by the US Department of Housing and Urban Development (HUD) allowed for the growth of urban neighborhood conservation. Programs offered limited funding and technical assistance to communities that wished to establish their own nonprofit, tax-exempt housing

services programs (URTF 1976). House-recycling programs, mini-home repair and rehabilitation services, and energy conservation measures targeted homeowners, as HUD shifted away from the construction of new rental housing aimed at low-income residents. The local approach to housing rehabilitation was the celebrated Pittsburgh Neighborhood Housing Services (PNHS), Inc., seen as the model for future groups. Between 1972 and 1974 the number of neighborhood housing services programs grew, with several developing under the umbrella of the Urban Reinvestment Task Force

In 1974, the Housing and Community Development Act consolidated its existing programs and began new initiatives. The goals of community development included: (1) eliminating slums and blight and preventing the deterioration of property; (2) eliminating conditions which are detrimental to health, safety, and public welfare; (3) conserving and expanding the Nation's housing stock; (4) expanding and improving the quality and quantity of public services; (5) achieving better use of land and other natural resources; (6) increasing the diversity and vitality of neighborhoods; and (7) restoring and preserving urban property of special value for historic, architectural or aesthetic reasons (USC 1974).

Local governments that participated in the block grant program undertook hundreds of thousands of preservation projects with this funding. Even with this financial assistance, however, residents often found it difficult to participate. By the mid-1980s, the declining direct government support for housing led to discussion about the need to increase privatization of nonprofit organizations' financing and the possibility of completely privatizing formerly public multifamily housing properties (Listokin et al. 1985).

The shift away from direct federal government support in providing more housing for the poor and toward insisting on more private sector support first became apparent in the 1970s. In an attempt to stop banks from discriminating against ethnic minorities and the poor due to the assumptions of poor credit risk, in 1977 Congress passed the Community Reinvestment Act (CRA). It declared that banks had a responsibility to meet the

---

[13] The 1934 National Housing Act created the Federal Housing Administration, allowing the government to underwrite and insure mortgages, and the 1937 Public Housing (Wagner-Steagall) Act involved the federal government in funding, building, and renting public housing to the poor (Radford 1996).

needs of the entire community, including the low and moderate-income residents in their service area.[14] Although this technique did spur some projects, progress was slow, particularly in documenting these activities.

In late 1993, low-income activists issued draft proposals to give CRA sharper teeth. Eugene Ludwig, Comptroller of the Currency, spearheaded the move to look closer at bank loans and leave behind the other services provided, such as ATMs, focusing on the loan to deposit ratio in certain low-income areas. The problem the Federal Reserve Bank reviewers encountered is that local banks might offer to make loans but in some areas the demand was weak or nonexistent (Hossain 2004; *Economist* 1993).[15]

Providing more funding was not the only problem, however, because many residents and their community development organizations lacked the financial expertise to assist the people in their neighborhoods. Following the leadership of the Local Initiatives Support Corporation (LISC), announced in 1980, a growing number of community development financial institutions were created to combine foundation support with assistance from corporations, and raise funds using federal and state tax legislation in a much more entrepreneurial spirit.[16]

At the same time, the federal government prepared to sell an increasing number of public housing projects, originally constructed for veterans returning from World War II, to local residential management corporations.[17] The Urban Revitalization Demonstration Act of 1993 retooled the earlier iterations of the "Housing Opportunities for People Everywhere" (HOPE) program, to form the largest intervention by the government in more than a quarter century by simultaneously spurring integration, income mixing, social service delivery, and good design. The latest iteration, HOPE VI, arose from a 1989 Congressional committee investigation intended to eliminate "distressed" housing by the year 2000. The areas targeted are characterized by entrenched crime, poverty, unemployment, and social dependency (Cisneros and Engdahl 2009). In 1992, Congress funded $5 billion in urban revitalization projects. A variety of grants support selective demolition, planning, revitalization, and main street intervention, so that administrators proudly claim to have initiated over 250 developments in the first seven years. Most of the schemes convert distressed public housing into mixed-income communities by demolishing high-rise towers and replacing them with low-rise townhouses or suburban units. The neo-traditional or "New Urbanist" forms and layouts provide some common space with market rate houses, subsidized rental units in town houses, and apartments in multifamily buildings (Popkin et al. 2004).[18] Hence, HOPE VI continues to serve poor residents while also providing market-rate homes for sale.

The HOME Program is a relatively new housing block grant program approved as Title II of in the 1990 Cranston-Gonzales National Affordable Housing Act.[19] It differs from other block grant programs for being devoted exclusively to low- and very low-income communities. Under the HOME initiative, states, counties, and municipalities are the participating jurisdictions that compete under a strict allocation formula for a share of the federal funds, intended to spur acquisition,

---

[14] The principal requirement was that a notice be posted in the lobby of the bank, showing that it complied with the regulations by means of a map showing the local service area being served. Members of the public could also access files with more information about the kinds of CRA services available, which include commentary made by evaluators who point out the positive and negative characteristics of the loans. "Good" banks advertise the results of these evaluations.

[15] Knowing where in the community banks are loaning money for residential loans is a positive step, but there is little comparable data for commercial activities.

[16] In 1991, LISC played an active role in the Rockefeller Foundation led initiative to create the National Community Development Initiative, now called Living Cities.

[17] The Housing and Community Development Act of 1988 spelled out the manner in which the transfers would take place.

[18] New Urbanism will be explained at greater length in Chapter 6.

[19] Also known as the HOME Investment Partnerships Act.

construction, or rehabilitation of rental housing. Over the first 20 years of its history, the program is credited with supporting about a half million affordable housing units. While some communities are providing rent subsidies, others are using a large proportion of the funds for gap financing for first-time homebuyers. Another large portion of the funds is dedicated to home owner renovation projects. Particularly helpful in this regard is the "HOME Program Tune-up Kit," which recognizes the importance of self-help in maintaining existing housing units (ICF 2004; Mallach 2009).

As the amount of federal, state, and local aid for residential programs continues to be strained, the other major financial tool has been to reform the tax codes to stimulate investment credits. This will be explored more thoroughly in the following chapters. In summary, the 1986 Tax Reform Act introduced the Low Income Housing Tax Credit (LIHTC) program, providing investors with a tax credit in return for investing equity in a rental project for low-income residents (Delvac et al. 1996; Escherich et al. 1996; Listokin 1995; Listokin and Listokin 1993). The most significant single program involving residential and commercial historic preservation, and the one for which the most comprehensive data is available, is the historic rehabilitation tax credit.[20] Again, hundreds of thousands of housing units have been provided by means of this program since the late 1970s, the majority of which are dedicated to low and moderate-income residents (Wallace 1995).

Hence, understanding the tools and initiatives used for housing renovation and rehabilitation is essential. It is particularly important to know the programs that are attempting to make housing more affordable because, as has been noted, the majority of our built heritage is residential.

A Broader Approach: National Heritage Area Redevelopment

Alongside preservation activities in a traditional historic district with either a commercial or residential emphasis, or both, a new approach has arisen with the identification and development of "heritage areas." The term "heritage" arose in the late 1970s to signify the wide range of historically-based activities that contributed to society's well-being. A heritage area usually involves economic and social integrated redevelopment with several different kinds of recognized historic properties, often in more than one governmental jurisdiction, guided by regional management. The preservation efforts combine public and private sector leadership and purposefully embrace environmental concerns and benefits. Typically a regional heritage area attempts to provide a balanced commitment to the protection of environmental and cultural resources, and it often encourages limited recreational development for tourism. This definition is intentionally vague in order to cover a broad and diverse range of initiatives, with a range of coalition members.

The National Park Service initiatives to establish and promote national heritage areas and corridors have a number of roots. Foremost are the remarkable social, economic, and physical developments that took place along canals and rivers. As the urban revitalization techniques developed during the 1970s grew, it became clear that this historical evolution could provide a unifying theme, involving a mix of public and privately owned land, addressing the recreational needs of populations in the metropolitan areas. Because the majority of the parks under the jurisdiction of the NPS and the open spaces in the hands of its sister agencies in the Department of the Interior are found in the western states, there is concerted effort to make more open space accessible to more people nationwide.

The NPS first began to address these needs with the Cape Cod National Seashore in Massachusetts, established by Congress in 1961. It contains both public and private properties in a patchwork of beaches and nature preserves mixed with residential and commercial property. An advisory commission composed of private citizens and government representatives that allows the localities a voice in decision making guides the Seashore staff. In a similar fashion, in 1972, Congress established both the Gateway and Golden Gate National Recreation Areas, attempts to provide federal "urban parks" in the New York City metropolitan and San Francisco Bay regions, respectively. In 1974, largely through the support

---

[20] Mentioned in Chapters 2 and 5

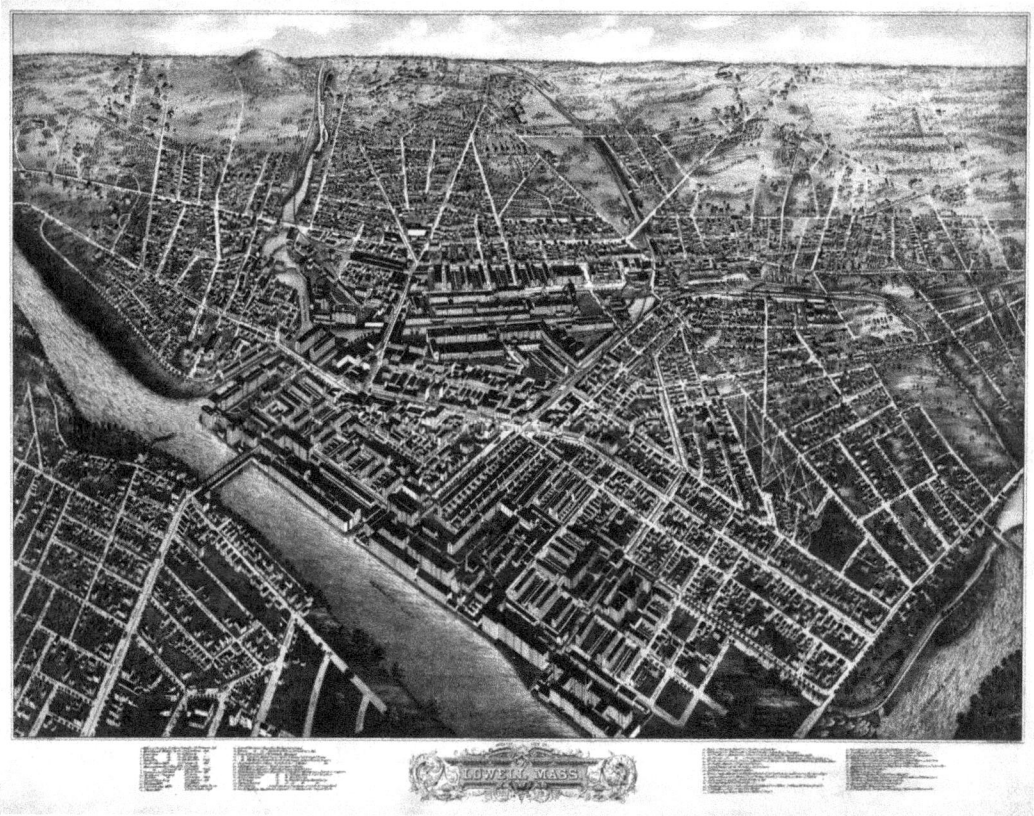

Fig. 4.3 Lowell, MA, birthplace of the Industrial Revolution in the United States, shown in the 1876 birdseye view, shrank in the twentieth century but attracted the attention of federal, state, county and local representatives, who backed the creation of the Lowell Historic Canal District Commission with an emphasis on economic revitalization. (Library of Congress)

of Akron, Ohio based Senator John F. Seiberling, the Cuyahoga Valley National Recreation Area was established to address the critical shortage of federal, state and local recreation facilities in that region (Cuyahoga 1974).[21] In this case, the Area combines about 12,000 acres of federal land with 14,000 acres of private land along an 18-mile river corridor incorporating existing municipal and multi-county parks and state land. The result is a much more ambitious effort at land management, largely within the high ravines spared much of the industrialization that characterizes Cleveland, but threatened by the relentless march of the suburbs and by the Cleveland Electric Illuminating Company that began constructing a high voltage power line through the Valley. Cape Cod's Commission was emulated in the thirteen-member Cuyahoga Valley National Park and Recreation Commission, appointed by local park officials, the Governor, and the Secretary of the Interior. The Commission must also include representatives from a conservation organization and a historical society, and at least five members of the public.[22]

The next developments occurred in Lowell, Massachusetts (Fig. 4.3). Whereas the Cape Cod

---

[21] Seiberling's first proposal, in 1971, failed for lack of support (Seiberling 1974; Naymik 2008).

[22] Although the Cuyahoga Valley contains important historic resources, most notably segments of the Ohio & Erie Canal, these features were not emphasized in the establishment of the recreation area. The authorizing legislation focused on creating recreational opportunities. Subsequent reconstruction of the Ohio & Erie Canal towpath and the rehabilitation of canal-affiliated structures led to the 1996 designation of the Ohio & Erie Canal National Heritage Corridor, which includes the Cuyahoga Valley National Recreation Area in its domain.

Fig. 4.4 Boott Mill Tower, one of the most notable elements on the skyline of Lowell's industrial waterfront, at the confluence of the Merrimack and the Concord Rivers. (Jack Boucher, photographer, Historic American Engineering Record, Library of Congress)

and the Cuyahoga Valley initiatives deviated from the NPS management norms, their focus on scenic and recreational resources remained well within the agency's traditional mission. With the Lowell National Historical Park, the NPS repeated the partnership of public and private entities in an urban area, but added an explicit emphasis on economic revitalization.

As one of the first planned manufacturing communities in the USA, Lowell's social history, technological advances, and industrial buildings are legendary. With the changes in textile production, however, the city also was one of the first to see the effects of deindustrialization. Social concerns arose in the 1960s that sparked a plan to revitalize the city based on preservation of its cultural and industrial heritage, leading to the mobilization of municipal officials and community and business leaders. Local programs were augmented by appealing

to the Commonwealth, resulting in the founding of Lowell Heritage State Park in 1974, the first such park in the state.

In 1975, the NPS established the Lowell Historic Canal District Commission, to create a plan for the preservation, interpretation, development, and use of the city's historic resources. Unfortunately, Lowell's problems seemed to worsen and funding was so limited that the results were difficult to evaluate. To meet perceived needs, and strengthen the state and local partnerships, in 1978 Congress established the Lowell National Historical Park. The legislation recognized that with a combination of government assistance and the private sector, the Federal property ownership would be kept to a minimum. Accordingly, the NPS acquired only seven key historic buildings and the canal system in its park unit. The preservation of areas beyond the official park zone fell to the newly established Lowell Historic Preservation District, overseen by a federally sponsored public–private commission with mostly local representatives. It administers a program of loans, grants, and technical assistance to acquire and rehabilitate properties within the preservation district. Thus, the project in Lowell went a step further than previous park efforts by having a commission that has greater influence on local decision-making in a drastically underemployed city (Stanton 2006) (Fig. 4.4).

The Cuyahoga Valley and Lowell initiatives were the principal experiments for the national heritage areas that followed. In both instances, a tremendous amount of time and care is invested in reaching a consensus before planning began. The chief fear on the part of local governments remains the loss of taxable land and increased federal oversight. On the other hand, the stark realities of de-industrialization almost forced many people to see hope in the idea of "making a silk purse from a sow's ear."

Like the other waterways constructed during Canal Era, hopes were high when the Illinois and Michigan Canal Commissioners began building the 96 mile link between Chicago and LaSalle in 1836. A number of new towns were platted along the route and a major stone industry flourished, mining local limestone bedrock. Within a decade of its opening, in 1848, the I & M Canal in northeastern Illinois helped industrialize the region.

As in Lowell, however, the I & M Canal was soon outdated as Chicago became a major rail hub. By the 1950s the state's neglect became so obvious that it eagerly began transferring land for transportation improvements, leasing property for industrial use, and selling parcels in piecemeal fashion. In response, in 1963 the Open Lands Project, a private conservation group, was formed, in part to press the Illinois governor to appoint a task force to study the feasibility of a park in the region.

In an attempt to protect the Lockport Prairie and oppose continued quarrying, members of the Open Lands Project, under the leadership of preservationist W. Gerald Adelmann, began a crusade to recognize the potential of the Canal corridor. This included 15 locks, 3 dams, and aqueducts, canal lock-tenders houses, and bridges. It also extended civic consciousness about the region's industrial heritage that included the Sanitary and Ship Canal, the steel mills, oil refineries, flour mills, coke ovens, stone works, and abandoned quarries. In 1971, a trail along the Canal was designated, stretching for approximately 60 miles from Joliet to LaSalle. Open Lands went further than many nonprofit organizations by contacting Congressional representatives to enlist support for funding a "concept plan" by the NPS. Adelmann also explained the idea of a linear park to industry leaders, enlisting them in the campaign to act on behalf of conservation and preservation interests. Most supported the proposal after they understood the rationale for the corridor and realized that no new environmental reviews would be required. As a final step, Open Lands solicited the support of the *Chicago Tribune* to explain the project to the public. A commission representing a wide range of local interests assumed management, with a staff to help plan and execute specific projects.[23]

As the examples at Cuyahoga, Lowell, and the Illinois & Michigan Canal demonstrate, it was important to have a broad base of support with both preservation and conservation-minded interests coming into play. Without Ohio's Department of Natural Resources, the Commonwealth of Massachusetts, and the Open Lands Project, the NPS would have had a much harder time. All three projects also benefited by the guidance provided by professionals, who helped to facilitate the projects.

The second of the fourteen original national heritage areas was the Blackstone River Valley National Heritage Corridor, established in 1986. It became the first to cross state lines, and thus required more than the usual amount of orchestration. Dozens of other heritage corridors followed.[24] Although the amount of funding made available in each instance varies from several thousand dollars to millions, the impact of these activities is striking. Of all the NHAs, the one that has received the most sustained funding is in southwestern Pennsylvania, where hundreds of millions of dollars have been invested.

In 1993, a group of public and private organizations convened in Washington, D.C. to discuss heritage area issues, including possible federal legislation to create a national program. This meeting led to the formation of the National Coalition for Heritage Areas, sponsored, in part, by the Countrywide Institute and the National Trust for Historic Preservation, with staff support

---

[23] Adelmann went on to found the Upper Illinois Valley Association in 1982, and it has since been transformed into the non-profit Canal Corridor Association.

[24] In order of their designation, the National Heritage Areas are: the Illinois & Michigan Canal National Heritage Corridor in Illinois (1984); the Blackstone River Valley National Heritage Corridor (1986); the Delaware & Lehigh Navigation Canal National Heritage Corridor and the American Industrial Heritage Area/Project, both in Pennsylvania (1988); the Quinebaug and Shetucket Rivers Valley National Heritage Corridor in Connecticut and the Cane River Creole National Heritage Area in Louisiana (1994); America's Agricultural Heritage Partnership in Iowa, the Augusta Canal National Heritage Area in Georgia, the Essex National Heritage Area in Massachusetts, the National Coal Heritage Area in West Virginia, the Ohio & Erie Canal National Heritage Corridor in Ohio, the South Carolina National Heritage Corridor, the Steel Industry Heritage Project in Pennsylvania; and the Tennessee Civil War Heritage Area (1996). Others have followed.

Fig. 4.5 Commercial
Slip, on the Buffalo
waterfront, is the western
terminus of the Erie
Canal, one of hundreds
of important elements in
the Erie Canal National
Heritage Corridor. Recent
preservation advocacy has
led to the archaeological
interpretation adjacent
to the Veteran's Park.
(Author's photograph)

from the NPS.[25] Subsequently, the Alliance for National Heritage Areas has taken on the responsibility of coordinating efforts between the designated areas and urging legislators to provide more financial support. Almost 100 regional heritage areas are in varying phases of development. These collaborative efforts protect the regional landscape, preserve historic resources, provide recreation, and stimulate economic development. Heritage Area tourism is not only creating jobs, but broader career opportunities, even supporting language training and educational options that allow individuals to develop special talents (Fig. 4.5).

The Economic Contribution of Heritage Tourism

In almost any economy that is service sector dependent, tourism will often play a strong role. Whether in a remote, undeveloped location, a formerly teeming city that has declined in size to a fraction of its peak population, or in a booming metropolis, tourists can play a significant role in supplementing the activities of a local economy.

Tourism is the movement of people to destinations outside their normal places of work and residence, together with the activities undertaken during their stay in those destinations. This includes the construction, renovation, and maintenance of the facilities created to serve their needs. Tourists—whether they are visitors to a location motivated by the desire to participate in leisure, business, family obligations, education, or cultural activities—may travel a considerable distance and stay hours or months at a time, but they draw on local goods and services in a different fashion from full time residents. Hence, tourism studies focuses on not only the visitors, but also those who are involved in the local and regional transportation and accommodation networks, water and food delivery systems, refuse collection, information services, and the host attractions, including natural and historic properties (McIntosh 1995; Morley 1990).

Because transportation industries are comparatively easy to monitor, attempts are made to relate tourism to travel statistics. Such linkages are often, at best, rough estimates. With that caveat, everyone recognizes that travel by car, bus, aircraft, and train is a huge industry. The Travel Industry Association (TIA) asserts that Americans traveling 100 miles or more from home spent $524 billion in 2004, up 6.8 % over the previous year (Travel 2006). In addition, foreigners are estimated to have spent $75 billion. The domestic portion of total travel in 2005 included more than

---

[25] A Maryland strategic planning and marketing firm, The Rosenbaum Group, provided assistance and the organization changed its name to the National Center for Heritage Development to reflect an expanded mission beyond only the heritage areas (Mastran 1994; Rosenbaum 1996).

1.9 billion trips to destinations 100 miles or more from home (Tourism 2007). Travel in the United States is composed of leisure travel (75%), business travel (25%), and combined leisure and business travel (25%).

Growth is expected to come from an increase in the number of leisure trips, as consumers seem to prefer long weekend getaways to lengthier vacations in distant locations. This may reflect the rise in the number of two-income households with more money but less free time. Overall travel data also suggests an increasing trend toward shorter duration trips—more day trips and one-night visits—and shorter distance trips. This may be due, in part, to the rising cost of fuel. Surprising to some analysts, notwithstanding the events of September 11, 2001, the cataclysmic weather conditions in the southern United States, and the widespread economic downturn that bottomed out in 2009, tourism as an industry has recovered relatively quickly (Riche et al. 2010).

The economic benefits of tourism include not only the immediate cash sales of products and services, but also the employment provided. Indirectly, tourism dollars affect both the income and sales taxes of residents as the assumption is that they spend more of their tourism-generated money in the local and regional economy. In addition, a community can raise revenue by targeting tourist hotels, motels, camping accommodations, and attractions with a "bed tax." Formally known as a transient occupancy tax, the revenue is dedicated to various community programs, some with an emphasis on historic preservation. Because of the inherent drain that the tourists place on a community's amenities, these taxes are spent first on public services and capital improvement projects.

Yet, not all tourists are alike. Heritage tourism is associated with heritage-related places, events, and activities. It includes visiting museums, historic sites and communities, cemeteries, and cultural landscapes, and participating in events, reenactments, religious and cultural performances. Like other forms of tourism, heritage tourism is both an individual and group activity. For example, thousands of visitors will travel considerable distances for sports events, but they differ from

cultural tourists, who are attracted to a wide range of historical, social, artistic, performing arts, and religious occasions and activities. This contrast is important to keep in mind because state and local governments often play a major role in all aspects of tourism, even indirectly supporting religious activities. They often go beyond providing promotional funding and regulating "camp sites" to become involved in actively marketing and encouraging the training of labor forces. In some cases, governments solicit experienced developers to become involved, offering considerable subsidies. In many cases, tourism requires enhanced fire and police protection, municipal water, waste removal, and a number of physical improvements. In short, governments often become investors in tourism, with an eye toward the economic return.

The long history of cultural tourism betrays its strong European roots. It comes as no surprise that the pilgrimages of various religious groups established the routes that the first large secular tours of the late nineteenth century followed. Hundreds of millions of people participate in ongoing, established rituals, stimulating the local hosts' economies to meet the needs and wants of visitors. Again, following European models, country house tours in the USA are another established social activity, with publications and tour guides to provide instruction. Places such as Natchez in Mississippi regularly raise funds for historic sites in this fashion, featuring gardens and landscaped grounds. As suggested at the beginning of this chapter, many people are interested in the political history of the country, and visit the preserved homes of presidents. The residences of Washington, Jefferson, Jackson, and Madison are all high on the list of oft-visited sites, attracting millions annually.

Military history plays a large role, involving thousands who become involved with reenactments. Sites associated with the Revolutionary and Civil Wars are remarkably important to the local and regional economy in several states (Johnson and Sullivan 1993; Kennedy and Porter 1999). In Virginia, the impact of travel to historic sites is crucial to the state's prosperity. The impact of Colonial Williamsburg alone on

Virginia's economy is estimated to be more than $0.5 billion a year (Virginia 1996).

The Civil War Preservation Trust, the nation's largest battlefield preservation organization, has saved over 25,000 acres from development in 18 states. To demonstrate the positive impact of its activities, the Trust commissioned a survey of nonlocal visitors to determine how much per day the average out-of-town person spends, focusing on two major battlefield sites, Gettysburg and Antietam. Surveyors found that many visitors planned to spend the night in the area, accounting for the remarkable $121 million contributed to the economy, with $51 million directly related to job creation (Peterson 2006).[26]

Heritage tourism compares well with trends in pleasure trips, and historic sites play a crucial role in fostering pleasure travel. As travel expert Arthur Frommer explains: "People travel in massive numbers to commune with the past.... [Y]ou cannot deny that seeing the cultural achievement of the past, as enshrined in period buildings, is one of the major motivators for travel" (McLendon et al. 2010, Chapter 3, p. 5).

Growing heritage tourism is also linked to other factors, from family finances to leisure time pursuits. Trips to historic sites tend to be less expensive than other types of vacations or pleasure travel. As family travel has increased, historic sites often offer something of interest to all family members. Families also are more interested than other travelers about adding educational opportunities to their vacations (Schiller 1996).

The national data on heritage tourism volume and spending is sketchy. One of the most commonly cited studies is the *Historic/Cultural Traveler* analysis conducted by the Travel Industry Association or TIA (Travel 2003). When examining both historic tourism and cultural tourism in 2002, it found that both were a large and growing spur to travel.

In 2002, heritage travel[27] was undertaken by 84.7 million of all US adults (of 211.6 million total) and 57.9% of all US adult travelers (146.4 million) (Travel 2003, p. 8).[28] Heritage travel in that year involved 143.5 million person trips (Travel 2003, p. 4)[29] or about one seventh (14.1%) of all 2002 person trip volume (of 1021.3 million total). The more aggregate historic/cultural travel market size (inclusion of a historic *and/or* cultural activity on a trip) was yet larger—involving 118.1 million US adults (55.8% of all US adults, 80.7% of all US adult travelers) and 216.8 million person trips (21.2% of all person trip volume).

Historic/cultural travel activity has grown over time, from 192.4 million trips in 1996 to 216.8 million trips in 2002, an increase of 13% or more than twice the 1996–2006 growth (5.6%) in all domestic travel (Travel 2003, p. 10) (Table 4.11).[30]

Among all 146.4 million adults who traveled in 2002, 59.5 million (40%) visited a designated historic site, such as a building, landmark, house, or monument (Travel 2003, p. 5). Other popular "historic travel" involved visiting a designated historic community or town (41.1 million adult travelers), a military museum (36.3 million adult travelers), or a historic military site, such as a battlefield (30.4 million adult travelers). Of note is the tremendous draw of ethnicity, a reflection of the growing diversification of the United States. Of all 146.4 million adult travelers in 2002, almost 50 million visited an ethnic area or ethnic culture exhibit. Combining historic and ethnic themes is a powerful subject for site interpreters.

Travelers often combine activities such as visiting friends/relatives or an ethnic site while also engaging in historic/cultural activities, but these

---

[26] At some sites as many as 73% of the participants had a college education, with an average age of 49.

[27] Defined as, "persons who traveled 50 miles or further from home who included at least one historic site, com-

munity, town, museum, military site, or memorial cemetery."

[28] Defined as "adults who have taken at least one trip of at least 50 miles one-way away from home, in the last year, not involving trips taken in regular commuting to and from work or school or trips taken as a flight attendant or vehicle operator."

[29] Defined as "one person trip includes one person on one trip 50 miles or more, one-way away from home or including an overnight stay."

[30] Separate historic trip volume is not available from the TIA.

Table 4.11 Historical/cultural travel market size, 2002. (Source: Travel Industry of America (2003))

	Number of US adults (million)	%	Number of adult travelers[a] (million)	%	2002 person-trip volume[b] (million)	%
Total	211.6	100.0	146.4	100.0	1021.3	100.0
Included an historic and/or cultural activity on a trip	118.1	55.8	118.1	80.7	216.8	21.2
Included a cultural activity on a trip	109.8	51.9	109.8	75.0	97.7	9.6
Included an historic activity on a trip	84.7	40.0	84.7	57.9	143.5	14.1

[a] Adults who have taken at least one trip of at least 50 miles, one-way, away from home, in the past year, not including trips taken in regular commuting to and from work or school, or trips taken as a flight attendant or vehicle operator
[b] Counts multiple trips and multiple people per trip

are very strong in their own right. About 40 % of historic/cultural travelers added extra time to their trip due to a historic/cultural event. Visiting a historic site was frequently the primary motivation for taking a particular trip.

By examining state-level tourism data in Arkansas, Florida, Massachusetts, Missouri, Ohio, Nebraska, New Jersey, and Texas over the past decade it is possible to see that heritage tourism comprises millions of annual trips (e.g., 3.3, 4.3, and 40.7 million in Arkansas, Massachusetts, and Texas, respectively). Heritage tourism ranges from a high of 17 % of total statewide tourism trips (in Massachusetts) to a low of 5 % (in New Jersey). The median was short: 5–10 %. This range is approximately similar to the Travel Industry of America's (TIA) finding that 14 % of US person trips involved heritage travel.[31]

Florida is often cited in tourism literature for its long-held dependence on out-of-state visitors, but the state is also notable for the amount of information it collects (McLendon et al. 2010). In 2000, the "Sunshine State" had some 72 million visitors, the lion's share (80 %) coming from within the United States. When domestic visitors to Florida were asked what were their primary activities, the top three responses were, not surprisingly, "beaches" (32.4 %), "shopping" (32.4 %)

and "theme/amusement parks" (26.5 %). About one-tenth (9.1 %), however, listed "historic places/museums" as their primary Florida travel activity.

Heritage travel is particularly important in some Florida communities, such as St. Augustine, Key West, Mount Dora, and Tampa-Bay City. St. Augustine epitomizes heritage tourism. The city's 14,000 residents host 3.5 million tourists annually, where they can relive the history of the nation's oldest continuously occupied city, while strolling along St. George Street, peering from atop the Fortress of Castillo de San Marcos, or driving across the Bridge of the Lions. The Economic Development Council of St. Augustine and St. Johns County Chamber of Commerce estimate that tourism brought in $490 million in 2000.

Other Florida cities are making a similar pitch. Heritage tourism has been a mainstay for Key West and Pensacola, as well as Tampa. Key West's Old Town and Hemingway House and Pensacola's Seville Historic District have attracted tourists for decades. Historic Mount Dora in central Florida is a charming mix of commercial and residential properties. The 9800 residents of the city host an estimated 1 million visitors annually, largely through a calendar filled with festivals built around the historic downtown shopping district. In Tampa, a resurgent Ybor City Historic District is drawing new heritage tourists. It is now a fashionable entertainment district, rediscovering its potential in the wake of massive destruction after the failed promises of urban renewal.

What is the profile of the heritage traveler? Relative to the average leisure traveler in the

---

[31] Although various attempts to offer a definition of the "historic" or "heritage" traveler have been provided, there is no industry-wide consensus. The Travel Industry of America (TIA) and Rutgers University reports were viewing different databases and, consequently, differed in how they flagged their "historic" or "heritage traveler".

United States, heritage tourists in this country are: somewhat older, less likely to be married, exhibit a smaller household size, disproportionately female, better educated, more likely to be in managerial/professional occupations, and earn higher incomes.[32] This characterization parallels some of the demographic changes earlier traced for the country as a whole, such as an aging population with a declining household size that is disproportionately female, and an economic shift away from manufacturing.

Trip characteristics also differ compared to the average leisure trip. The heritage trip is more likely to involve a stay at a hotel/motel, to last longer, and to include a larger party size. In part due to some of the above-cited statistics—such as heritage traveler higher income and heritage trip longer duration—there is higher spending associated with heritage tourism. The average heritage/culture traveler spent $623 per trip in contrast to a much lower $420 for the average leisure trip (Travel 2003).

The combination of the above factors means that heritage tourists are very desirable. In many jurisdictions in the USA, tourism ranks in the top five industries in terms of revenue. Since heritage travel is an important component of all travel, it constitutes an important economic prop for the state and local economies. Annual heritage travel outlays of $0.7 billion in Arkansas, $1.4 billion in Texas, $2.5 billion in Massachusetts, and $3.7 billion in Florida underline these points.

The Table 4.12 summarizes extensive survey information, demonstrating the differences and similarities between the types of travelers in age, education, annual household income, marital status, household size, and occupation. Going further, the types of accommodations, travel party size, trip duration, and total trip spending are shown.

Rural Heritage Tourism

While much of this chapter's discussion to this point has referred to how historic preservation spurs economic development in urban locations and nearby older suburbs, rural areas benefit as

well. For example, consider the contribution of preservation to the economy of Nebraska, one of the most rural states in the nation. Of the total $1.5 billion spent on the rehabilitation of existing residential and nonresidential building in this state between 2001 and 2005, $230 million, or 15%, was spent on historic properties. Of the total 9.5 million Nebraska overnight person trips in 2005, 546,000, or about 6% involved heritage travel. As elsewhere in the United States, Nebraska heritage travelers (on average) spend more than their nonheritage counterparts. Nebraska heritage travel amounted to about $100 million annually.

Nebraska is not alone in combining historic preservation and rural revitalization. There are many efforts throughout the rural United States to foster preservation-linked tourism. Southwestern Minnesota once had many family farms but these declined as the agricultural industry changed. In response, an agro-tourism initiative is being mounted to attract visitors drawn to the area's agricultural legacy such as the Olaf Swensson (homestead) Farm, the Minnesota Valley canning company (home of a Green Giant food processing plant), and the Minnesota Center for Agricultural Innovation, cited as the Midwest's largest collection of agricultural cooperatives (Spaeth and Parvis 2010).

Also deserving mention are programs specifically dedicated to combining historic preservation and rural development by maintaining historic barns and agricultural buildings as part of modern agricultural production. Illustrative is the conversion of the Scotch Hill Farm barn in Rock County, Wisconsin, from traditional beef cattle raising to a goat dairy and organic soap maker (Hoogterp 2007). A Rural Heritage Development Initiative has begun in the Arkansas Delta and Central Kentucky Heartland seeking to use heritage as a basis for revitalization.

No group in the United States is more rural than Native Americans and none is more impoverished. In 2000, the percentage of Native Americans living in poverty was twice that for the country as a whole. In part to combat this problem, many tribes throughout the country are promoting their history and culture as a strategy to foster tourism and economic development. The Alliance of Tribal Tourism Advocates, organized in 1992, assists tribes in the development of tourism codes

---

[32] Based on data from TIA and the Rutgers University studies.

Table 4.12 All, leisure, and historical/cultural traveler profile

Household demographic characteristics	All US travelers (Travel 2003)	US leisure traveler (Travel 2004)	Historic/culture traveler (Travel 2003)	Heritage traveler (CUPR, 1999–2003[c])
	556.7[a]	392[a]	113[a]	N/A
Age of household head				
18–34 years old	26%	27%	24%	25%
35–54 years	43%	41%	41%	37%
55 and over	31%	32%	35%	34%
Average age (years)	47	47	49	46
Education of household head				
High school education or less	20%	22%	18%	25%
Some college—no degree	25%	26%	24%	29%
College graduate	36%	35%	37%	28%
Graduate work	19%	17%	21%	21%
Annual household income				
Less than $50,000	43%	47%	44%	53%
$50,000–$74,999	22%	22%	23%	21%
$75,000–$99,999	16%	15%	16%	12%
$100,000 or more	19%	16%	17%	14%
Average income	$68,200	$63,600	$66,700	$59,475
Median income	$56,600	$52,600	$55,600	
Marital status				
Married	64%	63%	62%	60%
Never married	19%	19%	19%	18%
Divorced/widowed/separated	17%	18%	19%	22%
Household size				
One person	21%	21%	23%	23%
Two people	36%	36%	36%	39%
Three people	17%	18%	17%	15%
Four people	16%	15%	14%	14%
Five or more people	10%	10%	10%	10%
Occupation of household head				
Managerial/professional	39%	35%	37%	40%
Technical/sales/administrative	12%	12%	12%	15%
Service	5%	6%	5%	7%
Farming/fishing/forestry	1%	1%	1%	1%
Craftsman/repairman	6%	6%	5%	4%
Operator/laborer	7%	8%	6%	5%
Retired	16%	18%	20%	29% (others)
Other	14%	14%	14%	
Trip characteristics/preferences				
Accommodation type (person-night)				
Hotel/motel/B&B	55%	43%	62%	54%
Friends, relatives homes	38%	48%	36%	33%
RV or tent	5%	7%	6%	4%
Condo or time share	4%	5%	5%	3%
Other	8%	8%	8%	5%
Average hotel/motel/B&B (nights)	3.2	2.9	3.7	
Average friends/relatives (nights)	4.1	4.3	5.2	
Household travel party size/composition				
One	44%	33%	36%	20%
Two	31%	36%	38%	39%
Three	10%	12%	11%	9%

Table 4.12 (continued)

Household demographic characteristics	All US travelers (Travel 2003)	US leisure traveler (Travel 2004)	Historic/culture traveler (Travel 2003)	Heritage traveler (CUPR, 1999–2003[c])
	556.7[a]	392[a]	113[a]	N/A
Four	9%	12%	9%	16%
Five or more	6%	7%	6%	15%
Solo traveler	44%	33%	36%	
Multiple adults	32%	37%	39%	
Adult(s) with children	24%	30%	25%	
Total trip duration (%)				
Day trips	16%	15%	10%	no information
1 or 2 nights	39%	39%	30%	
3 to 6 nights	31%	31%	37%	
7 nights or more	14%	15%	23%	
Average duration (includes 0 nights)	3.4	3.4	4.6	
Average duration (excludes 0 nights)	4.1	4.1	5.2	
Total trip spending (%)				
Less than $100	26%	28%	16%	No information
$100–$249	28%	29%	23%	
$250–$499	18%	18%	21%	
$500–$749	12%	11%	15%	
$750–$999	4%	3%	6%	
$1000 or more	12%	11%	19%	
Average trip spending	$457	$420	$623	

NA Not applicable or available

[a] Base = Millions of Household-trips

[b] Wright 2000 (based on TIAA study on "Adventure Travel: Profile of a Growing Market" in 1994)

[c] The statistics for US heritage travelers are derived from the average of all available state heritage traveler data

[d] Wright 1996 (based on HLA/ARA Consulting Group's study on "Eco-tourism-Nature/Adventure/Culture-Alberta and British Columbia Market Demand Assessment")

and policies, and reservation packages to accommodate visitors to the reservations and cultural centers (Peterka 1992). The Cayuse, Umatilla and Walla Walla Tribes, which formed the Confederated Tribes of the Umatilla Reservation, have published a map presenting the homelands of their people with Tribal names and modern tourist attractions, linking interests along the path of the Lewis and Clark expedition (Denight 2005). The Northern Plains Tribal Arts Show and Market attracts almost 100,000 people and injects more than $10 million of economic activity into the area (Anderson 1999). At the same time, it is important to emphasize that many tribes hold a dim view of intrusive visitors, particularly when areas held sacred are declared "off limits."

Although travel statistics incorporate a considerable amount of data about civic cultural activities, conspicuously absent is any mention of cultural tourism related to religious activities and

events. Governments routinely shy away from collecting information about religion fearing that they may be perceived as favoring one faith over another, but a closer look at the activities of a community demonstrates the power of spiritually based economic development that is, in many instances, culturally-based expression. For example, the Hill Cumorah Pageant in rural West Palmyra, New York, presents the story of the founding of the Church of Latter Day Saints (Fig. 4.6). With seating for over 9000 people and thousands more camped on blankets on the hillsides, the mid-July performances are free and open to the public. Estimated attendance is over 100,000 people during the Pageant, and over 2 million visitors arrive every year (Hudman and Jackson 1992).[33] By providing customers for local hostelries and

---

[33] It should be noted that there is no required annual pilgrimage (Timothy and Olson 2005).

Fig. 4.6 The power of faith-based activities to stimulate cultural tourism can transform the local economy, as seen by the annual activities of the Church of Latter-day Saints, at Hill Cumorah, in Palmyra, New York. (Author's photograph)

businesses, these public narratives have boosted the local economy for nearly a century. In a similar fashion, Branson City, Missouri has attracted hundreds of thousands of visitors due to a handful of faith based, place-specific narratives. Harold Bell Wright's novel, *The Shepherd of the Hills,* led people to visit Marble Cave, imagining a supernatural subterranean world (Wright 1907). The novel spawned the creation of the Shepherd of the Hills Farm, host to hundreds of thousands of visitors annually. And Silver Dollar City, built over the Cave, emphasizes Christian values amidst specialty shops, attractions and rides, traditional musical shows, and scores of craft demonstrations (Ketchell 2007). Religious organizations throughout the country sponsor tens of thousands of festivals during feast days and holidays.

The Multiplier Effects of Preservation

Thus far, the discussion has focused on how historic preservation fosters housing creation, downtown commercial reuse, heritage area redevelopment, heritage tourism, and rural revitalization. Yet, these activities are interconnected. Thousands of examples show that, by preserving and rebuilding community life, local and regional economies can improve.

Property renovation has a stimulant effect; renovating one building encourages others. Reinvestment has a "multiplier effect," that is, as more properties are rehabilitated, lenders are more interested in making loans. Then, as more lenders compete for these loans, their rates and terms become more attractive. As additional financing becomes more readily available, appraisers adjust property values upward. As property appraisals increase, lenders are willing to extend further credit. Hence, the renovation of properties continues to improve the economic attractiveness of the neighborhood.

Some communities have adopted a "catalyst strategy" in the form of a "major development," such as a new festival marketplace or the rehabilitation and reuse of a large historic building to spur additional projects (Wagner 1993). A catalyst effect is also likely from historic district upgrading, as owners of properties in neighborhoods near the historic districts in which renovation is occurring are more likely to follow suit with improvements to their buildings. There is, in fact, fluidity to the process by which one neighborhood is designated as a historic district, encouraging rehabilitation in an adjacent neighborhood that may ultimately itself be designated, in turn stimulating more work in yet another area. This process is observed more anecdotally than statistically. In San Antonio, for example, historic designation of the King William area encouraged property renovations in, and ultimately designation of, neighboring areas. In New York City, historic designation of Brooklyn Heights encouraged rehabilitation in nearby Park Slope, the latter neighborhood ultimately designated as well (Abeles and Schwartz 1979). While there may be other forces at work in such cases (e.g., a revitalized New York City economy and a dearth of new residential construction), historic preservation has a positive effect.

Furthermore, the direct benefits associated with historic preservation, such as enhanced rehabilitation and heritage tourism spending, have advantageous multiplier effects. The latter incorporate what are referred to as indirect and induced economic consequences. Economists estimate these indirect and induced effects using an input-output model. The direct impact component consists of labor and material purchases made specifically for the preservation activity. The indirect impact component consists of spending on goods and services by industries that produce the items purchased for the historic preservation activities. Finally, the induced impact component focuses on the expenditures made by the households of workers involved either directly or indirectly with the activity. For example, lumber purchased at a millwork factory or hardware at a hardware store for historic rehabilitation is a direct impact. The purchases of the mill that produced the lumber are indirect impacts. The household expenditures of the workers at both the mill and hardware store are induced impacts.

To illustrate further, the total (direct and multiplier) economic benefits of the two historic preservation programs for which there is the most information—the national certified historic rehabilitation tax credit program and the state certified historic rehabilitation programs—and the state-level heritage spending provide data that is extremely convincing.

The total effects in both instances are estimated by means of a widely-used regional input-output (I-O) model developed by the Regional Science Research Corporation (RSRC). The model demonstrates economic impacts such as the following:

Jobs: employment, both part- and full-time, by place of work, estimated using the typical job characteristics of each detailed industry;

Income: "earned" or "labor" income, specifically wages, salaries, and proprietor's income;

Wealth: value added, the equivalent at the sub-national level of gross domestic product (GDP)

Taxes: revenues generated by the activity, collected by the federal, state, and local levels of government

Of further note is historic preservation's role as an economic pump primer vis-à-vis other non-preservation investments. Because construction is an important element of historic preservation, a common frame of reference is how well preservation, in the form of historic rehabilitation, compares economically to new construction. Table 4.13 shows the economic effects of the historic rehabilitation of different types of buildings (e.g., single- and multifamily properties) relative to new construction of the same types. The economic impacts include total (direct and indirect/induced) income, wealth, and tax consequences per standard increment of investment ($1 million) at both the national and state levels. The comparisons reveal that, across all building and investment types, historic preservation, defined in this instance as historic rehabilitation, is a slightly more potent economic pump primer than is new construction.

For instance, $1 million spent on nonresidential historic rehabilitation generates, at the national level, 38.3 jobs, $1,302,000 in income, $1,711,000 in GDP, and $202,000 in state and local taxes. By contrast, $1 million spent on nonresidential new construction generates nationally 36.1 jobs, $1,223,000 in income, $1,600,000 in

Table 4.13 Relative economic effects of historic rehabilitation versus new construction

Construction activity—historic rehabilitation and new construction

Geographic Level/ Economic Effect (in thousands)	Single-family		Multifamily		Nonresidential		Highway	Civic/Institutional	
	Historic rehabilitation	New construction	Historic rehabilitation	New construction	Historic rehabilitation	New construction	New construction	Historic rehabilitation	New construction
National									
Employment (jobs)	36.7	36.0	36.4	36.1	38.3	36.1	33.6	37.8	36.9
Income	1240	1206	1226	1213	1302	1223	1197	1285	1250
GDP	1672	1604	1661	1606	1711	1600	1576	1695	1626
State Taxes	106	102	105	102	110	103	101	108	105
Local Taxes	89	86	88	86	92	86	85	91	88
State									
Employment (jobs)	18.4	16.4	18.0	16.4	19.3	16.7	15.2	19.0	17.2
Income	623	578	623	577	685	600	600	675	616
GSP	937	811	915	814	964	827	806	946	843
State taxes	65	59	65	59	70	61	60	69	62
Local Taxes	55	49	55	49	59	51	50	58	52

GDP, and $189,000 in state and local taxes. The same size investment in new highway construction produces 33.6 jobs, $1,197,000 in income, $1,576,000 in GDP, and $186,000 in taxes. The historic preservation advantage in residential construction is much less but still apparent.

One other consideration of what constitutes a "good" investment is the relative comparison of historic preservation versus investment in nonconstruction sectors of the economy, such as book publishing, pharmaceutical production, or electronic component manufacturing. On this basis, historic preservation also shows some economic advantage, as illustrated in Table 4.14.

For this reason, the importance of historic preservation as an investment cannot be overestimated. As will become clearer in the following chapter, the fiscal impact of redevelopment extends into collateral real estate markets and affects job creation in ways that often become fully apparent only after a project is completed (Burchell and Listokin 1991).

Conclusion

This chapter demonstrated how the changing character of this country's population, location, and productivity are altering the prospects for our historic legacy. Rapid growth in some areas and shrinking populations in others propel economic forces that preservationists must understand as they attempt to influence the range of likely possibilities for reuse. Properties designed and built to support traditional agriculture, and others constructed for late nineteenth and early twentieth century industrial activity, are a significant part of the landscape, but to be reused, some must be adapted and integrated to fit in our predominantly service sector economy.

This fact underlines the need to understand society's anxieties about "obsolescence," paying more attention to the root causes of any disadvantages a particular property might suffer. Realtors might repeat "location, location, location" as the most important feature to determine the market value of a property, but that mantra leaves much to be desired in creating a preservation-minded solution. Market studies and fiscal analyses are needed to outline private and public costs, and estimate revenue, of a proposed redevelopment. Preservationists need to understand how projects can minimize damage to historic sites yet maximize profitability.

Private sector preservation programs have helped in downtowns and near suburbs. Thus far, the Main Street Program stands head-and-shoulders above all other initiatives designed to spur

Table 4.14 Economic impacts per million dollars of initial expenditure

Economic effect (National) (in thousands)	Residential historic rehabilitation[a]	Book publishing	Pharmaceutical production	Electronic component production
Employment (jobs)	36.7	35.3	28.4	30.9
Income	1240	1160	1045	1018
GDP	1672	1722	1546	1483
State taxes	106	103	93	87
Local taxes	89	86	79	74

[a] Single-family

revitalization. Its key to success lies, at least in part, in allowing each community to respond to its own challenges with creativity and determination. The National Heritage Area initiatives hold similar promise, but these programs must avoid fractious political preferences and constrained financing.

Most preservation programs designed to stimulate the economy and provide employment are based on tourism. This brings much-needed funding to even the most remote locations. In the United States, tourism ranks as the country's third-largest industry, contributing billions of dollars in spending to local economies. Assuming that the number of visitors is limited to a capacity the host community can accommodate, heritage tourism is particularly useful locally, not only for attracting visitors who are interested in an area's history, architecture, archaeology, and more, but also as more likely to attract visitors who will spend more, stay longer, and return again.

Beyond heritage tourism, many communities are searching for revitalization solutions that provide them with some competitive advantage, such as serving as centers of the arts, education, health care, and sporting events (Richmond 1989). Linking these ideas to the historic legacy of these communities, notably their older properties—such as underutilized commercial blocks and abandoned mills—will provide opportunities to multiply the effects of their projects in many ways (Cisneros 1996).

References

Aaron, M. H., & Wright, J. H. Jr. (1997). *The appraisal of religious properties*. Chicago: Appraisal Institute.

Abeles, P., & Schwartz, H., et al. (1979). *Economic and legal mechanisms for preserving residential buildings in historic districts*. Unpublished study, Abeles and Schwartz, New York.

Anderson, D. (1999). Northern plains tribal arts show and market a legacy. *Indian Country Today* (Oneida, NY), Sept. 13, p. C4.

Baranzini, A., Ramirez, J., Schaerer, C., & Thalmann, P. (Eds.). (2010). *Hedonic methods in housing markets*. New York: Springer.

Burchell, R. W., & Listokin, D. (1981). *The adaptive reuse handbook: Procedures to inventory, control, manage, and reemploy surplus municipal properties*. Rutgers: Center for Urban Policy Research.

Burchell, R. W., & Listokin, D. (1991). *Fiscal impact analysis. A manual and software for builders and developers*. Washington, D.C: National Association of Home Builders.

Caldwell, R. (1887). *A true history of the acquisition of Washington's headquarters at Newburgh by the state of New York* (pp. 21 ff.). Salisbury Mills: Stivers, Slauson and Boyd.

Campbell, L. (1995). *The restoration of market street*. Master of Arts thesis, Program in Historic Preservation Planning, Cornell University.

Census. (2009). *Current populations reports. Projecting the number of households*. Washington, D.C.: Bureau of the Census, U.S. Department of Commerce.

Cisneros, H. G. (1996). *Preserving everybody's history*. Washington, D.C.: U.S. Department of Housing and Urban Development.

Cisneros, H. G., & Engdahl, L. (Eds.). (2009). *From despair to hope: HOPE VI and the new promise of public housing in American cities*. Washington, D.C.: The Brookings Institution.

Clark, D. E., & Herrin, W. E. (1997). Historical preservation districts and home sale prices: Evidence from the Sacramento housing market. *Review of Regional Studies, 27*(1), 29–48.

Combal, M. (2007). *Program manager, home again program*. Lecture. Washington, D.C., Oct.

Cuyahoga. (1974). *Subcommittee on parks and recreation, hearings. Transcripts* (pp. 11–40). Washington, D.C.: Cuyahoga Valley National Recreation Area (March 1).

Dane, S. G. (1988). *New directions for urban main streets*. Washington, D.C.: National Trust for Historic Preservation, National Main Street Center.

Delvac, W., et al. (1996). *Affordable housing through historic preservation: A case study to combining the tax credits*. Washington, D.C.: U.S. Government Printing Office.

Denight, C. (2005). Tribes produce heritage map, driving tour CD. *Confederated Umatilla Journal, Supplement* (Pendleton, OR), May 19, p. 8.

Economist. (1993). Quotas by another name. *Economist* 329(7842), Dec 18, p. 7304.

Escherich, S., et al. (1996). *Affordable housing through historic preservation: Tax credits and the secretary of the interior's standards for historic rehabilitation*. Washington, D.C.: National Park Service.

ESD. (2011). New York State Empire State development, land bank program. www.esd.ny.gov/BusinessPrograms/NYSLBP.html. Accessed 2 March 2014.

Fisher, I. (1906). *The nature of capital and income*. New York: MacMillan.

Flechner, H. L. (1974). *Land banking in the control of urban development*. New York: Praeger.

Gerloff, S. (1995). Main street: The early years. *Historic Preservation Forum, 9*(3), 4–7.

Hanchett, T. (1996). U.S. tax policy and the shopping center boom of the 1950s-1960s. *American Historical Review, 101*(4), 1082–1110.

Hillier, A. E. (2005). Residential security maps and neighborhood appraisals: The homeowners' loan corporation and the case of Philadelphia. *Social Science History, 29*(2), 207–233.

Hoffman, M. (1989). New life for old buildings. *Christian Science Monitor.* March 6, p. 12.

Hoogterp, E. (2007). *Historic barns. Working assets for sustainable farms* (p. 14). Denver: National Trust for Historic Preservation.

Hossain, A. R. (2004). *The past, present and future of Community Reinvestment Act (CRA): A historical perspective*. Storrs: University of Connecticut Department of Economics.

Hudman, L. E., & Jackson, R. H. (1992). Mormon pilgrimage and tourism. *Annals of Tourism Research, 19*, 107–121.

Hurd, R. M. (1903). *The principles of city land values*. New York: Record and Guide.

ICF. (2004). *ICF Consulting, HOME program rehabilitation tune-up kit*. Washington, D.C.: U.S. Dept. of Housing and Urban Development.

Johnson, D. G., & Sullivan, J. (1993). Economic impacts of civil war battlefield preservation: An ex ante evaluation. *Journal of Travel Research, 32*(Summer), 21–29.

Joynt, J. H. (1989). Small towns are finding preservation is salvation. *Washington Post*, June 10, p. 1.

Kemp, R. L. (Ed.). (2000). *Main street renewal: A handbook for citizens and public officials*. McFarland: Jefferson.

Kennedy, F. H., & Porter, D. R. (1999). *Conservation fund, dollars and sense of battlefield preservation: The economic benefits of protecting civil war battlefields*. Washington, D.C.: Preservaortion Press.

Ketchell, A. K. (2007). I would much rather see a sermon than hear one. In P. Scranton & J. F. Davidson (Eds.),

The business of tourism. Philadelphia: The University of Pennsylvania Press.

Klein, R. (2011). The land bank model. *Mortgage Banking, 71*(9), 119–120.

Kula, E. (1998). *History of environmental economic thought*. New York: Routledge.

Listokin, D. (1995). *Rehabilitation and the building code: Recommended building code regulation of rehabilitation*. New Brunswick: Prepared for NJ Dept. of Community Affairs, Division of Codes and Standards.

Listokin, D., & Listokin, B. (1993). *Preservation and affordable housing: Accomplishments, constraints, and opportunities*. New Brunswick: Center for Urban Policy Research.

Listokin, D., et al. (1985). *Housing receivership and self-help neighborhood revitalization*. New Brunswick: Center for Urban Policy Research.

MacDonald, H., & Peters, A. (2011). *Urban policy and the census*. Redlands: ESRI.

Mallach, A. (2009). *A decent home. Planning, building and preserving affordable housing*. Chicago: American Planning Association.

Massey, D. (Ed.). (2008). *New faces in new places*. New York: Sage.

Mastran, S. (1994). Introduction: Heritage partnerships. *Historic Preservation Forum, 6*(7), 5.

McCoy, I. I. I., & Bill, W. (2008). *Introduction to commercial real estate sales*. Chicago: Dearborn Real Estate Education.

McIntosh, R., Goeldner, C. R., & Ritchie, J. R. B. (1995). *Tourism: Principles, practices, and philosophies*. New York: Wiley.

McLendon, T., et al. (2010). *Economic impacts of historic preservation in Florida*. Gainesville: Center for Governmental Responsibility, University of Florida and Center for Urban Policy Research, Rutgers University.

Moore, J. W. (2009). A history of appraisal theory and practice looking back from IAAO's 75th year. *Journal of Property Tax Assessment & Administration, 6*(3), 23–38.

Morley, C. L. (1990). What is tourism? Definitions, concepts, and characteristics. *Journal of Tourism Studies, 1*(1), 54.

Naymik, M. (2008). John F. Seiberling, 8 term congressman, dies. *Cleveland Plain-Dealer*, Aug 2

O'Brien, K. E., & Toth, K. (2005). *Best practices in land bank operation*. Cleveland: Cleveland State University, Maxine Goodman Levin College of Urban Affairs.

Opperman, J. K. (2008). Teaching preservation values. *Traditional Building, 22*(2), 122.

Pagourtzi, E., Assimakopoulos, V., Hatzichristos, T., & French, N. (2004). Real estate appraisal: A review of valuation methods. *Journal of Property Investment & Finance, 21*(4), 383–401.

Peterka, J. (1992). Tourism can empower tribes. *Indian Country Today* (Oneida, NY), Nov 2, p. C1.

Peterson, K. (2006). *Blue, grey and green. A battlefield benefits guide for community leaders*. Kennebunk:

Commissioned by the Civil War Trust (Prepared by Davison-Peterson Associates).

Popkin, S. J., Katz, B., Cunningham, M. K., Brown, K. D., Gustafson, J., & Turner, M. A. (2004). *A decade of HOPE VI: Research findings and policy challenges.* Washington, D.C.: The Urban Institute.

Virginia. (1996). *Virginia's economy and historic preservation: The impact of preservation on jobs, business, and community.* Staunton: Preservation Alliance of Virginia.

Radford, G. (1996). *Modern housing for America: Policy struggles in the new deal era.* Chicago: University of Chicago Press.

Riche, J. R. B., Molinar, C. M. A., & Frechtling, D. C. (2010). Impacts of the world recession and economic crisis on tourism: North America. *Journal of Travel Research, 49*(1), 5–15.

Richmond. (1989). *The importance of historical preservation in downtown Richmond: Franklin Street, a case study.* Richmond: Historic Richmond Foundation.

Rosenbaum, A. (1996). At the center.... *Heritage Links, 3,* Nov, pp. 1, 3–4.

Schiller, T. (1996). The travel market in the United States and the Third District. *Business Review,* Sep–Oct, pp. 11–21.

Seiberling, J. F. (1974). Cuyahoga valley's symbol of grace in a congested world. *National Parks and Conservation, 47,* 4.

Simpson, R. M. (2012). Land bank can help restore blighted areas. *Syracuse Post-Standard,* May 20.

Skelcher, B. (1990). *Economic redevelopment through historic preservation: The main street pilot project.* Doctoral dissertation, Southern Illinois University.

Smith, J. D. (1987). Measuring the informal economy. *Annals of the American Academy of Political and Social Science, 493*(6), 83–99.

Smith, K. L. (1995). Main street at 15. *Historic Preservation Forum, 9*(3), 51–52.

Spaeth, T., & Parvis, K. (2010). *Minnesota food production sector: Growing green jobs.* Minneapolis: Agricultural Utilization Research Institute.

Stanton, C. (2006). *The Lowell experiment: Public history in a postindustrial city.* Boston: University of Massachusetts Press.

Stein, R. G., et. al (1981). *Handbook of energy use for building construction.* Washington, D.C.: U.S. Department of Energy.

Stewart, N. (2006). Residents take a step to remain in Ivy city. *Washington Post,* June 4, p. C1.

Timothy, D. J., & Olson, D. H. (Eds.). (2005). *Tourism, religion and spiritual journeys.* New York: Routledge.

Tourism. (2007). *Tourism works for America. Travel industry snapshots 2007* (p. 7). Washington, D.C.: Travel Industry Association of America.

Travel. (2003). *The historic/cultural traveler, 2003 edition.* Prepared by The Research Department of the Travel Industry Association of America. Washington, D.C.: Travel Industry of America. Sponsored by *Smithsonian Magazine.*

Travel. (2004). The Historic/Cultural Traveler, 2004 Edition. Prepared by The Research Department of the Travel Industry Association of America. Washington, D.C.: Travel Industry of America.

Travel. (2006). *The Power of Travel 2006* (p. 5). Washington, D.C.: Travel Industry of America.

URTF. (1976). *Urban Reinvestment Task Force. Neighborhood partnerships-The urban reinvestment task force in 1976.* Washington, D.C.: U.S. Department of Housing and Urban Development.

USC. (1974). *United States Code, congressional and administrative news,* 93rd Congress, 2nd Session, Vol. 3.

USFNS. (2009). Winners Announced for Secretary of State's Florida Main Street Awards. *U.S. Federal News Service,* Sept. 23.

Wagner, R. D. (1993). Urban downtown revitalization. *Historic Preservation Forum, 7*(5), 53–58.

Wallace, J. E. (1995). Financing affordable housing in the United States. *Housing Policy Debate, 6*(4), 785–814.

Wight, P. A. (1996). North American ecotourists: Market profile and trip characteristics. *Journal of Travel Research, 34*(2), 2–8.

Wright, H. B. (1907). *The shepherd of the hills.* New York: A.L. Burt Co.

Wright, P. A. (2000). Sustainable ecotourism: Balancing economic, environmental and social goals within an ethical framework. In C Tisdell (ed) *The economics of tourism research* (pp. 533–549). Cheltenham: Edward Elgar Publishing.

Zangerle, J. A. (1924). *Principles of real estate appraising.* Cleveland: S. McMichael Publishing Organization.

Meeting the Financial Challenges

5

Introduction

It should be clearly understood that considerable financial resources are needed to rehabilitate and restore historic properties. A national study of historical societies and sister institutions in the United States, collectively housing 4.8 billion artifacts, found threats from water, fire, and other hazards that were significant (President 2005). An alarming share, about one third, of the most cherished properties in the country, those designated as National Historic Landmarks, are deemed landmarks under "watch," "threat," "emergency," or "lost" status (NPS 2004). Only about half of the historic structures under the stewardship of the National Park Service (NPS) are in "good condition" (NPS 2007, p. 101). While the NPS is spending about $200 million annually to stabilize, preserve, rehabilitate, and restore the resources is owns or controls, clearly a much larger investment is needed.

As noted in the previous chapter, census statistics and surveys of the county's older housing stock indicate a greater relative level of physical deterioration and widespread need for rehabilitation (Williams 2004; Listokin and Crossney 2005). According to one estimate, housing units built in 1939 or earlier require about $325 billion in renovations (Listokin and Crossney 2005).

It is important to be aware of the wide variety of financial incentives for rehabilitation. In some instances, the importance of a historic site will be widely recognized and direct government support follows. This can happen when public facilities, such as state capitals and city halls, are the object of restoration, renovation, and rehabilitation. A variety of private financial support, arising from corporate donations, family trusts, and a variety of nonprofit organizations, also contributes to many public projects, often on an ongoing basis. For properties that are in private hands, however, the financial inducements for preservation projects are even more varied. In addition to direct investment, several types of indirect subsidies exist, including below-market rate loans, density bonuses, property tax abatements, and tax incentives. Government assistance is often required with tax increment financing, industrial development bonds, and grants. Each is briefly considered in this chapter, with additional information provided in the citations.

A grant or low-interest loan would help the cash-strapped historic property owner launch a rehabilitation effort. Decreasing the operating costs of the income-producing landmark by lowering property taxes would have the same affect by strengthening the net operating income (NOI). A grant to help underwrite the restoration of an historic property would minimize the need to borrow for such purposes. Providing historic rehabilitation tax credits would have the same outcome, because investors would increase their equity contribution, reducing their need to borrow, in return for sheltering their federal and state taxable income.

The discussion below, organized by the described three categories, is not meant to be exhaustive. It includes the current primary finan-

M. A. Tomlan, *Historic Preservation*, DOI 10.1007/978-3-319-04975-5_5,
© Springer International Publishing Switzerland 2015

cial "bridge mechanisms," that is, the means by which funding is obtained to carry out historic preservation projects. First are the income tax credits. These include Federal historic rehabilitation tax credits (HTCs), and state HTCs specifically targeted to historic preservation projects. In addition, since 2000, New Markets Tax Credits (NMTCs) have carved out a promising role in financing preservation projects, although they are not preservation-specific. Second are property tax incentives. Although they do not having the high profile of the Federal and state HTCs or the NMTCs, creative application of a variety of property tax-based subsidies are important for preservation. These mechanisms range from tax-increment financing to outright reductions in the property taxes owed by historically designated properties. Third are the major nontax based financial supports. These are either directly targeted to historic preservation investment, including state bonds for historic renovation capital projects, or below-market rate financing.

Throughout the discussion that follows, the focus is upon preservation projects planned or executed throughout the United States in the recent past. These cases were chosen because they exemplify the rich mixture of resources available for doing one of the most challenging types of preservation, that of synthesizing the restoration and adaptive use of historic building while, at the same time, providing housing for low-and moderate income families.

The Nature of the Problem

Compounding the poignancy of the historic and older housing stock in their need for updating is the shortfall of resources to allow such investment. This financial shortfall, or gap, can take many forms for owners of both residential and income-producing properties. For instance, let us begin with an historic property worth $100,000 that needs $50,000 in renovation. If a resident household earning $40,000 annually owns this property, it would likely not have the $50,000 in savings to repair the home, nor be able to borrow the money because the debt load would be too

high. In a second situation, assume an income-producing historic property that has a minimal or negative NOI, i.e., the difference between building revenues and operating expenses for property taxes, utilities, management costs, and other ongoing nonmortgage outlays. In such a financially unattractive situation, the current owner or a prudent prospective investor would understandably hesitate to invest or purchase the property, and would surely question the advisability of renovating it. It is with these common scenarios in mind that a review of available financial tools is undertaken.

The Federal Historic Rehabilitation Tax Credit Program

As noted in the previous chapters, until 1976 the federal tax code in the United States favored new construction. The fastest depreciation schedule—a 200 % declining balance (DB) write-off—was available only for new construction, whereas existing buildings were limited to a 125 % declining balance schedule.[1] The 1976 Tax Act introduced some historic preservation–supportive measures, such as counting preservation easements as charitable donations, briefly described later in this chapter. Much more significant was the Economic Recovery Tax Act (ERTA) of 1981, which clarified the benefits for income producing properties. ERTA introduced a three-tiered investment tax credit (ITC). A 15 % ITC was allowed for the rehab of non-historic, nonresidential income-producing properties that are at least 30 years old; a 20 % ITC could be taken for the renovation of non-historic, income-producing nonresidential properties that are at least 40 years old; and a 25 % ITC was available for the rehabilitation of *historic*, income-producing properties, both residential and nonresidential. These ITCs could be applied against wage and investment income of affluent individual owners or, more likely, syndicates. Financially astute syndicators, who work

---

[1] This tax write-off schedule is twice the straight-line depreciation on the declining balance being depreciated. A higher depreciation shelters greater income.

Table 5.1 Federal Historic Rehabilitation Tax Credit Program, FY 1978–2011. (Listokin et al. 2012)

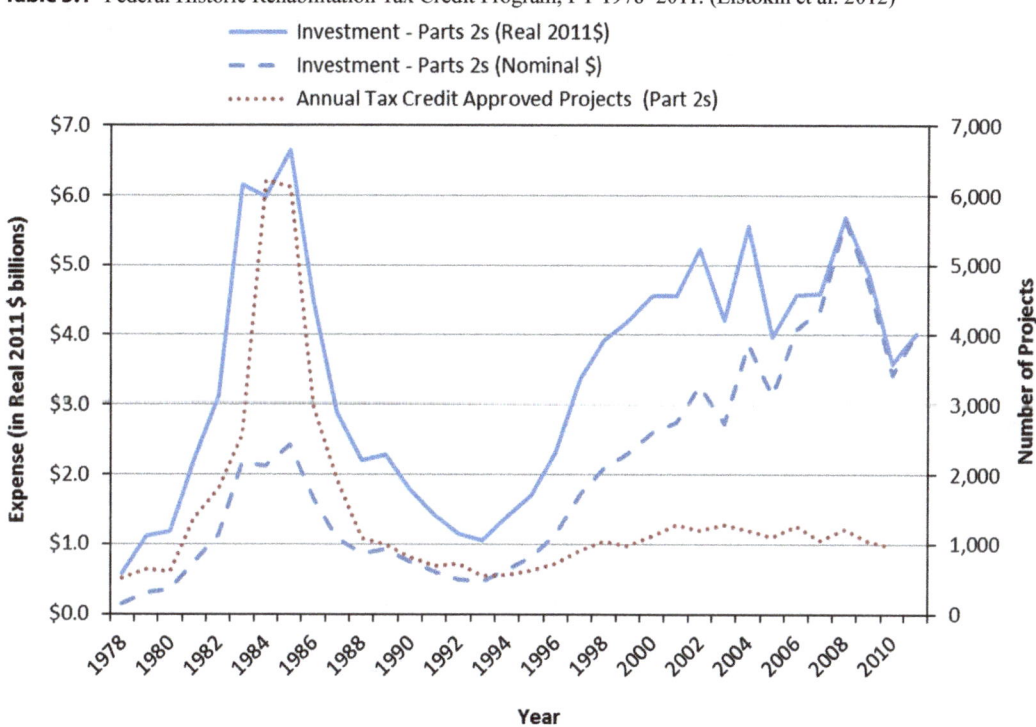

closely with the developers of preservation projects, often do the assembly and sale of ownership. For example, a $1 million rehabilitation of an historic apartment building could qualify for a $250,000 ITC, which investors could deduct dollar-for-dollar against their federal income tax liability according to their pro rata ownership of the historic renovation project.[2]

The 1981 historic preservation ITC was a powerful lure. Historic rehabilitation tax credit investment grew from $2.2 billion in FY 1981 to $3.1 billion in FY 1982, to $6.2 billion in FY 1983, and a high of $6.5 billion by FY 1985 (Tables 5.1 and 5.2).[3] The number of HTC projects more than doubled, exceeding 6000 in both FY 1984 and FY 1985.

The process of obtaining historic rehabilitation tax credits, developed in the early years of

the program, requires close attention to detail. To qualify for the 25% historic ITC, the rehabilitated property must be a "certified historic structure", that is, a building individually listed on the National Register of Historic Places, or located in, and contributing to, the historic significance of a registered historic district.[4] The "Part 1" certification requires the applicant to obtain the evaluation of the historic significance of the property from the State Historic Preservation Office (SHPO) and the NPS, with the clear mandate that the site will be recognized by the National Register before the conclusion of the project.

The "Part 2" is the description of the proposed rehabilitation work, which has to be "substantial," that is, $5000 *or* the adjusted basis of the renovated property, whichever is greater. In addition, both the SHPO and the NPS must approve the proposed work as being consistent with the

---

[2] "Pro rata" is simply in fixed proportion to the initial investment.

[3] These are computer inflation-adjusted 2011 dollars. The certified historic rehabilitation tax credit program is a multi-step application process, as explained below.

[4] A registered historic district includes both those districts listed on the National Register and any state or local historic districts in which the district and enabling statue are certified by the Secretary of the Interior.

Table 5.2 Federal Historic Rehabilitation Tax Credit Program, by year, FY 1978–2011. (Listokin et al. 2012)

Fiscal year	Investment (Part 2s) (in $millions)[a]	Cumulative investment (Parts 2s) (in $millions)[a]	Annual tax credit approved projects (Part 2s)	Cumulative annual tax credit approved projects (Part 2s)
1978	580	580	512	512
1979	1114	1694	635	1147
1980	1175	2869	614	1761
1981	2205	5074	1375	3136
1982	3123	8197	1802	4938
1983	6152	14,349	2572	7510
1984	5980	20,329	6214	13,724
1985	6648	26,977	6117	19,841
1986	4484	31,461	2964	22,805
1987	2877	34,338	1931	24,736
1988	2204	36,542	1092	25,828
1989	2273	38,815	994	26,822
1990	1782	40,597	814	27,636
1991	1419	42,016	678	28,314
1992	1145	43,161	719	29,033
1993	1056	44,217	538	29,571
1994	1398	45,615	560	30,131
1995	1697	47,312	621	30,752
1996	2304	49,616	724	31,476
1997	3378	52,994	902	32,378
1998	3914	56,908	1036	33,414
1999	4195	61,103	973	34,387
2000	4560	65,663	1115	35,502
2001	4557	70,220	1276	36,778
2002	5228	75,448	1198	37,976
2003	4214	79,662	1270	39,246
2004	5554	85,216	1200	40,446
2005	3962	89,178	1101	41,547
2006	4580	93,758	1253	42,800
2007	4597	98,355	1045	43,845
2008	5685	104,040	1213	45,058
2009	4858	108,898	1044	46,102
2010	3578	112,476	951	47,053
2011	4020	116,496	937	47,990

These figures are in inflation-adjusted terms (FY 2011 dollars)

[a] Data estimated from best available information

historic character of the property and, where applicable, the district in which it is located, using the Secretary of the Interior's Standards for Rehabilitation as a guide.

The "Part 3" step requires that the description and photographs of the completed work demonstrate that the proposed scope of work was executed in the manner deemed appropriate by the state and federal reviewers, who certify the result. These basic provisions and the process remain in place.

However, the 1986 Tax Reform Act (TRA) dramatically changed the provisions governing the ITCs. The 25% ITC for the rehabilitation of historic, income-producing properties was reduced to 20%. In other words, the $1 million rehabilitation of an historic apartment building would now qualify for a $200,000 credit, not $250,000, that investors could deduct dollar-for-dollar against their federal income tax liability according to their pro rata ownership of the project. In addition, the 1986 TRA severely

Table 5.3 Summary of the Historic Rehabilitation Tax Credit Program Statistics. (Listokin et al. 2012)

Dollar amounts are expressed in billions

Investment/Tax Credit Component[a]	FY 1978–2011				FY 2011
	Nominal \$[d]		Real \$[e]		Real \$[f]
	Total	Annual average	Total	Annual average	Total
Approved proposed (for tax credit) rehabilitation ("Part 2")	69.5	2.0	116.5	3.4	4.0
Certified (for tax credit) rehabilitation ("Part 3")	52.4	1.5	89.2	2.6	3.5
Total rehabilitation cost[b]	58.2	1.7	99.2	2.9	3.9
Federal tax credit[c]	10.9	0.3	19.2	0.6	0.7
Economic Impacts (see summary Exhibits 2 through 4 for details)	FY 1978–2011				FY 2011
	Total		Annual average		Total
Jobs (in thousands)	2215.8		65.2		63.9
Income	\$83.7		\$2.5		\$2.7
Gross domestic product	\$113.8		\$3.3		\$3.7
Output	\$230.5		\$6.8		\$7.3
Taxes-all government	\$33.5		\$1.0		\$1.0
Taxes-federal government	\$24.4		\$0.7		\$0.7
Taxes-state government	\$4.6		\$0.1		\$0.2
Taxes-local government	\$4.5		\$0.1		\$0.2

[a] Data estimated from best available information
[b] Equals all rehabilitation outlays—both "eligible"/"qualified" expenses and "ineligible"/"non-qualified" costs. The total rehabilitation cost is estimated by dividing the "Part 3" investment divided by 0.9. Case study investigation suggests that the "Part 3" amount is closer to 85% of the total rehabilitation cost, however we elected to apply the 0.9 factor to be conservative, that is to derive a lower rather than a higher estimate of the total rehabilitation expense.
[c] Assumes a 25% HTC in FY 1978–FY 1986 and a 20% HTC in FY 1987-FY 2011. These percentages are applied to the certified rehabilitation ("Part 3").
[d] In indicated year dollars–not adjusted for inflation
[e] In inflation-adjusted 2011 dollars
[f] Nominal and real dollars are the same for 2011

restricted application of the ITC against earned income. Investment in real estate limited partnerships was classified as "passive income." Under the "passive activity loss limitation," the passive ITC could generally not be applied against "non-passive" income (i.e., wages, interest, and dividends).[5]

Finally, instead of a 15–20% ITC for non-historic, income-producing nonresidential properties that were 30–40 years old, respectively, the 1986 Act reduced the non-historic ITC to 10% and applied it only to buildings built prior to 1939.

The result was that the changes in the 1986 Tax Reform Act caused investment to plummet. From a high of "Part 2" IITC investment (in inflation-adjusted 2011 dollars) of \$6.6 billion

in FY 1985, HTC activity dropped to a low of \$1.6 billion in FY 1993. The number of "Part 2" HTC projects fell similarly from about 6100 in FY 1985 to about 550 in FY 1993.

The program has subsequently rebounded, especially with respect to the HTC dollar investment, although less so with respect to the number of projects. The "Part 2" annual dollar investment (in inflation-adjusted 2011 dollars) exceeded \$3 billion by FY 1997, exceeded \$4 billion by FY 1999, and has hovered at the \$4 to \$5 billion annual amount from FY 2000 through FY 2011.

To date, from FY 1978 through FY 2011, there has been a cumulative total in inflation-adjusted 2011 dollars of \$116.5 billion "Part 2" IITC activity (in 47,990 total projects) and \$89.2 billion in "Part 3"[6] HTC activity (Table 5.3). An estimated \$99.2 billion of rehabilitation has occurred over

[5] It was precisely the ability to apply the ITC against wages, interest, and dividends that prompted wealthy individuals to invest in an historic rehab limited partnership. (This limiting provision does not apply to corporations).

[6] While the ITC is lower, the benefit remains quite valuable. Investors have paid anywhere from 80 cents to \$1,

the full span of the HTC program at a federal cost of an estimated $19.2 billion–proving it to be one of the most effective tools for historic rehabilitation.

To illustrate just how effective the program can be, consider the case of an adaptive use of a 1929 Neoclassical landmarked office building in Newark, New Jersey. This building had served as the corporate headquarters of a major publisher and as a school, but as the building aged it no longer was deemed fit for educational purposes. In 2000, a developer proposed reusing the building as a hotel with about 275 rooms. The estimated cost of the project was approximately $47 million or almost $170,000 per room. The Newark hospitality market at the time was so weak that it could not support that level of investment solely from conventional sources. As a result, the developer proposed a package that would draw on a first mortgage of about $32 million (about two thirds of the project cost), $7 million raised from the Federal HTC (about one seventh of the project cost), and the remaining $8 million from other sources. This project would not be feasible without the Federal Historic Rehabilitation Tax Credit.

The tax credit has served a similarly invaluable role in other historic projects. The $20 million renovation of the famous Apollo Theater in Harlem was made possible by the Federal HTC (NPS 2007, p. 3). The conversion of a former American Can Company complex in New Orleans into apartments and retail space, and the reuse of a 1929 Procter & Gamble soup factory as a 400,000 sq. ft. corporate office campus along Baltimore's Inner Harbor were similarly accomplish with the use of federal tax credits (NPS 2007, pp. 3–4).[7]

These cases demonstrate the valuable and varied application of the HTC. Since its inception, it has been available for both housing and nonresidential projects. One of the features distinguishing the HTC from the non-historic ITC is that the former can be used for housing while the latter cannot. In practice, the HTC has often involved housing or mixed-use projects. Although data are not readily available on the dollar distribution of HTC investment by category, the types of projects is a matter of record. The distribution indicates that about half of the HTC projects were exclusively housing and another 20–30 % were in mixed-use or other.[8] Table 5.4 illustrates the number of housing units produced with the support of the HTC. In the heady ERTA years, 15,000–20,000 housing units were created annually. That fell to 5000–10,000 units per year immediately following the 1986 Tax Reform Act. Activity has rebounded in the past decade (2000–2010) to a HTC production of about 10,000–15,000 units yearly.

Since the inception of federal historic preservation tax incentives, 440,052 housing units have been completed. Of that total, 260,835 or 59%, were existing units that were rehabilitated, and 221,222 or 41% were "newly" created housing

---

By way of background, both "Part 2" and "Part 3" rehabilitation statistics include only what are termed "eligible" or "qualified" items (or Qualified Rehabilitation Expenditures—QRE) for the tax credit as opposed to what are called "ineligible" or "non-qualified" costs. Examples of "eligible"/"qualified" items include outlays for renovation (walls, floors, and ceilings, etc.), construction-period interest and taxes, and architect fees; examples of "ineligible"/"non-qualified" costs include landscaping, financing and leasing fees, and various other outlays (e.g., for fencing, paving, sidewalks and parking lots). While the "ineligible"/"non-qualified" expenses do not count for tax credit purposes, they are practically a component of the total rehabilitation investment borne by the HTC-oriented developer and in fact, the total rehabilitation investment (including "ineligible"/"non-qualified" costs) help pump-prime the economy. Based on the best published data and through additional case studies conducted specifically for the purposes of the current investigation, the Rutgers University research estimates some of the "missing information" noted above regarding the cumulative HTC investment over FY 1978–2011.

[8] The remainder was commercial/office renovations.

---

and sometimes more, for every dollar of tax credit secured from the 20 % historic ITC.

[7] With respect to the HTC's dollar magnitude, the most complete data is for the approved proposed for rehabilitation tax credit investment ("Part 2"). The data is incomplete on the year-by-year certified rehabilitation ("Part 3") volume over the full FY 1978–2011 period. Only a portion of the "Part 2" rehabilitation is ultimately certified as "Part 3." Further, there is no information on the total rehabilitation investment associated with the HTC.

Table 5.4 Historic Rehabilitation Tax Credit Projects Involving Housing. (Listokin et al. 2012, p. 21)

Fiscal year	Total number of housing units completed	Number of units rehabilitated	Number of units created	Total number of low-/moderate-income units	Percent of total units completed that are low-/moderate-income
1978	6962	3876	3086	1197	17
1979	8635	4807	3828	1485	17
1980	8349	4648	3701	1435	17
1981	10,425	6332	4093	3073	29
1982	11,416	6285	5131	2635	23
1983	19,350	12,689	6661	3792	20
1984	20,935	16,002	4933	142	1
1985	22,013	16,618	5395	868	4
1986	19,524	12,260	7264	640	3
1987	15,522	11,306	4216	1241	8
1988	10,021	7206	2815	592	6
1989	11,316	7577	3739	2034	18
1990	8415	6098	2317	1993	24
1991	5811	4081	1730	1288	22
1992	7536	5523	2013	1762	23
1993	8286	5027	3259	1546	19
1994	10,124	6820	3304	2159	21
1995	8652	5747	2905	2416	28
1996	11,545	5537	6008	3513	30
1997	15,025	5447	9578	6239	42
1998	13,644	6144	7500	6616	48
1999	13,833	4394	9439	4815	35
2000	17,266	5740	11,530	6668	38
2001	11,546	4950	6596	4938	43
2002	13,886	5615	8271	5673	41
2003	15,374	5715	9659	5485	36
2004	15,784	5738	10,046	5357	34
2005	14,438	5469	8969	4863	34
2006	14,695	6411	8284	5622	38
2007	18,006	6272	11,734	6553	36
2008	17,051	6659	10,392	5220	31
2009	13,743	5764	7979	6710	49
2010	13,273	6643	6630	5514	42
2011	15,651	7435	8216	7470	48
Total	448,052	236,835	211,221	121,554	27

units resulting from the adaptive reuse of former commercial space.

Also important to understand is that these new units are serving a range of income levels. Of the total housing units completed using federal historic preservation tax incentives since the late 1970s, 121,554 or 28% were affordable to low- and/or moderate-income (LMI) families. That averages to about 3575 LMI units per year. In FY 2011, 7470 LMI units were produced with the HTC. While these figures are not large in an absolute sense, given national housing needs, they are noteworthy when compared with some better-known affordable housing production programs. For example, total national public housing in the USA averaged a gain of only 17,050 units yearly from 1975 through 1994; from 1994 through 2008, there was an annual average loss of about 18,000 units yearly, as shown in the previous chapter due to changes in policies and programs (Schwartz 2010). The HTC is largely invisible in the housing literature, yet it deserves much greater attention, given its total and LMI housing unit production. Just as important to note is that the LMI share of HTC housing units is growing. From FY 2005 through FY 2011, 39%, on average, of all HTC housing has been at LMI levels. In FY 2009, the LMI share of all HTC units reached a high of 49%.

Combining the HTC and LIHTC

One way that developers use the historic rehabilitation tax credits to create affordable units for low and moderate-income households is by "piggybacking," or combining the benefits of that program with other subsidies. Piggybacked financing packages can include many sources, but the most often used is the low-income housing tax credit (LIHTC). Created by the Tax Reform Act of 1986, the LIHTC gives states[9] the authority to issue tax credits to owners or developers who construct, rehabilitate, and acquire rental housing for lower-income households. Since its adoption, the LIHTC has been one of the most significant programs for the production of affordable housing in the United States, in recent years far exceeding that of direct housing subsidies administered by the US Department of Housing and Urban Development. From the beginning of the program in 1987 through 2008, the LIHTC has allocated $10 billion for federal tax credits granted for the production of 1,761,245 units of affordable housing. For 2008, the LIHTC allocation amounted to $932 million, resulting in the creation of 91,911 housing units (Danter 2012).

The tax credit is equal to a maximum of 9% annually over a 10-year period. To receive the 9% credit—equal to about 90% total over the

decade—the low-income units[10] must either be new or "substantially rehabilitated," and the property cannot otherwise be subsidized by the federal government.[11] The dollar amount of the tax credit available in any given project is equal to the tax-credit rate (up to 9% annually) multiplied by the dollar amount of the project's "qualified basis." This is increased in poor locations, known as "qualified census tracts" (QCTs) or in "difficult to develop areas" (DDAs).[12]

---

[10] To qualify for tax credits, project developers successful in the QAP-based selection process must reserve a specified proportion of units for lower-income households over a mandatory compliance period (a minimum of 15 years). The minimum set-aside within a given project must equal or exceed one of two possible targets: at least 20% of the units are reserved for households at or below 50% of the area median household income (the "20/50 Test"), or at least 40% of the units are set aside for households at or below 60% of the area median household income (the "40/60 Test"). Rents on the affordable units may not exceed 30% of household income. Investors may claim the credits annually against their federal income tax over a 10-year period, as long as the specified minimum number of units in the project are rented to low-income households within the rent limits described above for the entire compliance period.

[11] Substantially rehabilitated is taken to mean at least $3,000 in improvements per unit or 10 percent of the building's adjusted basis.

[12] The amount of tax credit available to a project is equal to the tax-credit rate (up to 9% annually) multiplied by the project's "qualified basis." The qualified basis is determined through a series of calculations. First, total (project) development costs (TDC) are calculated. Next, the eligible basis is determined by subtracting non-depreciable expenses (e.g., land, permanent financing expenses, rent reserves, and marketing costs) from the TDC. The eligible basis is increased by 130% if the project is located in either a qualified census tract (QCT) or a difficult development area (DDA). Finally, to determine the qualified basis, the eligible basis is multiplied by the applicable fraction, which takes into account the share of project units that are low-income (i.e., the percentage of low-income units to total project units). For example, a $1.2 million project that had $0.2 million in non-depreciable expenses (producing an eligible basis of $1.0 million), that was located in a DDA (therefore qualifying for an increase of 130% in the eligible basis), and was fully occupied by low-income tenants (producing a 100% applicable fraction) would have a qualified basis of $1.3 million. If the project involved substantial rehabilitation and was not receiving federal subsidies, its tax-credit rate would be 9%. Therefore, $0.117 million ($1.3 million × 0.09) in tax

---

[9] The LIHTC is jointly administered by the Internal Revenue Service (IRS) and state agencies. Awards are based on the project criteria specified in the Qualified Allocation Plan (QAP) prepared by each state, following IRS guidelines. QAPs take into account such factors as proposed project location, cost, amenities, and other characteristics. See the later discussion in this chapter.

As in the case of the HTCs, syndicators often sell the LIHTCs to corporations and individual investors seeking a tax shelter. Because the LIHTC tax shelter extends over a decade, unlike the immediate, 1-year benefit afforded by the HTC, investors pay less for the LIHTC credit.[13] Therefore, $1 million in low income tax credits would secure at least $800,000 in equity from investors in today's market.

According to a 2009 study of national LIHTC activity from 1995 through 2006, half of all LIHTC units were located in central cities, a third of all projects (six tenths in the Northeast) entailed rehabilitation, and about one third had a nonprofit sponsor. An earlier, 2000 study indicated that about 40% of all LIHTC projects nationally involved rehabilitation (Abt Associates, Inc. 2000). These characteristics suggest that the LIHTC can be tapped as a housing rehabilitation and historic preservation resource and is, indeed, the working reality.

There are at least two advantages of combining the LIHTC and the federal HTC. First, more equity can be made available to the project when the two tax credits are combined, reducing the amount of money borrowed and the overall risk. The risk is lower because the LIHTC provides subsidized rents that have a higher-than-average occupancy rate. Second, the combination of tax credits can offer a larger amount of investment to a single investor (Listokin and Listokin 2001b).

The gain in equity yielded from combining the LIHTC with the HTC is shown in Table 5.5. If one started with a $2.5 million mixed-use ($2 million housing, $0.5 million nonresidential) rehabilitation project, with the LIHTC alone, $1,147,550 in equity is created from the $2 million in housing rehabilitation. Combining LIHTC and HTC yields $1,368,000 in equity for the mixed-use project, or $220,500 more. Although the federal tax code requires that the credit from the HTC be subtracted from the hous-

ing expenditures in calculating the LIHTC, this is more than offset by two features of the HTC unavailable from the LIHTC: (1) the HTC is applicable to the non-housing portion of the project and (2) the HTC's credit allowance—20%—as noted, can be taken in the first year after project completion, whereas the LIHTC's maximum annual credit allowance—9%—is taken over 10 years.

Table 5.5 is a hypothetical example but such layering has made a significant difference in thousands of projects throughout the United States. To illustrate, let us turn to the rehabilitation of the historic Pacific Hotel in Seattle, Washington by a nonprofit Plymouth Housing Group (PHG) (Fig. 5.1).

Built in 1916, the Pacific Hotel traditionally provided transient housing and had closed by the 1980s. PHG, an advocacy group for the homeless, acquired the abandoned hotel and rehabilitated it to include 112 units. All of the units served low-income residents; there were 75 single-room-occupancy (SRO) units in one wing and 37 studio and one-bedroom apartments in another. The Pacific Hotel's total project cost was $8,534,694 ($2,113,092 acquisition and $6,421,602 rehab), or about $76,000 per unit. PHG's clientele could not afford the rents to amortize a $76,000 per unit mortgage, but rents were brought down to an affordable level using multiple sources. The $8,534,694 project expense was met by raising $3,656,085 in equity from combining the LIHTC ($2,708,079 in tax credit equity) and HTC ($948,006 in tax credit equity), and $4,878,609 in debt financing. The debt's cost and project operating expenses were reduced by subsidies received from the Federal Home Loan Bank, the Washington State Housing Trust Fund, the City of Seattle, and other sources. Other examples of projects from around the USA are briefly summarized below (Table 5.6).

---

credits would be available annually; $1.17 million in total tax credits would be available over the 10-year period.

[13] This is about $0.80 to $0.90 cents per every $1 of LIHTC, in comparison to $0.90 to $1.00 per every dollar of HTC (2006). A range is used because these amounts fluctuate depending on micro- and macro-economic factors.

Evaluating the Federal Historic Rehabilitation Tax Credit

The requirements and mechanics of the program certainly can be improved. The HTC was a more potent subsidy under its Economic Recovery Tax

Table 5.5 Example of Applying the HTC and the LIHTC Programs. (Escherich et al. 1996)[14]

Item	Amount	Equity
Historic Rehabilitation Tax Credit (HTC)		
Commercial basis	$500,000	
Rehabilitation credit %	20%	
HTC for commercial rehab	$100,000	
Housing basis	$2,000,000	
HTC %	20%	
HTC for housing	$400,000	
Total HTC	$500,000	
Equity yield for HTC	90¢	
Equity from HTC		$450,000
Low-Income Housing Tax Credit (LIHTC) Combined with the HTC		
Housing expenditures	$2,000,000	
Less HTC	<$400,000>	
Eligible basis	$1,600,000	
Low-income set-aside	75%	
Qualified basis	$1,200,000	
Annual LIHTC %	9%	
Annual LIHTC amount	$108,000	
Total LIHTC	$1,080,000	
Equity Yield for LIHTC	85¢	
Equity from LIHTC		$918,000
Combined equality		$1,368,000
LIHTC alone		
Housing expenditures	$2,000,000	
Eligible basis	$2,000,000	
Low-income set-aside	75%	
Qualified basis	$1,500,000	
Annual LIHTC %	9%	
Annual LIHTC amount	$135,000	
Total LIHTC	$1,350,000	
Equity yield for LIHTC	85¢	
Equity from LIHTC alone		$1,147,000
Additional equity from combined credit		$220,500

Act (ERTA) provisions in the 1981 through 1986 era than its Tax Reform Act (TRA) era (1986 to date). Table 5.7 demonstrates these stark changes.

Additionally, there are some major and often illogical differences between the HTC 20% credit and its sister 10% credit for commercial, non-historic rehabilitation—both authorized by Section 47 of the Internal Revenue Code—and the LIHTC credit authorized by IRC Section 42. Table 5.8 summarizes these differences.

In response to the 1986 changes, there have been calls to bring back some of the ERTA-era provisions of the rehabilitation tax credits, both to reduce the disparities between them and the LIHTC, and to remove structural impediments to the application of the credits. Major recommendations are summarized in Table 5.9. Some of these changes are contained in the Creating American Prosperity through Preservation (CAPP) Act, a bill introduced in 2011 (112th Congress). The broad themes of HR 2479 and S 2074 include provisions that would increase the 20% credit to 30% on "Main Street-scale" rehabilitations ($5 million in qualified rehabilitation

---

[14] The equity yield from the HTC has been increased from $0.85 on the dollar (1996 study) to $0.90 on the dollar. The equity yield from the LIHTC has been increased from $0.50 to $0.85 on the dollar.

Fig. 5.1 The Pacific Hotel in Seattle, WA, rehabilitated by the nonprofit entity Plymouth Housing Group, is one of hundreds of projects in communities throughout the United States to have used tax credit financing to rehabilitate properties. (Author's Photograph)

expenditures and under). Another provision provides a deeper credit (22%) if the rehabilitation project achieved at least a 30% energy efficiency improvement over a regionally adjusted baseline for similar buildings.

The CAPP Act provides for the indexing of the eligibility dates for properties that utilize the 10% rehabilitation credit, so that buildings 50 years or older would qualify. HR 2479 and S 2074 promote nonprofit sponsorship of HTC transactions by eliminating tax-exempt leasing rules that make it difficult for nonprofit organizations to access the historic tax credit. Finally, the bill contains several provisions that would increase the value of state HTCs when used in tandem with the federal HTC.

Another change would be to expand the applicability of the IITC to owner occupied properties, not just those that are income-producing. The proposed Historic Homeownership Assistance Act would have provided a credit of 20% for qualified rehabilitation expenditures up to $40,000 on owner-occupied historic homes used as a primary residence (HHAA 2011). This

would help families such as the one described at the beginning of the chapter. To allay fears that higher income households would take advantage of the credit even though it may not be needed, the homeowner credit was disallowed in locations where the local median income was double that of the state median income. To encourage use of the homeowner tax credit in lower income areas, the "substantial" rehabilitation requirement was reduced so that more modest investments would qualify.[15] Further, the homeowner rehabilitation tax credit could also be more flexibly applied than the standard income-producing historic credit.[16] Yet, while introduced numerous times, at the federal level the historic homeowner tax credits have never gained enough interest or support to be enacted.

An important question to address is whether federal financial aid to preservation—whether to investors or homeowners—should consist overwhelmingly of a tax mechanism (GAO 2012). Would more reliance upon a flexible financial aid program—one making available loans or even grants in cases of need—be more appropriate? A shift away from the current emphasis on tax incentives would offer the advantage of making the true public cost of preservation better known and controllable, as program outlays could be more readily projected and adjusted than can the revenue lost by a tax credit. Also, the soft costs involved with the HTC, such as syndication expenses, reduces the subsidy benefit of tax credits. However, a shift from an HTC to direct assistance may substantially increase governmental administrative costs, and the existing program has proved a very potent rehabilitation incentive.

In a time when all tax expenditures are being challenged, the search continues to find alternatives to financial assistance for preservation projects. For instance, with limited financial resources, it might be best to target tax incentive programs

---

[15] In distressed neighborhoods a minimum investment of $5000 would suffice as opposed to the current requirement of $5000 or the adjusted basis, whichever was greater.

[16] There were numerous flexible provisions, such as allowing developers—including nonprofit developers—to rehabilitate, sell, and pass the credit to purchasers, and providing an option to convert the tax credit to a mortgage credit certificate.

Table 5.6 Examples of HTC-LIHTC Projects

Historic building, construction date (year), and location	Description	Historic rehab
Katherine Court Apartments (1914), Macon, GA	Renaissance Revival, 28 unit apartment building, located in the Macon Historic District	$1.6 million rehabilitation investment retaining original detail (e.g., wood work and floor plans) while upgrading HVAC and other systems
Whitman Mills (1896, 1925), New Bedford, MA	Romanesque Revival mill complex important to the development of local textile industry. Listed individually on the National Register of Historic Places	A $22 million conversion into "Whalers Cove," a 120 unit assisted housing complex with 80% affordable apartments. The interior space was subdivided, but essential "historic" elements were retained (e.g., large mill windows and exposed tongue and groove ceilings)
Chamber Building (1915, 1923), Kansas City, MO	Prominent downtown office building individually listed on the National Register of Historic Places	$7.2 million rehabilitation into affordable loft housing. Important historic details were retained (e.g., terra cotta façade). Replacement of original historic Chicago-style wood and windows was allowed because of their extensively deteriorated condition
Carnegie Place Apartments (1912), South City, IO	Italianate three story library originally funded by Andrew Carnegie and listed individually on the National Register of Historic Places	$1.8 million adaptive use project to create twenty units of low-income housing. Most historic features retained, such as existing entry stair, atrium, wood columns, and plaster molding. The original eighty windows had deteriorated and were replaced with custom-made replicas with similar profiles and detail
Northern Hotel (1905), Fort Collins, CO	Four story hotel with added Art Deco ornamentation located in and contributing to the Old Town Fort Collins National Register District	$11.7 million rehabilitation conversion to mixed-use including 47 affordable apartments and first floor retail. The project combined both repair of existing salvageable windows and replacement of those that were badly deteriorated
Shelly School Apartments (1897–1919), West York, PA	Two former school buildings placed on the National Register of Historic Places for their cultural and architectural significance	$1.9 million adaptive reuse to seventeen apartments including five accessible units. The project encountered many code issues that were resolved, e.g., an architecturally significant open staircase was retained, but required installation of a 1-h fire rated wall

Table 5.7 Selected Provisions of Section 47 Compared

Selected provisions	ERTA-era tax credit (1981–1986)	TRA-era tax credit (1986+)	Comment
Tax credit percentages	15, 20, and 25%	10 and 20%	Higher percent worth more
Reduce depreciable basis by amount of credit	1981—no 1982—1986, reduce by 50%	Reduce by 100%	Lower reduction worth more
Apply tax credit to active income (for individuals)	Yes	With qualifications	Broader application (to active income) worth more

toward cases of greatest need. Under the present regulations, once the threshold tests of "certified structure," "certified rehabilitation," and "substantial rehabilitation," are met, the project qualifies for HTC assistance. No differentiation exists between projects that "need" federal tax support and those that likely would proceed without it. Perhaps a "but for" test should be added to the HTC (i.e., "but for" the credit, the project would not proceed). Perhaps, the 20% (or higher share,

Table 5.8 Comparison of the Section 47 and 42 Tax Credits

Selected provisions	Section 47—historic tax credit (20%) and commercial (10%) tax credit	Section 42—low income Housing tax credit	Comment
"Deep" (versus "shallow") subsidy	Shallow	Deep	Deeper subsidy worth more
Reduce depreciable basis by amount of credit	Yes	No	Lower reduction worth more
Boost credit by 130% in Qualified Census Tract (QCT) or Difficult to Develop Areas (DDA)	No	Yes	Boosted credit worth more
"Substantial rehab"	Greater of: $5000 or adjusted basis	Greater or: $3000 or 10% of adjusted basis	Higher "substantial rehab" requirement is harder to realize
Boost credit in small projects	No (but shallow subsidy)	No (but deep subsidy)	See above on "boosted credit"
"Act of God" triggers recapture	Yes	Limited	Recapture is a potential tax liability
Applies to income-producing housing	Yes—20% credit No—10% credit	Yes	Greater application worth more
Limited to properties built prior to 1939	Yes—10% credit	Not applicable	Age-restriction limits use

Table 5.9 Potential Strategies to Enhance the Support of the HTC

Strategy	Impact
Basis reduction—Eliminate or weaken the rule that lowers Federal LIHTC tax benefits dollar-for-dollar according to the amount of Federal HTC taken when combining the Federal HTC and LIHTC	This change would increase the tax benefit when using the Federal HTC and combining this tax credit with the LIHTC
Greater subsidy in socially distressed and/or high cost areas—Deepen the historic rehabilitation credit (e.g., increase it to 25–30%) in the most difficult to develop and disinvested locations	This change would provide greater tax benefits when effecting preservation in downtowns, deteriorated suburbs, and other high cost areas. It would parallel the *basis boost* (i.e., increasing the credit by 30%) awarded to *Difficult to Develop* areas and *Qualified Census Tracts* (low income areas) available in the LIHTC
More "workability" for small deals—Enrich the Federal HTC (e.g., increase the credit to 30–40%) for small projects (e.g., less than $2–3 million in total development costs)	Broadens the usefulness of the Federal HTC to modest size projects
More favorable tax exempt use rules—Ease the rules governing nonprofit deals so more community-oriented projects can use the Federal HTC credit	Would encourage more nonprofit participation
Promote secondary markets financing—Allow changes fostering a secondary market for Federal HTC credit projects	An enhanced secondary market for the Federal HTC would expand liquidity, i.e., make money more easily available, for preservation projects
Adjust the "substantial rehabilitation" test—Allow the Federal HTC to be used with less extensive rehabilitation. The current requirement is the *greater* of $5000 or the *adjusted basis*	Would broaden the application of the Federal HTC to include more modest-scaled preservation projects and promote preservation in areas with high real estate values

say 30 or 40%) HTC should be reserved for the most "needy" projects. That is the thinking behind the boosted credit recommendation for qualified (i.e., low income) census tracts (QCTs) and difficult to develop areas (DDAs). Yet it must be acknowledged that greater targeting of HTC assistance might add to governmental administrative delays and costs, and targeting inevitably favors economically viable projects over those that are less viable. Are we willing to tolerate the loss of a historic townhouse because its renovation did not satisfy a "but for" test and was located in a well-off neighborhood?

The use of the HTC to further preservation, especially preservation involving affordable housing, might be enhanced through more adaptation of the program on the part of the NPS and SHPOs. Tax certification regulations require that a project meet the Secretary's Standards to be eligible for federal historic tax credits. Real estate developers have noted that reconciling the Standards with market requirements, development costs, building efficiency codes, and other mandates can require considerable creativity, patience, and flexibility if they wish to use the HTC (Listokin and Listokin May 2001a). Tensions arise when it is not apparent to the developer at the outset what is considered historic material and should be retained, and what can be discarded. Small affordable housing projects can be especially difficult to make financially feasible because there are likely too few units generating too little income to cover the costs of rehabilitation and subsequent operating costs. For these small projects, the cost of the added preservation work effectively negates the incentives.

Fortunately, constructive dialogue on this and related subjects has been ongoing and there have been productive forums bringing together the preservation and development communities. Recommended reforms to the HTC review process will continue but there are no easy answers nor can set rules ever replace the need for context-sensitivity.[17]

State Historic Tax Credit Programs

Even before the 1986 Tax Reform Act, a few states had enacted their own investment tax credits for historic rehabilitation. Because the federal tax credits proved successful, it seemed appro-

priate to replicate them at the state level. After the early experiences with the 1986 Reform Act, even more states stepped into the breach. To date, approximately 30 states have adopted investment tax credit programs (Schwartz 2012, p. 4).

The perceived needs provide continued motivation for action. Illustrative is the situation described by individuals and companies knowledgeable about historic preservation in Ohio that were surveyed by Rutgers University in 2003 about their work and hurdles, even with federal credits (Lahr et al. 2003). This group worked well with the federal HTC but felt more was needed. The comments collected underscore the reasons for establishing a state tax credit program: [1] it would bolster a high risk investment in a depressed downtown; [2] it would provide additional equity in a project and lower the cost of capital; and [3] it would make it possible to meet the need for unforeseen engineering changes and providing additional finishes that benefit the rental units, and shorten the time involved searching for funding. Ohio ultimately adopted a state HTC (Schwartz 2012, p. 8; Lahr et al. 2003).

Variations in Tax Credit Level

The percentage of the rehabilitation investment against which a credit is granted for state tax purposes (e.g., individual income or corporate) ranges from 5% (Montana) to 50% (New Mexico). Many states mirror the current federal provisions and allow a 20–25% credit for income-producing properties (e.g., Colorado, Delaware, Indiana, Maryland, New York, and Oklahoma). Other states allow a 25% credit—the pre-ERTA federal incentive. States with a 25% preservation HTC include Connecticut, Georgia, Iowa, Kansas, Louisiana, Missouri, and Ohio. Some states provide different credits depending on the type of historic property. For instance, Delaware and North Carolina extend a 20% state tax credit for income-producing historic properties and a 30% state tax credit for homeowner-occupied historic buildings. Property location may also influence the credit. For example, Georgia allows an additional 5% credit (30 rather than 25%) for

---

[17] For further discussion of the Secretary of the Interior's Standards and the values underpinning preservation, the reader is referred to Chapters 6 and 7.

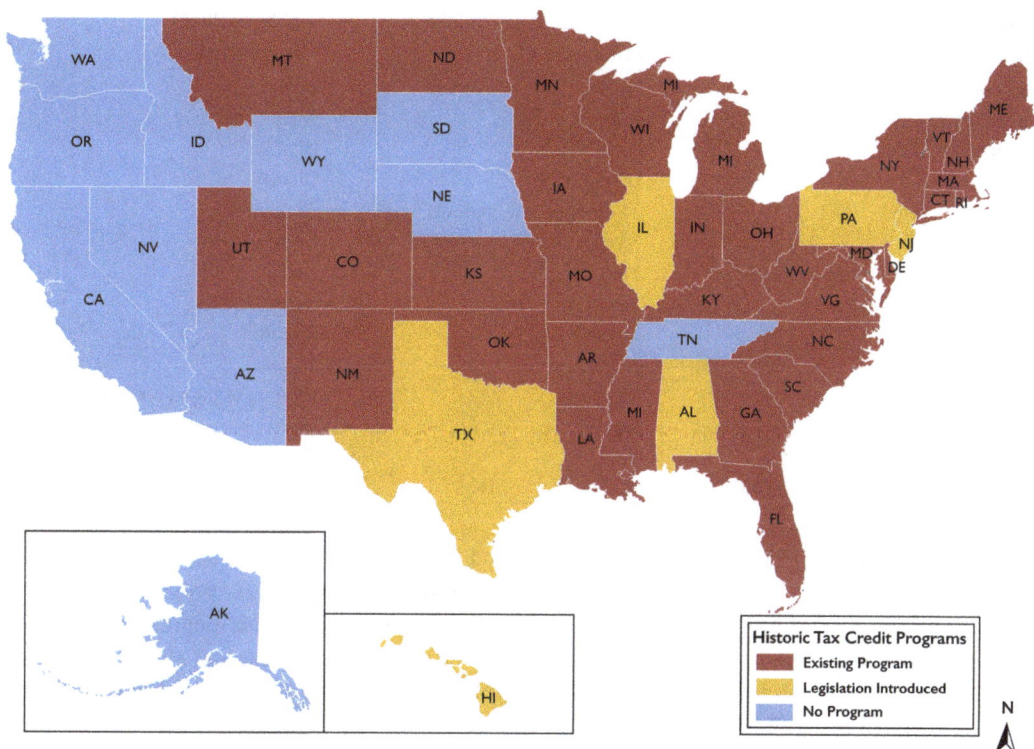

Fig. 5.2 Historic Tax Credit Programs exist at the state level, and legislation has been introduced and is pending approval in several other states. (Author's Illustration)

properties located in a HUD target area. Figure 5.2 indicates what states already have passed legislation and where it has been introduced (Listokin et al. 2011) (Fig. 5.2).

Applicability

This varies tremendously. The state historic tax credit (or state HTC) is often available to income-producing properties (just as the federal HTC), may be available to homeowner occupants (going beyond the current federal HTC), and may have further targeting, such as to farm buildings (Indiana and Iowa), downtown development districts (Louisiana), and archaeological sites (New Mexico).

Investment Requirements

Reflecting our country's dynamic federalism, investment requirements for state HTCs are quite disparate. States may require a minimum dollar investment (e.g., $5000 in Indiana, Kansas, Maryland, and Maine; $25,000 in Connecticut and North Carolina), may have no minimum dollar investment (e.g., Delaware, Georgia, Iowa, and Louisiana), may adhere to the federal HTC minimum investment (i.e., the greater of $5000 or the adjusted basis), or may revise the federal blueprint (e.g., the Rhode Island minimum investment is 50 % of the adjusted basis or $2000). While the federal HTC has no cap or maximum once its requirements are met, the less "deep pocketed" states often cap their state historic HTC. Caps may be imposed per project (e.g., $50,000 per property in Colorado and $30,000 per dwelling unit in Connecticut) and/or statewide (e.g., $2.4 million in Iowa, $3 million in Delaware, and $15 million in Maryland). States that allow a high credit percentage more often impose caps. For example, while New Mexico allows the nation's highest state HTC (50 %), that high percentage can be applied to a maximum project investment of $25,000 (outside arts

Table 5.10 Comparison of Federal and Missouri Historic Rehabilitation tax credits. (Shores 2012)

Characteristic	Federal credit	Missouri credit
Per-program maximum	None	None
Annual credit limitations	None	None
Commercial buildings	Qualify	Qualify
Residences	Do not qualify	Qualify
Restoration period	24 months or 60 months	24 months
Holding period	5 years	None
Reduction of basis by amount of credit	Yes	No
Recapture	Yes	No
Carry-back period	1 year	3 years
Carry-forward period	20 years	10 years
Partnership allocations	Pro-rata	Pro-rata or based on agreement
Transferable	No	Yes
Subject to post-issuance audit	Yes	No
Requires audit of expenses < $500,000	No	Yes

and cultural districts) to $50,000 (inside arts and cultural districts).

The state of Missouri has one of the most extensive state tax credits for historic rehabilitation. In this respect it can serve as a model for what is possible elsewhere. The Missouri program allows state taxpayers (except nonprofit entities) a 25 % state tax credit for costs associated with the rehabilitation of certified historic structures. As is evident from Table 5.10, the Missouri Historic Tax Credit (MHTC) is, in many respects, more generous than the historic tax credits offered by the federal government. In practice, the state and federal tax credits combined to create a powerful incentive that has prompted a considerable amount of historic rehabilitation, especially in the state's urban areas.[18]

From its inception in 1998 through fiscal year 2011, about $4.7 billion of historic rehabilitation has been completed under the auspices of the MHTC program.[19] The rehabilitation was often supplemented by new construction so that the total investment over the program's duration amounted to $6.1 billion. A 25 % state tax credit applied to the rehabilitation amounted to about $1.1 billion. The projects are located in St. Louis

and, to a lesser extent, Kansas City, Lexington, and Jefferson City. MHTC projects are concentrated in areas with higher population densities, significant minority presence, and lower household incomes. They are in areas that tend to have an older housing stock, higher vacancy rates, and lower owner occupancy than the state of Missouri as a whole. The Missouri Department of Economic Development classifies many MHTC locations as "distressed." Therefore, credit-inspired historic preservation investment in these areas was quite welcome.

The application of the MHTC to renovate landmark properties in downtown St. Louis is illustrative. As in many central cities, the core of this prominent riverside community had deteriorated as businesses and residents fled to the suburbs. Many iconic downtown landmarks, including the Old Post Office, the Statler and Lenox Hotels, and the Merchandise Mart, had closed or faced deterioration. The MHTC, along with other programs, aided the historic renovation of several of these downtown landmarks. The Gateway/Statler Hotel was built in 1917 and closed in 1989; the Lenox Hotel was built in 1922 and closed in the 1980s. They were rehabilitated in the late 1990s to create approximately 1100 first-class hotel rooms, which were key to supporting a nearby convention facility that itself has been built to help revitalize the downtown. Historic rehabilitation of the two hotels was neither easy nor inexpensive. Project costs amounted to about

---

[18] There have been changes in MHTC over time, such as recently imposed annual limits.

[19] Data provided by Mark A. Miles, Director and Deputy, Missouri State Historic Preservation Office, to David Listokin, April 19, 2012.

$200 million or $180,000 per room, with "hard" construction costs (e.g., building materials and labor) of $130 million, "soft" costs (e.g., interest and fees) of about $20 million, and the remaining amount for contingency, taxes, reserves, and preopening expenses.

The problem of financing a $200 million historic hotel renovation in downtown St. Louis became apparent when lenders would only offer about $90 million for a first mortgage, a modest 45% loan-to-value (LTV) ratio. This comparatively low LTV reflected a perception that investing in the city at the time—the late 1990s—was a risky proposition. With only a $90 million first mortgage, the developer had to find an additional $110 million from other sources—a daunting challenge that was met by layering subsidies. About $25 million came from investors seeking federal HTCs. An additional $12 million was obtained from Missouri investors taking advantage of the state's historic tax credits. A considerable sum, about $34 million, came from property tax increment financing (TIF), with another $25 million in the form of loan guarantees from the US Department of Housing and Urban Development's Section 105 program. Both the TIF and Section 105 will be discussed later in this chapter. Thus, the renovation of the downtown St. Louis historic hotels was made possible in large part by the federal HTC with a boost from the MHTC.

Over time, there have been changes to the MHTC (Missouri 2010). For example, the state has imposed annual limits on the program (Listokin et al. 2001). There are both annual total program caps as well as per project caps. Yet, even with these limits, annual rehabilitation activity associated with the MHTC has averaged about $450 million annually over FY 2009–2011, (Author's Papers 2012) although down from an annual $585 million average over FY 2006-FY 2008.

In 2002, another heartland state, Kansas, implemented an historic tax credit equal to 25% of eligible expenses on qualified historic structures used for either income-producing or non-income producing purposes (Listokin et al. 2010). The Kansas HTC (KHTC) is more flexible than the federal HTC. The KHTC provisions include: an ability to apply the credit to historic residences (the federal HTC is restricted to income-producing properties only); a more realistic minimum investment requirement (the federal requirements in this regard disqualifies many worthwhile projects); the right to transfer the state tax credits so as to make these more attractive to investors (prohibited in the federal HTCs); and the ability for nonprofit organizations to use the state HTC (severely limited with respect to the federal HTC).

The HKTC has markedly enhanced the HTC-based investments. In the 21-year pre-Kansas HTC period (FY1978–2001), a total of $114 million (inflation-adjusted 2009 dollars) was expended on federal HTC-assisted projects, or an average of about $5.4 million per year.

In the 8-year span (FY 2002–2009) during which the Kansas HTC has been in effect, there wasalmost a two and a half-fold increase in Kansas HTC projects (again both state-alone and state-and-federal-combined) to $271 million and the annualaverage project size rose six-fold to $33.9 million (all inflation-adjusted to 2009 dollars)

Relative to the state as a whole, the area (signified by zip codes) where KHTC activity has been implemented have the following characteristics:
1. Higher density (population per square mile)
2. Higher share of population classified as "urban"
3. Greater minority population (i.e., higher percentage of non-whites and Hispanics)
4. Lower median household income and higher economic distress (as measured by percentage in poverty and percentage unemployed)
5. Higher share of renter-occupied housing (as opposed to owner-occupied)
6. Similar housing value (for owner-occupied homes)
7. Greater housing affordability problem (as measured by households paying more than 30% of their income for housing expenses)

These characteristics of the local "hotspots" of KHTC activity strongly suggest that the program is aiding areas of higher distress and need.

Evaluating the State HTC

Overall statistics for the approximately 30 state HTC programs are not available, but the aggregate investment is likely quite large. In Missouri alone, the state tax credit-associated rehabilitation investment for FY 2011 totaled $465 million (Mark Miles 2012). It is likely that the aggregate rehab investment for all of the state programs amounts to billions of dollars per year, and it is conceivable that the aggregate state HTC volume is at least on par with the federal HTC activity.

Many of the pros and cons of the federal HTC also apply to the state preservation tax credits. Program technical requirements need to be constantly monitored, e.g., concerning the minimum investment and required holding periods, and the tax credits need to be creatively and flexibly administered by all involved parties. One can argue for steering more of the state HTCs to distressed areas and challenged property/property owner situations, but, in fact, the states already do this to a much greater extent than the federal HTC. The Vermont credit focuses on designated downtown areas; the Connecticut HTC is targeted to 29 needy municipalities in that state; and Louisiana's credit is limited to "downtown development districts." In general, the state HTCs are cauldrons of variation and experimentation, and are a model of creative federalism. While the federal HTC is a primary aid to historic preservation in the United States, state HTCs are a crucial supplemental support where it is most needed. The same is true of a relatively recent federal option, the New Markets Tax Credits.

Income Tax Bridge Mechanisms

The New Markets Tax Credit (NMTC) is offered by the Community Development Financial Institution (CDFI) Fund within the US Department of the Treasury and was authorized by the Community Renewal Tax Relief Act of 2000. The NMTC grants a 39% tax credit for investment in Community Development Entities (CDEs).

A CDE provides loans, investments, or financial counseling in "low income communities"

Table 5.11 NMTC from $1 Million Investment

Year	NMTC ($)
1	50,000
2	50,000
3	50,000
4	60,000
5	60,000
6	60,000
7	60,000
Total	390,000

(LICs), defined as census tracts with a minimum 20% poverty level or where median income is at or below 80% of the area median family income. CDEs may comprise various entities, including for-profit community development financial institutions, for-profit subsidiaries of community development corporations, and specialized small business investment companies. The CDEs, in turn, make "qualified low-income community investments" that can take various forms, including investing or lending to a "qualified active low-income community business" or a business located in a LIC with a "substantial connection to that location." CDEs can also help other CDEs, through investing, lending, or purchasing loans, or providing financial counseling.

The 39% tax credit is given for making a "qualified equity investment" (QEI) in a CDE. A QEI consists of purchase of stock or a capital interest in a CDE, thus helping capitalizing these entities. The investment must be held by the CDE for 7 years, constituting "patient capital," reflecting the fact that it often takes longer to secure a profit in a LIC. The NMTC is generally excluded from investment in rental real estate with some exceptions, e.g., when real estate is part of a mixed-use project.

The NMTC 39% tax credit is taken over 7 years (equal to about 30% in present value terms). The 39% is scheduled as follows: a 5% credit is allowed in each of the first 3 years and a 6% credit is extended in each of the final 4 years. Thus, an investor who committed a $1 million QEI to a CDE that makes qualified low-income community investments would receive the tax credits over 7 years as shown in Table 5.11, worth $1 for $1 against federal tax obligations. As with the HTC and the LIHTC, syndicators familiar

Table 5.12 New Market Tax Credit Allocations

NMTC allocation round	NMTC allocation year	NMTC amount allocated (billions)
Round 1	2003	$2.5
Round 2	2004	$3.5
Round 3	2005	$2.0
Round 4	2006	$4.1
Round 5	2007	$3.9
Round 6	2008	$3.5
Round 7	2009	$5.0
Round 8	2010	$3.5
Round 9	2011	$3.6
Total		$31.6

with the provisions of the NMTC provide investors with a pro rata share of the tax shelter according to their proportional investment.

It is instructive to point out differences between the Federal HTC and the NMTC beyond that of their primary missions—historic preservation for the former and economic development for the latter. While the Federal HTC is not capped in amount, the NMTC is, with the available amounts shown in Table 5.12.

Further, while the Federal HTC is an entitlement, i.e., the tax credits are automatically extended provided preservation-appropriate substantial rehabilitation is completed in certified historic structures, the NMTC is competitive. Entities first compete to be selected as CDEs on the basis of their business strategy, capitalization, management capacity, expertise in working with the disadvantaged, anticipated community impact, and other factors; only about 20% of applicants for CDEs created for NMTC purposes are chosen. Further, only about 10% of the tax credit dollars requested by the CDE finalists are awarded. In short, the NMTC involves a complicated multi-stage process for the CDFI Fund: choosing and allocating tax credits to CDEs; investors making QEIs in the CDEs; and, finally, the CDEs either directly or indirectly making investments to bolster economic activity in the low-income neighborhoods.

While it may be complicated, the NMTC has quickly become an important revitalization investment vehicle. A December 2010 analysis found that 57% of the NMTC investment to date was in communities with poverty rates exceeding 30% and that 60% of NMTC activity is located

in places where the median incomes are at or below 60% of area median (NMTCC 2010). As of February 2012, 644 allocation awards totaling $31.6 billion had been made to 632 CDEs.[20] While CDEs can make many types of investments, in practice the most typical investment has been a loan, typically for commercial real estate.[21] The NMTC tax credit allows an interest reduction on a loan equal to roughly 2.5–5.0% (Armistead 2005, p. 1). Besides a below-market interest rate, the NMTC allows borrowers to secure better loan terms, such as permitting a longer-than-standard period of interest-only payments or lower-than-standard origination fees.

While the NMTC is not directed to historic preservation *per se*, it has been a source of rehabilitation financing. The National Trust Community Investment Corporation (NTCIC), a CDE formed by the National Trust for Historic Preservation, reported that about 38% of National Register Historic Districts, 58% of the buildings within these districts, and 33% of all staffed Main Street programs are located in NMTC-eligible census tracts (Campbell and Leith-Tetrault 2006). While the exact number of NMTC projects that involve historic preservation remains unknown, indirect evidence suggests that preservation has been part of this program. When NMTC investors were asked what other government incentives they used besides the 39% credit, almost 30% cited the federal HTC (GAO 2007). Furthermore, the National Trust for Historic Preservation's CDE received one of the largest first round NMTC allocations ($127 million) and as of 2012 the NTCIC has been awarded a total NMTC allocation of about $383 million. According to a NTCIC study,[22] about 10% of NMTC transactions and about 20% of qualified equity investments in the first four rounds of the

---

[20] Some CDEs received multiple awards.

[21] Of the total NMTC loans and investment from fiscal years 2003 through 2008, 65% was used for the rehabilitation or construction of new commercial real estate, 22% was applied to business-related activities of QALICBs, and the remainder was used for various other purposes (GAO 2010).

[22] Data provided by John Leith-Tetrault of the NTCIC to David Listokin of Rutgers University, May 3, 2012.

Fig. 5.3 The recent rehabilitation of the Old Post Office in downtown St. Louis involved the use of New Market tax credits. Built from 1872 to 1884, this federal facility is listed on the National Register of Historic Places and is a National Historic Landmark. (Historic American Building Survey, Library of Congress)

NMTC program have involved a combination of the federal HTC and NMTC.

One of the most prominent examples of the use of NMTC funds was the restoration of the Old Post Office in downtown St. Louis (Fig. 5.3). Built in the Second Empire style over a 12 year period starting in 1872, this 242,000 sq. ft. federal facility is both on the National Register of Historic Places as well as a National Historic Landmark (NHL). By 1975, however, changing economic needs and a declining St. Louis downtown resulted in the cessation of operations. In an attempt to keep this acknowledged landmark open, the federal Government Services Administration oversaw a $16 million rehabilitation to adaptively reuse the space for retail purposes. That effort unfortunately failed and the building was ultimately reclaimed in a $51 million project completed in 2006. The Old Post Office now houses public courts, a private university, retailers, and other uses.

As in the St. Louis Gateway/Statler and Lenox Hotel historic renovations, private lenders were only willing to extend a relatively modest first mortgage for the Old Post Office project, about $8 million of the $51 million project cost. Downtown St. Louis was still a difficult market relative to the city's growing suburbs. Layered subsidies were assembled, with investors putting about

$18 million into the project, supplemented by the federal HTC and the Missouri state HTC. The additional NMTC attracted another $8 million in equity, for a combined $26 million in tax credits, 50% of the entire deal. Other sources included a Missouri Development Finance Board second mortgage of about $12 million, about $2 million in Community Development Block Grants, and the rest from private contributions (Armistead 2005, p. 37).

The renovated Old Post Office has benefited from these multiple financial aids and has returned to its former iconic glory, its many users thriving. With this downtown anchor secure, five adjacent historic properties have been rehabilitated, including the Frisco and Syndicate Buildings. These projects, combined, provide 400 market-rate and affordable housing units, 65,000 sq. ft. of retail, and 1130 parking spaces to serve the new residents and visitors.

The parking came at a cost, however, paid by the nearby Neoclassical Century Building, which was razed in order to build the parking garage. While the National Trust argued that pragmatism had to rule in this case to realize the larger goal of saving the Old Post Office and its historic neighbors, other preservationists were aghast and criticized the Century Building demolition as violating preservation's fundamental Hippocratic oath, to "first do no harm" (McKee 2005).[23]

Fortunately, other NTCIC projects have rarely involved a Sophie's Choice and instead have personified the successful layering of subsidies to save important historic resources. A brief glimpse of some typical NMTC and federal HTC projects (including some spearheaded by the NTCIC) follow below (NTCIC 2010; Table 5.13).

In short, while not designed specifically as a subsidy for historic preservation, the NMTC has become a useful resource for helping rejuvenate historic buildings. Because the NMTC is designed to assist low-income communities, it inevitably affects the treatment of underutilized properties frequently found in these neighborhoods. Much of the investment has taken the form of commer-

---

[23] The ethics of this case is discussed in Chapter 6.

Table 5.13 Combining the NMTC and HTC Programs

Project (Location)	Description	Total development costs (in million dollars)	Key project financing
American Brewery Building (Baltimore, MD)	Adaptive reuse of vacant former beer brewhouse (built 1877) to office and program space for nonprofit human service provider	22.8	$14 million NMTC-enhanced bank loan and $5.3 million federal HTC and NMTC
Carpenter Center for the Performing Arts (Richmond, VA)	Rehabilitation/conversion of former Loew's movie theatre (opened 1928, closed 1979) into performing arts center	85.5	$25 million grant from City of Richmond; $29 million in federal/state HTC and NMTC; $9 million Virginia state grant
DIA Art Foundation (Beacon, NY)	292,000 ft^2 manufacturing facility (1929) converted to avant-garde art museum	31.4	$28 million foundation and individuals; $6.3 million federal HTC and NMTC
First Street Lofts (Flint, MI)	Adaptive reuse of 1920s bank to mixed use loft apartments and office	6.3	$1.4 million bank loan; $1.9 million federal HTC, NMTC, and other tax credits; $1.5 million foundation and other grants
Helman Building (San Antonio, TX)	Adaptive reuse of 1907 hotel to headquarters complex	5.9	$2.1 million developer's equity; $2.0 million private loan; and $1.1 million federal HTC and NMTC
Pontchartrain Hotel (New Orleans, LA)	Adaptive reuse of hotel (built 1927) to service-enriched senior housing	20.5	$8.4 million bank loan; $5.2 million federal and state HTC; and $2.8 million NMTC

cial real estate loans with favorable terms, supporting commercial historic preservation projects. Although the exact magnitude of NMTC investment in historic properties is unknown, it is likely that, of the nearly $32 billion in NMTC allocations over nine years, at least 10 % or about $300 million annually involves preservation. At a 39 % tax credit, the NMTC is providing an annual subsidy for preservation of just above $100 million, or 39 % of $300 million.

Easements as Financial Tools

Related to the broad category of income tax incentives are the income and property tax benefits from creating an historic preservation easement. As seen in Chapter 3, this mechanism can be flexibly applied in a variety of preservation applications.

Since certain property rights are given away when a preservation easement is created, including the right to develop or modify the property at will, the argument to the Internal Revenue Service is that the diminished value should be considered a charitable deduction for Federal income tax purposes.[24] "The value of the easement is based on the difference between the approved fair market value of the property prior to conveying an easement and its lower value with the easement restriction in place" (NPS 2007, p. 2). For instance, compare the Philadelphia Land Title Building, worth $5,000,000 without the easement and the same structure at a market value of $4,000,000 with the easement. In that case, the diminished difference in value, $1,000,000, could then be counted as a deduction (not a credit) against income taxes, as would any charitable donation.[25]

---

[24] The deduction may also be taken on other Federal taxes such as gift and estate levies, and state tax benefits may also be available.

[25] The old technique of using a percentage of the value is no longer recognized as valid, although there is no appar-

Table 5.14 Local General Revenue, by Source, 1980–2008 (in billions)

Year	Total	Inter-gov-ernmental	Total own-source	Own-source					
				Taxes					Charges and miscella-neous
				Total	Property	Individual income	Sales, other income	Other	
1980	232,452	102,425	130,027	86,387	65,607	4990	12,072	3718	43,640
1990	512,322	190,732	321,599	201,130	149,765	9563	30,815	10,987	120,469
2000	888,865	349,894	538,971	332,696	238,182	17,088	44,188	33,238	206,275
2005	1,160,466	452,099	708,367	447,900	324,437	20,676	71,682	31,105	260,466
2008	1,401,341	524,737	876,603	548,764	396,994	26,254	90,166	35,350	327,839

State and Local Government financing for the years indicated (US Census data)

The preservation easement charitable contribution was recognized by an Internal Revenue Service ruling in 1964 and was formalized by Congress in 1976 (Roddewig 2011). A 2006 pension reform law made certain changes, such as requiring the donor to provide more detailed documentation to substantiate the value of the donation, eliminating deductions for conservation-affected land areas in registered historic districts, and imposing a new reduction for easements on structures that have also qualified for the Federal HTC (PL 2006). State revenue agencies are also providing guidance for land conservation and preservation easement donations. In California, state enabling legislation allows the cities that adopt the Mills Act to work with the owners of historic properties, entering into easement contracts for 10 years, whereby a special assessment formula is applied to the property, resulting in a 50% or more tax deduction.[26]

An Introduction to Property Tax Rates

The property tax is a levy on wealth held in the form of property. Property is divided into two main categories—real and personal. Real prop-

ent, widely-accepted technique being applied. Still, with an increasing number of easements being granted, more documentation is assembled, so that actual real estate "comparables" can be used as reference.

[26] Named for California State Senator John Mills, the act was passed in 1972 in an attempt to help save the Coronado Hotel in San Diego. In 1976, California voters passed a constitutional amendment; over 80 communities have adopted this law.

erty consists of land and the improvements on it, including structures. All other property is considered personal property. In most instances, the property tax is based primarily on real property.

The property tax is a major source of funding for local governments (Hy and Waugh 1995). Sources of revenue for local government in the United States over the 1980–2008 period are detailed in Table 5.14. In 2008, for instance, local general revenues in the United States amounted to $1,401 billion. Of that total, $525 billion (37%) was supported by intergovernmental (state and federal) aid and $876 billion (63%) was derived from local own source revenues. Of the latter, the property tax contributed $397 billion; fees and miscellaneous, $328 billion; sales and corporate income taxes, $90 billion; and the rest from individual income taxes and other sources. The property tax was thus the single most important source of local income supporting local governments. It generated almost three tenths of all local government general revenue, almost half of every dollar of own source (i.e., non-intergovernmental) general revenues, and an even higher share, nearly three-quarters, of local tax income. In 48 of 50 states, the 2008 property tax yield alone is larger than the combined yield from all other local government taxes (e.g., sales and income); in 36 of 50 states, the property tax exceeds the total revenue from the sum of all fees and miscellaneous revenue.

It is important to realize, however, that within the national profile are significant state and regional variations. While nationally the property tax contributed about 28 cents of every dollar of local general revenues, in Arkansas *ad valorem* income amounted to 10 cents, but in Connecticut it was 56 cents. Noticeable regional variations exist in the reliance placed on the property tax. In the Northeast it is about 35 % of the local government's revenue, in the Midwest it is 32 %, in the South only 15 %, and in the West is 18 %.

In all areas, the property tax rate of a given jurisdiction is obtained by dividing the tax dollars gained by the jurisdiction's total property valuation. The dollars raised from the property tax is equal to total local government spending less the sum of all other nonproperty sources of local revenue. For example, if a local government spent $5 million and received $1 million in inter-governmental revenue and $2 million in nonproperty taxes, then it would have to raise $2 million from the property tax. If that community had an aggregate $100 million market value tax base, then the property tax rate is $2.00 per $100 of valuation. This rate may alternatively be expressed as $20 per $1000 of valuation, or 20 mills or 0.0200, or 2 %. This percentage nomenclature is widely understood. In the example community, a house valued on the open market at $100,000 would be obligated to pay $2000 in annual property taxes. This community has a 2 % effective property tax rate (EPRT).

How the Property Tax Affects Preservation

According to the 2000 decennial census, the average EPTR in the United States was 1.27 %. While preservation is undertaken anywhere, it is more likely to take place in cities. Yet, these often have the highest property tax burdens. While the average national EPTR was 1.27 %, it was 1.33 % in central cities and only 1.10 % in nonmetropolitan locations.

In addition, the average EPTR on housing built before 1939, the stock most likely to be designated as historic, was 1.41 %, whereas for the youngest housing stock (units built between 1996 and 2000), it was a much lower 1.10 %.

These disparities are even greater in those states that rely more heavily on the property tax, particularly those in the Northeast. New Jersey

is a case in point. While the average EPTR in this state as of 2000 was 2.38 %, its central cities had an average EPTR of 2.78 %. In New Jersey, housing units built in 1939 or earlier had an average EPTR of 2.56 %, noticeably higher than the 2.05 % for the newest housing stock (units built 1996–2000).

This condition is not unique. The average EPTR in Maryland's cities in 2000 was 2.02 %, double the 1.00 % rate in the state's nonmetropolitan areas and far above the average 1.32 % EPTR for the state as a whole. Maryland's older housing stock (i.e., units built in 1939 or earlier) in 2000 had a noticeably higher property tax rate (1.44 %) when compared to the EPTR (1.16 %) of this state's newest housing units (i.e., units built 1996–2000), which were typically built in the suburbs and exurbs.

In short, in New Jersey, Maryland, and other states, the property tax burden is highest just in those locations (i.e., cities) and on that portion of the existing stock (i.e., older buildings) where preservation is most likely to be effected. This higher burden is magnified if the historic resource is rehabilitated. Since the property tax mirrors value, an investment that adds to value increases the annual property tax obligation.

To illustrate, a $300,000 New Jersey historic home located in a central city would pay annual average property taxes of $8340 (2.78 % of $300,000). An extensive $150,000 renovation would raise the annual tax bill to $12,510 (2.78 % of $450,000). Given the above situation, the homeowner might find it hard to pay the already high annual property taxes and would be discouraged from improving the property because it would make the tax burden even worse. Situations such as this, writ large, poses a common fiscal constraint to preservation.

Property Tax Incentives

In response, many states have enabled local governments to offer property tax incentives to encourage historic preservation. Three types of programs are currently available: property tax exemption or reduction for historic properties, property tax rehabilitation incentives, and dedicated use of property taxes for preservation purposes.

Property Tax Exemption/Reduction

Property taxes can be exempted (no property taxes are paid) or reduced on historic properties. These provisions do not require investment (e.g., rehabilitation) but are extended solely on the basis that preserving a landmark is socially desirable and a property tax break is one means to advance the cause of preservation. To illustrate, Connecticut allows tax exemption or reduction where tax relief is necessary to permit continued operation or maintenance. Alabama's Constitutional Amendment No. 373 classifies historic buildings as Class III structures, a category assessed at 10% of fair-market value. Without this special provision, certain types of Alabama landmarks, such as nonresidential structures or residential buildings that are not owner-occupied, would be assessed at 20% of fair-market value. Amendment No. 373 thus reduces the assessment and therefore the property taxes of designated historic structures by one half.

Property Tax Rehabilitation Incentives

A number of states offer favorable property-tax treatment to historic buildings, specifically buildings undergoing renovation. Provisions range from reducing the existing property taxes (*rehabilitation refund*), to not reassessing (*rehabilitation assessment*), or only partially increasing the assessment of the rehabilitated property (*rehabilitation abatement*). All of these treatments convey property-tax relief, meaning that although rehabilitating the historic property improves its value (and should result in an increased, rather than a decreased/frozen, assessment/tax obligation), the taxes do not increase as they otherwise would.

About 15 states provide some type of rehabilitation incentive. Five permit refunds. New Mexico Statue δ18-6-13, for example, provides

that "local, city, county and school property taxes assessed against the property shall be reduced by the amount expended for restoration, preservation and maintenance." The amount of the refund varies across jurisdictions. New York allows a credit against taxes equal to almost the full amount expended on rehabilitation. In contrast, Maryland limits the refund to 10% of rehabilitation expenditures. The time span varies over which the refund is in effect, with a range of five years in South Dakota and Maryland to a generous 12 years in New York.

Rehabilitation refunds are quite expensive since the taxing jurisdiction is not only precluded from any gain in assessment/taxation due to rehabilitation, but suffers an absolute loss in its tax base for varying periods of time. It is perhaps for this reason that rehabilitation incentive and abatement programs are more popular; they have been adopted in about 10 states. These statutes typically allow a period during which the rehabilitated historic building either will not be revalued or else is reassessed by only a fraction of the true value added by the renovation. Some states combine rehabilitation assessment/abatement provisions. Maryland provides a 2-year period after rehabilitation of a landmark when there is no increase in assessed value. Afterwards, the following schedule is maintained: in year three, the upward reassessment is limited to 20% of the improvement; in year four, 40%; in year five, 60%; in year six, full upward reassessment is permitted. Other combinations are possible. New York, for example, combines a rehabilitation assessment and refund.

Earmarking Property Taxes for Preservation Purposes–Tax Increment Financing (TIF)

The objective of this third group of strategies is to turn the "lemon" of property taxes, especially high taxes that can discourage investment, into the "lemonade" of a resource that can support investment, whether for preservation or for other purposes. A prime example is tax increment financing (TIF). A TIF is a popular tool to finance new development or redevelopment (rehabilitation and new construction) by capturing the property appreciation and associated higher property tax payments resulting from the development or redevelopment.[27] The mechanism works as follows.

1. The area within which the development/redevelopment is to occur is designated as a TIF district
2. Property values for standard property taxation purposes are then frozen in the TIF district for a given period of time (e.g., 10–20 years).
3. As property values from the frozen levels increase over time, the appreciation (or "increment") is used for development or redevelopment purposes. The amount captured is equal to the increment in property value multiplied by the property tax rate (the full rate or a portion, such as the municipal but not the school property tax rate).

For example, a Maryland city with an EPTR of 2% creates a TIF to benefit preservation. If the TIF district appreciated $10 million in value from the frozen base, then $200,000 (2% of $10 million) in preservation assistance would be made available annually.

There are many TIF variations, such as a "bond TIF" (where the city issues bonds to raise money for up-front project purposes with the bonds to be repaid from projected TIF revenues) versus a "pay-as-you-go TIF" (where annual TIF revenue is made available as per the district's valuation increment). Since developers often need assistance up front to launch a project, a bond TIF is more desirable, albeit riskier if the value increment is not secured. Because all TIFs involve some risk, this mechanism typically requires state enabling authority for the effecting local entity. Further, the type of area eligible for a TIF may be limited to "blighted," "redevelopment," or other financially challenged locations.

In addition, a TIF scheme may require a report showing that "but for" this finance mechanism the proposed project could not proceed. In practice, however, "blight" and "redevelopment" are themselves broadly applied, as is satisfaction of a "but for" requirement (Johnson and Man 2001).

Almost all of the states have passed enabling legislation to allow cities to use TIFs, and they have been used for a variety of desirable purposes. California has the greatest number, but other heavy users include Illinois, Minnesota, and Missouri. California TIFs have financed affordable housing as well as a new baseball stadium for the San Diego Padres. The $5.2 million adaptive reuse of the 1893 Belvidere, Illinois High School into 57 housing units benefited from a $300,000 TIF. In the cold Minnesota climate, pedestrian skyways and underground garages have been financed in the Twin Cities with the TIF mechanism (Lefcoe 2011). The successful renovation of the historic Gateway/Statler Hotel in St. Louis, a $200 million project described earlier, used $34 million secured by TIF.

In other instances, the TIF is smaller yet nonetheless part of the preservation financing toolkit. The $3.4 million investment in revitalizing the 1909 St. Luke's School in Two Rivers, Wisconsin benefited from $200,000 in TIF funds. In Tulsa, Oklahoma, a TIF provided over $1 million in support for historic preservation in that city's Brady Village. These monies have spurred other efforts, such as the renovation of the Tribune Building and Lain's Ballroom in Brady Village.

To understand TIFs better for their application to historic preservation, consider the activities in Chicago. In Illinois, all cities are allowed to use a TIF scheme to generate property tax dollars for economic development purposes in specifically designated areas. This permits the city to invest all new property tax dollars generated from the designated TIF district (property value appreciation from the frozen tax base multiplied by the property tax rate) for as long as 23 years.

Illustrative is Chicago's North/Central Loop TIF zone, the first and largest (both in terms of land area and value of property) such zone in the city and one of the largest in the United States. In order to revitalize the declining downtown area,

---

[27] The financing mechanism was initially devised in 1952 by Los Angeles bond counsel Jim Beebe, who spearheaded enabling legislation in California. Two years later Sacramento's Redevelopment Agency was the first to benefit; by 1990, over 40 states had adopted similar legislation (Wyatt 1990).

Chicago initiated the program in 1984. The original North Loop TIF area covered about 32 acres valued at about $53 million. In 1997, a considerably larger Central Loop extension was added to this area. Today, the entire district is referred to as the Central Loop. It currently covers 171 acres of land and incorporates 22 redevelopment agreements where TIF subsidies were paid. Since its inception, the total dollar amount of TIF allocations has been about $273 million, of which $183 million were developer subsidies and $91 million were public works or infrastructure expenditures. The total amount of private investment in the North/Central Loop TIF has been $1.153 billion. Some of this area's major projects included renovation of the historic Blackstone Hotel and Palace Theater (in which a $65 million private investment was aided by a $17 million TIF) and the historic rehab of the Chicago Theater (where a $42 million private investment was aided by a $16 million TIF). The Chicago North/Central loop is not alone but is joined by almost 130 other TIF locations in the city, comprising 30% of Chicago's land area.[28] In short, this financing device has been vital to the redevelopment of the "Windy City."

Evaluating Property Tax Bridge Mechanisms

Property tax incentives provide considerable room for creating subsidies. Nationally, billions of dollars are collected each year. As indicated earlier, the states in the Northeast and Midwest depend on this revenue more than those in the South and West. The linkage is also clear between higher tax cities and older suburbs. These are important factors to keep in mind when considering ways to improve tax mechanisms to benefit preservation.

One measure of evaluation is to consider the empirical evidence on the effectiveness of financial inducements, such as property tax reduction to foster investment. That evidence is mixed.[29] A survey of 34 factors prompting business to invest in a given area found that financial incentives were not as important as a city's general business climate or distance to customers (Schmitt et al. 1987; Wolkoff 1985). On the other hand, regression analyses have found that property tax incentives were a statistically significant positive investment influence (Bartik 1991).

Moreover, property tax exemptions and reductions, rehabilitation incentives, and TIFs—while arguably necessary to spur preservation in a given situation—nonetheless remove property tax income from the city's coffers that would ordinarily be available to the community at large. Because a community's tax rate is directly influenced by its overall property tax base, removing property from the base through a TIF or other means inevitably puts increasing pressure on the tax rate for nonproject businesses and residents. In practice, frequently the justification is made that the fiscal pressure is temporarily bearable for the ultimate good of the community. Yet, the question remains who is affected by the lack of funds that are diverted into the TIF scheme.

If 5% of the current property tax levy were taken and used for a TIF, the shortfall would have to be made up from other sources. Since added state and federal aid is unlikely, making up the loss would require increases in locally generated revenues, perhaps instituting or raising city income or sales taxes. Assuming a city's budget adjusted for inflation remains the same, the expenses remain the same. This means there is no "free lunch" from a property tax break. In fact, some jurisdictions are contracting or even disallowing property tax incentives. California, for example, rescinded the ability of its community redevelopment agencies from using TIFs (NYT 2012). There has been growing controversy in Chicago concerning TIFs, with headlines-grabbing charges of TIF abuses and a lack of accountability. Other jurisdictions are also rethinking

---

[28] http://www.cityofchicago.org/city/en/depts/dcd/provdrs/tif.html (accessed March 3, 2014) provides up-to-date information about the status of TIF projects throughout the city (Gibson 2003).

[29] A considerable amount of literature has been generated, often coming to different conclusions (Austrian and Norton 2002; Chirinko and Wilson 2008).

their property tax incentive measures (Youngman 2011).

If, as is likely, property tax incentives continue to be applied to support preservation and other objectives in some form, how can they be improved? Among the ways that might be considered are to allow greater flexibility. This might include varying the amount of the reduction that is allowed, the development product to which it can be extended, and the geographic area in which the property tax incentive can be granted.

For example, it was previously noted that Alabama's Constitutional Amendment No. 373 reduces the property taxes on landmark nonresidential structures or residential buildings that are not owner-occupied by one half. Yet, even paying 50 cents on the dollar of property taxes owed may be too much to have an impact on pioneer preservation in very challenging locations, e.g., the first historic property being renovated in an inner city neighborhood.[30] In this instance, the need to establish a viable market in an area suffering from decades of disinvestment may require a higher property tax reduction. Conversely, a lower property tax reduction may suffice in more promising preservation situations, such as the renovation of luxury housing in a sought-after historic district. Perhaps the Alabama historic property tax incentive, and others like it, should incorporate a "but for" test, i.e., "but for" the tax reduction, the preservation investment would not be viable, that would be rigidly applied and, once that test is satisfied, varying property tax reductions would be allowed as per the need.

Programmatic and Other Bridging Tools

The third category of financial aid to preservation is the federal and, increasingly, state programmatic aids that contribute funds and provide important bridge mechanisms. Other entities, including local governments and preservation organizations, also offer assistance. Some are relatively well known, but their limitations are not well understood.

Federal Program Assistance

The Historic Preservation Fund (HPF) provides a federal contribution that must be matched dollar-for-dollar by non-federal sources (e.g., state contributions) to support survey and planning activities, regulatory review (e.g., Section 106, NEPA, and rehabilitation tax credit reviews) and "bricks and mortar" activities. Created by the National Historic Preservation Act, the HPF was and is supposed to receive $150 million annually from outer continental shelf oil lease revenues. The rationale of this pairing was to use the resources from the depletion of a non-renewable natural resource, oil, to fund the continued renewal of historic resources. In fact, however, only a fraction of this nominally dedicated revenue was actually appropriated, leaving to date a $2.8 billion unexpended balance. Recent HPF annual appropriations have generally ranged from about $70 to $95 million (NCSHPO 2009; NPS 2011).

As is evident from Table 5.15, a large share of the HPF goes to SHPOs (SHPOs)[31]. This SHPO funding rose from about $0.1 million in 1968 (the first year of appropriations) to about $50 million in 1979. Funding was then slashed, reaching a nadir of about $20 million in 1986. Funding for SHPOs from the HPF plateaued at approximately $30 million annually from 1990 to 2000, and in recent years, with one exception (FY 2001), has hovered at about $35 million.[32]

---

[30] A further constraint is the relatively low EPTR in Alabama, thus reducing the benefit from a property tax subsidy in this state.

[31] Ten percent of the HPF funding to states is transferred to local units of government with preservation programs in place called "Certified Local Governments" (CLGs), as noted in Chapter 3. Tribal Historic Preservation Officers (THPOs) also receive funding from HPF.

[32] The SHPO funding from the HPF was about $47 million in FY 2001. This increase was due to efforts to enact the Conservation and Reinvestment Act (CARA). CARA would have funded the HPF from oil leases at the authorized annual amount of $150 million and guaranteed that funding for 15 years. CARA was not enacted, but SHPOs

Table 5.15 Recent HPF Support (in millions). (NCSHPO 2009; NPS 2011)

Component	Fiscal year							
	2001	2002	2003	2004	2005	2006	2007	2008
SHPOs	$46.6	$39	$33.7	$34.5	$35.4	$35.7	$35.7	$35.7
THPOs	5.6	3.0	3	3	3.2	3.9	3.9	3.9
SAT	30.0	30.0	30	33	29.5	30[a]	12.6[d]	10
HBCUs	6.8	0.0	0	3	3.47	2.9	2.9	0
Sites		2.5	2	0.5	0	0	0	0
PA	[b]	[b]	[b]	[b]	0	5[a]	12.6[d]	10
Inventory	[b]	[b]	[b]	[b]	[b]	[b]	[b]	4
Total	$94	$74.5	$68.7	$74	$71.57	$72	$55.6	$63.7

SAT Save America's Treasures, *HBCUs* Historically Black Colleges and Universities, *Sites* Presidential Sites, *PA* Preserve America

[a] 5 million set-aside for Preserve America

[b] Program not in place

[c] Funding for all government program for FY07 was done through a continuing resolution—H.J.R.20—which is based on FY06 levels and an elimination of earmark projects

[d] 12.6 million for both Preserve America and the competitive grants of Save America's Treasures. Save America's Treasures earmark funding was eliminated

[e] President's budget.

When the HPF had more resources, SHPOs would use a share of their federal allocation to support local preservation activities, including grants for bricks and mortar projects (NCSHPO 2009). Over the last three decades, with pared down federal funding and constrained state support, SHPOs have been forced to use the HPF to fulfill their mandated review activities.

Programmatic support for "bricks-and-mortar" projects is available from the HPF through the Save America's Treasures (SAT) program. Launched by President Clinton in his 1998 State of the Union address, the SAT provides matching grants to federal agencies, units of state and local governments, federally recognized tribes, and nonprofit organizations to preserve the nation's most significant historic and cultural resources.[33] This aid is typically dedicated to threatened, privately owned National Historic Landmarks, as well as NPS sites and collections in need of additional funding. SAT support has hovered at

about $30 million annually, though that amount was halved in recent years.

To date, the SAT has helped hundreds of projects, particularly over 230 NHLs. It is also important for assisting about 20 projects on the National Trust for Historic Preservation annual "most endangered list" (PCAH 2006). In addition to famous properties, important artifacts have benefited. Some of the most celebrated efforts are the restoration of the iconic flag that flew at Fort McHenry, known as the Star-Spangled Banner; the restoration of the US Constitution; and restoration of the rusted bus that carried Civil Rights advocate Rosa Parks in 1955, by the Henry Ford Museum and Greenfield Village (PCAH 2006). Beside support for SHPOs and the SAT, other HPF aid goes to Historically Black Colleges and Universities, and other recipients.

A much greater amount of programmatic support for preservation comes from a surprising source, federal assistance to transportation. As mentioned in Chapters 2 and 3, federal transportation actions were often antithetical to preservation. Begun in 1956, the Interstate Highway System spawned a ribbon of concrete that doomed many historic neighborhoods in the United States. By 1987, it was apparent that the original intent of the highway legislation had largely been accomplished, so that the Highway Builders Associa-

---

received a one year boost in funding (by about $12 million) from their prevailing $35 million to $47 million in FY 2001 (NCSHPO 2009).

[33] Other partners include Heritage Preservation, the National Endowment for the Arts, and the National Park Foundation.

tion, trucking industry, and the American Association of State Highway and Transportation Officials (AASHTO) began to exert pressure for a new wave of projects.[34] President George H. W. Bush adopted the idea of an even larger highway system in February, 1991 (Fehr 1991). The problem the pro-highway coalition faced was that the old political consensus to fund road infrastructure, a product of the Cold War era, had dissolved. President Ronald Reagan's New Federalism devolved many responsibilities to the states, and state officials often had different goals than city representatives. In order to form a new political consensus, Senator Daniel Patrick Moynihan held hearings to gather support for shifting transportation policy away from dependency on the automobile while offering the highway lobby support by ensuring that individual Congressional representatives could sponsor their special road projects (Hodson 2000). In the end, everyone got something. More importantly, the underlying transportation philosophy broadened the predominant transportation paradigm by encouraging "intermodalism," where funding was available to encourage many forms of travel, including mass transit, bus, bicycle, and pedestrian.

The Intermodal Surface Transportation Efficiency Act (ISTEA) of 1991, familiarly known as "ICE TEA," and its successor in 1998, the Transportation Equity Act for the twenty-first century (TEA-21), led to the Safe, Accountable, Flexible and Efficient Transportation Equity Act–A Legacy for Users (SAFETEA-LU) in 2005. All of the above were transportation funding behemoths: ISTEA funded at about $155 billion; TEA-21, about $220 billion; and SAFETEA-LU, about $280 billion (Brown 1991).

The largest and most flexible component of these three bills was the Surface Transportation Program (STP), which provided federal block grants to states for non-national highway purposes (Costello and Schamess 2006). In turn, 10% of the STP was dedicated to what are referred to as Transportation Enhancement Activities (TEAs), which are both directly and indirectly supportive of preservation. The TEA resources are very significant—involving billions of dollars—so monies going from this pool to preservation are large sums, especially relative to the much smaller amounts available from other federal programmatic support.

To receive TEA funding, a project must (1) be related to surface transportation *and* (2) must include an eligible enhancement activity. There are currently 12 eligible activities (Table 5.16).[35] For example, the National Scenic Byways Program was begun in 1992, allowing several state DOTs to join their sister natural resources agencies, preservation offices, and tourism departments in programs that recognize the intrinsic qualities of transportation corridors, be they scenic, historic, natural, recreational, cultural, or archaeological.

In brief, of the $9.87 billion distributed in TEA support over this 19-year span, the activities that have received the most funds are pedestrian and bicycle facilities ($4891 million or 50%), landscaping and other scenic beautification ($1863 million or 19%), and rehabilitation and operation of older historic transportation infrastructure ($926 million or 9%).

Of the 12 eligible activities, numerous investments are directly supportive of historic preservation. These include acquisition of scenic or historic sites, historic preservation, rehabilitation and operation of historic transportation infrastructure, and archaeological planning. The other activities are indirectly helpful to the preservation of historic or older areas. For instance, an historic downtown might benefit from such TEA-funded assistance as enhanced pedestrian and bicycle facilities or removing unsightly billboards. Further, the requirement that TEA funding must be "related to surface transportation (RST)" can, at least technically, be easily accommodated by most preservation projects because the RST man-

---

[34] The Surface Transportation and Uniform Relocation Assistance Act of 1987 (STURAA) was generally seen in Congress and the transportation community as the last authorization bill of the Interstate era. Its Congressional conference report stated it "will provide the states sufficient funds to complete the system."

---

[35] Not all of the 12 listed activities were eligible for funding throughout the FY 1992–2006 period. For instance, ISTEA had 10 eligible activities.

Table 5.16 Transportation Enhancement Activities: Eligible Activities and Funding, FY 1992–2010

The term Transportation Enhancement Activity means any of the following as they relate to surface transportation	Funding (in millions)		
	Total	Annual	%
1 *Pedestrian and bicycle facilities:* New or reconstructed sidewalks, walkways, curb ramps, bike lane striping, paved shoulders, bike parking, bus racks, off-road trails, bike and pedestrian bridges and underpasses	4891	257.4	49.6
2 *Safety and educational activities for pedestrians and bicyclists:* Programs designed to encourage walking and bicycling by providing potential users with education and safety instruction through classes, pamphlets, and signs	33	1.7	0.3
3 *Acquisition of scenic easements and scenic or historic sites, including historic battlefields:* Acquisition of scenic land easements, vistas and landscapes, including historic battlefields; purchase of building in historic districts or historic properties	218	11.5	2.2
4 *Scenic or historic highway program including tourist and welcome center facilities:* Construction of turnouts, overlooks, visitor centers, and viewing areas, designation signs, and markers	548	28.8	5.6
5 *Landscaping and other scenic beautification, including pedestrian streetscapes:* Street furniture, lighting, public art, and landscaping along street, highways, trails, waterfronts, and gateways	1863	98.1	18.9
6 *Historic preservation:* Preservation of buildings and facades in historic districts; restoration and reuse of historic buildings for transportation-related purposes; access improvements to historic sites and buildings	343	18.1	3.5
7 *Rehabilitation and operation of historic transportation buildings, structures, or facilities:* Restoration of historic railroad depots, bus stations, canals, canal towpaths, historic canal bridges, and lighthouses; rehabilitation of rail trestles, tunnels and bridges	926	48.7	9.4
8 *Preservation of abandoned railway corridors and the conversion and use of the corridors for pedestrian or bicycle trails:* Acquiring railroad rights-of-way; planning, designing and constructing multi-use trails; developing rail-with-rail projects; purchasing unused railroad property for reuse as trails	713	37.5	7.2
9 *Inventory, control, and removal of outdoor advertising:* Billboard inventories or removal of nonconforming billboards	40	2.1	0.4
10 *Archaeological planning and research:* Research, preservation planning and interpretation; developing interpretive signs, exhibits, guides, inventories, and surveys	47	2.5	0.5
11 *Environmental mitigation to address water pollution due to highway runoff or to reduce vehicle-caused wildlife mortality while maintaining habitat connectivity:* Runoff pollution mitigation, soil erosion controls, detention and sediment basins, river cleanups, and wildlife crossings	100	5.3	1.0
12 *Establishment of transportation museums:* Construction of transportation museums, including the conversion of railroad stations or historic properties to museums with transportation themes and exhibits, or the purchase of transportation related artifacts	148	7.8	1.5
Total	$9.870	$519.4	100%

date itself is flexible and includes environmental protection, community preservation, and livability (Costello and Schamess 2006).

TEAs can provide critical financial assistance. TEA funded a total of 3782 projects at $1.52 billion from FY 1992 to FY 2010 (NTEC 2012). Figure 5.4 provides a visual representation of the kinds of preservation projects by sub-type that have been supported in the last several years.

In practice, states—the entities that decide on the ultimate TEA investments—have varied in the degree to which the TEA program in their jurisdiction has been used for preservation. Some traditional engineers are simply not com-

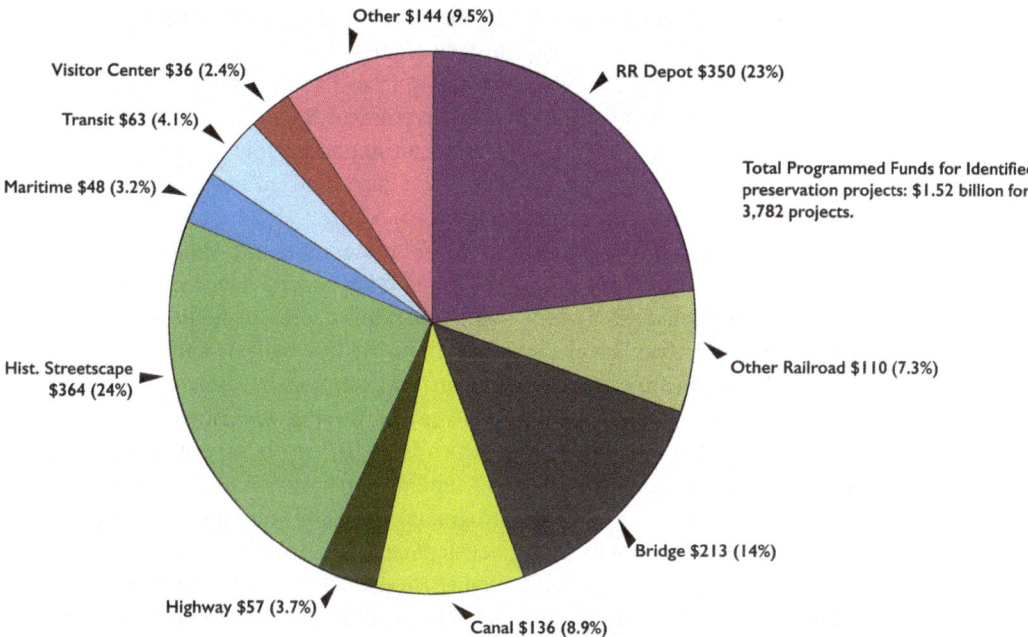

Fig. 5.4 Historic preservation projects of several kinds have been supported by transportation funding, as this pie-chart demonstrates by subtypes, from FY 1992 to FY 2012, in millions of dollars. (Author's Illustration)

Fig. 5.5 San Francisco's Ferry Terminal, a prominent waterfront Beaux Arts structure listed on the National Register, was completely rehabilitated as a multimodal center with several million dollars of transportation funds. (Author's Photograph)

fortable with the integration of transportation with preservation. Some narrowly interpret the TEA program and will fund preservation as a transportation activity, but only if it involves an historic bridge, tunnel, or similar piece of transportation infrastructure. In part through advocacy and education, many preservation projects have benefited handsomely from ISTEA, TEA-21, and SAFETEA-LU. San Francisco's Ferry Terminal, a prominent waterfront Beaux Arts structure listed on the National Register, was completely rehabilitated as a multimodal center with several million dollars of transportation funds (Costello and Schamess 2006) (Fig. 5.5). Because the majority of the funding is made available through the state departments of transportation and their regional offices, it is important to become familiar with their plans. This is particularly essential as preservationists focus more upon the re-discovery and rehabilitation of historic roads (Marriott 1998).

Besides the HPF and TEA, other federal programs can either directly or indirectly assist historic preservation. As indicated in the previous chapter, many housing, community and economic development programs sponsored by the US Department of Housing and Urban Development (HUD) are helpful. Prominent examples are Community Development Block Grants (CDBG)—funds that can be flexibly applied for housing, community and economic development projects—and the HOME Investment Partnership, which provides housing grants that can be used for both new construction and rehabilitation. Both are large programs: CDBG funding is funded at about $4 billion annually and HOME at about $2 billion per year (HUD 2010). Both programs have numerous components. For instance, CDBG encompasses Section 108 loan guarantee assistance, the Neighborhood Stabilization Program, and economic Empowerment Zones/Enterprise Communities. Both CDBG and HOME have been tapped for historic preservation and rehabilitation purposes. A portion of the funds that St. Louis committed to help revitalize the Old Post Office came from its CDBG allocation. The $200 million rehabilitation of the Gateway/Statler Hotel, also in St. Louis, benefited from $25 million in HUD Section 108 assistance, a CDBG program. The $7.6 million rehabilitation in historic downtown Journal Square was facilitated by a $500,000 CDBG grant to Jersey City, as well as $1.2 million in Urban Enterprise Zone assistance—aid given for economic development in distressed areas—and other HUD and state assistance. The $1.9 million adaptive reuse of the Shely School in West York, Pennsylvania utilized $340,000 in HOME funds.

HUD is far from the only federal agency of potential benefit to preservation. Others offer direct or indirect aid, including federal financial regulators and their sister agencies. For example, the Federal Home Loan Bank offers subsidized funds in an Affordable Housing Program that has been used to help finance below market rate historic housing units. Favorable homeowner financing from Fannie Mae and Freddie Mac—two Government Sponsored Enterprises (GSEs) playing an important role in the mortgage market—have also assisted borrowers with historic properties.

While preservationists should be aware of HUD and other federal agencies, they must recognize that this source of funding is decreasing. Over time, HUD's budget authority has shrunk in constant dollars as have the number of HUD-aided public housing and other affordable units (Schwartz 2010). In fiscal year 2011, Congress cut funding for low-income housing and related programs by $800 million, with community development aid suffering a cut of about $1 billion (Rice and Sard 2011). The future assistance for such purposes will be challenged by constraints posed by the multi-trillion dollar federal deficit. The bursting of the "housing bubble" in 2008 has affected other federal agencies that had provided assistance for affordable housing, most notably the dramatic reversal of the financial fortune of the GSEs (Fannie Mae and Freddie Mac), from financial behemoths to entities that had to be placed under federal conservatorship. The good news is that in a system of creative federalism, state governments have become invigorated funders of housing and community development as well as offering direct assistance for preservation.

State Programmatic Assistance

In addition to the several ways in which states offer incentives through tax preferences, they often have developed direct programmatic support for preservation. For instance, states use their ability to issue tax exempt (or taxable) bonds and/or tap general revenues to raise funds for outright grants or below-market interest rate financing for the improvements of historic resources. In the 1990s, a New Jersey $60 million bond served to leverage a total of nearly $400 million in historic rehabilitation investment. The projects included the renovation of the New Jersey State House, revolutionary battlefields, and the Cape May Point Light House (Listokin and Lahr 1998). These properties are some of New Jersey's defining historic resources, and are also important tourist attractions.

In a similar fashion, over the past 30 years Florida used both state general revenue and bonds to create one of the largest state pools of funds for preservation, awarding $10 to $20 million annually. From FY 1996 through FY 2008, the program was responsible for about $900 million (in 2008 dollars) of preservation activity, including $315 million in grants and $585 million in matching loans (McLendon et al. 2010). Several sites have benefited. The 1891 Key West Custom House, abandoned in 1974, was adapted to a historical museum with the assistance of $1.25 million in state aid (Florida 2002). The museum attracts 150,000 tourists annually. In Historic Pensacola Village, the rehabilitation of the Old City Hall and the restorations in surrounding Escambia County have been aided by almost $7 million in state grants. Other preservation projects in Florida, ranging from saving Art Deco landmarks in Miami Beach to restoring the Governor Stone Schooner at the Appalachia Maritime Museum, have similarly benefited from Florida state aid, secured from state bonds and general revenues.

States have tapped a variety of "creative sources" to secure assistance for preservation. Some of these sources include lottery funds (Arizona and Iowa), gambling taxes (Colorado), and real estate transfer taxes (Arkansas) (Beaumont 1996). "Creative source" preservation financing is appealing because it neither raises taxes nor draws down rationed state bonding capacity. If the new revenue is derived from real-estate activities, it is possible to rationalize the funds as being complementary, as new home construction is sometimes perceived as a threat to preservation.[36] Yet, creative source preservation funding is often far from painless. Legalizing gambling in Colorado mountain towns, for instance, generates preservation funds, but the voracious appe-

tite of gambling parlors for casino space and hotel rooms sometimes threatens historic resources.

States may also support (or challenge) preservation through their housing and community development policies and funding. To start, states often help guide where federal monies for this purpose, e.g., LIHTC or CDBG, are spent, and the state's decisions in this regard can further (or impede) preservation. This can be seen in the state's role in the LIHTC, previously described, which is jointly administered by the federal government (Internal Revenue Service) and the states. LIHTC awards are based on the project criteria specified in what are referred to as a Qualified Allocation Plan (QAP) prepared by each state following IRS guidelines. These include requirements related to low-income occupancy of the LIHTC units as well as general categories of selection criteria, such as project characteristics and location. A state QAP includes the federal mandates and specific criteria that reflect each state's affordable-housing priorities. The synthesis of the federal and state requirements is used to evaluate project applications. As many developers compete for the LIHTC, the QAP scoring criteria are crucial.

Countervailing influences affect how state QAP criteria either encourage or discourage LIHTC projects that include rehabilitation as opposed to new construction (Barr 1998; Gustafson and Walker 2002; Listokin 2005). A total of 13 states award QAP preferences for rehabilitation applications; at least eight states give extra points for historic rehabilitation, in addition to the points awarded for rehabilitation in general (Indiana, Louisiana, Oklahoma, Rhode Island, Texas, Vermont, Virginia, and Washington).[37] In contrast, other QAP scoring criteria can favor LIHTC new construction as opposed to tax credit rehabilitation-preservation developments. These

---

[36] Recall the complementary nature of the oil lease revenues funding the HPF.

[37] Other QAP scoring criteria that may encourage rehabilitation or historic preservation include points for small scale projects (the rehabilitation-preservation LIHTC applications tend to contain fewer units than their new construction counterparts) and points for location in challenging areas, such as lower-income Qualified Census Tracts (QCTs) or Difficult to Develop Areas (DDAs), both of which may disproportionately include rehabilitation-preservation activity.

include points specifically for new construction or points for the lowest cost per housing unit (rehabilitation or preservation may be more expensive because of the amenities provided).[38] Thus, when states act as gatekeepers of where federal housing and community development funds are spent, they influence resources available to historic preservation. Sometimes there is a prod for states to be more preservation-centric in this role. For instance, the 2008 federal Housing and Economic Recovery Act requires that states include "the historical nature of the project" as part of their required selection criteria for the LIHTC QAP.

States have also blossomed as important housing and development funders in their own right, and their actions in this arena affect preservation. Every state has a housing finance agency (HFA) with some, such as New York, having multiple such entities. HFAs can issue tax exempt bonds, which can be used for housing and other purposes (Schwartz 2010, p. 218). Using housing bonds and other programs, such as HOME and Section 8 monies from HUD and the previously described LIHTC, HFAs have to date financed 2.9 million low and moderate income rental units and have provided 2.6 million below-market interest rate mortgages for home purchase (NCSHA 2014). In addition, many of the HFAs have state housing trust funds—money for affordable housing from such sources as property transfers or deed registration—while others administer state housing tax credits of their own that may, or may not, be modeled on the federal LIHTC.

These and other state programs can help finance preservation. The adaptive use of the 1894 Burnham Factory in Irvington, New York, a $4.6 million project, was assisted, in part, by $400,000 advanced from the New York State Housing Trust Fund and a financially favorable

$500,000 loan from New York State. Other subsidies, including the federal HTC and LIHTC ($2.4 million) and HOME ($900,000) were also used. The $3.8 million conversion of the historic Far East Building in Los Angeles from the single unit occupancy units into affordable housing for families utilized $500,000 in assistance from the California Department of Housing and Community Development and $200,000 in support from the California Housing Finance Agency. These state funds supplemented aid from the LIHTC ($700,000), federal HTC ($600,000) federal Economic Development Administration ($300,000), and local sources described below.

In short, states have become increasingly important in funding historic preservation. In addition to allowing local units of government to be supportive and influencing how federal resources are allocated, states are financial dynamos in their own right. They have made available general tax revenues, general obligation bonds, creative sources, and an array of HFA resources.

Other Bridge Mechanisms for Preservation

Although it is impossible to describe every means of bridging the financial gap to make a project possible, assistance from two other sectors, local government and preservation organizations, deserve at least brief mention. In much the same way that states came to the fore as federal spending for housing and community development was cut, local governments have assumed an invigorated role in this sector.

That is especially the case for larger units of local government, the populous counties and cities. These entities sometimes decide how federal funds, such as CDBG and HOME, are spent and additionally offer resources from their own coffers. Many of the projects previously cited have used some local assistance. The adaptive reuse of the historic Burnham Factory in Irvington benefited from Westchester County making available $900,000 of its federal HOME grant, $100,000 from the County's Housing Implementation Fund, as well as $200,000 from the Village of Ir-

---

[38] Other QAP criteria that may favor new construction LIHTC applications by including points for "ready to go" projects (rehabilitation-preservation development is inherently complex and may have higher costs and regulatory barriers) and points for large (e.g., three bedroom) units or developments with central air conditioning (characteristics that may not be included when dealing with existing buildings).

vington. The $3.8 million adaptive reuse of the Far East Building in Los Angeles supplemented the LIHTC ($700,000), federal HTC ($600,000), and various state assistance previously detailed ($700,000) with $4.2 million in local monies from different local sources, including the city's housing ($500,000) and economic development departments ($400,000, and development authority ($300,000).

Preservation organizations sometimes offer some financial assistance to individual property owners and to nonprofit organizations working with historic building and districts. As the nation's chief preservation nonprofit, the National Trust for Historic Preservation makes available such funds. These include preservation loan funds for preservation planning and educational purposes, which must be matched on a dollar-for-dollar basis; area-targeted funds, for the Eastern Shore of Maryland, small towns, New York City, and other locations; and special purpose funds, dedicated to battlefield preservation and emergency intervention after a national disaster. In addition, mentioned earlier is the National Trust Community Investment Corporation, which provides historic real estate equity (NTHP 2014). A number of statewide preservation organizations have similar programs. Perhaps the largest is Indiana Landmarks, which offers to nonprofit organizations "endangered places" grants for professional architecture and engineering studies, loans to buy and/or restore historic properties, legal defense grants, and preservation education grants.

In short, assistance is offered by many entities: governments at all levels (federal, state, county, and local), and the private and nonprofit sectors as well. The challenge is to learn about each of the sources of support in order to mix and match them in a way that satisfies the investors and the community in which the property is located.

Conclusion

This chapter began by considering the financial investment needed to maintain, repair, rehabilitate, and restore the old and historic properties in the USA. While that exact number remains elusive, it is likely that the difference between the amount of money required and the resources available for such purposes is, conservatively, many tens of billions of dollars

Ideally, the preservation community should bolster its efforts to monitor these financial needs and the financing gap; otherwise the pleas for enhanced funding resemble the summer camper's postcard request to "send money." This enhanced monitoring and accounting can build upon past efforts to evaluate the condition of NPS designated properties. To begin to understand and come to grips with the gap, this chapter has sketched out many bridge mechanisms. An estimate of the resources that are currently being used is detailed in Table 5.14, the total of which is approximately $2.2 billion annually. This is clearly much less than the tens of billions that, at a minimum, is needed.

Of this $2.2 billion, about $1.6 billion, or about three-quarters of the total aid, is available in the form of tax credits: HTC, LIHTC, and NMTC.[39] The American response to subsidizing preservation has decidedly embraced a tax-credit strategy. That is largely the case with respect to affordable housing as well, in the form of the LIHTCs. There are many advantages to this. It reflects the private sector ethos of the United States, capitalizes on the talents of the many participants involved (e.g., developers, syndicators, and lenders), and builds on years of success. Many in the worldwide preservation community study and are envious of the tax-credit system subsidizing preservation as it has developed.

Yet, as discussed earlier in this chapter, there are shortcomings to the tax credit vehicle. A private-sector driven approach does not always make the right decisions, nor is it necessarily more efficient. Bringing together many parties can create its own strains and the tax credit's past success does not necessarily mean it should be the exclusive template for the future (Table 5.17).

---

[39] The share from a tax-based system would be yet greater had this chart included the additional, considerable subsidy to preservation from property tax reductions, TIFs, and similar programs.

Table 5.17 Order of Magnitude Estimate of Major Federal and State Subsidies and Funding

Support	Estimated Annual Support for Preservation	
Income tax credits		
Federal HTC	$700 million[a]	
State HTC	$700 million[b]	
LIHTC	$28 million[c]	
NMTC	$160 million[d]	
Preservation easements	*Unknown*	
Subtotal income tax credit	±$1600 million	
Programmatic federal support (selected)		
HPF total	$72 million[e]	
Bricks and mortar portion		$29 million[f]
NPS	$190 million[g]	
TEA	$80 million[h]	
CDBG	$100 million[i]	
HOME	$100 million[j]	
State		
From housing supports	$60 million[k]	
Subsidies for preservation from bonds, general tax revenues, "creative" and other sources	*Unknown*	
Subtotal programmatic	±$600 million	
Other (local/other)		
Property tax incentives, including TIFs		
Aid from local government, preservation organizations and others	*Unknown*	
Total of all estimated sources	±$2.3 billion	

[a] Derived as follows:

Approximate $29.6 billion total HTC over the past 5 years (FY 2000–2008), or about $3.7 billion per year

Federal subsidy $3.7 billion annual investment × 20% credit or about $0.7 billion annually

[b] This is a very gross order of magnitude estimate

[c] Derived as follows:

Approximately $5.6 billion in federal LIHTCs were allocated over 2000–2008 or about $700 million per year

Approximately 40% of LIHTC activity involves rehabilitation, or about $240 million annually ($0.7 billion × 0.4)

Approximately 10% of all rehabilitation in the USA involves historic buildings (based on work done by Rutgers University in ten states, which indicates that generally about 5–15% of all rehab in each location was effected in buildings on or eligible for the national, state, or local historic registers)

Therefore, the annual LIHTC activity associate with historic preservation is estimated at about $28 million ($280 million × 0.10)

[d] Derived as follows:

Approximately $31.6 billion in NMTC tax credit authority was allocated over the 2003–2011 periods or an average of about $4.0 billion per year

While about 30% of NMTC investors used the Federal HTC, this may not translate into a proportional share of NMTC investment because the historic preservation projects may be smaller on average. It is assumed 10% of NMTC investment has involved historic resources implying an annual NMTC- preservation activity of about $0.4 billion ($4.0 billion × 0.1)

Applying the 39% NMTC credit to the $0.4 billion in annual NMTC preservation activity implies an annual subsidy for preservation from the NMTC of $160 million ($0.3 billion × 0.39)

[e] Average annual funding for all HPF purposes FY 2001–2008

[f] Average annual funding for two HPF components most related to bricks and mortar purposes over FY 2001–2008 (Save America's Treasures and Preserve America)

[g] Average annual funding for NPS spending to stabilize, preserve, rehabilitate, and restore historic structures under NPS stewardship over FY 2006–2007

[h] Average annual funding over FY 2010 for the four transportation enhancement activities associated with historic preservation as analyzed by the National Transportation Enhancements Clearinghouse

Table 5.17 (continued)

Support	Estimated Annual Support for Preservation

[i] From FY 2001–2006, a total of $7.0 billion of CDBG funds was spent on housing assistance or about $1.2 billion per year. Such CDBG funding is predominately for rehabilitation, about $1.0 billion annually. An estimated 10 % of the $1.0 billion, or $100 million, is expended on historic building (see note c)

[j] HOME funding is approximately $1.8 billion annually, of which about 60 % or about $1 billion yearly is spend on rehabilitation as opposed to new construction. An estimated 10 % (see note c) of the $1 billion, or $100 million, is expended on historic buildings

[k] From 1968 through 2004, all states cumulatively funded a total of $55 billion in mortgage revenue bonds for multi-family housing or about $1.5 billion per year. If 40 % of this aid was used for rehabilitation (mirroring the LIHTC rehab share), this would represent support of $0.6 billion annually. An estimated 10 % of the $0.6 billion or $60 million might be invested in historic multifamily buildings (see note c)

References

Abt Associates, Inc. (2000). *Updating the low income housing tax credit (LIHTC) database*. Washington, D.C.: U.S. Department of Housing and Urban Development.

Armistead, J. P. (2005). *New markets tax credits: Issues and opportunities* (p. 1). Brooklyn: Pratt Institute Center for Community and Environmental Development.

Austrian, Z., & Norton, J. (2002). *Strategies and tools in economic development practice*. Cleveland: Cleveland State University.

Author's Papers. (April 2012). Transcript. Mark A. Miles interview by David Listokin.

Barr, A. (1998). *Under one roof: Combining affordable housing and historic preservation*. A joint policy research project prepared by Preservation Action, the Boasberg Historic Preservation Fund and the Center for Preservation Initiatives. Washington, D.C.: National Conference of State Historic Preservation Officers.

Bartik, T. J. (1991). *Who benefits from state and local economic development policies*. Kalamazoo: W. E. Upjohn Institute.

Beaumont, C. (1996). *Smart states, better communities* (pp. 76–86). Washington, D.C.: National Trust for Historic Preservation.

Brown, W. (28 Nov 1991). Reaping the big benefits of the transportation bill; wide variety of firms expected to be winners. *Washington Post*, D1.

Campbell, A., & Leith-Tetrault, J. (2006). *The new markets tax credit*. Washington, D.C.: New Market Tax Credits Coalition.

Chirinko, R. S., & Wilson, D. J. (2008). *Tax competition among U.S. states*. San Francisco: Federal Reserve Bank of San Francisco.

Costello, D., & Schamess, L. (2006). *Building on the past, traveling to the future: A preservationist's guide to the federal transportation enhancement provision* (2nd ed., p. 22). Washington, D.C.: Federal Highway Administration and National Trust for Historic Preservation.

Danter. (2012). *Statistical overview of the LIHTC program, 1987 to 2008*. The Danter Company. http://www.danter.com/taxcredit/stats.htm. Accessed 3 March 2014.

Escherich, W. F., et al. (1996). *Affordable housing through historic preservation: A case study guide to combining tax credits*. Washington, D.C.: National Trust for Historic Preservation.

Fehr, S. C. (1991). Highway plan shifts costs to states. *Washington Post*, Feb 14, p. A1.

Florida. (2002). *Economic impacts of historic preservation in Florida* (p. 26). University of Florida Center for Governmental Responsibility and Rutgers University Center for Urban Policy Research, Sept.

GAO. (Jan 2007). *Report to Congressional Committees. Tax policy. New market tax credit appears to increase investment by investors in low-income communities, but opportunities exist to better monitor compliance* (p. 36). Washington, D.C.: U.S. Government Accountability Office.

GAO. (Jan 2010). *Report to Congressional Committees. New markets tax credit. The credit helps fund a variety of projects in low income communities, but could be simplified* (p. 11). Washington, D.C.: U.S. Government Accountability Office.

GAO. (2012). *Limited information on the use and effectiveness of tax expenditures could be mitigated through congressional attention*. U.S. Government Accountability Office-12-262, Feb 29.

Gibson, D. (2003). Neighborhood characteristics and the targeting of tax increment financing in Chicago. *Journal of Urban Economics, 54*, 309–327.

Gustafson, J., & Walker, J. C. (2002). *Analysis of state qualified allocation plans for the low-income housing tax credit*. Washington, D.C.: The Urban Institute.

HHAA. (2001). *Historic Homeownership Assistance Act*. H.R.1172, S. 920, 107th Congress.

Hodson, G. (2000). *The gentleman from New York. Daniel Patrick Moynihan, a biography* (pp. 329–334). Boston: Houghton Mifflin Company.

HUD. (2010). *FY 2010 Budget–Road map for transformation* (p. 41). U.S. Department of Housing and Urban Development.

Hy, R. J., & Waugh, W. L. (1995). *State and local tax policies. A comparative handbook*. Westport: Greenwood Press.

Johnson, C. L., & Man, J. Y. (Eds.). (2001). *Tax increment financing and economic development: Uses, structures, and impacts*. Albany: State University of New York.

Lahr, M., Listokin, D., & Francisco, F. N. (2003). *Economic impacts of historic preservation in Ohio*. Newark: Rutgers University Center for Urban Policy Research for Heritage Ohio and Downtown Ohio, Inc.

Lefcoe, G. (2011). Competing for the next hundred million Americans: The uses and abuses of tax increment financing. *Urban Lawyer, 43*(2), Spring, 427.

Listokin, D. (2005). *Best practices for effecting the rehabilitation of affordable housing: Volume II-Technical studies*. Washington, D.C.: U.S. Department of Housing and Urban Development.

Listokin, D., & Lahr, M. L. (1998). *Partners in prosperity: The economic benefits of historic preservation in New Jersey* (p. 170). Trenton: Rutgers University Center for Urban Policy Research for the New Jersey Historic Trust.

Listokin, D., & Listokin, B. (2001a). *Barriers to the rehabilitation of affordable housing: Volume I Finding and analysis* (p. 118). Washington, D.C.: Office of Policy Development and Research, U.S. Department of Housing and Urban Development.

Listokin, D., & Listokin, B. (2001b). Historic preservation and affordable housing: Leveraging old resources for new opportunities. *Housing Facts and Findings, 3*(2), 1.

Listokin, D., Lahr, M., & St. Martin, K. (2001). *Economic impacts of historic preservation in Missouri* (pp. 122–128). New Brunswick: Rutgers University Center for Urban Policy Research for the Missouri Downtown Association.

Listokin, D., Crossney, K., et al. (2005). *Best practices for effecting the rehabilitation of affordable housing-Volume I: Framework and findings*. New Brunswick: Rutgers University Center for Urban Policy Research for the U.S. Department of Housing and Urban Development.

Listokin, D., et al. (2010). *Economic benefits and impact of historic rehabilitation tax credits in Kansas*. New Brunswick: Rutgers University Center for Urban Policy Research for the Kansas Preservation Alliance.

Listokin, D., et al. (2011). *Second annual report on the economic impact of the federal historic tax credit* (p. 38). New Brunswick, NJ and Washington, D.C.: Rutgers University Center for Urban Policy Research and National Trust Community Investment Corporation.

Listokin, D., Lahr, M., & Heydt, L. (2012). *Third annual report on the economic impacts of the historic tax credit* (pp. 10–13). New Brunswick: Rutgers University Center for Urban Policy Research.

Marriott, P. D. (1998). *Saving historic roads. Design & policy guidelines*. New York: Wiley.

McKee, B. (31 March 2005). When preservation equals demolition. *The New York Times*.

McLendon, T., et al. (2010). *Economic impacts of historic preservation in Florida*. Gainesville, FL and New Brunswick: Center for Governmental Responsibility, University of Florida and Center for Urban Policy Research, Rutgers University.

Missouri. (30 Nov 2010). *Report of the Missouri Tax Credit Review Commission* (p. 33). Jefferson City: Missouri Tax Credit Review Commission.

NCSHA. (2014). National council of state housing agencies website. http://www.ncsha.org/about-hfas. Accessed 4 March 2014.

NCSHPO. (2009). *The Historic Preservation Fund Annual Report*. Washington, D.C.: National Conference of State Historic Preservation Officers and U.S. Department of the Interior, National Park Service.

NMTCC. (2010). *The New Markets Tax Credit 10th Anniversary Report* (pp. 1–2). Washington, D.C.: New Markets Tax Credit Coalition.

NPS. (2004). *Improving the administration of the federal historic rehabilitation tax credit program*. Washington, D.C.: National Park Service.

NPS. (2007). *Budget justifications and performance information. Fiscal year 2008*. Washington, D.C.: National Park Service.

NPS. (2011). *The Historic Preservation Fund Annual Report*. Washington, D.C.: U.S. Department of the Interior, National Park Service.

NTCIC. (2010). First annual report on the economic impact of the federal historic tax credit. National Trust Community Investment Corporation, The Historic Tax Credit Coalition, and Rutgers University Bloustein School of Planning and Public Policy, March.

NTEC. (2012). *Transportation enhancements spending report FY1992–FY2011* (p. 21). Washington, D.C.: National Transportation Enhancement Clearinghouse.

NTHP. (2014). National trust for historic preservation website. http://www.preservationnation.org/resources/find-funding/preservation-funds-guidelines-eligibility.html. Accessed 4 March 2014.

NYT. (11 April 2012). Uncertain fate for urban projects in California. *The New York Times*.

PL. (2006). Pension Protection Act of 2006. Public Law 109–280, 109th Congress.

President. (2005). *Saving America's treasures. Preserving the legacy of our national experience*. Washington, D.C.: President's Committee on the Arts and Humanities.

PCAH. (2006). President's committee on the arts and humanities. Press release. Sept 22.

Rice, D., & Sard, B. (23 June 2011). *Unbalanced approach to deficit reduction could cripple housing and community development programs*. Washington, D.C.: Center for Budget and Policy Priorities.

Roddewig, R. J. (2011). *Appraising conservation and historic preservation easements*. Chicago: Appraisal Institute.

Schmitt, N., et al. (1987). Business climate attitudes and company relocation decisions. *Journal of Applied Psychology, 72*(4), 622–628.

Schwartz, A. (2010). *Housing policy in the United States* (p. 126). New York: Routledge.

Schwartz, H. K. (2012). *State tax credits for historic preservation*. Washington, D.C.: National Trust for Historic Preservation.

Shores, L. K. (2012). Defending the historic preservation tax credit. *Missouri Law Review, 77*(1), 199–234.

Williams, B. (2004). *These old houses: 2001. Current housing reports H12/04-1*. Washington, D.C.: U.S. Census Bureau.

Wolkoff, M. J. (1985). Chasing a dream: The use of tax abatements to spur economic development. *Urban Studies, 22*, 305–315.

Wyatt, M. D. (Nov/Dec 1990). The TIF smorgasbord: A survey of state statutory provisions of tax increment financing. *Assessment Digest*, pp. 2–9.

Youngman, J. (May 2011). TIF at a turning point: Defining a debt down. *State Tax Notes*, p. 321.

Introduction

Some of the most important contributions that preservationists make are contained in their alternative visions of the future. The challenge is to extend the legacy while accommodating current and future needs. In this chapter, preservation solutions are primarily discussed as built designs: documenting existing properties; considering contextual issues; and imaging the range of appropriate changes.

Whether the problem is an existing structure and landscape above ground or an archaeological site below grade, and whether the property is in a rural, urban, or suburban location, efforts must begin with a thorough historical investigation. Documentation involves greater-than-average attention to urban and suburban development, landscape, architecture, interiors, decorative arts, and material culture. It also includes observing and recording the contemporary social and environmental scene. Only with a thorough knowledge of what exists is it possible to appreciate the value of what is significant. The preservationist serves several roles: provider of images and historical texts, aesthetic critic, socially minded contributor to civic discussion, and end-user.

Using an open public platform, two standard approaches to developing acceptable design solutions are to offer community design assistance and mount a design competition. In some situations, more careful, intensive design review is required, when the changing nature of the aesthetic context requires specialized knowledge. In this regard, the changing nature of twentieth century design ideas is reviewed in some detail. In addition, interest in what is termed "sustainability" is particularly instructive, as it can have different meanings in different contexts, not all of which are sympathetic to preservation concerns.

The preservation treatment options discussed include "marking time" with stabilization, restoration, reconstruction, and rehabilitation, each of which have their own challenges as the examples show. Often, more than one treatment is appropriate for a property, especially in cases where large or complex sites are adapted to more than one new use. By considering these properties—e.g. baseball stadia, railroad corridors, and military bases—it is possible to envision tackling almost any problem. This is especially true in the in face of natural and man-made disasters, where preservationists have a role in assisting recovery, mitigating harm, and planning for the next calamity, protecting life and property.

Designing Begins with Observation and Documentation

In any instance in which a new design is being proposed, the starting point for those involved lies in a period of observation and documentation. This statement cannot be overemphasized. Using one's eyes, ears, nose, and senses of touch and taste to investigate the characteristics of the world in which a property is located is an essential first step. Some of these experiences are

M. A. Tomlan, *Historic Preservation*, DOI 10.1007/978-3-319-04975-5_6,
© Springer International Publishing Switzerland 2015

positive, while others are negative. The early twentieth-century philosopher John Dewey argued that ordinary activities, when considered as a continuum, provided numerous opportunities for an aesthetic experience (Alexander 1987). Dewey's view of art included not only what is contained in museums and art galleries, but also whatever object or environmental context embodied or communicated human meaning (Dewey 1934).

Similarly, millions of people discover for themselves the characteristics of their cities and suburbs simply by walking to work, or running or bicycling for recreation and fitness. To celebrate the legacy of urban thinker, writer, and activist Jane Jacobs, "Jane's Walks" have spurred thousands of people to get to know each other and their neighborhoods by getting out and walking (Soderstrom 2008). With simple informal observation, mental recording is taking place every day. Others "learn" about their neighborhoods and cities using a more systematic approach, by following the routes laid out for garden and historic house tours.

By looking closely and noticing details over time, it is straightforward to take the important first step of creating a record of change. Often the idea follows that deliberate documentation is a simple task, accomplished with the quick identification of a building's date, style, or function. Although this kind of easy categorization seems to collect important details, and while it might provide a reference point, much more is needed for a full understanding (Longstreth 1984). This comprehensive approach may cause the preservationist to repeatedly return to the evidence, so that access to the property or site is critical.

Features that the eye captures and the mind begins to question must be discovered and rediscovered to be understood as significant and treated sympathetically. And the observations should be made repeatedly, at different scales, during various times of the day and different seasons of the year. Of course, who is involved in noticing details will make a considerable difference to the outcome.

Fragments of objects, buildings, and landscapes both above and below ground can also play a role because they often help to complete a mental image of a larger site. Observing the gaps where structures or buildings once stood may show a pattern or define a space. Foundations below grade, pieces of an abandoned railroad bed, or earthen ramps alongside long-vanished structures that were used to for loading or unloading are pieces of the picture that can provide a fuller understanding of the range of activities that took place in an agricultural, industrial, or extractive mining process (Andrzejewski and Rachleff 1998).

Often the novice asks "Just how much documentation is desirable?" The simple answer might be "as much as possible," within the limitations of time and money. If the existing building will be completely replaced with a new structure, the question may arise, "why bother?" The impending demolition of a property could be seen as requiring less information than what is required for a complete restoration. Or the rehabilitation of a single room might suggest only that a particular room be measured and drawn. Experience has frequently proven otherwise. Studying comprehensively is always helpful, as it provides an understanding how the past and current physical conditions came to be, culturally, socially, and economically.

Another danger for the preservationist is to suppose that earlier historical research is complete, making it only necessary to review and accept the previous narratives or attempts at documentation, without investigating why the work was done or questioning its conclusions (McAlester and McAlester 1984; McVarish 2008; Whiffen 1969). This may lead to problems because the knowledge gained in the process of documenting the current state of a property contributes to our broader understanding. The process of learning should never be foreshortened or taken for granted.

As indicated in Chapter 2, the National Park Service established the first widely-accepted approaches to documentation during the early twentieth century with the Historic American Buildings Survey. It continues to rely on highly educated personnel to record buildings of all kinds, as does its sister program, the Historic

American Engineering Record. In 2000, the National Park Service formally established the Historic American Landscape Survey (HALS) program to document historic landscapes. Its first survey project was the Marsh-Billings-Rockefeller National Historic Park in Vermont (Dolinsky 2010; Auwaerter 2005).[1] Spurred by the American Society of Landscape Architects, a framework is now in place for examining landscapes that vary in size from small gardens to vast national parks and landscapes of almost every kind. (Fig. 6.1)

The operating procedures for all of these federal programs are established in recordation standards. Traditionally they rely on measured drawings, large-format rectified photographs, historical records, and written contemporary observations, regardless of whether they are above or below-ground sites, buildings, engineering structures, districts, objects, or landscapes (FR 1983).[2] Stereo images, used in photogrammetry, capture even more information with the advantage of increasing the accuracy of the drawing (Borchers 1977; Burns 1992; Lagerqvist 1996; Carbonell 1989). The HABS, HAER, and HALS programs have studied thousands of properties, so that the existing conditions are known before even simple repairs are started, or before demolition begins.

In recent years, more advanced electronic documentation tools have become available. Distances and dimensions formerly only measured by steel tapes are now verified with and, in some cases, being supplanted by, lasers, often saving time and effort in gathering information that formerly took a traditional team months to gather (APT 1990). Millions of points are scanned that can be digitally rectified and linked to computer aided drafting (CAD) programs.

Fig. 6.1 The first survey project of the Historic American Landscape Survey (HALS) program was the documentation of the Marsh-Billings-Rockefeller National Historic Park, in Vermont. Spurred by the American Society of Landscape Architects, the framework involves recording landscapes from small gardens to vast national parks and landscapes of every kind. (Historic American Landscape Survey, Library of Congress)

Electronic scanning can also be helpful in documenting interiors, which are typically overlooked because the effort requires so much time and attention to detail. With the exception of Broadway live theaters, opera houses, movie theaters, some government buildings, subway stations, libraries, and comparatively few religious buildings, the number of interiors that have been designated and recorded to the prevailing standards is very small. Even professionals who are charged with examining the complete historic and aesthetic significance of a property often reduce the "inside story" to single-sentence room descriptions and a few photographs. Yet, whether documenting a subway station in anticipation of the changes needed for handicapped accessibility, or the interior of a battleship that is about to become a museum, the need to identify all elements of the historic fabric is the first step to designing for a new use (Waterloo 2010).

It is precisely because documentation takes a considerable amount of time and attention to detail that the use of electronic measurements as a substitute for hand measuring raises the risk of limiting the knowledge gained in the process, leading to an inappropriate new design. Simply put, those involved with design simply *must* take

---

[1] Following the example set by HABS, a Memorandum of Understanding has been established between the American Society of Landscape Architects (ASLA), the National Park Service (NPS), and the Library of Congress (LOC). The work of HALS is seen to be an extension of the Historic American Landscape and Garden Project (HALGP), which created over 40 records between 1935 and 1940 in Massachusetts.

[2] Field instructions are available from the NPS to guide professionals involved in assembling and presenting this information.

the time to understand thoroughly the value of the entire building, not just what can be easily measured.

Those involved with documentation also often recognize subtle differences that provide evidence of the changes in the property, suggesting several periods of significance. It is important to keep in mind that the interior is often remodeled more often than the exterior (Winter and Schulz 1990). In fact, almost all domestic interiors, kitchens and bathrooms in particular, have seen nearly continuous change. It is helpful to remember that museum curators involved with the removal and installation of complete rooms often assemble teams of historians, architects, decorators, and craft specialists to work on recording an important historical interior.

How do we collect information when physical evidence is lacking? By using the methods of the anthropologist and ethnographer, the patterns of everyday life reveal significance. Those involved in daily, weekly, and yearly life cycles can often contribute to understanding a place in very important ways. Whether documenting Native American tribal sites or properties important to under-represented minorities, the information contained in the memories of community members requires special attention (Emerson et al. 1995).

Documenting tangible and intangible cultural resources has been tremendously helped by consumer electronics. The advent of personal computing led to the development of a wave of useful software programs. Digital video recording can be integrated with geographic information systems (GIS) to allow artifacts anywhere on the globe to be located, compared, and evaluated. Yet, because often only a partial picture is all that remains, distribution patterns are important in order to "see" the complete picture. In addition, because documentation is also the first step when working with archaeological ruins above or below ground, or underwater, it is possible to correlate information about sites across boundaries, linking museums and private collections.

Language and literature are extremely important when documenting anything, as they inherently carry the conceptual frameworks that allow

comparison and evaluation. Just as documentation of buildings in this country often begins with the study of the classical language of architecture (Summerson 1969; Sturgis 1989), and proceeds to an examination of a broad range of building elements, the documentation of vernacular sites and settings requires acquiring the knowledge of local interpretations of building traditions. Historic landscapes often require the study of agricultural literature and sometimes include learning the proper botanical names to identify trees and plant materials, even an examination of fish and wildlife. In these cases, care must be taken to appreciate the changing seasons to determine the periods in which individual features were introduced or removed. Preservationists must also understand the local juxtaposition of plants, in that the languages of tribes, immigrants, and recent settlers may not have had a familiarity with Linnaeus's system of classification. Without corroborating the historical record with the physical evidence, it may be difficult to attribute any significance to what is observed or the changes that have taken place (Longstreth 2008).

Although collecting this information remains an essential first step, contemporary large scale documentation project often makes use of satellite imagery in mapping, positioning, and boundary marking. This broader view can be electronically enhanced, so that it is possible to make discoveries that would have eluded earlier investigators. GIS hold enormous potential (Huxhold 1991; Jones 2004),[3] and sonic recording makes it possible to compare audible character-defining noises and sounds, pinpointing their regularity and duration so that the recognition of a place can go well-beyond visual, material, and historical documentation (Gunderlach 2006; Smith 2004). These techniques are increasingly used as the number of recording of intangible cultural heritage broadens.

---

[3] Practical temporal geographic information systems, designed to store changes over time, still lie in the future.

Organizing Information for Preservation Planning

Proactive historic preservation planning begins with knowing the full range of historic resources available in an area. In the twentieth century, a considerable amount of time, effort, and funding went into creating a range of comprehensive surveys and analyses of existing cultural resources and their conditions. In many respects the information collected was often similar to that contained in surveys of residential, industrial, and commercial buildings. More recently it became obvious that, while these were important, a number of other important aspects of the landscape were being omitted, which led to a search for other approaches.

As noted in Chapter 2, the first survey of Charleston, South Carolina called for each historic property to be recorded on a separate card, noting its name, location, owner, use, and condition. The documentation included a few photographs and comments about the character of the neighborhood (favorable, mediocre, adverse, or inharmonious) and period (defined as Prerevolutionary, Postrevolutionary, Ante Bellum, or Modern). This led to a "quality rating" (Mention, Notable, Valuable, Valuable to City, or Nationally Important) (Weyeneth 2000).[4] Perhaps most interesting was a "subject" classification that included the options of dwelling, garden, church, cemetery, public building, square, park, and accessory building, with "scenic," "isolated," and "extensive" indicated as modifiers. Today it might seem odd that commercial and recreational properties were not included, but in 1941, this information was collected for 1380 properties.

After World War II, locally supported historic buildings surveys became more commonplace. The first aim of the College Hill Study in Providence, Rhode Island was to develop a system for "rating" historic architecture. Using as a point of departure the criteria devised by the National Trust for Historic Preservation and the National Park Service, the College Hill survey staff chose seven characteristics to be scored, and weighted them according to a system of priorities. The seven features and the maximum number of points obtainable for each were: Historical Significance (30); Architectural Significance: As an Example of its Style (25); Importance to the Neighborhood (15); Desecration of Original Design (8); Physical Condition of the Structure; (10), Condition of the Grounds (4); and Condition of the Neighborhood (8), for a maximum total of 100 points. Any property receiving over 70 points was considered to be exceptional (Hayward 2006).[5]

Notably, both in Charleston and Providence preservationists borrowed the techniques of art historians, who defined styles by combinations of form, materials, detail, color, and context, combining it with local historical information. This information was placed in a framework similar to a housing conditions survey, going property-by-property to create an inventory and render a preliminary judgment about the importance of each site.[6]

Recording information should not imply an evaluation of the merits of a property, but the very act of recording does mark the site as one worthy of investigation, distinguishing it from others that are ignored. This concept became more important in planning as the preservation movement grew, because survey areas frequently marked the boundaries of public concern. Meanwhile the survey *process* broadened to include more people and, thus, built a constituency for collective and individual action.

The pioneering attempts at inventory and analysis in Charleston and Providence were widely imitated. Their survey framework is, in general, the template followed in local preservation plans, master plans, revitalizations plans, Main Street revitalization projects, and

---

[4] Helen Gardner McCormack recorded the information; Frederick Law Olmsted, Jr. served as consultant.

[5] See Chapter 2 for the context in which this survey was undertaken.

[6] It is worthwhile noting that the term "survey" was associated with the first efforts to examine the environment for sites of historic and architectural merit, while the term "inventory" was added later. They are often used interchangeably although the National Park Service distinguishes one from the other.

recommended in some growth-management legislation (White and Roddewig 1994; Cambridge
1965). Nevertheless, this survey approach has
weaknesses. First, the rating system provides
little or no differentiation between buildings that
are exceptional in some particular respect from
those that are merely very good. Second, the inclusion of "desecration" as a scored criterion in
the Providence survey led to a number of odd
results because the integrity of the design that
remained was often confused with the condition
of the property. Third, the results were often in-
flexibly locked into a system with fixed criteria,
and the values assigned to the various elements
of the system created a process that was increasingly difficult to implement in subsequent years
(Kahlman 1976). For example, broad landscape
features were rarely mentioned. Fourth, any attempt to evaluate archaeological information,
even in the same locations, often remained un-
addressed even when data was available. It is as
if whatever exists below grade was never connected to whatever remains standing.[7]

Today, cultural resource surveys generally
avoid "rating" properties as unwise and premature. In part because the efforts often encompass
thousands of resources in suburbs, on military
bases, or in the path of gas pipeline or electrical power projects, crossing state lines, and several political divisions. For example, the effort
to survey Route 66, "The Mother Highway,"
cuts across several states in its 2448 miles from
Chicago to Los Angeles, with several "miracle
miles" outside of other cities along the way (Liebs
1985; Rutgers 2011).[8] The effort to survey the historic timber roadhouses along the roads and highways in Alaska—built for prospectors and used
as hunting lodges, stage coach stops, and highway contractors' depots—similarly cuts across
several hundred miles (Phillips 1986). (Fig. 6.2)

Fig. 6.2 The Rapids Roadhouse, a remarkable survival
on the Delta River, 231 miles from Valdez, AK, was established in 1902 as a log cabin that continued to increase
in size and change with the various uses it has served.
(Photograph: Casey Woster)

Experience has shown that valuation is highly
context-dependent.

Preservation planners generally agree that a
survey should be designed to serve present needs
as well as those in the future.[9] Questions arising
today and tomorrow demand that the process
and the results be flexible enough to accommodate changing conditions and changing values.
The relative significance of a property varies
every time another property is built, altered, or
demolished. For example, a structure that appears
to be ordinary might be elevated to a position of
importance when others of its kind are destroyed.
Also, as more people research and write about a
period, style, designer, engineer, or property type,
the values associated with the particular object,
location, or activity often change. The relatively
new interest in industrial archaeology, landscape
design, late-twentieth century architecture, and
early twenty-first century sites can increase the
appreciation of a particular structural innovation,
park vista, or artistic approach. In the same vein,
a newly discovered archaeological site will throw

---

[7] The first urban archaeology programs are noted in
Chapter 2. These begin with the efforts in Alexandria,
Virginia.

[8] Route 66 has gained increasing attention, thanks to the
passage of the National Route 66 Corridor Preservation
Act in 1993, with a program overseen by the National
Park Service.

[9] Efforts to create an appropriate set of common, over-
arching chronological and thematic context statements
began anew in the early 1980s with the introduction of
the Resource Planning Protection Process (RP3), outlined
by the National Park Service. Unfortunately, little funding
was made available to stimulate this approach to assembling and analyzing information (Aten 1978).

into high relief previously overlooked properties of a similar period, forcing the reevaluation of all of the existing artifacts. Unfortunately, the amount of time and money to do a comprehensive survey that is continually updated is rarely available, so that each state and many cities have been left to their own devices to find adequate resources. Large areas of potential interest remain unexplored. .

Theoretically, the idea of designing a survey to accommodate change seems possible by using the most advanced computerization, digitization, and communication techniques. Only two elements seem necessary: a long and open-ended list of criteria, and a variable point allocation scale. After the criteria have been selected and the points allocated to each item, the scores can be totaled or, with additional information, recomputed. The advantages of such a system seem obvious: the selective retrieval feature could allow the evaluations to be made by vicinity or by any other appropriate categorization depending upon future developments, and original survey data could be updated as research unearths new information, or as demolitions or alterations occur. In this way, the researcher could repeatedly recheck the data bank for the earliest extant examples of a style, or for streets with unaltered vistas, or could correlate archaeological remains with fragments in museums in any location.[10]

Practically, however, problems immediately arise given that who decides what criteria are applied will provide a variety of results. In a commonly accepted variant of the system, objects to be rated are not simply passed or failed, but receive a verbally descriptive grade or grades. The nomenclature varies. Sometimes it is borrowed straight from the schoolroom (excellent, good, fair, poor); it may be translated into everyday English (extremely high, high, average, low); or expressed in more specialized jargon (of national significance, of major significance, of importance, of value as part of the "scene," an objectionable "imposition," or of no importance). These grades may be assigned to

the building as a whole, or attached separately to each of a series of criteria.

The only reasonable path and the one currently followed in most communities is a "strategic planning" approach, whereby the political, financial, and practical concerns help to form the framework within which the survey is conducted.[11] In the United States , the best-known framework for conducting a survey is provided by the National Park Service, working through the State Historic Preservation offices and the local certified governments. More often than not, the criteria used are those for determining the eligibility of properties for listing in the National Register of Historic Places, and the state and local registers.[12]

The chief purpose of the survey and evaluation process is to look to the future. In the late twentieth century, the analysis of the survey results often led not only to the creation of an historic district but also provided guidance about the character-defining features of the properties and sites in that district. This, in turn, provides direction in the form of recommendations about what can be added or altered, that is, what properties would be targeted for future treatment, such as restoration or rehabilitation. The process also provides information for educational programs, cultural tourism, and other economic development initiatives discussed in other chapters.

The Roles of the Preservation-Minded Designer

Because preservationists are striving to extend the usefulness of existing cultural resources, both implicitly and explicitly they become involved in the design process at many levels. Designers are needed who can easily envision and translate

---

[10] The mathematics of this has been studied (Bussan 1986).

[11] Strategic planning, arising from military applications, first became the preferred approach in the 1980s and 1990s.

[12] The National Register guidelines call for evaluating seven characteristics—integrity of location, design, setting, materials, workmanship, feeling, and association—before determining eligibility to be listed (NRB 1991).

ideas into graphic representations and images that are acceptable to the broader public. In addition, it is essential to have design critics involved who can see both the advantages and difficulties with each scenario.

Many younger architects are educated to begin from nothing and create a design that is innovative and appealing to the client, whether it is for an individual or a corporate client. Interior designers also often begin in the same fashion, with a "blank" computer screen. Landscape architects are restrained somewhat, as they begin with ideas about the land and what grows upon it. "Urban design" is conceived as big architectural projects with groups of buildings and public spaces, sometimes with artistic arrangement and massing. Generally, studio courses assume that well-financed individuals, developers, and governments will have the ability to bring the scheme to fruition. More often than not, the design studio emphasizes newness in bold, exciting strokes.

Preservation-minded designers are different. They see that history is not a label or an option to be accepted or rejected. Rather, they are professionals who see themselves as curators. Their vision begins with a different set of assumptions. Rather than suppose that little of merit exists in the region, city, neighborhood, or parcel that is worthy of retention, they start with a careful examination of the cultural landscape and all its features, above and below ground, studying the character-defining features, the historical context, and the social groups in an area. They accept as worthy of study the buildings and landscapes around them, including the available archaeological evidence. The existing interiors are closely examined too, for they can contain a considerable amount of merit. In this way, surveys of existing cultural resources are critical, and often provide additional starting points for the analysis of a range of design alternatives. This is where the sense of responsibility to the existing history of a place begins (Tomlan 1994).

Preservation-minded designers are also distinguished because they feel a sense of responsibility to the community. The designer should work with the client or clients to incorporate the collective vision of everyone who contributes to the final outcome (Forum 1988–1989). The

work may be at a broad urban level, but more often it focuses on a neighborhood, reinforcing all aspects of its social usefulness. Encompassing an assessment of all of the social and economic activities of the residents in an area, preservation design requires respect for the environment before new aesthetic ideas are introduced. This approach also recognizes from the start that design intervention is needed more in some areas than in others. Understanding the importance of restraint is often the key to a successful scheme because the goal is to intervene only to the degree necessary. Design restraint is very important.

Preservation-minded design accepts and embraces diversity. Ideally, the approach should be concerned with people of all ages and all ethnic groups, holding forth a vision to include all economic classes. It supports variety in housing, education, commerce, and industry, with mixed land-uses and a range of open spaces.

Just as preservationists are proactive socially, preservation-minded designs also pay attention to how people arrive at the site, circulate around, and leave it, emphasizing access for all. The connections between places and spaces are important elements, in paths and walks that reinforce the underlying social norms of the community. As indicated previously, walking is important. Sidewalks are essential, even in the suburbs, a basic prerequisite for comfort. Bicycles, motorbikes, and buses play an important role as well, often providing a more economical and immediately viable alternative to geographically constrained rapid-transit systems.

While economic incentives and legal restrictions provide a carrot-and-stick approach to design, preservationists must accommodate reasonable alternatives, particularly when the ideas and values of community members and groups aren't formally recognized or go unheard. The need to be familiar with design vocabulary and participate with a critical view of the process is important because often the obvious path can be improved. Working with a group of recent immigrants and first-generation Chinese who consider site design principles involved in *Fengshui*, for example, will provide a completely different set of ideas than working with South Indians concerned with the principles of *Vaastu Shastra*, or the values and cultural norms of Haitian immigrants. Preserva-

Fig. 6.3 One of the earliest and best "how to" manuals ever produced, *Rehab Right: How to Rehabilitate Your Oakland House without Sacrificing Architectural Assets*, provides tips on architectural elements and practical approaches to common repair problems. (Courtesy of the Oakland (CA) Planning Department)

tionists can make an enormous contribution to the manner in which the existing character of a place is treated by helping newcomers understand the contributions of those who arrived earlier.

Community Design Assistance

Creating an organization that can regularly assist a community with design issues is often a desirable goal. Whether spurred by a city agency, a nonprofit organization, or a local foundation, the vision of a better future through design is often realized one building at a time. In some neighborhoods or suburbs, planners, preservationists, and urban designers work collaboratively to provide guidance to individuals, developers and others. Professional design assistance frequently provides information in the planning stages that saves time later. In many instances, sketches and studies aided by photography and digital representation plays an important role, with overlays that provide alternative schemes and vision. In cases where municipal staff members encounter questions that are repetitive, "how to" manuals or booklets are provided. One of the most well-known publications that proved helpful was published by the Oakland, California Planning Department: *Rehab Right: How to Rehabilitate Your Oakland House without Sacrificing Architectural Assets* (Kaplan and Prentice 1978). A combination of architectural awareness pointers and practical tips on solving everyday repair problems, the illustrated "common sense" approach was understandable to people faced with similar problems in neighborhoods throughout the country (*PN* June 1979). (Fig. 6.3)

More generally, dozens of nonprofit organizations have been established to assist in designing in-fill buildings, new additions, and in making repairs. Community design assistance centers, composed of architects, landscape architects, planners, and preservationists, often offer their services on an affordable, fee-for-service basis.[13] The primary goal of these centers is to engage local residents and community groups that would not otherwise participate in the process of improving their physical environment. Among the oldest are the Pratt Institute Center for Community and Environmental Development, in Brooklyn, and the Community Design Center of Pittsburgh. Both arose to meet the need for guidance in small, low-income housing projects. About half of the nation's approximately 80 community design assistance centers are connected or affiliated with university programs in architecture, planning, and preservation, and draw on their faculty and students to work with a network of volunteers (ACSA 2000). Many of these organizations are members of the Association for Community Design, which holds annual meetings to share knowledge and evaluate the progress of initiatives.

In several communities, the role of these professional organizations is very helpful. The chapters of the American Institute of Architects, American Society of Landscape Architects, and the American Planning Association often provide referrals. In still other instances, the Mayor's Institute on City Design, based in Washington, D.C., provides helpful advice on design, planning, and financing for mayors of small and medium-sized cities.

In suburban areas, where the commercial activity is declining, the standard approach is often to increase density, building on former parking lots and constructing parking garages (Dunham-Jones Williamson 2009). Yet, this is not the only answer to revitalization. Avoiding natural features and conserving open spaces should be respected, if possible. The history of the planned unit development, cluster subdivisions, "loop" streets, and the townhouse arrangements of post-World War II suburbs demonstrates the reaction of many in the housing industry to the monotony left behind by speculative builders.

In more remote areas, the challenge may be greater. In these cases, student service-learning projects can be helpful. In that regard, state legislators might ask university and program administrators to provide public assistance in targeted areas. Indeed, in some locations, these efforts are the only assistance communities are likely to see.

Design assistance is also important in the wake of natural disasters, and these events often draw professionals from hundreds of miles away. In the wake of hurricanes, tornadoes, floods, fires, and earthquakes, dozens of organizations have provided help. This is particularly important in an economically distressed community, when crime and property vandalism follow the neglect of properties, as will be discussed later in this chapter. After a natural disaster, outside design assistance and other aid can be very welcome when local residents and community representatives appear to lack hope or vision.[14]

The Role that Design Competitions Can Play

Design competitions can help historic preservation projects by involving the local community in a discussion with a wide range of professionals to outline a path of action. The artists, architects, botanists, ecologists, landscape architects, planners, preservationists, and real estate developers that become involved all contribute to this

---

[13] Although local organizations of all kinds are vehicles for designing in a socially-responsible fashion, it is important to distinguish community development corporations (CDCs), which are chiefly concerned with affordable housing, from centers providing community assistance in design. For more on CDCs, HUD-sponsored Community Outreach Partnership Centers with 2 and 4-year colleges and university programs, and Community Development Financial Institutions (CDFIs), see Chapter 4. To increase local service delivery, parallel discussions have emerged regarding the role of community-based organizations in tourism.

---

[14] The discussion about the possibility of displacement is treated in Chapter 7.

alternative vision of the future, one that incorporates the existing fabric. Preservationists must keep their "eye on the prize," however, as the competition is only one means to an end.

Competitions often originate when exploring the range of problems and opportunities for a particular site, neighborhood, city, or region. Although there are many ways to hold a competition, some basic concerns should be kept in mind. The entries in the competition should be judged by respected professionals and nonprofessionals, people who have no stake in the outcome and who have no personal agenda. An important preservation concern is to avoid the expense and caprice of any proposed "signature" design that ignores the existing cultural resources (Nasar 1999; Witzling and Ollswang 1986). This should be part of the competition program. This issue can *also* be addressed, in part, by removing the names of those competing, so that any hint of favoritism can be avoided. Some provision should be made to remind the jurors to seek a balance between originality and a strikingly ambitious scheme that ignores one or more basic conditions for acceptance (Lewis 2009).

Assuming that the competition is properly framed, and adequate information provided to the competitors in either a one or two stage process, potential solutions can be identified and the client will accept the decision of the jury. It is important to keep in mind that the competition is often viewed as the beginning of a public discussion that leads to a design that is worth pursuing, rather than *the* design that will be constructed. Then, with sufficient media attention, government representatives and potential sponsors will endorse the competition and promote even more public discussion.

The National Endowment for the Arts (NEA) has played a significant role in framing and helping to sponsor competitions, many having to do with important historic sites and prominent locations. For example, the 1979 Provincetown, Massachusetts Playhouse Competition was a regional charette to determine the range of options for the structure, which had been burned by vandals two years earlier (Pittas 1985). Competitions have long been used to create memorials and in this regard the NEA played an important role in initiating and funding the Vietnam Veterans'

Fig. 6.4 The winning design in the competition for the Wesleyan Methodist Chapel at the Women's Rights National Historical Park, in Seneca Falls, NY, called for a treatment that recalled the Vietnam Memorial, with the remnants of the original wall exposed to the outdoors. (Authors's photograph)

Memorial Competition, ultimately designed by Maya Lin, on the Mall in Washington, D.C.

In a similar fashion, museums often sponsor competitions to attract attention and to garner funding for new construction. The Museum of Modern Art, the Metropolitan Museum of Art, the Guggenheim Museum, and dozens of others have enlarged their facilities in recent years, and the design alternatives have often been accompanied by considerable public discussion (Newhouse 1998).

Competitions can also produce less-than-desirable results for preservationist, however, even when sponsored by preservation-minded organizations and agencies. The design for the treatment of the Wesleyan Methodist Chapel at the Women's Rights National Historical Park in Seneca Falls, New York, provides an example of how a preservation problem sparked a community crisis. (Fig. 6.4) The Chapel, dedicated in October 1843, was one of the oldest religious structures in the village. More importantly, on July 19, 1848, it was the site of the signing of the Declaration of Sentiments, an important moment during the Women's Rights Convention. Subsequently, however, the size of the religious congregation declined and the building was sold and served a number of other purposes: as an opera house, movie theatre, automobile dealership, athletic club, two stores, a public hall, and, lastly, as a laundromat and apartments.

In 1979, through the efforts of the Elizabeth Cady Stanton Foundation and Judy Hart, then a legislative specialist, the National Park Service approved a study of a proposed Women's Rights National Historical Park. The following year, President Jimmy Carter signed the bill creating the Park. In 1982, the Foundation bought the nearby Elizabeth Cady Stanton House and gave it to the NPS, and Ms. Hart became the first Park Superintendent.

Although the Stanton House was a source of pride, the all-but-abandoned laundromat remained an embarrassment to the community and those interested in celebrating the history of Women's Rights. Its future was also uncertain because no known photographs of the entire Chapel were readily at hand and a physical examination of the property produced only fragmentary evidence of the original church. Despite Hart's best efforts, neither the National Park Service nor the community were enthusiastic about the building.

To focus the attention of everyone on the property, Hart adopted the idea of holding a national design competition, jointly sponsored by the National Park Service and the NEA. The competition was announced on March 30, 1987, and the winning design was selected in October from among over 200 entries: a wall similar to the Vietnam Memorial, which would make use of the remaining elements of the original Chapel. The construction contract was awarded a year later. (Ithaca 1988).[15]

In the following months, however, several questions arose about the Women's Rights Convention and the Chapel. First, historian Judith Wellman came forward with information based on her research that showed that the activities of the Convention were not spontaneously generated in one location, the Chapel; instead, there were several events in a much longer story. Second, the technical aspects of the design were raised by members of the local historic preservation com-

Fig. 6.5 After several years, the National Park Service rejected the winning design and used the available evidence to construct a replica of the Wesleyan Methodist Chapel, which allows for year round interpretation. (Author's photograph)

mission and other officials, including the Mayor. It appeared that the idea was to demolish most of what remained of the Chapel to create an outdoor park. Third, because the archaeological investigation continued after the winning competition entry was announced, when the final draft historic structures report became available in 1990, it was apparent that much more information was available about the physical fabric of the Chapel than was previously assumed. In fact, the location, dimensions and materials of the building's foundation, walls, roof, chimneys, and 20 windows on the east and west elevations all could be determined with certainty. In short, little documentation had been provided to the designers who competed, leading to an awkward situation where the integrity of the existing structure was likely to be severely compromised (Wellman 2004). Were the documentation completed first, and all of the information gathered been made available at the beginning, the results would have been different, and the decision-making process would not likely have fractured the community.

What finally happened provided another curious turn in the story. A few years after the award-winning design was erect, the scheme was altered. A replica of the Chapel was built on the site, reportedly because the exposed walls of the competition winning design could not withstand the harsh weather. (Fig. 6.5)

[15] Announced by the Associated Press, the cowinners of the competition, Harvard architectural students Ray Kinoshita and Ann Wills Marshall, were hired by the Stein Partnership for the project, expected to cost $9 million (Ithaca 1987).

Fig. 6.6 Architect Toshiko Mori won the competition to design the new visitor's interpretation center, part of the effort to restore and interpret Frank Lloyd Wright's Darwin D. Martin House in Buffalo. The model shows the relationship between the new pavilion, the house and the grounds. (Author's photograph)

Fig. 6.8 The excellent documentation available on the Martin House property, and the talent of the new architect, who was respectful of the existing design but not subservient to it, won the design widespread recognition. The work of neighborhood residents, local and regional Frank Lloyd Wright advocates continues to the present time. (Author's photograph)

Fig. 6.7 The visitor-orientation space, interpretive galleries, education spaces, and a museum shop are included in the Eleanor and Wilson Greatbatch Pavilion, set back from the street, while a considerable amount of attention is paid to the landscape. (Author's photograph)

By contrast, another competition held slightly later resulted in a better solution by respecting the historic fabric from the outset. The competition for a visitor's interpretation center became a principal initiative of the Martin House Restoration Corporation, established in 1992 to restore and interpret the Frank Lloyd Wright-designed Darwin Martin House in Buffalo (Quigley 2002). In this case, New York-based architect Toshiko Mori, then chairwoman of the Department of Architecture at the Harvard Graduate School of Design, was selected to design the new building,

which includes a visitor-orientation space, interpretive galleries, education spaces, and a museum shop (Woodward 2009).[16] (Figs. 6.6 and 6.7) Despite the subsequent funding difficulties that truncated part of the construction program, the ability of the contemporary architect to respect the existing design, and yet not be subservient to it, won acclaim and awards from local observers and visitors (Buckham 2008, 2010). In this case, the tremendous amount of documentation that was available, the sustained work of neighborhood residents, local and regional Frank Lloyd Wright advocates, and representatives of the state historic preservation office—all of whom were familiar with the context and the talent of the architect—led to a successful solution. (Fig. 6.8)

Working on a much larger scale, with several properties that are undervalued historically, aesthetically, and economically, the Urban Land Institute's Gerald D. Hines Annual Competition provides a more commonly encountered sce-

---

[16] Mori worked with Hamilton Houston Lowrie Architects, restoration architects for the Martin House project, and Christopher Chadbourne and Associates, Boston-based museum planning and exhibition designers, to provide a solution that not only respects the house and grounds, but is suitably scaled and detailed to fit comfortably with the surrounding residences.

nario. This competition requires graduate student teams composed of architects, engineers, lawyers, finance majors, real estate specialists, landscape architects, planners, and preservationists to collaborate as they solve a problem in an existing city neighborhood.[17] Teamwork is necessary to produce the most successful solution, treating the existing conditions of the properties and proposing economically viable alternatives. Hundreds of students from dozens of universities participate, creating redevelopment proposals that serve as catalysts for broader concerns. These include the community space, transportation hubs, and the need for job incubation; in all, being as inclusive in every dimension as possible. The results of these initiatives, both good and bad, are available online.

Design Review in Neighborhood Conservation and Historic Districts

The work of a preservationist may intersect the process of design and design review in several ways. As noted earlier, information about the character of historic resources gathered in a survey can become the basis for design review guidelines that help to govern the alterations and new structures built within a neighborhood or an historic district. The preservationist may play an active role by contributing to the development of these guidelines and participating in design review to maintain the existing character of the area. This can include stipulations about the size, scale, setback, roof forms, materials, doors, and fenestration pattern of the principle building on the lot, as well as the nature of auxiliary structures.

The preservationist may also work for the municipality, county, or state government to administer these guidelines, assisting planning, zoning and public works staff, review board members, applicants, and the general public in understanding the review. In some cases this process extends over several months. Or, the preservationist may work directly for or with the client to help develop a project wherein the alterations or new construction will be sympathetic to the existing historic fabric and acceptable to the reviewers and the public.

Problems often arise whenever a change is proposed in a district and the roles and responsibilities of individuals and groups involved in the review process are not clear. This can occur among members of the community and the general public, and among the historic district commission board members and staff (Scheer and Preiser 1994).

For those who have never encountered any form of government review, design review procedures can be very confusing. In part, this is because design reviews can take place under the jurisdiction of several boards or commissions, including those that deal with planning, urban design, historic preservation, and zoning. Often these seem to have overlapping authority affecting an historic district or site. And design review often affects dozens of projects that are not considered or designated "historic." Hence, the novice might find that the advice about a proposed design seems contradictory. For example, a zoning code may allow a much taller structure on a lot, while the planning commission would prefer a lower height, and an historic district commission might prefer that the height remain unchanged. Which should prevail? Or a subdivision design review might differ from historic preservation commission review in the degree to which they advise or regulate signage, and in the manner in which they weigh-in on the effort to preserve the existing fabric. In addition, as we have seen in previous examples, differences of opinion between representatives of the National Park Service, state preservation office, or local preservation organizations will sometimes need to be resolved. Only with a great amount of patience and study can one begin to understand the differences. In dealing with all of these issues, a well-educated and experienced preservation planner can be enormously helpful (Beasley 1992; Lightner 1993; Stamps and Nasar 1997).

In some cases a community design-assistance center can provide assistance, but more often the process begins when the project designer[s], i.e.,

---

[17] At least three of these disciplines must be included in the teams.

the client or the client's representative, meets the staff member who will guide the case through the process (Bowsher 1978). Design review begins with informal conversations and information sharing, and continues in the formal public evaluation of schemes for private and public projects, a process that reviews the quality of the additions and alterations, including those that involve the landscape.

The individuals selected to sit on the commission that conduct the reviews should be chosen with the appropriate mix of backgrounds, interests, and abilities, and be provided with adequate information about the nature of the schemes being set before them. Complementing the usual list of people with backgrounds in archaeology, architecture, history, real estate, planning, and urban design, those with a particular sensitivity to ethnic issues, oral history, and the value of traditional practices can be very helpful. Criticisms of the design review process often center on the limited ability of those participating in the discussion of the merits of the project to share information and communicate effectively (Brolin 1980; Smeallie and Smith 1990; Byard 1998). This is particularly noticeable when an attempt is made to introduce a new design in an historic district and little information about it is made available to assist those involved in decision-making. Only about half the hundreds of existing historic preservation commissions use design guidelines, which are often needed on the very first day a decision comes before the newly formed body (Wilkinson 2003).

The keys for effective design review begin with the survey and documentation that is available to provide a context for decision-making. Going beyond that, the recent literature on planning as "communicative action" can be helpful in making design review decisions. This shows that by monitoring meetings, conducting interviews, reviewing cases and associated public and internal documents, people can be better informed. The "rules" or guidelines should be applied consistently, whether considered from the point of view of designers, the commission members, the City's administrative officers, local media personnel, or the public. It is also helpful to avoid presentations that rely on conceptual language favored by designers. For example, a speaker who wants to "create a dialogue between building X and building Y" so as to provide a rationale for a design scheme will only confuse people unfamiliar with design studio critiques.

Boston provides a good example. The city has nine historic districts, each with a separate commission that makes decisions based on their respective resources and each with different guidelines. What may not be permissible in the Beacon Hill Historic District, for example, may be easily allowed in another district. Problems can arise because many design guidelines are duplicated from previous models with different cultural resources and an unusual social and political constituency. As a result, it is not the guidance provided by the State Historic Preservation Office, or the reliance upon the Secretary of the Interior's Standards that are at issue, but the lack of initiative on the part of the local preservation community to provide what should be seen as reasonable alternatives, thoughtfully framed before a "problem" arises. The preservationists must be forward-thinking, going beyond the designation of landmarks and defining the edges of historic districts, or creating conservation districts overlaid on the pre-existing zoning. They must create enforceable guidelines that are appropriate reflections of the local historical context, cultural norms, and attitudes, and that the residents of the area can willingly, and even enthusiastically, endorse.

The Changing Nature of Aesthetic Contexts

In addition to the need for adequate documentation and open discussion about alternatives, preservationists and, particularly, preservation-minded review commissions should be well-enough educated about aesthetic sensibilities to make suitable decisions. In some cases, the general characteristics of a style or period are relatively well known. In many other cases, they are not. Just as important, the rationales being used by designers are often obscure to the public so that those responsible for making decisions need to be able to explain these ideas, and state their reasons for agreeing or disagreeing with them in a consistent and rational fashion.

In this regard, the International Style of modern architecture provides a particularly challenging problem. Until the twentieth century, the concept of space was simply explained by the emptiness between solids. Objects were put into a void and the distance between objects was measured in feet and inches. Buildings contained "space" only if they enclosed it in rooms or chambers. With the advent of modern art, "space" was given another definition: it became a means by which to create objects and environments. For most modernists, space was defined not as a void, but a vast environment made dynamic by design (Arnheim et al. 1966). Accordingly, some of the proponents of modernism in architecture argued that buildings should be designed consistently, from the inside out. Because the spaces inside a building were initially conceived primarily in relationship to one another, the front façade was not accorded the importance it had once possessed. This can be seen as a characteristic of many late-twentieth century buildings in the United States: there is little difference between the front and side elevations, and the entrances are not immediately apparent.

Although the historic district commission is generally only concerned with exterior appearances, it is important that some of these modernist ideas be thoroughly explained and understood. In addition, the preoccupation with a similarly abstract landscape design, if partially obscured or ill-maintained, might be met by the commission members with less than enthusiastic interest. The problem this presents for most historic preservation review commissions and the public is that these aesthetic sensibilities are often seen as academic, esoteric, and thus comparatively unimportant.[18]

Fig. 6.9 The Seagram Building on Park Avenue, here seen under construction in January, 1957, was one of the first International Style skyscraper commercial structures to feature glass walls, in marked contrast to the properties around it. (Gottscho Shleisner, Inc. photograph, Library of Congress)

By contrast, other aspects of modern architecture are generally well appreciated. For example, late twentieth century buildings (spaces) were enclosed with "skins," or membranes of glass, metal, or concrete. The care and treatment of the Seagram Building in New York City provides a good example. (Fig. 6.9) If an uncaring tenant begins to substitute an inappropriate heat-absorbing, opaque glass for the transparent bronze originally specified, the character of the building would be considerably altered. This kind of concern is more easily equated to the changes that buildings of other periods may undergo, destroy-

---

[18] Further complications arise because the concepts of space that are under discussion here are those that arose in the Western tradition of art and architectural history.

The concepts of space often held by designers in the Far East or Africa are much different. This will be addressed further in Chapter 7.

ing their character-defining features. The uneven understanding of a particular style or a particular structure will inevitably have a bearing on how it is regarded and how it is treated.

Given the disdain with which Jane Jacobs and some other leaders in historic preservation viewed International Style modernism and post-World War II urban renewal planning, it is little wonder that some preservationists continue to be skeptical of the design community today (Birch and Roby 1984). Yet, designers who agreed with Jacobs had to find an alternative way to express their ideas. Robert Venturi's *Complexity and Contradiction in Architecture*, published by the Museum of Modern Art in 1966, is sometimes seen as the first critique by a contemporary designer of the corporate modernism that characterized downtown redevelopment of the preceding decade. *Learning from Las Vegas*, a Yale University architecture studio study led by Robert Venturi, Denise Scott Brown, and Steven Izenour, first published in 1972, went further by legitimizing the study of strip architecture, often deemed antithetical to designers who felt commercial imperatives poisoned their creative talents (Vinegar 2008). Ironically, in succeeding years, the big box stores dubbed as "decorated sheds" by this Yale architectural studio group became the most common form of all the new retail space being built in this country. Now decorated sheds are often lying abandoned in the suburbs, alongside early shopping centers.

In 1977, modernism was declared "dead," although the heroic tradition continued as a few architects and urban designers completed some major commissions (Huxtable 1978). Critics such as Brent Brolin and Peter Blake pointed out the repeated failure of modernism to satisfy the public, the architect's clients, and the design community alike (Brolin 1976; Blake 1977).[19] Although it was not clear what term could be applied to the styles or manners of design that would characterize the years ahead, several alternatives were tried

(Huxtable 1978). Then, in March 1978, architects Philip Johnson and John Burgee unveiled their design of the proposed AT&T Building in New York, which *New York Times* architecture critic Paul Goldberger proclaimed as the first monument of the "post modern" movement. Whether or not it was actually the first might be debated, but it was a large building that physically differed in several respects from previous skyscrapers. With a 30 foot tall "Chippendale" pediment, rather than a flat roof, it provided a distinctive shift in profile in a city of tall contemporary buildings (Goldberger 1978). More to the point, it was the first time that most people outside of the design professions learned about "postmodern" architecture.[20]

The period of reassessment continued. In architectural circles, although designers often agreed more on what they did not like than what was best, postmodernism came to accept and adopt a wide range of historical styles, and openly accepted previous ideas that contained elements of regionalism, popular culture, and urban context. While confirmed modernists such as then recently-retired Columbia University Professor James Marston Fitch condemned the new use of historical references in contemporary design as a sham (Brown 1982), many designers enthusiastically embraced the additional freedom to explore sources previously ignored. A renewed emphasis on shape, size, scale, mass, and materials stimulated designers to make creative use of traditional architectural references. A renewed respect for a broad range of historical precedent, the classical language of architecture, and a re-examination of the Beaux-Art techniques of teaching gave rise to a "new classicism," championed by architects Robert A. M. Stern, Allan Greenberg, Thomas Gordon Smith, Elizabeth Plater-Zyberk, and Andres Duany (McLeod 1989).

---

[19] Many people outside of the design professions learned from Tom Wolfe in a series of his articles that were published in *Harper's*, collected under the title *From Bauhaus to Our House* (Wolfe 1981).

[20] Goldberger's was not the first time the term "postmodern" had been used, nor did Venturi coin it, as has sometimes been assumed. In Susie Harries's magnificent biography, *Nikolaus Pevsner: The Life* (Harries 2011), it is clear that this imminent historian applied the term to his own thinking as a modernist, when, in the face of the new designs of 1956, he found himself "out of date."

As the recession of the 1970s gave way to the economic recovery of the early 1980s, with amazing rapidity postmodern historicism became the accepted norm in both the city and suburb. James Rouse's inner city festival marketplaces often sported the new traditional styles, as did the latest corporate facilities and oversized suburban "McMansions."[21] Historic preservationists embraced postmodern ideas because, for the first time in a generation, architects and designers would willingly explore an approach that was more sympathetic to the existing context. Additionally, largely due to the Tax Reform Act of 1976 and its amendments during the early 1980s, historic preservationists had the opportunity to play a meaningful role when working with designers on rehabilitation projects. For a time, it seemed that many architectural designers were working "in synch" with historic district commissions (Tomlan 1992).[22]

Not all postmodern designs were accepted as "good design" because some seemed too indiscriminately historicist, but the opportunities for the discussion of acceptable alternatives appeared to increase (King 2011). This became more obvious 10 years later with the rise of "Deconstructivism," the next fashion in architectural circles to display a range of decorative allusions, with designers continuing to take pride in the manner in which they would defy all structural and material logic.[23]

Just as important to historic preservation, the rise of postmodernism also gave birth to a renewed interest in saving modern structures of all kinds, including "roadside architecture," and mid-twentieth century properties, leading to a renewed sense of purpose among younger preservationists (Liebs 1980; Lynch 1991; Longstreth 1991; Tomlan 1990). By the 1980s, context was beginning to be redefined to include works of international modernism that was no longer seen as a break with tradition. Modernism became part of tradition, accepted as part of the stylistic canon alongside other types and subject to a broad range of contemporary reinterpretations. In fact, the affection for modernism increased as a younger generation grew up in its presence, leading to another chapter in the history of historic preservation (Rappaport 1998).

In the same fashion in which international modernism lost favor, the reaction to sprawl led to a wave of reassessment in contemporary suburban design. Much of this was labeled "new urbanism," the principal ideas of which involved bringing people to locations with mixed uses, in new mixed-income communities, with increased density and, whenever possible, less dependence on the automobile. The "father" of new urbanism was the postmodern architect Andres Duany, a condominium developer, who was inspired to become a more environmentally responsible urban designer (Redmon 2010). Duany and his partner Elizabeth Plater-Zyberk formed their firm, DPZ in 1980, specializing in small suburban layouts, such as Seaside, Florida, using historical town plans with buildings in "new" traditional forms and materials.

Although preservationists decried the continuing trend toward suburbanization, some seemed to admire the manner in which historic idioms were used in contemporary design to set the tone for new town planning. Celebration, the Disney new town established in central Florida in 1994, is one example (Celebration 1995). Designed to evoke a sunny, festive atmosphere, it was purportedly developed as an education-minded and health conscious community. Protected by a 4700-acre greenbelt that contains wildlife, with views of the natural landscape, the corporation that manages it proclaims "small town architecture is back," using images that recall small, southern nineteenth century public squares and

---

[21] The term refers to the well-known fast-food franchise that emphasized oversized ground beef sandwiches on a bun. Further discussion regarding the rise and fall of the house type, and its incipient need for preservation, is provided in Chapter 7.

[22] The term "postmodern" is retained throughout this work for the sake of consistency.

[23] Philosopher Jacques Derrida is credited with the introduction of the term but the principal architects associated with the ideas was Peter Eisenman and later, Daniel Libeskind. The 1988 Museum of Modern Art Exhibition brought together the then-current examples, which variously displayed some debts to early twentieth century Russian Futurism and Constructivism.

railroad towns. Sports facilities offer many op-portunities for recreation, and trails, bicycle and jogging paths encourage neighborly socializ-ing. To provide added visual variety, the archi-tects of the master plan, Robert A. M. Stern and Jaquelin Robertson, made sure that every type of architecture was available in six classic pre-1940 American styles. The largest homes on a third of an acre began selling for $750,000, offering es-tate-like possibilities, while the townhouse lots, village lots, and cottage lots offer other options. The smallest accommodations are the downtown apartments over the first story shops. All theo-retically follow design guidelines that specify the "do's" and "don'ts" to insure a cohesive image is maintained (Lassell 2004). As with the early "new urbanist" designs, critics noted that the new housing appealed to a segment of the population that was financially secure and well educated (Edgell 1995; Talen 2005). As a result, it is un-likely that low-income groups will be comfort-ably accommodated.

Broadening the concerns expressed by new ur-banists, in 2000 architect and urban designer Peter Calthorpe and planner and author William Fulton introduced their approach to "understand[ing] the relationship between the block and the metropo-lis as a whole, and to illuminat[ing] for all of us how this relationship affects the way we live our lives" (Calthorpe and Fulton 2001, p. xiii). To re-duce sprawl and the emphasis on the automobile as the principal mode of transportation, Calthor-pe and Fulton proposed a framework that takes advantage of the neighborhood and the region. To reform the neighborhood, planners would fol-low the new urbanist ideas of traditional urban design, emphasizing walking. In addition, to change the framework for the region, public of-ficials would develop and adopt policies that pro-mote social and economic opportunities, as well as diversity, human scale, and preservation. In their thinking, the suburbs remain linked to the city core for their regional amenities, economic opportunities, and tax income. The "Regional City" is also an ecological unit, complete with watersheds and habitat conservation (Calthorpe and Fulton 2001, pp. 45–48, 51).

To those familiar with early twentieth century planning ideas, the combination of city, urban, and regional planning recalled the initiatives of the Regional Planning Association of America. These were promoted by Lewis Mumford, Clar-ence Stein, and Henry Wright, and embraced earlier proposals of conservation planner Benton MacKaye, particularly his Appalachian Trail (Anderson 2002). Although new urbanists claim that theirs is fundamentally an anti-sprawl move-ment, which preservationists who are interested in conserving the existing urban and suburban public infrastructure might applaud because it encourages more mixed use with greater density, this approach primarily promotes new construc-tion. As a result, it often works against using the existing, under-utilized built environment more effectively.

In addition, some of the ideas proposed by new urbanists deliberately undermine the integ-rity of the existing physical infrastructure. For example, the cul-de-sac, a Garden City inven-tion widely believed to have been introduced in the late 1920s at Radburn, New Jersey to allow driveways to penetrate a community from its cir-cumference, became a character-defining feature of hundreds of mid-twentieth century American suburbs. State and local government planning templates often preferred the cul-de-sac because it was considered by home builders and home owners alike as the safest place to live (Wood 1931). Recently, however, the cul-de-sac has been linked to suburban sprawl and thus has been held in disfavor. Virginia Governor Timothy M. Kaine made a name for himself when he began a campaign to reducing traffic and pollution, and emphasized the need for greater land-use effi-ciency when providing transportation funding. The Governor stated that the escalating cost of maintaining all of the suburban roads seemed to be excessive, and in 2009 he announced and succeeded in pushing through new transportation regulations that banned cul-de-sacs (Weiss 2009). Although some new urbanist designs use both the more ubiquitous grid layout *and* the cul-de-sac (Cozens and Hillier 2008), it appears that hun-dreds of residential subdivisions built around a prominent suburban feature in Virginia are likely to be unsuccessful in when it comes to maintaining this disparaged feature of their streets.

The Renewed Emphasis on "Sustainability"

The idea of "sustainability" was used by futurists during the late 1950s and 1960s, linked to the large and seemingly intractable problems of feeding the rapidly expanding global population, the majority of which were poor and relatively uneducated. In addition to these social problems, others challenges demanded attention: the environmental destruction manifested in deforestation and the pollution of the air, water, and soil; the need for more efficient sources and uses of energy; the possibility of nuclear war; and the uneven funding of public infrastructure. Scientists, design professionals, public administrators, and politicians seemed to be held spell-bound, for example, when inventor and futurist R. Buckminster Fuller addressed all of these challenges to our "spaceship earth" (Fuller 1969, 1971).[24]

The vision of ecological disaster as a "Hell on Earth" went only so far in changing daily habits. The shift in the public's thinking became more immediate when the 1973–1974 Arab oil embargo forced automobile and truck drivers in the United States to reassess a livelihood that once seemed invincible (Roeder 2005). Environmental and historic preservation advocates found in this "temporary adversity" an opportunity to explain the advantages of conserving existing properties, using traditional construction techniques to rehabilitate old buildings and to design new properties (Olkowski 1979; Butti and Perlin 1980). The National Trust for Historic Preservation and several state preservation organizations held sessions at their annual conferences and published a variety of works on the these topics (Energy 1981). In addition, the Advisory Council on Historic Preservation released a report on "embodied energy" and ways to better assess conservation efforts

(Advisory Council 1977), and the National Park Service redoubled its efforts to explain how energy could be saved (Smith 1978; T. Vonier Associates 1981), sometimes working with the US Department of Housing and Urban Development and the American Planning Association (Jaffe and Erley 1980).[25] The need to guide local design review often played a role in stimulating these works. Landscaping, awnings, shutters, porches, storm windows, and overhangs gained more technical significance in these reviews, and solar collectors were reconfigured and relocated to be less obtrusive on historic properties. Today, some are even the "character-defining features" of the existing historic fabric.

The education campaign even included some public school systems, as biology, chemistry, and physics teachers enlisted the help of young adults to determine the advantages of wind power, biofuels, and solar energy, while at the same time examining the ills of the "appliance explosion." Other experiments displayed the advantages of additional insulation and energy-saving window treatments (NY Energy Education Project 1977).

Weighing the costs of investing in alternative energy against their economic return, architects and engineers worked with economists to develop techniques to measure their "life-cycle." Life-cycle costing takes into account the higher initial costs to implement changes that insure long term results, and questions the idea of "built-in obsolescence" held by manufacturing circles (AIA 1977; Stevens 1979). This often tended to rely upon economic incentives to change consumer behavior. It posited that the public's interest in saving energy—i.e., money—was the most important motivation and, by extension, saving existing materials would follow.

Discussion of the life cycle evaluation of historic properties gave increased legitimacy to keeping the existing fabric, while considering carefully any replacement options. More people began comparing the environmental impact of a salvaged product with a new product, which

---

[24] Chapter 2 provides more background on the federal and state legislative responses to these social and environmental problems.

[25] It is worth noting that the National Bureau of Standards also played an active role (Petersen 1974; Rossiter and Mathey 1978; Rubin 1978).

would reduce energy consumption by saving on the energy used to move new materials from the manufacturing site to the construction or rehabilitation site. For the first time, materials needing little remanufacturing effort were evaluated, allowing for an extended comparison. Results show that the environmental impact is significantly reduced when local salvaged materials—often requiring minimal remanufacturing or preparation—are selected over new materials, especially when imported from a considerable distance (Webster and Bronski 2005). In addition, the number of local jobs could be maintained or increased, rather than pay for nonlocal labor to manufacture new products.

The extraction and fabrication of building materials, the assembling and ease of construction, and the ability to reuse the property are all considerations in design, every bit as important as the use of energy to operate and maintain it. As historic properties also show, natural lighting, heating, and ventilating can achieve substantial savings, and insulation of all kinds saves energy.

What is more, this kind of design is imaginative. It requires creativity that is every bit as artistically sensitive and mechanically and structurally advanced as new construction, incorporating natural materials and, where appropriate, new synthetics. During the 1980s and early 1990s, measuring thermal performance and energy use shifted from the gross calculations to more sophisticated, localized, computerized calculations, often coupled with a renewed interest in solar-energy applications (Ayers and Stamper 1995).

In comparison to the earlier, largely reactive environmental initiatives, the most recent redefinition of sustainability was generated in Northern Europe in a proactive manner, causing considerably more discussion and debate. According to the 1987 World Commission on Environment and Development, the world faces "interlocking" crises in the environment and in the economy that threaten the future of humanity. "Sustainable human progress" can be achieved only if environmental protection and economic growth are treated as inseparable. The dangers to air, water, and soil that threaten life on the planet has to be addressed at the same time that poverty, hunger,

population growth, and the unequal distribution of wealth has to be corrected. Echoing many of the same themes discussed by a previous generation of environmental advocates, the emphasis on economic development as the most essential aspect of the solution was, in 1987, seen as a "first" (Shapecoff 1987).

The 1987 publication of *Our Common Future*, popularly known as the Brundtland Report, was named for Gro Brundtland. Dr. Brundtland, a Harvard-educated physician, was then the Prime Minister of Norway and chairman the World Commission that sponsored the report. Its release proved very well timed because, as the world's economy slowed, it allowed world leaders the time to reassess their goals (Brundtland 1987). The fundamental tenets of the report held that environmental consciousness, social equity, and economic viability had to be kept in balance if development was to be sustainable. Because the report was published by the United Nations, it offered the first widely-distributed definition of "sustainable development." Subsequent discussion and promotion broadened this deceptively simple term and preservationists who remembered the earlier environmental campaigns understood that the concepts were not new (Revkin 2007; Dalibard n.d.).

Raising the visibility of this discussion, in 1992 the United Nations sponsored an international conference in Rio de Janeiro, later dubbed the "Earth Summit," attended by representatives of more than 150 nations and environmental groups. The purpose was to raise concern for global environmental issues, including atmospheric change, the effects of pollution, and the loss of natural resources and the flora and fauna that characterizes much of the world.

These European-based initiatives had comparatively little resonance in the United States, however, because this country's construction industry is very large and influential and political consensus on global warming and climate change is deeply fractured. Here, "sustainability" took on a different meaning, holding more resonance in the private sector. Moreover, like the developing ideas in environmentalism in the 1960s, the discussion about sustainability in the USA left behind any substantial concerns for social equity.

In Washington, the American Institute of Architects reformulated its Committee on Energy in 1990 to create a Committee on the Environment (COTE). Its purpose was to advocate for best practices that integrated knowledge of the built and natural environment into design practice. Through COTE, the AIA began to work with the Environmental Protection Agency (EPA) to produce the annual publication, "Environmental Resource Guide," providing a basis for comparing the environmental impact of building materials, products, and systems, and assessing the environmental impacts of building materials from their original extraction and manufacture to their final disposal or reuse.

The Birth and Development of the US Green Building Council

All of this was a prelude to what became the most successful and popular American effort at "going green." In October 1992, two Washington lobbyists and a developer formed a nonprofit organization, initially called The United States Green Manufacturers Building Council, later known as the US Green Building Council (USGBC). The founding principal, David Gottfried, stated that the chief goal was to promote the services and products of major corporations and institutes that displayed clear environmental sensitivity. The USGBC set out to attract a broad range of industry and research representatives (Gottfried 2004). One of the first initiatives was to create a set of standards or guidelines for building materials and products, a kind of "Good Housekeeping Seal of approval." Using the American Society of Testing Materials Green Building Subcommittee as the launching point, these ideas became codified in the "Leadership in Energy and Environmental Design" (LEED) Green Building Rating System, introduced in 1998. The greater the number of points awarded, the higher the rating, the highest being platinum, followed by gold, silver, and certified. In this fashion, LEED was intended to be a nationally accepted benchmark for the de-

sign, construction, and operation of "high performance" buildings.

From the outset, the LEED system was controlled by a consensus-based committee of a nonprofit organization not directly connected to any federal agency or government department. As the initial organizers realized, not until large corporate backers became involved would it have sufficient funding and legitimacy in the building industry to gain widespread acceptance. The breakthrough came when Johnson Controls came to the table, signaling acceptance to thousands of other companies seeking to demonstrate the "greenness" of their products.

Despite being a private initiative, public decision-makers have generally understood the "branding" of LEED as a good first step in responsible stewardship, and public agencies have adopted the LEED standards to guide them. At the federal level, the General Services Administration and the Environmental Protection Agency have adopted LEED thresholds in new construction. Several other systems have been developed. The US Army created its own "green" rating tool in 2001 to include operation and maintenance concerns, and to allow for future building modifications (Army 2009).[26] Similarly, state and local governments have used the LEED rating system or similar home grown variants as guidelines to determine eligibility to earn benefits. Oregon and New York provide tax credits for new buildings that meet green standards, the latter state being the first to provide an incentive for "environmentally sound" apartments and commercial buildings. Portland, Oregon has distinguished itself by adopting the LEED rating system in January 2001 so that new construction and major renovations receiving city funding or private sector funding incentives are required to obtain LEED certification (Call 2002).

The concept of awarding points and issuing certifications would in no way be the exclusive right of USGBC, or the agents of the federal, state, or local governments. Seeing the advantages of appealing to a broader market, in 2007

---

[26] The Army launched the Sustainable Project Rating Tool (SPiRiT).

the National Association of Home Builders (NAHB) introduced its initiative to "go green" with criteria termed the National Green Building Standard (NGBS). In an "Emerald-certified home," for example, water and energy usage is reduced by more than 50%. In summary, there are now dozens of "green" rating systems, all well intended, but with few shared characteristics (Jackson 2010). Ironically, as the monitoring of the actual performance of these buildings has begun to show, some are by no means as efficient as anticipated (Miner 2009).

With the initial focus on new construction, in 1999 that LEED discussions turned to "Existing Buildings: Operations & Maintenance" (LEED EBOM). The emphasis on groups of buildings and campus projects turned around questions regarding solid waste management, green cleaning, and occupant comfort. Because the generally accepted feeling among green advocates is that existing buildings consume about 40% of America's energy, at first glance it seems natural to assume that more attention would be paid to historic structures (McKinsey 2009). Remodeling and renovation have played a minor role, however, because data can be difficult to collect and there is bias by green building advocates to construct new buildings that incorporate sophisticated electronics.

The question that arises is how the preservation community evaluates an appropriate response when, for example, a property owner in an historic district wants to remove the building's original windows and install new, high performing substitutes that promise to save energy. Again, the context is important. First, most sustainable building practices are evaluated based on limited comparisons of the up-front cash cost alone. Rarely are the future costs weighed, over an extended period. Second, the specifics of the proposal can make a considerable difference. For example, what kind of window is being proposed? If the answer is a style or type that will seriously affect the visual characteristics of the structure, alternatives should be considered. Third, what is the means by which the work will be done? Do the costs of improving the existing structure with local materials and labor significantly outweighed installing new windows from a distant source? (Leimenstoll 2010).[27]

Because so many of the issues vary with the scale of the project—from a particular site to neighborhoods, cities and regions—even if the algorithms are developed to account for and sort through the features, other environmental factors should be weighed. These include the manner in which the natural habitat is disturbed in open areas and the effects of collecting water, allowing for drainage and disposal of sewerage. All this will continue to challenge the USGBC, and what it means for preservationists for years to come.

"Marking Time" as a Treatment

It is important to consider the timing of the decision-making. Often, "marking time," i.e., doing comparatively little, can be the best approach in the short term. Although preservation issues often seem to demand an immediate response, it is crucial to provide everyone involved with enough time to study all the options.

The best first step is often stabilization or "mothballing" the property by taking protective measures while further investigation is taking place. For buildings and archaeological sites, this often includes installing temporary roofing and drainage to shelter the site against water, ice, snow, and wind. The protection may include temporary shoring or structural support. It may also include placing temporary plywood covering with louvers over the windows for ventilation and security. (Fig. 6.10) It might also include adding a ventilation fan to prevent damage from condensation, installing temporary fire detection and security systems, and building a perimeter security fence. These temporary measures may be in place for much longer than originally intended, but organizations such as Indiana Landmarks that regularly become involved with taking temporary custody to save properties have gained considerable experience in the techniques (Indiana 2010). By providing researchers with

---

[27] Similar questions arise when the property owner indicates that he or she wishes to place solar panels on an existing roof. When placed against the plane of a roof with a slight slope, solar panels can be well hidden.

Fig. 6.10 The stabilization of the hospital buildings on Ellis Island involved securing the buildings and allowing sufficient light and ventilation in a very humid location. The documentation of the volunteer labor of Cornell students and alumni and other groups allowed the National Park Service to argue more effectively for financial support to continue to the work. (Author's photograph)

more time to assess the nature of the problems, through the completion of historical research, a comprehensive historic structures report, landscape analysis, and extensive archaeology, the resulting solution will surely be improved.

If one is marking time, however, communicating with the public about the present and future steps to get to a permanent solution is vitally important. Uninformed observers may view the temporary measures as an end in itself and question the decision-making process. Often the comments are misplaced. When the story is explained fully, is it possible to understand whether the intent, and proposed solution, is satisfactory.

Restoration: Easily Understood, Often Impossible to Achieve

For critics like John Ruskin, restoration is impossible to achieve, largely because the action requires turning back the clock to live in conditions no longer acceptable. Yet, "restoration," defined by the National Park Service as "the act or process of accurately depicting the form, features, and character of a property as it appeared at a particular period of time," removing elements that were added and reconstructing missing features from the restoration period (Standards 2001), remains the ideal that many people see as a chief focus of preservation efforts. Museums, particularly house museums, may claim to be undertaking a restoration, although they are not, strictly speaking, restoring a house, with servants or slaves, devoid of all modern conveniences. Rather, most are serving a didactic purpose, displaying what some aspects of life were like at a particular time.

The "restoration" of Montpelier, President James Madison's home, was one of the most stunning transformations of the early twenty-first century. (Fig. 6.11) Begun as an eighteenth century slave plantation that grew to 22 rooms during his lifetime, by the late twentieth century the original form of the structure was no longer evident. This was the result of deliberate actions by successive owners. Particularly after being purchased by William duPont in 1901,

Fig. 6.11 The "restoration" of Montpelier, the plantation of President James Madison, was one of the most stunning transformations of the early twenty-first century. The eighteenth century estate that grew to twenty-two rooms during his lifetime and, after being purchased and expanded by the millionaire William DuPont, became a grand twentieth century estate. (Author's photograph)

Montpelier was expanded by the family into an imposing mansion, with 55 rooms and 12 bathrooms, all under a long, almost flat, roof, with walls covered in pink stucco. The grounds included horse tracks, stables, a cockfighting ring, a bowling alley, and dozens of outbuildings (Conroy 1989).

The decision to restore the house to Madison's time was not an easy one. Preservation advocates pointed out that the duPont chapter of the property's story was certainly worthy of recognition and should not be destroyed. On the other hand, the justification for the restoration lay in the difficulty that members of the Montpelier Foundation had in maintaining and interpreting the greatly enlarged property relative to President Madison's life. While both Mt. Vernon and Monticello are immediately recognizable icons for the homes of Washington and Jefferson, Montpelier was not (Downey 2005; Kennicott 2006).[28]

Enlisting some of the research staff of Colonial Williamsburg, all of the sources of available documentary evidence were collected and analyzed.[29] Researchers were surprised to find that much of the original fabric still existed, including some of the doors and windows, and the original hearthstone from a fireplace in Madison's main parlor. The most difficult compromise, however, was the decision as to which of Madison's houses the final result would resemble. The house that Madison inherited from his father was small in comparison to the house in which he died decades later. In fact, the Montpelier that was restored was a duplex, one half of which was occupied by the President's parents, with a large portico added and two brick wings on either side. Ultimately, having spent over $20 million by the time the site reopened in 2009, the restoration to

the period between 1815 and 1836 has removed all evidence of the post-Madison decades to present a clearer interpretation of the property's primary period of significance.[30]

Reconstruction: Replication for a Reason

Montpelier illustrates yet another approach: reconstruction. The National Park Service has defined this as "the act or process of depicting, by means of new construction, the form, features, and detailing of a non-surviving site, landscape, building, structure, or object for the purpose of replicating its appearance at a specific period of time and in its historic location." In Montpelier, once the decision to "restore" was made, it was logical to replicate features needed to complete the appearance of the period. At times a current feature will be hidden inside the old form. Modern plumbing, electrical systems, air conditioning, and security equipment can be disguised behind cornice molding profiles or located in out buildings.

The ethical question is how much reconstruction should be permitted and for what purpose? Those who propose reconstruction often demonstrate the amount of documentation that has been assembled, including archaeological evidence, to assure those in doubt that every detail has been considered. Yet, a reconstruction often has the least authenticity because it depicts an historical period using new materials. The question then arises whether the rational for reconstruction is being taken too far. Colonial Williamsburg is an example where the justification for reconstruction rests primarily in its role as an educational organization.

Reconstruction in a religious context might be perfectly reasonable, particularly if a church,

---

[28] Both Mount Vernon and Monticello have garnered considerable amount of funding for restoration work in recent decades.

[29] These included Edward A. Chappell, Willie Graham, Carl Lounsbury, and Mark R. Wenger. Wenger worked with Myron Stachiw, with help from Willie Graham, Peter Sandbeck, and others. Joining them were Montpelier staff members John Jeanes, Ann Miller, and Alfredo Maul. The architectural firm Mesick, Cohen, Wilson, and Baker provided a schedule and cost estimates (Chappell 2008).

[30] In archaeology, the demand to interpret to the general public the ruins of a site or structure leads to what is termed "anastylosis," that is, rebuilding by reassembling and reerecting the fallen parts, incorporating new materials when deemed necessary. Far more difficult is the idea of landscape restoration.

mosque, synagogue, or temple were severely damaged by an earthquake, flood, or other natural disaster. Actively practicing religious groups have every reasonable expectation of addressing these problems. This is especially true, for example, in some non-Western cultures, such as Native American, which places more emphasis on preserving the process that creates the historic resource than the resource itself.

An increasing range of composite/synthetic materials can duplicate the appearance and performance of original organic materials and fabric. What is the philosophical and practical basis for deciding what and how much to substitute or replace? How much synthetic material can be used and still retain authenticity? Some of these issues are addressed in the case studies found in Chapters 7 and 8.

Rehabilitation: A Term with Special Meaning

The word rehabilitation, or "rehab," has undergone a considerable transformation over the years. Beginning with the very first major inner city waterfront industrial conversions, Ghirardelli Square in San Francisco and Quincy Market in Boston, the word rehabilitation has become synonymous with substantial changes of use and considerable investment in new interior construction. In the early 1970s, those who regularly became involved in preservation practice informally redefined the terms "remodeling" and "renovation." *Remodeling* retains some of the pre-1966 aura of home improvement and continues to mean updating and improving, with or without professional guidance. *Renovation* became a more deliberate effort, often associated with commercial work. To these yet another word, "rehabilitation" was added. This adopted a special meaning, particularly when preceded with the term "certified rehabilitation" as discussed in previous chapters.

The shift occurred because of the growing amount of housing rehabilitation taking place. Specifically, a request for help in developing appropriate assistance for professionals involved in rehabilitating low income housing led to a request by the US Department of Housing and Urban Development to the Advisory Council on Historic Preservation and the National Park Service for more specific guidance in how to proceed with work involving historic properties. Too many difficulties arose when what was an acceptable treatment of an historic property by one agency was not considered appropriate to one of the others. The ensuing discussion about appropriate treatment led to drafting the first national guidelines for historic preservation projects. Under the 1974 Emergency Home Purchase Act, the National Park Service created "Guidelines for Rehabilitating Old Buildings," which were made generally available in 1976 (HUD 1977).

Shortly thereafter Congress passed and President Gerald Ford signed the Tax Reform Act of 1976, which stipulated that "certified" historic properties that underwent "certified rehabilitations" were eligible for new financial benefits. The regulations regarding the implementation of the Tax Reform Act issued by the National Park Service in 1977 further stipulated that the Secretary of the Interior had to determine that the rehabilitation met "certain standards with respect to the historic integrity" of the property. Hence, HUD's "Guidelines" were recast and expanded to become the first rehabilitation "standards" (Morton 1995).[31]

As a result, the word rehabilitation took on a new meaning, almost unique to the United States, largely because of the review process that the Rehabilitation Standards were intended to guide to meet the provisions of the tax code. It is extremely important to remember that W. Brown Morton III, coauthor of the Secretary of the Interior's Standards, defined the ten rules as "… a code of ethics—as general statements that apply to all preservation work and which articulate an attitude or set of values against which a specific action or plan can be evaluated" (Morton 1995, p. 2).

Because the National Park Service is the principal federal agency concerned with setting

---

[31] Other countries have followed this approach (Foo 1996).

policy, implementing programs, and supporting restoration and rehabilitation activities, all the state historic preservation offices took notice. With the passage of state tax code provisions, the Secretary of the Interior's Standards for Rehabilitation were often "readopted" as the working platform for evaluation, and applied increasingly at the local level. Unfortunately, the initiative to frame more appropriate local standards for historically sympathetic work has waned among preservation advocates, preservation commission members, and their staff.

Largely overlooked was the discordance between some of the ideas that international modernism contributed to the Standards and the development of alternatives that have become more commonplace in recent decades. In architecture and urban design circles, Standards Nine and Ten contain language that are considered the most relevant, for both are concerned with the relationship between what has been built and any proposed new construction.

Standard Number 9 states "Contemporary design for alterations and additions to existing properties shall not be discouraged when such alterations and additions do not destroy significant historical, architectural or cultural material, and such design is compatible with the size, scale, color, material, and character of the property, neighborhood or environment" (NPS 1983). That is, Standard 9 may be interpreted as encouraging the design of new structures as long as they did not promote demolition and remained sympathetic to their site and surrounding. The original understanding was that frank, new construction is desirable in a contemporary style, clearly differentiated so that a false appearance is not created. Jarring juxtapositions were argued to be the most appropriate at the very time that international modernism was declared "dead." Subsequently, the acceptance of historical idioms of any period were accepted as the contemporary style, so that the question arises again: what mode of expression is most helpful given the context?

Standard 10 states "Wherever possible, new additions or alterations to structures shall be done in such a manner that if such additions or alterations were to be removed in the future,

the essential form and integrity of the structure would be unimpaired" (NPS 1983). Although the words "wherever possible" sidestep the question of just when it would be permissible to violate the standard, the basic understanding remains that the action should "do no harm" to the property. The integrity of the original should not be compromised by the new.

More practically, changes have been made to the manner in which a certified rehabilitation is evaluated in the field. For example, in the Revenue Act of 1978, the National Park Service and the Internal Revenue Service were much more specific about the conditions that had to be met by the rehabilitation for it to be certified, especially for projects that involved merely facade retention or a "gut rehab." The Standards were not altered, but a "walls test" was introduced in the Internal Revenue Code, whereby at least three-quarters of the exterior walls of a building had to remain intact for the project to be certified (Duerksen 1983).[32] Unfortunately, even this attempt at setting boundaries has proven difficult to enforce.[33]

As can be seen, the aesthetic considerations in historic preservation can never be completely freed of the existing physical conditions, the contextual situation, and all of the historical considerations. The intent of guidelines and standards is not to hamstring creativity, but to provide boundaries against which rationales can be tested and the best interpretation made. Designing with sensitivity to human comfort and a respect for the fabric is an exciting challenge, leading to some remarkable solutions.

---

[32] This was understood to mean at least the principal facade and the two side elevations would remain intact.

[33] Even the then-president of the National Trust for Historic Preservation sided with the developers that these regulations were too onerous when a 1983 Congressional subcommittee considered technical corrections to the procedures (Ainslee 1984). The tendency to accept "facadism" is discussed at greater length in Chapter 7.

Rehabilitating Properties that Seem Impossible to Reuse

Large train stations, factories, church complexes, and office parks are often seen as too large to be reused. Hundreds of examples are available for those who wish to rehabilitate properties to provide working and living spaces, and places for worship. Less well known are the ways in which recreational facilities are treated. Team sports, specifically baseball, football, basketball, cricket, wrestling, swimming, and track and field, are a major component of every school, college, and university, and the professional leagues. Their facilities are major long-term investments whose design and rehabilitation require a considerable amount of attention.

To anyone who knows baseball, Boston's Fenway Park is a recognized part of the history of the sport (Stout and Johnson 2004). (Fig. 6.12) Constructed in 1912, it is the oldest major league baseball stadium in the country and the Boston Red Sox enjoy a tremendously loyal regional following. Yet, keeping up with the expectations of the team's owners and the needs of the fans has been no easy task. In the late 1950s attendance stopped growing and plans to modernize Fenway called for taking over the adjacent street, adding viewing stands, and increasing parking. Because the team's owners expected the government to pay for the improvements, and the government disagreed, nothing happened. As attendance declined, Fenway became threatened with demolition and replacement. The Boston Red Sox management gave a number of reasons for wanting a new ballpark, most of which centered on their inability to collect adequate revenue. Other teams, such as the Chicago White Sox and the Detroit Tigers, announced they were moving into new facilities, so it seemed inevitable that Fenway would face the wrecking ball.

Sensing an immediate threat, a nonprofit organization, Save Fenway Park!, was formed in early 1998 to champion its preservation.[34] Working with representatives of the local commu-

nity, the Fenway Action Coalition, the activists attempted to raise awareness about the threat to the ballpark, while calling for a more transparent planning process. By offering a series of design proposals in a public forum, they demonstrated that renovation could meet the needs of the owners, the team, and fans.

Ultimately this paved the way for a better outcome because a change in attitude took place in 2001, when the Red Sox team was purchased by owners sympathetic to the preservation of the Park. To be able to describe precisely what was considered valuable, the first step was to determine a list of character defining features, both on the interior and the exterior. On the interior, the field configuration had to be maintained, which meant its irregularity and the wall heights. The location of the hand-operated scoreboard was important, as was the slope and configuration of the grandstand, right and left field pavilions, and the bleacher pavilion. Views were also deemed important. The ability to see the Prudential Tower and the Citgo sign were added to the list. The approach to Fenway was also important, so the Gate A lobby, the ticket booths, and the turnstiles had to be retained. Outside, the 1912 brick Yawkey Way façade and the side street facades were listed, as well as the light towers.

The key to the successful rehabilitation arose during the advocates' discussions with Chicago architect Howard Decker, who proposed treating each element of the Park differently, recognizing varying levels of significance within the overall context. Each component—the bleachers, the pavilions, the score board, etc.—was treated as a separate project.[35]

What effect has the Fenway project had on the area and other attempts to save sports facilities? A number of other advocates around the country have become more interested in saving recreational facilities. In Detroit, the threat to the "The Corner," so named for its location at Michigan Avenue and Trumbull Avenue, gave rise to an or-

---

[34] Bill Steelman, Steve Rubin, and Dan Wilson were the first to serve on the board.

[35] Additional members of the team included Boston architects Jack Glassman, Tom Lingel, architectural intern Travis Vaughan, and preservationists Jeffrey Harris and Kim Konrad Alvarez.

Fig. 6.12 As the oldest major league baseball stadium in the country, Boston's Fenway Park is intimately tied to the history of the sport. Its superb rehabilitation respects each of the periods of its construction, and maintains the popularity of the venue and the character of the place. (Author's photograph)

ganization that attempted to save Tiger Stadium, the Old Tiger Stadium Conservancy. The structure was declared a State of Michigan Historic Site in 1975 and listed on the National Register of Historic Places in 1989. After the Tigers baseball team left the stadium, several redevelopment and preservation efforts were attempted, then discarded. The city approved its demolition, which took place in September 2009, despite having no plans for the site (Gallagher 2009). In Portland, by contrast, the nomination to the National Register of the Memorial Coliseum was the first signal that the city would rededicate its multipurpose arena, rather than demolishing it for a new facility.

Reevaluating Elevated Transit Corridors

Historically, the growth of new transit corridors has served to reorient community life. Whether following the development alongside rivers and ports, or along turnpikes and roads, or railroads, people have moved their activities, at times relocating communities to entirely new locations. Almost no aspect of life in America has been left untouched by a new means of access. As indicated in Chapter 2, the construction of a system of superhighways in the late 1950s and early 1960s provoked intense emotion, often precipitating interest in local preservation action. Highways often ripped through neighborhoods, and, when completed, acted as a social barrier by interrupting movement on existing streets and sidewalks (Mohl 2008).

Not everyone in the country believed that the best path to future development lay in providing more highways. The "freeway revolt" began in San Francisco. By the late 1940s highway engineers knew that the city's waterfront was the best route for a freeway connecting the Golden Gate and Bay bridges. An elevated highway could be built over level land in the industrial zone comparatively easily, with a number of access ramps to the Embarcadero Freeway link. To the surprise of the California Highway Department, almost as soon as the first concrete was dry in 1953, several civic groups and local public agencies objected to the plan (Johnson 2009). Months of heated discussion followed around the future of the Embarcadero and the state's plans to build a highway through the western neighborhoods of the city; in June 1956 the Board of Supervisors voted to cancel all aspects of the plan. Still, as a state project, over the next two years highway construction began, creating two thick concrete ribbons, constructed 70 ft. in the air, nearly a mile long and 52 ft. wide. As a result, the city was cut off from the water and, at the water front, the Ferry

Fig. 6.13 Submerging the central arterial highway in Boston in a project that became known as "The Big Dig" began in 1991 and continued until 2008, a massive project. Existing buildings, subway lines, and highways had to be safeguarded as the tunneling proceeded, the results of which allowed residents and visitors to walk to and from Government Center, on the left. (Author's photograph)

Building was overshadowed along its 660-ft. length by the highway. Oddly, the two stub ends went nowhere (Canty 1963).

Although other issues superseded the "freeway revolt" in the San Francisco during the ensuing years, the idea of demolishing the Embarcadero continued to surface. In 1980, the Northeast Waterfront Plan called for a pedestrian-oriented neighborhood, and in the following years the recommendation to remove the highway that went nowhere gained the unanimous approval by the Board of Supervisors. In 1986, voters considered an unsuccessful ballot initiative to tear it down. However, it was the Loma Prieta Earthquake in October 1989 that began the demolition, as chunks of the freeway fell to the ground (King 2004). The formal demolition took place in 1991, but the plan to revitalize the area did not begin in earnest until the funding was assembled eight years later (Adams 1998). When completed, the new waterfront, centered on the Ferry Building, became only a "union station" for streetcars, buses, ferry boats, Amtrak, bicycles, and pedestrians, but it increased the number of ferry slips, codified the existing plaza for more public use, and allowed the Market Street

corridor to reconnect to the waterfront (Epstein 2000).[36] Chapter 5 discussed the importance of transportation funding in the treatment this historic property. (Fig. 5.5)

The story of elevated highway demolition in Boston is similar, but the regenerative vision was more daring and the results more impressive. There the Central Artery was built in the 1950s with the idea of improving traffic flow, even though it was quickly understood that it severed and blighted several neighborhoods (Keyhoe 1991). Facing near continuous maintenance headaches, the idea of creating an alternative began in the 1980s with the initiative to construct a third highway tunnel under the Boston Harbor. The project then grew into a more ambitious proposal to (a) replace the elevated Central Artery with an underground highway, (b) extend Interstate 90 east under Boston Harbor to East Boston and Logan Airport, and (c) replace the Interstate 93 bridge north of the inner city. Over seven miles long, it was a daunting undertaking, which required a vast amount of design input

---

[36] The largest single improvement was the new San Francisco Giants' home, which opened in 2000.

from architects, engineers, landscape architects, planners, preservationists, and urban designers (Luberoff and Altshuler 1996). (Fig. 6.13)

Construction of what became known as "The Big Dig" began in 1991 and continued until 2008, although the final elements of the project were less finished in some areas than originally planned, despite the $24 billion price tag. Existing buildings and facilities such as the subway lines had to be shored up and underpinned as tunneling took place. Alternative power, water, sewer, communication, and transportation routes were created to allow continuous service during construction. To ensure vibration and blasting was minimized, seismic monitors were installed. In the process, the project created an unprecedented opportunity to examine Boston's archaeological past, from the time of the Native American residents through the Industrial Revolution to the present (Lewis 2001).

Where a highway stood for decades, now a mile-long green space exists with benches, fountains, and trees. Where the highway cut off the waterfront neighborhoods from the city, now pedestrians have clearer views of the Boston Harbor, the Italian North End, and the wharfs. Because the state decided that 75% of the land created as a result of the tunnels should be left as open space, the resulting greenway is divided into four parks, totaling 10.5 acres. The southernmost part, close to Chinatown, sports a red entrance gate, with fan-shaped paving stones and bamboo planting. The South Station garden is next, an entrance to the city. The Aquarium gained a circular plaza and a large fountain, and the northernmost park, which connects the North End's famous Italian restaurants, has a long pergola. Named the Rose Fitzgerald Kennedy Greenway, the parks have opened up possibilities for recreation, and buildings that had sealed off their windows overlooking the highway can now reopen them. A former warehouse has been converted to condominiums (Goodnough 2008). Hence, while critics occasionally complain that the Greenway remains less actively used than the streets and spaces alongside it, visually the improvement is remarkable and the process of sewing together the city has begun (Campbell 2011).

Fig. 6.14 The abandoned elevated tracks of the New York Central Railroad along 10th Avenue became the High Line linear park, providing remarkable views of the city and waterfront from Chelsea Market through the Meatpacking District in western Manhattan. (Author's photograph)

The influence of these remarkable visions in San Francisco and Boston has not been lost on community-minded politicians, professionals, and advocates in other locations. They have been inspired to follow suit in New Haven, Seattle, Baltimore, Syracuse, and several other cities (Kuther 2011; Yardley 2011). Just how these cities attempt to knit their neighborhoods back together remains an open question, but demolition should never be the only option. More generally, as the "hub and spoke system" that characterized the early years of the Interstate highway goes beyond the "spider web system" that is failing to solve the problems many cities and suburbs experience, additional opportunities will arise for reconfiguring transportation routes and nodes.

Transportation corridors above ground also provide opportunities in the same way. Several bridges declared surplus or inadequate for heavy traffic have become pedestrian-only thoroughfares. More recently, Manhattan has celebrated the complete transformation of a railroad corridor, the "High Line," keeping in place a former "industrial artifact." (Fig. 6.14) From the Chelsea Market through the Meatpacking District on the western side of Manhattan, the old elevated tracks of the New York Central Railroad were designed in the early twentieth century to relieve congestion on 10th Avenue. The snake-like route facilitated direct access to the abutting warehouses and factories, but the line was abandoned by the early 1980s. Although a few people thought the line could be put back into use, most saw the rusting steel superstructure, elevated 20–30 ft. above the ground, as an unsightly intrusion that should be removed. Mayor Giuliani even signed a demolition order.

Joshua David, a writer, and Robert Hammond, a painter, took exception to the view that the High Line should be demolished. They met at a community board meeting in 1999 and discovered their mutual interest in saving the abandoned elevated rail corridor, forming the Friends of the High Line. David and Hammond saw the possibility for an elevated linear park that would serve as a catalyst for the rehabilitate the West Side of Manhattan. The Friends were led by real estate developer Philip Aaron, who knew the importance of convincing property owners and was familiar with bureaucratic hurdles. As a result of the Friends' advocacy, the City took ownership of the property in 2005. The unusual dimensions, seven acres 20–30 ft. wide and 1.45 miles long from Gansevoort to 34th Street, provided an unusual design challenge (Pogrebin June 8, 2009; David and Hammond 2011).

The idea was to offer a bucolic retreat from the street life below, featuring views of the Hudson River and the city.[37] Yet, the railroad bed and some of the tracks remain in their original location, reminding the pedestrians of the indus-

trial origins of that portion of the city. The same wild grasses that grew between the rusted rails and platforms now create a green corridor, interspersed by sundeck chairs and benches, a occasional water feature, and an amphitheater at the 10th Avenue crossing.

Designed by James Corner Field Operations and Diller Scofidio and Renfro, the scheme includes more than 100 species of plants, in stark contrast to the surrounding landscape.

The first two sections of the High Line cost $152 million, $44 million of which was raised by Friends of the High Line. In mid-2009, media mogul Barry Diller and his wife, fashion designer Diane von Furstenberg, offered a $10 million challenge grant to the walkway project, and another couple quickly volunteered to match it, requiring the Friends of the High Line to raise an equivalent amount (Pogrebin June 1, 2009). The city justified its investment by citing more than 30 new projects under construction alongside the walkway, including condominiums, hotels, and offices, and the rising nearby property values that rival those around Central Park.

Just as the interstate highway projects in San Francisco and Boston spurred rethinking in other cities, the High Line Project has stimulated communities to reexamine their elevated rail lines. In Chicago, the Friends of the Bloomingdale Trail, a three-mile long elevated railroad spur on the city's northwest side, is fighting a battle to reuse a corridor that could help transform several neighborhoods (Kamin 2011). In St. Louis, the Iron Horse Trestle has been purchased by the Great Rivers Greenway District to become a segment of the interconnected parks and trails that will encircle the city and environs. The renovation of the 25 ft. wide and 25 ft. high deck is planned to provide exciting new views (Gregorian 2011). In Philadelphia, the Reading Viaduct is being re-thought as a "linear version of Rittenhouse Square," one of the original parks in the city (Saffron 2011).[38] In all of these cases and more, what was formerly inconceivable is being seriously considered as an achievable goal.

---

[37] The Promenade Plantee, an old train viaduct renovated in Paris, provided the Friends with inspiration.

[38] The idea of regenerating the Atlanta Beltline follows a similar scheme for urban revitalization.

Our Military Legacy: Redesigning it to Fit Current Needs

Revolutionary War and Civil War battlefields have long held a prominent place in this country's historic preservation movement, and memorials to the world wars and regional conflicts have been erected by patriots in many parts of the globe. Yet, the United States Armed Forces oversee far more property than the sites set aside as memorials, in dozens of locations across the country and abroad. In that regard, the largest historic preservation effort ever supported by the federal government was initiated, in large part, to mark the 50th anniversary of World War II. The original legislation was supported by Senators Daniel Inoyee of Hawaii and Robert Dole of Kansas, both veterans. The Legacy Resource Management Program was established by Congress in 1990 to provide financial assistance to the Department of Defense (DoD) to protect and enhance this nation's natural and cultural heritage, while supporting military readiness. Three principles guided the Legacy program: stewardship, leadership, and partnership. Stewardship initiatives assisted the DoD in safeguarding its irreplaceable resources for future generations. To demonstrate its leadership role, the Department provided models for respectful use of natural and cultural resources with hundreds of millions of dollars of support. Through wide-ranging partnerships, the Legacy Program intended to gain access to the knowledge and talents of individuals outside of DoD.

In order to implement these principles, the Program adopted an ecosystem approach that insisted in maintaining biological diversity and the sustainable use of land and water resources, and implemented a multi-disciplinary approach to stewardship of both natural and cultural resources on installations. Broad regional initiatives, for example in the Gulf Coast, Great Basin, and Chesapeake Bay, oversaw habitat preservation; protecting the migratory patterns of animals, fish, and birds; archaeological investigations; and the preservation of cultural resources. Because of overarching geographical concerns, several levels of government and negotiations with Native American tribes became commonplace. Surveys of cultural resources, including those on army posts, air force facilities, navy and coast guard bases, led to the recognition and designation of dozens of historic sites, properties, and objects. This allowed the military to evaluate the changes that had taken place during and after the Cold War era.

One of the most striking changes within the armed forces is the shift in housing, away from the wooden and brick barracks of a largely-male, conscripted military toward an all-volunteer force that has become family oriented. Some of the wooden barracks are considered historic and are in need of rehabilitation. Surveying the post-World War II housing for military personnel made apparent the problem of rehabilitating federally-built structures constructed during the Cold War-era (1946–1989), if only by their number. From 1950 to 1964, approximately 250,000 married personnel housing units were constructed in two waves, built to meet temporary needs. Considered a limited success at the time, many units were subsequently renovated, while others were not maintained and became referred to as "slums" (Baldwin 1996). Studies suggested that many of the units did not meet National Register criteria at either the national, state, or local level, for they were not directly related to the military missions of the bases on which they were constructed. When examined in 1994, about 194,000 of these units were still standing, with about 70% found inadequate for an all volunteer Army; completely rehabilitating all of them seemed unfeasible. After a lengthy review, Army installations were free to follow a wide range of options—including maintenance and repair, rehabilitation, layaway and mothballing, renovation, demolition, and transfer, sale, or lease out of federal control—when dealing with the family housing, associated structures, and landscape features, all without further Section 106 consultation (USAEC 2004). The Air Force and Navy followed this path with their own residential structures, spurring additional ideas for addressing future needs.

Fig. 6.15 The long history of the Presidio as a military facility was recognized when it was designated a National Historic Landmark in 1962. Here, the Presidio and Fort Winfield Scott while in active military use, c. 1919. (Library of Congress)

Once Military, Now Put to Civilian Use

The move from "Cold War readiness" to peacetime military preparedness has had remarkable consequences, affecting the future of how we understand our military history. Major bases were closed between 1977 and 1988 as the end of the Cold War brought about reductions in defense spending. More active demilitarization began to occur with the Base Realignment and Closure Act of 1988, which was extended and improved through 1995 (DAABCRA 1988). In the process, decisions were made to close 97 of the country's 495 major domestic military installations (Kirschenbaum and Marsh 1993).[39]

Although the fear of closing is often linked to the loss of jobs in an area, once the base, camp, post, or port has been closed, and only caretaking personnel remain, environmental cleanup follows. Assuming a clean bill of health is given, the property becomes open for inspection and possible reuse to other branches of the federal government, and the state and local governments in turn. The process of transferring property for community reuse then begins. Generally, a redevelopment plan has several preservation elements, but the first rule of thumb is to ensure that any local development agency that controls the property should be party to any agreement or memorandum of understanding that states that historic resources are to be protected. The second rule of thumb is to facilitate historic resources

surveys where they have not been done, remembering that the inventory of real property being transferred may not indicate whether the site is considered historic.

Often it is important to put in place easements and covenants protecting historic structures when the property is transferred. The transfer of Fort Monroe, near Hampton, Virginia, is a particularly noteworthy example of the care needed, as it was one of the largest facilities closed and a designated National Historic Landmark. With deeds dating to 1798 that stipulate it would be returned to the Commonwealth when it was given to the federal government for military use, the cleanup and transfer became a complicated effort, in part because the state did not want the property (*Post* November 1, 2011).

What can be done with all this former military land? In most cases, bases are ideal sites for commercial and residential development, as well as for use as parks and open space. Dozens of properties have found new life (Lockwood 1993).

Sitting at the entrance to San Francisco Bay, the Presidio is naturally sited to provide one of the most sweeping views ever of water, land, and islands. (Fig. 6.15) First populated by native tribes, the Ohlones, the area was claimed by the Spanish in 1776 by Captain Juan Bautista de Anza, and the Presidio became the northern-most fortified Spanish site on the coast of California. In 1846, the settlement was captured in the Bear Flag Rebellion, and for the next 150 years the installation remained under the control of the Army (Trelstad 1997). After the end of the Korean War, however, the Presidio began to face the prospect of closure. In 1955, the Eisenhower Administration

[39] Largely because of the post World War II military emphasis in the Pacific, California is the state most affected by the reductions.

Fig. 6.16 The very active discussion in the city about the future of the Presidio consumed thousands of hours, but in the end the Planning Areas were mapped, suggesting the manner in which new functions would be inserted. (Author's photograph)

recommended the post be decommissioned, but it was actively maintained through the Vietnam War. After the Cold War ended, however, the sweeping need to reduce the number of facilities renewed the effort to decommission the property.

As a result, the Presidio's transformation from the country's oldest military facility to a 1480-acre park in the National Park Service presented a remarkable opportunity. The agency could design an approach that might guide the future redevelopment of other large-scale public properties, such as insane asylums, prisons, and poor farms. This approach involved extensive discussion with all interested parties, treating the entire site as an historic landscape. NPS remained sensitive to the combination of the site's natural resources and its history of human activities, retaining and reusing both, yet allowing for new design in specific areas so as to introduce new constituencies to the extensive site.

In general, the local commandants welcomed city residents and, as the number of visitors increased, the soldiers planted what would become shady forests of pine, acacia, oak, cypress, and nonnative eucalyptus trees and, in time, grass, lupine, and barley to control the erosion and provide themselves and visitors with pleasant environs. The Presidio's beautification in the early twentieth century is reflected in the Spanish Colonial style buildings reminiscent of early missions, exemplified by the colored stucco of Fort

Winfield Scott, constructed on the property beginning in 1907. (Fig. 6.16) During World War I, the base developed Crissy Airfield along its coastline, although the need to land larger planes that required longer airstrips quickly doomed the facility. What "saved" the Presidio was the decision to take advantage of its position to build Golden Gate Bridge through the property during the Depression. This action accelerated the public accessibility of the post, particularly after World War II, when residents became more concerned about the environmental quality of the city. In the early 1960s a move to allow a portion of the Presidio to be developed was thwarted by pushing for a National Historic Landmark district designation, granted by the Department of the Interior in June, 1962 (Barker 1997). This federal recognition underscored the special history of the place, its remarkable topography and natural advantages, and the revival architecture.

The threat to establish two public schools on the Presidio grounds and the rising concern for a wide range of natural and historic areas in the area led to the formation in 1971 of a broad coalition called the People for a Golden Gate National Recreation Area, led by advocates John Jacobs, Amy Meyer, and Sierra Club president Edgar Wayburn. The resulting Recreation Area includes the shorelines of San Francisco, Marin, and San Mateo Counties, with a variety of natural features, such as woods, beaches, seashores, and military property, including the Presidio. Given that the scheme was already used to establish the Gateway National Recreation Area in New York and New Jersey, the legislation for both "urban parks" was passed by Congress and signed by the President in late October, 1972 (Meyer 1999).

In 1980 the NPS released a General Management Plan for the Presidio lands showing that, whereas the agency would decide policies, a more cooperative and flexible style of management would be needed, particularly in an era of reduced federal funding. In essence, if the Presidio were to become a national park, the uses of the land would need to generate the capital needed to manage and maintain it.

In 1988 the Base Realignment and Closure Commission deemed the Presidio surplus proper-

Fig. 6.17 Today, the buildings of the Main Post at the Presidio have been provided with a number of new purposes, including museum interpretation. (National Park Service, Draft General Management Plan, p. 13.)

ty so that, with the military presence all but completely gone, the garrison seemed to have a ghost town feel (NYT May 18, 1993). In part because the site was designated a landmark, unlike many other former defense properties that were transferred to the General Services Administration for disposal, the Presidio was destined to come into the hands of the National Park Service.

The following year the NPS kicked off the planning process with a conference "Think Big," and several subsequent "visioning" workshops led to the consideration of several themes. The extensive public hearings, widespread publicity, and considerable attention paid to the housing and business interests in the area meant that when the draft plan and environmental impact statement became public in early 1993, few surprises remained. The plan acknowledged the multiuse character of the Presidio in the 13 planning areas, differentiating the forest, beach, and bluff from the historic Main Post, Fort Scott, and east housing area. (Fig. 6.17)

Generally, the NPS is not equipped to manage large numbers of deteriorating buildings and it is not considered an agency that supports cutting-edge design (Reilly 2000). In fact, because many residents of the area around the fort feared that the real estate might be sold to the highest bidder, Congresswoman Nancy Pelosi drafted a bill to create the Presidio Trust, a government corporation, to manage the park. The Trust was formed in 1997, based on a similar private-public controlled corporation, the Pennsylvania Avenue Development Corporation in Washington, D.C.[40] The charge given the Presidio Trust was to create a self-sustaining property by 2013.

As part of the transition, an amendment was prepared to the General Management Plan of the Golden Gate National Recreation Area (GGNRA)

---

[40] As noted in Chapter 2, the Pennsylvania Avenue Development Corporation was formed in 1972 to revitalize Pennsylvania Avenue in the District of Columbia. The PADC completed its work about 30 years later.

to determine what type of park the Presidio should contain. An interdisciplinary team was assembled to undertake a 2-year planning effort to chart a course for the future (Feierabend 1991).[41] The former fort contains both cultural and natural resources, so that the cultural landscape analysis had to convey the complex and integrated system, rather than be treated as a collection of isolated buildings, roads, and natural resources. The identification of significant discrete features, as well as overall patterns, also provides an opportunity for sensitive integration of the new with the old.

Because the Presidio was built to meet military needs largely independent of the city and county of San Francisco, it is a "city within a city" that grew up around it. The overall objectives of the initial study worked to knit the two cities together while respecting the social, economic, and physical integrity of each. The planning and design process sought to understand the evolution of the setting by tracing the landscape components, conducting a conditions assessment of the components, identifying a level of sensitivity for change in each of the subareas, and determining what characteristics should be maintained and preserved, and where others would be considered for removal before any additional planning began.

The initial step involved exploring and identifying the development of the landscape, to understand the components as the post evolved from 1776 to 1990, making use of military and civilian records, maps, photographs, and documents. The principal landscape elements included: the boundaries; surface water found in springs, ponds, creeks, and lakes; tree cover; structures, including the wharves, earthworks, dams, storage tanks, reservoirs, fences, walls, bridges, tunnels, and coastal defense batteries; circulation systems for pedestrians, vehicles, and animals; buildings; topographic changes; and utility systems, paying attention to the evolution of land uses.

Over 400 buildings were found to be historically significant, including two hospitals, a major research institute, 1200 housing units, a golf course, a national cemetery, the 1920s airfield, a range of harbor and coastal defense structures, a Mission Revival style artillery post, a Coast Guard station, and varied support facilities. The natural resources include a mature forest dominated by eucalyptus, Monterey pine, and Monterey cypress planted in the 1880s; the last free-flowing creek in San Francisco; federally- and state-listed rare, threatened, and endangered plant and animal species; remnant native plant communities; and potentially significant archeological resources (Blind et al. 2004).

The second step involved assessing the condition of each of these components in order to make a preliminary assessment of their integrity. Primary and secondary landscape components were examined for each of the subareas in the Park, including the native plants, historic vistas and views, integrating the architecture, engineering, archaeology, and historic contexts to determine significance. The manner in which the archaeological investigation proceeded was particularly noteworthy, for each week new artifacts were featured and explained, and efforts are made to make use of the ongoing projects to educate young people (Cox 2005).

After the resource information was mapped and analyzed, the next step involved the rating of subareas to determine its level of sensitivity to change. Some components were found more compromised than others, which become instrumental in planning the manner in which the subareas would be treated, redeveloped, and managed. A key concern was the perpetuation of the land use patterns to retain the visual relationships of building clusters and their related small features, so that their meaning could be easily understood and appreciated. The restoration and enhancement of the historic circulation entryways and networks was anticipated when upgrading the safety of roads and walks. Additional information about the fauna and flora was integrated with the forest management planning so that the natural resources, drainage, and water systems could be enhanced as well. All of this provided

---

[41] The Presidio Planning Team worked with the firms Land and Community Associates and Architectural Resources Group to conduct the cultural landscape analysis of the Presidio. The work began in the fall of 1990 and was completed about 18 months later.

the ability to weigh alternatives because the cultural landscape components and character-defining features offer a holistic basis upon which to make informed decisions.

The Presidio Trust Management Plan, adopted in 2005, called for some changes. To make way for future development, the Trust decided to demolish some of the buildings and to allow the construction of sympathetically designed new structures when they were needed (GGNRA 1994). The decision to lease 900,000 square feet of the Presidio's Letterman Hospital complex for 99 years to Lucasfilm was the first major decision to be questioned.[42] Of the three finalists for redeveloping the old Letterman Hospital site, Lucasfilms' was the lowest bid, but the Presidio Trust board of directors decided this firm would be a better tenant (Levy 2005). The advantages are obvious. The new home of Lucas entertainments provides San Francisco with a major state-of-the-art studio that employs about 1500 people connected by fiber optic cable to share sound and images. Income from the Lucas firm was, at the outset, a significant percent of the Presidio's budget.

---

[42] Originally, the Letterman/LAIR complex was to be converted to an animal research center. That plan fell through and a much broader "Request for Qualifications" (RFQ) was prepared by the Trust and sent to nonprofits, developers, and other businesses. It suggested that "prospective tenants might also include those involved in ... biotechnology, multimedia, computer graphics, telecommunications, film production, internet-based research, computer software...." (Scott 1999). The founder of the Preserve the Presidio Campaign, Joel Ventresca, found that "these fours areas [telecommunications, multimedia, biotech, and health sciences] are industries incongruent with a national park setting." Local environmental and historic preservation groups called on the President's Advisory Council on Historic Preservation to review the design of the new four-building proposal, claiming the scheme was too big. Although the staff of the National Park Service stated that the "overall size, scale, materials, detailing and siting" were incompatible with the National Historic Landmark district, and the National Trust for Historic Preservation weighed-in noting the adverse impact of the proposed project, as it gave the appearance of a "private, suburban office enclave," the Presidio Trust claimed the scheme conformed with the plan and federal guidelines.

How could this new use fit into the landscape? Although the Lucas buildings have strict security, the tree-dotted area designed by landscape architect Lawrence Halprin is open to the public during the day, assumedly allowing residents continued access to the site. Almost all of the parking is underground. Halprin worked with the architects of the tile-roofed red and white complex to site the new buildings on six acres, which included landscaping a sloping meadow that follows a man-made creek to run between the two clusters of buildings (Whiting 2005).

Critics were unhappy that a large office complex is being rented to support the activities in a national park (Enge 2001; Levy June 26, 2005), but the grounds remain open to the public. The Trust was counting on the income provided by the four buildings of the new digital arts center to provide a significant amount of operating capital (Andelman 2000). The fear was that the Lucas proposal would be precedent setting, guiding other leases and their developments, and work against the agreed-upon goals that called for "a global center dedicated to addressing the worlds most critical environmental, social and cultural challenges" (Scott 1999). The project was to be compatible with the Plan, which sought to complement the existing facilities in the area to promote education, arts, scientific research, healthcare, philanthropy, international relations, and environmental studies.

It is evident that the National Park Service had problems determining the scope of acceptable activities, and this was reflected in its proposal to introduce new clusters of uses that the complex would host. It is also apparent that this was a far cry from the days when residents whose property was seized for a National Park were discouraged from staying, and in some cases evicted to allow the property to return to a "natural state" (Olson 2008). In the Presidio, designing for people to occupy the Park and use it appropriately in specific zones made it possible to accomplish goals that are more ecologically sound, socially equitable, and economically feasible. Perhaps more important,

Fig. 6.18 One of the largest open spaces in the San Francisco, the former Crissy Airfield accommodates for recreation of all kinds. (Author's photograph)

the vision the Presidio exemplifies is a viable model for similar federal, state, and local public facilities.

Today, the Presidio's thousands of civilian residents share the 1480-acre National Park with Bay Area citizens and visitors who hike the trails, bike the paths and roads, or play golf on the 18-hole golf course. Even by 2005 the Trust had leased out 90% of the Park's apartments, duplexes, townhouses, and single-family homes, providing more than half the Presidio Trust's operating budget.[43] The feeling of safety and the closeness to the ocean and the trees are attributes often noted by residents living in the housing, with a landscape more like a rural college campus or a neighborhood in a small town, including a National Cemetery, rather than part of a bustling city (Levy June 26, 2005). (Fig. 6.18)

On the other side of the country, the Philadelphia Naval Yard provides another excellent example. (Fig. 6.19) It is a 1200-acre site

located along seven miles of waterfront at the confluence of the Schuylkill and Delaware Rivers. After the Defense Department announced in 1996 that it no longer required the property for ship building, the problem arose of how to make best use of the dozens of structures, dry dock facilities, and airfield (Hess et al. 2001). The site had a distinguished history, producing major ships for the Navy, but the project required an imaginative spark to be transformed into a useful part of the greater community. The Navy retained a limited presence on-site and concentrated on long-term research and development projects, while the federal government transferred control of about five-sixths of the 1200-acre stretch of land to the city, which, in turn, delegated the redevelopment responsibility to the Philadelphia Industrial Development Corporation (PIDC), a not-for-profit corporation founded to promote economic development. Like many industrial development agencies, the first reaction was to make use of the waterfront in the original manner. In 1996, a public-private partnership was formed with the city, the state, the federal government, and a Norwegian company, Kvaerner. In addition, PIDC found commercial tenants to move into seventeen newly renovated historic buildings. (Fig. 6.20) Vitetta, an architectural and engineering firm, led the way in August 1999, even before PIDC formally acquired ownership. The site gained a boost when the city and PIDC announced a new master plan that called for a mixed-use approach to the 525 acres of land east

---

[43] Rents are market-rate and vary depending on the neighborhood, the most expensive being the three houses where generals once lived. The row of officers' quarters, built in 1862, is the oldest, followed by the officers' family homes on Infantry Terrace, constructed above the Main Post in 1909–1911. Next to appear were the neat Pilots' Row houses near the Golden Gate Bridge, built in 1921; and the more modest enlisted family housing complex, erected at the beginning of the Depression. The Baker Beach apartments, constructed during the Korean conflict, add to the remarkable range of housing options.

Fig. 6.19 The Philadelphia Naval Shipyard, a 1200-acre site located along seven miles of waterfront, is slowly being revitalized by the Philadelphia Industrial Development Corporation (PIDC), a not-for-profit corporation created to promote economic development. (Library of Congress)

Fig. 6.20 The Supply Department Building 624 is just one of several substantial structures in the Philadelphia Naval Shipyard, many of which have been put to civilian uses. (Author's photograph)

of Broad Street, which includes a mile and a half of waterfront. Also included in the initiative is the Corporate Center, a 72-acre, 1.4 million Sq. ft. office campus setting developed by Liberty Property Trust and Synterra Partners. With convenient access to the Philadelphia International Airport, 30th Street Station, and Interstates 95 and 76, its status as a key urban site is guaranteed. Additionally, Urban Outfitters, Inc., owner of such stores as Urban Outfitters, Anthropologie, and its wholesale division, Free People, has embraced

the Navy Yard as its new corporate headquarters (Wong 2005).

In summary, these two examples provide some insight into the different goals of large projects. The first began with a general management plan that accepted the need to generate funds, using income from an office park and housing to provide public access to a remarkably scenic and historic landscape. The second took a more economically distressed situation and planned for the renewal of the working waterfront, respecting the naval heritage of the area. Large projects of this kind are increasingly found throughout the country.

Preparing for Natural Disasters

Disasters are violent interruptions of daily life, nightmares that can cause death, injury, disease, widespread distress, and property damage. A natural disaster can affect social relations and economic activities hundreds and even thousands of miles away. Because of improvements in mass communication, warnings are ever timelier. This might suggest that the next disaster occurrence will be met with more immediate and appropriate action. Yet, of the hundreds of disasters that occur each year, few receive much attention and the institutional memory of the unaffected public is surprisingly short. In addition, the technological advantages that help to predict disasters have not made much of a difference for the thousands of people affected by them.

Natural disasters can destroy all types of property, but their effect on cultural sites is particularly serious. Earthquakes, fires, floods, droughts, landslides, tsunami, tornadoes, and other disasters continually threaten culturally significant sites, buildings, objects, and collections. These disasters are untimely events that can last for seconds, but their effects take weeks, months, or years to recover from. Because disasters can never be completely predicted or avoided, the need exists everywhere for preservationists to become involved with disaster planning. Equally important for the people in any location that has been affected is their ability to see hope for a complete recovery. Again, context is important.

Disasters are characterized by the need for rapid decision-making in a chaotic environment, so that the goal of a preservationist should be to avoid or minimize damage to resources, reduce the chaos, and speed decision-making appropriately by providing accurate and up-to-date information. Oftentimes, only the prior thinking about mitigation and contingency alternatives makes the difference between continued destruction and appropriate damage assessment, salvage, stabilization, and repair.

Disaster planning involves varying federal, state, and local government agencies, volunteer organizations, and private insurance companies. Established in 1978, the Federal Emergency Management Agency (FEMA) serves as the lead agency for disaster relief, federal preparedness, and civil defense. FEMA sponsors a wide range of state and local preparedness, mitigation response, and recovery programs and activities (Krimm 1986). In disaster relief, Federal money and services only become available after it is determined by a state that the effort required to mitigate the effects exceeds its abilities. FEMA programs provide a wide range of support, including low interest loans and grants, temporary housing, unemployment assistance, legal assistance, and crisis counseling.

A brief overview of a few recent hurricanes that have affected our country's most recognized historic cities demonstrates widespread differences in the nature of the storms, the manner in which they affect people and property, the challenges of disaster preparedness, and the length of time needed for recovery.

The potential for a catastrophic loss of Charleston's cultural resources has long been known. However, in one recent instance a catastrophe *did not* occur, largely attributable to the preparation activities within the city and by various collection holding institutions, and the swift, organized response of the city's cultural resource managers.

The land upon which Charleston was laid out consisted of low tidal flats crossed by several streams. Land reclamation began almost as soon as the peninsula was settled, as shown in the 1704 plan. (Fig. 6.21) The streets of frame buildings gradually were joined by brick structures, particularly as fire continued to destroy sections of the city throughout the eighteenth and nineteenth centuries (Ludlum 1963). The history of the storms that have crossed the region makes abundantly clear that the people in the region should expect natural disaster. The hurricane of 1686 is the earliest storm recorded to have hit Charleston, although the "Great Hurricane" of 1752 was

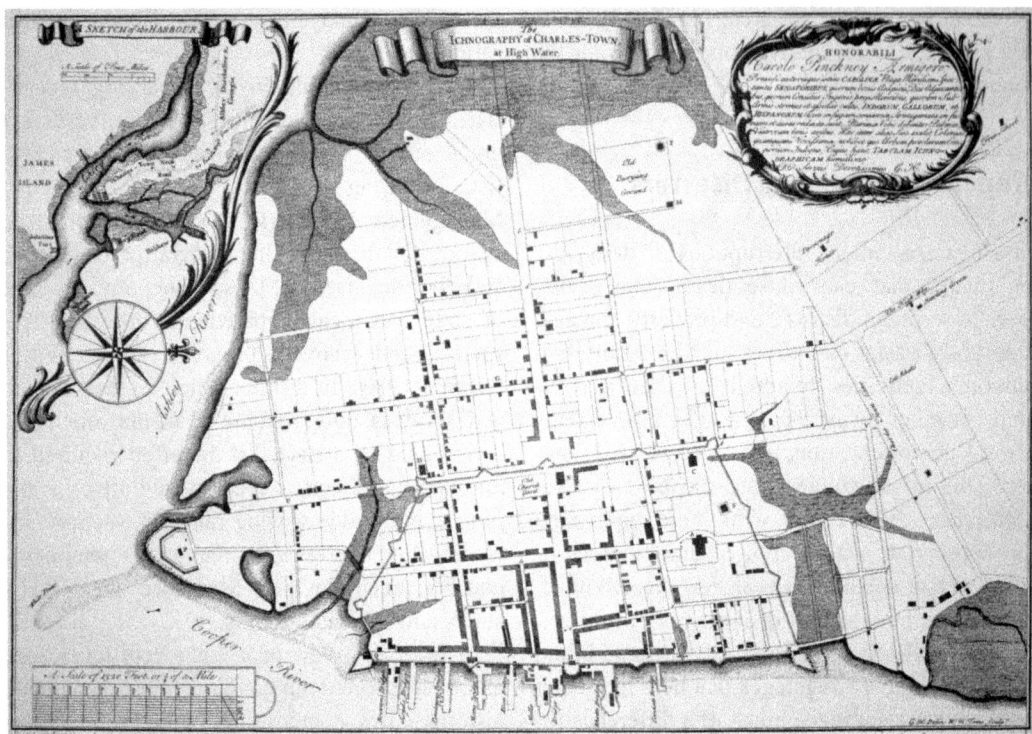

Fig. 6.21 Charleston was laid out on a peninsula of low tidal flats crossed by several streams. Land reclamation began almost as soon as the peninsula was settled, as shown in the 1739 plan, but the "High Water" tidal markings demonstrate the low-lying coastal lands subject to flooding. (Author's photograph, Courtesy of Historic Urban Plans, Inc.)

more memorable. Less destructive were hurricanes in 1804, 1822, and 1881, but then the hurricane of 1893 was a major force (Huger Smith and Huger Smith 1917). More than a dozen major hurricanes crossed over South Carolina during the twentieth century, the closest to Charleston being Hurricane Gracie, in 1959, which passed over nearby Beaufort. An estimated $14 million of damage occurred in Charleston County as a result (Davis 1960).

On September 21, 1989, Hurricane Hugo made landfall just outside of Charleston, with winds of 138 miles per hour and a sea surge of over nineteen feet over mean sea level. The storm carved a wide path of destruction from the Caribbean and across the Carolinas, with a total cost of over $7 billion. (Fig. 6.22)

Hugo's storm caused widespread flooding in Charleston. Over 25% of the city's tree cover was lost and 89 buildings suffered total collapse, 278 incurred severe structural damage, and over 400 suffered moderate structure damage. Much of the damage was due to the loss of roofing and gutter drainage systems, with some chimney and parapet wall failure. It was discovered that wooden buildings performed as well as masonry structures (Vitanza 1990).[44]

However, advanced preparations by city government laid the framework for effectively mitigating Hugo's damage. A week before its arrival, the Mayor's office contacted area cities for advice on the best actions to take. And city departments were asked to make contingency plans, locating large quantities of supplies, including sandbags, plywood, and plastic, to board-up buildings. The Mayor and the Governor of South Carolina declared a state of emergency,

---

[44] Less than a month after Hugo, the Loma Prieta earthquake in the San Francisco area occurred, stretching the ability of preservation professionals on two coasts.

Fig. 6.22 Hurricane Hugo landed in Charleston Harbor on September 21, 1989, having already done significant damage in Puerto Rico and other islands in the Caribbean, with gusts of more than 100 miles per hour tearing off roofs and felling trees. (Photograph: Charles Uhl)

mobilizing the National Guard to aid in the possible evacuation, ordered on September 21.

The city staff, including the city engineer, stayed in the emergency command post and devised the initial responses, closing down the city to visitors and authorizing a dawn to dusk curfew, enforced by the Police Department and the National Guard. City maintenance and park crews, assisted by the National Guard, began clearing transportation routes immediately, and building inspectors began their initial inspections of the city's damage. On the whole, Charleston exemplifies the striking benefits of reducing exposure to property losses by proactive preventative programs of action. As investigations of the resiliency demonstrated by cities show, disasters reveal the ability of government to meet the challenges posed by natural disasters, reaching out to resources beyond the affected area and doing more than rebuilding the physical losses of a city (Vale and Campanella 2005).

As noted in previous chapters, the romance associated with New Orleans, given its architecture, music, food, and festivals, has gained world-wide recognition. The culture based on family, neighborhood activity, faith, and local economic and social conditions is one of the most distinctive in the United States. In part, this culture is linked to the Delta region and to the Mississippi River. In fact, the river continues to change course, despite almost continuous efforts during the nineteenth and twentieth centuries to improve flood control and navigation (Barry 1997).

On August 29, 2005, Hurricane Katrina reached Louisiana and, in its wake, over 1300 lives were lost and thousands of buildings and structures were damaged or destroyed. The repair work cost billions of dollars, and the effects are still being measured, almost a decade later.

Although most residents of New Orleans are aware that they are living in a city surrounded by water, not until one of the levees is breached or one of the pumps fail is everyone reminded that 80 % of the population is living below sea level. As historic surveys show, in some areas, the city is as much as 12 ft. below normal water levels (McPhee 1989). (Fig. 6.23) Some scientists claim that climate change has intensified storms, or made hurricane development more frequent, arguing that more should be done to protect the coastal areas of the southern United States, including New Orleans. Whether or not that is accepted as sufficient motivation for change, because gas, oil, and water are being pumped out of the soil and rock under the Delta, the city is sinking and its sea-wall defenses are sinking with it. Meanwhile, the level of the Mississippi is rising, so the prospect for repeated flooding is ever more obvious (ASCE 2007).

Historically, New Orleans was constrained by the wetlands and Lake Pontchartrain on the north, the Mississippi River on the south, Jefferson Parish on the west, and Lake Borgne and more wetlands on the east. A number of studies were conducted to provide suggestions for introducing adequate protection. With more effective pumps

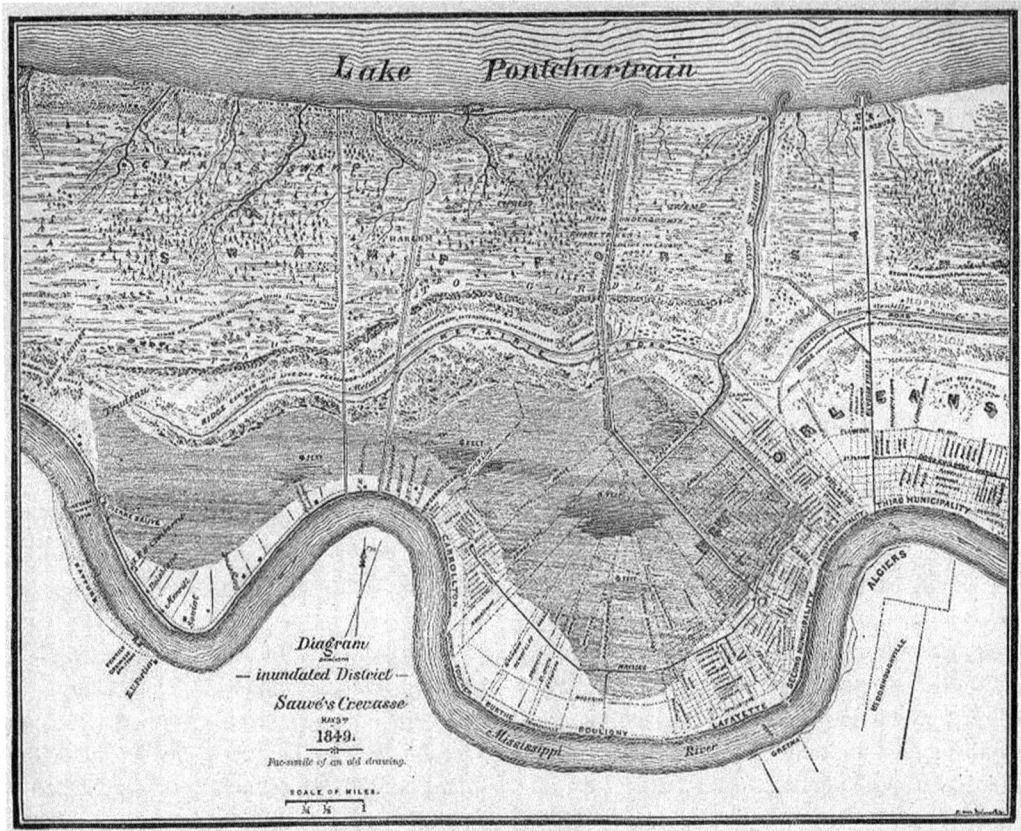

Fig. 6.23 Residents of New Orleans are living in a city surrounded by water, in some areas as much as 12 feet below normal water level, often affected by hurricanes. As this 1849 plan shows, flooding has caused extensive damage in the past, often breaching the dike walls. (Library of Congress)

and higher levees, building on the former wetlands was accepted as possible, so that by the 1970s, suburban expansion was well underway (Lewis 2003).

Unfortunately, in the wake of Hurricane Katrina, the waters entered New Orleans through the back door, that is, by breaking down the levees on the north. The flooding left thousands of buildings in polluted water, and demonstrated what can occur when land development continues in an area where there is a lack of public concern for natural hazards. The immediate problems of rebuilding the levees, pumping out the water, and evaluating the damage were hampered by the absence of many residents, leading to concerns for safety and security. The magnitude of the damage in the city and the region meant that qualified

personnel were in short supply and, given the difficulties of the federal, state, and local government to provide timely financial assistance, the options for those who did not have the means were very limited (Lubell 2006).

The displacement of people due to disasters is often overlooked, but it is an equally important characteristic to evaluate because, without residents, cities cannot survive. This goes beyond the immediate neighborhood problem of abandoned real estate. The dislocation of the residents of New Orleans to Houston and Baton Rouge continues to characterize areas of those cities and, to a lesser extent, other communities in the region. Over 150,000 New Orleans residents still live in Houston, although news about Louisiana remains important to the former resi-

Fig. 6.24 Hurricane Katrina left 80% of New Orleans under water, necessitating years of rebuilding, importing personnel and materials for years to come. (Courtesy of the National Oceanic and Atmospheric Administration)

dents of the Crescent City (Foster 2011; NOTP 2011). Not every population subgroup has left in equal number, as the poor and less well educated are the most likely not to return. The barbers and beauticians, housecleaners and dishwashers, the jobs in small stores that have gone unfilled, have had a significant impact on the heavily depopulated and hardest hit St. Bernard's and Plaquemines Parishes. Thanks to rebuilding efforts, job loss in the Greater New Orleans area is less than it might have been, but the area's median household income has not increased since Katrina (Plyer and Ortiz 2011).

With the absence of these people, the context in which New Orleans' residents work, play, worship, and play is changing. The rebuilding of the city takes place incrementally. Is it possible to improve the infrastructure in and around the city to guarantee its protection in the immediate future? Engineers might say yes, assuming political and social support for a multi-year, multibillion dollar project. Preservationists should shout out affirmatively that it is not only possible, but critical. The Preservation Resources Center in New Orleans has taken a particularly active role in home restoration and rehabilitation, purchasing and renovating vacant and blighted properties, targeting areas in the Holy Cross and Esplanade Ridge/Tremé

Fig. 6.25 Hurricane Sandy struck New Jersey and New York coastlines with an enormous amount of wind and water. Here, the typical result, in Union Beach Borough, Monmouth County NJ. (Courtesy of the New Jersey State Historic Preservation Office, 2012)

neighborhoods. However, the disaster preparedness of the region was woefully inadequate, and it remains so, even with so much stark evidence of thousands of damaged properties. In part, the conflict about what to do is being clouded by well intended outsiders with their recommendations for rebuilding, which residents deem unacceptable.[45]

---

[45] Several other organizations sponsored conferences and meetings about the issues and provided reports with

In yet another recent instance, Hurricane Sandy battered the northeastern United States. In this case, the loss of life and nearly $20 billion damage has put Sandy only second to Katrina in effect. (Fig. 6.24, 6.25) The impact of natural disasters can be mitigated, however. As Charleston demonstrated, assuming that residents and representatives of governments at all levels *can* agree on the vision and the necessity of improvement, it is possible to effect change to everyone's benefit. In New Orleans, the loss of the wetlands due to land reclamation projects can be controlled and reversed, the flood protection system can be rebuilt, and an effective evacuation and relocation plan can be adopted and tested (Giegengack and Foster 2006). That this has not been the path chosen is all the more remarkable when compared to the deliberate and extensive large-scale planning for the conversion of dozens of military bases around the country.

Conclusion

While preservationists showed remarkable vision after the passage of the National Historic Preservation Act in 1966, even more dramatic preservation projects have become reality in the recent past. Although the challenges ahead sometimes seems ever more daunting, the manner in which preservation activity is being incorporated in small and large projects is a resounding testimony to the efforts of literally tens of thousands of people.

Just as obviously, to reach a successful preservation solution, these visions begin with observation and documentation. The simple necessity of walking on the property and its surroundings, observing the changes that provide its character, is the first basic lesson. The time invested in surveys that put properties in their historical context is essential.

suggestions. These included the American Institute of Architects, American Planning Association, Brookings Institution, National Trust for Historic Preservation, Preservation Resource Center, and World Monuments Fund.

The second necessity is to work with the communities that will assume custody of the property, not only to recognize and adapt to immediate needs, but also to ensure a common understanding for preservation success into the future. Unless sufficient public discussion about alternatives takes place, any design review can prove to be more difficult than it need be. Preservationists must make sure that what they mean by "appropriate treatment" is widely understood, in the local language, making sure their literature and views are widely available.

Third, it is necessary that preservationists not avoid contemporary design, but, by engaging in an exploration of alternatives, bring to the table information that inevitably influences the results, and extends our common legacy in a more sympathetic fashion.

Lastly, emergencies will continue to arise that present challenges. It is well to remember that the same approaches and techniques that have provided us with guidance in successful projects can be advanced to anticipate the need for disaster recovery in the future.

References

ACSA. (2000). *ACSA sourcebook of community design programs*. Washington, DC: Association of Collegiate Schools of Architecture.

Adams, G. D. (29 June 1998). Massive waterfront make over to begin. Embarcadero plan will transform area. *San Francisco Examiner*.

Advisory Council. (1977). *Assessing the energy conservation benefits of historic preservation*. Washington, DC: Advisory Council on Historic Preservation. http://www.achp.gov/1979 %20-%20Energy%20Conserv%20 and%20Hist%20Pres.pdf. Accessed 5 March 2014.

AIA. (1977). *Life cycle cost analysis: A guide for architects*. Washington, DC: American Institute of Architects.

Ainslee, M. L. (1984). Statement concerning an alternative percentage of walls test. In R. Keune (Ed.), *The historic preservation yearbook* (pp. 371–373). Bethesda: Adler & Adler, Publishers, Inc.

Alexander, T. M. (1987). *John Dewey's theory of art, experience, and nature. The horizons of feeling* (p. xi). Albany: State University of New York Press.

Andelman, K. (11 Dec 2000). The Presidio's power player. *Recorder*, 1.

Anderson, L. (2002). *Benton MacKaye: Conservationist, planner and creator of the Appalachian Trail*. Baltimore: Johns Hopkins University Press.

Andrzejewski, A. V., & Rachleff, A. (1998). The significance of fragmentary landscapes in cultural landscape preservation. In M. A. Tomlan (Ed.), *Preservation of what, for whom?* (pp. 181–191). Ithaca: National Council for Preservation Education.

APT. (1990). Special issue: Cultural resource recording. *APT Bulletin, 22* (1–2).

Army. (2009). First army sustainability report outlines environmental efforts. *Army Logistician, 41*(2), 47.

Arnheim, R., Zucker, W. M., & Watterson, J. (1966). Inside and outside architecture: A symposium. *Journal of Aesthetics and Art Criticism, 25*(25), 3–15.

ASCE. (2007). ASCE Hurricane external review panel. *The New Orleans Hurricane protection system: What went wrong and why*. Reston: American Society of Civil Engineers.

Aten, L. (1978). *The resource planning protection process*. Washington, DC: Heritage Conservation and Recreation Service.

Auwaerter, J. E. (2005). *Cultural landscape report for the Mansion grounds, Marsh-Billings-Rockefeller National historical park. Vol. I: Site history*. Boston: National Park Service, Olmsted Center for Landscape Preservation.

Ayers, J. M., & Stamper, E. S. (1995). Historical development of building energy calculations. *ASHRAE Journal, 27*(2), 47–55.

Baldwin, W. C. (1996). *Four housing privatization programs*. Washington, DC: US Army Corps of Engineers, Office of History.

Barker, L. (1997). The Presidio within the Presidio: Historical archaeology in a NHL. *CRM, 20*(9), 38–40.

Barry, J. H. (1997). *Rising tide: The Great Mississippi flood of 1927 and how it changed America*. New York: Touchstone Press.

Beasley, E. (Nov 1992). Design guidelines: A preservation perennial. *Historic Preservation Forum*.

Birch, E. L., & Roby, D. (1984). The planner and the preservationist: An uneasy alliance. *Journal of the American Planning Association, 52*(2), 194–207.

Blake, P. (1977). *Form follows Fiasco: Why modern architecture hasn't worked*. Boston: Little, Brown.

Blind, E. B., et al. (2004). El Presidio de San Francisco: At the edge of empire. *Historical Archaeology, 38*(3), 135–149.

Borchers, P. E. (1977). *Photogrammetric recording of cultural resources*. Washington, DC: U.S. Department of the Interior.

Bowsher, A. M. (1978). *Design review in historic districts. A handbook for Virginia review boards*. Washington, DC: The Preservation Press.

Brolin, B. C. (1976). *The failure of modern architecture*. New York: Van Nostrand Reinhold.

Brolin, B. C. (1980). *Architecture in context. Fitting new buildings with old*. New York: Van Nostrand Reinhold.

Brown, P. L. (Nov 1982). Curator of the built world. *Metropolis*, 18–19, 26.

Brundtland, G. H. (1987). *Our common future*. Oxford: Oxford University Press.

Buckham, T. (24 Oct 2008). Martin house assimilates change. *Buffalo News*.

Buckham, T. (8 April 2010). More recognition for Martin House. *Buffalo News*.

Burns, J. A. (1992). New techniques for recording historic structures. *CRM, 15*(6), 13–17.

Bussan, M. M. (1986). *Formalizing urban aesthetics*. Doctorial dissertation, Department of City and Regional Planning, Cornell University, Ithaca.

Butti, K., & Perlin, J. (1980). *A golden thread. 2500 years of solar architecture and technology*. New York: Van Nostrand Reinhold.

Byard, P. S. (1998). *The architecture of additions design and regulation*. New York: Norton.

Call, W. (28 July 2002). Portland becomes trailblazer of "Green Buildings." *San Diego Union-Tribune*, A8.

Calthorpe, P., & Fulton, W. (2001). *The regional city: Planning for the end of Sprawl*. Washington, DC: Island Press.

Cambridge. (1965). *Survey of architectural history in Cambridge. Report one: East Cambridge*. Cambridge: Cambridge Historical Commission.

Campbell, R. (15 May 2011). If you don't build it, they won't come. *Boston Globe*.

Canty, D. (Oct 1963). The fight to tame the urban freeway takes a positive new turn. *Architectural Forum, 119*(4), 69–72.

Carbonell, M. (1989). *Photogrammetry applied to surveys of monuments and historic centres*. Rome: ICCROM.

Celebration. (1995). Small town architecture is back. *Celebration Chronicle, 1*(1), 1–2.

Chappell, E. A. (March 2008). The restoration of James Madison's Montpelier. *Colonial Williamsburg, 6*(7).

Conroy, S. B. (16 July 1989). The once and future Montpelier. *Washington Post*, F10.

Cox, B. (9 July 2005). After the dig: Archaeology open house. *Project Updates*.

Cozens, P., & Hillier, D. (2008). The shape of things to come: New Urbanism, the grid and the Cul-De-Sac. *International Planning Studies, 13*(1), 51–73.

DAABCRA. (1988). Defense Authorization Amendments and Base Closure and Realignment Act, 102 Stat. 2623, Public Law 100-526, 10 U.S.C. S 2687 note.

Dalibard, J. (n.d.). New clothes for an old scarecrow. http://arc.library.carleton.ca/sites/default/files/scarecrow%20low%20qual.pdf. Accessed 4 March 2014.

David, J., & Hammond, R. (2011). *High line: The inside story of New York City's Park in the sky*. New York: Farrar, Straus and Giroux.

Davis, W. R. (Feb 1960). The Hurricane season of 1959. *Weatherwise, 13*, 23–25.

Dewey, J. (c.1934). *Art as experience* (p. 4). New York: Minton, Balch & Company.

Dolinsky, P. (2010). The intimate and the epic. *Common Ground, 15*(2), 2.

Downey, K. (29 Oct 2005). Authentic Madison; Today's architectural restorations follow a controversial path to the past. *Washington Post*, F1.

Duerksen, C. J. (1983). *A handbook on historic preservation law* (p. 464). Washington, DC: Conservation Foundation and National Center for Preservation Law.

Dunham-Jones, E., & Williamson, J. (2009). *Retrofitting Suburbia: Urban design solutions for redesigning suburbs*. Hoboken: Wiley.

Edgell, D. L. (1995). *John Nolan and the new Urbanists in Florida: The cases of Venice, Seaside and West Palm Beach*. Master of Arts thesis, Program in Historic Preservation Planning, Cornell University, Ithaca.

Emerson, R. M., Fretz, R. I., & Shaw, L. (1995). *Writing ethnographic fieldnotes*. Chicago: University of Chicago Press.

Enge, M. (28 Jan 2001). Activists protest base's conversion for development; Environmentalists Want Bay Area Famed Presidio to become urban park, not a commercial property. *Washington Post*, A–4.

Energy. (1981). *New energy from old buildings*. Washington, DC: Preservation Press.

Epstein, E. (17 June 2000). Ceremony opens an era of optimism for S.F. Embarcadero. *San Francisco Chronicle*.

Feierabend, C. (1991). The Presidio of San Francisco's cultural landscape. *CRM, 14*(6), 11–13.

Foo, C. C. (1996). *A tax incentive scheme for quality rehabilitation of historic structures in Singapore*. Master of Arts thesis, Program in Historic Preservation Planning, Cornell University, Ithaca.

Forum. (1988–1989). Historic preservation as a design strategy. *Preservation Forum, 3*(2), 2–5.

Foster, M. (16 Sept 2011). Mayor wants to stop New Orleans killings. *Houston Chronicle*.

FR. (29 Sept 1983). Secretary of the interior's standards and guidelines for archeology and historic preservation. 48 *Federal Register, 190*, 44730–44731.

Fuller, R. B. (1969). *Utopia or Oblivion. The prospects for humanity*. New York: Bantam Books.

Fuller, R. B. (1971). *Operating manual for spaceship earth*. New York: E.P. Dutton & Co.

Gallagher, J. (25 Sept 2009). Agency may soon seek ideas. *Detroit Free Press*, A15.

GGNRA. (1994). Golden gate National recreation area. *Creating a park for the 21st century: From military post to National park. Final General Management Plan Amendment* (p. 14). San Francisco: Presidio Trust.

Giegengack, R., & Foster, K. R. (2006). Physical constraints on reconstructing New Orleans. In E. L. Birch & S. M. Wachter (Eds.), *Rebuilding urban places after disaster. Lessons from Hurricane Katrina*. Philadelphia: University of Pennsylvania Press.

Goldberger, P. (31 March 1978). A major monument of post-modernism. *The New York Times*.

Goodnough, A. (24 Feb 2008). Boston has high hopes now that the dig is done. *The New York Times*.

Gottfried, D. (2004). *Greed to green. The transformation of an industry and a life* (pp. 63, 88, 100). Berkeley: Worldbuild.

Gregorian, C. B. (13 May 2011). Old railroad trestle may become a park. *St. Louis Post-Dispatch*, A1.

Gunderlach, J. (2006). *Sound, a character defining feature of historic places: Listening in Chatham Village,*

Pittsburgh, PA. Master of Arts thesis, Program in Historic Preservation Planning, Cornell University, Ithaca.

Harries, S. (2011). *Nikolaus Pevsner: The life* (p. 650). London: Chatto & Windus.

Hayward, N. A. (2006). *Preserving College Hill through urban renewal: The role of the providence redevelopment agency in the implementation of the College Hill demonstration study*. Master of Arts thesis, Program in Historic Preservation Planning, Cornell University, Ithaca.

Hess, R., et al. (2001). *The closing and reuse of the Philadelphia Naval Shipyard*. Santa Monica: Rand Corporation for the National Defense Research Institute.

HUD. (Jan. 1977). *Guidelines for rehabilitating old buildings. Principles to consider when Planning Rehabilitation and New Construction Projects in Older neighborhoods (pp. 5, 22). Prepared in cooperation with the Office of Archaeology and Historic Preservation, National Park Service*. Washington, DC: U.S. Department of Housing and Urban Development.

Huger Smith, D., & Huger Smith, A. (1917). *Dwelling houses of Charleston, South Carolina*. Philadelphia: J.B. Lippincott.

Huxhold, W. E. (1991). *An introduction to urban geographic information systems*. New York: Oxford University Press.

Huxtable, A. L. (31 Dec 1978). Architecture view. *The New York Times*, D21.

Indiana. (June 2010). Old Republic reclaims status. *Indiana Preservationist*, 17.

Ithaca. (22 Oct 1987). Ithacan wins monument design contest. *Ithaca Journal*, 3A–5A.

Ithaca. (24 Oct 1988). Women's rights monument gets architectural contract. *Ithaca Journal*.

Jackson, M. (2010). Green home rating systems: A preservation perspective. *APT Bulletin, 91*(1), 13–18.

Jaffe, M., & Erley, D. (1980). *Residential solar design review: A manual on community architectural controls and solar energy use*. Washington, DC: U.S. Department of Housing and Urban Development.

Johnson, K. M. (Feb 2009). Captain Blake versus the Highwaymen: Or, how San Francisco won the freeway revolt. *Journal of Urban Planning History, 8*(1), 47–74.

Jones, C. L. (2004). *It's about time: The use of geographic information systems for historic preservation planning*. Master of Arts thesis, Program in Historic Preservation Planning, Cornell University, Ithaca.

Kahlman, H. (1976). An evaluation system for architectural surveys. *APT Bulletin, 8*(3), 3–22.

Kamin, B. (2 Jan 2011). Will Chicago think big after Daley? *Chicago Tribune*.

Kaplan, H., & Prentice, B. (1978). *Rehab right: How to rehabilitate your Oakland house without sacrificing architectural assets*. Oakland: Oakland Planning Department.

Kennicott, P. (13 Aug 2006). Madison's makeover. *Washington Post*, N1.

Keyhoe, C. (1991). *The history of the Central Artery Expressway in Boston, Massachusetts, 1907–1990*. Master of Arts thesis, Program in Historic Preservation Planning, Cornell University, Ithaca.

King, J. (17 Oct 2004). 15 seconds that changed San Francisco. *San Francisco Chronicle*.

King, J. (5 Oct 2011). Postmodern architecture poised for revival. *San Francisco Chronicle*.

Kirschenbaum, J. F., & Marsh, D. S. (1993). *War games. Evaluating the California military base conversion process*. Berkeley: University of California, Berkeley, Institute of Urban and Regional Development.

Krimm, R. (1986). Federal response measures to natural disasters. In B. G. Jones (Ed.), *Protecting historic architecture and Museum collections from natural disasters* (pp. 429–440). Boston: Butterworth Publications.

Kuther, J. (2 March 2011). Downtown need a makeover? *Christian Science Monitor*.

Lagerqvist, B. (1996). *The conservation information system: Photogrammetry as a base for designing documentation in conservation and cultural resource management*. Goteborg: Goteborg University.

Lassell, M. (2004). *Celebration. The story of a town*. New York: Roundtable Press.

Leimenstoll, J. R. (Dec 2010). Going green: Applying a sustainability lens to historic districts. *Forum*.

Levy, D. (26 June 2005a). City life, Country setting. *San Francisco Chronicle*, J1.

Levy, D. (26 June 2005b). Lucas' Presidio premiere. *San Francisco Chronicle*.

Levy, D. (3 July 2005c). Lucas has another hit. *San Francisco Chronicle*.

Lewis, A.-E. H. (Ed.). (2001). *Highway to the past: The archaeology of Boston's big dig*. Boston: Massachusetts Historical Commission.

Lewis, P. F. (2003). *New Orleans: The making of an urban landscape* (p. 76). Santa Fe: Center for American Places and Charlottesville: University of Virginia Press.

Lewis, R. K. (2009). The case for architectural competitions. *Chronicle of Higher Education, 6*(34), B24.

Liebs, C. (1980). The meaningful assessment of American roadside architecture. *The [SAH] Forum, 2*(1), 1–2.

Liebs, C. H. (1985). *Main street to miracle mile: American roadside architecture*. Boston: Little, Brown, and Company.

Lightner, B. C. (1993). *Planning advisory service memo. Survey of design review practices*. Chicago: American Planning Association.

Lockwood, C. (1993). Tour of duty. *Architectural Record, 181*(10), 96–97.

Longstreth, R. (1984). The problem with style. *Society of Architectural Historians Forum, 6*(1–2), 1–4.

Longstreth, R. (1991). The significance of the recent past. *APT Bulletin, 23*(2), 16.

Longstreth, R. (Ed.). (2008). *Cultural landscapes: Balancing nature and heritage in preservation practice*. Minneapolis: University of Minnesota Press.

Lubell, J. (2006). Housing displaced families. In E. L. Birch & S. M. Wachter (Eds.), *Rebuilding urban places after disaster. Lessons from Hurricane Katrina*. Philadelphia: University of Pennsylvania Press.

Luberoff, D., & Altshuler, A. (1996). *Mega-project. A political history of Boston's multibillion dollar artery/tunnel project*. Cambridge: Harvard University Press.

Ludlum, D. M. (1963). *Early American Hurricanes: 1492 to 1870* (p. 41). Boston: American Meteorological Society.

Lynch, M. F. (1991). What are we going to do with the recent past in the not too distant future? *APT Bulletin, 23*(2), 3.

McAlester, V., & McAlester, L. (1984). *A field guide to American houses*. New York: Knopf.

McKinsey, R. (2009). *Unlocking energy efficiency in the U.S. economy*. New York: McKinsey & Company.

McLeod, M. (Feb 1989). Architecture and politics in the Reagan era: From postmodernism to deconstructivism. *Assemblage, 8*, 22–59.

McPhee, J. (1989). *The control of nature*. New York: Farrar, Straux & Giroux.

McVarish, D. C. (2008). *American industrial archaeology: A field guide*. Walnut Creek: Left Coast Press.

Meyer, A. (May 1999). Establishing the golden gate National recreation area. *SPUR Newsletter*.

Miner, C. (4 Sept 2009). LEED seeks to beef up its credentials. *The New York Times*.

Mohl, R. A. (April 2008). The interstates and the cities: The U.S. department of transportation and the freeway revolt, 1966–1973. *Journal of Policy History, 20*(2), 193–226.

Morton, W. B. III (1995). *The secretary of the interior's standards for historic preservation projects: Ethics in action. In Ethics in preservation*. Ithaca: National Council for Preservation Education.

Nasar, J. L. (1999). *Design by competition: Making design competition work*. New York: Cambridge University Press.

Newhouse, V. (1998). *Towards a new museum*. New York: Monacelli Press.

NOTP. (15 Sept 2011). Hurricane Katrina Evacuees in Houston still connecting. *New Orleans Times Picayune*.

NPS. (1983). *The secretary of the interior's standards for rehabilitation and guidelines for rehabilitating historic buildings* (p. 6). Washington, DC: National Park Service, U.S. Department of the Interior.

NRB. (1991). How to apply the National register criteria for evaluation. *National Register Bulletin #15*. Washington, DC: U.S. Department of the Interior, National Park Service.

NY Energy Education Project. (1977). *The 1977 young adult assessment of energy. A National assessment of educational progress*. Albany: State University of New York.

NYT. (18 May 1993). Golden Gate guardian ends a long mission. *The New York Times*, A10.

Olkowski, H., et al. (1979). *The integral urban house: Self-reliant living in the city*. San Francisco: Sierra Club Books.

Olson, K. (2008). *A window of opportunity: Cades Cove and The National Park service*. Master of Arts thesis, Program in Historic Preservation Planning, Cornell University, Ithaca.

Petersen, S. R. (1974). *Retrofitting existing housing for energy conservation: An economic analysis*. Washington, DC: U.S. Department of Commerce.

Phillips, W. T. (1986). *Roadhouses of the Richardson highway.* Anchorage: Alaska Historical Commission.

Pittas, M. J. (1985). Design competitions. *Urban Design International, 5*(2), 4.

Plyer, A., & Ortiz, E. (Aug 2011). *New Orleans index at six. Measuring greater New Orleans' progress toward prosperity.* New Orleans: Greater New Orleans Community Data Center.

PN. (June 1979). Awards. *Preservation News, 19*(6), 6.

Pogrebin, R. (1 June 2009). $10 million donate to high line project. *The New York Times.*

Pogrebin, R. (8 June 2009). Renovated high line now open for strolling. *The New York Times.*

Post. (1 Nov 2011). Obama signs proclamation designating fort Monroe in Virginia a National Monument. *Washington Post.*

Quigley, K. (Nov (2002). Mori selected for visitors' Center at Wright's Darwin Martin house. *Architectural Record, 190*(11), 25.

Rappaport, N. (1998). Preserving modern architecture in the US. In A. Cunningham (Ed.), *Modern movement heritage* (pp. 59–65). London and New York: Taylor & Francis.

Redmon, K. C. (2010). The man who reinvented the city. *Atlantic, 305*(4).

Reilly, W. (7 June 2000). Presidio's park survival depends on its self-sufficiency. *San Francisco Examiner,* A23.

Revkin, A. C. (8 May 2007). 20 years later, again assigned to fight climate change. *The New York Times.*

Roeder, J. (2005). What we learned from the oil crisis of 1973: A 30-year retrospective. *Bulletin of Science, Technology & Society, 25*(2), 166–169.

Rossiter, W. J. Jr., & Mathey, R. G. (1978). *Criteria of retrofit materials and products for weatherization of residences.* Washington, DC: U.S. Department of Commerce.

Rubin, A. I. (1978). *Window blinds as a potential energy saver–A case study.* Washington, DC: U.S. Department of Commerce.

Rutgers. (2011). *Route 66 economic impact study: Executive summary.* New Brunswick: Rutgers University.

Saffron, I. (17 June 2011). A park on high. *Philadelphia Inquirer,* E01.

Scheer, B. C., & Preiser, W. F. E. (Eds.). (1994). *Design review: Challenging urban aesthetic control.* New York: Chapman & Hall.

Scott, D. (28 Dec 1999). Presidio for sale. *Albion Monitor,* 3–4.

Shapecoff, P. (27 April 1987). Pollution and economic growth. *The New York Times.*

Smeallie, P. H., & Smith, P. H. (1990). *New construction for older buildings.* New York: Wiley.

Smith, B. (1978). *Preservation brief No. 3: Conserving energy in historic buildings.* Washington, DC: U.S. Government Printing Office.

Smith, M. M. (Ed.). (2004). *Hearing history. A reader.* Athens: University of Georgia Press.

Soderstrom, M. (2008). *The walkable city. From Hausemann's Boulevards to Jane Jacobs' streets and beyond.* Montreal: Vehicule Press.

Stamps, A. E., & Nasar, J. L. (1997). Design review and public preferences: Effects of geographical location, public consensus, sensation seeking, and architectural styles. *Journal of Environmental Psychology, 17,* 11–32.

Standards. (2001). *Standards for restoration and guidelines for restoring historic buildings.* National Park Service. http://www.nps.gov/hps/tps/standguide/restore/restore_index.htm. Accessed 5 March 2014.

Stevens, A. J. (1979). *The economics of buildings. Life cycle costing.* Master of Science, University of Cape Town, South Africa.

Stout, G., & Johnson, R. A. (2004). *Red Sox century: The definitive history of baseball's most storied franchise.* New York: Houghton Mifflin.

Sturgis, R., et al. (1989). *Illustrated dictionary of architecture and building.* New York: Dover Publications. (Reprint).

Summerson, W. (1969). *The classical language of architecture.* Cambridge: MIT Press.

Talen, E. (2005). *New urbanism & American planning. The conflict of cultures.* New York: Routledge.

Thomas Vonier Associates, Inc. (1981). *Energy conservation and solar energy for historic buildings: Guidelines for appropriate designs.* Washington, DC: National Center for Architecture and Urbanism.

Tomlan, M. A. (1990). Identifying and evaluating the landmarks of tomorrow. Lecture given at *Preservation Challenges of the 1990s: A Conference for Public Officials,* sponsored by the National Park Service, the Advisory Council on Historic Preservation, and the General Services Administration, Washington, DC, June 5–7.

Tomlan, M. A. (1992). Preservation practice comes of age. In A. J. Lee (Ed.), *Past meets future: Saving America's historic environments* (pp. 73–79, 240–242). Washington, DC: Preservation Press.

Tomlan, M. A. (1994). Historic preservation education: Alongside architecture in academia. *Journal of Architectural Education, 47*(4), 187–196.

Trelstad, B. (1997). *The Presidio trust legislation: Privatization or preservation?* (p. 1) Berkeley: University of California, Institute of Urban and Regional Development

USAEC. (2004). Capehart-Wherry housing compliance action complete. *USAEC Environmental Update, Winter,* 1.

Vale, L. J., & Campanella, T. J. (Eds.). (2005). *The resilient city. How modern cities recover from disaster.* New York: Oxford University Press.

Vinegar, A. (2008). *I am a monument. On learning from Las Vegas.* Cambridge: MIT Press.

Vitanza, T. A. (1990). NPS surveys yield data on the effects of Hurricane Hugo. *CRM, 13*(1), 12–14.

Waterloo, E. (2010). *Under the big apple: A retrospective of preservation practice and the New York City subway system.* Master of Arts thesis, Program in Historic Preservation Planning, Cornell University, Ithaca.

Webster, M. D., & Bronski, M. B. (2005). Green salvage solutions: Reusing roofing and structural materials. *Construction Specifier, 63*(1), 58.

Weiss, E. M. (22 March 2009). No Cul de Sacs. *Washington Post*, 1.

Wellman, J. (2004). *The road to Seneca Falls: Elizabeth Cady Stanton and the first women's rights convention.* Urbana: University of Illinois Press.

Weyeneth, R. R. (2000). *Historic preservation for a living city: Historic Charleston Foundation, 1947–1997* (pp. 26–27). Columbia: University of South Carolina Press.

Whiffen, M. (1969). *American architecture: A guide to the style.* Cambridge: MIT Press.

White, B. J., & Roddewig, R. (1994). *Preparing a historic preservation plan.* Chicago: American Planning Association.

Whiting, S. (22 May 2005). A part of the landscape. *San Francisco Chronicle*, 19.

Wilkinson, D. (May–June 2003). The what, why, and how of design guidelines. *Alliance Review*, 4–6.

Winter, T., & Schulz, P. (1990). A systematic approach to historic structures reports. *APT Bulletin, 22*(1–2), 142–148.

Witzling, L., & Ollswang, J. (1986). *The planning and administration of design competitions.* Milwaukee: Midwest Institute for Design Research.

Wolfe, T. (1981). *From Bauhaus to our house.* New York: Farrar Straus Giroux.

Wood, E. E. (1931). *Recent trends in American housing* (p. 167). New York: The Macmillan Company.

Woodward, R. B. (21 May 2009). Buffalo's Wright stuff. *Wall Street Journal*, D9.

Wong, E. (4 Oct 2005). After being shut down. *Daily Pennsylvanian.*

Yardley, W. (9 April 2011). Seattle Ponders (some more) the wisdom of replacing a roadway. *The New York Times.*

Advocacy and Ethics

7

Introduction

When preservation problems are relatively modest in scale the efforts taken to solve them often do not attract much attention. Millions of people are involved in saving properties simply by maintaining them. Repainting, re-roofing, or re-glazing decisions are not generally subject to much public notice or scrutiny. People also gradually change their social and cultural practices and activities to meet the current norms, altering their expressions, language, and customs. Introduce large changes quickly, however, and fear will often be the result.

In a similar fashion, as preservation projects increase in size and complexity, the changes are more significant or noticeable, and more people become involved. Often an extended discussion ensues, sometimes reported in the media, especially if the project or program is costly. Although preservation efforts may begin as a relatively limited crusade, as they become a matter of more widespread concern, questions arise about the ethics that should guide and shape the treatment of the people and places.

As discussed in earlier chapters, the ethics involved in current historic preservation activity were re-formed in the late twentieth century against a background of the rising environmental movement, modernism, and social and economic reform. The rationales for preservation at issue—aesthetic, social, historic, economic, and spiritual—typically surface when the future of a property is at stake. But there may be a conflict between the perceptions of what is needed and what is possible, stemming in large part from who is speaking for whom. These discussions frequently trouble policy makers and local officials. The disputes are also disconcerting for those who seek guidance and direction. In addition, conflicts also occur within the preservation community, often diverting attention and foiling attempts to build a common understanding about the best solution or path to follow. That, too, often serves to sound the death knell for a property. Hence, advocacy and ethics are worthy of more extended study.

Broadly understood, professional ethics are simply an extension of the social values held by society. Indeed, without a generally understood concept of normative behavior and a belief in "fair play" between individuals and groups, it is difficult to establish more specific laws, regulations, and guidelines. Temptation and coercion often threaten good judgment. A high salary and benefits may prove enticing to young professionals, just as the offer of government or corporate funding can turn the heads of advocacy groups. The genteel atmosphere in the preservation movement sometimes works to keep the discussion about ethics relatively private, restricting full disclosure.

By contrast, an examination of advocacy and ethics provides both advocates and professionals with a common starting point. These extend into every area of preservation activity, whether considering the smallest object in a museum context or entire landscapes, multiple properties below or above ground, in or on the sea, or in the sky.

M. A. Tomlan, *Historic Preservation*, DOI 10.1007/978-3-319-04975-5_7,
© Springer International Publishing Switzerland 2015

In this chapter examples are chosen to demonstrate the challenges being faced, the problems that arise, and the losses that follow, with concluding thoughts about taking better stock of our experiences and the limitations of our existing social values and ethical norms.

Culture and Social Values

Given that historic preservation is a social movement directed at saving and caring for our cultural heritage, it is worthwhile to consider just what culture is, why it continues to exist, and, when it is threatened, what happens in different societies. From the Latin word "cultura" the idea arises that we cultivate people. Hence, culture is composed of the patterned manners of thinking, feeling, reacting, and acquiring associations. These include beliefs, attitudes, and values. All are shared and learned among people who, in turn, create and shape objects and the property they occupy. Cultures, then, are distinctive characteristics of human groups (Murdock 1961), and the achievements of these groups can be measured and compared.

Assumptions among people give rise to common ideas and beliefs passed along within the group and these, in turn, give rise to activities that produce "artifacts." In historic preservation, these are often termed "cultural resources." In this fashion, members of the group share culture largely because the individuals carry similar ideas about how they interact with Nature and one another. The artifact is the tip of the proverbial cultural "iceberg." (Fig. 7.1)

This definition indicates that culture is not instinctive or inborn, but learned through interaction with the environment and other people. Guidance about what is appropriate behavior begins with one's parents and extended family. Language, religion, and government or organizational structures strengthen the patterns. Narratives, whether oral, pictorial, or written, further reinforce ideas in a culture because they pass along information learned from previous generations.

Language plays a remarkably important role in transmitting culture, in part because it conveys and defines the way in which groups view

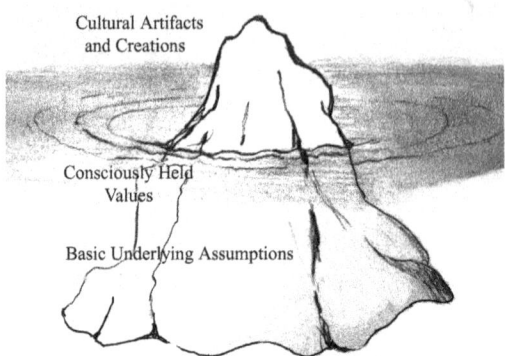

Fig. 7.1 The interest in and concern for cultural artifacts and expressions, sometimes thought of as tangible and intangible heritage, rest on consciously held values, but those, in turn are based in underlying assumptions and beliefs, some of which are unconsciously held in common by members of a group. (Author's illustration)

the world. Although language does not constrain thought, it does have a role in conveying attitudes, values, beliefs, and behaviors that relate to one another (Bonvillian 2011). So it should come as no surprise that some societies fiercely protect their language as a key to safeguarding their culture.

Religion is also important for it reflects attitudes and beliefs traditionally shared by groups that are difficult to measure (Inglehart and Baker 2000). As will be discussed in Chapter 8, religion has variously benefited from and been hampered by government support, but the degree to which people in a country tolerate religious freedom is an important measure of the possibility of conflict between different creeds. Recognizing the importance of a wide range of religions depends on openness.

The concept of a "national" culture is often characterized by language, government and legal system, religion, and education, reinforced by concepts of self-identity. One example is the First Nations of North America, with their pockets of distinct cultures, in contrast to the prevailing overall culture of the United States. National sovereignty remains an important feature in these cultures, as it does in most countries around the world. Because nations are social systems, they have cultures that become part of the mental programming of individuals (Hofstede 1983, 1991).

Given this basic definition of culture, it is possible to describe the values most deeply held in the United States, bearing in mind that its values are ever changing. The country is principally an English-speaking Judeo-Christian society, which has considerable national pride in its form of representative democracy. More fundamentally, however, it is a society that sees time in a linear fashion, making it is more likely to place value on the present and future rather than the past. In a similar fashion, if time is seen as limited, action is taken as soon as possible, rather than viewed as part of a continuum in which performance can be measured over lifetimes. If our society feels it should control the environment, channeling rivers, and capturing solar power, it is likely to insist on significant physical changes. By comparison, a people who strive to be in harmony with Nature are more likely to be less invasive on the Earth. As we have seen in previous chapters, preservationists engaged in winning popular support regularly test the public's values, and may find, to their dismay, that the prevailing views and beliefs will result in needless demolition.

This approach can also be misleading, however, because the dominant view is not monolithic. There are dozens of subcultures in any country, some of which are viewed as more important than others. This is precisely where preservationists can go wrong: by not recognizing the presence of subcultures within an area, and by ignoring the variation, conflict, and dissent that exists within a culture. Appropriately trained preservationists must be more sensitive than most people to cultures and their artifacts. Because they care, it is often the role of preservationists to negotiate the conflicts that arise between values and attitudes of various social groups, maintaining a suitable humility in the process.

Ecology, Environmental Ethics, and Historic Preservation

As a social movement, historic preservation has a considerable number of features in common with the advocacy for major environmental concerns, such as the need to protect the quality of our air, water, and soil, and the need to safeguard fauna, flora, and wildlife. Just as the damage to open space and natural habitats spurred activists, urban preservationists' objected to the destruction of the physical fabric of cities and the social disruption of communities. All of these protests called into question larger land-use decisions, and pointed to the need to conserve energy and materials.

Rachel Carson's appreciation of the connections of all life systems included human advancement (Carson 1962). Her ecological thinking argued for policies that are not confrontational but cooperative. The approach was flexible and capable of being tailored to fit varying circumstances. In the same fashion, Jane Jacobs' appreciation for the diversity of housing and the manner in which "unslumming" takes place indicates that our thinking must be informed by the wide variety of needs in people's lives. Failing to understand their competing desires leads to policies that are out of sync with local residents, and diminishes the prospects for winning the public and political support necessary to effect change.

For years, environmentalism was largely pollution-based and law driven. As a movement, it disapproved of human activities resulting in economic growth because of their harmful pollution and other side effects. Central policy control depended on a set of command and control mandates. Likewise, historic preservation legislation was reactive and depended upon early recognition of the value of the resource and extensive use of mitigation. Even the most stringent preservation provision, in transportation legislation, stipulating that every "prudent and feasible alternative" be explored, allowed for a considerable amount of damage to occur.

On a theoretical level, a natural union exists between the conservation of natural resources and the preservation of our built environment. President Jimmy Carter attempted to realize this union in the late 1970s by combining agencies within the Department of Interior, including the National Park Service, with departments dedicated to natural resources. The rise and demise of the Heritage Conservation and Recreation Service, however, demonstrated that a forced partnership between the two interests was not going to work.

In part this was due to the prevailing political climate that called for decentralization and devolution of responsibilities to the state and local governments. Without a clear outside threat, a unifying political agenda, and economic support, it became impossible to forge a stable alliance. The unification failed because the supposed substitute—public-private partnerships—depended upon businesses that would provide government with much needed public investment. In another 10 years the economy had fluctuated so markedly that it was apparent that businesses could not shoulder the burden alone (Tomlan 1992).

As the effects of the 1976 Tax Reform Act became noticeable, the preservation movement gained the ability to sit at the table as development and redevelopment decisions were planned and executed. And, as a result of the preoccupation with the "business" of preservation, the distance from the goals of the environmental movement—also affected by the idea of economic incentives—led to an almost complete loss of unity. Although both movements begin with the idea of protection, for preservationists interested in supporting the social needs of communities, the preferred alternative is the continued use of historic properties. But for some conservationists, continued use is less than a desirable choice. True, there is a wide diversity of opinion among environmentalists about how much can be saved. It is equally true, however, that when preservationists moved to embrace the development community during the 1980s, their actions spurred the use of more oil, gas, and wood. Further, as preservationists increased their inherent bias toward urban and suburban concerns, alliances with conservationists seemed less fruitful.[1]

By the 1990s, the idea of "comprehensive planning" faded, and the fragmentation that "strategic plans" caused became even clear. Targeting specific properties sometimes produced spectacular results. As historic preservation projects became more ambitious, they also became more complex and involved more debt-financing. And, as the

funding from the federal government was redirected and local organizations have had to fend for themselves, organizational fragmentation has increased. As a result, the relationship between preservation legislation and environmental law continues to be a difficult one because rather than be goal-oriented, each has developed its own compliance culture, with evaluative measures, permits, emission levels, and standards that are reduced to a check-list of considerations, which are variously interpreted and enforced.

The Need for Ethical Coherence in the Face of Change

Although most preservation activity is reasonably well-defined by a number of goals, charters, principles, laws, regulations, and guidelines, the broader concerns that lie outside of the field often are difficult to understand to those unfamiliar with them. The rationales for saving—the historic, aesthetic, social, economic, and spiritual—sometimes seem inadequate, or seem in competition with one another. As other ideas become more important in time, the motivations of the advocate are clouded. When does the aesthetic rationale or the historic over-ride the economic rationale, or when does the contemporary social concern for low income housing become more compelling than the aesthetics of the property or district? Does a spiritual need trump them all? The answer lies chiefly in how well we understand the need to conserve all our resources: appreciation of the historic property or site, respect for the lives and activities of the people involved, and the broader community goals. For, if the definition of anything is also the definition of a good thing of that kind, and if the best use for a property is the function or functions for which it was originally intended, it follows that the best approach is the one that serves current and future generations.

Unfortunately, people who become involved with preservation projects of all kinds routinely combine two different objectives: the preservation of our legacy and the enhancement of our physical environment (Striner 1995). As amply

---

[1] This was clearly reflected in the results of a nationwide survey conducted by the National Trust for Historic Preservation (Wood 1987).

demonstrated in the opening chapters, preservation and a wide range of similar social goals are often compatible and mutually reinforcing. However, historic preservation projects are, by their very nature, distinguished by the attempt to save the useful life of existing properties and ensure their ongoing, sympathetic uses. The primary thrust of historic preservation is to go beyond esthetic enhancement, to see beyond the immediate creative act.

Problems can arise when preservationists knowingly abandon their first goal—to save resources and serve as curators of places and people's activities—and instead express their various aesthetic preferences. Frequently a preservation commission or state historic preservation office becomes preoccupied with the elements of a new design before addressing their primary ethical responsibility to safeguard the existing site. Whether the review occurs at the local, state, or federal level, preservation advocates need to be continually mindful of this distinction, and alert to the occasions when this might occur.

In a similar fashion, the idea that sprawling suburbs often contain miles of "uninspiring" designs has occupied some preservationists for a number of years (Moe and Wilkie 1997). Granted, several legitimate reasons exist for opposing sprawl. Existing resources are often overlooked and undervalued in the transition from undeveloped land to low density schemes. With that said, it is important to remember that, once they are built, these same suburban developments are all candidates to be evaluated as worth saving. They are a significant part of the social history of the country.

The pioneering sociologist Herbert Gans, who conducted his research by living in a post-WWII Levittown, implied that mass produced houses lead to mass produced consumption and monotonous lives. Gans also observed, conversely, that the suburbs were a good place to live and they remained popular (Gans 1967, 1991). Today, the majority of this country's built fabric and social activities are suburban-based. Now pockets of disinvestment are seen in dozens of these locations and they lie outside of the scope of most urban-based preservation organizations.

A few preservation initiatives are being taken to go beyond surveying the suburbs to address disinvestment and social relocation. For example, the First Suburbs Housing Initiative in northeastern Ohio has provided a model outside the urban core that can easily be extended into the second and third ring suburbs. The idea behind this initiative is to reinvent the post-War bungalow and the two-family house so as to improve the desirability of neighborhoods suffering disinvestments, like Parma, Maple Heights, Garfield Heights, Fairview Park, Cleveland Heights, Lakewood, and Shaker Heights. Home maintenance cooperatives help insure that property values do not decline with the support of incremental and continuous improvement (Schwartz 2002; Ott and O'Malley 2007).[2] What is more, these programs continue to attract new residents, and strengthen the school system's tax base.

In reality, suburbia, far from being a calm and boring place to live, often displays all of the scars of battles over race, class, and politics found in urban areas (Kruse and Sugrue 2010). It is where the hopes and dreams of the majority of Americans are played out, and controversies have repeatedly erupted. During the 1980s it was very noticeable that whenever the wealthy built houses in the suburbs, they were larger and more ostentatious than the existing housing. Home builders and mortgage bankers understood this, and they aided the construction of a new wave of "monster" houses, designed on colossal proportions. The schemes gained attention particularly when backed by celebrities, such as Bill Gates and Ted Koppel, but the trend was countrywide. While the term "trophy house" cropped up, the word "McMansion" seemed to be most appropriate. Architects Andres Duany and Elisabeth Plater-Zyberk castigated McMansions as pretentious and isolated, a "cartoon version of country living," but did little to formally identify the trend (Duany and Plater-Zyberk 1992). They used the term disparagingly in 1992, even as it became a buzzword in popular journalism, and increasingly

---

[2] Cleveland's reputation nationwide has led Kent State University's Urban Design Collaborative to address this issue (Ott 2006).

questions were raised as to the appropriateness in size and density of these new "monuments" (Parshall 1996; Cheever 1998; Musante 1998; Knight 1997; Blum 1998; Salant 1999).

Although they could be built on "greenfields," McMansions could also replace "tear downs," the existing, smaller houses purchased with the expressed intent that they would be demolished. Many were on small lots, and the new designs were relatively devoid of any landscaping that would hide their size so that they appear even more grandiose than they are. Vaguely classical pillars, columns, pilasters, and huge Palladian windows adorn the vinyl-clad fronts, sometimes with a nonfunctional "widow's walk" at the peak. Alternatively, if the McMansion is a medieval chateaux, it will have a large tower or turrets providing sweeping views and a faux stone profile. Regardless of the style, a three or even four car garage with a broad driveway provides access, while the grounds are lit by a security system and watered by an automatic sprinkler system (Mc-Guigan 2003). The floor area, often in excess of 15,000 sq. ft., becomes more impressive as one moves through the house, from the two story entrance foyer with its spacious staircase, to a family room or "great room," moving on to the formal dining room and to the enormous "gourmet" kitchen, with granite counters and the most expensive collection of large appliances available. A media room, perhaps with a wall-sized plasma video screen, a home office, or a workout room, or all three, completes the first floor. Upstairs, among the several sleeping areas, the master bedroom is a special feature, as it often has dual master bathrooms with a jacuzzi.

As the specter of more McMansions rose in the public's mind and the attempts to halt more tear downs mounted, preservationists and neighborhood activists led the charge to control their construction (Warren and Armour 2001; Nasar et al. 2007). Yet, almost as soon as the public trashing and bashing of McMansions peaked, the 2008 economic downturn caused would-be owners to question the value of their prospective investments (Tribune 2010). As banks became wary of making loans on large houses with questionable resale values, the number of new McMansions being constructed slowed. In 2010, the McMansion era had come to an end, marked by the conversion of some to other uses (Perlman 1998; Weinberg 2001; Szold 2005). Saving McMansions, already part of our recent past, is similar to preserving the great "white elephant" estates of the nineteenth and early twentieth centuries. Consequently, the possibility arises of converting a McMansion to multifamily housing or other forms of residential occupancy (McGrew 2008).

Just as the population in urban areas is changing, the population in the suburbs is no longer homogenous, if it ever was. As studies of the Levittowns have shown, the idea that a stay at home mother, breadwinning father, and two point five children raised in front of a television has been replaced by a wide variety of new and more mobile family configurations (Kelly 1993; Lucy and Philips 2000). More fundamentally related to the "makeover" of the American suburbs is their changing social and ethic composition. With changes in immigration legislation and preferential quotas in particular, well-educated Asians—including physicians and technology specialists—have benefited. Asylum has also been given to less well educated, lower income newcomers. Enclaves of immigrant-owned residences and businesses, called "ethnoburbs" (Li 2009), are a significant aspect of the new suburbia. With over a million ethnic Chinese in California, about a half million in New York, and at least 120,000 in Texas, on the surface this trend appears to be part of America's traditional melting pot of assimilation.

Preservationists tend to support small, locally-owned retailers, but they should think about the role of shopping at every scale. If the future of malls as retail centers is a matter of concern, it is, as Wal-Mart has shown, to re-create the functional equivalent of a department store, selling everything imaginable under one roof, including groceries. Assuming that sustaining the existing facility or increasing the retail capacity of a location is not a viable option, some suggest it is necessary to demolish everything and rebuild the property with a denser, more traditionally mixed use (Hudnut 2004).

The rise of the department store in the nineteenth century was followed by the development of the shopping center, the first of which is generally thought to be that developed by J.C. Nichols, in the Country Club Plaza in Kansas City, Missouri, which opened in the early 1920s. This new model was followed by the enclosed suburban mall, at first supported by an "anchor" department store to reach the expanding middle class. Architect Victor Gruen's Southfield, Michigan example set the tone for thousands of similar malls. Whereas only 49 shopping centers were constructed in 1949, over 11,000 had been built by 1965 (Gossling 1976). By the mid-1970s, however, the rate of construction slowed and competition intensified as the number of anchor tenants decreased. By 2005, industry specialists wondered whether the shopping mall was dead, and the end of an era seemed to be nearer when one of the largest mall operators in the United States, General Growth Properties, declared bankruptcy in 2009 (Pristus 2005; Stabiner 2011; WSJ 2011).

In a similar fashion, the suburban "corporate campus" seems dated. In light of the current emphasis on providing a less automobile-dependent society and the rising cost of gasoline, the exclusive and remotely located research and office park is being questioned. What began as a 1951 invention of Stanford University to capitalize on federal defense contracts and spur private sector entrepreneurs in the new high-tech industry is being reexamined (Findley 1993). The park-like settings with well-manicured lawns now often are a luxury. For example, United Airlines moved from its 1 million sq. ft. Elk Grove Township headquarters in the suburbs to the Willis (Sears) Tower, shifting hundreds of workers to the center of Chicago (Tribune 2011).

Yet, demolition of seemingly ubiquitous properties should never become the first and only option. Commerce has given way to new uses like education, medicine, and religion. A community college or branch university campus often finds that an underutilized shopping center or mall will provide appropriate classroom space, considerable parking, and easy access to students. For example, the thriving Shelton State Community College in Tuscaloosa, Alabama, used this "shopping center" solution to meet its need for more space. Health care once provided by hospitals is also available in the mall. As patients are also often consumers who shop for the best care, including alternative therapies, they are attempting to speed-up the pace of treatment, closer to home (Sloane and Sloane 2003). Religious groups of all kinds have also found the shopping center or mall to be a desirable start-up location for worship and social service activities.[3]

As we have seen, context is important, and making improvements in the world around us is always necessary. By the same token, theoretically every property does need an advocate, to bring together a team that documents, analyses, and considers the options. Who the advocate is, and what techniques are employed is the subject of the following sections.

The A, B, Cs of Advocacy

Because historic preservation is fundamentally a social campaign, advocacy is absolutely essential. Whether defending a person, a community, a place, or an object, advocacy requires a public expression that states the case for extending the life of our legacy. This pleading is similar to defending a case in court. More often than not, because there are so many more preservation amateurs than professionals, it is the nonprofessional who first becomes aware that a problem exists. Whether amateur or professional, preservation requires raising one's voice in any suitable venue to gain public attention. Alerting neighbors, civic associations, and city, township, and county officials is a first step, followed by contacting existing organizations that could lend assistance and help discover all the available information about the proposed project (Warren and Warren 1977; Robin 1990).

For those unfamiliar with advocacy campaigns, the learning curve can be steep and time consuming. Even in the simplest disputes— learning how to do the research; consulting

---

[3] Chapter 8 suggests that these are a logical development and stimulating aspect of "ethnoburbs".

Fig. 7.2 The Community Awareness Kit of the Historic Resources Committee of the American Institute of Architects offered examples of press releases from around the country to provide local chapter advocates with models of how to alert the public to current issues. (Author's collection)

architects, planners, public servants, government officials, attorneys, and accountants; working with the press and organizing public information campaigns; gaining a working knowledge of the local political connections; and testifying at the appropriate hearings, sometimes repeatedly—often stretches the determination of even the most dedicated preservationist (Schmickle 2007). Learning about the options for a lawsuit, how to stage a community charette to generate acceptable design alternatives, or evaluating the pros and cons of a negotiated settlement, all also takes considerable effort.

The first steps in advocacy often involve providing the public with information (Fig. 7.2). If historic preservation planning is orderly, this often begins with the survey process, working with the neighborhood group to determine the history and activities of the area, and sharing the results with the residents. Millions of hours of volunteer labor have gone into these surveys, followed by enumerable committee meetings and public hearings as landmark designation is discussed. Published surveys have broadened our understanding of African American history, commercial properties, highway bridges, and adobe structures, in addition to districts and landscapes.

The Antoinette Forrester Downing Award for the best published survey, first announced at the 1987 annual meeting of the Society of Architectural Historians, celebrates this type of study (SAH 1986).

In some cases, historic preservation planning efforts include reaching out to economic development agencies and tourism departments. As noted in Chapter 2, radio and public television broadcasting programs in the 1970s introduced rehabilitation ideas to a broad segment of the population, thoughts that were restricted to do-it-yourself magazines of the previous generation. During the 1980s, the introduction of the History Channel and television programming by the National Geographic Society further stimulated historical thinking, some of it done in conjunction with preservation organizations. In places like New York, the History Channel has even contributed funding to the City's official History Center, and donated videos to public school libraries (Paskin 2004). In Boston, the public radio station PRX sponsors the listener call-in show "About Your House," in an "ask the expert" format.[4]

Advocacy campaigns are often launched by historical societies and historic preservation organizations, but also by ad-hoc groups, particularly when more established organizations are seen by a younger generation as doing little to advocate for a particular historic site. Indeed, thanks to the viral SMS or text message phenomenon, a relatively small initiative by two or three vociferous advocates can become a massive call for action. Young preservationists' organizations sometimes form when the conventional organizations have not been given the opportunity to participate. Whether directed to the young or old, advocacy events can be very important and helpful when building a network to address preservation issues. Historic Landmarks of Illinois sponsors "pub crawls" in Chicago neighborhoods, linking the stories told in the communities to historic bars and restaurants. The St. Louis Landmarks Association sponsors "anti-wrecking

balls," where local bands vie for the attention of participants in important locations. Membership organizations are often strengthened by these activities.

Although 11th-hour appeals will always arise and campaigns to save relatively unknown and undocumented properties will continue to be launched, preservationists have become more pro-active by calling attention to the difficulties with significant historic properties. The National Trust for Historic Preservation launched the "Eleven Most Endangered" list in 1988, one of its most successful national media campaigns. Begun as part of the campaign to dramatize the plight of the Manassas Battlefield in Virginia, the program featured sites that faced not only inadequate protection but also incompatible development (PN 1988). Beyond endangered battlefields, including Antietam National Battlefield Park, Cedar Creek Battlefield, Custer Battlefield National Monument, and Reno-Benteen Battlefield Memorial, in Big Horn, Montana; other sites such as the West Mesa Petroglyphs near Albuquerque, New Mexico, and the Vieux Carre in New Orleans have been featured. Increasing and improving advocacy rests on publicity that highlights distinctive properties with appropriate narratives. The stories need to be appealing to the media. Syndicated articles, radio, and television programs are useful in dramatizing the plight of landmarks on the brink of extinction, thus bringing the problems and their advocates to the attention of millions who would otherwise be unaware of the issues (Berke 1992; Humstone 2001).

Several state-wide and city-wide organizations immediately adopted the Trust's approach.[5] The "ten most endangered" or "seven most threatened" properties featured by preservation organizations has proven a remarkably effective advocacy tool by simultaneously gaining publicity for the site and attracting sponsors and developers interested in rehabilitation. For example, the Providence Preservation Society's

---

[4] PRX or Public Radio Exchange is a major distribution center for public radio programming. http://www.prx.org/pieces/51221-about-your-house-with-bob-pat-yapp.

[5] Statewide advocacy groups in Arizona, Colorado, Illinois, Iowa, Maine, Massachusetts, Minnesota, Missouri, New York, North Carolina, North Dakota, Tennessee, Texas, and Virginia maintain such initiatives.

Fig. 7.3 Alongside the Rhode Island State Capitol, the Masonic Temple was once featured by the Providence Preservation Society as an "endangered property" before it was rehabilitated to become the Renaissance Hotel. (Author's photograph)

endangered property campaign, begun in 1994, selected the long-abandoned Masonic Temple in downtown, just a few blocks west of the Rhode Island State Capitol and north of a planned shopping mall (Fig. 7.3). By centering attention on this endangered Neoclassical monument and convening a local stakeholder meeting with a design charette in 1997, the community decided a hotel would likely be the best possible use (Smith 1997). Subsequently, a sympathetic developer was found, the project expanded, and the Providence Renaissance Hotel opened in 2007 (DuJardin 1997; Smith 1998).[6] With the city's new waterway, downtown park space, esplanades, and bicycle and walking paths, the project fit into the transformation of the urban core (Bunnell 2002).

Some problems may arise with this approach when there is not sufficient attention paid to the property's disposition and one or more sites remain "endangered" more or less indefinitely. The goals may not be immediate rehabilitation of a particular property, however. When the entire state of Vermont was declared endangered,

for example, the effect was intended to be more political than physical. Regardless, using an endangered properties approach does focus preservation effort, working with the media to dispel misconceptions and create a more proactive preservation message to gain public attention.

Advocacy for historic preservation at the federal level, in Congress and the Executive branch of the federal government, was once considered to be solely the province of organizations like the American Scenic and Historic Preservation Society or the National Trust for Historic Preservation. However, because the National Trust has been unwilling or unable to take up causes for a variety of reasons, other organizations have been formed to push nationwide legislative agendas. Most prominent is Preservation Action (PA), the brainchild of Washington lawyer Tersh Boasberg, who launched the new organization at the National Trust annual meeting in San Antonio in 1974. Boasberg hired Nellie Longsworth as the chief advocate in the fall of 1975, and together they developed a network of preservation advocates across the country, with a board of 100 members, at least two in each state (Glass 1987; Miller and Longsworth 2001; Fig. 7.4). This grassroots network was linked through a small, Washington-based

---

[6] The State of Rhode Island provided at least $500,000 toward the project, but the private investment was in excess of $50 million.

staff to the members of Congress and their staffs. Preservation Action directors and members advance preservation interests by informing themselves about the issues and making strategic connections in the committee assignments and responsibilities of Congressional representatives. Lobbying is the central activity of PA[7] and, although it has launched some initiatives that have not gained widespread national acceptance, such as an historic homeowners tax credit, the visibility its gives to preservation issues in Washington is essential. PA has also provided specific guidance on how to build an effective lobbying team: assessing the level of interest of potential advocates; recruiting new team members; identifying issues that will arise during the legislative calendar; developing an easily understood and expressed message; and delivering results at the local level whenever possible.

Advocacy at the state government level is also important. Early statewide preservation groups, such as the Association for the Preservation of Virginia Antiquities, and the Association for the Preservation of Tennessee Antiquities, continue to serve as influential groups, even as a new wave of organizations formed in the wake of the 1966 National Historic Preservation Act. As noted in earlier chapters, the official state-level historic preservation activity came about largely because of early federal initiative. NHPA stipulated the designation of state liaison officers by their respective governors. Without them, no state historic preservation programs were possible. The growing needs of these state officers led to the creation of the National Conference of State Historic Preservation Officers (NCSHPO), organized in August, 1969 (PN 1969). With 30 representatives already in place, the organization could ably testify before Congress that the partnership between the federal and state governments was working, an important step as the funds from the Department of Interior began to be distributed to the states and the National Trust for Historic Preservation. In the early years, increasing

Fig. 7.4 Nellie Longsworth was the first executive director of Preservation Action, the nation-wide grassroots network explicitly created to work with the members of Congress and their staffs. (Author's collection)

funding for survey and planning, grants-in-aid, Section 106 archaeological review, and technical assistance on building issues occupied the attention of SHPOs, but later concerns often turned to the administration of tax advantaged rehabilitation. The NCSHPO also played an important role by assisting local historic district commissions, particularly as the idea of the certified local government became a reality with the 1980 NHPA amendments, and as serving as a model for the tribal historic preservation officers (THPOs).

The National Association of Tribal Historic Preservation Officers (NATHPO) formed to represent the interests of the officially designated individuals representing the tribes. As with NCSHPO, the requirement to assume responsibility for Federal undertakings that affect historic properties and archaeological sites requires cooperation inside governments at all levels. Therefore, NATHPO assists their members by seeking the approval of their programs and technical training in all aspects of cultural heritage work on and off reservations, including advocating for funding. By their very nature, THPOs give more emphasis to the importance of protecting "traditional cultural properties," those properties that are eligible

---

[7] As such it maintains a different Internal Revenue Service status than nonprofit organizations and is a registered lobbying organization.

to be included on the National Register of Historic Places because of their association with cultural practices and beliefs that are rooted in their community's history. The THPOs often have difficulty defending and maintaining the traditional beliefs and practices of their people in the face of outside pressures. For example, Dakota Indians attempted to block a state highway that would destroy an oak grove that held tribal burial platforms; while the Quechans near the Fort Yuma Reservation in California confronted plans for an open pit gold mine that violates ancient ceremonial circles and footpaths used by the Creator. Similarly, Narragansett leaders attempted to halt an off ramp to a shopping mall that would rip up a burial ground that was at least 4000 years old (Claiborne 1998).

As the preservation network grew, the idea that a local commission could be delegated some of the responsibilities of the SHPO was very attractive to cities distant from state capitols. In this regard, the support NCSPHO provided in 1982 for the creation of the National Alliance of Preservation Commissions (NAPC) proved critical to improving the make-up of local commissions (PN 1982). Much of the credit for the vision of this new organization rests with G. Bernard Callan, Jr., who extended his work in Maryland, where he started a statewide association of local historic district commissions (Callan 1981). The advocacy of the NAPC became most evident as it strengthened the guidance provided to new members of local historic governing bodies with manuals and newsletters that addressed previously overlooked topics (Malone and Cassity 1994). From about the time the Alliance was created in 1983 until 1993, the total number of commissions more than doubled. In addition, their variety increased as more county- and parish-wide bodies were created, and the number of commissions in cities with a population of 50,000 or less blossomed, constituting the majority of the membership. Just as important, an increasing number of small commissions began to enjoy more professional support when administering their respective ordinances and assisting communities (Crimmins 1990).

Underlying all advocacy efforts is the necessity to become not only the voice of resistance, but a positive force for change at the local level. Assuming the historic preservation organization is as deeply concerned as it should be in the political process, it will sponsor public forums during election periods. For example, New York City's Historic Districts Council hosts forums, provides candidate questionnaires, and issues press releases highlighting important concerns in each individual voting district. The Council's Concerned Preservation Voters Initiative aims to gather community groups within the City's historic neighborhoods into coalitions that are active during elections in their voting district around preservation and development concerns. The over-arching goal of the initiative is to educate political candidates about these issues during the campaign and beyond. This project and its community coalitions are nonpartisan and will not endorse any particular candidate for political office. On the other side of the country, the Los Angeles Conservancy has taken to reviewing the 89 jurisdictions of the County and "grading" their preservation performance by reviewing how many properties have been designated, whether a certified government program is in place and operating effectively, and whether local ordinances are being enforced (CPDR 2006).[8]

The Need for Sound Professional Preservation Thinking

While advocacy is essential, because many decisions require more information and experience, people with specialized knowledge are consulted. Those with specialized knowledge are often professionally educated in preservation and allied fields. They are characterized by their particular knowledge, the result of long and patient study, and their activities are best described by a distinctive vocabulary. As opposed to the academic, who often studies a topic for its own sake,

---

[8] The Los Angeles Conservancy was the winner of the 2006 Daniel Burnham Award from the American Planning Association, in part because of this initiative.

the professional applies knowledge, regardless of whether the skills are primarily intellectual or physical. The most important feature of a professional, however, is the service provided to others, either as individuals or as members of a group. In fact, the education of the professional focuses on not only providing the student with a solid knowledge base, but investigating a number of case studies of an increasingly complex nature. This develops in the individual the ability to define the nature of the problem and to solve it. In this regard, experiential learning is essential.

The other features common to most professions are stipulations about registration, licensing, and certification. The public is to some degree assured that professionals have certain credentials, but it is important to recognize that licensing is neither necessary nor sufficient to define an occupation as a profession. Many people who act in a professional capacity do not hold licenses issued by a state, country, or local government. For example, many accountants are not certified, nor are many designers, but each can provide professional services. The growing tendency to collaborate with a wide range of people, each of whom has specialized knowledge, works against the domination of any one discipline, regardless of the recognition it might be granted by a government entity.

Because historic preservation activities repeatedly challenge the predetermined path of action, questions arise about the difference between the current goals and the fundamental values of the movement. Whether preservationists come to grips with them or not, the success or failure of a project and of the field in general depends on the answers being developed. This is not simply an issue of public policy because, as constraints grow on government employees, the tendency to hire consultants increases. In essence, this encourages professionals for hire and the expectation that they will present evidence to support a predetermined result.

In this situation, client confidentiality is one concern, particularly in cases where the information is privileged or personal. A preservationist inside or outside of government, who learns about an impending property transfer, is privileged and that information could be sold to someone seeking to either promote or halt further development.

The professional apologist is more worrisome. Companies or individuals sometimes will want an independent, unprejudiced answer to the question "Is this property or site eligible for the National Register?" or "Can this structure be rehabilitated?" On the other hand, what the client is often really seeking is a confirmation of a preconceived notion and it expects the hired gun to not provide findings to the contrary. The consultant can accept the assignment with one of two understandings: that the client's wishes will be supported or that the recommendations will depend upon the investigation's findings. Only the latter approach is appropriate.

Experts for sale can occurred when a middleman is used. Frequently a property owner will hire a lawyer to assemble a team of experts who are charged with facilitating approvals in the public review process. For example, the attorney will call for an expert on materials or structural systems, which happens to be one of the consultant's areas of expertise. Problems arise when the consultant makes guesses based on limited experience rather than taking the time to investigate thoroughly. Questions may arise regarding the history of the property, the landscape, or the archaeological potential, any of which will be affected by and should affect the proposal. Collateral topics and issues may crop up that go beyond the knowledge of any single consultant (Longstreth 1998). In short, the consultant should not accept an assignment if the project is not fully understood or lies outside an area of one's expertise.

Consultants willing to support either side of a case can be "hired guns," and travel considerable distances for an assignment. The transactions in the overheated property markets of New York, Washington, D.C., Chicago, and Los Angeles are often capitalized at a level high enough to hire some of the most articulate spokespeople. The more ethical position is to determine from the client or lawyer during the initial contact whether it is possible to spend several hours becoming familiar with the basic facts of the case before becoming deeply involved. This allows the consultant to be able to determine whether the client's best interest can be served. It is important to show not only competence in the required field, but also a distinct level of impartiality. Although the testimony is being paid for, it must be based on the facts, not on who is paying the bill.

Consultants are not the only ones who face ethical questions. Employees in government, corporations, and nonprofit organizations encounter improper behavior and are troubled by whether they should be the whistle blower. This question may hinge on whether the employee's supervisor is accessible and open to discussion. In these instances, the problems of confidentiality loom large, especially if there is fear of retribution. That said, an employee should first turn to those who have oversight responsibility. Only if that course is unavailable should other paths be explored. For example, a staff member working for a development company that requires kickbacks from subcontractors awarded construction contracts might not find sufficient internal support to correct a troubling informal practice. In fact, the employee may be fired. In one instance, an employee who provided information to the Internal Revenue Service resulted in a government audit that disclosed irregularities in the developer's activities, allowing outside prosecutors to follow-up with formal legal charges.

Demolition: Salvation in Salvage

Were preservationists to have a choice, restoration or rehabilitate of an historic property would always be preferable to its demolition. In urban and suburban locations that are continually declining, however, demolition takes place all too frequently. In some larger cities, at least a half dozen demolition permits are issued every day. For a number of reasons, but especially the depopulation and decline of rust belt inner cities, this scenario is not likely to change in the near future. Concern about the future of an historic property or a neighborhood can lead to rising general anxiety in an entire community. In response, advocates may launch a campaign to educate the public about the merits of preservation, gathering

information, and disseminating press releases. Questions can arise over whether the site has sufficient merit to be designated "historic" or, if it has achieved a level of recognition, whether the cost and complexity of preservation measures is inappropriate. This discussion is generally aired publicly at hearings of the local historic preservation commission, planning commission, and/or the zoning boards. In some cases, the elected representatives of the community become involved, in which case the discussion often is much wider in scope. If the decision is not favorable, it may be appealed to a higher body or to the courts. After a court fails to overturn the decision, the preservation community is faced with demolition and the campaign to save the property falters. At that point, advocates experience frustration, making it difficult to be creative about options for the future. After all, what recourse is there? As the demolition crew begins to clear the site, perhaps some advocates begin to reflect on where they went wrong, but it is often difficult to revisit the issues and face, again, the loss. In addition, when this scenario repeat itself week after week, month after month, it is increasingly difficult to care.

In locations where the decisions are repeatedly negative, the preservation community is sometimes reluctant to do what is necessary to prepare for a building's demise. To staunch advocates, demolition is often regarded as an embarrassment. While neither federal nor local legislation provides much guidance, experience and common sense should return the preservationist to the renewed importance of documentation. At a minimum, recordation is critical and should be required.

It is wise to avoid "building wrecking" and demolition experts who facilitate the quickest and most efficient manner of property disposal (Colby 1972; Pledger 1977; Horwitz 1982). For example, blasting is often preferred because it is much quicker and therefore less expensive than disassembly. Due to increased sensitivity to the environmental hazards associated with asbestos and toxic materials, engineers and safety experts are paying an increasing amount of attention to "controlled demolition." In this approach, damage during the process is much more exacting.

The basic questions associated with even controlled demolition involve whether or not there is anything of value in the tons of material taken to the landfill.

"Salvage" means selling the building materials for reuse, so that planning for the demolition of an historic site is as crucial as predevelopment planning for rehabilitation. The first consideration is the legal issues surrounding demolition. Federal, state, and local legislation has a particular relevance, as demolition is both an environmental and a life-safety issue, and is subject to both local interpretation and political influence. Assuming demolition of some kind is to occur, a number of physical issues need to be considered, including the correct procedures for recording, salvaging, and caring for the remnants.[9]

Assuming demolition will take place, it is wisest to seek a local depository for the elements. If one disperses "the remains" regionally or further afield—sold for commercial purposes or educational—the intrinsic cultural value of the artifact is diminished (Bonnette et al. 2006).[10] An extreme example underlines the point: dismantling a New York Dutch barn so that the wood can be shipped to California for a beach house is not a move any preservationist should support.

Assuming the debris is destined for the landfill, the question arises as to what criteria are useful to select what is recorded and collected. One approach is to save only those pieces that are unique: the unusual or rare historic, structural, or aesthetic elements. The larger question remains: to what degree can elements of the landscape be saved, and at what cost?

Building components may be assembled and interpreted in architectural study collections. Although these can be located some distance from the original site, they may be the best home for the artifacts, as they educate professionals and the public. Virtually every state has at least one study collection, often in a State museum, and a number of regional and national organizations maintain them (Bevitt 1993a, b).[11]

Facadism: Another Name for Demolition

Perhaps no other late twentieth century discussion has been so intense in preservation circles than the manner in which new buildings have been erected behind fragments of existing structures. During the 1960s and early 1970s, when many inner cities were being abandoned, property values declined and demolition was commonplace. Although property values remain depressed in a number of communities across the country, in locations where the economy is expanding, the prospect exists of making money by enlarging the income producing activities on a site that has been deemed historically significant. In such cases, "partial" demolition may be proposed as a compromise. This is "facadism," or the demolition of the vast majority of a structure, saving only the facade.

The term "facadism" is not an old one, but in architectural circles it had a negative connotation from the start. During the Depression, proponents of Modernism coined the word to decry the tendency of some traditional architects to design buildings with facades that were unrelated in style to their interiors and contemporary needs. Designers seemed to switch the face of a building to suit a client, although what was behind it remained the same (Walcott 1936).[12] By 1964, architectural historians used the term facadism to

---

[9] In addition, a number of questions should be answered regarding the site after the structure is removed. For example, how long does the land sit vacant? What are its associated costs and legal responsibilities, and how does the lack of a structure affect the surrounding properties?

[10] After Hurricane Katrina, the Preservation Resource Center (PRC) in New Orleans and the National Trust for Historic Preservation worked with MerciCorp to encourage deconstruction over demolition. The PRC also has established a sizeable salvage store (Alweiss 2010).

[11] For example, major collections exist under the care of Colonial Williamsburg, the Smithsonian Institution, and the National Park Service Independence National Historic Park, in Philadelphia.

[12] Historian Nikolaus Pevsner may have been the earliest person to notice that "England was the first country in the 18th century … to break the unity of interior and exterior and wrap buildings in clothes not made for them but for buildings of other ages and purposes" (Harries 2011).

describe the pretentiousness of the "Queen Anne front" when compared to the "Mary Ann back," a reference to Frank Lloyd Wright's disgust with the Victorian era schemes he encountered when beginning as a young architect in Oak Park (Ames 1964). In an era when the Queen Anne style was only beginning to attract serious scholarly attention, facadism was not encouraged.

In September, 1982, a new meaning was added when the *Washington Post* architectural critic Benjamin Forgey used the term "facadism" to describe the trend of massing "… new construction behind an ensemble of older buildings." As Forgey noted, "In practice this does not often lead to the best of all possible worlds." Builders wanted to build as high as possible because property was valued based on the density allowed by the local zoning legislation. The frequent result became a "… tremendous discrepancy in scale, with the new structure towering ominously over the old … a sort of instant 'facadism' that serves neither preservation nor architecture with distinction."

On balance, however, Forgey saw a number of urban design benefits to this approach because it provided a welcome relief to the boring speculative office buildings erected in the District of Columbia during the previous two decades (Forgey 1982). Design critics did not rise up against the trend toward "partial" demolition because most of their discussion centered on how to improve the visual appearance of the city, particularly the urban core. For architectural critic Peter Blake, the treatment of the facade was merely a "polite deception" (Blake 1980). Behind the front elevation of an older building, a high rise of any size could be built. Blake reasoned that throughout European history facades had often been disassembled, moved, and rebuilt. In the United States, however, there were comparatively few examples, the earliest being the 1803 Albany State Bank, moved in 1930 to be incorporated into a new sixteen story building (Root 1929; Cobb 1930; Fig. 7.5). As North America was spared bombing during World War II, rebuilding inside of old shells was rare. Modernist architectural critic and preservation educator James Marston Fitch, who had visited the "phoenix

Fig. 7.5 In 1926, when the Albany State Bank directors decided to build a new 16 story office building, they asked their architect Henry Ives Cobb to keep the original 1803 façade with the result that it was jacked up and moved to its new location, to form the entryway. (Author's collection)

city" of Warsaw in 1963, sided with Blake and accepted facadism with total impunity because the pedestrian rarely noticed the difference. "The streetscape is what the ordinary citizen sees and knows" (Fitch 1982).[13] Urban design commentator Ronald Fleming also believed there is nothing phony in keeping the facade when it enlivens the streetscape and he sought to demonstrate a variety of approaches to justify his position (Fleming 1982, p. 9).

Most modernist design professionals followed this view and a cluster of projects demonstrated how facades or architectural elements could be reinstalled as artistic elements. In Philadelphia, all but the Egyptian Revival front of the Pennsylvania Fire Insurance Company was

---

[13] The date of Fitch's visit to Warsaw is derived from his passport and subsequent articles (Tomlan 2001). Fitch reiterated this view on at least one other occasion (WSJ 1984).

removed to make way for the Penn Mutual Life tower, a 21 story office building designed by Mitchell/Giurgola architects, erected in 1971–1974 (Fig. 7.6). The facade, designed by John Haviland in 1835, serves as a four-story, free-standing sculpture defining the new building's entrance plaza (Webster 1981; Mitchell and Giurgola 1983).[14] Likewise, the Carter Dry Goods Building in Louisville, Kentucky, remained a warehouse until the mid-1970s, when the mayor convinced the city to issue bonds and buy the building for a Museum of Natural History. Architect Jeffry Points' design called for retaining the original facade and building a shiny aluminum front behind it. A 16 foot deep entranceway separates the two, ensuring that the contrast between the old and new is obvious (CJLT 1976; Morton 1978; Smith 1980). In Salt Lake City, the Zion Commercial Mercantile Institution founded by Brigham Young and other members of the Church of Latter Day Saints, sported a single cast and sheet iron storefront. In 1971, the church's business and real estate corporation decided to replace the department store with a new commercial mall, but was persuaded by the Utah Historical Foundation to save the front. The corporation, convinced by a flood of letters threatening to cancel charge accounts, decided to reconstruct the facade on steel supports in front of the new mall. When reassembled, however, the facade was only a small stage-set; the new building was much wider than the old. The shopping mall architect Victor Gruen was not interested in becoming involved with the cast iron front (Fleming 1982, pp. 80–82).

As the real estate investment in urban areas boomed, more incentives were provided to clear as much of the site as possible. At times, the designation of a landmark proved helpful in saving more than just the front wall. In Manhattan, the fronts of the McKim, Mead and White-designed Villard Houses were grafted onto the towering Helmsley Palace Hotel (Shopsin and Broderick 1980; Morton 1981; Smith 1981). The restoration of the interiors was so extraordinary that virtually

Fig. 7.6 All but the Egyptian Revival front of the Pennsylvania Fire Insurance Company was removed to make way for the Penn Mutual Life tower, a 21 story office building erected in 1971–1974. It serves as a four-story, freestanding sculpture defining the new building's entrance plaza. (Author's photograph)

no discussion arose of what was lost at the rear of the property (Fig. 7.7).

By contrast, a classic battle erupted in Boston when, in 1979 and 1980, the 88-year-old Boston Stock Exchange, designed by the local architectural firm of Peabody and Stearns, was scheduled for demolition so that Olympia-York, a Toronto-based company, could erect a new office tower. While the Boston Landmarks Commission rushed to put together a report so that designation would prohibit the alteration of the facade or the height of the roof, the company began its own campaign. It maintained that failure to construct the building as designed would cost the city over $100 million in taxes over the next 50 years, 2000 construction jobs in the near

---

[14] Facadism continues to be proposed in Philadelphia (Saffron 2013).

Fig. 7.7 In Manhattan, the fronts of the McKim, Mead and White-designed Henry Villard Houses were grafted onto the Helmsley Palace Hotel. The restoration of the interiors was so extraordinary that virtually no discussion arose of what was lost in the rear of the property. (Author's photograph)

future, and 6000 permanent jobs. Their argument was persuasive to decision-makers, resulting in a structure that became "… a kind of mask, slicing much of it off but leaving the front part as a kind of historic bill board" (Globe 1979; Brown 1979; Fig. 7.8).

At the same time, when architectural critic Benjamin Forgey first encountered facadism in Washington, D.C., he thought it would be short-lived. In fact, the opposite has proven true: more facadism has taken place in that city than any other place in the world. The reasons lie in the Congressionally-mandated height limit and the problems regularly encountered in building in a tidal plain. These factors, combined with an almost continuously overheated market for office space, have contributed to more than one hundred examples. The mania began in the mid-1970s, when the local preservation advocacy organization, "Don't Tear It Down," began to object to several "partial" demolitions.[15] The most egregious was the proposal fostered by George Washington University, which purchased a group of nineteenth century town houses on the south side of Pennsylvania Avenue with the intent of

Fig. 7.8 By contrast, "a classic battle" erupted in Boston when in 1979 and 1980 the 88-year-old building, designed by the Boston architectural firm of Peabody and Stearns to house the Boston Stock Exchange, was scheduled for demolition so that Olympia-York, a Toronto-based company, could erect a new office tower. (Photograph: Thomas Richmond)

developing the properties for rental income. "Our land is our endowment" said the university's president. The university fought and eventually won the battle to erect an eleven story office high-rise behind all of them, with a shopping mall-like atrium below. The group of buildings was renamed "Red Lion Row" (Swallow 1986; Fig. 7.9).

The public's perception of this project was positive because it was a relief from the prevailing design mode at the time: unrelieved, undistinguishable reinforced concrete office buildings constructed to the property line. Red Lion Row "emerged as an unexpected tourist attraction," as numerous visitors were caught short by the sight

---

[15] See Chapter 2 for the origins of this organization.

Fig. 7.9 George Washington University's "Red Lion Row," a group of nineteenth century town houses on the south side of Pennsylvania Avenue, were in disrepair when the prospect of redeveloping the entire block became a reality. (Historic American Building Survey, Library of Congress)

Fig. 7.10 Each of the buildings in Red Lion Row were deliberately "facadimized" to build a much larger structure that would generate rental income, with some doors and windows that are simply used as decoration. (Author's photograph)

of the facades, bereft of their buildings, being supported by a heavy grid-work of I-beams. After being informed that the facades were being saved at great expense due to their landmark status, many onlookers were full of praise (DC Tribune 1982). Indeed, the use of technology to preserve the facades of a building seemed impressive. The innocent observer cannot help but be amazed by the extent to which architects and engineers will go to ensure a satisfactory result (Bumbaru 1989; Fig. 7.10).

As Post-Modernism came to the fore in the early 1980s, however, the context for judgment changed. Younger critics, less vested in the Modernist approach, joined preservationists who found facadism abhorrent. Robert Campbell, the architectural critic for the *Boston Globe*, questioned the practice of "… amputating part of an old building and grafting a new building in its place," terming it "prosthetic architecture" (Campbell 1980). The controversy was brought to a nationwide popular audience in 1985 when *Newsweek* featured the most recent examples. "Faced with developers interested in prime locations and preservationists intent on saving old buildings, many civic leaders are allowing modern structures to be built behind preserved facades.... More often than not, facadism is unattractive, with distortions in scale and volume." At best, it appeared that facadism could be lighthearted and carefully avoid compromising the dignity of the original structures. Neither preservationists nor developers were pleased by the compromises, and "Several cities are standing firm against facadism. Savannah and San Francisco, for example, have ordinances establishing height limits that discourage out-of-scale development" (Stevens 1985).

Historians who sought to reaffirm the views of the modernists noted that the history of western architecture includes a number of monuments that contain old building elements. The Arch of Constantine, the facades of Siena and Orvieto Cathedrals, and dozens of structures all incorporated pieces of earlier structures when they were constructed. Preservationists countered by noting that facadism is not an exercise whereby long abandoned archeological fragments are woven into a new fabric, but a practice whereby existing old structures suffer almost complete demolition to serve as decorative elements for big, new buildings erected above and around them. Unfortunately, preservationists in the United States opposed to facadism were slow to consult European conservation specialists, who were even more aghast at the rising practice.[16]

By August 1983, an editorial in *Preservation News* stated flatly, "Saving facades only is not preservation." Red Lion Row and the row of Meeting Street commercial buildings in Charleston that lost their backs for a convention center parking project were cited as the most egregious examples. "The most nearsighted laymen can

detect a Disneyland-style fraud when they see one. The results speak poorly of the entire movement" (PN 1983). Indeed, this is obvious in some locations where the doors have no hinges and the handles are inoperable.

By 1985, the number of examples had risen to the point that a trend, if not a style, was apparent. New York architectural critic Paul Goldberger brought the issue to light when learning of a proposal to build a 19 story apartment tower behind three brownstones on East 79th Street (Goldberger 1985; NYT 1985; McGuire 1985). The building at 712, with three floors of windows by the French artisan Rene Lalique, was especially noteworthy for its artistic glasswork. The solution was to use the facade of glass as an atrium for the tower, "a doormat ... a small stoop cowering before a ponderous skyscraper of entirely different scale."

In the Midwest, the story has been similar. In the heart of Chicago's financial district, a 37 story office tower was built above a four story terra cotta building by architects Holabird and Root at 10 South LaSalle Street. Above the white lower cladding arose a bright green stone veneer, a jarring contrast (Tribune 1985).[17] Milwaukee and Minneapolis have both seen similar schemes. In Wisconsin's largest city, the 1913 Jung Brewery was scheduled for demolition by the owner, the Carley Capitol Group of Madison, which proposed saving six fronts to a depth of 20 ft. along Water Street (Berke 1984). In Minneapolis, the downtown Nicollet Mall has been similarly inserted behind a row of buildings (Freeman 1988).

In general, local landmarks commissions remain ill equipped to cope with these design issues because economic development is desirable, particularly in cases where the local economy is weak. Decrying the attempt to use narrowly constructed local historic preservation legislation as a growth management tool, the former dean of

---

[16] Sir Bernard Feilden warned "there is a danger of deception when only townscape values are considered" (Feilden 1982). English county planner and archeologist David Baker wrote that the practice of reusing the facade in this manner is "another form of demolition" (Baker 1983). Stephen Trombley wrote "'Facadism,' the process of saving only the front of a building to grace a modern structure, is particularly execrable. The most serious danger of this fashion is that it obstructs history by preventing the creation of new structures, and may leave a legacy of bastardized buildings that betray the age's lack of confidence" (Trombley 1985).

---

[17] The discussions with the architects, Moriyama & Teshima Planners Ltd. of Toronto, in conjunction with Chicago-based Holabird & Root, designer of the original 1911 structure, resulted in the decision to preserve the historic four-story terra-cotta and granite-base façade, a solution that was "a first for Chicago."

Vanderbilt University Law School, John Costonis, wrote "Beauty is off the mark as a force behind aesthetics laws [used in the preservation field.] In its place I propose to substitute our individual and social needs for stability and reassurance in the face of environmental changes that we perceive as threats to these values" (Costonis 1989). He divided the built environment into two classes of objects, in a way that discussions by preservationists often take. First, there are icons, structures invested with a special character. They have certain architectural, historical, or social values that confirm our sense of order. Second, there are aliens, those that threaten icons and their values. In essence, Costonis argues that preservationists must capture a sense of *community values* to protect our icons and better defend them in court. Again, ultimately, preservation is a social campaign, requiring people to learn about and understand the value of extending our legacy.

Although heated comments are made on both sides of the issue, facadism continues. The press cites examples, both good and bad, without discrimination. Instances of facadism are reported, but the trend goes unexamined. The widespread confusion in the preservation community about facadism has generally led to silence in hearings and public forums. Some architectural critics, in turn, have interpreted this as ambivalence. "Preservationists have always been somewhat ambivalent regarding the issue of erecting new buildings behind historic facades. On one hand, the practice has allowed developers to build financially viable structures that maintain an existing streetscape." On the other hand, "some of these projects have resulted in contemporary behemoths that overwhelm their delicately scaled antecedents" (AR 1985).

By the end of the 1980s, a number of journalists chose to interpret this ambivalence about aesthetic and urban design issues as a sign of successful compromise.[18] Unfortunately, the tendency to trade pieces of buildings increased in some communities. Just as it was becoming common to

sacrifice all but the façade of the historic building, some preservationists decided that they would back down altogether. Instead, they would only support the designation of that part of the buildings that could be re-hung or relocated on the new high rise, or that piece of a site that contained the "most significant" elements, overlooking the context. In essence, this is acknowledging that demolition can take place without opposition from the organization or agency created to safeguard preservation interests.

The trend can infect the nomination process, which lies as the core of the movement. Perhaps the most shocking example occurred in Chicago. In March of 1987, when the Chicago Landmarks Ordinance was revised, the Commission declared an end to the practice of designating parts of buildings. Yet, in early November 1988, when faced with the objections of the owners of the Tribune Building, the Commission approved an agreement for a partial designation of the tower, limited to the west (Michigan Avenue) facade, 85% of the northern and southern facades, the east facade above the 23rd floor, and the first floor of the lobby (LPCI 1989). Not included as critical features were the eleven-story annex or the adjoining court. All of this assumed that a new structure would be built to absorb the pieces of the old, maintaining only a "view corridor" toward the Tribune Tower from Lake Shore Drive (Kamin 1989; Fig. 7.11).

When the Property Does Not Seem to Exist, Demolition Follows

While partial designation is problematic, cases also arise where the city's decision-makers have dreams of economic return that completely preclude the local landmarks commission from determining whether a property is worthy of official recognition. In such cases "people's public hearings" are held to raise the public's awareness that the designation process is being frustrated, a reminder that the elected representatives in a community hold the ultimate decision-making authority.

---

[18] "Developers, Activists Find Common Ground," reads the headline in a Washington, D.C., commercial real estate article (Lebovich 1989).

In New York, Columbus Circle, at the southwest corner of Central Park, was a difficult territory to negotiate whether on foot, bicycle, or in a vehicle. Even today, proposals for its redesign and reinvention occur frequently (Goldberger 1988; NYT 1998). Style is important in that area, so a reasonably apt solution in the form of a 10 story marble clad arcaded museum stirred talk. Designed by architect Edward Durell Stone for the collector Huntington Hartford, the Gallery of Modern Art at 2 Columbus Circle opened to considerable fanfare in 1964 (Huxtable 1964). *New York Times* architectural critic Ada Louise Huxtable found it less controversial than other experiments at the time, commenting that the exterior resembled "a die-cut Venetian palazzo on lollypops." She went on to note that the "interior planning is the building's conspicuous success," for within the irregular shape, the large and small galleries were effectively organized around the service core. In all, it seemed to suit perfectly its "functions, purposes and patron." Record throngs of over 4000 visitors visited during the opening week, and Huntington Hartford soon used it to launch his campaign to salvage the ancient Egyptian temples at Abu Simbel from inundation by the waters captured by the Aswan High Dam (NYT 1964a, b).

By 1969, however, Hartford's A&P grocery store fortunes had suffered and the Museum, which had always cost the patron hundreds of thousands of dollars a year to operate, was closed. The property was given to Fairleigh Dickinson University to be reopened as the New York Cultural Center, with mixed success (Gluek 1969). Gulf and Western Industries bought the building in 1975 and, in 1980, presented it to the city, which used it for the Department of Cultural Affairs and the visitor's bureau.

The circuitous path by which the property came into the possession of yet another museum was used as justification for not holding a pubic hearing under the city's uniform land-use procedure. Gulf and Western gave the building to the city with the understanding that it would be used as a visitors' center and cultural affairs office for 30 years. The successor to Gulf and Western, the Viacom Foundation, in exchange for

Fig. 7.11 Anticipating facadism, only some parts of Chicago's Tribune Building are designated. The western façade of the tower along Michigan Avenue, most of the north and southern facades, the east façade above the 23rd floor and the first floor of the lobby are deemed significant, while the remaining elements are not. (Author's photograph)

tax benefits, transferred this interest to the New York City Economic Development Corporation (NYCEDC), a nonprofit organization that operates as a large economic development agency under an agreement with the city. Since the building no longer was operating as it was intended, the NYCEDC exercised its reversionary rights and took title, with the consent of city officials (Dunlap 2003). Because New York City anticipated the sale of the property to a big corporate taxpayer, as critic Tom Wolfe wrote, "every time the question of a hearing on 2 Columbus Circle came up, the landmarks commissioners... dove under their desks, clapped their hands over their ears, cried out to their secretaries to shove history and the concept of landmarks preservation itself through the shredder, and hid" (Wolfe 2003). No sale was forthcoming, however.

In June, 2002, Mayor Bloomberg announced that the city would sell 2 Columbus Circle to the American Craft Museum, which pledged to spend at least $30 million to return its use to galleries for art and various performances. The president of the NYCEDC indicated the Museum was to complement the redevelopment of Columbus Circle, along with the AOL Time Warner Center, the Central Park Gateway, and the Trump International Hotel and Tower.

To remake the image of the Circle and mark the new beginning for the facility—renamed the Museum of Arts and Design—the façade of the building would need to be changed (Dunlap 2002; Fig. 7.12). Although the building had never been a design favorite, tastes had changed and it gained a number of admirers for its role in the development of modern architectural thinking and the evolution of architect Stone's work. Still the Landmarks Commission would not hold a hearing.

In early November, 2003, three preservation organizations filed suit to stop the sale to the Museum. These included Landmark West, a preservation group on the Upper West Side; the Historic Districts Council, which helps neighborhoods pursue landmark designation; and the New York-area chapter of an international preservation group DOCOMOMO.[19] They charged that the Landmarks Preservation Commission failed to hold a public hearing on designating the property a landmark because the City wanted to sell the building and allow it to be remodeled. They demanded that a new environmental impact statement be prepared on the proposed alterations (Barron 2003). The National Trust for Historic Preservation and the Preservation League of New York State filed *amicus* briefs in support of the petitioners, arguing that New York City had an obligation to go to the Keeper of the National Register, given the lack of a decision by the state.

Fig. 7.12 The famed "Lollipop Building" on Columbus Circle could not be landmarked because the New York City administration blocked the Landmarks Commission from holding a hearing, despite the appeals of local preservation organizations. (Author's photograph)

Meanwhile, the National Trust for Historic Preservation made an appeal directly to the Keeper of the National Register, since the State Historic Preservation Officer would not take the initiative to make a determination of eligibility on the building.

Still, the Landmarks Commission balked at holding a hearing. The frustration of supporters gained some outlet when City Councilman Bill Perkins convened a "people's hearing" in July 2004, at which the evidence was aired. Perkins introduced a bill in August to give the City Council the power to direct the Landmarks Commission to hold hearings as a first step toward correcting the lack of action (Dunlap 2005). Curiously, the case against designation was most succinctly stated in July of 2005 by a former Landmarks Commission member, Sherida E. Paulsen, who went on record, writing that "In order to be considered a landmark in New York City, a building must meet certain criteria. It must be at least 30 years old, and it must have contributed to the city's development in the fields of architecture, history or culture." She went on: "2 Columbus Circle fails all but the age test" (Paulsen 2005). Paulsen stated that 2 Columbus Circle was "not

---

[19] The name is an acronym for "Documentation and Conservation of Buildings, Sites and Neighborhoods of the Modern Movement." Founded in 1990 in the Netherlands, DOCOMOMO claims chapters in 40 nations. The chapters in the United States are located in New York, Chicago, and San Francisco.

one of Stone's notable works,"… [it was of] "little consequence historically and culturally," and the Museum's design did not influence other architects. She went on, "The review of 2 Columbus Circle has been conducted under the stewardship of three different chairmen and reflects the opinions of 19 commissioners, including six architects, four historians, two planners and three realtors," suggesting that the entire issue of holding a hearing was closed (Paulsen 2005).

As the end of the building seemed to be drawing nearer, some members of the Landmarks Commission became willing to vocally disagree with the "official" position. Whereas in 1996 the decision not to consider designation seemed reasonable, time had passed and views had changed. Professor Sarah Landau of New York University, one of the four commissioners who recommended in 1996 not to hold a hearing, now joined three other commissioners to suggest that holding a hearing was appropriate (Dunlap 2005). In addition, Stephen Raphael, one of the Commissioners who wished to hold a hearing, noted "Some of us neither participated in this [earlier] decision nor were we asked to acquiesce in it," and the decision then should not be considered a binding precedent. Meanwhile, three former chairs of the Landmarks Commission let it be known they supported the call for a hearing, in contrast to the position of Laurie Beckelman, a former chairwoman, who was involved with the new program for the Museum that would re-clad the structure.

Unable to mount a successful campaign to stop the project, New York City preservationists lost the battle to save Stone's design, although the first floor "lollipops" are still visible behind the new façade. Oddly, even the critic Ada Louise Huxtable equivocated in her review of the replacement façade and there seems to be little to suggest the story will not repeat itself in a just few years (Huxtable 2008; Gardner 2008).

When Preservation Organizations Disagree, Demolition Follows

Rehabilitation in some cities is more difficult than in others, particularly in case where the declining population leads to declining income levels. In some instances, local preservation organizations take strikingly different views, each holding its view as more "progressive" than the other. As discussed in Chapter 5, among the most economically distressed inner cities is St. Louis, Missouri, where the community is less than half its former size and designated landmarks are always endangered. Chief among the important historic properties is the Old Post Office and Customs House, declared surplus by the General Services Administration in 1975, and renovated from 1978 to 1982 for commercial reuse. Unfortunately, it was all but completely empty of tenants by 1990. Studies of the downtown area repeatedly identified the importance of the enormous structure so that, in 2001, when city officials announced they had chosen a development team to renovate the property for the Missouri Eastern District Court of Appeals and a Webster University extension, the move could be seen as a positive step.

As discussed previously, the development team proposed demolishing the adjacent Century Building to build a parking garage. The Century Building had its own history, playing an important role in the downtown commercial and social scene, even though it had not yet been listed on the National Register. It served as the home of the Equal Suffrage League when it planned the National American Women's Suffrage Convention in the city in 1919. It provided a home to a prominent department store, a famous architectural firm, and dozens of other businesses (Duffy 2004; Fig. 7.13). Looking into this case study in greater detail provides a useful illustration of what happens when preservation organizations disagree.

The Landmarks Association of St. Louis, a group instrumental in saving the Old Post Office in the 1960s, objected to the demolition of the Century Building and the decision that its removal was necessary to insure the economic viability of the rehabilitation project. Ample parking already existed on nearby lots and other developers suggested alternatives, including the rehabilitation of the Century. Unfortunately, the city administration would not change direction. When the redevelopment plan became public, it was natural for the Landmarks Association to appeal to the National Trust for Historic Preservation,

Fig. 7.13 The Century Building in St. Louis, located at Ninth and Olive Streets, opened with great fanfare in 1896. It had a long and distinctive history before being threatened with demolition, at which point the Landmark Association of the city enlisted the help of the National Trust for Historic Preservation. The regional office challenged the developers to find a better alternative. (Photograph: Michael Allen)

which joined the local preservationists to oppose demolition of the Century. The Midwest Regional office director, Royce Yeater, challenged the developers to find a better alternative than demolition. At the same time, because the rehabilitation of the Old Post Office again involved federal funding, a Section 106 review was conducted and the case was heard in Washington. There the Advisory Council sought a "compromise." It held that, as part of the mitigation agreement between the developers, the city, the State, and the National Trust, the Century Building could be demolished to ensure the financial feasibility of the project. The National Trust, finding that the city, the state, and the Advisory Council had reached an agreement, rationalized that the restoration of the Old Post Office was paramount. Soon the Trust changed its position and, by January 2002, backed the demolition of the Century and the construction of a parking garage on the site.

St. Louis preservation advocates felt betrayed. Yet, in an even greater affront to those who sought to save the Century, the National Trust decided to provide nearly $7 million in New Market Tax

Credits to the project to close a gap in financing. Although it might be expected that the National Trust would only promote innovative adaptation of existing structures, and spur local officials to act as good stewards of their properties, in fact the organization chose to facilitate demolition.

As over 3500 preservation advocates across the country began signing a petition to protest the National Trust's actions in June 2004, the organization attempted to justify its position more publicly. President Richard Moe released a statement claiming that the demolition of the Century Building for a parking garage was the key to revitalizing the entire downtown area (Moe 2004). While the rationale developed was extensive, preservationists were not convinced. Even when a session was mounted at the Trust's 2005 annual convention in Portland, the majority of those who heard about the case were shocked.

The Trust then issued a 63 page rebuttal, attempting to explain its position yet again.

President Moe said the Trust was only helping to finance the $45 million Old Post Office project. Yet, St. Louis preservationists were expected to overlook their loss and focus on what remained (Prost 2004). The local newspaper seemed to back the project, claiming that "something extraordinary" was taking place with all of the human activity in the blocks around the site, as hard-hats were seen everywhere. Indeed there was. Late at night on October 20, 2004, bulldozers began demolishing the Century Building, sections of which were donated to the St. Louis Building Arts Foundation (SLPD 2004; Fig. 7.14). In its place rose a parking garage, vaguely modeled on the previous structure. By March 2006, the construction crews finished their work on the Old Post Office, and the building was rededicated (Evans 2006).

The Landmarks Association expected that, when it took a stand and asked for help, the National Trust would be a constant and faithful ally. Hanging in the balance was not only the immediate costs and benefits to St. Louis and the surviving historic resources, but also the damage inflicted on preservation activities across the country when a widely recognized national organization, charged with the responsibility of serving as an advocate for historic properties, deliberately changed course and decided to back the opposition. The fact that the National Trust benefited financially as a broker of the New Market Tax Credits only underscored the point and undermined confidence in its purpose. That the general public observed the public dispute and learns that the Trust continues to support high style Victorian architecture over what it claimed was an expendable building only works against broadening the preservation movement. Lastly, the success of the project has by no means been proven to be the economic stimulus to the downtown that was promised.

Whose History Is More Important?

Before the invention of photography, artists held unparalleled sway over the public by producing paintings that captured people, events, and activities. Landscape sized canvasses were common enough for those who could afford them, but panoramic views that stretched to 360 degrees

Fig. 7.14 When the Century Building issue came to the attention of the National Trust leadership in Washington, D.C., however, that organization ultimately allied itself with the developers and not only acceded to the demolition but also financially assisted the project's backers. (Photograph: Michael Allen)

became familiar to the public only in the mid-nineteenth century. Enormous oil-on-canvas works depicting battles and religious scenes provided a three dimensional effect by positioning the viewer in the center of the action, on a platform. Such "cycloramas" often had special buildings constructed to accommodate the viewing public. The "Cyclorama at Gettysburg," originally painted by French artist Paul Philippoteaux in 1883 for a site in Boston, was "restored," and assembled at the battlefield for the 50th anniversary celebration of the Civil War in 1913. Depicting the central battle, "Pickett's Charge," it illustrated the actions of July 1, 2 and 3, 1863 in a 400 ft. long, 50 ft. high panoramic view. It was a remarkable work, relying on contemporary material, photographs, and interviews with survivors for its accuracy. In 1913, however, those who remembered the battlefield site and returned for the celebrations remarked, "Oh, it's all changed," and "Everything is different" (NYT 1913; Huyuk 1962). The landscape had changed to the degree that it was difficult to understand as it had existed in 1863.

Just as the National Park Service had taken on responsibility for the stewardship of the Gettysburg Battlefield, it purchased the painting just after World War II, and stored it. In 1955, anticipating the battlefield's centennial, the agency

Fig. 7.15 The changing interpretation offered by the National Park Service at Gettysburg led to the demolition of architect Richard Neutra's Cyclorama, in March 2013. Built to provide the visitor with an unparalleled vantage point, the modern building was termed an intrusion and an obstacle to the planned battlefield restoration. (Author's photograph)

launched its "Mission 66" program, designed to provide the public with the best possible facilities in "visitor's centers." Most of these structures were designed and planned by National Park Service staff, but prominent architects designed five of the Mission 66 centers. Modern architect Richard Neutra was one of the best-known, chosen to create a structure that would serve several purposes: visitors' services, exhibition space, administrative offices, a lecture venue, an observation platform with "sweeping views," and the new home for Philippoteaux's "Battle of Gettysburg." The Cyclorama painting was prepared for installation by restoring and repairing sections that had deteriorated. In the meantime, the agency also installed in Neutra's new drum-shaped structure the wooden ring to mount the panorama.[20] At the dedication, at which former President Dwight D. Eisenhower spoke, both the public and professional critics immediately recognized the design as a remarkable success (Huyuk 1962; Van Trump 1962).

In the mid 1990s, the National Park Service adopted a policy that called for the restoration and rehabilitation of Ziegler's Grove, located south of the town of Gettysburg and an important part of the battlefield. In 1995 and 1996, the NPS draft development concept discussion and

a request for proposals for a visitor center and museum facilities carefully avoided the mention of the building's demolition, but took the position that the modern structure was an intrusion and an obstacle to the planned restoration. In 1999, however, the agency publically admitted it sought the removal of the Neutra building (Fig. 7.15).

The rationale for demolition hinges on the need to "restore" the landscape so that visitors can better appreciate the setting in which the battle took place. "The only way to protect the historic landscape," argued Civil War historian and Superintendent of the Park John Latschar, "is to remove the building." He added that the Cyclorama building does an inadequate job of protecting the painting, which is designated a National Historic Object. "Nothing in the building has worked, virtually from Day One. Neutra's gizmos never worked", Latschar stated, referring to the original features, including sun-activated aluminum louvers in the front facade, a rooftop waterfall and fountain, and an flexible rostrum, none of which were maintained by the NPS (Hine 1999). Richard W. Segars, the Park's historical architect, corroborated the view that the building never seemed to work properly, and cited the fact that the handicapped access ramp does not meet current standards. And the Gettysburg Park staff gained an ally in Richard Moe, another Civil War historian and President of the National Trust for Historic Preservation. When speaking before

---

[20] Reduced in size, the painting is 359 feet long, 27 feet high, and weighs an estimated 3 tons.

a Senate subcommittee in 1998, Moe remarked "There is no question that serious mistakes were made in the placement and construction of facilities at Gettysburg decades ago," and he urged that the site be returned to its original condition (Hine 1999). In 1999, in a memorandum of agreement between the National Park Service, the Pennsylvania State Historic Preservation Office, and the Advisory Council on Historic Preservation seemed to spell the end for the Cyclorama building. The Council sided with the Park Service's scheme, saying the vast majority of the millions of people who had visited the park since it opened came to see the battlefield and not Neutra's architecture. "There are other Neutra buildings; there is only one Gettysburg Battlefield," the Council wrote, and the Gettysburg NPS staff broke ground on a new building site, a mile away.

However, continued external pressure led the Keeper of the National Register to declare the Cyclorama as eligible for listing for "its exceptional historic and architectural significance," noting it as the work of a master architect and the Center as a rare example of Neutra's government work. The National Park Service staff also recognized the growing need to examine and carefully evaluate Mission 66 properties, convening a Mission 66 Research Work Meeting in Washington, in late May, 2003. It became clear to all present that, not only was there a considerable amount of research already underway, but also a number of state preservation officers were becoming involved in reviewing Mission 66 properties (Allaback 2000). Historian Ethan Carr demonstrated how Mission 66 visitors centers were key to their programmatic layout, which included a deliberate strategy to develop interpretative facilities as close as possible to the viewing areas, quite in opposition to the current thinking.[21]

Despite the growing recognition outside and inside the National Park Service that Mission 66 designs were worthy of saving, the plans to demolish the Cyclorama building proceeded apace. The agency closed the Cyclorama Center on November 22, 2006, and the process of removing and restoring the panorama for installation in the new building continued. As a result, the Recent Past Preservation Network, a nationwide nonprofit organization dedicated to the preservation and understanding of the modern built environment, and Dion Neutra, the architect son of Richard Neutra, sued to stop the demolition. In their view, it was clear that the NPS had not followed the procedures spelled out by the national environmental and historic preservation legislation. The court agreed and asked the agency to conduct a study of alternatives, which it released in 2012. The NPS bureaucracy did not wish to stand down, however, and demolition of the structure began shortly thereafter (Worden 2008; Prudente 2011; Stansbury 2013).

Better Public Education or Historic Preservation?

No one who has ever had the responsibility of raising a child makes a deliberate choice to enroll him or her in a substandard school when a better alternative exists. In fact, the construction of new schools at the periphery of urban areas continues to be one of the most important factors behind sprawl. Yet "smart growth" advocates, sustainability planners, and most members of the preservation community generally ignore the role of school boards in land-use planning. Parents regularly choose their residences to have access to the best available school district, providing a compelling rationale for large school bus systems and athletic facilities in counties, boroughs, and parishes across the United States. In addition to the high standard of the teaching, one of the most important factors in the parents' decision-making is the quality of the school facilities (Varady and Raffel 2010).

The goal of developing the best possible schools lies behind much of the assumed wisdom regarding school construction and reconstruction, the product of decades of thinking that "bigger is better" through centralization. Although this process began in the late nineteenth century in Massachusetts, centralization was accelerated considerably during the Depression as standard

---

[21] Meeting notes from Timothy Davis, NPS Historian, "Mission 66 Research Work", May 28–29, 2003.

design templates were followed to construct enormous "consolidated" school district facilities with gymnasia, auditoriums, laboratories, and cafeterias on mini-college campuses (Gumbert and Spring 1974).[22]

Today, while small, rural schools may provide better teaching and connect their students to their community to enhance existing ethnic or racial ties, they are unable to access the funds needed to build larger, more modern facilities (Swedberg 2000). Several state and federal policies follow the "bigger is better" thinking, without promoting and supporting a more integrative approach using the old along with new elements. For example, the so called "20–60" rule holds: if the cost of renovating an old school totals 60% of the cost of a new facility, no state money can be used to reimburse a school district, while if the repairs to an existing building total more than 20% of the price of replacement, likewise no reimbursement is possible (Pittsburgh 1998). The inevitable solution by the school board is to choose a new site further at the periphery and depend on a fleet of buses to carry students across the metropolitan area. And these policies do nothing to improve the facilities in inner cities, where the needs of students are often the greatest.

School athletic facilities are also affected. For example, a controversy developed over the Memorial Grandstand of the Bainbridge Island High School, built between 1947 and 1951, probably one of the largest structures ever constructed by high school manual training students. This intact timber structure, complete with plaque bearing the names of the Bainbridge Island men who died in World War II, was demolished by the local school board over the objections of the community, despite the fact it had been placed on the state register of historic places. A $350,000 concrete and aluminum stadium now stands on

the site, largely because state education funds were available for new construction, but not for maintenance.[23]

School administrators concerned with policy, the implementation of new programs, budget difficulties, and personnel procedures are unlikely to have the time to consider the impact of schools on land use in their communities. Likewise, the city, town, and county planners, and locally elected representatives, are not likely to become involved with school affairs, although their transportation systems, food services, athletic and health care facilities may be the largest in the immediate area.

One of the most controversial preservation efforts of the early twenty-first century in Los Angeles revolved around the proposal to convert the Ambassador Hotel to school use, a struggle that ended in defeat but at least provided an incentive to change the manner in which educational facilities are regarded (Fig. 7.16). The Ambassador was famous for being one of the first luxury tourist hotels in the country. Opened in 1921, it came to exemplify the glorious nature of the Southern California lifestyle, frequented by notable film and stage stars. Equally important, it was the site of the 1968 assassination of Senator Robert F. Kennedy. Due to the special nature of its architecture and social history, the Los Angeles Conservancy nominated the hotel as a Los Angeles Historic-Cultural Landmark in 1983, but the nomination was never approved by the City Council because of the uncertainty about its future. Sitting on 23.5 acres of land in the Mid-Wilshire Boulevard area, an increasingly congested portion of the city, the question of the Hotel's survival as a hostelry became more acute as visitors to the city went elsewhere. In 1987, the owners announced that the main building would be closing because they were operating at a deficit and were not willing to invest in the improvements that the city code required (LAC 1987).

Fearing that demolition would take place before an alternative plan for the property was developed, the Los Angeles Conservancy again

---

[22] In 1932, 58% of the 245,940 school buildings in the United States were one-room school houses. During the Depression, the Public Works Administration helped to finance 70% of the school construction, with over 6300 classroom building projects, 2100 auditoriums, 1700 gymnasiums, and hundreds of libraries, shops, laboratories, and cafeterias, leading to passage of the 1941 Lanham Act and the 1946 George-Barden Act.

[23] Communication by R. Elfendahl, President, Bainbridge Island Historical Society, to the author, October 22, 1988 and May 14, 1990.

Fig. 7.16 The Ambassador Hotel was famous for being one of the first luxury tourist hotels in the country. Opened in 1921, it came to exemplify the glorious nature of the Southern California lifestyle, frequented by notable film and stage stars. In addition, it was the site of the 1968 assassination of Senator Robert F. Kennedy. (Tom Zimmerman, Historic American Buildings Survey, Library of Congress)

proposed designation and the local chapter of the American Institute of Architects began to consider future uses for the site. Then, in what was termed a "precedent setting agreement," local city councilman Nate Holden proposed an alternative: the Los Angeles Conservancy would not press for landmark designation, while the hotel owners agreed not to demolish the hotel for up to a year while trying to find a preservation-minded buyer. This agreement was endorsed by the City Council in late July (Harris 1987).

However, over 12 months passed and efforts to find an owner who wished to rehabilitate the hotel failed and the property fell into the hands of a bankruptcy judge. In the year that followed, the Los Angeles Unified School District began seriously eyeing the site for new facilities. As a result, in 2001, when a Beverly Hills housing developer offered to pay $15 million more than the LAUSC, Mayor James Hahn joined school district officials to criticize any plan for putting commercial interests ahead of the education of the children of the community. The die was beginning to be cast: the property would be dedicated to educational use (LA Times 2001; Hayaski 2002).

Throughout most of 2003 the plans ranged from razing the hotel to converting the seven-story building into a school complex with splendid new facilities. In some scenarios the hotel's famous Cocoanut Grove nightclub would become an auditorium and the Embassy Ballroom turned into a library (Helfand 2003). In an added twist in the controversy, the widow and children of Senator Robert F. Kennedy made it known that the Los Angeles Unified School District should demolish the Ambassador and replace it with school buildings as a more fitting memorial (Pool 2004). While one community group, calling itself RFK-12, asserted that turning the hotel into a school would be too expensive, requiring demolition, another, named A+ (Ambassador plus), called for saving the majority of the key elements of the property (DiMassa 2003; Merl 2004a).

After years of debate and study, in the fall of 2004, school Superintendent Roy Romer chose a compromise plan costing $318.2 million that called for razing most of the hotel to make way for a 4200 student K-12 complex (Merl 2004b). The Los Angeles Board of Education narrowly voted to back the plan, which saved the Cocoanut Grove nightclub and a coffee shop, and parts of the Embassy Ballroom ceiling, but little else. Dissatisfied, the Los Angeles Conservancy and a group of seven other organizations—including the Art Deco Society, the California Preservation Foundation, and the Korean Culture Center— filed lawsuits contending the School Board had not complied with state environmental quality law (DiMassa 2004).

At the end of July 2005, a Los Angeles County Superior Court judge dismissed the claims of the preservation-minded groups. Instead of appealing that decision, the Conservancy and all of its allies approached school district officials with the idea of setting aside their differences and allowing the District to demolish the Hotel for a new school complex in exchange for a financial contribution to the future preservation of educational facilities in the city. "We will always believe that the Ambassador Hotel represents a tragic missed opportunity," said Conservancy Executive Director Linda Dishman. "But having fought the good fight and lost, we decided to create something lasting." A $4.9 million contribution from the District to a newly established independent nonprofit Historic Schools Investment Fund was supplemented by $100,000 as a "sign of good faith" from the coalition of preservation groups. Going forward, the interest from the $5 million would be spent on meeting rehabilitation and preservation needs in the 50 district school buildings identified as historic in a 2002 Conservancy survey (Rubin 2005; DiMassa 2005).

Could the Ambassador Hotel have served as a meaningful element of the Los Angeles School District's educational facilities? Theoretically, yes, especially if the funding were available to integrate the old and the new. Was the Ambassador "worth" the $4.9 million the School Board paid? Certainly, it was worth far more because of the tangible and intangible values of the property. It is understood, however, that the Conservancy and the other leading community organizations that joined the coalition to create a new vision for the future of the Ambassador Hotel learned immensely about the challenges involved and the benefits of working together to present a united front.[24]

---

[24] Examples abound. In California, the Mendez Fundamental Intermediate School was constructed on a site that shares space with a renovated shopping center parking structure. The Santa Ana residents also benefited from the redevelopment of the site. And in the Central Valley, the Center for Advanced Research and Technology, jointly constructed and operated by Clovis Unified and Fresno Unified in a manufacturing building, serves hundreds of

When Is Encouraging Heritage Tourism Inviting Difficulty?

As discussed in previous chapters, tourism and the outside visitors it attracts is an important source of income for many people involved with historic and archaeological properties. Cultural tourism stimulates the local economy and raises tax revenues, while encouraging the exploration and interpretation of past cultures, directly and indirectly helping the locality. Because tourism is no longer a pastime for the rich, but enjoyed widely by the middle class, the growth in the number of visitors has stimulated governments at all levels to pay closer attention to this industry.

Encouraging some interest in a property on the part of outsiders may be desirable, but too much of a good thing can be destructive. Even beginning to plan to promote tourism at a site affects how it is perceived, well before any advertising begins. Rumor of an anticipated influx of visitors often spurs speculation, which makes land more valuable and the existing improvements on the surrounding properties are reevaluated immediately for their economic potential.

Tourism is an "invisible" industry for not having a single, identifiable workforce or building type. It encompasses transportation, lodging, and various forms of activity and attractions, including visiting religious and civic sites, and entertainment venues. Unfortunately, the motivations for promoting tourism are not often studied or measured. Few historic site managers have the time to study their visitors. Why they visit is often somewhat of a mystery. Few hoteliers know why visitors have chosen their location, or how visitors spend their time while visiting, or the stops they plan to take when leaving. Tour operators may have a better idea of what visitors do, but the information is rarely compiled meaningfully or shared with the host communities.

As travelers explore more regenerated urban cores and more remote destinations, many

---

part-time high school students. These students are also enrolled in comprehensive high schools where they participate in sports and other activities provided by traditional high schools.

government-backed projects to accommodate or attract them are dubbed "economic development." Inevitably, the number of "tourist bubbles" increases, with some of them bound to pop (Urry 1995; Judd and Fainstein 1999; Alsayyad 2001). The critique of what was at first termed the "heritage industry" began in the 1970s in England, when rapidly de-industrializing cities, such as Lancaster, attempted to improve their formerly sooty image by attracting cultural venues such as art galleries, music venues, and publishing businesses (Hewison 1987). For those interested in history, the prospect that these former industrial communities would be transformed by cultural attractions seemed to overlook their past importance and offered a questionable economic future.

In the United States, attempts to attract cultural venues in the coastal cities continued to be successful, although rust belt cities such as Detroit and Buffalo saw comparatively little change. Publicly backed cultural tourism efforts in places such as Lowell, Massachusetts, have been helpful, but not always as positive as might be first portrayed (Norkunas 2002; Stanton 2005). As the number of critiques by anthropologists and advocates has increased, many focusing on the inequity of the financial investments relative to the costs and benefits felt by the local population, the excesses of heritage tourism seem more egregious.

Tourism of any kind affects the location and the people in it. There are environmental effects, physical impacts on properties, and economic and social costs. All need to be carefully considered. In the same way that market studies, environmental impact statements, and social impact statements have been designed to evaluate and mitigate the anticipated results of various projects, tourism impact studies have attempted to forecast difficulties, including the host community's reactions to seasonal visitors (Ap and Crompton 1998).

A large influx of outsiders will place pressures on the environment as land is cleared and spaces filled to accommodate improved roads, bridges, parking areas for busses, cars, and campers, restroom facilities, hotels, restaurants, and other food service. Infrastructure changes may include water and sewer systems, gas and electricity, sidewalks, paths with handicapped accessibility, and require improved safety and medical facilities. Animal life, fauna, and flora are affected by the increasing human presence. In Florida and parts of the coastal south, for example, pressure continues to fill-in swamps to create more "usable" land, damaging the ecosystem, affecting the salinity of water further inland, and degrading animal habitats in the water, air, and on land. With more visitors more goods are imported and more waste is produced, so that the enlarged capacity for food service and trash disposal becomes a major concern.

One important question is whether the site was ever intended to receive large numbers of visitors and whether, today, it can physically withstand them. As thousands of people travel through cultural landscapes, assemble for re-enactments, cross bridges, walk over paths and over thresholds, walk up and down staircases, and explore fragile auxiliary structures, the wear and tear takes its toll. If visitors are permitted to touch objects and finished surfaces, the costs escalate. The fluctuations in temperature and humidity levels make a considerable difference even on collections housed indoors. Physical "improvements" and reconstructions are often made to assist the interpretation, host events, and re-create rituals and dances in order to attract and entertain the visitor (Rothman 1998, 2003). Any of these can cause difficulties. Setting aside the question of how "authentic" the portrayal or interpretation of the property might be, docents, guides, and maintenance personnel are needed to meet the expectations of visitors.

The economic ramifications of tourism are also of major concern. The types of jobs made available and who gets employed has a tremendous effect on the population makeup of the area and the family structure. It may be pleasant to think that cultural tourism provides more secure, better paying jobs than other type of tourism. However, no guarantee exists that this is the case. In New Orleans, for example, of the 16,000 people employed in the tourism industry, the vast majority work at the low end of the wage scale. A major hotel might employ 700 people, but over 90% will earn under $15,000 annually (Greenhouse 1998). While some individuals will find jobs in a new hotel or transportation company, others will create new jobs for themselves. The sale of items by local people can pop up quickly wherever tourists appear; children selling reproductions of ancient artifacts, bead necklaces, or local chilies. In the same way, an entire informal industry can appear with local food service on street corners and in shops, as guides, and offering transportation.

Although heritage tourism can be promoted, it should not be seen as a panacea. Local economies dependent on visitors will be severely affected by natural disasters or human catastrophes. As described in the previous chapter, Hurricane Hugo destroyed millions of dollars of real estate in Puerto Rico and Charleston, crippling their tourist-dependent economies with 140 miles per hour winds in September, 1989. Sixteen years later, Hurricane Katrina crossed southern Florida and moved into southeast Louisiana, causing severe damage to life and property in New Orleans and the Lower Mississippi Basin. In such cases, cultural tourism comes to complete stop as travel is interrupted and accommodations, water, and food are in short supply. Terrorist attacks and local conflicts will also keep tourists away from particular locations for extended periods of time.

The competition for tourist dollars often leads public officials to promote their city in an attempt to gain attention nationally and internationally, and this initiative often affects land use decisions. In the late 1990s, Philadelphia city officials took the position that heritage tourism would be the springboard to spur economic growth, and that more hotel rooms were needed to accommodate more visitors, which would also allow the city to compete for large conventions. The goal of the planning and development staff was to create 2000 new hotel rooms by the year 2000. The business community and the city-wide historic preservation organization backed the initiative. Sensing opportunity, the amount of construction quickly doubled the target number, as several former banks and underutilized office buildings in downtown were adapted. Within a few years, the private sector had added some 6000 hotel rooms to the city. In retrospect, all who were involved in the initiative admitted that the result was difficult, if not impossible, to control and for years after the demand took some time to meet the supply.[25]

Tourism can also have severe social impacts on a community, and historic districts and properties can suffer disproportionately, as residents live with tourists on a daily basis.

For example, Charleston, South Carolina, with its 1785 acre historic district, attracts millions of visitors to its core, filled with reminders of its early colonial history and eighteenth and nineteenth century structures. In a 1999 study in which a random sample of residents in four neighborhoods—South of Broad, Harleton Village, Downtown and Ansonborough—were surveyed, overall the community seemed neutral to the negative side of tourism. Significant differences appeared between neighborhoods, however, because some were more closely tied to and affected by the tourism activities than others (Harrell and Potts 2003).

Despite the belief that responsible tourism can be planned and implemented, not all tourists are likely to act responsibly and purchase suitable tourist products, choose environmentally friendly transportation, or consider the views of the destination communities. Considerably more education and awareness-raising is needed to put words into actions (Budeanu 2007). Any local or traditional activity or use of a location will be affected by visitors. For example, prayers will be interrupted by visitors with flash cameras coming into sacred spaces, churches, synagogues, and temples. The timing of the visitors is, in fact, one of the greatest sources of inconvenience for local residents.

Heritage tourism marketing is designed to create a demand in a particular location. However, if the host population is not receptive to a part of its history, it may be difficult to recognize and interpret. For example, the trauma of an assassination may prove too much for a community to accept the designation of the site as "historically important." As in the case of the Ambassador Hotel, the site of the assassination of Robert Kennedy, the trauma associated with the assassination of Martin Luther King Jr. at the Lorraine Motel in Memphis, and the murder of John F. Kennedy at the Dallas Book Depository seems to have been internalized by the local populations and stymied official recognition. Research conducted in the mid-1980s indicated that, at the time, Memphis

---

[25] Public comments at City Hall by Barbara Kaplan, Philadelphia City Planning Commissioner, October 1, 1999.

Fig. 7.17 The San Francisco Peaks, a volcanic mountain range north of Flagstaff, AZ, are not only 12,000 foot high scenic wonders used for outdoor entertainment, but also sacred to the Indian tribes in the region. (Author's photograph)

and Dallas had no streets, schools, or government buildings named after the hero who had died in their city. However, both cities had named streets, schools, and buildings to recognize heroes assassinated in the other location (Pennebaker 1990; Neumann 2001).

Collective shame and embarrassment are not the only motivating factors for host populations to reject tourism. Minority communities may see the activities of the visitors as actually profaning a site that is considered by some a sacred place. Since 1979, the Hopi Tribe has been fighting the United States Forest Service over its issuance of a special permit that allows a growing resort, the Arizona Snow Bowl, to develop 777 acres of federal land to operate a ski operation outside Tribal lands but within the *Nuvatukya'ovi*, the San Francisco Peaks (Fig. 7.17). The Hopi and seven other tribes consider the mountains sacred and deserving of protection. Although the courts have minimized the effects of the Snow Bowl as representing only 1 % of the Sacred Peaks and found that the skiing facility placed no burden on the practice of religion, the fact that the majority of the visitors are from Phoenix seems to have been an unwritten basis for the decision (Dougherty 2005; Wilson 2008).

The social repercussions often have political dimensions. Governments or private developers that want to relocate groups of people to make way for tourism facilities may find resistance from local residents who fight to retain their land. Transportation, security, waste management facilities, restaurants, and hotels have an effect on population density as people move to areas where employment opportunities are greatest (Milman and Pizam 1988), but the increased allure of tourism-related jobs can draw workers away from other businesses, such as agriculture. Political repercussions result when governments choose to remove "undesirable" activities or types of structures that might be part of the local heritage.

Therefore, while heritage tourism can be helpful to the local economy and might increase the likelihood that a depressed neighborhood can be revitalized, it is important to study the positive and the negative effects, and learn from previous efforts how to ensure that any scheme, if implemented, will cause minimal harm to people and properties.

Urban Regeneration or Displacement? Is Preservation "White Blight"?

Although controversies often arise around the reuse of public property and commercial buildings, housing rehabilitation continues to lie at the center of the historic preservation movement because the majority of people understand the importance of maintaining and improving their

homes. Granted, the majority of housing rehabilitation does not occur in historic districts. The
prospect arises, however, that by preserving and
upgrading old and historic residences, the low-
income residents of an area may be priced out of
the housing market. Regardless of whether there
is any correlation between historic preservation
efforts and what is often termed "gentrification,"
it is worth examining if for no other reason than
the social and political importance of the question.

Confusion often arises when the word gentrification is used as a generic description of neighborhood revitalization, because the meaning has
changed over time. The term was first coined in
1964 to characterize the changes in London's
neighborhoods during the previous decade (Center for Urban Studies 1964). In Great Britain,
the term "gentry" refers to the ruling class or
aristocracy, who often reside in outlying rural
locations. The implication is that outsiders with
more wealth, power, and prestige than the local
residents will purchase homes in the city. In the
United States, the number of gay men and lesbian women who began to move into inner city
neighborhoods in the 1960s was followed by
some working- and middle-class city residents
who relocated and reinvested in locations such
as Brooklyn, Savannah, and Pittsburgh. "Sweat
equity," that is, one's own labor, often went into
these early rehabilitation efforts. With a decrease
in crime, more urban revitalization took place,
some with the assistance of community development block grants as nonprofit organizations
began to work more with banks and local lenders. Most of their effort was dedicated toward increasing neighborhood stabilization and reinvestment (McKinnish et al. 2008).[26]

Early studies pointed to the rapid social and
economic changes in historic neighborhoods by
examining census data. By comparing neighborhoods in Philadelphia, including Society Hill,
from 1950 to 1970, it became clear that the economic and racial profiles changed significantly
in that historic district (Smith 1996). A similar

comparison of neighborhoods in Washington,
D.C., focusing on Georgetown, demonstrated
that the population shifted from nonwhite to almost entirely white, while the median family income increased dramatically; the percentage of
owner-occupied housing units rose markedly at
the expense of the rental stock; and median house
values showed a hefty appreciation. As the oc-
cupational profile in the area changed from blue-
collar workers to managerial and professional,
the poorer, less-educated residents left the historic neighborhoods (Smith and Williams 1986).
In the late 1970s, for example, in the Quaker Hill
district of Newark, Delaware, 20% of the residents were not there one year after being interviewed. Follow-up surveys indicated that a large
share of those moving did so involuntarily because of rising rents, rental units being converted into condominiums, and smaller apartments
being combined into fewer large ones (Barnekov
and Caron 1980).

Some of the reinvestment opportunities that
were marketed to and attracted young, urban
professionals, who enjoyed two incomes, of-
fended long time residents. As tax assessments
rose and the local service industries and restaurants changed to accommodate the new residents, the poor pointed out that "gentrification"
of some areas made them seem like foreigners
in their own city. Increasingly, gentrification became a "dirty word," referring not only to social
changes in housing, but also in commercial and
recreational activities. The new health clubs and
fitness centers attracted to the area seemed to be
one of the final insults.

In Baltimore, for example, the housing improvements in neighborhoods such as Harwood,
Charles Village, Union Square, and Patterson
Park appeared to be displacing the local residents. To counter the fear of displacement, before what was seen as a trickle could become a
flood, a considerable amount of attention was
given to assistance programs that helped working
class families wrest their homes from absentee
property owners and purchase them (Quayle and
Crolius 1978; Goodman and Wiessbrod 1979).
Less attention was paid to the private sector investments made by commercial entrepreneurs, as

---

[26] Community development and neighborhood revitalization were introduced in Chapter 2.

they attempted to appeal to an upscale market. Gentrification became the inevitable result of efforts by developers who wished to convert empty, former industrial buildings in the Baltimore Harbor to higher income housing, sometimes using the historic rehabilitation tax credits to help with financing (Pietila 2004). Although it could be argued that no one was being displaced in these industrial zones, the media often reported an overly simplified story of displacement, and the problems with perceptions continued (Baltimore 1994; Hopkins 2006).

By the 1980s, with an increasing number of studies centering on the social effects of housing improvements, the results became clearer but more complex. The evidence showed that gentrification had taken place in some neighborhoods in San Francisco and Boston. For all the marketing and popular press, however, when compared to all the work being done in urban neighborhoods, the substitution of one class of resident for another was relatively minor, very uneven, and most of it due to inner city relocation common in most similar locations (Palen and London 1984). Case studies continued to demonstrate that the central city newcomers were often not dissatisfied suburbanites who were throwing off their commuter lifestyles for a return to the excitement and culture of city life. Many who relocated in the city were simply people who were improving their home neighborhood, or one nearby, some returning from stints in school or from living in other towns in the region. For example, observations in East Boston indicated that second and third generation residents living in inherited houses, upgraded them with the intent of remaining in the neighborhood. The elderly have often moved within a city as they grew older in anticipation of becoming more dependent on others. In short, the picture of revitalization was a much more complex kaleidoscope than anyone had imagined, while many areas of the inner city continued to suffer disinvestment and the urban improvements did not stem the tide toward investing in the suburbs.

While the number of historic districts being nominated slowed during the 1990s, the discussion of gentrification and dislocation increased, particularly in locations like Harlem, fast losing its former identity as an African American enclave in the face of development pressure. The planned eighteen acre expansion of Columbia University into West Harlem is but one example of luxury housing replacing lower income residents (Bailey 2008), while the planned historic district designation remained on hold since the mid-1990s. Overall, the most current, refined data from the 1990 and 2000 Census provided new evidence that, while the in-migration of relatively young, white college graduates without children was a prominent characteristic of "gentrification," there is not a disproportionate exit of less well educated or minority residents. Instead, gentrifying neighborhoods seems to retain its black high school graduates (McKinnish et al. 2008).[27] In addition, in parts of the country where whites are already in a majority, the economic reinvestment is spurred by Asians and other groups that wish to invest in their new neighborhoods.[28]

Claims that historic district designation might precipitate displacement continue to surface, but some of these arise due to lack of communication on the part of those spearheading the survey and nomination process. Preservation advocates who fail to become involved in neighborhood concerns and work with the community will allow others to frustrate the nomination process. One such instance took place in Brookland, an area of about 500 acres in the northeast quadrant of Washington, D.C., east of Catholic University (Barton 2009; Fig. 7.18). Named for Col. Jehiel Brooks, the area was rapidly subdivided in the last decades of the nineteenth century, and developed into subdivisions of modest one and two story bungalows and cottages shortly thereafter. Always principally a working class community, by the early 1930s the neighborhoods in Brookland began to attract African-American residents, many of whom worked for the federal

---

[27] Research confirms the premise that gentrification is a residential phenomenon, not a commercial one.

[28] Asian investments in cities throughout the country have led to dozens of enclaves. The rise and fall of Chinatowns in the United States has been well studied (Kwong and Miscevic 2005).

Fig. 7.18 Named for Col. Jehiel Brooks, "Brookland" is composed of working class subdivisions of modest one and two story bungalows and cottages in Northeast Washington, D.C., home to many African-Americans who worked for the federal government. (Photograph: Thomas Richmond)

government. When threatened by the development of the Metro transportation system, and again by the proposed North Central Freeway, the residents organized to halt the planning process, proving themselves responsible and efficient citizens. The fact that over 75% of the residents are homeowners, and that many are well-educated professionals made a difference. In the late 1990s, when the future of the Brooks Mansion was in question, it was no surprise to see widespread support. Studies had shown that the special character of the area was worthy of local designation, and in 2000 preservation advocates planned to embrace representatives of local community organizations. However, despite the volunteer time spent surveying and the assistance of professionals and the staff of the State Historic Preservation Office, opposition developed by those uninvolved with the designation late in the process, claiming it would lead to gentrification and property speculation. The opposition, making use of hundreds of listserv postings and anonymous posters, effectively raised fears that the advocates found impossible to overcome, sidelining the nomination process.

It is important to place the foregoing comments in perspective. Most applications of historic preservation are thoughtful, and those involved in historic property designations must meet legitimate concerns to protect a community's historic resources. Yet, it is also important to keep in mind that community involvement and diversity is essential so that, whether the claims

of gentrification are real or imaginary, they can be overcome during the public discourse. Dissent serves as an important reminder that people of all income levels are needed for a vibrant community, and all activities and lifestyles need to be incorporated into historic preservation activities (Lees et al. 2008).

Conclusion

Over the course of the last several decades, preservationists continued to expand the scope of their interest, largely at the behest of people who believe their lives are being threatened by sudden change. Frequently these changes are proposed by decision-makers in government, individuals who have made assumptions about what is the best interest of everyone. Just as often, little communication takes place beforehand to explain why change is necessary. Little explanation is provided about what their role might be in the process, or how they will be affected. As a result, decisions are made based on social norms that are imperfectly understood.

For those working at the local level the need to integrate preservation in every aspect of decision-making has been evident for decades. It is clear that to be successful the first principles should be listening to and learning about the social values of the immediate community. Measuring them is important. As John Costonis stated, only by capturing a sense of community values is it possible to defend them successfully. The trend in land use planning and zoning is to lump together the need for sustainability, affordable housing, efficient transportation, and handicapped accessibility. All are legitimate concerns to be weighed as community interests, but they stand alongside the need for historical sensitivity and the respect for social coherence that underlies continued use.

Assuming that those representing the preservation community can agree on the basic need to speak coherently, with one voice, on behalf of those who feel threatened by change, the nature of future activities may be changed for the better. Failing to deal with differences, bringing to light a thoughtful solution, is likely to result the loss of both the constituency that is willing to support preservation activities and the demolition of the historic resource. Differences between preservation organizations, particularly when one stands to gain financially by the demolition of an historic property, are particularly disastrous.

If we learn anything from our mistakes, it should be apparent that nothing should be taken for granted. What is possible in one community often is not viable, or even desirable, in another. It is also clear that what is socially acceptable for the majority in the United States will sometimes overpower the views of the minority. An Indian tribe or ethnic enclave will often hold a different set of values and cultural norms that may be difficult to understand, much less accommodate. Negotiation that fails to recognize these broader ethical constructs is more than likely to lead to failure. This indicates that, looking ahead, as the country becomes more diverse the need for cross-cultural study is more of a necessity.

References

Allaback, S. (2000). *Mission 66 visitor Centers: The history of a building type*. Washington, DC: Government Printing Office.

Alsayyad, N. (Ed.). (2001). *Consuming tradition, manufacturing heritage*. New York: Routledge.

Alweiss, M. (Oct 2010). Preservation salvage store adds extended outdoor sales area. *Preservation in Print, 37*(7), 19.

Ames, W. (Oct 1964). Queen Anne vs. Eastlake. *Journal of the Society of Architectural Historians, 23*(3), 155.

Ap, J., & Crompton, J. L. (1998). Developing and testing a tourism impact scale. *Journal of Tourism Research, 37*(2), 120–130.

AR. (Sept 1985). To preserve and protect an architectural legacy. *Architectural Record, 173*(10), 53.

Bailey, N. (13–18 Nov 2008). Activists call for mobilization to halt displacement. *New York Amsterdam News*, 13.

Baker, D. (1983). *Living with the past: The historic environment* (p. 49). Bletsoe: David Baker.

Baltimore. (26 April 1994). Editorial. Accelerating change in Pigtown. *Baltimore Sun*, 10A.

Barnekov, T. K., & Caron, J. (1980). *Quaker Hill: Reinvestment displacement in an historic district*. Newark: College of Urban Affairs and Public Policy, University of Delaware.

Barron, J. (8 Nov 2003). Groups Sue to prevent sale of Columbus circle building. *The New York Times*.

Barton, C. L. (2009). *Brookland: A case study in historic district planning*. Master of Arts thesis, Program in Historic Preservation Planning, Cornell University, Ithaca.

Berke, A. (April 1984). Milwaukee Brouhaha? *Preservation News, 27*(4), 1, 10.

Berke, A. (July/Aug 1992). The endangered list: Our National advertisement. *Preservation News, 32*(7–8), 6.

Bevitt, E. (Ed.). (1993a). Architectural study collections: Material worthy of a second life. *CRM Bulletin, 16*(8), 1–28.

Bevitt, E. (Ed.). (1993b). Second lives: The survey and use of architectural study collections in the United States. Washington, DC: National Park Service, Preservation Assistance Division.

Blake, P. (1980). *The architecture of courtesy. Old & new architecture* (pp. 92–93). Washington, DC: National Trust for Historic Preservation.

Blum, J. (1 March 1998). In Loudoun, class of views Amid the Hills. *Washington Post*, B1.

Bonnette, S., Gallas, W., & LeBreton, A. (Oct 2006). Preservationists explore deconstruction as last alternative to demolition. *Preservation in Print, 30*(8), 24.

Bonvillian, N. (2011). *Language, culture and communication*. Upper Saddle River: Pearson Prentice Hall.

Brown, B. (23 Nov 1979). Battlelines drawn to save 53 state street. *Boston Ledger*.

Budeanu, A. (3 Aug (2007). Sustainable tourist behavior: A discussion of opportunities for change. *The International Institute for Industrial Environmental Economics, 31*(5), 499–508.

Bumbaru, D. (Oct/Dec 1989). Le Facadisme: Le Decor A L'Envers! OU Less is Decor! *ICOMOS Information*, 4, 11–18. (English translation provided to the author by Bumbaru).

Bunnell, G. (2002). *Making places special: Stories of real places made better by planning*. Chicago: Planners Press, American Planning Association.

Callan, B. Jr. (Dec 1981). Item. *Preservation News, 21*(12), 16.

Campbell, R. (21 Dec 1980). Blending the old and new. *Boston Globe*, B3.

Carson, R. (1962). *Silent spring*. Boston: Houghton Mifflin.

Center for Urban Studies (Ed.), Glass, R., et al. (1964). *London: Aspects of change*. London: MacGibbon & Kee.

Cheever, B. (27 Aug 1998). Close to home. *The New York Times*.

CJLT. (26 Dec 1976). Louisville's 'New' museum. *Courier-Journal and Louisville Times Magazine*, 4–5.

Claiborne, W. (28 Nov 1998). U.S., Indians fight over role in protecting sacred sites. *Washington Post*, A2.

Cobb, H. I. Jr. (Feb 1930). 1803 Facade moved as a unit becoming Central Motif of Modern Bank building in Albany, N.Y. *American Architect, 137*(2580), 60–61, 84.

Colby, J. P. (1972). *Building wrecking*. New York: Hastings.

Costonis, J. J. (1989). *Icons and Aliens: Law, aesthetics, and environmental change* (pp. 11, 61). Urbana: University of Illinois Press.

CPDR. (2006). Los Angeles Conservancy's Linda Dishman. *California Planning & Development Report, 21*(2), 1–2.

Crimmins, T. J. (Summer 1990). NAPC: A brief history. *Alliance Review*, 4–5.

DC Tribune. (3 May 1982). Out like a lion. *Washington Tribune*, 1.

DiMassa, C. M. (21 Nov 2003). Los Angeles Group opposes bid to preserve Ambassador Hotel; neighborhood organization calls for a New Building, saying that conversion into a School would be too costly and take too long. *Los Angeles Times*, B3.

DiMassa, C. M. (24 Nov 2004). Lawsuits filed to prevent razing of Ambassador. *Los Angeles Times*, B4.

DiMassa, C. M. (2 April 2005). Ambassador Hotel is spared as suit goes on. *Los Angeles Times*, B3.

Dougherty, J. (31 March 2005). Sacred hypocrisy. *Phoenix New Times*.

Duany, A., & Plater-Zyberk, E. (Winter 1992). The second coming of the American small town. *Wilson Quarterly, 16*(1), 19–49.

Duffy, R. (31 Oct 2004). Century building dies a senseless death downtown. *St. Louis Post-Dispatch*, B01.

DuJardin, R. C. (14 Aug 1997). Luxury Hotel chosen for Masonic Temple. *Providence Journal-Bulletin*.

Dunlap, D. W. (21 June 2002). 2 Columbus Circle will be a museum again. *The New York Times*.

Dunlap, D. W. (23 May 2003). Blocks; Fate of 2 Columbus Circle is hidden behind Marble Walls. *The New York Times*.

Dunlap, D. W. (18 Aug 2005). For 2 Columbus Circle, a growing fan club. *The New York Times*.

Evans, T. (16 March 2006). Old Post Office is new again. *St. Louis Post-Dispatch*, C01.

Feilden, B. (1982). *Conservation of historic buildings* (p. 5). London: Butterworths.

Findley, J. M. (1993). *Magic lands*. Berkeley: University of California Press.

Fitch, J. M. (1982). *Historic preservation: Curatorial management of the built world* (pp. 158–159). New York: McGraw-Hill.

Fleming, R. (1982). *Facade stories. Changing faces of main Street Storefronts and how to care for them*. Cambridge: The Townscape Institute, Inc., Hasting.

Forgey, B. (4 Sept 1982). New after old. *Washington Post*, D1, D6.

Freeman, A. (Dec (1988). Linear complex strung along a downtown Minneapolis Mall. *Architecture, 77*(12), 96–97.

Gans, H. (1967). *The Levitowners*. London: Allen Lane.

Gans, H. (1991). *People, plans and policies: Essays on poverty, racism, and other National problems* (p. 140). New York: Columbia University Press.

Gardner, J. (25 Sept 2008). Bring back the Venetian Lollipops. *New York Sun*.

Glass, J. A. (1987). *Interview with Nellie L. Longsworth. Guide to the National historic preservation Program, Oral Histories, 1986–1987*. Ithaca: Cornell University Archives.

Globe. (19 Nov 1979). A classic battle at 53 State. *Boston Globe*, 12.

Gluek, G. (16 July 1969). Huntington Hartford's museum is given to Fairleigh Dickinson. *The New York Times*, 1, 42.

Goldberger, P. (15 July 1985). Facadism on the rise: Preservation or illusion? *The New York Times*, B1, B3.

Goldberger, P. (19 June 1988). Architecture view; why Columbus Circle should go back to square one. *The New York Times*.

Goodman, A. C., & Wiessbrod, R. (1979). *Housing market activity in South Baltimore: Immigration, speculation and displacement*. Baltimore: The Johns Hopkins University Center for Metropolitan Planning and Research.

Gossling, D. (1976). *Design and planning of retail systems*. New York: Whitney Library of Design.

Greenhouse, S. (18 Aug 1998). Labor eyes a prize: Hotels of New Orleans. *The New York Times*.

Gumbert, E. B., & Spring, J. H. (1974). *The Superschool and the Superstate: American education in the twentieth century, 1918–1970*. New York: Wiley.

Harrell, R., & Potts, T. D. (Summer 2003). Tourism planning in historic districts. Attitudes toward tourism development in Charleston. *Journal of the American Planning Association, 69*(3), 233–244.

Harries, S. (2011). *Nikolaus Pevsner. The life* (p. 492). London: Chatto & Windus.

Harris, S. (1 Aug 1987). Council supports private effort to save Ambassador. *Los Angeles Times*, 1.

Hayaski, E. (27 Jan 2002). Learning what the public wants at Ambassador land use. *Los Angeles Times*, B3.

Helfand, D. (17 June 2003). L.A. unified unveils 5 plans for Ambassador site. Historic hotel property is to house up to three schools. Public will have 60 days to review. *Los Angeles Times*, B3.

Hewison, R. (1987). *The heritage industry: Britain in a climate of decline*. London: Methuen.

Hine, T. (21 Feb 1999). Art/architecture; which of all the pasts to preserve. *Philadelphia Inquirer*.

Hofstede, G. H. (1983). The cultural relativity of organizational practices and theories. *Journal of International Business Studies, 14*(2), 75–89.

Hofstede, G. H. (1991). *Culture and organizations: Software of the mind*. London: McGraw-Hill.

Hopkins, J. S. (25 July 2006). Gap gives city its chance; forces now favor growth, but major challenges persist. *Baltimore Sun*, A1.

Horwitz, E. L. (1982). *How to wreck a building*. New York: Pantheon.

Hudnut, I. I. I., & W., H. (2004). *Halfway to everywhere. A portrait of America's first tier suburbs*. Washington, DC: Urban Land Institute.

Humstone, M. (2001). *Threatened treasures: Creating lists of endangered historic places*. Washington, DC: National Trust for Historic Preservation.

Huxtable, A. L. (25 Feb 1964). Architecture: Huntington Hartford's Palatial Midtown museum. *The New York Times*, 33.

Huxtable, A. L. (10 Dec 2008). Setting the record straight about Ed Stone and Brad Cloepfil. *Wall Street Journal*.

Huyuk, D. B. (6 May 1962). Gettysburg's gain. New $1 million visitor center to give tourists clearer picture of battle. *The New York Times*.

Inglehart, R., & Baker, W. E. (2000). Modernization, cultural change, and the persistence of traditional values. *American Sociological Review, 65*, 19–51.

Judd, D. R., & Fainstein, S. S. (Eds.). (1999). *The tourism city*. New Haven: Yale University Press.

Kamin, B. (25 Feb 1989). Tribune, Landmark panel agree. *Chicago Tribune*, 2C.

Kelly, B. (1993). *Expanding the American dream*. Albany: The State University Press.

Knight, D. (19 Oct 1997). Make way for McMansions. *Boston Globe*.

Kruse, K., & Sugrue, T. (2010). *The new suburban history*. Chicago: University of Chicago Press.

Kwong, P., & Miscevic, D. (2005). *Chinese America*. New York: The New Press.

LA Times. (29 Nov 2001). Editorial. The schools gain ground. *Los Angeles Times*, B14.

LAC. (Jul–Aug 1987). Ambassador hotel. *Los Angeles Conservancy Newsletter, 9*(4), 11.

Lebovich, W. (15 May 1989). Developers, activists find common ground. *Legal Times*, S15, S19.

Lees, L., Slater, T., & Wyly, E. (2008). *Gentrification*. New York: Routledge/Taylor & Francis Group.

Li, W. (2009). *Ethnoburb. The New Ethnic Community in Urban America*. Honolulu: University of Hawaii Press.

Longstreth, R. W. (1998). *History on the line: Testimony in the cause of preservation*. Ithaca: National Council for Preservation Education.

LPCI. (Jan–Feb 1989). Partial designation returns to Chicago. *Landmarks Preservation Council of Illinois, 10*(1), 1.

Lucy, W. H., & Philips, D. L. (2000). *Confronting suburban decline. Strategic planning for Metropolitan renewal*. Washington, DC: Island Press.

Malone, C., & Cassity, P. (1994). *The United States preservation commission identification project*. Athens: National Alliance of Preservation Commissions.

McGrew, A. (2008). *Repurposing the suburban McMansion*. Master of Arts thesis, Florida State University, Florida.

McGuigan, C. (27 Oct 2003). The McMansion next door. *Newsweek*.

McGuire, J. (27 July 1985). Letters. Adrift, confused and without scale. *The New York Times*, A22.

McKinnish, T., Walsh, R., & White, K. (2008). *Who gentrifies low-income neighborhoods* (pp. 2–3). Cambridge: National Bureau of Economic Research.

Merl, J. (2 April 2004a). The group offers the L.A. School District alternatives to razing. *Los Angeles Times*, B3.

Merl, J. (1 Oct 2004b). Kennedys call for knocking down the Ambassador hotel. *Los Angeles Times*, B1.

Miller, P. P., & Longsworth, N. (Winter 2001). Nellie Longsworth: Champion for historic preservation. *Public Historian, 23*(1), 9–26.

Milman, A., & Pizam, A. (1988). Social impacts of tourism on Central Florida. *Annals of Tourism Research, 15*(2), 191–204.

Mitchell, E. B., & Giurgola, R. (1983). *Mitchell/Giurgola Architects* (pp. 76–79). New York: Rizzoli International Publications.

Moe, R. (14 July 2004). Saving landmark buildings can require tough trade-offs. *St. Louis Post-Dispatch*, B07.

Moe, R., & Wilkie, C. (1997). *Changing places: Rebuilding community in the age of Sprawl*. New York: Henry Holt & Co.

Morton, D. (May 1978). Industrial aesthetics. *Progressive Architecture, 59*, 82–85.

Morton, D. (Nov 1981). The best of both worlds? *Progressive Architecture, 62*(11), 29, 96–101.

Murdock, G. P. (1961). The cross-cultural survey. In F. W. Moore (Ed.), *Readings in cross-cultural methodology* (pp. 45–54). New Haven: HRAF Press.

Musante, F. (15 Nov 1998). Can big houses be too big? *The New York Times*.

Nasar, J. L., Evans-Cowley, J., & Mantero, V. (Oct 2007). McMansions: The extent and regulation of super-sized houses. *Journal of Urban Design, 12*(3), 339–358.

Neumann, T. (2001). *Preservation of assassination sites: Interpreting Trauma in Dallas and Memphis*. Master of Arts thesis, Program in Historic Preservation Planning, Cornell University, Ithaca.

Norkunas, M. (2002). *Monuments and memory: History and representation in Lowell, Massachusetts*. Washington, DC: Smithsonian Institution Press.

NYT. (4 July 1913). Pickett's charge fifty years after. *The New York Times*.

NYT. (2 April 1964a). 4,719 at modern gallery set attendance record. *The New York Times*.

NYT. (11 Nov 1964b). First meeting held. *The New York Times*.

NYT. (25 July 1985). Letters. Hiding New York's tomorrow behind the facade of yesterday. *The New York Times*, A22.

NYT. (29 July 1998). New hope for Columbus circle. *The New York Times*.

Ott, T. (23 Aug 2006). Cuyahoga to offer cities house renovation Loans; Shaker heights to borrow $250,000. *Cleveland Plain Dealer*, B4.

Ott, T., & O'Malley, M. (24 Aug 2007). Housing downturn hits suburbs just as hard; Foreclosures jump outside Cleveland. *Cleveland Plain Dealer*, A1.

Palen, J. J., & London, B. (1984). *Gentrification, displacement, and neighborhood revitalization*. Albany: State University of New York Press.

Parshall, G. (30 Dec 1996). Buzzwords. *U.S. News & World Report, 121*(26), 80.

Paskin, W. (8 Dec 2004). Gotham will take a page out of history. *The New York Times*.

Paulsen, S. E. (30 July 2005). The black hole of Columbus Circle. *The New York Times*.

Pennebaker, J. W. (1990). *Opening up: The healing power of confiding in others*. New York: William Morrow.

Perlman, E. (April 1998). The McMansion Moratorium. *Governing, 11*(7), 16.

Pietila, A. (19 July 2004). Mill development divides Woodbury. *Baltimore Sun*, 1A.

Pittsburgh. (30 June 1998). Editorial. Preservation lesson: Make it easier to remodel and reuse old school buildings. *Pittsburgh Post-Gazette*.

Pledger, D. M. (1977). *A complete guide to demolition*. Lancaster: Construction Press.

PN. (Oct 1969). State Liaison officers vote to create National Council. *Preservation News, 9*(10), 6.

PN. (April 1982). Commissions form National alliance. *Preservation News, 22*(4), 8.

PN. (Aug 1983). Saving facades only is not preservation. *Preservation News, 24*(8), 4.

PN. (Sept 1988). The Endangered Eleven: Landmarks near the edge. *Preservation News, 28*(9), 3.

Pool, B. (9 Oct 2004). A clash of two passionate forces. *Los Angeles Times*, B1.

Pristus, T. (2 March 2005). Shopping malls adopting new strategies to survive. *The New York Times*.

Prost, C. (14 Oct 2004). Renovation of 120-year old landmark will get underway. *St. Louis Post-Dispatch*, B01.

Prudente, T. (10 Dec 2011). End near for controversial cyclorama? *Evening Sun*.

Quayle, V. P., & Crolius, J. T. (March 1978). Is preservation bad for the poor. *Preservation News, 18*(3), 12.

Robin, P. (1990). *Saving the neighborhood*. Rockville: Woodbine House.

Root, E. W. (1929). *Philip Hooker. A contribution to the study of the renaissance in America* (pp. 85–94, Figs. 30, 44–47). New York: Charles Scribner's Sons.

Rothman, H. (1998). *Devil's Bargain, tourism in the twentieth-century West*. Lawrence: University Press of Kansas.

Rothman, H. (Ed.). (2003). *Culture of tourism, the tourism of culture. Selling the past to the present in the American Southwest*. Albuquerque: University of New Mexico Press.

Rubin, J. (30 Aug 2005). Deal Struck to Raze Ambassador Hotel. L.A. Conservancy Gives Up Its Bid to Save Historic Structure. *Los Angeles Times*, B1.

Saffron, I. (23 Nov 2013). Changing Skyline: Theater owners seeking to gut their historical landmarks. *Philadelphia Inquirer*.

SAH. (15 Nov 1986). Press release. *The SAH Award for Excellence in Published Architectural Surveys*. Society of Architectural Historians.

Salant, K. (2 Oct 1999). Goodness gracious, that's awfully spacious! *Washington Post*, G11.

Schmickle, W. E. (2007). *The politics of historic districts*. Lanham: Alta Mira Press.

Schwartz, T. (2002). First suburbs renewing housing, preserving neighborhoods. *CUDC Quarterly, 2*(3–4), Fall.

Shopsin, W. C., & Broderick, M. G. (1980). *The Villard houses. Life story of a landmark*. New York: Viking Press.

Sloane, D. C., & Sloane, B. C. (2003). *Medicine moves to the mall*. Baltimore: Johns Hopkins University Press (in association with the Center for American Places, Santa Fe, NM and Harrisonburg, VA)

SLPD. (23 Oct 2004). Demolition begins. *St. Louis Post-Dispatch*, 14.

Smith, M. A. (Sept 1980). Revitalizing main street: Museum of natural history and science, Louisville, Kentucky. *Museum News*, 59, 58–61.

Smith, C. R. (March/April 1981). Palace intrigues. *Historic Preservation*, 54–58.

Smith, N. (1996). *The new urban frontier: Gentrification and the Revanchist City* (pp. 119–139). London: Routledge.

Smith, G. (30 April 1997). Almond invites ideas for Masonic temple. *Providence Journal-Bulletin*.

Smith, G. (28 Oct 1998). New plan for Masonic temple: A '4-Star' Marriott renaissance. *Providence Journal-Bulletin*.

Smith, N., & Williams, P. (Eds.). (1986). *Gentrification of the city*. Boston: Allen & Unwin.

Stabiner, K. (21 Jan 2011). New lives for 'dead' shopping malls. *The New York Times*.

Stansbury, A. (10 Jan 2013). Locals have mixed opinions about Cyclorama Demolition. *Evening Sun*.

Stanton, C. (Dec 2005). Serving up culture: Heritage and its discontents at an industrial history site. *International Journal of Heritage Studies, 11*(5), 415–431.

Stevens, M. (30 Sept 1985). Putting on a good face. *Newsweek, 106*(76–77).

Striner, R. (1995). Historic preservation and the challenge of ethical coherence. In M. A. Tomlan (Ed.), *Ethics in preservation: Lectures presented at the annual meeting of the National Council for preservation education, Indianapolis, Indiana, Oct 23, 1993*. Ithaca: National Council for Preservation Education.

Swallow, W. (18 Oct 1986). Historic fronts preserved with more finesse. *Washington Post*, E1, E10.

Swedberg, D. (2000). Maintaining respect for the past and flexibility for the future: Additions and renovations as an integrated sequence. In S. Dewees & P. Cahape

(Eds.), *Improving rural school facilities: Design, construction, finance and public support*. Charleston: AEL.

Szold, T. S. (Spring 2005). Mansionization and its discontents. *Journal of the American Planning Association, 7*(2), 189–202.

Tomlan, M. A. (1992). Preservation practice comes of age: Recent trends in the movement. In A. J. Lee (Ed.), *Past meets future: Saving America's historic environments*. Washington, DC: Preservation Press.

Tomlan, M. A. (Sept 2001). James Marston Fitch (8 May 1909–10 Dec 2000). *Journal of the Society of Architectural Historians, 60*(3), 381–382.

Tribune. (26 May 1985). New 37-Story Office Tower preserves its historic Façade. *Chicago Tribune*, C1.

Tribune. (29 Aug 2010). Americans close the door on the McMansion Era. *Chicago Tribune*, 7.

Tribune. (20 June 2011). United airlines bringing 1300 jobs to Chicago. *Chicago Tribune*.

Trombley, S. (Oct 1985). Stifling history. *History Today, 35*, 3–5.

Urry, J. (1995). *Consuming places*. New York: Routledge.

Van Trump, J. D. (1962). Circular history: The visitor center and Cyclorama at Gettysburg, Pa. *Charette, 42*(10), 223.

Varady, D. P., & Raffel, J. A. (2010). *Selling cities: Attracting homebuyers through schools and housing programs*. Albany: State University of New York Press.

Walcott, R. (Nov 1936). Facadism. *Architectural Record, 80*(5), 385–389.

Warren, E., & Armour, T. (15 July 2001). Preservationists build hope despite Winnetka Teardown. *Chicago Tribune*, 2.

Warren, R. B., & Warren, D. I. (1977). *The neighborhood organizer's handbook*. Notre Dame: University of Notre Dame Press.

Webster, R. J. (1981). *Philadelphia preserved. Catalog of the historic American Buildings survey* (p. 88). Philadelphia: Temple University Press.

Weinberg, P. J. (March 2001). Monster homes: How big a house is too much? *Zoning and Planning Law Report, 24*(3), 17–22.

Wilson, S. J. (12 Aug 2008). Forest service, Snowbowl Win. *Navajo Hopi Observer*.

Wolfe, T. (13 Oct 2003). The building that isn't there, con't. *The New York Times*.

Wood, E. J. S. (1987). *Historic preservation in American communities. Appendix* (p. 9). Washington, DC: National Trust for Historic Preservation.

Worden, A. (4 Nov 2008). Temporary reprieve for Gettysburg building. *Philadelphia Inquirer*.

WSJ. (18 Jan 1984). Builders' mix of old and new angers some preservationists. *Wall Street Journal*, 31.

WSJ. (3 May 2011). One expensive Bankruptcy case. *Wall Street Journal*.

Introduction

Almost every community in the world recognizes religious sites and properties as being critically important to its people. The meetinghouses, churches, mosques, synagogues, temples, worship sites, and faith-based properties are immediately recognized as important to a country's social, economic, and religious history. They are also important because they connect people who share beliefs and ideas to other people, crossing state and national boundaries. These sites are distributed throughout the country, in urban, suburban, and rural settings, some in very remote locations. Open spaces and landscapes often have sacred meaning as well. In the United States, an Indian tribe may consider a mountain or stream significant, a Mormon group could hold a grove sacred, or a Roman Catholic parish can find an open parking lot used for outdoor "drive-in" services a very special church. These faith-based places provide anchors in overlapping social networks and meeting places of special merit. At the same time, owing in part to mass media and personal communication, centers of religious thought and practice have the ability to reach individuals at home, anywhere.

The discussion of the role that religion plays in civic affairs is often controversial, polarizing political discussions, social views, and economic decisions, all of which influence how a property is treated. Under the First Amendment to the US Constitution, often interpreted as the "separation of church and state," many Americans prefer to ignore the presence and impact of almost all religions, even their own. Influenced by the Protestant Reformation, the country's Founders insisted on religious freedom, outlawing an established religion so that citizens could practice any religion, or none, as they chose. This founding principle has resulted in a pluralistic society that practices many religions and holds many different beliefs, but many choose not to discuss religion and few people have a clear idea how many aspects of society are affected by it.

How can a country that has such a rich set of traditions, with a amazing range of historic faith-based sites, and such a vibrant religious life, put at arm's length the public recognition of so much of what characterizes the life of its people? Certainly the contributions the various religions are worthy of recognition. In addition, if we acknowledge that the country has a bias toward Protestant Christianity, what are the implications for the care of properties not only of those traditions but also for those of different religious views and ethical values?

The answers lie in our history and our current thinking. Whether or not religious properties are officially designated as historic or architecturally significant, or as possessing archaeological importance, or as sites of notable events, if preservation is a social campaign that seeks to guide the recognition and treatment of properties important to our society, the role of religion in preservation and revitalization cannot be ignored. Support for the preservation of religious structures and landscapes should not simply stem from an interest

M. A. Tomlan, *Historic Preservation,* DOI 10.1007/978-3-319-04975-5_8,
© Springer International Publishing Switzerland 2015

in their historical, artistic, architectural, or physical characteristics. It must include the broader program of the religious organization that is the steward of the property and the approach must respect the viewpoints of all those who are involved.

In order to have a complete picture, preservationists must attempt to understand the rituals and practices of religions other than their own. This chapter attempts to expand historic preservation in this underdeveloped arena by providing historical background about the predominant religious currents in our country. To be able to appreciate the special nature of these places—their uses and changes over time—this chapter reviews the way in which the changes in belief and practice affected the physical layout of the grounds and buildings. The discussion continues, reviewing the extent to which the religious unit is growing or shrinking in size, and how this affects the approaches that might be used to extend their legacies. As will become evident, inside and outside of religious denominations, remarkable preservation partnerships are being forged in ways that almost defy programmatic definition (Drinan 2004).[1]

Religion's Role in Social Revitalization

To begin to understand religion as a positive force for revitalization, it is important to put aside thoughts or feelings relative to the great harm has been done to people, groups, and communities in the name of religion. That said, if religion is defined as a social system in which participants profess a belief in a supernatural being whose approval is often sought to guide individual and collective behavior, it becomes possible to distinguish these broader beliefs from those that are held personally, which often lie behind the problems with any faith (Dennett 2006, pp. 9–11). This is important because,

regardless of whether an individual holds that religion should have more, or less, influence in public affairs, if the preservationist wishes to understand and become involved with religion's powerful regenerative ability, he or she must enter, explore, and become familiar with how faith-based societies are organized. These social groups may, at first, seem foreign.[2] However, rather than take the position that religion is too difficult to understand, the preservationist must study and evaluate the alternatives that faith presents.

For millions of individuals, a significant portion of their time and energy are dedicated to some sort of religious activity: rituals such as daily prayer and regular attendance at ceremonies punctuate the calendar. These activities are often a sacrifice, if only because they demand time. They also often require supporting a spiritual leader, which can be a considerable expense for a small group of followers. The construction and maintenance of elaborate buildings and properties is yet another major expense (Dennett 2006, p. 75). Less traditional folk religions also have practitioners and their ceremonies—defined by chants, song, dance, and music—allow the transmission of ideas and their gradual transformation (Bohlman et al. 2005). All of these are part of the intangible heritage of the people of a particular place and affect the locations in which their activities are practiced.

The motivations for religion are generally believed to be to comfort those who are suffering and allay a fear of death, to explain things that are not otherwise understandable, and to encourage group cooperation in the face of adversity (Boyer 2001; Dennett 2006, p. 103). Hence, religion matters for several reasons. It provides solace for those facing suffering, disease, and death, often relieving anxieties. Its rituals and practices serve to bridge the "trauma" of being uprooted or dislocated, whatever the context. Conscious that most religious groups have been ostracized or condemned in the past or even the present, most faith-based organizations have long assisted

---

[1] Although this chapter does not focus on material outside of the United States, linkages to activities in other countries is apparent by the global reach of many religions (Wuthnow 2006).

[2] It is worth noting that the sociology of religion has only recently developed as a field of study.

refugees. Religions also provide a narrative for natural phenomena, the origins of which are often obscure. Wherever scientific explanations are inadequate, often faith can provide an answer, offering a view that presumes a positive outcome that is essential for well-being.

Religion also provides a year-long and life-long social structure, marking the passage of time. Aid and support for the needy is also a significant aspect of religious belief. Aside from providing food and clothing, shelter is critical. When disaster strikes or people have experienced loss, faith-based initiatives provide the basis for regeneration. Last and most important, religion provides a moral framework for behavior, often stronger than any civil code. In short, because people often embrace ideas that go beyond reason or positivist thinking, religion can provide an alternative path to guiding behavior. Relics, graves, cemeteries, and battlefields are preserved as reminders of the honored dead, to renew the memories, stir stories, and strengthen habits of mind.

The Importance of Religion in Our History

Many of our goals are morally generated and our religions play a vital role in supporting our view of the world around us. The Native tribes throughout the country each hold views of the spirit world that often connect them socially to the natural elements, including the earth, sky, water, animal life, fauna, and flora. Often the beliefs of the members of the clan or tribe form part of their social connectivity, and their interactions are often characterized by these closely held ideas. For years, the policy of the white majority toward Native Americans was to force them to be Christianized and become citizens by splitting tribal lands held in common into family farms owned by individuals (Dawes 1887; Fig. 8.1). During the colonial period, both Catholic and Protestant colonization had an impact on religious expression, which, in turn, transformed Native American religious sites. Only recently has the story of American Indians who have

resided in urban locations for generations, attracted by jobs and military service, begun to be shared. Many migrated to Chicago, e.g., where they formed the backbone of an urban community whose numbers swelled following implementation of the Indian Bureau's controversial "relocation" program (LaGrand 2002). The US government acknowledges over 550 Indian tribes, including 223 village groups in Alaska.[3] Federal recognition signifies a relationship of trust between the two parties, often established by treaties, Constitutional provisions, legislation, and the Federal Acknowledgement Process, established in 1978. These "Procedures for Establishing that an American Indian Group Exists as an Indian Tribe" outline what must be done to prove the group has genealogical, social, and political traditions, however imprecise they may be. The kind or practice of religion is not part of that discussion, but decisions are inevitably influenced by beliefs, necessitating special attention for those who become involved with assisting tribes (Miller 2004).[4]

More familiar to many Americans are the deep-seated European religious convictions that often characterized early settlers. The long connection to Roman Catholicism in the former French and Spanish colonial regions of the western and southwestern portions of the United States is carried forward in the place names of missions, presidios, and pueblos. History demonstrates that rivalry and suspicion was common among members of the Judeo-Christian religions. Along the East Coast, settlements associated with one Protestant group often excluded many others. Catholics were particularly subject to exclusion whenever Protestants predominated. Equally, in the principal colony founded by Catholics, Maryland, non-Catholics were forbidden from settling in its earliest years. The views of the

---

[3] For details see http://www.bia.gov/WhatWeDo/index.htm.

[4] A significant issue is the ability of, and the manner in which, the federal government is privileged in its role of validating who is a member of an acknowledged tribe by their "Indian-ness." Some Indians are more visible in society than others.

Fig. 8.1 Acoma, New Mexico, where the church of San Esteban stands over the remarkable landscape, witness to the Catholic presence amidst the Indian tribes since its founding about 1630. (Author's photograph)

early religious leaders were influential. As a result, although the Founding Fathers used strong language in the Bill of Rights to guarantee religious freedom, the states of Connecticut, Massachusetts, and New Hampshire had "established" churches even after adopting the Federal Constitution. Massachusetts gave up its tie to the Congregational Church only in 1833 (Ervin 1983).

It is also axiomatic that religious freedom was a key factor in influencing settlement patterns. Given the birth and death rates of the Colonies, the speed at which a location would grow was often linked to religious tolerance. A town that could accommodate people who held different faiths would certainly expand quickly, even if it was ethnically segregated.

One outcome of tolerance is that sacred sites and places are relatively well-marked and recorded, although it takes time to understand their distribution and extent, and there is no single source of information or point of reference. With better understanding of the geographical and social transformations of a religion, we take the first step in knowing something about its organizational structure and the importance of its architectural objects, forms, and spaces.

Just as important as the historical geography of religious settlement patterns is the manner in which religion continues to guide education. When we recall that the medieval church gave birth to the university, it is no surprise to find that religious preferences were closely linked to higher learning in colonial America. The Court of the Massachusetts Bay Colony established Harvard in 1636 with the idea of promoting the prevailing Puritan philosophy. The minister John Harvard of Charleston, for whom the College was named, left his library and half his estate to the institution. In the South, a convention of the clergy of the Church of England in Virginia spurred the founding of the second oldest educational institution in the nation, the College of William and Mary. The Virginia General Assembly sent Reverend James Blair to England to request a charter for a college from the King and Queen, which was granted in 1693. Yale began as the Collegiate School in the home of its rector, Abraham Pierson, in 1701 (Nessenbaum 1972). The civic leadership in hundreds of colonial communities was influenced to some degree by the moral views of early educational institutions as their graduates moved to other parts of the country.

After the American Republic was well established, education remained tied to the study of religious affairs. To foster a religious view of life, early academies emphasized Bible study and sometimes even made it compulsory. College administrators and faculty cherished the idea that every member of the student body would be an active member of the denomination by graduation day. As the Christian denominations spread over the continent, their doctrinal positions were

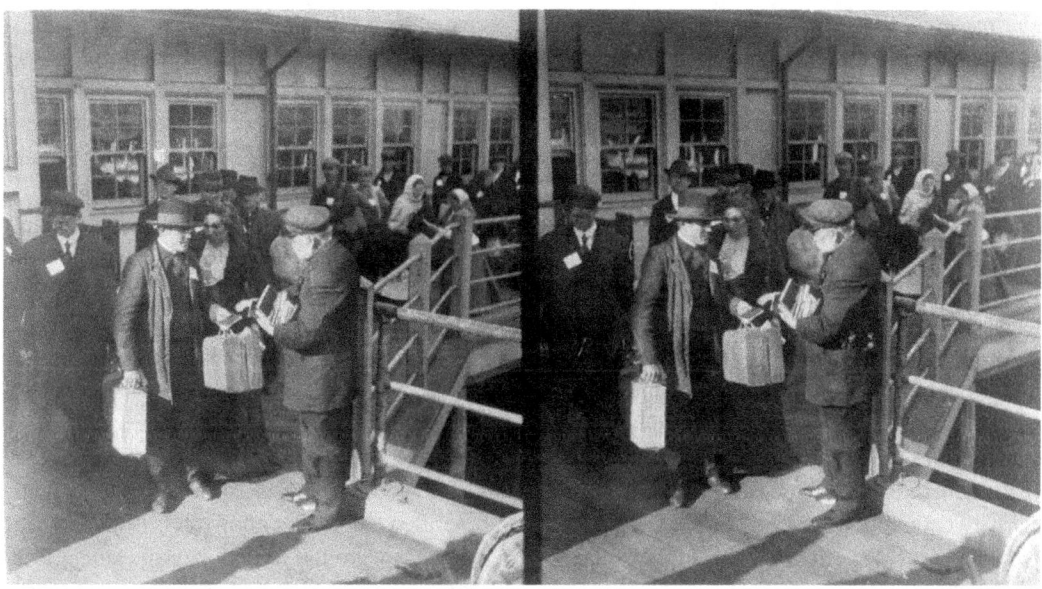

Fig. 8.2 The New York Bible Society distributed Bibles and other religious literature to emigrants at their arrival on Ellis Island, here in 1911, attempting to impart fundamental viewpoints to be held in common. (Library of Congress)

reinforced. In areas of the country where education leadership was lacking, church-sponsored academies often were established. By the time of the Civil War, about 6000 such institutions operated. Further, in 1869, of the 247 colleges in the United States, only 17 were state institutions (Fig. 8.2).

The social guidance that faith-based educational institutions provided earlier generations has often been overlooked, in part due to the rise of public support for learning in succeeding years. This becomes clear when the role of African American clergy is considered in providing alternative views and independent facilities (Murphy 2001). The concept that Biblical justice would prevail undergirded the instructional and financial support provided to African-American students and to adults who wanted self-improvement. Primary and secondary schools and dozens of colleges transformed thousands of lives. For example, between 1879 and 1919, the African Methodist Episcopal Zion Church sponsored at least 11 secondary schools, and between 1880 and 1917, it supported at least 9 secondary educational institutions. The Baptists were even more successful: between 1867 and 1902 they

founded at least 13 secondary schools. Earlier, the African Methodists founded Wilberforce College in Ohio, 1856; Allen University in South Carolina, 1881; Morris Brown in Georgia, 1885; Livingston College in North Carolina, 1889; and Lane College in Tennessee, 1889. The African Baptists began institutions such as Selma University in Alabama, 1879; Arkansas Baptist College in Arkansas, 1884; State University in Kentucky, 1873; Virginia Theological Seminary in Virginia, 1891; and Morris College in South Carolina (Holmes 1934). Because of the dearth of opportunities in the early nineteenth century, these efforts had a tremendous effect. The educational achievement of African Americans in the 50 years following emancipation was even more substantial than that of European Americans, as their literacy rate rose from 10 % in 1880 to 50 % in 1910, all laying the groundwork for the Civil Rights movement (Ng 2001).

During the late nineteenth century, faith-based education still prevailed, but students learned that more information and knowledge was explainable by human reason and scientific thought. The Christian framework in teaching broke down as the amount of science-based education increased and research opened new disciplines. This was due to government sponsorship, most notably with the Morrill Act, which promised each state a federally supported educational institution dedicated to agricultural and technology. This sparked the flame of the "modern university," going well beyond classical languages and Biblical texts. For example, as early as 1884 Cornell University's first president, Andrew Dickson White, wanted to establish a course in which the social questions associated with pauperism, intemperance, crime, and insanity could be addressed (White 1905).[5] In 1886, when the first instructor was appointed to teach this course, the class became the largest in the department of history and political science. Early twentieth century Progressive Era thinking would soon widely embrace the study of the social sciences.

Sociology based on Christian values reinforced broad social reform in the United States. Educators such as Charles Ellwood became known for reconstructing religion in light of social science, stripping away much of the divisive aspects of Protestant theology, particularly those forms offensive to non-Christians, with whom cooperation was desirable (Ellwood 1922).[6] The late nineteenth century replacement of theology and philosophy with humanistic philology permitted history, archaeology, anthropology, and other specializations and disciplines to grow and develop (Turner 2003).

Although scholars led the way in reforming higher education, equally important was the education of children. The public school movement, pushed by reformers like Horace Mann, emphasized the importance of every child being able to read, write, and do arithmetic unconnected to any religious context (Cubberley 1920). As high schools spawned junior high schools, and as biology, chemistry, and physics emphasized the exciting deductive logic of the scientific method, religion was sidelined. Protestant leaders quickly recognized that young people were being

prepared to participate in a more secular, industrial society. The Victorian era embraced physical improvements, fashionable amusements, and outdoor entertainment, even on the Sabbath, as a positive sign of progress, all of which was anathema to a faith-based code of ethics.

By the late nineteenth century, however, almost all Protestant denominations established their own "bible schools" (Burroughs 1917b; Wardle 1918; Lynn and Wright 1980), or, as Northern Baptists and Methodists preferred to call them, "church schools" (Miller 1917). The rise of the urban social gospel movement, so important in Methodist and Baptist circles, extended the Protestant reach into the working classes in the quickly growing cities, often embracing immigrants (Fig. 8.2). The Methodists were the leaders in establishing Protestant Sunday schools and youth organizations, although in some locations they were less noticeable than the Lutherans, Baptists, and Presbyterians. Church-sponsored summer camps extended the Gospel and explained the Parables to provide object lessons in daily life. As more Irish, German, and Italian immigrants entered the country and became established, their families supported Catholic parishes which, in turn, established parochial schools, serving neighborhoods and wards in many cities.

As the number of better educated, more scientifically-minded young people increased, religious leaders became alarmed. The conflict between the old and the new was not identical in each faith, but the social attitudes awakened were much the same. The advocates of the older religious order exhibited loyalty to traditional Christian values but, when they acted, it was often to change ritual, creed, and policy in a reformative manner. Protestants debated whether they should make the past authoritative over the present, or set the present and future free to reorganize religion in response to living needs.

The modern use of the term "Fundamentalism" in religion dates from 1910, when two wealthy laymen backed the publication of millions of copies of a tract entitled *The Fundamentals, A Testimony to Truth* (Cole 1931). Edited first by Amzi Clarence Dixon, one of the best known biblical scholars of the day, certain beliefs

---

[5] Cornell University, established in 1865, is the country's earliest nonsectarian institution of higher learning.

[6] Charles Elwood attended these first classes in social problems at Cornell.

were emphasized among Protestants that gained particular emphasis. The Virgin Birth, the physical resurrection of Christ, the inerrancy of the scriptures, the substitution theory of atonement, and the imminent second coming of Christ were the basic tenets, all or some of which led to tribunals in various quarters to judge those who varied from the path.

Fundamentalists fought for their views in convention halls of religious gatherings and on the floors of half of the state legislatures, where they attempted to have laws enacted that prevented or at least limited the teaching of evolution in public schools. Both sociologists and religious leaders realized that the nature of Protestant congregations was changing rapidly during the post-WWI era, but were conflicted about what to do about it.

Sociologist H. Paul Douglass found that "rather than [to] associate themselves with the lot of strange Negroes or foreign immigrants or people from the farms…," often the church moved. Instead of facing social challenge, "… the group takes it for granted that its duty is to reproduce its own religious culture for its children and to preserve the social ties and sympathetic interests of its women" (Douglass 1926). In short, the prevailing policy was to search for the conditions equivalent to those that allowed for the church's original success, supporting *de facto* segregation rather than demonstrate commitment to a specific location or any broader social and civic responsibility. If a compromise developed, whereby the religious body divided the original ministerial work in the older location and the newer elements moved elsewhere, the suburbs gained the upper hand in management.

The antievolution campaign reached its height when John Scopes, a public school teacher, was charged with willfully disobeyed Tennessee law by teaching that Man was descended from the lower order of animals and denied the story of the Divine Creation. The constitutionality of the law was upheld in 1927, but the decision against Scopes was later reversed (Grebstein 1960; Israel 2004). More important, this antiscience view declined with the onset of the Depression and World War II. "Creationism" did re-emerge later alongside more liberal and ecumenical approaches in the late twentieth century. The range and development of contemporary religious thinking is reviewed in the sections that follow.

Being Able to Distinguish Between Faiths: An Important First Step

If society believes in a supernatural force or Supreme Being, it is important to distinguish beliefs held in common and those held personally (Dennett 2006). This is because, before anyone can evaluate what actions might appropriate for a group, he or she must be familiar with and understand the beliefs, patterns, and activities that give rise to views held in common about objects, structures, and landscapes of a particular faith.[7]

It is also important to keep in mind that curiosity about religion does not necessarily lead to a pantheistic understanding. Freed of the need to study or encounter faith-based organizations of any kind, most Americans became increasingly naïve to and unaware of the wide variety of religious traditions in their own country, and the connections that faith provides to people around the world. Even individuals with degrees in religious studies or sociology are unlikely to have but a cursory knowledge of faiths aside from their own. This may be related to the bewildering variety and personal predisposition that religions present. It may also be due, in part, to a growing number of young people raised in a secular household, allowed to choose what religion or moral code to follow.

Yet, if preservationists wish to assist religious groups, they must have an understanding of the basic beliefs of each faith, how the followers practice their beliefs, and how each faith is changing. Both the dogma and the cultural rituals of each religious tradition are important, because much of a faith can be expressed with little physical imprint. There are also differences between each individual denomination. Considerable attention

---

[7] American philosopher and cognitive scientist Daniel Dennett holds that religion "… is a human phenomenon composed of events, organisms, objects, structures, patterns."

must be paid to the degree to which the religion is socially organized. Some, like Roman Catholicism, are hierarchically organized, while others, such as the Buddhist sects, are deliberately less structured. Traditional Protestantism deserves even more study by preservationists in the United States, if only because of the links to the country's prevailing democratic idealism. Baptist, Methodist, and Lutheran beliefs are everywhere evident in our thinking and in the landscape. Offshoots of Protestantism, such as the Seventh-day Adventist Church, the Church of Jesus Christ of Latter-day Saints (LDS), and the Church of Christ, Scientist, are "American inventions," influencing religious thought in other parts of the world. Some faiths are growing and seek to expand beyond their existing facilities, while others are undersubscribed and likely to abandon their properties. Waves of immigration and widespread population shifts make a considerable difference to both decline and growth, and perhaps decline again. In Detroit, Buffalo, St. Louis, Memphis, and Atlanta, the striking decline in the center city's population and the growth in the suburbs led to the devaluation and abandonment of properties, including religious sites. In cities that have relatively stable population growth, such as New York, a city may experience such rapid in and out-migration that turnover is relatively commonplace, and shared facilities are likely. In cities in the Sunbelt region, some of which are growing at least 2–3 % a year, expansion of the religions' functions and related activities have an impact on their sites and surrounding neighborhoods. And faith-based facilities such as hospitals and schools can be as important as the primary religious property for worship or ritual use.

The church, meeting house, temple, mosque, or mountaintop that is the site of religious practice; the school, nunnery, or monastery; the burial mound, graveyard, or cemetery all have special characteristics. Almost all religions—with the possible exception of the Puritans, Shakers, and a few other fundamentalists—have given their believers a cornucopia of beauty, with remarkable displays of architecture, music, and ceremony. It is not necessary to be a believer to be entranced by a Gothic cathedral, an Islamic mosque, or a Buddhist, Hindu, or Shinto temple. The appreciation of their beauty should be linked to understanding what faith caused these structures and their surroundings to be designed and built, and changed. In short, the character defining features of a denomination are religious, social, economic, and physical.

Of the billions across the world who claim some religious affiliation, about one third are Christian, with about half of those Catholic. Muslims are nearly equivalent in number to Catholics, with Hindus not far behind, and Buddhists compose the next largest group. This stands is stark contrast to the groups in which most of the fundamental values and morals are based on Judeo-Christian teaching. Yet, regardless of their faith and contrary to the views expressed in the media, the number of people in the United States who are attending religious services continues to be higher than in many other countries, contributing to the upkeep of their facilities without direct government financial support (Finke and Stark 1992).[8] Given the roots of the majority of Americans, it is no surprise that our currency states "In God We Trust" and, since 1947, Christmas has been recognized as a federal holiday. A more balanced view requires acknowledging the holidays of every major religion, but the majority opinion will likely remain predominant in the foreseeable future.

The following review centers primarily on the Judeo-Christian religions, with less attention paid to faiths with smaller numbers of adherents in the United States, including hundreds of tribal religions. Largest among all religions are the Catholics, who are growing in number. These are followed in size by the Baptists, Methodists,

---

[8] Across the globe, state-supported religion is more common than many Americans know. In Great Britain the historic role of the Church of England has provided it with certain advantages. Overlooked is that fact that the financial support was authorized for educational programs sponsored by a wide range of Christian religions in 1907; this was later expanded to include Catholicism, and now includes Muslim programs. Some nations actively promote religions, while others discourage religious thinking. In Saudi Arabia, for example, every resident recognizes the supremacy of the Qur'an (Koran). Beyond this discussion is the indirect financial support provided by government supported tax advantages.

Lutherans, Presbyterians, and the Church of Latter-day Saints. Each has had strong representation in different parts of the country, and the changes in their relative strength provide suggestions as to what preservation opportunities and challenges lay ahead. The focus is first on the declining influence of what is no longer a Protestant majority, itself indicative of a profound shift in religious thinking in the United States (Dart 2008).[9] A brief review of the alternatives outside of the majority view completes this picture, before proceeding to preservation initiatives involving this tangible and intangible heritage.[10]

The Roman Catholics

The Roman Catholic tradition first became firmly established in Colonial Maryland and in the Spanish missions and French outposts in the country's interior. Catholicism has always been pervasive in those areas (Fig. 8.3). Immigrants from Ireland, Germany, Italy, Poland, and southeastern Europe provided additional ethnic adherents during the nineteenth and early twentieth century, characterizing neighborhoods with their churches, parochial schools, and hospitals throughout New England and the Great Lakes regions (Walch 1989).

Like many Protestant denominations, the Roman Catholic Church did not always allow religious freedom for everyone in its parish domains. For centuries the Church held to the conviction that governments should be required to discourage and even ban non-Christian religions and any version of Christianity different from Catholicism, but remarkable changes occurred during the first half of the twentieth century as

parishes across the country became more socially secure, less ethnically insular, and more mobile (Chinnici 2004). The emphasis on family, respect for the dignity and prerogatives of labor, and a greater understanding of the need for reasonable discipline in governance in the Church became more apparent after World War II (Catholic 1943). The Church was troubled, however, by its apparent irrelevance in contemporary thinking. Dozens of conferences, Eucharistic congresses, and retreats in the United States during the 1940s and 1950s prepared the way for reform, as Catholics sought a way to renew their worship services. In 1965 the Second Vatican Council radically altered doctrine in several respects, so that now the Catholic Church firmly states that any governmental coercion of individuals to adhere or not to adhere to any religion is wrong.

Just as important, Vatican II removed many of the differences between Catholics and the Protestant majority, allowing more communication and collaboration. A considerable number of liturgical changes took place as well, causing facilities to be altered. English became the preferred language of prayer, not Latin, and the roles of the laity and the clergy were redefined. As the sacrament of penance was changed, small rooms that served as confessionals were abandoned. The number of statues was reduced. The cruciform plan, characterized by long naves with center aisle as the principal axis, often with the high altar separating the priest from the congregation by a communion rail, was transformed to seem less "distant" from the parishioners. As altar rails were removed, the altar tables became more accessible when serving the Eucharist. In fact, as the Mass invited those attending to witness the celebration more closely, the altar itself was often brought into the center of the nave. The architects and designers practicing in the Catholic tradition, formerly severely restricted in new design, were allowed much more variety (Kervick 1962). In fact, the experimental designs of the 1960s and early 1970s often damaged the art and architectural patrimony. Yet, today the desire to return to pre-Vatican II conditions is spotty. Parishioners expect contemporary comfort and convenience with air conditioning and heating, cushioned

---

[9] Researchers estimated that in the 2000s, about 3700 churches closed each year, up to half of which are new churches. Admittedly, however, some congregations decline very slowly, so that the small number of churches that actually close is not a clear indication of the strength of the religion in any area (Olsen 2008).

[10] This work does not detail the role of Jewish and Episcopalian views in the United States, although both faiths have stimulated nascent preservation efforts within their faiths.

Fig. 8.3 When the Roman Catholic Archdiocese of Los Angeles announced plans to abandon the Cathedral of St. Vibiana and construct a new cathedral, the future of the historic structure was clouded, in part, due to the extent of the damage from the Northridge Earthquake. With help from the University of Southern California School of Architecture, the Los Angeles Conservancy, and others, the property continues in use as an arts and entertainment center. (Photograph: Jeffrey Chusid)

pews, and acoustical assistance, with adequate lighting for every occasion (DeSanctis 2002).

Although neoconservatives reacted to the "liberalization" of Catholic practices in the early 1970s—they missed the Latin mass and the ritual that characterized the faith—the majority within the Church embraced the changes (Time 1974; Bromley 1991). Messages were issued by the Church to guide new construction and renovations of religious facilities.

Many of the other functions of the Catholics were less affected by Vatican II. For example, the role played by the church's primary social services organization, Catholic Charities, and by hospitals and schools, continued with little interruption. This is important because, while other denominations may tithe a greater amount to their religious group's activities, or contribute more to their respective missions, the Catholics' financial support is larger than the proceeds of their collections plate. This is evident in their support for parochial schools, often including volunteer time, which provides an important alternative to public education in cities and suburbs (Gabert 1973).

The most severe problems for the Catholic Church are seen in the Northeast and Great Lakes regions, where the decline in the number of priests and the number of adherents has forced bishops to close parishes, mothballing and selling churches, schools, rectories, and monastic buildings. Recent lawsuits against sexually abusive priests have not helped attendance or financial support. Comparisons with the conditions a century or more ago are striking. For example, in 1900 the Diocese of Burlington included about 150 priests in parishes across Vermont; a century later, less than half that number remains (NYT April 8, 2004). In recent years, the growing problem of surplus churches and other real estate has gained more attention and, because the ownership of these properties generally rests with the dioceses, they have tried to respond. From 1985 to 2004, for example, the Archdiocese of Boston trimmed the number of parishes from 404 to 357, but this was insufficient to stem the tide as expenses mounted while parish support declined. In May 2004, Archbishop Sean O'Malley announced that he intended to close one sixth of the parishes in Boston, the fourth-largest Catholic diocese in the nation. Closing 65 parishes seemed necessary because many Catholics had moved to the suburbs, attendance at Mass had dwindled in inner city churches, and many of the buildings were in poor repair. In addition, several priests were over 70 years old and the Diocese saw no replacements in sight. Catholic seminaries are not recruiting or graduating enough young priests (Paulson 2004). Unfortunately, often parishioners who are immigrants bear the brunt of these changes because they live primarily in the inner city parishes slated for closure and have less to contribute to finding possible solutions. Nevertheless, a fifth of the 65 parishes actively resisted (Paulson and Kurkjian 2004; Abelson 2004). In South Boston, an appeal for help at the Gate of Heaven Church almost overnight tripled its attendance, and the parish appealed to politicians and other clergy to intervene in what was otherwise a diocesan administrative decision. In short, in dozens of parishes faced with closure, Catholic parishioners renewed their dedication to their neighborhood church, reinforcing the widely-held view that believers in a certain geographical area should attend mass locally.

Catholic churches in the North are also successfully avoiding shutting their doors by adapting in remarkable ways. The Church of the Ascension in Manhattan is distinguished by featuring three completely different services, each addressing a segment of its parish. The physical differences are as notable as the music produced. The morning service begins with tapping drums, highlighted by horns, and the band sings in Spanish. A few hours later, a more operatic performance is presented in English, with incense. In the evening, a three piece jazz combo pumps out a lively song (Medina 2008). These changes arise from the ministry dedicated to Latino immigrants, the Columbia University community, and a growing body of affluent young professionals in the Amsterdam Avenue at 107th Street neighborhood, over 1500 members in all. Rev. John P. Duffell, the pastor, takes the view that "You have to observe and respond to what you have and see," reaching out to first time visitors at the end of services by asking where they are from, then leading the parish in a round of applause to be sure they feel welcome. Regardless of age, race, gender, or sexual orientation, all are encouraged

to attend and become involved. As a result, to the Dominican and Puerto Rican parishioners have been added a range of Euro-Americans, Peruvians, Mexicans, and Ecuadoreans, and the parish council is considering the idea of adding bilingual services, to more closely integrate Spanish and English speakers.

The ideas that parishes such as this are embracing may reflect the Catholic Church in the United States as a whole, suggesting the way in which the physical facilities should be assessed and adapted. The approach is important because, as striking as the decline of the Roman Catholic Church is in some areas of the country, the growth in the South and Southwest is just as impressive. Largely due to the influx of Hispanics, the Catholic Church remains the largest denomination in the country. Increasingly suburbanized, evangelical Catholics are transforming worship spaces, and are often returning to the traditional cathedral and church designs whenever a new structure is needed (Flott 2011). Here, too, the largest problem being faced is the increasing difficulty of leadership, as the rising number of adherents is not being met by a growing number of priests (Schoenherr and Young 1993). An effort to meet the demand for prayers has led the Vatican to outsource the task to priests in Kerala, India (Rai 2004).

The Baptists

The position the Baptists developed is a familiar one in Protestant thinking: because the early New Testament churches gradually saw the elder or spiritual leader become less of a servant and more of a master of the people, increasingly the chief pastor became a bishop, an position that wielded such influence that corruptions was a concern (Christian 1922). As the idea that the human body was evil and its natural emotions must be repressed if the soul is to attain spiritual growth gained increasing acceptance in the early thirteenth century, ascetic monasticism came to rule the Church. Christians persecuted Christians for their dissenting views, while the dissent from within the Church hierarchy was even more disruptive. The story of the Reformation is well

Fig. 8.4 In 1862, map and atlas maker H.H. Lloyd and Co. produced this *Pictorial Pilgrim's Progress* to show more explicitly the average Christian the correct Protestant theological path to salvation. (Library of Congress)

recognized by almost all Protestants, but especially relevant for those whose faiths rely on the teachings of Martin Luther, Ulrich Zwingli, and John Calvin. In Protestant thought, the need to separate church and state was immediate and unmistakable, and had significant consequences in the British Colonies.

Critics of the Baptists saw them as having a separate set of beliefs from traditional Protestants. Their overriding ideas were that salvation was a gift of God, not given by the church, and that Christianity was corrupted when Baptism became "procurative rather than declarative." If properly administered, Baptism required complete immersion, common in the Church until the sixteenth century, when the practice of the sacrament was gradually supplanted by pouring water into a container and then simply sprinkling it. Infant baptisms were unthinkable to Baptists because they placed the ritual in the hands of the church, not in the individual who could make a credible profession of faith (Torbet 1963).

Perhaps the most important seventeenth century Baptist thinker was John Bunyan, arrested and imprisoned for 12 years for preaching the gospel in Bedford, England. His *Pilgrim's Progress* ranked, next to *The Bible*, as the most published text, translated into several foreign languages (Fig. 8.4). During the eighteenth century, Dr. John Gill, a well-known Baptist scholar, wrote hundreds of pages that advocated a brand of Calvinism that held that Christ made atonement only for the elect (Rippon 1838). In the English Colonies in North America, Roger Williams is the most prominent early minister, settling in Rhode Island among the Narragansett tribe. His colony was the first where the charter guaranteed the complete separation of church and state, although the Baptists held a majority. On the ever-expanding frontier, the English Bible, made readily available because of advances in the printing press, led to an increasing number of interpretations, each ably explained and defended by charismatic leaders.[11]

All of these people are featured in the history of this denomination but it, too, spawned reform. The early nineteenth century Baptist preacher Alexander Campbell was particularly convinced that his interpretation was more correct, preaching throughout Ohio, Indiana, Illinois, and Kentucky. His followers believed Baptism was essential to Salvation, as immersion is the act of conversion. This split the Baptists, and added to the growing list of distinctive Protestant faiths with the Church of Christ or Disciples of Christ. By the 1840s, the slavery controversy arose, furthering dissention. The Baptists discussed the issue at the Triennial Convention of 1844, which went on record as being neutral, although its Executive Board was opposed to appointing a missionary who owned slaves, thus providing the Southern brethren with the basic platform that led them to withdraw. While the three main denominations, African Methodist Episcopal, African Methodist Episcopal Zion, and Baptist, differed in their

---

[11] English scholar William Tyndale was the first to translate the complete Bible into English, which was later built upon and revised by others to become the King James version in 1626 (Daniell 1994: Nicholson 2003).

Fig. 8.5 The famous Sunday School Board, headquartered in Nashville, is long recognized as the major center for Baptist publications. The Executive Building still stands alongside the Printing Building and other structures that connected them to distribution centers in the country. (Author's photograph)

organizational structure and theological positions, their ministers and preachers went on to influence not only other faiths but all of society, reforming attitudes in millions of households, neighborhoods, and communities.

Much of the activity took place outside of church, in missionary work. In May, 1845, the Southern Baptist Convention (SBC) was established with two boards of governance, the first for domestic missions and the second for foreign missions. The Bible Board, launched at the same time, gave birth to the Sunday School Board in 1863, located in Nashville, Tennessee in 1891, subsequently the principal center of Baptist publications (Burroughs 1941)[12] (Fig. 8.5). Bible schools, such as the institute established by Rev. Dwight L. Moody, produced a steady stream of graduates who came from the same social class as many Baptists, insuring that there was a sym-

pathetic match and the right combination of evangelicalism and mission (Miller 2007).

The simplicity of the early wood frame Baptist meeting houses in Boston, Charleston, and Philadelphia is remarkable (Newman 1894). In time, they became more substantial, two story brick structures and later, with the "Great Awakening," a period of religious revival during the nineteenth century, the number of Baptist associations in the South increased. Sunday school lessons conducted in a Christian home would allow the children to be instructed apart from the sacred place in which the adults worshipped. Later, rooms were set aside inside the meetinghouse for Bible instruction. Following the Methodists, the Baptists adopted the auditorium church plan in the mid-nineteenth century and, when the means permitted, added a school and social hall with kitchen, and sometimes a gymnasium. While some Baptist congregations have moved as they became more prosperous, others have worshipped in the same location for two centuries (Fig. 8.6).

By the late nineteenth century, even very modest Baptist churches were laid out in a rough square with auditorium seating and a platform on the diagonal. Classrooms were frequently arranged at the perimeter, often with sliding or rolling partitions so that the rooms could be joined to the auditorium. The plans often had to fit on the lot selected. When a corner lot was chosen, the option arose of placing a bell tower to mark the location more visibly. During the last decade of the nineteenth century, however, the Baptists began to reconsider the fundamental linkage between the Early Christians and the classical temple. After the World's Congress of Religions in Chicago, held in 1893, a Neoclassical temple exterior was considered to be more in keeping with early Baptist thinking, a position favored by some associations until the present time (Hanson 1894).

Because the sacrament of baptism is so central to this religion, and immersion requires a large container on the platform, the baptistery remained the center of the church, at or near the platform. This allows everyone to witness the event, focused on the pastor and the person being baptized. After World War I, the baptistery is often

---

[12] The Baptist Young Peoples' Union, later known as the Baptist Training Union, was established about the same time.

Fig. 8.6 The Sinking Creek Baptist Church, founded in 1772 on the Elizabethton Highway in what has become Johnson City, TN, is reportedly the oldest church of any denomination in the state. (Author's photograph)

on the right, with the communion table to the left of the preaching platform, to provide almost equal emphases. The decorative treatment of the interior is most elaborate around these three foci, sometimes enhanced with a flowing water scene in the wall above and controlled lighting to reinforce the drama (Burroughs 1917a, pp. 184–189; Burroughs 1927).[13]

American Baptists, deriving their governance from the Northern Convention, number about two million members. For decades they have experienced comparatively slow growth, particularly in the Snow Belt region. Their lack of expansion accounts, in part, for the relatively limited financial resources at their disposal and a slow attrition due to the megachurch growth in the center of the country. By contrast, the SBC claims a slowly growing membership (approximately 2% per year) and, at the beginning of the twenty-first century, it can lay claim to being the largest Protestant denomination in the country. It has particularly strong roots in the South and extends into the North Central and Western states. Atlanta, Houston, Dallas, and Nashville are its major urban and suburban centers. The Cooperative Baptist Fellowship is a national body that

emerged from the Southern Baptist Convention as that group became more politically active, supporting conservative candidates in the 1980s and 1990s (Wayne 1997).

The Methodists

The Methodist Episcopal Church organized in the United States in 1784, breaking its ties with England. Methodists embraced the idea of freedom of religion as one of the key tenants of democracy, essential to their growth and the expansion of the nation. Indeed, Methodism became known as the quintessential American denomination during most of the nineteenth and early twentieth centuries because its developing moral consciousness spurred the social and economic movements that forever changed the country (Tucker 2001). Concerned with the needs of Africans and African Americans, the Methodist Church was vitally involved with the question of slavery and the cause of Emancipation, and later, the importance of temperance and women's suffrage. Methodists also played an important role by spreading the Gospel among the rising urban population of the country with the establishment and growth of the Young Mens' Christian Association (YMCA) and the Young Womens' Christian Association (YWCA). Millions of people learned about the importance of leadership, teamwork, and tolerance in these

---

[13] Architects favored by the Southern Baptist Convention during the late nineteenth and early twentieth century included R.H. Hunt of Chattanooga; C. W. Bulger of Dallas; Frank L. Smith of Lexington; and George Kramer of New York.

Fig. 8.7 The Methodist Camp Meeting was well organized and designed for maximum effect. Here the characteristic camp tents ring the meeting area, with a simple stage to provide a focus. (Author's collection)

remarkable recreational organizations (Morse 1913; Mjagkij and Spratt 1997).

The Methodist worship services drew inspiration from the views of evangelical Anglican John Wesley and centered on the Lord's Day service. They reinforced Sunday as the holy day socially and, indirectly, legally, providing the basic structure and uniformity for life on the Sabbath in many communities. Methodism remained a religion that avoided formal teaching and conceited attitudes, while emphasizing fiery preaching, testimonies, ardent prayer, and hymn singing. Whether on the frontier in camp meetings, or in vast urban temples, there was considerable freedom of expression.

Organized loosely but governed by a conference of bishops, only gradually during the late nineteenth and early twentieth centuries did a series of orders begin to introduce uniformity in public worship in the Methodist Episcopal Church and the Methodist Episcopal Church, South. Much of the twentieth century strength of this religion rests in the heartland of the country, in the near-suburbs. The current United Methodist Church is the result of a 1968 merger of Methodist and Evangelical United Methodists, designed to increase the support of their mission by drawing on its suburban strength.

The design of the plain log houses and unadorned meeting houses of the eighteenth and nineteenth century were transformed by increasingly wealthy Methodists into substantial churches. Regular Sunday services led by a resident preacher became the norm in most growing cities, and the log buildings with simple benches were replaced by frame, brick, and stone structures with regular pews. After the congregation gained sufficient wealth to construct a belfry, bells were hung to ring out the call to prayer. The rectangular interior was fitted out with a central pulpit or desk on a raised platform for preachers, sometimes with three chairs for the minister, visiting preacher, and song leader, taken to represent the Trinity. The Communion table was set in front of the pulpit and surrounded by a rail. By mid-century, the issue of slavery and the perceived need for additional financial resources led to a heated discussion over the policy regarding pew rents, some believing that free seats were more in keeping with the purity of early Christianity. Yet another dispute arose over the promiscuousness of allowing men and women and entire households to be seated together (Tucker 2001).

The emphasis on preaching and teaching make a difference in the Methodist Church. Early camp meetings gathered people from considerable distances, even in the rural South, sometimes in a ring surrounded by tents and wagons (Gorham 1854)[14] (Fig. 8.7). After the Civil War the most

---

[14] The first camp meeting was held in 1799 in Kentucky.

Fig. 8.8 The First Methodist Church, Akron, OH, built in 1866, contained the first "Akron Plan," widely copied by other Protestant denominations for more than 50 years. The interior view shows the partitions that separated the classrooms. (Hendricks Ellwood, *Lewis Miller*, 1925, illus., opp. p. 146, Author's collection)

advanced congregations adopted an auditorium arrangement, with seats on a modest slope, arranged on a diagonal inside of the plan so as to provide the preacher with maximum advantage. Angled and curved pews directed the attention of the faithful, focused on the platform and pulpit, often with galleries similarly fashioned to direct the attention of the audience. Lest those attending forget the link between God and country, the national flag was displayed to remind the audience of their patriotic duties (Jaeger 1984).

The introduction of Uniform Sunday School lessons, whereby all classes studied the same lesson under the direction of a main superintendent, regularized the programmatic needs that led to a specific architectural response. Akron Sunday school superintendent Lewis Miller was the first to insist on a building that satisfied these teaching needs, wherein the classrooms opened into a two story central space with a platform and desk, at which the exercise and worship were introduced and, at the end of the class instruction period, concluded in prayer. The First Methodist Episcopal Church in Akron became the Sunday school model widely emulated across the country for being both multi-functional and economical, and came to represent the preferred approach until after World War I (Fig. 8.8). The

later introduction of the separate, graded religious classrooms set aside the Uniform Lessons and made the flexibility provided by the Akron Plan less necessary (Kilde 2002).

Although Methodists were slower than some other religious groups to adopt pointed arched sash and stained glass windows, memorial donations spurred their acceptance. By the second half of the nineteenth century, urban churches often sported grained woodwork, decoratively papered walls and ceilings, and carpeted floors with cushioned seats and elaborate chandeliers. Central furnaces heated the interiors, while visible organs with grand pipes provided a backdrop for the costumed choir.

By the early twentieth century, the artistic merit of Methodist churches vied with those of the Episcopalians. Although architect Ralph Adams Cram may have preferred to design for Anglicans, his Gothic designs were often very inspirational to suburban Methodists whenever the congregation was expanding (Tucci 1995). Elbert Conover, director of the Bureau of Architecture of the Methodist Episcopal Church and later director of the Interdenominational Bureau of Architecture, provided many Methodists with a considerable amount of design guidance, writing that "worship spaces utterly failed if they did not inspire, comfort or create humility of mind" (Conover 1924). After World War I, the Akron plan was deemed unnecessary and the divided chancel plan, with the altar on the far end of the nave and the preachers' and choir seats on either side of the chancel, became the favorite arrangement. The pulpit and lectern were on opposite sides of the entrance, and the Baptismal font placed near the entrance to the nave or slipped in near the chancel.

As the country became less rural, abandoned Methodist properties began to be noticed. By 1920 it was commonplace to find unused churches becoming stores, automobile garages, and apartment buildings. It was suggested that the National Board of Missions hold these properties and prevent deterioration, perhaps using them as missions. It was also observed, however, that the deserted churches were surrounded in urban areas "by teeming multitudes of Negroes and

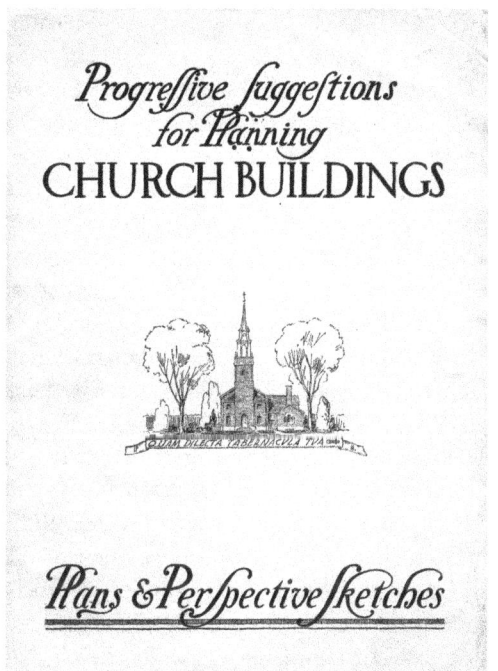

Fig. 8.9 *Progressive Suggestions for Planning Church Buildings*, published by the interdenominational Home Missions Council in New York, provided a fashionable range of examples by architects throughout the country during the 1920s. (Elbert M. Conover (Ed.). (1920). *Progressive Suggestions*, 1920, title page. Author's collection)

industrial workers," while those in rural areas were "surrounded by share-croppers and others." By the early 1940s, it was clear that "Abandoned churches, therefore, in nearly every instance, represent the failure of Methodist evangelism to reach and influence persons of the very type among which the early Methodist movement originated and flourished" (Garber 1941).[15]

By contrast, suburban Methodists actively left behind the simplicity of design of their predecessors. Even those who held that Gothic design could potentially undermine the value of preaching and the traditional Protestant emphasis on the Scriptures, when they chose any alterative, be it Georgian or Colonial, it was equipped in

considerable comfort and style, with an elegant community center on a generous lot (Conover 1948)[16] (Fig. 8.9). After World War II, the nature of Methodist structures changed again with thousands of new facilities and the gradual renovation of older properties. Because ownership of most Methodist facilities is vested in the Quarterly Meetings, when the local congregation seeks a new facility or wishes to make major changes to existing property, it must seek permission. The National Division of the Board of Missions offers advice and guidance in design, construction, and financing (Murphy 1965). By the late twentieth century, then, large roofed sanctuaries and simplified modern design become the norm for the new buildings and modern additions, often in striking contrast to the earlier, more "churchlike" structures.

The Lutherans

The religion that bears Martin Luther's name arrived in the New World in select locations with some of the earliest settlers. Lutherans settled in New Sweden, in the Delaware Valley, and both the Dutch and English colonial governments allowed Lutherans to practice their faith without persecution, served by circuit riding pastors sent from Europe. Henry Melchior Muhlenberg is generally considered the church father of Lutherans in the United States. His arrival in 1742 signaled the beginning of the structural organization of the German, Swedish, and other Lutheran churches, and he served congregations from New York to Georgia for over four decades. By the late 1780s, 31 ministers worked with congregations totaling about 100,000 members, the majority in Pennsylvania (Gritsch 2002).

Worship consisted of prayers, hymns, Scripture readings, confession or absolution, preaching, and the Lord's Supper, with considerable variation, a reflection of the differing interpretations on teachings during the nineteenth century. As the number of congregations

---

[15] Paul N. Garber, the Dean of the Divinity School at Duke University, noted that 492 Methodist societies in the Southeastern and South Central Jurisdictions had no churches at all.

[16] lbert Conover, author of *The Church Building Guide* (1948), is an exhaustive work on the subject.

grew, assemblies or "synods" increased, with some holding views and traditions that separated them from others. During the Civil War, five Southern synods withdrew from the General Synod and, even after Emancipation, they remained segregated as the United Synod, South, formed in 1886. Additional Danish, Norwegian, and Finish immigrants formed ethnic synods in Iowa, Illinois, Minnesota, Missouri, the Dakotas, and Wisconsin, and some turned their attention almost exclusively to foreign and domestic missionary work rather than strengthening the Lutheran unity in the United States. The synods also established seminaries, colleges, and universities to promote and strengthen views on many widely debated topics.

Unlike the Methodists and Baptists, most Lutherans did not readily embrace the broad humanitarian urban gospel movement. Lutherans insisted on using the language of their country of origin in relatively rural, isolated locations in the center of the country, and firmly held to their conservative political and economic views. They did continue to foster their own "Inner Mission" work, however, which centered on reinforcing their piety and mercy under the influence of the Gospel with charitable hospitals, orphanages, and old peoples' homes to address the problems of individuals (Svendsbye 1967).[17]

The Missouri Synod became distinguished as the most religiously conservative, emphasizing the use of German in their worship services. This worked against it in the twentieth century (Gritsch 2002, pp. 192–97). In 1914, Germans in the United States generally supported Germany in its war against Great Britain until this country entered the war. Some Lutheran pastors had sworn an oath of allegiance to the Kaiser, who was legally the head of the Lutheran Church. As anti-German feelings rose, streets were renamed, artists and musicians were forbidden to perform certain works that were seen as seditious, and music records by German composers were broken. Several Lutheran parochial schools were forced to close and even German books were burned. At the cessation of European hostilities,

some Lutherans gained a reputation by leading the crusade for world peace.

The post-World War II history of the Lutherans can be seen as a series of attempts at ecumenical cooperation and union, expansion, and gradual contraction. The formation of the Lutheran Church of America took place in 1962, with the union of the American Evangelical Lutheran Church, the Augustana Evangelical Lutheran Church, the Finnish Evangelical Lutheran Church, and the United Lutheran Church in America (Gilbert 1988). Then, the Evangelical Lutheran Church in America (ELCA) was created in 1987 with the merger of the American Lutheran Church, the Lutheran Church in America, and the Association of Evangelical Lutheran Churches. The total population of the ELCA peaked in 1968, with 5.9 million members (Linder 1969), and it is generally acknowledged inside and outside of the Lutheran church that the decline in membership continues ((Lutheran March 2009a; Lutheran May 2009b), particularly in the Snow Belt regions of the country.

The rise and decline of the number of adherents is paralleled by the amount of funding Lutherans have dedicated to church facilities. In the 1950s the Lutheran Laymen's Movement for Stewardship raised money for new, suburban church campuses, parish houses, and remodeling work. Through the efforts of these businessmen and professionals—nearly 3000 of whom were dedicated full time to the church—more than $10 million was raised from 1954 through 1958 (NYT, October 15, 1958). Since the early 1970s, however, giving declined and capital stewardship campaigns in congregations suffered, so much so that the group was abandoned in 2003 for lack of interest (ELCA 2003). Attempts to explain the decline in giving to the synods and the national ELCA have revealed no link between the congregations' dissatisfaction to the decisions made by the larger bodies. Rather, the laity seems to have become disinterested in the organizational dynamics of the church. Instead, the congregations tend to respond to more immediate, local needs (RRR 1994; Century 2007). With the decline in the number of Lutherans, and the decrease in the amount of funding and personnel available to help distressed congregations, the future of these

---

[17] An exception was the Pittsburgh Synod, which did develop its social programs.

Fig. 8.10 In San Francisco, CA, St. Johannes Evangelical Lutheran Church has been successfully transformed into the Hua Han Zang Si Temple, opened in 2004, in the thriving Mission district. (Author's photograph)

story level. Exteriors occasionally made use of the classical language of architecture but, until after World War II, most Lutheran churches were Gothic-inspired and favored lancet sash and towers. Most have traditional, ritually oriented naves with center aisles featuring a large organ, first introduced by the Swedish, with pipe arrangements often more striking than the altar. Lutherans were almost always adverse to anything that might be considered papist. Few churches displayed crucifixes and fewer still had statuary or displays of iconographic symbolism. The relative simplicity of the interior that distinguished the Lutheran worship space was easily expressed by modern architecture, often in suburban campus settings. As will be discussed later, the best hope for some declining Lutheran congregations appears to be to promote the shared use of their facilities by other religious groups.

The Church of Latter-day Saints

Although hundreds of religions have been spawned in what is now the United States, few have grown to have a worldwide following. The noteworthy exception is The Church of the Latter-day Saints. Its birthplace is generally accepted to be in Ontario and Wayne Counties, in upstate New York. On a hill rising about 150 feet above a small plain near the small community of Manchester, the angel Moroni—whose human form is believed to have been responsible for burying the American record of the ancient Gospel in golden plates in the early fifth century— appeared in the 1820s to make the Christian texts available to the prophet Joseph Smith. The location, the "Golden Bible Hill," or Hill Cumorah as it became known after the publication of the *Book of Mormon* in Palmyra, New York in 1829, remains a primary center of pilgrimage for believers (Porter 2000; Fig. 8.11). The subsequent history of Smith's activities in New York and Pennsylvania was not widely known to the general public until comparatively recently. At the impetus of the contemporary Mormon Church, two properties—the Joseph Smith Farm, near Palmyra, and the John Whitman Farm, near

historic churches, parsonages, and parochial schools is in jeopardy. Although predictions of the decline of a religion are often grossly premature and adversity may strengthen the resolve of a group of adherents, without significant support, Luther's beliefs have an uncertain future in the United States (Fig. 8.10).

It is important to note that the evolution of the Lutheran religious spaces, while not as dramatic as other faiths, is very distinctive. Colonial Lutheran church interiors exhibit some architectural characteristics of their Scandinavian and German predecessors, but they were increasingly molded by the building programs of growing ethnic congregations, and later affected by the remodeling schemes that were in vogue at various periods. In the eighteenth and nineteenth centuries, commonplace changes including the addition of towers and insertion of galleries at the second

Fig. 8.11 Hill Cumorah, near Palmyra, NY, the site where an angel appeared before prophet Joseph Smith in the early 1820s, is one of the most important pilgrimage sites for the Church of Jesus Christ of Latter-day Saints. (Author's photograph)

Fayette, the site where the church was formally organized in 1830—have been considerably restored and received increased public attention. It was not long after the new faith was founded that the legendary pilgrimage west began. The two story temple in Kirtland, Ohio, is the first permanent Mormon monument, a mix of styles similar to the examples of meeting houses commonplace in central New York and found in the land opened for settlement by the Connecticut Land Company in the Western Reserve of Ohio (Slaughter and Landon 1997)[18] (Fig. 8.12).

Early Mormon leaders often warned church members not to discuss what took place in the temple so that most published accounts refer to the activities only in general terms. This is because the ritual, termed the "temple endowment," is considered sacred and the ceremonies or "ordinances" provide the sanctification to members. The leaders take pride in having performed ostensibly the same ceremonies for decades, with the same gospel and the same authority administered by the prophet Joseph Smith. In fact, some Mormon leaders have pointed to the change taking place in other religions as evidence of moral weakness. More recently, while under

construction, Mormon temples have been open for inspection by the public so that it is possible to see the remarkable religious consistency of the arrangement of the properties. Having taken the Temple of Solomon as a starting point, Smith's divine inspiration was considerably less detailed than an architect might have preferred, but his first references to an "upper court" and a "lower court" fixed the idea of two principal rooms (Givens 2007).

By 1838, however, Smith was forced to leave Ohio and move westward. Nauvoo, Illinois, then the largest city in the state, provided a suitable location for a number of years, but strife developed within the church when Smith revealed to the leadership his doctrine of plural marriage. Many of the faithful challenged him, some of whom left the church and denounced him as their leader.[19] His position as leader fell to Brigham Young, who, in early 1847, led an advance party that reached a pass on the western slope of the Wasatch Range, later known as Emigration Canyon. By July, the new Zion was well established and 10 acres was designated for a new Tabernacle, larger than any

---

[18] The first Mormon temple is currently under the jurisdiction of the Community of Christ, and as such is the only such structure whose interior may be visited by non-Mormons.

[19] His troubles were compounded when he was arrested on a charge of attempting to assassinate the Governor of Missouri. While Smith won acquittal, a new indictment for treason caused him to be jailed and, while awaiting trial, he and his brother Hyrum were killed by a mob in June, 1844.

Fig. 8.12 Joseph Smith moved his church to Kirtland, OH, in 1831 and they constructed their first temple from 1833 to 1836, a major monument at the time. The site served as the headquarters for the Mormons until the majority left in 1838 for locations in the West. (Historic American Buildings Survey, Library of Congress)

previously attempted, which set the tone for hundreds of buildings like it.

Most established religions are aware of the importance of their history, but few are comparable to the record of the Church of Latter Day Saints, which considers historical investigation as key to salvation, even for the deceased. The Mormon Historic Sites Registry is continuously being updated by the Mormon Historic Sites Foundation, formed in 1992 to preserve and create the Ensign Peak Park in Salt Lake City, Utah. The Foundation next became involved with the restoration of the historic Kirtland village, including a major road relocation project. Just as important, the growth of the Mormon religion is striking, due to the higher birth rate of the adherents and the success of their missions. In 1996, for example, the Mormons fielded over 50,000 missionaries, more than the total of all of the Protestant groups. Just as significant is the fact that, with limited change

in their beliefs over time, the layout of the religious facilities remains consistent.

The Presbyterians

As with other Protestant denominations, Presbyterians mark their beginnings with the early Christian church and transformation as a result of the Reformation. John Calvin and John Knox are key figures, and religious activities in Scotland, Ireland, and England provide much of the story behind why the first Presbyterians arrived in the East Coast Colonies. The first presbytery was formed in Philadelphia in 1706, quickly growing and reorganizing as four presbyteries and one synod in 1716, as immigrants continued to arrive (Gillett 1864).

The notable evangelical influence among the American Indian tribes and African Americans magnified the role of this denomination in civic affairs. For example, Jonathan Edwards, a pastor of a Congregational Church, was not only one of the most notable missionaries to the Native Americans, but also was invited to become president of Princeton, a Presbyterian theological stronghold. Just as important, the view regarding leadership, whereby congregations elected representatives to presbyteries that constituted a general assembly, reinforced the democratic principles of the early republic.

Although the simple meetinghouse near the town's center became an icon for Protestant faiths in the Northeast, in the Trans-Appalachian region Presbyterians held revivals and awakenings. The influence of Charles Grandison Finney, pastor and later professor and president of Oberlin College, was widely acknowledged, and it was the first American educational institution to admit women and African Americans. The intellectual leadership of the Presbyterian clergy was a matter of great pride, their assemblies thought to be less emotional than some other faiths. The Presbyterians' growth allowed them to give birth to the Disciples of Christ and the Cumberland Presbyterian Church, although differences over slavery before the Civil War caused more divisions.

Fig. 8.13 The Modernist Neo-Gothic design for the National Presbyterian Church in Washington, D.C. demonstrates how this denomination can embrace an elegant traditional limestone exterior form, with a rich array of stained glass windows. (Author's photograph)

The shift from meetinghouse to the word "church" was but one indication of the growing trend of Presbyterians to display their prosperity. Commenting on the growing attention to the physical expression of buildings, in 1868 the *United Presbyterian* wrote: "We cannot believe that it is pleasing to (God) to have so much of the money of the church buried in extravagantly costly buildings, when it is so much needed to support her benevolent agencies." It was not only a waste of money, but it also brought on "costly worship, operatic singing, worldly-mindedness in the attendants, expulsion of the poor, and what is worse, the exclusion of the precious influences of the Holy Spirit" (Advocate 1868).

By comparison to more ritual-bound denominations, Presbyterians were concerned less with the ceremony associated with the Holy Eucharist, resulting in a de-emphasis on the communion table. Their alternative was to treat the communion table as an altar and view it more as an aesthetic piece of furniture (Drummond 1934). Presbyterian baptisteries are also diminished in scale. On the other hand, as architect Harold E. Wagoner's Modernist Neo-Gothic design for the National Presbyterian Church in Washington, D.C. shows, like other liberal Protestants, the Presbyterians often embraced traditional ritualistic paradigms, with a splendid array of stained glass windows (Fig. 8.13). In the early twentieth

century, a chancel aided worship, it was believed, because it added a devotional tone.

Post World War II Presbyterian church building was often influenced by the thinking of the Department of Church Building and Finance of the Board of American Missions, which was, at times, involved with a joint effort of relocation. Alternatively, the Church Architectural Guild might provide suggestions for the new Modern designs that included only vague historical references, with broad roof spans, a considerable amount of glazing, some abstract symbolism, and a centrally planned sanctuary. The suburban lot provided enough set-back to admire the two story church and the adjacent community hall and offices, sometimes with a memorial garden, but most likely without a cemetery. The tower is represented by a tall spire atop the facing gable of the church, ornamented by a cross (Leitch 1957; Seth 1960). Remodeled Presbyterian churches often contented themselves with similar modifications, but the trend was clearly to provide more light and air conditioned comfort whenever possible.

More Religions from Abroad: Not all That "Foreign" any More

The United States has remained largely composed of believers in the Judeo-Christian tradition, with a gradual shift from Protestant to Catholic beliefs.

Fig. 8.14 The remarkable interior of the Amitabha Buddha Hall, second floor, Hau Han Zang Si Temple, formerly St. Johannes Evangelical Lutheran Church, the exterior of which is shown in Fig. 8.10. (Author's photograph)

This overall image is being affected by another feature of immigration. In 1965, the quota system that had favored European immigrants and restricted Asians and Africans was readjusted, allowing for a sharp rise in non-Europeans, including peoples from Asia and the Middle East. What began as a small number of immigrants who practiced their religions in their own homes followed the age-old pattern (Levitt 2007). As the number of adherents following the Buddhist, Hindu, and Islamic traditions increase, their religious properties grow in number and size, expanding the boundaries of religious pluralism to an extent undreamed of only a few decades ago.

The relatively recent growth of Asian immigration has introduced their temples and mosques to the landscape. Sometimes a house is converted to religious use, while in other instances an existing church or a synagogue is remodeled. This process can be complex because the functions are so distinct. For most Asian religions sitting at floor level is the norm, rather than sitting on pews with kneelers. The number of people who can be accommodated in what might at first glance be taken for an ordinary bungalow or suburban tract house, devoid of any interior furniture, is surprisingly large.

The Buddhist tradition traces its origins to India in the sixth century BCE, with the teacher Siddhartha Gautuam, also known as the Buddha or "Awakened One." His insights into human suffering and the way to relieve it influenced followers to develop practices that spread from India to China, Japan, Korea, and throughout Southeast Asia (Alba et al. 2009). Buddhist thinking first entered the United States primarily through Hawaii during the nineteenth century with the earliest Japanese and Chinese immigrants. The differences in Buddhist ideas can be rather striking, however. For example, in Theravada Buddhism, God does not exist, prayers and worship are not important, and devotees do not vow to be reborn in the Buddha Lands but to attain Nirvana individually. In Mahayana Buddhism, especially the Pure Land Sect, God and divine being exist but are not Supreme, chanting prayers like "Namo Amitabha" and praying to Bodhisattva to seek spiritual help and getting rid of suffering is encouraged, and the devotees vow to be reborn. (Fig. 8.14). In addition to these Buddhist branches, the Japanese Zen, Tibetan Vajravana, and Soka Gakkai traditions are seen in various locations in the country. These ties are important to assess closely: Cambodian-American Buddhists are making considerable contribution to temples in Cambodia, although their religious facilities in the United States are relatively modest.[20]

---

[20] Field observations in the early twenty-first century in Battambang Province in Cambodia support this claim. New temples in the region often have doors, lintels, and columns thanking donors and are marked "USA."

One of the most powerful linkages religion makes is the connection between the home and the place of worship. Many religious practices take place in the home, so it can be considered a sacred site. The hearth serves as the center of the religious ceremony just as it is the center of social activity, often around food preparation and eating. Today, even in house construction, many continue to employ the ideas of *Fengshui* and *Sthapatya veda*, which discern different spiritual energies and claim to improve health and rest (Cox 2000).

By comparison to Buddhism, Hinduism has grown quickly in the United States in the wake of the 1965 immigration changes. The major sects, Saivism, Vaishnavism, and Skaktism have attracted a sufficient number of followers to support temple construction in several locations. In Saivism, Lord Shiva is the chief deity and regarded as the Supreme Braham. Followers of Vaishnavism worship Lord Vishnu as the creator, while the followers of Shaki consider the Mother Goddess as the universal self. Because the maintenance of Indian heritage is important, and many Indian immigrants are well-educated professionals, it is common to see their religious festivals and functions publicly marked and celebrated. After years of worship in private homes and community meeting halls, the Hindu Society in America is advising local groups to purchase a property that can, over time, be quickly changed to display the success of the adherents. The earliest Hindu temple in the United States is reputed to be the Maha Vallabha Ganapathi Devasthanam, in Flushing, Queens, consecrated on July 4, 1977, but dozens of others have been built in the suburbs, in California, Hawaii, Illinois, Maryland, Tennessee, and Texas (Saran 1985; Worth 2003; Kayal 2004; Newman 2008; Capecchi 2009; Fig. 8.15).

The Islamic faith begins with the prophet Mohammed, the visit of the angel Jibral (Gabriel) in about AD 610, and the words contained in the *Quran*, the holy book that his followers, the Muslims, believe are the revealed word of God. The *Quran*, revealed by Allah to Mohammed over 22 years, is designed to be recited as an act of worship, a fundamental aspect of the faith. There

Fig. 8.15 The Maha Vallabha Ganapathi Devasthanam, in Flushing, Queens, is the oldest Hindu temple in the country, largely constructed of imported materials and assembled by artisans from India. (Author's photograph)

is no mention or prescription for a building to house the religion, but every Muslim is bound to observe the five daily salat prayers, at dawn, midday, afternoon, sunset, and late evening. In addition, Friday is the weekly day of midday communal worship, incumbent on all adult male Muslims. The prayers consist of recitations with several movements, including standing, sitting, bowing, kneeling, and prostrating, denying the need for any furniture. "Masjid," the Arabic word for "prostrating," is often the term most associated with the place of worship, always with an orientation toward Mecca. With the exception of the minbar, or pulpit, used by the Prophet to give sermons, and the mihrab, or prayer niche in the qibla wall, facing Mecca, the structures are relatively devoid of overt furnishings whether in the Mediterranean, the Middle East, or South Asia. (Bukhari et al. 2004).

Fig. 8.16 The Mother Mosque in Cedar Rapids, IA, completed in 1934, continues to serve as the home of a variety of religious activities. Its membership spawned the establishment of the first Muslim Nation cemetery in the southwestern portion of the city. (Photograph: Caitlin Kolb)

Some evidence exists that Islam was practiced in the British Colonies in North America by Africans brought to the New World as slaves. In the United States, evidence exists of regular Muslim worship in scattered locations in the country during the late nineteenth century, but little sustained public interest is evident and references to Mohammed and the *Quran* appear largely in reference to Christianity (Washburn 1894). Early immigrants lacked the funds to build what might have been recognized as a mosque, so that Muslim religious buildings were often converted from other uses. Many were seen as social halls and cultural centers, and most, indeed, served those purposes (Smith 1999). Highland Park, Michigan, claims to have been the first place to have built a mosque, in 1919 (Krupa 2009), followed by Michigan City, Indiana, five years later, but in both cities those early structures have been demolished. The earliest extant mosque was completed in 1934 in Cedar Rapids, Iowa, and is recognized as a site of historic importance by denominations of all kinds and the public (Fig. 8.16). Although the property was sold in 1970 and was allowed to deteriorate, the Islamic Council of Iowa repurchased it in 1990. A recognized historic site, this renovated "Mother Mosque" began offering services again in 1993. Although damaged in the 2008 flood that put 1300 blocks of Cedar Rapids under water, the property was reclaimed and continues to offer religious services (Huffstutter 2008).[21] One recent survey of the country counted over 1200 mosques, or "masjids," about three quarters of which were built for another function before they were converted to religious use (Bagby 2001).[22]

Although the importance of Islamic cultural centers grew, Muslims were hardly noticeable until the 1960s, when the charismatic leader Elijah Mohammed led inner-city African Americans to embrace the religion as a means of reform. His son, Warith Deen Mohammed, continued to lead the Nation of Islam, practicing Sunni Islam and integrating it with the broader tenets of the faith. Most immigrant Muslims held a completely different vision of their role in life, however, because most were relatively well-educated, holding professional positions, and moved in completely different social circles than the inner-city African Americans. Today, most Muslims are a

---

[21] This Cedar Rapids Mosque has been added to the National Register of Historic Places. In 1948, Muslim businessman William Yahya Aossey Sr. gave the group six and a half acres of land to establish the first Muslim Nation Cemetery just outside of the city.

[22] The 2012 statistics show a growth to over 2000 mosques nationwide.

mix of African Americans and Arab and South Asian immigrants, about equal in number, gravitating to live in the suburbs. Characterized by their devoutness and the recognition of centralized authority in which an executive committee or council makes decisions for the mosque, an imam or president wields considerable influence. Residents of the United States have gained an increased familiarity with the Muslim faith following the attacks of September 11, 2001, for the first time paying attention to the differences between the Sunni and the Shia and the African American Muslims, among others.

In sum, a deeper knowledge about the differences among religions can provide understanding that leads to interreligious dialogue and to the exploration and development of common agendas. In a similar fashion, the understanding of the location of significant events and the role of the beliefs helps explain why places look they way they do. All of this makes it possible to forge links to specific historical, architectural, and artistic religious legacies. The power of each religion also relates to the role of particularly persuasive leaders, who sometimes fashion faith in what others might find relatively unorthodox manners, as discussed next.

Evangelical Regeneration and Preservation

As we have seen, religious groups often reform themselves, proselytizing their views. The power of outstanding preachers to attract thousands of followers from considerable distances has transformed people and places. The fiery evangelist Dwight L. Moody, the young Rev. J. Wilbur Chapman, and his younger-still colleague Billy Sunday were often invited by the union of Methodist, Baptist, and Presbyterian ministers to join a revival. This occurred in a rented opera house or a farmer's field in Iowa, Minnesota, Nebraska, Indiana, and Illinois. These crusades also attracted vast crowds in the nation's largest cities, where the evangelists' appearances would be followed by press conferences and dinners. Leading women also gained attention. For example,

Aimee Semple McPherson's Angelus Temple in Los Angeles opened in 1923 and quickly gained a sizable following. Several thousand people would attend a single service or event (Fig. 8.17). During a revival "Sister" Aimee saw a vision of four creatures reminiscent of a lion, a man, an ox, and an eagle, a symbol of perfection, which became the creed of her "Foursquare Church." Two years later her Pentecostal group claimed 32 branch churches, and at least four dozen more wished to affiliate. The "mother church" was Angelus Temple, centered on a 5000 seat auditorium, featured in radio broadcasts with performers, choirs, and musicians (Lately 1959).

While comparatively well-established congregations often published a mimeographed newspaper and sponsored religious dramas and re-enactments to provide additional spiritual and social appeal, the evangelical reach was considerably enhanced with the advent of electronic media. Radio opened up new ways of proselytizing and provided an additional vehicle for physical relocation and change. Testimonials and gospel reading were offered over the radio almost from the introduction of the medium, connecting people over hundreds of square miles (Roberts 1924).[23] Rev. Samuel Parkes Cadman is recognized as having been the first, beginning to broadcast from the Central Congregational Church in 1923. Dr. Ralph Sockman established his Manhattan-based National Radio Pulpit soon thereafter (Melton et al. 1997). As pulpit broadcasting became a more broadly accepted facet of Protestant religious life, preachers were encouraged to hire "radio men" to assist them in reaching the "unchurched." Soon, complaints arose from the pastors of smaller rural churches about this "poaching" or "competing for sheep," to which they attributed the loss of membership, but the difficulties faced by rural churches in the face of widespread growth in urban and suburban locations were far more complicated than radio broadcasting. In 1924, at least 28 churches from Boston to Tacoma owned and operated their own

---

[23] Rev. Clifford L. White, known as the "Radio Parson," notes the role of Nashville and early religious broadcasting stations in the country (White 1924).

Fig. 8.17 The Angeles Temple, in Los Angeles, CA, was made famous by one of the most popular women preachers of the twentieth century, Aimee Semple. (Author's photograph)

stations, in addition to the congregations that were sending their services over the air through an arrangement with another broadcasting studio (Management 1925). The Baptists and Presbyterians led the way. By the start of the Depression, the Federal Council of the Churches of Christ in America reported that 531 Protestant services were conducted over the National Broadcasting System, representing 20 different denominations.

In the post-World War II era, as soon as television broadcasting was possible, religious programming was evident. In the 1950s and 1960s evangelist Billy Graham held leaders and the general public spellbound for hours during his televised sermons. More than any other Christian preacher Graham extended the global reach of Christianity through televised crusades in sports stadiums and arenas with his charismatic power, reaching millions. For Roman Catholics, the radio and television personality, scholar Bishop Fulton Sheen, provided moral guidance in an era when the Church was attempting to be more relevant to its believers. Mention of both of these leaders is appropriate for they inspired other preachers (Pollock 1966; Sheen 1980; Lippy 1989; Bruns 2004).

As in previous decades, a stark difference remains between the power of the large church and the problems of the small church, which often depends on meager financial resources and part time personnel. The "megachurch," a congregation with more than 2000 in attendance on a weekend, is, by definition, not a Catholic church or Jewish synagogue. In addition, the sheer size of the organization stands in stark contrast to most Protestant denominations with deep historical roots (Chaves 2004).[24] Most of the current megachurches are thought to have begun in the 1950s, perhaps because many of the most prominent examples began during that decade (Thumma and Travis 2007). As they outgrew their domestically scaled facilities and sought newer suburban locations with large parking lots and room for extensive community facilities they began to be noticed more often. Currently over 1300 megachurches have been identified, and about a third make extensive use of radio, television, and the internet (NYT 2007a).[25]

Some megachurches are "pastor-based," i.e., they center on a charismatic leadership that possesses the gift of the Spirit, often celebrating healing, much in the fashion of the conservative Assemblies of God and the Church of God in Cleveland, Tennessee. Often the wives of the pastors play an active role in leading the group.[26] Other groups are more liberal, purposely

---

[24] Scholars suggest that the general trend is toward an increasing number of small churches and very large churches.

[25] Although episodic experiments were launched by the United Methodists in 1983, the Presbyterian Church launched the first continuously sponsored network, "Presbynet," in 1985.

[26] Prominent examples are Randy and Paula White in the Church without Walls in Tampa, FL; Creflo and Tafi Dollar of World Changing Ministries in College Park, GA; Keith and Deborah Butler of The Word of Faith International Center, Southfield, MI; and Mac and Lynne Hammond of Living Word Christian Center, Brooklyn Park, MN.

reshaping their message to help reconnect people to what God is already doing in their lives. All have expanded during the 1980s and early 1990s.

Recent studies confirm that evangelical or born-again Americans make up 34% of all American adults and 45% of all Christians and Catholics. Researchers have found that 18% of Catholics consider themselves born-again or evangelical, and nearly 39% of established Protestants prefer those labels. Studies have also found signs of a growing influence of churches that either don't belong to a denomination or don't emphasize their membership in a religious group. They are less interested in supporting choirs or church-like activities, and even celebrate communion less frequently.

Generally they are composed of more young people than other churches, and they have more diverse audiences. The attendees of megachurches are always free to choose their level of involvement, but they are continually urged to step-up and volunteer, serving in as many diverse ministries as possible, rather than simply sitting on the sidelines as a passive observer.

As the surveys of megachurches are demonstrating, some are becoming *de facto* replacements for denominations as they adopt bureaucratic structures. The Vineyard Churches and the Calvary Chapels have expanded beyond their respective founding megachurch locations to become quasi-denominations with nationwide appeal (Century 2008). Some of the fastest growing Protestant congregations are the megachurches that are part of the World Changers Ministry, which have planted satellite facilities in dozens of locations in the country and abroad (NYT May 16, 1992).

Because many of these fast-growing new churches have recently built their suburban facilities, preservation is not yet a major concern. Some have already outgrown their properties, however, and could provide more urban and suburban regenerative capacity with ample financial support. Therefore, their investments make a difference. Examples can be found where a growing megachurch brings new life to an unused industrial facility, an undervalued shopping center, or a surplus school. In Charlotte, North Carolina,

the University Park Baptist Church bought the 0.5 million square foot Merchandise Mart to be remodeled for church and new business activities. Commercial activities are, in fact, essential to the development of these enterprises. At least ten megachurches own and operate shopping centers and some are adding residential developments with upscale homes, retail offices, sports facilities, food distribution centers, restaurants, lending institutions, and housing for the elderly (NYT 2007b).

As in the case of many religious groups, radical change can lead to a considerable amount of dispute. With the rehabilitation of old "megachurches," concerns have arisen when the leadership proposes updating the facilities or improving the grounds. In the case of the Angelus Temple in Los Angeles, the Church's new pastors, Ed and Ivy Stanton, proposed to drop a new, flat ceiling beneath the sanctuary's remarkable dome, cover the historic 40 foot mural over the proscenium, and build a superstructure to cover the sanctuary's Kimball organ pipes. They cited the need to improve acoustics; over 200 members of the congregation opposed the changes. Enlisting the help of the Los Angeles Conservancy, a portion of the congregation worked to redirect the project plans and the results are more pleasing to the whole group and sympathetic to the Temple, one of the city's important National Historic Landmarks (Bernstein and Sandmeier 2001). Today the pastors celebrate the history of their spiritual and physical legacy (Fig. 8.18).

Interfaith Cooperation

In the United States, evangelical activity has continued to be one of the most powerful reasons for interfaith cooperation. On the frontier, organized religions often helped one another. Missionaries of one faith would put aside their denominational differences to assist another. The assistance between Protestant leaders in spiritual matters often extended to physical help. In some instances this cooperation begins with the construction of the first church in a village or city when a more established congregation would permit a smaller

Fig. 8.18 The interior of the Angelus Temple can hold 5000 people, making it one of the earliest "megachurches." In addition, satellite churches in other locations broadcasted to thousands more by radio. (Author's collection)

religious group to meet in its basement or sanctuary while the younger organization was constructing its new building.

During the late nineteenth century Protestant leaders of all major denominations banded together at the local, national, and international level in the Evangelical Alliance (Douglass 1930, pp. 41–44), which promoted faith-based activities and social service. In many regards, this allowed Protestants to band together to advance common political agendas, including temperance and women's rights. Following the World's Congress in Chicago, the first formal step for sustained contact took place in 1908, with the formation of the Federated Council of Churches of Christ.

In addition to support for evangelical activities, federations of Protestant denominations supported joint social service work. However, the growth of the number of local federations was slowed during WWI, and afterward the Federal Council of Churches saw considerable differences between federations of Protestant denominations in various cities. In the south and south

central states they were practically non-existent while in the Great Lakes and western states considerable cooperation existed.

As the number of church building programs accelerated during the 1920s, the financial aspects of the expanded religious missions even led to the creation of the National Association of Church Business Administrators.[27] On closer examination it becomes clear that, because the federation was a voluntary organization, denominations that asserted a considerable amount of independence often criticized the role of group activities and the limited participation of some denominations worked to undermine effectiveness. Some federations excluded religious bodies that were not constitutionally proscribed. More to the point, even though African American churches were included by charter and many were characteristically evangelical, only in rare instances did one actively participate with the two dozen

---

[27] The journal of this organization, *Church Management*, begun in 1924 and edited by William H. Leach, continues to be produced today by *Clergy Journal*.

or more white denominations. Non-English-speaking congregations were also notably absent (Douglass 1930, p. 91).[28]

Because federations depended in part on the contributions of their church denominations, the Depression adversely affected joint activities. The practical needs of ministering to the needy remained higher than normal until after World War II. Reorganization took place in 1950 when the Federal Council of Churches merged with the International Council of Religious Education, formed in 1905, to give birth to the National Council of the Churches of Christ in the United States (often abbreviated the National Council of Churches or NCC). Its denominations, conventions, and dioceses include a broad variety of Protestant and evangelical communities, representing an estimated 45 million followers. While the efforts to alleviate poverty and hunger in Asia, Africa, and the Americas were impressive, the Churches' attention to the living and working conditions of migrant workers, Indian tribe housing, and urban dislocation and immigration influenced government thinking (Sartain 1960). When, during the 1960s, urban renewal programs gained strength, a loose coalition of religious leaders, housing reformers, planners, and federal officials became convinced that the modernization of cities was destroying neighborhood churches, adversely affecting their social service programs, particularly those needed by inner city African American residents. The Johnson era "War on Poverty" was fought by "creative federalism," a term used to describe federally-financed, locally conducted activities. During this period the working cooperation of church groups was deemed essential to reach low income residents, particularly in riot-torn neighborhoods. Yet, even the government admitted that the needs far outstripped the ability of any single religious group or any outside agency. The NCC, particularly the departments of United Church Women and Education for Mission, took a leading role (Schaller 1967).

A marked change in interfaith cooperation came about in the 1960s with the willingness of Protestants and Catholics to speak and work with one another outside of troubled inner cities. In the Midwest, seminarians studying at Presbyterian institutions were allowed to take courses in Lutheran and Catholic theological schools. While on the streets of a city such as Detroit, the Metropolitan Council of Churches sponsored radio dialogues of informal conversations with all local religious leaders, Jewish, Catholic, and Protestant, just as much discussion was taking place behind the scenes within the dominations themselves (Presbyterian 1965a, b, pp. 28–29).

Traditionally, a "community" defined by ethnicity and geography supported the practice of religion in a particular place. As indicated earlier, Catholics defined a parish with boundaries that embraced adjacent neighborhoods. As the number of Irish, Polish, Italian, and French Catholics grew, often in close proximity to one another, each group supported its own churches and related facilities. Assuming a certain amount of language and customs survive, the parish had the ability to sustain religious and material life by providing all of the goods and services close at hand and yet be connected to other parishes with similar interests around the world. In a similar fashion, Protestant groups have worked together. In 2005, the United Methodists made news by approving an agreement to share the Eucharist with the Episcopal Church and the Evangelical Lutheran Church, allowing the three religions to take the first step in recognizing one another's sacraments. The Methodist tradition includes the African Methodist Episcopal, African Methodist Episcopal Zion, and Christian Methodist Churches (Century 2005).

This is by no means the only use of the term "community." When a religious leader declares it is necessary to consider the needs of the "community," the definition can be interpreted as a "community of interest," i.e., a group of adherents who come together by a common set of beliefs rather than located in close proximity to one another. They can be motivated by religion, but also by common interests such as class, language, race, recreation, or any human connection. Communities of interest are often seen as the vehicle through which social groups build

---

[28] Relatively few Roman Catholics participated as well.

constituencies for political change. Religions often question contemporary society, warning against the tendency to acquire material goods and waste natural resources. Almost all faiths attempt to reframe the measures of fundamental progress not in terms of acquired wealth, but by insisting on a reinterpretation of daily activities by focusing on human well-being. As diffuse as the faith-based efforts are, they remain remarkably consistent with the concept of sustainability, defined by the balanced goals of ecological respect, economic prosperity, and social equity.[29]

It can come as no surprise, then, that a growing number of faith-based organizations have embraced ideas about sustainability. The position being maintained by the majority of religious leaders is not to reject science or recent social changes that have improved the lives of an increasing number of people, but to balance true human worth with what is considered progress.

Religion has not, until comparatively recently, embraced environmental thinking. Sporadic discussion of ecological thinking and its connections to religion took place in the 1960s; however, Evangelical Christians have begun to focus on caring for the earth, calling for more respect for Nature. The Evangelical Environmental Network, founded in 1993, calls on God's people to educate, inspire, and motivate to "tend the garden." Not only has the Network addressed the problems of global warming, it has taken the additional step of providing step-by-step information about how to care for church properties, including the landscaping and grounds, and how to construct "creation-friendly buildings" (Krueger 1995).[30]

The Interfaith Center on Corporate Responsibility established a Global Warming Working Group concerned with the need for action to prevent the damage caused by climate change. Cooperating with corporations that are responsible for greenhouse gas emissions, electricity, oil and gas production and distribution, automobile and appliance manufacturing, the group urges monitoring and measurement to reduce emissions.

Faith-Based Community Development

As a first step in determining what a neighborhood, village, town, or city needs, a survey must be taken to determine just how many community services are already in place, and how well they are being provided. Some religions have a long standing tradition of assisting people of their own faith and some others. This often begins with providing housing, health care, and schools. For example, in 1926, St. Louis had 45 specialized denominational enterprises, including 28 children's, old people's, and other homes, eight hospitals, and nine schools of major importance.

After World War II, the general rise in the number of new church facilities provided a burst of activity. One of the ideas suggested to help make churches relevant to their urban communities was the "cathedral ministry." This concept, put forward by Rev. Gaylord B. Noyce in 1975, offered a framework for churches located in downtown areas to reshape their ministry programs in order to better serve the increasingly geographically dispersed, commuter-following. The cathedral ministry proposed to reconfigure outreach programs and ministry to appeal to and accommodate the "every day but Sunday" congregation. Influenced by the traditional European model of the Church often controlling and managing the hospitals, orphanages, almshouses, and hospices, the cathedral ministry called for a renewed commitment to providing social services (Noyce 1975; Baskerville 1994, pp. 38–51). Because cathedral building was such an extensive social and economic enterprise, it involved the leadership of the community and the wealthy, the skilled crafts and guilds, as well as the labor of the poor.

Even the most outspoken advocates of the cathedral ministry concept were aware that the medieval institution was not going to be duplicated. The idea persists, however, that a church, synagogue, or temple should respond not only to the needs of the local adherents, but also to

---

[29] Sustainability is treated in more detail in Chapter 7.

[30] Founded by Professor Calvin DeWitt, in 1994 the Evangelical Environmental Network issued "An Environmental Declaration on the Care of Creation."

diverse social constituencies, with soup kitchens, child day care centers, organ recitals, and arts events. One of the most notable examples in the Northeast is the Allen A.M.E. Church, a growing congregation of over 10,000 members in Queens, New York, dedicated to improving the spiritual and physical conditions of the area (Cohen 1997; Fig. 8.19). The Church is named for the African American spiritual leader Richard Allen, who escaped slavery and later organized the Bethel A.M.E. Church in Philadelphia in 1794. The Allen A.M.E. Church began in 1834 in the area of Queens known as Jamaica, and grew in the nineteenth and early twentieth century as more members migrated from the South (Ebony 1971). A new sanctuary, built in the 1960s, was fire-bombed in 1969, but the congregation held fast to their location. By the early 1980s, the charismatic leader Reverend Dr. Floyd H. Flake, a former professor and dean, began to attract attention for having re-introduced the social gospel. He subsequently ran for Congress and won, forging ties with the Irish, Jewish, Italian, and Hispanic communities, being re-elected for six terms.[31] Just as important, Reverend Flake brought national attention to the role of faith-based initiatives in the 11 years he served in Congress, before leaving political life to become President of Wilberforce University.[32]

Allen AME Church is a cathedral church that serves not only its adherents but the larger geographic community with a number of programs. Church sponsored schools accept students from outside the congregation. As the same time, a

Fig. 8.19 Allen A.M.E. Church, Jamaica, Queens, is one of the most remarkable "cathedral ministries" in the nation, with tens of thousands as members, involved with dozens of activities that serve the neighborhood, the region and well beyond. (Author's photograph)

vibrant community center, a Head Start program, and a number of community action activities involve the church members and others during every day of the week. Even before Rev. Flake was called to the Church, the community recognized that providing decent, affordable housing was an important part of revitalizing the area. The experience with senior citizen housing projects led to the organization of the Allen Housing and Development Corporation. This entity constructed a 300-unit apartment facility using Section 8 funding and built on land cleared by urban renewal. At the same time, the Allen Neighborhood Preservation Corporation, created in 1978 to rehabilitate and renovate vacant houses, assists owners to make repairs and upgrade their property. ANPC has also sponsored new affordable, infill housing. In 1985 alone, 62 new duplex houses were built on land formerly owned by the City of New York. By constructing, financing, and selling the units to people who are not members of the church, residents in the neighborhood understand the Church is not favoring any faith, race, ethnicity, or gender preference, but providing access to all. One of three major employers in the borough, it is an undeniably effective revitalizing force in the area.

---

[31] Floyd Flake was one of 13 children raised in a disciplined Christian family in Houston, TX. He distinguished himself by preaching throughout his college days at Payne Theological Seminary in Ohio. He served as associate dean at Lincoln University from 1970 until 1973, when he was called to be the director of the Martin Luther King Center and assistant dean of students at Boston University. His wife, Margaret McCollins Flake, an educator and minister, has provided leadership alongside him in a number of capacities.

[32] The Community Renewal Act of 1995 encouraged the involvement of voluntary community organizations in addressing social needs, and recognized faith-based nonprofits as legitimate partners in urban redevelopment. Rev. Flake believed that both Democrats and Republicans must recognize the value of the approach being taken at Allen Church.

African American Methodists are by no means the only ones to lay a claim to abandoned or underutilized inner city real estate. In 1990, the talented songwriter and producer Kenny Gamble returned to the blighted neighborhood around 15th and Christian Streets in South Philadelphia, promising to make a difference. Gamble founded a nonprofit organization, Universal Companies, which began to purchase abandoned properties and build new in-fill housing for low- and moderate-income families. The area's proximity to the center city and the initial low property values were obvious advantages. A decade later, about 200 units were completed, a remarkable record. This progress was not without problems. Short of cash and plagued by construction delays, the Universal Companies took longer than expected to complete rehabilitation projects (Lin 2005). Seen from the perspective of many nonprofit organizations, however, this is by no means uncommon and the effort to create affordable housing did serve as the springboard for other property owners to take an interest in upgrading their properties. Every block resounded with hammers and power saws, as well as talk about the advantages of investing in real estate. An early partner with the Philadelphia Housing Authority in redeveloping the King Public Housing, the Universal Companies also worked with high-end housing developers to diversify the income levels in the area (Lin 2006). One of the most significant aspects of Gamble's work, however, is that it centers on a African American Muslim community. Gamble, also known as Luqman Abdul-Haqq, and his wife founded the company, which has grown to include four charter schools and provides support services for welfare recipients and public housing residents.

Communities Making Secular Use of Religious Space

Wherever the future of a religious property does not lend itself to further use for worship, the prudent course may be to convert it to another use, at least in the short term. Among religious groups there is considerable variation about what is acceptable, but it is important to keep in mind that secular activities have long taken place in churches, temples, and synagogues. They have often included providing sanctuary and shelter for the homeless or traveling pilgrim, but the list also includes sleeping, eating, drinking, teaching, dancing, and assembly. Peddling and some sales of services has been commonplace, too, especially the sales and distribution of food and clothing (Davis 1968). In fact, the re-use of a former religious property is often possible only be examining the options in the immediate neighborhood.

One example of dozens is seen in northern New Jersey. The 1967 riots in Newark's Central Ward deeply moved William Linder, a young resident priest (Linder 2008). To meet the challenge of rebuilding the community and creating institutional strength to serve local needs, Linder and his parishioners formed a new board that included the leaders of the African American community. This signaled the formation of the New Community Corporation (NCC). The state-commissioned investigation to determine what caused the riots laid out three primary reasons: police brutality, lack of political representation, and poor social conditions, the most important aspect of the latter being insufficient and deteriorating housing. As a result of these findings, New Community set as its first objective the creation of permanent and affordable housing for residents. NCC raised over $100,000 by symbolically selling land in the Central Ward for $5 per sq. ft., which allowed it to purchase two acres of land and construct 120 apartment units, which opened in 1975 (Mumford 2008; Tuttle 2009).

This early work continued so that currently NCC owns over a dozen properties in Newark, housing over 6000 people. The developments include both rentals and homeownership opportunities, providing a range of affordable options. The organization's activities, however, extended beyond housing. It also owns and operates Babyland, which offers daycare to hundreds children in several nurseries and seeks to provide employment opportunities. When the Newark Roman Catholic Archdiocese closed a neighboring parish, St. Josephs, NCC purchased the property with the intention of increasing the community's private health care by offering doctors the opportunity to rent office space, so that local residents did not have to travel to suburban medical centers. With the campus of the University of Medicine and Dentistry of New Jersey abutting the area, the opportunity was too good to ignore and the NCC launched into its first commercial venture. The rehabilitation of the old brownstone church into 18,000 sq. ft. of professional office space and a 3500 sq. ft. restaurant began in 1980 and was substantially complete four years later. The project, called St. Joseph's Plaza cost about $1.75 million and was financed, in part, through $1.2 million in tax exempt bonds issued by the State's Economic Development Authority in view of the expected job creation (Depalma 1983).[33] The central nave of the church, with its high ceiling and exposed wooden trusses, became a three-level atrium connected to the other floors by a winding staircase and a glass-enclosed elevator. The clustered columns, arches, and stained glass windows all remain in place, while the side aisles were enclosed and divided into several offices on two levels.

Subsequent community work by NCC included opening Harmony House, which cares for the homeless, and building PathMark and Shop-Rite grocery stores to improve food service and provide employment at a supermarket training facility (Narvaez 1987; Teltsch 1991; Stewart 1996; Carter 1998). Linder's "city of hope" is an organization with over 1600 employees and still remains committed to its community oriented mission.

Partnerships: The Importance of Sharing Space

Partnerships in sharing spaces can be forged between religious bodies, or with other non-profit charitable organizations with a social service mission. In many cases the union can be mutually beneficial and program partnerships can develop that go beyond sharing the same facility.

Where a strong leader is enlisted and transforms the organizational dynamic of the religious group, it often expands to engage more social programs in the community. This growth and expansion provide strength. Such a transformation in leadership or the continued growth of the denomination is not always possible, however, so that another approach is needed to address problems that arise when a religious group's property is too large and its membership declining.

In these instances, as the nationwide nonprofit Partners for Sacred Places and other organizations have repeatedly shown, forming partnerships to make better use of underutilized facilities can be an important key to reducing expenses. Partnerships with other religious organizations arise when another declining church or an expanding young group agrees to support the maintenance and care of the facility. Usually the host church owns the property and the guest congregation contracts to make use of it at different times. Provided care is given to the financial arrangements, the host church benefits from the income while the guest church contributes to the maintenance and upkeep. Often schools, day-care programs, food pantries, and homeless shelters find homes in underutilized space (Mosher 1994; Hopkins 2011).[34]

One of dozens of examples of a parish that is being transformed is St. Catherine's Catholic Church in southwestern Houston, built in the late 1960s by middle-class Anglos who, in the fashion of many whites, fled from the African American and Hispanic working class in the center city. As the local economy declined in later years, Vietnamese, Mexican, Philipino, Indian, Nigerian, and other immigrant groups moved to the surrounding suburban neighborhood. Because the Church was not growing, the diocese agreed to allow people of other faiths to make use of the facilities. No fewer than seven distinct immigrant groups share the amenities, forming parallel congregations, with their own festivals and Church-sanctioned social

---

[33] Architect Roz Li of New York was responsible for the sympathetic design of the property, which is listed on the National Register of Historic Places.

[34] Religious institutions must take care when partnering with for-profit entities because properties may be reassessed as taxable.

occasions. Regardless of their ethnicity, however, most of the adherents reside within the parish boundaries and thus share the same concerns (Ebaugh et al. 2000).

The Al-Noor Islamic Mosque in north Houston displays the same kind of close community. The Sunni Muslims in the area have considerably more latitude to worship in other locations, but most of the members of the mosque have deliberately chosen to attend religious services in this place, as they feel at home in the community.

Members of some faiths live at considerable distances from their places of worship, however, and can be termed "communities of interest." The Jyothi Hindu Temple, 30 miles south of Houston, is supported by a group of worshippers who will drive 20 to 30 miles from anywhere in the metropolitan area. Although there are nine temples in Greater Houston, this is the finest local example and the first in the United States to be dedicated to a goddess. It is important to emphasize the fact that membership in this temple is considered a sign of deep commitment to Hindu identity, although the frequency of attendance is not as regular as, perhaps, other religions might require. In the same fashion, spatial distribution studies show that the Zoroastrians, chiefly Parsis, and the Greek Orthodox communities, may live considerable distances from where they worship, as many of their members are comparatively well-educated and prosperous.

In short, the social ties often are just as important as faith for seeking a place to gather. In between the extremes, other faiths display a combination of organizational arrangements, some of which appear to be operating as geographically constrained but are not, while in other cases the reverse is true. Looking at a neighborhood, a parish may seem to be underpopulated, but it may also maintain multigenerational ties that provide significant strength from family members that live outside the boundaries but maintain an active interest in local affairs.

Nondenominational "Custodial" Partnerships

Faith-based organizations of all kinds have become familiar with the activities of non-sectarian preservation groups that provide an increasing amount of fiscal and personnel support for the rehabilitation and repair of religious properties. For years, because the general public valued historic properties owned by religious organizations, government funding has been quietly channeled to non-profit organizations that shepherded the restoration and repair of churches, meeting houses, synagogues, temples, and several other kinds of religious buildings. As early as 1971, the National Trust for Historic Preservation awarded grants and loans to fund a restoration plan for a 1852 adobe Roman Catholic Church in Albuquerque, New Mexico, and to develop a strategy for reusing a Jewish synagogue in Denver as a performing arts center (Hoffman 1989). In this way, the separation of church and state remained clear because the studies did nothing to promote religion, or prefer one faith over another. As the same time, the preservation organization served to guide the work, occasionally helping with fundraising.

Ironically, it was during the Presidency of the born-again Christian Jimmy Carter that controversy arose about providing funding for this kind of bricks and mortar project. By the late 1970s, while many Protestants and some Catholics attempted to forestall the increasing decline in their memberships, many of whom were scattering to the suburbs, the problem of being able to raise sufficient financial support for repairs was dire. In response to the widespread call for help, during the 1980s some special preservation organizations dedicated to working in partnership with religious groups began to blossom (Baskerville 1994, pp. 13-14).

In 1982 the New York [City] Landmarks Conservancy created a Religious Properties Program to assist religious property owners and managers across the state with restoration, rehabilitation, and maintenance. Fundraising provided mini-grants to jump-start projects. In 1984, the organization of what became the nonprofit Save Our Universalist Landmark (SOUL) considered how to raise money to support the restoration of the Fourth Universalist Society in New York City. This was one of the first attempts to combine fundraising with restoration work (Dunlap 1988; Partners 1991). David Dunlap, business manager for the Society, worked closely with the Landmarks Conservancy to raise funds from corporations and foundations, reaching their goal of $500,000 in three years.

In 1983 Philadelphia followed suit. The Philadelphia Historic Preservation Corporation (PHPC) instituted a Historic Religious Properties Program, focusing on needs in the city and in neighboring Camden, New Jersey, and emphasizing the benefits of shared uses. Again, PHPC helped by providing technical assistance and small grants, the latter used for feasibility studies and historic structures reports that prioritized conservation problems in order to guide cost estimating and fundraising.

In 1986, Historic Boston, Inc. (HBI) began with a similar intent, largely as an outgrowth of its mediation effort in a dispute between the Jesuits of Immaculate Conception Roman Catholic Church and the local landmarks commission. Like the two older groups, HBI provided case study examples to demonstrate the alternatives to abandonment and demolition.[35]

In the same manner as the late nineteenth century Los Angeles-based Landmarks Society approached saving the historic California Missions, preservationists took the initiative a century later to renew Roman Catholic properties in New Mexico. In 1985, the New Mexico Community Foundation (NMCF), dedicated to developing more self-reliant communities in the state, began helping the small churches in rural areas (PNM 1987). Working with the New Mexico State

Historic Preservation office, the Foundation identified adobe churches as key elements in the state's communities, about 700 in all. Because government funds could not be used to restore or rehabilitate the properties, donations of materials, money, and labor were solicited to re-mud the walls and secure the roofs. Working closely with the Archbishop of Sante Fe's Committee on Historic Churches, the Foundation backed preservation plans for eight communities.

The challenges associated with San Jose Mission Church in Upper Rociada, a ten-family village in the Sangre de Cristo Mountains, 50 miles north of Taos, proved exceptionally difficult because the cement coating applied years earlier trapped moisture within the walls, accelerating the adobe wall decay (Sweeney 1990). Seeing that the difficulties needed the services of an organization that did not yet exist, in 1986 Churches: Symbols of Community or C: SOC—later renamed Cornerstones Community Partnerships—was founded in Santa Fe, New Mexico (PNM 1994–1995). First led by Sam Baca and Barbara Zook, Cornerstones provided hundreds of Hispanic and Native American communities with technical assistance to rehabilitate their historic buildings. Relying on financial assistance from the New Mexico Community Foundation to help support a paid staff, the majority of the work depends upon a loyal and diverse group of volunteers. Cornerstones Community Partnerships has addressed the needs of parishes that care for both the great monuments of the region and everyday structures. Whether at San Estevan del Rey at Acoma Pueblo, or smaller churches such as San Rafel in Tajique, the need to work in adobe, stone, and mud plaster continues. The restoration work at San Jose De Rociada Arriba Mission, a condemned adobe church, took six years.

At the San Jose Mission, it was recommended that vigas (ceiling timbers) and corbels be uncovered, cement stucco removed, and the adobe walls repaired. Those who become involved were divided on whether they had the energy or finances for this project. While the small community was deciding, a horizontal crack in the wall expanded and it took a Christmas Eve effort by community volunteers and C: SOC staff to shored up the

---

[35] In 1988, Chicago became involved when the Midwest Regional Office of the National Trust for Historic Preservation launched a three year pilot project, called Inspired Partnerships. In 1991 it began to operate independently, working to maximize the use of space in religious properties by finding other organizations to share the challenges of maintenance. Unfortunately the organization did not survive (Brink 1992).

roof. The wall completely collapsed four months later and a final decision on whether to save or demolish the church was necessary.

A very difficult meeting was held. Many community members were elders with little physical capacity or money to support such a project. The church was built by their ancestors, however, and served as their community and spiritual center. One community member, Antonio Martinez, encouraged people to look to their children and extended family for help with labor and financial support. Finally a vote was taken and the decision was made to proceed with the restoration, lead by the newly formed San José Mission Restoration Committee.[36]

Committee member José Martinez wrote a fundraising letter from his home in Littleton, Colorado, and sent it to all the former residents of the community he could trace. Local residents contributed what they could, many averaging $300 a family, and in the first year $8000 was raised for building materials. Over the course of the multiyear building project more than $13,000 was donated. Additionally, businessman Jerry Sanchez of Rio Abajo Adobes donated 4000 adobe bricks.

The restoration began with a committed group of six residents working every day over the first summer. These workers were supplemented by entire families of former residents from Idaho and Wyoming who worked on the church during their vacations. Other residents cooked meals for the workers each day, including Encarnacion Martinez, who provided lunch for all the workers during the first two summers. It was a model community effort. The intense community spirit was evidenced one day when an older woman visited the site and asked if she could lay just one adobe brick so that she could be part of helping to restore the church. During the first year 50% of the fallen wall was replaced. In the second year the other half was completed. However, each new phase of the restoration uncovered more damage. Two rotted ceiling *vigas* were replaced, caves were extended, and a new subsurface drainage system was installed on the interior and exterior.

Over the next four summers, a new electrical system was installed, the roof was patched, interior plastering was completed, doors and window frames were replaced, and the floorboards—which cover the burial sites of thirteen townspeople—were replaced, sanded, and refinished. Rebuilding and stabilizing the exterior walls used over 13,000 adobe bricks.[37]

As this example shows, religious buildings can represent an entire community, going well beyond a place of Sunday worship. With this in mind, in 1988, the first nationwide "Sacred Trusts" conference was held, which reinforced the need for a nationwide organization parallel in many respects to the English groups dealing with "redundant churches." The new network was established the following year by Diane Cohen and A. Robert Jaeger, who came together with interested members of the clergy to form Partners for Sacred Places, based in Philadelphia (Levinson 1991). Providing an information clearinghouse was an important first step. The directors and their staff visited dozens of religious properties and their leaders. In the first five years, 13 workshops were held across the nation, allowing Cohen and Jaeger to design a model workshop curriculum to be delivered in four locations each year, emphasizing the stewardship of both people and properties (PSPN 1991). To meet more immediate crises, Jaeger proposed a team approach, which he put to work in Oakland and Detroit. At the same time, the organization assembled the largest single collection of books, studies, films, and periodicals on religious property stewardship, supported by a board of directors representing almost all of established faiths. By the mid-1990s, Partners had begun to assist the Cleveland Restoration Society and the Pittsburgh History and Landmarks Foundation in structuring their own religious property initiatives, in essence re-tooling the local non-profit organizations to

---

[36] The members were Flora Martinez, Ted Martinez, José Martinez, Joe Trujillo, and Antonio Martinez.

[37] A statewide survey in New Mexico revealed that that the characteristics of churches built before 1815 differed from those constructed from 1880 until 1930, influencing the manner in which they could be restored or reused (PNM 1986). The Santa Fe firm of Johnson-Nestor conducted the survey of more than 200 churches (Johnson-Nestor et al. 1989).

address immediate needs more directly (PSPN 1995). Partners also worked with Preservation North Dakota and the Mountains/Plains Office of the National Trust for Historic Preservation to launch a program called "Prairie Churches of North Dakota," and with the Preservation Trust of Vermont to sponsor conferences for religious leaders facing constrained budgets and deteriorating properties. Partners begin any preservation effort by trying to assist the people in the buildings, not simply focusing on the structures alone. As Jaeger states, "If you believe that the whole range of services that religious institutions provide is important, in fact essential, to a healthy city, then this is not a tactic but a necessary first step in the preservation of our sacred sites."[38]

It is important to remember that changing the nature of partnerships will affect relationships within that partnership. In some cases the organization providing assistance to the religious group will change, while in other instances the religious organization will alter its stance. Disagreements can become very uncomfortable and public, as illustrated in the case of the Holy Trinity Church in Brooklyn, a widely recognized landmark. Completed in 1848 to the design of architect Minard Lafever, the church exterior is an impressive Gothic Revival design, and the interior features plaster vaulting and more than 7000 sq. ft. of early stained glass by artist William Jay Bolton. The declining number of adherents in the area led to closing Holy Trinity in 1959, but when the adjacent St. Ann's Church also closed, the two were combined in the current structure. Recognizing the importance of the architect's work, the church's history, and Bolton's stained glass, in 1979 the non-profit New York Landmarks Conservancy intervened and helped spawn the St. Ann Center for Restoration and Arts. Thanks to this new organization and partnership with the church, the chancel was renovated, 64 stained glass windows restored, and the exterior fence repaired. With additional support from the World Monuments Fund, a conditions report led to a successful application for funds from the New York State Environmental Bond Act to restore the roof.

In 1995, however, a crisis arose when the boiler broke. Paying for the repairs exposed the shaky financial position of the parish and, alarmed at the prospect of declining support and donations, the rector recommended that the building be closed. A new rector, Rev. Wilson-Kastner, appealed to the diocesan officials who initially concurred the building was in danger of collapse, and thought that money for the restoration might have been improperly funneled to the arts program. The charge also surfaced that the content of the arts center's programs was disturbing to some in the parish. Hence, with the backing of the Diocese, an order was issued to evict the Center for the Arts and Restoration, which had operated in partnership with St. Ann's for more than a decade.

Rising to the defense of the Center were former pastors, as well as diocesan officials who stated that the defiance directed at them by the elected parish leaders was motivated by racism. Meanwhile, the parish vestry charged that the Bishop and their rector wanted to sell the property and two nearby brownstones to reap the profits in the gentrifying Brooklyn Heights neighborhood.

A truce was called and an agreement reached two years later when the bishop, head of the Episcopal Diocese of Long Island, allowed the pastor to leave and the shrinking parish to elect a new vestry (Rohde 1997). In July 2000, however, the Center announced that disagreements over the terms of its lease with the parish led it to leave the facility and search for another venue (Gootman 2000).[39]

---

[38] Private conversation held on August 15, 1991 between A. Robert Jaeger, Co-Director of Partners for Sacred Places, and the Author.

[39] The arts group earned a reputation for its innovative Arts at St. Ann's performances, which have included such disparate shows as a Velvet Underground reunion, a jazz suite featuring Elvis Costello and Debbie Harry, and operas with crooning puppets. The church's stained-glass windows, the first created in this country, served as a backdrop when Lou Reed and John Cale reunited for an Andy Warhol tribute and when the cartoonist Art Spiegelman's "Three-Panel Opera" had its debut. The partnership of church and arts center was lucrative, with the Center raising more than $4 million over the years to restore the church building.

A Final Resting Place?

In the same fashion that religious beliefs influence life, they also affect funeral customs. The preparation of the remains for burial or cremation; the approaches to embalming and encasement; the inclusion of grave goods; the celebrations, wakes, and mourning services; the processions and assemblies; all are part of the variety of cultures that are revealed in burial locations. While some Native American tribes will favor building mounds, others will prefer exposure to Nature. Many Christian religions take the position that death is followed by resurrection and, as a Christian nation, many of the burial laws and customs followed in the United States make this assumption. As in life, religious belief also affects the manner in which the remains are regarded, and treated in the future. As a result, the connection between religions and burial customs is an important concern for preservationists. Early religious life often extended beyond the walls of the meeting house or church into the immediate landscape.

No one knows the number of all of the burial places in the country, largely because many family burial grounds are unrecorded, and not all states regulate burials. The location of a cemetery, whether in the center of the city or at its periphery, can be an important indication of its age and character. Given the settlement and migratory patterns of American Indian tribes, and the population distribution of European settlements in the Colonial period and the early decades of the Republic, it is no wonder that cemeteries are found in what today seems some of the most remote locations. Today, family and clan graveyards abound, although many relatively isolated burial sites remain unconnected to the generations of families that followed. As the activities and land uses around the plots and cemetery yards and "hills" changed, they were often seen as impediments to development and commercial improvement (Sloan 1991).

The cemetery can provide a remarkable amount of historical information about a community. For some individuals, it is the only permanent record of their existence and their ac-

complishments. Many of the markers go beyond political and military history to provide social commentary about the moral innocence of children, the activities of women, and suggestions of domestic relationships, the use of animals, the problems with diseases, famine, and financial difficulty. The languages, expressions, symbols, and tools of professionals and skilled workmen, the musical instruments and artistic products are displayed for anyone to see (Meyer 1989; Fig. 8.20).

Going beyond family or communally owned plots and church yards, in some municipalities public land was set aside to bury paupers. As the early nineteenth century opened, however, a new model arose. A voluntary association of individuals, chartered to serve the families from the entire community, became more commonplace. The New Haven Burial Ground, for example, set aside land to bury the poor, "Negroes," and strangers, with the remainder separated into family lots (Sloan 1991, pp. 32–33). The diversity of ethnicity, class, race, and gender was as varied as the time, effort, and expense of the burial (Mitford 1963).

As cities grew, pressure increased to disregard burial plots. Disinterment became more common and involved moving mausoleums, monuments, hundreds of thousands of headstones, footstones, and markers, as well as the buried remains (Zollman 1916). Other forces tended to make burial places, once established, more permanent. Generally under-recognized is the degree to which Protestant faiths that had objected to the idea of life insurance before the Civil War began to accept the idea that a life was worth money. Thereafter, the amount of funds made available at the death of a wealthy person stimulated a number of substantial memorials being constructed in a fitting cemetery "neighborhood" (Zelizer 2009). In addition, as immigrants from Asia died and their families wished to bury them in public cemeteries, there was the tendency of the white majority to further segregate the dead. The burial rituals of Chinese, following the same rules of *fengshui* that applied to houses, placed the dead in harmony with Nature (Chung and Wegars 2005).

A remarkable change in the amount of attention paid to the design of a burial ground

Fig. 8.20 The Cemetery of Old First Congregational Church, Bennington, VT (1805), was designated by the state legislature as "Vermont's Sacred Acre" in light of its importance to religious history. (Author's photograph)

Fig. 8.21 The first romantically designed cemetery in the country, Mount Auburn, in Cambridge, MA (1831) broke away from the traditional cemetery grid and set the tone for many others in the North and Midwestern States. (Author's photograph)

became evident with the first romantically designed "rural" cemetery, Mount Auburn, in Cambridge, Massachusetts, which was laid out in 1831 (Fig. 8.21). Its chief promoter, Dr. Jacob Bigelow, was concerned with the dangers of disease often associated with the weedy, smelly urban cemetery, and insisted a new burial ground should be located outside Boston. The Massachusetts Horticultural Society took up the responsibility to produce one of the most rustic pleasure grounds ever created, complete with artificial water bodies, specimen trees, and exotic plants. Laurel Hill in Philadelphia, Green Mount in Baltimore, Green-Wood in Brooklyn, and Mount Hope in Rochester all followed in quick succession. At least 30 other rural cemeteries were laid out by the close of the Civil War, all of them designed with a remarkable amount of care to their landscapes (French 1974).

The introduction of the rural cemetery provided a socially desirable alternative to city owned cemeteries and broke the lock that religious denominations had on burials. In addition to graveyards and rural cemeteries, the nineteenth century also saw the addition of another fashionable concept, the "memorial park." A part of the broader movement to establish parks of all kinds, the memorial park was seen as a suburban alternative that contained sections consciously developed for various religious, civic, or ethic groups. As a group they functioned as memorial gardens, often more practical than romantic rural cemeteries, with fewer horticultural specimens and stricter controls that required markers to be kept within boundaries, or to lie flat with the ground, permitting lawn mowing machines to trim the grass. Indeed, nature was a backdrop in the landscape, with more open space and lower overall maintenance than the landscaped rural cemetery. In the case of Mount Auburn Cemetery, the master plan recognizes the growth of the property, as it should. The plan treats each section as an expression of the time, noting the gradual shift from a meandering romantic landscape to a denser, geometric plan (Berg 1992). The 175-acre cemetery has more than 40,000 monuments for over 94,000 people buried there; its management was recognized by the National Trust for Historic Preservation for its excellence in stewardship.

The planting of memorial trees and the practice of cremation challenge traditional beliefs of death because the modern emphasis on bolstering the spirits of the survivors and not dwelling on the process of dying or the accomplishments of the dead has led to a de-emphasis on the burial place. For the poor, who do not have the financial ability to choose, these characteristics become more obvious. But even the middle class have seen the cost of burial rise. Reflecting the premium on their property, some cemetery superintendents are raising prices. In Cambridge's Mount Auburn Cemetery, a two-person grave with a headstone went from $1000 in 1999 to $13,000 in 2013. A four-person plot spiked from $3000 to $37,000 (Diaz 2005).

The threats to human burials arise in several different forms. In some areas of the country grave digging continued to be a problem, much as it was before Congress passed the Antiquities Act in 1906. Indian tribes continue to face these challenges. As discussed in previous chapters, hundreds of Indian tribes have seen their burial locations and sacred sites desecrated. In a gruesome twist in nineteenth century medical history, the search for bodies for teaching and dissection by anatomists led to spates of grave robbing.

Other struggles to save cemeteries arise chiefly due to development and neglect. To overcome the threat of being seized in the public interest for a road or other infrastructure, often religious groups are the only advocates. During development, the prospect of encountering a burial site may not be considered and, if discovered, the re-

mains can prove to be difficult to identify, which hinders the ability to determine who is responsible for their care. In Manhattan, the African Burial Ground was uncovered in 1991 during construction of a federal office building at Broadway and Duane Street (Fig. 8.22). Termed the largest black colonial graveyard ever excavated in the country, with an estimated 20,000 graves, archeologists exhumed 419 human skeletal remains and scores of artifacts for study at Howard University in 1993. To the disappointment of many, the project stalled during the 1990's as research continued but no individuals were identified. In 2001, the US General Services Administration took definitive steps to move forward on the project and determined to set aside a portion of the property so that the remains of the seventeenth and eighteenth century slaves could be returned to the site and re-interred in a memorial next to the adjacent 34 story tower (Shipp 1991; Harrington 1993; Kilgannon 2003; Perry et al. 2009; Fig. 8.23).

People who care about cemeteries and burial grounds have organized. The best-known group is the Association for Gravestone Studies, the first organization founded for the purpose of furthering the study and preservation of gravestones. Its international representation, publications, conferences, workshops, and exhibits expand public awareness of the significance of historic grave-markers, and encourage individuals and groups to record and preserve their location. Just as often, religious groups are alone fighting to stop the bulldozer. In a response to Chicago's attempt to seize land for an expansion of O'Hare International Airport, St. John's United Church of Christ in Bensonville sued the larger neighboring city, claiming irreparable harm would come to a graveyard in which over 1300 of its church members have been laid to rest since 1849 (Rozak 2002). The most significant aspect of these conflicts is not only that they continue to arise, but their number increases.

Preservation initiatives also are often proposed by religious groups that affect the remains left in their care. When excavating the grave sites in and around Bruton Parish Church in Williamsburg, Virginia, at the turn of the last century, the

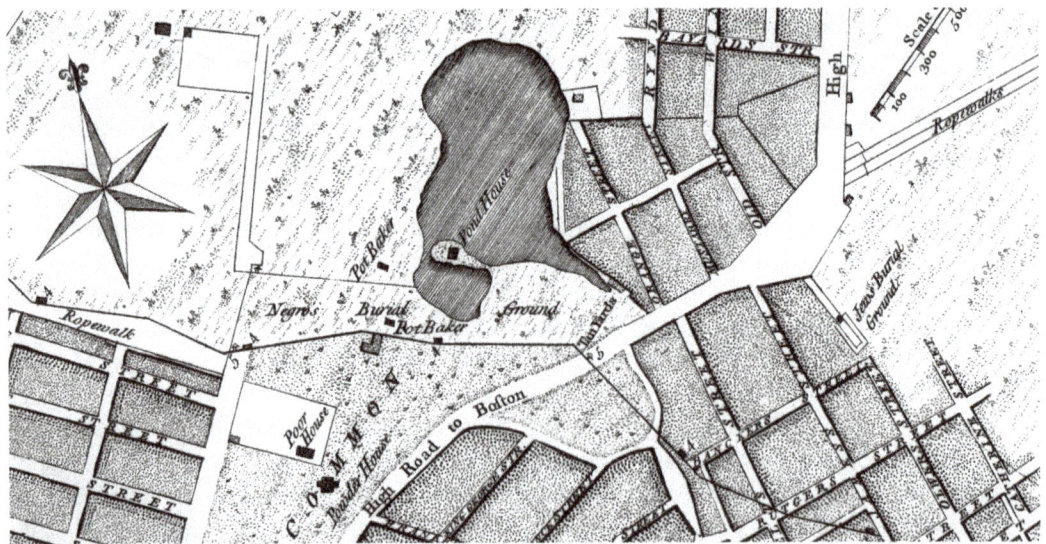

Fig. 8.22 The "Negro Burial Ground," formerly outside the walls of the city of New York, came to light in 1991 when excavating for a new federal office building. Originally but five and a half acres in size, it was the only co-lonial era cemetery for thousands of Africans and African decedents until it closed in 1794. (Author's photograph, Courtesy of Historic Urban Plans, Inc.)

Fig. 8.23 In 1993, the African Burial Ground was designated a National Monument and the remains were re-interred, with appropriate below and above grade interpretation. (Author's photograph)

discovery of the tombs inside and outside the building led to a massive relocation process to "restore" the property to its current state, thereby "beautifying" the grounds.[40]

As noted in the opening chapters, largely due to the Civil War, state and federal governments expressed concern about the treatment of battle-fields and the interment of veterans. This concern passed to the National Cemetery Administration, which provides admirable amount of mainte-nance for the tombs of those who have served in the armed forces. Cemetery preservation efforts

---

[40] See Chapter 2 for more about the church and the resto-ration in Williamsburg.

increased during and just after WWII and the Korean War. Since that time, however, individual headstone and burial plot maintenance has declined and been left to a groundskeeper, especially with the introduction of long-lasting artificial flowers and less interest by families in the annual graveyard holiday. In the last several decades, however, several "friends of" cemetery groups have arisen in Philadelphia, Rochester, New York, Mobile, Atlanta, and dozens of smaller cities and villages to take corrective action, cleaning and repairing deteriorating stones, and giving tours.[41]

Museum groups have also taken an active role in cemetery preservation activities. For example, the Santa Cruz County Museum of Art and History, in Santa Cruz, California, owns and operates the Evergreen Cemetery as an historic site with an active volunteer group. The Museum's Evergreen Cemetery docents teach members about the maintenance of the property and conduct presentations on the lives of the most prominent permanent residents, aided by obituaries, newspaper articles, and other historical information. As more volunteers participated, they initiated individual studies of such issues as the history of epidemics, suicides, women's history, and comparative social and ethnic studies with other cemeteries in the county.

Government-funded preservation planning for cemeteries is not common, but it has had considerable effect. At a state level, the preservation guidelines for municipally owned historic burial grounds and cemeteries produced for the Massachusetts Department of Environmental Management stands above other efforts, winning national recognition (Walker-Kluesing Design Group 2002). In the South, when Georgia's residents were asked at public meetings what historic resources they thought were most at risk, cemeteries rose to the top of the list, even ahead of public buildings. Since that state has over 100 cemeteries listed in the National Register of Historic Places, from family plots to municipal fields, an application to the federal program, Save America's Treasures, garnered $60,000

from the National Park Service for a wide range of activities (Kaplan 2007). The fundamental requirement that matching funds are required for the government money provides a convenient reminder of the importance of cooperation between religious groups and the broader community to advance common interests.

Conclusion

For the majority of the population in the United States, faith-based activities are part of life. Regardless of one's experience with the roles religion plays, the appropriate stance for preservationists is clear: faith must be recognized as an important motivating social and personal force. Regardless of doctrine or any specific issues, religions provide primary cultural characteristics that continue traditions, often essential to maintain sites of archaeological, artistic, architectural, historical, and social importance. By working with religious denominations, preservationists become better connected with a broader constituency, one that is balanced ethnically and more representative of the country as a whole. Just as important, if a preservationist is to do his or her job appropriately, having a sense of what is considered sacred in any location better equips one to assist the people and the properties in their care.

If government at any level takes an active role in supporting religious groups, preservationists should recognize that the funds can be spent wisely (Henriques and Lehren 2007). If government representatives maintain that they cannot be supportive—that their hands are tied by the Constitution—the fact remains that all religions are being supported to the degree that their properties are tax exempt. This includes seminaries, monasteries, cemeteries, and hospitals, as well as a significant number of residential buildings.

In a similar fashion, as is their right, some faiths are deeply involved with social issues and attempt to minister to those who are less fortunate, sometimes through missionary activities. Other religions may be less responsive to the social problems around them, taking only a

---

[41] The role that funeral homes have played in cemetery care is generally overlooked (Laderman 2003).

peripheral role in urging their members to care for people outside of their congregation.

Regardless of differences in denominations, religion has played a powerful role in our country's history, leading the way in its contemporary social consciousness for decades. The crusade for Civil Rights and Women's Rights were primarily faith-based. Today leadership in the most economically depressed areas of the country depends upon religious involvement for guidance, offering solace and charity that regenerates in a fashion that preservationists cannot help but celebrate as well.

References

Abelson, J. (5 Apr 2004). Parish makes a case. *Boston Globe.*

Advocate. (1868). Costly churches. *Christian Advocate, 43*(7), 52.

Alba, R. D., Raboteau, A. J., & DeWind, J. (2009). *Immigration and religion in America. Comparative and historical perspective.* New York: New York University Press.

Bagby, I., et al. (2001). *The American Mosque: A national portrait* (p. 15). Washington, D.C.: Council on American-Islamic Relations.

Baskerville, J. L. (1994). *Churches as effective partners in community revitalization: New initiatives for building restoration and community involvement.* Master of Arts thesis, Program in Historic Preservation Planning, Cornell University.

Berg, S. P. (1992). Approaches to landscape preservation treatment at Mount Auburn Cemetery. *APT Bulletin, 24*(4), 52–58.

Bernstein, K., & Sandmeier, T. (2001). Preservation issues in the news. *Los Angeles Conservancy Newsletter, 23*(23), 3.

Bohlman, P. V., Blumhofer, E. L., & Chow, M. M. (Eds.). (2005). *Music in American religious experience.* New York: Oxford University Press.

Boyer, P. (2001). *Religion explained. The evolutionary origins of religious thought.* New York: Basic Books.

Brink, P. (1992). President's column. *Preservation News, 32*(1), 6.

Bromley, D. (Ed.). (1991). *Religion and social order: Vatican II and U.S. Catholicism.* Greenwich: JAI Press.

Bruns, R. (2004). *Billy Graham: A biography.* Westport: Greenwood Press.

Bukhari, Z. H., et al. (2004). *Muslims' place in America's public square.* Walnut Creek: AltaMira.

Burroughs, P. E. (1917a). *Church and Sunday-school buildings* (pp. 184–189). Nashville: Sunday School Board, Southern Baptist Convention.

Burroughs, P. E. (1917b). *The present-day Sunday school.* New York: Fleming H. Revell Company.

Burroughs, P. E. (1927). *How to plan church buildings.* Nashville: Sunday School Board, Southern Baptist Convention.

Burroughs, P. E. (1941) *Fifty fruitful years, 1891–1941.* Nashville: The Broadman Press.

Capecchi, C. (29 June 2009). In Minnesota, big moment for a Temple for Hindus. *The New York Times.*

Carter, B. (1998). Agency hopes to double job-placement numbers. *[Newark] Star-Ledger,* Feb 10.

Catholic. (1943). Preparing for post war life. *Catholic Action,* March, pp. 5–8.

Century. (2005). Methodists OK sharing communion with ELCA and Episcopal church. *Christian Century, 122*(11), 13.

Century. (2007). ELCA reports drop in membership. *Christian Century, 124*(17), 14.

Century. (2008). Flexible megachurches rival denominations. *Christian Century,* Oct 7, p. 14.

Chaves, M. (2004). *Congregations in America.* Cambridge: Harvard University Press.

Chinnici, J. P. (2004). The Catholic community at prayer. In J. M. O'Toole (Ed.), *Habits of devotion: Catholic religious practice in twentieth-century America.* Ithaca: Cornell University Press.

Christian, J. T. (1922). *A history of the Baptists, together with some account of their principles and practices.* Nashville: Sunday School Board of the Southern Baptist Convention.

Chung, S. F., & Wegars, P. (Eds.). (2005). *Chinese American death rituals: Respecting the ancestors.* Lanham: AltaMira.

Cohen, A. (1997). Feeding the flock. *Time,* Aug 25, p. 47.

Cole, S. G. (1931). *The history of fundamentalism.* New York: R.R. Smith.

Conover, E. M. (1924). Building a seven-day-a-week church. *American Architect [and] the Architectural Review, 126*(2453), 179–180.

Conover, E. M. (1948). Planning the church community center. *Architectural Record, 103*(5), 127–128.

Cox, K. (2000). *Vastu living: Creating a home for the soul.* New York: Marlowe.

Cubberley, E. P. (1920). *The history of education.* Boston: Houghton Mifflin.

Dart, J. (2008). Church-closing rate only one percent. *Christian Century, 125*(9), 14–15.

Dawes. (1887). *General [Dawes] Allotment Act,* 24 Stat. 388, Ch. 119, 25 U.S.C. 331, Feb 8.

Daniell, D. (1994). *William Tyndale: A biography.* New Haven: Yale University Press.

Davis, J. G. (1968). *The secular uses of church buildings.* London: S.C.M.

Dennett, D. C. (2006). *Breaking the spell: Religion as a natural phenomenon.* New York: Penguin Viking.

Depalma, A. (1983). A new life for an old church. *New York Times,* April 17.

DeSanctis, M. E. (2002). *Building from belief: Advance, retreat and compromise in the remaking of catholic church architecture*. Collegeville: The Liturgical Press.

Diaz, J. (2005). After 375 years, times grow tight under local sod. *Boston Globe*, Oct 30.

Douglass, H. P. (1926). *1000 city churches*. New York: George H. Doran Company.

Douglass, H. P. (1930). *Protestant cooperation in American cities* (pp. 41–44). New York: Institute for Social and Religious Research.

Drinan, R. F. (2004). *Can god & caesar coexist? Balancing religious freedom & international law*. New Haven: Yale University Press.

Drummond, A. L. (1934). *The church architecture of protestantism* (pp. 210–213). Edinburgh: T & T Clarke.

Dunlap, D. A. (1988). The personal history of a church's fundraising effort. *Inspired*, May 3, pp. 6–7.

Ebaugh, H. R., et al. (2000). The social ecology of residential patterns and membership in immigrant churches. *Journal for the Scientific Study of Religion, 29*(1), 107–117.

Ebony. (1971). *Ebony history of Black America* (Vol. I, pp. 165, 171). Nashville: Southwestern Publishing Co.

ELCA. (17 Apr 2003). Lutheran Laity movement to cease operations May 31. *Evangelical Lutheran Church in America News*.

Ellwood, C. A. (1922). *The reconstruction of religion: A sociological view* (pp. 305–307). New York: Macmillan.

Ervin, S. (1983). The constitution and religion. *Free Inquiry*, Summer, p. 13.

Finke, R., & Stark, R. (1992). *The churching of America 1776–1990. Winners and losers in our religious economy*. New Brunswick: Rutgers University Press.

Flott, A. (2011). Trending to the traditional. *National Catholic Register*, June 7, p. 1.

French, S. (1974). The cemetery as cultural institution: The establishment of mount auburn and the "Rural Cemetery Movement". *American Quarterly, 26*(1), 37–59.

Gabert, G. (1973). *In Hoc Signo? A brief history of catholic parochial education in America*. Port Washington: Kennikat Press.

Garber, P. N. (1941). *The methodist meeting house* (p. 95). New York: Board of Missions and Church Extension, Methodist Church.

Gilbert, W. K. (1988). *Commitment to unity: A history of the Lutheran Church in America*. Philadelphia: Fortress Press.

Gillett, E. H. (1864). *History of the Presbyterian church in the United States of America*. Philadelphia: Presbyterian Publication Committee.

Givens, T. L. (2007). *People of Paradox: A history of mormon culture* (pp. 105–110). New York: Oxford University Press.

Gootman, E. (20 July 2000). After squabbling, arts center is leaving its historic church. *The New York Times*, p. B3.

Gorham, B. W. (1854). *Camp meeting manual: A practical guide for the camp ground; in two parts*. Boston: H.V. Degen.

Grebstein, S. N. (Ed.). (1960). *Monkey trial: The state of Tennessee vs. John Thomas Scopes*. Boston: Houghton Mifflin.

Gritsch, E. W. (2002). *A history of Lutheranism*. Minneapolis: Augsberg Fortress.

Hanson, J. W. (Ed.). (1894). *The World's congress of religions. The addresses and papers delivered before the parliament, and an abstract of the congresses held in the art institute*. Chicago. Philadelphia: Houston.

Harrington, S. P. M. (1993). Bones and bureaucrats: New York's Great Cemetery Imbroglio. *Archaeology Magazine*, March/April.

Henriques, D. B., & Lehren, A. W. (13 May 2007). Religious groups reaping share of Federal Aid for Pet projects. *The New York Times*, p. 1.

Hoffman, M. (1989). Uplifting efforts to save edifices. *Christian Science Monitor*, May 19, p. 13.

Holmes, D. O. W. (1934). *The evolution of the Negro College*. New York: Teachers' College, Columbia University.

Hopkins, B. R. (2011). *The law of tax-exempt organizations*. New York: John Wiley & Sons.

Huffstutter, P. J. (2008). Salvaging hope at Iowa Mosque. *Los Angeles Times*, July 1.

Israel, C. A. (2004). *Before scopes: Evangelism, education and evolution in Tennessee, 1870–1925*. Athens: University of Georgia Press.

Jaeger, A. R. (1984). *The auditorium and Akron Plans: Reflections of a half century of American Protestantism*. Master of Arts thesis, Program in Historic Preservation Planning, Cornell University.

Johnson-Nestor, et al. (1989). *A survey of historic churches of Northwest New Mexico, 1988–89*. Santa Fe: New Mexico Community Foundation and the New Mexico Historic Preservation Office.

Kaplan, P. (25 Jan 2007). Cemeteries' resurrections: Six regions get Federal cash for graveyards. *Atlanta Journal-Constitution*.

Kayal, M. (7 Feb 2004). Religion Journal. *The New York Times*.

Kervick, F. W. W. (1962). *Architects in American in the Catholic Tradition*. Rutland: C.E. Tuttle.

Kilde, J. H. (2002). *When Church became theatre: The transformation of Evangelical architecture and worship in nineteenth-century America*. New York: Oxford University Press.

Kilgannon, C. (2003). Public lives; unearthing the past, then burying it with respect. *The New York Times*, Oct 2.

Krueger, F. W. (1995). *The Lord's house: A guide to creation careful management of Church facilities*. Macalester: Macalester Park Pub Co.

Krupa, G. (13 May 2009). Oldest Mosque in Michigan celebrates 70 years. *Detroit News*.

Laderman, G. (2003). *Rest in peace: A cultural history of death and the funeral home in twentieth-century America*. New York: Oxford University Press.

LaGrand, J. B. (2002). *Indian metropolis: Native Americans in Chicago, 1945–75*. Urbana and Chicago: University of Illinois Press.

Lately, T. (1959). *The vanishing Evangelist: The Aimee Semple McPherson kidnapping affair*. New York: Viking Press.

Leitch, J. E. (1957). Five dedications featured in June. *United Presbyterian, 115*(25), 12–13.

Levinson, N. (10 June 1991). Getting out in the field and spreading the word. *Preservation News, 31*(6).

Levitt, P. (2007). *God needs no passport: Immigrants and the changing religious landscape*. New York: New Press.

Lin, J. (2005 Nov 21). Rehabbing effort falls short of its ambitions. *Philadelphia Inquirer*, p. A1.

Lin, J. (2006 May 1). Nonprofit developer appears to move upscale. *Philadelphia Inquirer*, p. B1.

Linder, E. W. (Ed.). (1969). *Yearbook of American & Canadian Churches*. Nashville: Abindon Press.

Linder, M. W. J. (2008). Witnessing history. *The Clarion, 25*(8), 1.

Lippy, C. H. (1989). *Twentieth century shapers of American popular religion*. New York: Greenwood Press.

Lutheran. (March 2009a). Downside of Worship. *Lutheran*.

Lutheran. (May 2009b). Worship attendance is falling. *Lutheran*.

Lynn, R. W., & Wright, E. (1980). *The big little school. Two hundred years of the sunday school*. Birmingham: Religious Education Press.

Management. (1925). Broadcasting churches. *Church Management*, Feb, p. 232.

Medina, J. (2008). Changing with times, Parish prospers. *The New York Times*, April 16.

Melton, J. G., Lucas, P. C., & Stone, J. R. (1997). *Primetime religion: An Encyclopedia of religious broadcasting*. Phoenix: Oryx Press.

Meyer, R. E. (Ed.). (1989). *Cemeteries and grave markers: Voices of American culture*. Ann Arbor: UMI Research Press.

Miller, E. A. (1917). *Making the old Sunday school*. New York: The Methodist Book Concern.

Miller, G. T. (2007). *Piety and profession. American Protestant theological education, 1870–1970* (p. 411). Grand Rapids: William B. Eerdmans.

Miller, M. E. (2004). *Forgotten tribes: Unrecognized Indians and the Federal acknowledgement process*. Lincoln: University of Nebraska Press.

Mitford, J. (1963). *The American way of death*. New York: Simon and Schuster.

Mjagkij, N., & Spratt, M. (Eds.). (1997). *Men and Women Adrift: The YMCA and YWCA in the city*. New York: New York University Press.

Morse, R. C. (1913). *History of the North American young men's Christian associations*. New York: YMCA Association Press.

Mosher, M. P. (1994). Space-sharing arrangements in Houses of Worship. *Inspired Partnerships, 6*, 1–26.

Mumford, K. (2008). *Newark: A history of race, rights and riots in America*. New York: NYU Press.

Murphy, B. P. (1965). *The building and care of Methodist Church property*. New York: National Division of the Board of Missions, Methodist Church.

Murphy, L. (2001). *African-American faith in America* (p. 50). New York: Facts on File, Inc.

Narvaez, A. A. (1 Nov 1987). Housing group rebuilds in Newark. *The New York Times*.

Nessenbaum, S. (Ed.). (1972). *The great awakening at Yale University*. Belmont: Wadsworth.

Newman, A. H. (1894). *A history of the baptist churches in the United States*. New York: Christian Literature.

Newman, A. (26 May 2008). Breathing life into Gods. *The New York Times*.

Ng, K. (2001). Wealth redistribution, race and southern public schools, 1880–1910. *Education Policy Analysis Archives, 9*(16), 16.

Nicholson, A. (2003). *God's secretaries: The making of the king James Bible*. New York: HarperCollins.

Noyce, G. B. (1975). *Survival and Mission for the City Church*. Philadelphia: The Westminster Press.

NYT. (15 Oct 1958). Lutheran laymen list aid to church. *The New York Times*.

NYT. (16 May 1992). More Megachurches. *The New York Times*, 9.

NYT. (8 April 2004). Catholics consolidate in Vermont. *The New York Times*.

NYT. (23 Oct 2007a). Where Megachurches are concentrated. *The New York Times*.

NYT. (22 Nov 2007b). Branching out. *The New York Times*.

Olsen, D. T. (2008). *American church in crisis: Groundbreaking research based on a national database of 200,000 churches*. Grand Rapids: Zonderyan.

Partners. (1991). *The complete guide to capital campaigns for historic churches and synagogues*. Philadelphia: Partners for Sacred Places.

Paulson, M. (26 May 2004). 65 Parishes to be closed. *Boston Globe*, p. A–1.

Paulson, M., & Kurkjian, S. (4 Mar 2004). Fifth of Parish groups reject closing. *Boston Globe*.

Perry, W. R., Howson, J., & Bianco, B. A. (2009). *The New York African burial ground: Unearthing the African presence in colonial New York, Vol. 2: The archaeology of the New York African burial ground*. Washington, D.C.: Howard University Press.

PNM. (1986). Historic church survey completed. *Preservation New Mexico, 3*(4), 1.

PNM. (1987). New Mexico community foundation. *Preservation New Mexico, 4*(3), 1.

PNM. (1994–1995). Cornerstones founded. *Preservation New Mexico, 11*(1), 10.

Pollock, J. (1966). *Billy Graham, the authorized biography*. New York: McGraw-Hall.

Porter, L. C. (2000). *A study of the origins of the Church of Jesus Christ of latter-day saints in the states of New*

York and Pennsylvania, 1816–1831. Doctoral dissertation, Brigham Young University.

Presbyterian. (1965a). Church leaders meet on ecumenicity. *Presbyterian Life, 18*(16), 29.

Presbyterian. (1965b). Chasm narrows between Protestants, Roman Catholics. *Presbyterian Life, 18*(16), 28–29.

PSPN. (1991). Welcome! *Partners for Sacred Places Newsletter,* 1(1), 1–2.

PSPN. (1995). Two new programs. *Partners for Sacred Places News, 4*(4), 7.

Rai, S. (2004). Short on Priests, U.S. Catholics outsource prayers to Indian clergy. *The New York Times,* June 13.

Rippon, J. (1838). *A brief memoir of the life and writings of the late Rev. John Gill, D.D.* London: Bennett.

Roberts, P. I. (Ed.). (1924). *Radio preaching: Far Flung Sermons by pioneers in broadcasting.* New York: Fleming H. Revell Company.

Rohde, D. (1997). Truce calms a Torn church. *The New York Times,* March 16, p. 11.

Rozak, D. (2002). Church sues to save cemetery. *Chicago Sun-Times,* Nov 13.

RRR. (1994). Giving trends in the Evangelical Lutheran Church in America. *Review of Religious Research, 36*(2), 238–244.

Saran, P. (1985). *The Asian Indian experience in the United States.* New Delhi: Vikas Publishing House.

Sartain, G. (1960). The national council of churches: The first ten years. *Presbyterian Life, 13*(23), 24–25.

Schaller, L. E. (1967). *The churches war on poverty.* New York: Abingdon Press.

Schoenherr, R. A., & Young, L. A. (1993). *Full pews, empty altars: Demographics of the priest shortage in the United States Catholic Dioceses.* Madison: University of Wisconsin Press.

Seth, M. (1960). New designs for church building. *Presbyterian Life, 13*(4), 11–13.

Sheen, F. J. (1980). *Treasure in clay.* Garden City: Doubleday.

Shipp, E. R. (9 Aug 1991). Black Cemetery yields wealth of history. *The New York Times.*

Slaughter, W. W., & Landon, M. (1997). *Trail of hope: The story of the Mormon trail.* Salt Lake City: Deseret Book Co.

Sloan, D. C. (1991). *The last great necessity: Cemeteries in American History.* Baltimore: The Johns Hopkins University Press.

Smith, J. L. (1999). *Islam in America.* New York: Columbia University Press.

Stewart, B. (1996). Bill Linder and his city of hope. *The New York Times,* Feb 18.

Svendsbye, L. (1967). *The history of a developing social responsibility among Lutherans in America from 1930 to 1960* (pp. 10-44). Doctoral dissertation, Union Theological Seminary.

Sweeney, T. W. (1990). New Mexicans save Beleaguered Adobe churches. *Preservation News,* Dec, pp. 1–2.

Teltsch, K. (1991). Newark Priest wins a "Genius" award. *The New York Times,* June 18.

Thumma, S., & Travis, D. (2007). *Beyond megachurch myths: What we can learn from America's largest churches.* San Francisco: Jossey-Bass.

Time. (1974). The new counter-reformation. *Time,* July 8, pp. 32–33.

Torbet, R. G. (1963). *A history of the Baptists.* Valley Forge: The Judson Press.

Tucci, D. S. (1995). *Ralph Adams cram: Life and architecture.* Amherst: University of Massachusetts Press.

Tucker, K. B. W. (2001). *American methodist worship.* New York: Oxford University Press.

Turner, J. (2003). *Language, religion, knowledge, past and present* (pp. 111–115). Notre Dame: University of Notre Dame Press.

Tuttle, B. R. (2009). *How Newark became Newark: The rise, fall and rebirth of an American City.* New Brunswick: Rivergate Books.

Walch, T. (1989). *Catholicism in America: A social history.* Malabar: Robert E. Krieger Publishing Co.

Walker-Kluesing Design Group. (2002). *Preservation guidelines for municipally owned burial grounds and cemeteries* (2nd ed.). Boston: Massachusetts Department of Environmental Management.

Wardle, A. G. (1918). *History of the Sunday school movement in the Methodist Church.* New York: Methodist Book Concern.

Washburn, G. (1894). *Points of contact between Christianity and Mohammedanism. World's Congress of Religions* (pp. 491–504). Chicago: John C. Winston & Co.

Wayne, M. N. (1997). *A critical evaluation of the historiography surrounding the southern Baptist Convention, 1979–1996.* Doctoral dissertation Trinity Evangelical Divinity School.

White, A. D. (1905). *Autobiography of Andrew Dickson White.* New York: The Century Co.

White, R. C. L. (1924). The message of the radio. *Church Management,* Nov, pp. 67–68.

Worth, R. F. (2003). A Hindu temple of discord. *The New York Times,* Dec 5.

Wuthnow, R. (2006). *Saving America? Faith-based services and the future of civil society.* Princeton: Princeton University Press.

Zelizer, V. A. R. (2009). *Morals & markets: The development of life insurance in the United States.* New Brunswick: Transactions.

Zollman, C. (1916). Church cemeteries in the American Law. *Michigan Law Review, 14*(5), 391–398.

Conclusion

As we have seen, all of the rationales for saving places continue to motivate people throughout the United States. The social utility, economic advantages, historical memory, aesthetic accomplishments, and the religious significance of sites motivate individuals and groups to step forward and take action. This conclusion synthesizes the major points raised in the chapters and provides guidance about challenges ahead.

The United States is principally, but not exclusively, an English-speaking, Christian society with considerable pride in its form of representative democracy. The Positivist view prevails that we can improve our destiny. The ideas are intimately connected to several common beliefs, principally that all citizens are free and equal, and everyone has a right to life, liberty, and the pursuit of happiness. This implies the free use of one's property and improving property generally signifies progress.

Early preservation advocates understood this. In some instances, when faced with demolition, preservation pioneers not only openly questioned the prevailing norms and attitudes, but they took steps to avoid what seemed to be the inevitable. Similar to preservationists today, early advocates had an interest in history, art history, anthropology, archaeology, and architecture, disciplines that developed remarkably during the nineteenth and early twentieth century.

Some scholars have held that the Romantic ideals of the period played a role. The rejection of the evils of industrialization in favor of the arts and crafts of a previous era was important to some preservationists as they banded together, putting aside personal goals to advancing the common good. Yet, others were very pragmatic. Regardless, by 1900 it was clear that, if the preservation movement was to succeed, the government had to be pressed into action. Soon the federal government set about saving "antiquities," and the National Park Service was formed to care for the parks and monuments, but its goals of controlling poaching and pot-hunting were far from an instant reality. Progress was more of a threat in urban locations, as the majority of the country's population was moving to the industrializing cities. With the rise of local zoning and planning legislation, urban preservation advocates believed they had more leverage, particularly if steps were taken to survey and defend what was deemed significant. The stories of Charleston and New Orleans are legendary, and their ordinances remain very instructive for later preservation advocates.

Equally important is the growth of federal government activities during the Depression and World War II. In the late 1940s, it became clear that there was more need for government intervention in housing, as new homes were sorely needed to accommodate returning veterans. With the rise of the Cold War, civil defense was the rationale for the construction of superhighways that aided suburbanization. The country's population, always mobile, began to move to the new centers of productivity in the service industries, and away from the former centers of heavy industry. Change was afoot everywhere, as the United States experienced the longest sustained

M. A. Tomlan, *Historic Preservation*, DOI 10.1007/978-3-319-04975-5

period of growth in its history. When the federal government and some state governments cleared "slums" and "obsolete" properties for highways, this idea of progress sparked a reaction.

Today, with decades of preservation activity behind us, it is possible to see that almost all of the policy recommendations contained in the 1965 report to Congress, *With Heritage So Rich*, have been achieved, even if some are not fully realized. An organizational structure "capable of providing leadership, information, standards and criteria, and technical and financial assistance" is in place.[1] The government agencies involved—the National Park Service, Advisory Council on Historic Preservation, state historic preservation offices, and local commissions—have done a remarkable amount of work, assisted by the National Trust for Historic Preservation and a host of other national, state-level and local nonprofit organizations. All of these are involved in various forms of advocacy, surveys and nominations, review and compliance projects, and funding.

However, the financial commitment at all levels of government remains uneven. The National Historic Preservation Act assumed that federal authorization would naturally allow Congressional appropriations to flow to the National Park Service, the states, and, eventually, the cities to provide financial support for projects. A modest amount of funding became available in the early 1970s. The National Trust and the state historic preservation offices at first blossomed. However, more funding is needed and a concerted effort to ramp up federal support remains difficult to sustain.

To those who became involved in framing the NHPA, only the barest hint of *indirect* funding was suggested. After the 1976 Tax Reform Act was fully implemented in the early 1980s, private funding became available as never before, and the projects became larger and more numerous. In the twenty-first century, one of the most noticeable features of the preservation effort is the manner in which funding provided by the state

and federal tax codes has made a difference. In that regard, historic preservation and low income housing tax credits have weathered scrutiny and done comparatively well. Looking ahead, more revisions to the tax codes are inevitable. With that in mind, it is important to gather the statistics and supporting information to demonstrate the case—repeatedly if necessary—that the use of historic rehabilitation investment tax credits, particularly in low income projects, are among the wisest use of our economic resources.

Thousands of hours have been spent by representatives of the national organizations analyzing the difficulties with the current federal preservation program, most recently in the face of drastic budget cuts. A report released by a group of well-known preservationists in 2011 called for "realigning" the efforts of the public sector, private partners, and nonprofit organizations. This would provide "a leadership role in job creation, energy independence, better international relations… heritage conservation, and the forging of efficient and effective public-private partnerships…"[2]

The primary recommendation is to establish a new deputy director of historic preservation and heritage in the National Park Service. The report further recommended that, with an expanded staff dedicated to economic development, energy efficiency, and sustainability, a better case could be made for the truly significant role of historic preservation in the American economy.

This was a commendable effort, and the new initiatives are consistent with the ideas in this textbook, but the recommendations sorely need a plan for implementation, one that is developed iteratively and incrementally with stakeholders *outside* of Washington. Given the discussions in Congress, calls for the expansion of any federal program are not likely to be feasible in the near future. As we have seen, the historic preservation movement lacks sufficient numbers and the financial backing needed to influence Congress. Tactical legislative initiatives have been more

---

[1] United States Conference of Mayors, Special Committee on Historic Preservation, *With Heritage So Rich. A Report*. New York: Random House, 1966, p. 210.

[2] Preservation Action et al., *Alligned for Success: Recommendations to Increase the Effectiveness of the Federal Preservation Program*. Washington, D.C.: Federal Historic Preservation Task Force, 2011, p. iv.

successful. In addition, they might be more so, particularly given the repeated and very obvious need—stimulated annually by Nature—to respond to emergencies and disasters, and to prevent damage to life and property. Ramping up preservation units inside of federal and state level disaster relief agencies would help both the public and the preservation community both in the short term and in the long run. By contrast, the lion's share of the attention given to preservation by the National Park Service is likely to continue to be dedicated to the care of the national parks and monuments, which are growing in number, despite a lack of any significant increase in funding.

Locally, preservationists continue to rise to defend important sites using the standard rationales in discussions with historic preservation commissions, and in zoning, planning, and economic development boards and agencies. Because further research and broadening attitudes have changed the definition of local significance, the inclusion of that section in the National Historic Preservation Act continues to be relevant. This is the genius in the Act. It provides the framework for continuous education, at all levels, across the country. By making amendments in 1980 and 1992, the scope was broadened and, as a result, we are able to understand our historic properties even better. Considering the sites of Indian tribes and under-represented minorities is a natural extension of our preservation ideals, seeds of which first bore fruit supporting neighborhood preservation, empowering a wider range of people to challenge the prevailing decision-making.

More could be learned from the Main Street programs, as they provide the closest link to people in the businesses community. Their inclusiveness and adaptability have helped many downtowns and near suburbs. The National Heritage Area initiatives hold similar promise, but more attention needs to be paid to the role of heritage tourism, for it presents both opportunities and challenges, particularly to high visitation sites.

To defend a place and be part of a transformation that will respect its historical development, it is necessary to understand who lives there today, how it came to be, and how it has changed. Taking the time to look, listen, and understand the character of the people and of the place is the first step in creating an adequate record, which must be tied to a thorough investigation of historical sources. Adequate documentation is needed not only to contribute to our knowledge, but also to educate others. At a larger scale, the preservation planning techniques developed in Charleston and Providence, Rhode Island remain viable for both creating a record and engaging people to learn more by participating in surveying. Incorporating the aesthetic and historical context is also important if only to discover the limits of ideas about sustainability and trends such as "new urbanism." The aesthetic context is as important as the historical significance in designing a suitable response. Again, open discussion is needed to understand treatment options—reconstruction, restoration, or rehabilitation—and how any and all of them may become part of the solution. If recent preservation practice has proven anything, it is that there are no properties that are impossible to reuse. The adaptation of all aspects of the Presidio in San Francisco—a city within a city—amply illustrates this.

Nevertheless, differences arise, even among preservationists, about the perceptions of what is needed for the public good. Inherent in the democratic process, power relationships often play a decisive role. It is also important to keep in mind that the cognitive frame of reference for parts of society or for an individual may differ completely from that held by the majority. The thinking of Native American tribes is but one of many instances of different ways of thinking, for very understandable reasons. To respect all cultures, in fact, one has to appreciate the limits of the dominant culture. After all, our advocacy is an expression of our American society.

This was demonstrated in Chapter 7 to a degree, but much more attention should be paid to how politics has a bearing on preservation policies and programs. Although it may seem that political organizations lie outside the scope of preservation concerns, the reverse is true. Our elected officials pass laws and make decisions for all of us. In many instances, a non-partisan league will prove to be an important sounding board. This is where individuals concerned about preservation issues, and the local, state, and national level preservation organizations, should become much more involved.

The long-held ideas that historic preservation is primarily an "artifact-centered" crusade and that preservation is predominantly engaged in resisting change will continue to be put forth, however. These ideas are inaccurate, as demonstrated by the way in which the preservationists have embraced the cultural significance of religious places and properties, extending their understanding of how people are linked to places. Religion played a key role in our settlement patterns, and profoundly influenced our educational growth and social development as a nation. Yet, as in other issues facing the country, each faith is changing. In the Northeast, Catholic parishes have insufficient adherents supporting what has become an overabundance of churches and facilities, while their numbers are growing in the South and Southwest. Baptists are also experiencing comparatively slow growth, while the Latter-Day Saints are expanding well beyond their Rocky Mountain base. All of these changes suggest that there is an increasing need to form partnerships to help to make more efficient use of existing properties. In this regard, advancing interfaith cooperation is important. Preservationists' understanding of the importance of religions other than their own should serve to expand the appreciation of our country's many cultures. It is also important to respect the variety of traditions in the transformation of religious properties, including open landscapes that appear to some as "empty."

In addition to these suggestions for future action, renewed effort should be placed in promoting what was formerly termed "built environment education," and later heritage education. This was largely a secondary school initiative that was originally sponsored by the American Institute of Architects and later by the National Endowment for the Arts. Teaching young people in school settings about preservation and architectural history undoubtedly strengthened preservation organizations in the late twentieth century. Although museums carry on a broad range of educational programming for young people, much more has to be been done to foster this early training in the twenty-first century, even becoming involved in discussions about school reforms at every level of government.

To inspire and invigorate the movement, its recent history should be studied. This includes important contributors, women such as Antoinette Downing, Joan Maynard, Elizabeth Barlow Rogers, Nellie Longsworth, Loretta Neumann, Mary Means, Frances Edmunds, and Eileen Rhea Brown. The list of men includes Arthur Ziegler, Reid Williamson, Wesley Wallace Law, as well as many of those who led preservation agencies and organizations. These people are "living treasures" who should be celebrated for their lifelong contributions. This is important because, as a social campaign, historic preservation's leaders deserve recognition so that others entering the field can follow their examples and become active in extending our legacy.

Index

A

Aaron, Philip, 244
Abandoned Shipwreck Act, 106
About Your House (radio show), 273
Absinthe House, New Orleans, 30
Abyssinian Baptist Church, New York City, 102
Academy of Arts and Sciences, 20
Academy of Design, 5
Ad Hoc Committee on Federal Office Space, 81
Adams, Samuel, 98
Adelmann, W. Gerald, 159
Adler, Dankmar, and Sullivan, Louis, 55
Adler, Emma, 75
Adler, Lee, 52, 75
Adverse effect, 106, 110, 116
Advisory Council (Pennsylvania Avenue), 81,
Advisory Council on Historic Preservation (ACHP), 100,
    105–107, 113, 232, 238, 289, 292
Advocacy, 271–276
Advocacy and ethics, 265 ff.
Advocacy and public expression, 271, 285–288
Advocacy at the community level, 71–76
Advocacy at the state level, 275
Aesthetic experience, 214
Aesthetic preferences, 269
Aesthetics and economics, 124–126, 129
Aesthetics and social preference, 149
Affordable Housing Program, 204
African American, 24, 28, 44, 49, 71, 72, 74, 75, 77, 89,
    98, 272, 300, 311, 331, 335, 336, 338, 339, 340
African American Methodists, 338, 339
African American Muslims, 332, 339
African Baptists, 311
African Burial Ground, 347, 348
African Methodist Episcopal Zion Church, 311
African Methodists, 311
Age, sex, and household composition, 145
Agency preservation officer (APO), 104
American Institute of Architects Historic Buildings
    Committee, 56
Air and Space Museum, 77
Air Force, United States, 245
Akron Plan, 332
Alabama Historic Preservation Alliance, 135
Alabama Religious Freedom Amendment, 135

Alamo,
    restoration of, 31
Alamo Monument Association, 31
Alamo property, 32
Alaska, 67, 76, 215, 309
Albany (NY) State Bank, 276, 280
Albright, Horace, 33, 34
Albuquerque, New Mexico, 46, 273, 341
Alcoa Building (San Francisco), 57
Alexandria (Virginia), 48, 53, 215
Aliens (vs. Icons), 285
Alinsky, Sol, 59
Allen A.M.E. Church, 338
Allen Housing and Development Corporation, 338
Allen Neighborhood Preservation Corporation, 338
Allen, Richard, 338
Allen University, 311
Allen, William Slater, 50
Alliance for National Heritage Areas, 160
Alliance of Tribal Tourism Advocates, 164
Allied military forces, 37
Al-Noor Islamic Mosque, 341
Ambassador Hotel, 293–295, 297
American Academy of Fine Arts, 5
American Anthropological Association, 17, 47
American Antiquarian Society, 3
American Association of State Highway and
    Transportation Officials (AASHTO), 200
American Automobile Association, 63
American Can Company, 178
American Church Review, 17
American Civic Association, 18
American Commission for the Protection and Salvage
    of Artistic and Historic Monuments in Europe
    (ACPS), 37
American Council (English National Trust), 11, 12
American Council of Learned Societies, 37
American Craft Museum, 287
American Defense-Harvard Group, 37
American flags, 43, 322
American Indian artifacts, 2–4, 16, 17, 39, 69, 104, 111,
    200, 219, 249, 266, 297, 347
American Indian religions, 111
American Indian Religious Freedom Act, 111
American Indians, 17, 111, 136, 309; see also tribes by
    name

M. A. Tomlan, *Historic Preservation*, DOI 10.1007/978-3-319-04975-5
© Springer International Publishing Switzerland 2015

GPSR Compliance
The European Union's (EU) General Product Safety Regulation (GPSR) is a set
of rules that requires consumer products to be safe and our obligations to
ensure this.

If you have any concerns about our products, you can contact us on

ProductSafety@springernature.com

In case Publisher is established outside the EU, the EU authorized
representative is:

Springer Nature Customer Service Center GmbH
Europaplatz 3
69115 Heidelberg, Germany